BERNARD SHAW

His Life, Work and Friends

ST. JOHN ERVINE

Bernard Shaw
His Life, Work and Friends

WILLIAM MORROW & COMPANY, NEW YORK, 1956

© 1956 by St. John Ervine
All rights reserved
Printed in the United States of America

Library of Congress Catalog Card Number: 56-9717

TO
THE MEMORY OF CHARLOTTE

FOREWORD

MY INTENTION in writing this book is to tell the story of Bernard Shaw's life from my personal knowledge of him, with such additions of fact as are essential to proper understanding of his career. I began to write it long before his death, but put it aside because I had work of my own to do; but he knew that I had begun it, had, indeed, read what I had written, and he hoped that I would one day finish what I had begun because, so he said, 'You will understand the Irish side of me better than anybody who is not Irish.'

The Life of a man who lived for more than ninety-four years, and was not only world-renowned as a dramatist who had written about fifty plays in addition to other works, but had been a brilliant musical critic, an even more brilliant dramatic critic, a critic of books and a critic of painting, and also extensively and influentially engaged in political affairs of an advanced and revolutionary character, cannot be compressed into a small space. The fact that he was a founder of the Labour Party is sufficient in itself to show how varied and extensive his life was. His correspondence alone would fill many volumes, and the task of editing it will not be enviable. But when it is accomplished, readers will be amazed by the care and trouble he spent on the least of his letters; which were not surpassed by the care and trouble he took over his major works. There must be, scattered about the world, thousands of letters and postcards, many of them in his handwriting, which are full of wit and wisdom. The man who undertakes the task of collecting them will have to dedicate his life to it.

I knew G.B.S. intimately for more than forty years, and I felt an affection for him that was proof against all mischance or misunderstanding. He could say what he liked to me without hurting my feelings, not only because he was an exceptionally kind man, but also because I would not allow myself to feel hurt. He had the privileges of a friend who was my senior by twenty-seven years, and I had his confidence because he knew that I would not betray it. In the whole of our friendship, I never quoted his words without his consent; and it was this fact which made me, I think, better acquainted with his mind than most people. That happiness was increased by the fact that Mrs Shaw, too, received me, and even more than me, my wife, into her affection.

Few things in my life have given me so much happiness as the friendship of Bernard and Charlotte Shaw, and I find myself bereft without them. Their kindness, and his in particular, was beyond measure, nor was it diminished by the fact that I did not share their views, especially on politics. Of all the men I have known in my life, none was so full of grace of mind and spirit as G.B.S. His generosity was almost incredible. A legend has grown up since his death that he was mean about money. There never was uttered a greater lie about anyone than this. Sir Desmond MacCarthy was fond of telling a story of the response to an appeal he had made to G.B.S. for some cause in which he was interested: it was so large that MacCarthy returned half of it!

The number of books about Shaw is already large, and is likely to become larger. The first biography was the late Holbrook Jackson's:[1] it was published in 1907 when G.B.S. was 51 and still had a great part of his work to do. It has had many followers, including the monumental Life by Professor Archibald Henderson, a most useful quarry for other biographers to dig in, and a characteristic and brilliant commentary by G. K. Chesterton, which is the best book on Shaw that has been written and will probably be the best that will ever be written. The reader, with my statement in his mind, may well wonder why I have written this book. The answer is, first, that I wanted to write it, which is sufficient in itself, and, second, that G.K.'s book was written in 1910, forty years before G.B.S. died. Chesterton pre-deceased him by fourteen years, and much that G.B.S. wrote, including, probably, *Saint Joan* and *Heartbreak House*, was unknown to that most likeable man. Memoirs and biographies of other people have been published since G.K.'s death, many of which include accounts of Shaw or references to him; for his interests were numerous and uncommonly varied. It is inevitable, therefore, that all the books about him, written before his death, should suffer from insufficiency; and that the whole life should call for description.

I am deeply in debt to many people in connexion with this book, a debt which is deeper than appears from the footnotes in the book. My obligation to Mr Ivo L. Currall, a close friend of G.B.S., who lent me his numerous volumes of press cuttings about him, is great. This is a debt I have no hope of repaying. Mr Currall, who lives at Luton, was of immense service to G.B.S., when, after the accident which ended in his death, he was taken to Luton and Dunstable Hospital. Mr R. F. Rattray, whose work, *Bernard Shaw: a Chronicle*, is invaluable to the student of Shaw, has been generous with his time in answering questions and giving me information not easily obtainable. Without his aid and Mr Currall's I should have been heavily handicapped. Professor Henderson, too, has been generous with his

---

[1] But there is some biographical material in the late H. L. Mencken's *Shaw and His Plays*, which was published in New York in 1905.

wide knowledge, and I owe many thanks to the Public Trustee and the Society of Authors, by whose permission as copyright owners I have been able to make use of much unpublished material. I am also grateful to Miss Blanche Patch for permitting me to make use of her transcription of Shaw's shorthand diaries, to the National Trust for leave to reproduce illustration material at Shaw's Corner, and to Mr Harold White, of the Leagrave Press of Luton for the loan of illustrations from the work published by B. & H. White Publications Ltd: *Bernard Shaw through the Camera*. I am also in debt to Mr G. P. Wells and Mr Frank Wells for permission to quote their father.

I have the happy fortune to number among my friends, Mrs Georgina Musters, who is the grand-daughter, by his second marriage, of G.B.S.'s maternal grandfather. She was, until her marriage, G.B.S.'s secretary. Their close relationship, cemented not only by affection from G.B.S., but also from Charlotte, lasted until his death. She has not spared herself in answering my importunate questions on points where I was uninformed or insufficiently informed, especially in regard to his family. Mrs Musters lived for many years with G.B.S.'s mother, and was familiar with many of the figures mentioned in these pages. I owe her gratitude for reading and correcting my proofs, gratitude which is also due to Mr Ivo Currall and Mr R. F. Rattray who read the book in typescript.

I am also in debt to Sir Max Beerbohm for permission to quote his works, and to the Executors of the Passfield Trust for letting me make large quotations from the works of Sidney and Beatrice Webb. In some cases, I have sought and failed to obtain consent, either because the author cited is dead and I have no knowledge of any person from whom consent should be sought, or, as in the case of Mr W. P. Barrett—see page 500—because my letter has been returned by the Post Office as delivery cannot be made. I hope I shall be forgiven if I seem to have been lacking in courtesy to some of my authorities. Failure to obtain permission is entirely due to my inability to find the author.

My last, but not my least debt, is due to my former secretary, Miss Philippa Drake, now Mrs Simon Wills, who patiently disentangled my ill-typed and disorderly script and replaced it by one that was seemly; and I am also indebted to Miss Cecilia Nicholls for secretarial assistance.

Honey Ditches, Seaton, Devon   ST JOHN ERVINE
1952–56

ILLUSTRATIONS

Between pages 148-149

G.B.S.

An early photograph of mother and father with
George John Vandeleur Lee

Lucy (sister) and G. B. S. (1876)

Birthplace, 33 Synge Street, Dublin (Courtesy *New York Times*)

Jenny Patterson

Annie Besant (Courtesy *Picture Post* Library)

Beatrice Webb (Courtesy *Press Portrait Bureau*)

Sidney Webb (Courtesy *Press Portrait Bureau*)

An early portrait of Mrs. Bernard Shaw

Barrie, Galsworthy, G.B.S. and Granville-Barker
(Courtesy Alvin Langdon Coburn)

G.B.S. and H. G. Wells (Courtesy Alvin Langdon Coburn)

Pastel portrait of Charlotte by Sartorio

G.B.S. in his forties

G.B.S. and Mrs. St. John Ervine at Torquay, about to start for
one of his long walks (Courtesy Stuart Black, Newton Abbot)

Helen Keller, G.B.S. and Lady Astor (Courtesy *New York Times*)

Mrs. Patrick Campbell

Ellen Terry

G.B.S. and Ellen Pollock's son (1934)

G.B.S. at work in his garden hut

G.B.S. in his garden on his 90th birthday

BERNARD SHAW

BERNARD SHAW

GEORGE BERNARD SHAW, the only son and youngest of the
three children of George Carr Shaw and his wife, Lucinda
Elizabeth Gurly, was born at 3 Upper Synge Street, now
numbered and renamed 33, Synge Street, Dublin, on Saturday,
July 26, 1856. He died at Shaw's Corner, Ayot St Lawrence, Hertfordshire, on Thursday, November 2, 1950, at a minute to five in the
morning. His age was ninety-four years and fourteen weeks.

I

Ireland, at the time of his birth, was suffering severely from the
effects of the Famine of the Forties, which is still known among
country people as The Great Hunger. It was not the first famine
Ireland had suffered, nor was it the last or worst in its immediate
results. Between 1727 and the year of the Union, 1800, there had
been eight that were disastrous; and there were numerous failures
of the potato crop between 1817 and 1839, some of them partial,
some of them complete, each bringing with it sinister attendants of
pestilence and death.[1]

But Ireland was not the only country which suffered from famine,
though the Irish generally talk and write as if it were. The harvest in
England failed for fourteen years in succession during the French and
Napoleonic Wars, and there were bread riots throughout the country.
Famine, indeed, like plague in the Middle Ages, was endemic everywhere, and vast numbers of people could be said, as we say to-day
of the Indians, to have been hungry all their lives.

But the Famine of the Forties had a far different effect on the
Irish than any that had preceded or followed it. For the first time in
their history, they panicked. They had been deprived suddenly of
their main supply of food, and the loss had been accompanied by a
plague. A man would walk down a street and suddenly collapse and
die. The retail trader hesitated to open his door in the morning lest
the dead body of someone who had leant against it during the night
should fall into his shop. The spectacle of men and women trying to
stem the pangs of their hunger by eating grass could sometimes be seen.

[1] Dr George O'Brien gives a detailed account of them in his valuable work: *The
Economic History of Ireland from the Union to the Famine*, pp. 225–31.

3

The frightened Irish went away in vessels that were soon to be called coffin-ships, most of them to America, where many of them died in the Southern swamps. They were called the Shanty Irish, because, being poor and accustomed to hovels, they took to shanties as if they were the natural habitation of people in distress. Some of them crossed the Irish Sea to Scotland and England where they were ill-received by working-men because they reduced the standard of life by taking low wages; though they were innocent of mean intention when they let themselves be thus exploited: for the wages they were offered seemed wealth to them. In a few years, the population of Ireland, which had almost doubled in the first forty years of the Union, rising from about 4½ millions to more than 8 millions, began to drop more rapidly than it had risen. To-day, despite the establishment of a republic, despite, too, a substantial increase in the population of the Six Counties, the population of all-Ireland is less than it was in 1800, and is still declining. In 1851, four years after The Famine had ended, the population, which had been 8,175,124 in 1841, had dropped to 6,552,385. More than 1½ million people had either perished in the Great Hunger or fled their country.

There were other elements of Irish life more deeply affecting Shaw's life than the recent Famine. He belonged to the ascendant minority, the Irish Protestants, who had been planted in the country and were in possession of landed property that had formerly been owned by the older and Roman Catholic population. This fact involved him in a deep social division from the mass of the people, a division which was not only created by difference of racial origin and religion, but by a long, haunting recollection of deprivation and robbery.

Ireland was, and still is, populated by three highly dissimilar groups of men and women whose intercourse is considerably less than that of any groups in, say, England. They are the Roman Catholics, most of them poor and agricultural; the Ascendancy, most of them Protestant and prosperous, though less so to-day than they were, and in any case, rapidly dwindling in number; and the Ulster Protestants who founded and maintain practically the whole of the industrial system of Ireland.

These three highly individualised groups despite the political and social changes in the last fifty years, still dominate the Irish scene. They prevailed with such severity when Bernard Shaw was born that they were, for the most part, strangers to each other. He belonged to the Southern Ascendancy, but to a socially declining section of it; and this fact had a profound influence on his whole life.

2

Lytton Strachey is said to have begun the singular biographical custom of treating a man's ancestors as if they were irrelevant to his career and character, and were generally unfit to be mentioned. This is a nonsensical custom since all of us are affected far more than we realise by our ancestors; and it will not be followed in this book, especially as Bernard Shaw, whom I shall call G.B.S. hereafter, to distinguish him from his father, was deeply influenced in mind and character by the remarkable collection of distinctive and dissimilar people from whom he sprang.

His parents, two totally incompatible people, brought remarkable strains into his immediate ancestry, strains so strong and diverse that it is a miracle he was not burst asunder by them. The Shaws gave him his wit and power to write,[1] as well as his business ability and his freedom from conventional attachments; and the Gurlys gave him his assurance of his own rightness and his disconcerting indifference to other people's opinions. It was from the Gurlys, not from the Shaws, that he drew the strain of hardness that was sometimes, surprisingly, found in his exceptionally generous mind and heart.

The Irish people, outside Ulster, despite their assumption of pseudo-democracy, are more class-conscious than any other race; and they possess in a high degree the form of inferiority complex which makes a subject people profess superiority to other and better men and women. This is the result of their history.

When a country is inhabited by a large group of people who have been deprived of their power and property, and a small group who have climbed to wealth and authority through conquest and confiscation, snobbery is certain to prevail in both; the first remembering the place from which they have been thrust, the second remembering the place from which they have sprung. When their division into a small group of expropriators and a large group of expropriated is allied to a deeper division, that of religious belief, the ground for separation by snobbery is enormously increased.

We shall see presently how humiliated G.B.S. felt when he was sent to a school in Dublin where the majority of the pupils were Papists. His humiliation was so profound that he not only refused to remain in the school, but concealed the fact that he had ever attended it until after the death of his wife, when he purged the gnawing

[1] 'My mother . . . had no comedic impulses, and never uttered an epigram in her life: all my comedy is a Shavian inheritance.' G.B.S. in the preface to *Immaturity*. He adds, however, that she 'had plenty of imagination'.

5

secret from his breast by public confession in *Sixteen Self Sketches*. This spirit was inherited from the proud Shaws and the prouder Gurlys.

3

The first Shaw to settle in Ireland was William, a captain in the army of William of Orange. He landed in the island about the year 1689, and was a man of mingled English and Scottish blood. William Shaw's grandson, Robert, became the owner of an estate, called Sandpits, in County Kilkenny, and this Shaw's great-grandson became the father of G.B.S.

The Shaws, who were remarkably prolific even in a period of excessive proliferation, were essentially middle-class and professional people, unlike the Gurlys, who belonged to the landed gentry, though their possessions in land were smaller than those of some of the Shaws, most of whom were lawyers, bankers, civil servants and clergymen; though they laid claim to distinguished ancestry which, however, could not be sustained. They thought they had descended from Oliver Cromwell and Shakespeare's Macduff!

The Gurlys considered them dull, but as the Gurlys were poor and unstable and not notably intelligent, they invented this misbelief to console themselves for their financial inferiority to people whom they considered socially beneath them, although they were, in fact, small fry among the landlords and were far less important, socially, politically, and professionally, than the Shaws.

The Shaws were far from dull. Some of them were exceptionally able, all of them were highly idiosyncratic and inclined to flout routine opinions. Their claim to have descended from the Thane of Fife who slew Macbeth amounted to no more than the claim any clansman in Scotland might make to be related to his chieftain; and their seemingly more substantial and certainly more interesting claim to descent from Cromwell through the marriage of his daughter Bridget to General Fleetwood, has been disproved.[1] The most unorthodox of G.B.S.'s relatives were the parsons. Two of them became notorious for their rebellious interference in public affairs.

One, the Rev. George Whitmore Carr, associated himself prominently with a Roman Catholic priest in a temperance crusade. It is true that the priest was Father Mathew, a sanctified man, superior to sect; but a Protestant minister was expected to be careful in associating with a priest who was not only compelled to doubt the validity of his orders, but had to regard him as an interloper in Irish life and immorally possessed of Roman Catholic property.

[1] In an article in the *Bath and Wilts Chronicle*, April 28, 1949

The second of the rebellious parsons was the Rev. William George Carroll, curate of St Bride's in Dublin,[1] who was G.B.S.'s uncle by marriage, in addition to being his second cousin. Carroll was the first minister of the Episcopal Church of Ireland to become a Home Ruler and a Republican, a conversion which required a great deal of moral courage in a man of his creed and cloth, and one, Mr Shaw told his son, which cost him the bishopric to which he could reasonably expect to have been appointed. He was reputed to have written leading articles in the Nationalist daily paper, *The Freeman's Journal*. Carroll was intimately associated with G.B.S.'s early life, for he not only celebrated the marriage of Mr and Mrs Shaw, and baptised their children, but taught G.B.S. the first Latin he learnt, the only Latin he remembered.

These unorthodox curates and turbulent rectors saved the Shaws from the conventionality which might have been expected to stultify a family so solidly and successfully founded. They brought healing into the pool of Bethesda by disturbing it.

In G.B.S.'s childhood, the Shaws, like minor luminaries, revolved round a great light. This was their rich bachelor relative, Sir Robert Shaw, the banker-baronet, who held court at his fine estate, Bushy Park, Rathfarnham, which was then outside Dublin, but is now one of its suburbs. Sir Robert, the second baronet, was the son of a notable father, also Sir Robert, who had represented New Ross in Grattan's Parliament, and had refused to be bribed into support of the Union. He eventually became member for Dublin in the Imperial Parliament. It was he who founded the Royal Bank of Ireland.

The second baronet, plump and wealthy, looked, according to Charles McMahon Shaw in *Bernard's Brethren*, like 'a truculent bear disturbed out of a doze,' and combined 'an arrogant air' with 'a curious look of assurance, like one who arms his sensitivity with a cruel exterior. It was certainly only an exterior cruelty, for he was a kind and honest gentleman.'

When he died on October 26, 1866, Bushy Park and the title passed to his brother Frederick, a very able and eloquent man, who was renowned for his integrity. He was Recorder of Dublin and sat in the Imperial Parliament as member, first, for Dublin, and second, for Dublin University, which is better known as Trinity College. In 1846, Peel offered him the post of Chief Secretary for Ireland, but ailing health forbade him to accept it. His second son married a

---

[1] The parish in which the church stood was formerly fashionable, but when its population ceased to be Protestant and opulent, and became Roman Catholic and poor, the purpose of the church as a church was over, and it was diverted to a secular function. Its registers, in which the marriage of G.B.S.'s parents and the birth of his sisters and himself were recorded, were removed to the Four Courts for safe custody, but they perished in the flames which destroyed that building during the Civil War in 1922.

Frenchwoman, became a General, and was the father of Flora Shaw (Lady Lugard), a famous correspondant of *The Times*.[1] Bushy Park remains in the possession of the Shaws, whose coat of arms carries the motto, *Te ipsum nosce* (Know thyself) an injunction which was better observed by G.B.S. than by any of his relatives.

4

George Carr Shaw, who was born on December 30, 1814, and died on April 18, 1885, was the eighth of the fifteen children borne in twenty-two years to Bernard Shaw by his wife, Frances, one of the numerous children of the Rev. Edward Carr, rector of Kilmacow, Co. Kilkenny.

This Bernard Shaw, according to his grandson and namesake, was 'a combination of solicitor, notary public, and stockbroker that prevailed at that time' in Dublin; and he inherited the original home of the Shaws, Sandpits. He became High Sheriff of Kilkenny, and seems, thereafter, to have neglected his profession in his ardour to perform his shrieval duties, for he was ruined when his partner decamped with, it is said, £50,000 of his money, together with large sums belonging to their clients. The shock was too much for the High Sheriff, who collapsed and died while he was seeking spiritual consolation from his brother, the Rev. Robert Shaw, leaving his widow and large family almost destitute.

It was fortunate for her children that their mother was made of sterner stuff than their father. She was a woman who could face adversity with fortitude, and was disinclined to run moaning to the Almighty with complaints about misfortune she herself had caused: a woman of vigorous mind and determined character, as her powerful and prominent nose denoted. How she maintained herself and her large family is not now known, but she retired from the grandeur of Sandpits and a shrieval life to a cottage with Gothic windows at Roundtown, near Terenure, not far from Bushy Park, which, like Rathfarnham, is now a Dublin suburb; and there, at the age of eighty-eight, she died in 1871.

The cottage was let to her rent free by Sir Robert, whom she is reputed to have refused in marriage, both before she became a wife and after she had become a widow; and it is possible that he made her an allowance, though G.B.S. thought that enough money was recovered from her husband's ruined estate to enable her to live unbeholden to anybody. Whatever her means of subsistence may have been, her eldest son, William Bernard, was able to enter Trinity College, Dublin, and to take holy orders.

[1] See her Life, *Flora Shaw*, by E. Moberly Bell.

George Carr Shaw who was twelve years old when calamity came upon his parents, grew up to be a genial, but ineffective man with a sardonic sense of humour and anti-climax: a gift which he transmitted to his son. Disaster, especially if it were financial, gave him a fit of the giggles. Like Charles Lamb, he could say, 'Anything awful makes me laugh!' He may never have been in danger of expulsion from a wedding service, as Elia was when Hazlitt married, but he came very near to misbehaving at a funeral, saving himself, unlike Lamb, just in time. He thought that funerals were funny, as, indeed, in those days, they were, when, that is to say, they were not frightful. He had little capacity to cope with the general traffic of existence, and as he considered himself to be a member of the Irish aristocracy and, therefore, under no obligation to earn his living in base and almost menial occupations, such as shop-keeping and retail trade, his relatives had difficulty in knowing what to do with him.

Having failed to impress two employers with his ability as a clerk, he decided that it was the duty of the Government to keep him in the style to which he considered he should have been accustomed; and so, through the influence of Sir Robert, he obtained a sinecure in the Dublin Law Courts, which did not impose upon him the ungentlemanly necessity of knowing anything about the law he was supposed to administer or even involve him in strict and regular attendance at his office.

Here he would probably have remained for the rest of his life had not unmannerly demagogues made such a row about his job that the Government abolished it in 1850. He was consoled for its loss by a pension of £60 a year, which was immediately commuted for £500. The money thus realised was invested in a corn mill, a wholesale, and therefore respectable, business, of which he knew even less than he had known of the law. His partner, a cloth merchant named George Clibborn, was as ignorant of corn milling as he was; and the result of their joint incompetence was that the firm of Clibborn and Shaw, with offices and warehouses in Jervis Street, Dublin, and a water mill at Dolphin's Barn, which never flourished at any time, almost foundered through the bankruptcy of its largest customer.

This disaster drew tears from Mr Clibborn's eyes, but Mr Shaw had his usual fit of the giggles. Impending bankruptcy, he thought, was almost as funny as a funeral and far funnier than a wedding. The mill, however, survived its peril, maintaining Mr Shaw, but not Mr Clibborn, for the rest of his life. Clibborn had wisely married a wealthy woman, and retired from all trade, wholesale or retail, living like a gentleman on his wife's income.

Mr Shaw was still short of thirty-eight when he met a wilful girl of twenty-one, who had a cold, unloving heart, a ferocious chin, and

9

a peculiar sense of humour which might be said to be no sense of humour at all; an unbiddable young woman whose face became less amiable as she grew older, as, indeed, it well might, considering how precarious and socially distressing her life with her husband, as Mr Shaw soon became, turned out to be. A disparity of nearly seventeen years between husband and wife is deplorable: it should either be much greater or much less; and when the disparity is between a slight and inefficient middle-aged man and a hard and unemotional girl, disillusionment and unhappiness seem certain to follow.

5

Lucinda Elizabeth Gurly, was born on October 6, 1830, and died on February 2, 1913.[1] She was the daughter of an improvident country gentleman with a small estate in County Carlow which was deeply embogged in debt. Walter Bagnal Gurly, who could never make up his mind about the correct spelling of his middle name, might have stepped out of the more fantastic pages of Charles Lever or Samuel Lover: a red-haired and unscrupulous sportsman who was better able to spend money than to save or earn it. He lived on mortgages, and was steadily descending to the lower level of Irish squireens.

Apart from sponging on his relatives or on anyone who was willing to lend him large sums of money on no security and with little or no prospect of repayment, the only means of living he knew was marriage. So he looked around for a respectful rich girl who was unlikely to ask awkward questions about her fortune after it had been dissipated.

His glance lit on Lucinda Whitcroft, one of the five successive Lucindas who figure in the Shaw history, whose father, John Whitcroft, of Highfield House, Rathfarnham and Kilree House, Co. Kilkenny, a property of 2,267 acres, differed in almost every respect from the traditional Irish landlord. He was wealthy, but not wasteful, a careful, acquisitive, but not ungenerous man, whose two daughters, as well as his son, would be dowered, not with debts, but with substantial sums. There was a romantic mystery about his birth. He belonged, it was said, to a very high-up family, but his parents had omitted to legalise their union.

How deeply he differed from his neighbours, and especially from Walter Bagnal Gurly, who was then living near him in Rathfarnham, will appear from the fact that, in addition to be a careful and efficient

[1] I am indebted to Dr F. E. Loewenstein, G.B.S.'s bibliographer, who made careful research into his genealogy, for this information, and also for the date of birth and death of George Carr Shaw on page 8. The Gurlys came originally from Cumberland, where their name was probably Gourlay. The first Gurly, like the first Shaw, to settle in Ireland was a Williamite.

landlord, he was also a semi-secret pawnbroker, although he was now withdrawing his name from several of the pawns he possessed.

Whitcroft's name was boldly advertised over a large pawnshop at 16, 18 and 19 Winetavern Street,[1] in Dublin, part of which stands and is still a pawn, although it is no longer in the possession of any member of Whitcroft's family: a cause for regret to some of them, who feel that it would be a valuable asset in these hard times.

Gurly, whose only previous contacts with pawnbrokers had probably been made while he was pledging portable property, was a-moral about money, and felt certain that thrifty people were cads. The purse of Croesus would not have been long enough or deep enough for him. He could have emptied the Bank of Ireland in a month. Whitcroft must have spent large sums in delusive efforts to keep him solvent; and he continued the struggle long after his daughter had perished in the attempt. He did what he could to safeguard Lucinda by forcing Gurly to assign his property in and around Carlow to trustees as part of her marriage settlement; and we shall presently see how he arranged a bequest to his grand-daughter, G.B.S.'s mother, and her children so that Gurly should not be able to dissipate it.

But this late Roman father had little respect for contracts and deeds, and took the simple view that his children's property, as well as his wife's, was his to dispose of as he pleased: a delusion which, fortunately for G.B.S. many years later, was successfully dispelled by a lawyer, though not before Gurly had made away with a substantial portion of it.

Lucinda, who was gentle and pretty, subservient and devoted to her extravagant and chronically impecunious husband, died on January 14, 1839, at the end of ten years of marriage. She was 37, and she left her husband one son, Walter John Gurly, the Rabelaisian uncle who figures so largely in G.B.S.'s reminiscences of his childhood, and one daughter, the firm-willed Lucinda Elizabeth, who had been schooled, according to her son, in a manner that made her virtually illiterate:

> 'Though she had been severely educated up to the highest standard for Irish "carriage ladies" of her time, she was much more like a Trobriand islander as described by Mr Malinowski than like a modern Cambridge lady graduate in respect of accepting all the habits, good or bad, of the Irish society in which she was brought up as part of an uncontrollable order of nature. . . . She had been tyrannously taught

[1] No. 17, which was the original portion of the shop, has been demolished and replaced by a brick building, differently used. There is a statue, looking very like that of Justice, except that the figure holds up three brass balls, outside 18 and 19. It bears the date, 1820, on its base, the year in which the business was founded at 17, the present buildings dating only from the year 1834.

French enough to recite one or two of Lafontaine's fables; to play the piano the wrong way; to harmonize by rule from Logier's Thoroughbass; to sit up straight and speak and behave like a lady, and an Irish lady at that. She knew nothing of the value of money nor of housekeeping nor of hygiene nor of anything that could be left to servants or governesses or parents or solicitors or apothecaries or any other member of the retinue, indoor and outdoor, of a country house.'[1]

Gurly's chief, perhaps his only, virtue seems to have been his love for his wife, whose nature was such that it would have been hard for anyone not to love her; and he remained a widower for twenty years, although he did not amend his wasteful ways. At the end of these twenty years of widowhood, he married Elizabeth Anne, the daughter of an insolvent neighbour, Simeon Clarke, a miller, who had nearly ruined him by failing to meet a bill which Gurly had foolishly backed.

Lucinda Elizabeth, by this time, had removed from her father's bailiff-infested house to live in Dublin with her mother's only sister, Miss Ellen Whitcroft, a hunchback with a pretty face and a fierce puritanical temper. Miss Whitcroft, whose means were less ample than her niece imagined, lived in a small, yellow-brown brick, two-storied house with a basement, in Palmerston Place, which still retains its faint air of gentility. It was to this pleasant, almost dainty place that Lucinda Elizabeth fled from the shabby pretences of her detested father's house: from the mortgages and duns, the writs and bailiffs, the wholy shoddy traffic of a collapsing house, owned and mismanaged by a feckless fool whose acres were swiftly disappearing in a quagmire of debt.

The pretty hunchback, serenely dreaming of a grandeur she herself would never enjoy, but which the firm-minded Lucinda Elizabeth, who had no nonsense about her, would obtain with ease if she would accept the guidance of her forceful aunt, laid plans for the conquest of a well-appointed peer. Her niece should never be escorted to balls and parties by penniless and untitled young men, no matter how brilliant and clever they might be. If a member of the nobility even though he were only an Irish peer and not entitled to a seat in the House of Lords, could not be persuaded to call for her in his well-sprung coach, driven by a man in magnificent livery and drawn by superb horses, champing at their bits, she should, at least, go to them escorted by a harmless, ineligible poor fellow with a squint, undoubtedly a gentleman, but in no way likely to stir the emotions of a spirited girl of twenty-one. This was George Carr Shaw.

It was a bitter blow to Aunt Ellen when she heard that Lucinda Elizabeth and he had become engaged to be married. Her vehement temper broke, and she stormed at her niece, who remained impeni-

[1] See Preface to *London Music in* 1888–9, Standard Edition, pp. 7–8.

tent until she received a revelation that startled and disturbed her. She had not been daunted when Aunt Ellen had threatened to cut her out of her will, but she was shattered when told that her intended husband was a notorious tippler. She flew to his lodgings—he was living in Lennox Street on the other side of the Liffey, close to the Grand Canal—and taxed him with his vice which he indignantly denied.

He was, he protested, a strict teetotaller, a statement which he believed to be true, since he not only tippled, as he thought, in secret, but was morbidly ashamed of his habit when he was sober. He belonged to the generation which imagined that port wine was a temperance beverage, innocuous as milk and very suitable for the refreshment of Rechabites; and he had convinced himself that when he slipped into a spirit-grocery shop and took half a glass of whiskey, he was not as those drunkards were who brazenly boozed in public-houses and were not ashamed to be seen drinking porter in open bars.

Lucinda Elizabeth, who found life in her Aunt Ellen's austere rooms almost as desolating as her life with her father had been, and was eager for a home of her own, believed him; and the engagement was maintained, despite Aunt Ellen's wrath and cancelled will.

Why did she engage herself to this elderly detrimental who had no qualities that could attract a young girl: an insignificant and entirely footling man? She did not love easily, if, indeed, she could love at all, and it is very certain that she had no feeling for George Carr Shaw that could be called love or even ordinary affection. Ireland was then, and still is, a country in which, outside Ulster, the passion of love is lightly esteemed. Money in marriage is the first and, frequently, the only passion. It is not unusual to meet, as the writer has done, a couple whose first meeting was at the altar on the day they were married. Lucinda Elizabeth could not have been affected by this absence of ardour in Irish wooings, for she was a Protestant gentlewoman, not a Roman Catholic peasant, and her lack of love, therefore, must have been due to some defect inherent in her nature. She was a cold girl, and she became a cold wife and mother.

Her refusal to break her engagement made the quarrel between her and Aunt Ellen complete; and she removed from Palmerston Place to the house of relatives in Stillorgan. Aunt Ellen sent for her lawyer and revoked her will, nor was she appeased when, a few years later, Lucinda Elizabeth took her small son to see her. The wrathful old lady died in January, 1862, and was buried beside her father and sister in Whitechurch graveyard. Her age was fifty-eight, and she left about £4,000, a much smaller fortune than G.B.S. had imagined she possessed, though it was a substantial sum in her time. None of it was bequeathed to her rebellious niece. G.B.S.'s first effort to conquer people by his personal charm had lamentably failed.

6

This was not the only quarrel Lucinda Elizabeth had at this time. There was another, almost as bitter, with her father. But in this quarrel, she was entirely innocent. Having heard that he was about to marry again, she casually mentioned the matter to her uncle, John Hamilton Whitcroft, a member of the Irish Bar, who had inherited a large part of his father's property, including the pawn-shops, and was as quick-tempered and arbitrary as his sister, Aunt Ellen. He became violently angry with his brother-in-law, whose impending marriage seemed to him worse than irresponsible: it was wanton, for he was not only deeply in debt to Whitcroft, who had undertaken the hopeless task of trying to keep him solvent, but was about to marry a woman without a penny piece to her name, the daughter of a man almost bankrupt and the cause of a financial crisis in Gurly's affairs.

So great was John Hamilton's fury that he had Gurly arrested for debt on the morning fixed for his wedding: an act which infuriated the bridegroom, now fifty-two years old, not against his brother-in-law, but against his daughter, who had, he believed, betrayed him to prevent the marriage. Whitcroft seems to have relented almost immediately, and the marriage was celebrated on May 25, 1852, at St Peter's Church in Dublin. Gurly's wrath with his daughter, however, was not instantly appeased, though it became cool enough for him to witness her marriage in the same church three weeks later, on June 17.

Aunt Ellen did not attend it, but she sent her niece a wedding present: a bundle of IOUs signed by her father, who, when they were shown to him, promptly put them in the fire. That debt discharged, he forbade his daughter to enter his house, a ban which did not much disturb her, for she had no desire to see the place again. He went further than forbidding her his house. He tried to deprive her of the bequest under her grandfather Whitcroft's will, by which her children, if she should have any, were to receive £5,000 between them.

Lucinda had what lawyers call a power of appointment over this bequest. It allowed her to use the interest on it and, with the consent of her children, to spend the capital sum as each of them came of age. By means which must have amounted to fraud, Gurly diverted £1,000 of the bequest to his own needs, and would have diverted the entire sum had not the solicitor consulted by Lucinda convinced him that he would land himself in gaol for a long period if he did not amend his monetary manners. He was shocked to hear that a man could not sequester his child's fortune when the fancy took him! . . .

Gurly figures in these pages no more. His second wife bore him a son, who died an infant, and six daughters. He lived uneventfully and, no doubt, on his old resource, the mortgage, until December 20, 1885, when he died at Monacurragh in County Carlow at the age of eighty-five. He had survived his son-in-law, George Carr Shaw, by eight months, but had not seen his daughter for at least fourteen years.

7

It is certain that Lucinda did not love her husband. But did he love Lucinda? He must have had some affection for her, but his nature was too slight for him to feel much emotion about anyone. Her unhappiness in her father's house and her Aunt Ellen's lodgings had made her eager, almost desperate, to escape from her thraldom. She was sharp-witted enough to realise that Miss Whitcroft's romantic hope that she would marry a peer was so improbable that it was certain never to be fulfilled. Mr Shaw, she believed, had a pension of £60 a year from the Government, and he was part owner of a corn mill.

The pension seems small to us. We toss that sum to an errand boy with apologies for offering him so little a wage. But it was a substantial sum in Ireland in 1852, where the scale of grandeur was so low that G.B.S. himself, when he wrote *Cashel Byron's Profession* in 1882, thought that thirty acres formed a large estate. Did not Miss Nora Reilly, in *John Bull's Other Island*, regard herself in 1904, as a great catch because she had a private income of £40 a year, a sum which, she was surprised to learn from Mr Larry Doyle, would not pay the wages of a cook in London?

A pension of £60 a year, in 1852, would certainly have seemed to a girl of twenty-one a very useful addition to the earnings of a wholesale corn miller. Lucinda did not know that the pension had been commuted so that the mill could be bought, nor did Mr Shaw feel obliged to mention the fact. The discussion of money with a refined and delicate female was distasteful to a well-bred man. He preferred to let her find out the facts of finance for herself when it was too late for her to do anything about them, or to leave such discussion as might be necessary to lawyers who had no delicacy about mentioning money or anything else. Lucinda, being the daughter of an Irish landlord, was accustomed to casual habits, especially where incomes and debts were concerned, and she took it for granted that a person of her sex should not soil her mind with squalid thoughts about cash.

Like Thomas Hardy, she had a horror of being touched; a horror of which her son was well aware when he came to write *You Never Can*

Tell and depict the character of Mrs Clandon. Demonstrations of affection were distasteful to her. She had the morbid delicacy which Clare Dedmond, in John Galsworthy's tragi-comedy, *The Fugitive*, possessed to a ruinous extent. She kept herself fastidiously to herself, yielding embrace neither to husband, child nor friend. Mr Shaw, always ready to retire to the corner, was an exceptionally undemanding man, who seldom asserted himself or fussed about anything. He must have seemed very restful to a girl who had endured an anxious and distressing life with her father and a cramped life with Aunt Ellen. The question of love did not enter into her marriage: the questions of escape and security and a home of her own, did.

Disillusionment was swift and dire. During the honeymoon, which was spent in Liverpool, a resort not usually sought by lovers in the first raptures of romance, the bride, opening a cupboard in the bedroom of the hotel, was horrified to find it full of empty bottles. This discovery, confirming Aunt Ellen and convicting Mr Shaw of lying, sent her running, almost frantically, to the Liverpool Docks with a vague intention of obtaining a job as stewardess on an Atlantic liner; but the familiarities she received from unmannerly dockers unnerved her, and sent her back in haste to her husband. The return to Dublin, we may surmise, was unhappy. The cold, hard young heart became colder and harder, and she announced herself an atheist.

Mr Shaw had rented a squat, two-storied house with a basement in Synge Street, a short distance from his lodgings, a house about the same size and shape as that in Palmerston Place where Aunt Ellen rented her rooms. It, too, was on the confines of Dublin, so near to them that fields still confronted half the street, though these were soon to be hidden from the residents by a hoarding which advertised, among other advantages of civilization, the benefits of pills, potions and porter.

In this shabby-genteel home, her dreams of freedom and splendour with the pensioned cousin of a wealthy banker-baronet were all dispelled; and here, in four years, her three children were born Lucinda Frances Carr, commonly called Lucy; Elinor Agnes, sometimes called Yuppy, the only member of the family who looked like a Gurly; and George Bernard, known as Sonny, though his father, when he was a baby, had called him Bob. It was a graceless house, ill-managed and impecunious. 'The adult who has been poor as a child', G.B.S. remarked late in life, 'will never get the chill of poverty out of his bones.' But he and his sisters had a sharper chill than poverty to bear: a home in which there was no love and little affection. It was ruled by a disillusioned young woman who had neither taste nor talent for domesticity, and was married to a furtive drunkard whom she despised: a 'throughother' house, as the Irish say, where

16

the meals were erratic and ill-cooked and monotonous, and the children were brought up in an untidy kitchen by slatternly servants. They had a nurse, even a peripatetic governess, Miss Caroline Hill, a distressed gentlewoman who was paid by the hour; education by piece work. Those were the days when servants were overworked and underpaid. The Shaws paid theirs £8 a year, three shillings a week, plus bed and board. The pay was small, but the services rendered for it were not worth their reward.

These children had no love from their mother, who felt such contempt for her husband that she may have withheld her love from them because they were *his*. The fact that her son physically resembled his father seemed to make her more antipathetic to him than she was to his sisters. Once, in a rare mood of bitterness, G.B.S. asserted that he had been begotten after a brawl when his father was fuddled with drink. If this were true, his conception must have been a humiliation to the proud, hard-natured mother. Yet she had some particle of common tenderness for her child; for Lucy, going through her effects after her death in 1913, found 'the cap I used to wear as a baby', G.B.S. wrote to Mrs Patrick Campbell, adding, 'Had anyone suggested such a possibility, I should have laughed him (or her) to scorn. We never know anything about our parents.'[1]

'Technically speaking,' her son wrote in the preface to *London Music*, 1888–1889, 'I should say she was the worst mother conceivable, always, however, within the limits of the fact that she was incapable of unkindness to any child, animal or flower, or, indeed, to any person or thing whatsoever:' a statement which seems to suggest that neglect and incompetence and a total lack of love and affection are not culpable and need not be denounced.

But a person who dislikes apples is not virtuous because he never rifles an orchard.

Lucinda Elizabeth may have been incapable of unkindness to any creature, but she was also, her son asserts by implication, incapable of positive kindness. 'She did not hate anybody,' he says in *Sixteen Self-Sketches*. 'The specific maternal passion awoke in her a little for my younger sister, who died at 20; but it did not move her until she had lost her, and then not noticeably.' She was, in short, devoid of human qualities. 'We children', G.B.S. says in *London Music*, 1888–1889, 'were abandoned entirely to servants who . . . were utterly unfit to be trusted with the charge of three cats, much less three children. I had my meals in the kitchen, mostly of stewed beef, which I loathed, badly cooked potatoes, sound or diseased as the case might be, and much too much tea out of brown delft teapots left to "draw" on the hob until it was pure tannin.'

[1] *Bernard Shaw and Mrs Patrick Campbell. Their Correspondence.* p. 111

Such was the home in which the Shaw children were reared. It had, undoubtedly, happy times, for children are extraordinarily resilient and snatch eagerly at happiness, no matter how determined their parents are to prevent them from enjoying it. We come across references to such times in odd places. In a letter to Mrs Patrick Campbell, G.B.S. says 'I used to write letters for Irish servants when I was a child,' obviously from dictation, as the sample he sends her demonstrates. 'Dear mother I hope you are well as this letter leaves me at present thank God for it dear mother I saw Bridget on Friday and she desires to be remembered to you dear mother I hope you got the flannel petticoat safely dear mother! . . .'[1]

This habit denotes some warmth of feeling between him and the servants: he would not have been asked to write the letters if there had not been any warmth. But his childhood was starved of affection, and the mark it left on his mind was dark and deep. He seldom refers to his infancy without bitterness. In a note to Mrs Ada Tyrrell written in 1942, when he was eighty-six, he still remembered it unhappily. 'The way we were brought up, or rather not brought up, doesn't bear thinking of,' and in an earlier note to her in 1928, he tells her that 'except in my secret self, I was not happy in Dublin; and when ghosts arise from that period, I want to lay them again with the poker.' Writing to Ellen Terry when he was over forty and still living with his mother, bitter remembrance of it made him cry out, 'Oh, a devil of a childhood, Ellen, rich only in dreams, frightful and loveless in realities.' Sixteen years later, writing to Mrs Campbell, he recurs to his childhood:

> 'What was done to me in my childhood was nothing at all of an intentional kind. I wasn't spoiled; and I wasn't helped. No direct ill treatment was added by anybody to the horrors of the world. Nobody forbade me to discover what I could of its wonders. I was taken—and took myself—for what I was: a disagreeable little beast. Nobody concerned himself or herself as to what I was capable of becoming, nor did I. I did not know I was different from other people (except for the worse); far from being conceited, I hadn't even common self-respect. I have discovered all my powers from the outside, with incredulous astonishment, or rather I have discovered that everybody else hasn't got them. My shyness and cowardice have been beyond all belief.'[2]

The kindest thing he said about Dublin appeared in a quarterly review entitled *Courier*, where he wrote 'There's nothing wrong with it except its slums with their shocking vital statistics and the perpetual gabble of its inhabitants.'

[1] *Bernard Shaw and Mrs Patrick Campbell. Their Correspondence.* p. 48.
[2] Ib. pp. 52–3.

Can we feel surprised at his denunciation of mothers in his plays? When *Man and Superman* was first publicly performed in England, audiences were shocked and horrified by John Tanner's outburst against them, and every time the play is revived, there is an uneasy movement in the theatre when he delivers his complaint. The heart knows its own bitterness, and G.B.S., despite the curious and dispassionate admiration he felt for his mother, expecially in her later years, never forgot for a moment the misery of his childhood or her responsibility for it. The testimony of those who knew her when he was a boy, supports his, which is sometimes thought to be overdrawn and dramatised. Lady Thompson, who was a playmate of the Shaw children, her mother being Mrs Shaw's friend and resident in the next street to Synge Street, informed the writer that 'Lucy and her brother held their mother in veneration, but with no love. Lucy used to tell us her mother was shrewd and fearless, but difficult to love.'

In justice to this extraordinary woman, it must be stated that her step-niece, Mrs Musters, who lived with her for a number of years, had great affection for Mrs Shaw and is distressed by suggestions that she was cold, hard, unloving and unlovable. It is indisputable that she had charm and grace which overcame even those who encountered her casually. Sydney (afterwards Lord) Olivier, in his autobiography, refers to her with admiration, and G.B.S., in an extraordinary letter to Mrs Patrick Campbell, written immediately after Mrs Shaw's cremation, tells a story which confirms the feeling Mrs Musters felt for her.

> 'The undertaker approached me in the character of a man shattered with grief; and I, hard as nails and in loyally high spirits (rejoicing irrepressibly in my mother's memory), tried to convey to him that this professional chicanery, as I took it to be, was quite unnecessary. And lo! it wasn't professional chicanery at all. He had done all sorts of work for her for years, and was actually and really in a state about losing her, not merely as a customer, but as a person he liked and was accustomed to. And the coffin was covered with violet cloth—not black.'

What a singular woman she was, able to stir liking in a casual tradesman, unable to give any love to her son. She developed some sort of maternal feeling late in life, and Mrs Musters enjoyed the benefit of it; but there appears to be little doubt that G.B.S. and his sisters never received any of the love that is a child's right. The explanation is simple: a cold woman with a deep aversion from all demonstration of affection, her natural dislike of such demonstrations intensified by her deep disdain for her shiftless husband and her disgust at the thought that she had conceived children by him. It turned her away from her son and daughters as surely as it turned her away from her husband.

8

The gentility of their home was overpowering. If the Shaws mixed with their neighbours at all, they did so only on clearly defined terms of condescension. The easy-going, unassertive father was not less strict on this subject than the firm-minded and emphatic mother. Catching his son in conversation with the child of a retail ironmonger, Mr Shaw rebuked him severely. The fact that the ironmonger was a richer man than the wholesale corn miller aggravated his offence. It was subversive of all civilised society that a man who probably sold tenpenny nails across his counter, should be better off than one who claimed to be descended from the Thane of Fife and the Lord Protector of England, and was, indisputably, related to the second baronet, Sir Robert Shaw.

But the characteristics of this ill-assorted house were not all disadvantageous. If the meals were casual and ill-cooked and likely to be composed of decaying cabbage, dubious potatoes, emetics and tea, and if there was no love or ordinary affection in the house, there were music and good conversation. Like Caliban's island, it was full of noises, sounds and sweet airs that gave delight and hurt not; and every person who frequented it could sing or play an instrument. The Shaws were known to be musical, though there was nothing remarkable about them, either as instrumentalists or as persons of musical taste, but there was no history of any culture, and certainly none of music, among the Gurlys. They were merely small landowners, little more than large-scale farmers; and there is nothing in her ancestry to account for the remarkable love of music Mrs Shaw possessed.

There was undesigned advantage, too, in being neglected, though there was none in being badly fed. These children, almost totally disregarded by their mother, who might have imposed her powerful personality upon them and made them too dependent upon her, and avoiding a father who was almost certain to return from his mill muzzy with drink, were compelled to develop their character themselves and to make their own lives and minds. Like Leonardo da Vinci, Shakespeare, Sheridan, Byron, Shelley, Dickens, Thackeray, Florence Nightingale, Queen Victoria, Edward VII, Ibsen and H. G. Wells, Bernard Shaw found his feet because he had feckless or neglectful parents. If there is any lesson to be derived from family history, it is that a child who receives insufficient care and love is as likely to become a genius as a child who receives too much. It was better to be Bernard Shaw than John Ruskin. William Morris was certain that of all the guardians a child could have, its parents were probably the worst. In this belief, G.B.S. concurred.

What do our eugenics amount to if genius can be born to people seemingly so unfitted to be parents as George Carr and Lucinda Elizabeth Shaw?

9

Mr Shaw's tippling habits seem not to have been noticed by his son until the boy was well past the age at which they would certainly have been observed by a less remarkable child. One evening, he took Sonny for a walk along a bank of the Grand Canal, and, feeling jocular, threatened to throw him into the water, and, in a clumsy pretence, very nearly did. This incident opened Sonny's eyes. 'Mamma,' he said on his return home, 'I think papa is drunk!' and was amazed to hear her reply, 'Ah, when is he anything else?' The disillusionment of a child is a bitter experience, and is never forgotten.

Many years later, when sentimentalists accused him of dishonouring his father, G.B.S. retorted angrily that neither his mother nor her children had ever thought intoxication funny. His memory of his father's tippling was long and deep, and it made him a fanatical teetotaller.

Once, while scrambling over rocks in the West of Ireland, he slipped on wet seaweed and twisted his ankle. His wife hurried off to the village for a doctor, and was unfortunate enough to meet one who had recently read *The Doctor's Dilemma*, and was in no mood to put himself out for its author. Luckily for himself, however, he agreed to accompany her to the rocks; luckily, because Charlotte would have torn him limb from limb if he had not. They went by boat, because Charlotte thought it would be easier to bring G.B.S. back by sea than by land. Lest his pain should be too much for him, she bought a small bottle of brandy to stimulate him; and was almost overwhelmed by his wrath when she suggested that he might relax his rule of total abstinence for once. Yet he tasted her wine, though he swallowed none of it, because, he said, his palate was purer than any carnivorous person's could possibly be, and he was able, therefore, to save her from being poisoned by a mixture of red ink and corrosive acid. His talk about drunkenness might sometimes be wildly comic, and often was, but never for a second of his life after that day of dreadful discovery by the Grand Canal, did he think that it was funny in itself.

Mr Shaw's chronic intoxication made Dublin a desert for his family. Amiable enough when he was sober, the miller lost his temper easily when he was drunk, and could not endure contradiction. A doubt or an enquiry was enough to make him smash anything breakable that might be lying about; and this habit rendered him unwelcome at parties, even at those given by his relatives. Because he was excluded from them, his wife and children felt themselves obliged to be excluded, too. The two girls and their young brother huddled apprehensively in the kitchen, hoping that their father would be sober when he came home from his mill.

But there was music in the house. Lucinda Elizabeth, who possessed a mezzo-soprano voice of remarkable purity, had become acquainted with a lame musician, George John Vandaleur Lee, a teacher of voice production by unorthodox methods, and the leader of a Dublin orchestra. Because of his unorthodoxy and the frankness with which he spoke of his routine rivals, he was generally unpopular; but his adherents treated him with great respect and deference. Lee lived with an invalid brother and a tyrannous housekeeper, old Ellen, in Harrington Street, the main thoroughfare off which Synge Street runs. The house was only a few minutes' walk from the Shaws'. It was he who produced Mrs Shaw's fine voice, and it was because of his success with her, no doubt, that The Method—the term always used by his followers in referring to his system—was mentioned in her house in hushed tones that could not have been more reverential if they had been applied to the holy and undivided Trinity.

He had a limited vogue in G.B.S.'s childhood, but is now known only because he is mentioned in several of G.B.S.'s prefaces. There is no account of him in any biographical work of reference, not even in Grove's *Dictionary of Music and Musicians;* and all efforts to obtain information about his birthplace and nationality have failed. Lee was, undoubtedly, a man of some authority among musicians in Dublin, but he had little or no authority elsewhere. He played a considerable part, however, in the early life of G.B.S.

There was another family in Harrington Street, Shaws, too, but unrelated to G.B.S.'s family, with whom Lucinda Elizabeth became friendly: Dr and Mrs G. F. Shaw. This Mrs Shaw, G.B.S. wrote to her daughter Ada or Addie, in 1940, was:

'A very remarkable woman who would have filled a larger place in a larger world than that into which she dropped. Her scale of values was not that of Harrington Street. Also she was a siren, and, as such, could not be confined within the ordinary circle of home interests. Apparently, your father could not reconcile himself to being only one among so many men whom she interested and in whom she was interested; and so the household went to pieces, leaving her in freedom which was rather barren because she had not duties enough to balance her privileges. But why bother about her? Children never know anything about their parents; and I don't think their occasional attempts to reconstruct them after death are ever quite successful. I do not remember any characters in my books and plays modelled consciously on your mother. I always had a vision of her as the mother of Cashel Byron in an early novel of mine, called *Cashel Byron's Profession* (he was a prizefighter); but it was a visual impression mostly. Still, now you mention it, I daresay the visual impression led to a touch of caricature from the living model here and there. . . .

My life has rushed through very quickly: I have seen very little of anyone who has not worked with me. Except with my wife, I have no companionships: only occasional contacts, intense but brief. I spring to intimacy in a moment, and forget in half an hour. An empty life is peopled with the absent and the imagined: a full one has to be cleared out every day by the housemaid of forgetfulness or the air would become unbreathable. Those who see me now are those who shove and insist and will not take no for an answer, with, of course, the great people who must be seen because they have earned a right of entry everywhere. . . .'

The friendship between G.B.S.'s mother and Mrs G. F. Shaw was repeated in a friendship between his elder sister, Lucy, and Mrs Shaw's eldest daughter, Ada, commonly called Addie, whom Lucy generally addressed as Barnacle.[1]

This friendship began with a brawl about washing. The two families employed the same laundress, and a table-cloth belonging to the Harrington Street Shaws had been sent in error to the Shaws of Synge Street. Addie, the eldest daughter of the Shaws in the superior street, whose age was twelve, was sent to reclaim it, but G.B.S.'s sister, Lucy, also aged about twelve, resisted the claim, and there was a fight on the doorstep. Nevertheless, a friendship was begun which lasted for life, and the two families were familiar as long as they both lived in Dublin, and continued in some association thereafter.

Addie Shaw's daughter, Lady Hanson, repeating her mother's reminiscences of this period, remarks that G.B.S.'s mother was 'rather inscrutable', and that Lucy was 'the master mind of the group of young people' with whom she played, 'daring and independent'.

'There was a little boy—George Bernard. He wore a holland tunic and went by the name of Sonny. He was always rather apart from the others and would be seen sitting at the piano, picking out airs with one finger or absorbed in the construction of a toy theatre.'

[1] Addie married Professor Robert Yelverton Tyrrell, Regius Professor of Greek in Trinity College, Dublin. She died at Budleigh Salterton at the house of her daughter, Lady Thompson, on January 1, 1955, in her 101st year.

The least conspicuous member of the Synge Street Shaws was the second daughter, Agnes, who, Addie, when she was a very old woman, remarked, 'was plain, with ugly red hair and a dry humour at times, but, as a rule, quiet', the only member of the family who was a Gurly in looks, resembling her Uncle Walter, the Rabelaisian doctor. But Yuppy was already 'delicate', as the Irish say of the consumptive, and her life was to be short.

10

Music was the chief entertainment, almost the chief occupation of the Shaws of Synge Street, and here, especially on Sunday nights, people came to sing and play. Lee was in control, and Protestants and Roman Catholics mingled melodiously.

'My first doubt as to whether God could really be a good Protestant,' G.B.S. wrote in T. P. O'Connor's weekly paper, *M.A.P.* (Mainly About People) for September 17, 1898:

> 'was suggested by the fact that the best voices available for the combination with my mother's in the works of the great composers had been unaccountably vouchsafed to Roman Catholics. Even the Divine gentility was presently called in question; for some of these vocalists were undeniably shopkeepers. If the best tenor, undeniably a Catholic, was at least an accountant, the buffo was a frank stationer. There was no help for it: if my mother was to do anything but sing silly ballads in drawing rooms, she had to associate herself on an entirely unsectarian footing with people of like artistic gifts without the smallest reference to creed or class. She must actually permit herself to be approached by Roman Catholic priests, and at their invitation to enter that house of Belial, the Roman Catholic Chapel, and sing the Masses of Mozart there. If religion is that which binds men to one another, and irreligion that which sunders, then must I testify that I found the religion of my country in its musical genius, and its irreligion in its churches and drawing rooms.'

The final statement is made in disregard of the fact that his mother found the tolerance in a *church* of a creed that was not her own. She might well have wondered whether a Roman Catholic mezzo-soprano would have been permitted by her spiritual director to sing in a Protestant church.

The Shaws had, at this time, an affectation of indifference to class and creed which they believed to be sincere. Lucinda Elizabeth had abandoned the faith of her fathers and declared herself an atheist. By the time G.B.S. was ten, all pretence of church going had ended in his family, and he had begun to hear a great deal of very frank conversation and debate not only on sectarian dissensions, but on the

Christian faith itself. The shocks his mother had sustained since her flight from Aunt Ellen's genteel lodgings had discomposed her in many different ways, and she was a deeply disappointed young woman.

'My mother', her son was to write of her, 'was embittered because she expected money to be left to her and it didn't happen, and we all suffered for it.' But they would not have had to suffer for it, had her marriage been a happy one. The disparity in age between a girl of twenty-one and a man of thirty-eight is far greater than the disparity between a woman of forty and a man of fifty-seven; and when the man is insignificant and a tippler, it is greater still. The single consolation Lucinda Elizabeth had in the first years of her marriage and maternity was her music, of which, until she met Lee, she seems not to have been much aware.

In this upheaval of beliefs and habits, the fact that a good tenor or a fine pianist was a Roman Catholic when a discriminating deity might have been expected to make him a sound Episcopalian, became unimportant. But only to a limited extent. For although the Papists came to Mrs Shaw's house to musical parties, Mrs Shaw did not go to theirs. It is doubtful, indeed, if she or any of her children ever entered the house of a Roman Catholic in Dublin as a guest; though her children probably were taken into the home of their Roman Catholic nurse. The social separation of the sects was as rigid as that of Christians and Moslems in Syria.

But the consolations of music did not come immediately after Lucinda Elizabeth's marriage. She had babies to bear. Lucy was born on March 26, 1853; Agnes in 1855;[1] and G.B.S. on July 26, 1856. When their son was old enough to be present at the musical parties, he seemed to his elders to be a quiet, unobtrusive and studious boy who listened so attentively to what he heard that he was able to boast, before he was fifteen, that he 'knew at least one important work by Handel, Mozart, Beethoven, Mendelssohn, Rossini, Bellini, Donizetti, Verdi, and Gounod from cover to cover.'

His formal education, apart from his instruction by Miss Caroline Hill and the Latin he learnt from his clerical uncle, Mr Carroll, was, he fiercely declared in after life, entirely useless.

In 1867, when he was eleven, he entered the Wesley Connexional School, now known as the Wesley College, on the south side of St Stephen's Green, where he was 'generally near or at the bottom of the class', and seemed to his preceptors, most of whom were filling in the time before ordination as Methodist ministers, to be an incorrigible dunce, 'a source of idleness in others, distracting them from their

[1] Mr John O'Donovan discovered the date of Lucy's birth in *Saunders's News-Letter* of March 29, 1853, but all efforts to find the date of Agnes's birth have been unavailing.

studies by interminable comic stories' about a character called Lobjoit which he himself had invented, although the character's name was taken from a tale in Dickens's magazine, *Household Words*.

This pastime does not indicate unhappiness in school. A miserable boy does not enliven his schoolmates by telling them funny stories. Nor was he always at the bottom of the class. Because of his uncle Carroll's instruction, he knew more Latin than any boy in his first form at Wesley; and there was an occasion when he jumped up suddenly to the second place because of an unexpected display of Biblical knowledge. This was the occasion when he revealed his own character very clearly by telling the dazed master that he did not want the second place, as it merely proved that there was a boy who knew more than he did.

His industry in occupations where his attention was stimulated was immense. He was invariably at the top of his class or close to it when he went, later on, to a school in Aungier Street. He was not idle in his study of music or pictures. A Dublin musician, Joseph Robinson, allowed him to borrow, a volume at a time, Duchesne's outlines of the old masters, about twenty of them, and when he had the money, he bought the Bohn translation of Vasari's volumes. This application was inherited from his mother, who was utterly inefficient in matters which did not interest her, but worked hard at matters which did: music, for example.

There was no labour in music which she was not glad to undertake. Lee:

> 'taught her to sing; and she sang for him; copied orchestral parts for him; scored songs, etc., for him (she had learnt thoroughbass from old Logier); led the chorus for him; appeared in operas he got up (she played Azucena in Il Trovatore, Donna Anna in Don Giovanni, Margaret in Gounod's Faust, and Lucrezia Borgia in Donizetti's opera of that name): and as they were all rehearsed in our house, I whistled and sang them from the first bar to the last whilst I was a small boy, not to mention all the oratorios got up by the musical society. . . .'[1]

She sang in church choirs, and she is said to have composed the music for several drawing-room ballads, although I have not been able to trace them. Both Lady Hanson and Lady Thompson can recall songs she composed, one of them being entitled *Silver Music Ringing*. Lady Hanson, when I enquired about these compositions, wrote to me that she was quite sure that Mrs Shaw composed and published songs. 'I could this moment play for you one of her compositions which my aunt Constance Shaw often sang to my accompaniment. It finished "Love is God's bell ringing Thro' the spirit night," ' a singular con-

[1] Extracted from a letter to Archibald Henderson and published by him in *Bernard Shaw: Playboy and Prophet*, p. 45.

clusion to be made by a woman with so little love as Lucinda Elizabeth possessed.

G.B.S. and his mother were exceptionally industrious in matters which absorbed them, but inert and diffident in matters which did not. 'I cannot learn anything that does not interest me,' he says in the preface to *Immaturity*. But he was antlike in his eagerness to master the things that did.

Despite the harsh report of his masters at Wesley, he was, in several respects, more cultured, better educated and more widely read than any other person, teacher or pupil, in the school. In music alone, he was superior to them all, and he had seen the pictures in the National Gallery of Ireland so often that he 'knew enough of a considerable number of painters' to recognise their work at sight. His father, who read nothing but newspapers, encouraged him in his liking for literature, and he read not only those that a normal lad generally reads: Scott's novels, *The Pilgrim's Progress*, Dickens, and *The Arabian Nights;* but also works which a normal lad would denounce as dull or unreadable. These included William Robertson's *History of Charles the Fifth* and his *History of Scotland*. On hearing a school-fellow boast that he had read Locke's *On the Human Understanding*, he decided to surpass him by 'reading the Bible straight through', and got as far as the Pauline Epistles before he broke down in disgust at what appeared to him their inveterate crookedness of mind: though this disgust was, we may believe, an afterthought in later life.

His entrance to Wesley College had been preceded by a change for the better in the economic circumstances of his home. Mr Shaw's income was small. His son never knew what it was, but surmised that it must always have been about 'three figures': an estimate which may mean anything between £99 and £1,000, and certainly did not mean the latter sum. It was probably between £200 and £300 a year, and nearer to the second sum than the first.

About the year 1866, when G.B.S. was ten, Lee, whose invalid brother, much to Lee's distress, had died, proposed to the Shaws that he and they should share a larger house in a more select street, and they thereupon removed to No. 1, Hatch Street, a four-storied house with a basement, which was a short distance from the two-storied basement house in Synge Street, but nearer to the centre of the city and close to St Stephen's Green. Here they were joined not only by Lee, but by Lucinda Elizabeth's brother, Walter, now a ship's surgeon, who lived with them between voyages. A walk of less than fifteen minutes would have brought G.B.S. to Merrion Square, where a boy, two years his senior, lived in a very grand house. This was Oscar Wilde, whose acquaintance, however, G.B.S. did not make until about twenty years later in London. Oscar's father, Sir William

Wilde, had operated on Mr Shaw's squint, but had only shifted it from one side of the eye to the other. This was the sole contact the Shaws had with the Wildes in Ireland, and it did not make for cordial relations.

Lee also bought Torca Cottage at Dalkey, which the Shaws were invited to inhabit whenever they liked. It overlooked Killiney Bay, and was well within view of the Wicklow and Dublin Mountains: a very beautiful and delightful place in which to live; and here G.B.S. first became aware of natural beauty and was exalted by it, though its influence did not last into his manhood, when his mind became increasingly concerned, almost to the exclusion of all other beauty, with intellectual activity. In a letter written to a lady in 1907, he says, 'I dare say Dalkey is actually and really and prosaically a stupid little suburban seaside place, but to me it is wonderland. Though you would not suppose so from my present appearance, I was once a boy, apparently disreputable and worthless, but a prince in the world of my own imagination. . . . When I was in those gardens they commanded all the kingdoms of the earth, all the regions of the sky, and all the ages of history. I once described the place to an English lady in such terms that she went to Ireland to see it, and was unspeakably disgusted at the piffling reality that confronted her.' But what child has not transformed some such place as Dalkey into romantic dreamland!

By this time, the vague atheism which Lucinda Elizabeth had announced, had become vaguer. Church-going ended, but dabblings in spiritualism began. Her atheism had not prevented her from having her children baptised, though they were never confirmed. This, however, was probably more deference to convention than to religion. Yet the planchette she manipulated when her son was ten—it was one of the first planchettes to be seen in Ireland—seems to suggest a belief in another life, and her preoccupation with the spirits continued throughout the rest of her life.

How far she was genuinely dissevered from Christianity is hard to determine. The stone over the grave of her daughter Agnes in the churchyard of Ventnor ends with the inscription, 'With Christ which is far better', one which certainly does not indicate that the person responsible for it was either an atheist or a recusant from Christianity. It may be that Mr Shaw had the stone erected, but as he did not attend his daughter's funeral and never visited Ventnor in his life and was not himself a pious man, this possibility seems unlikely. The young girl's death may have evoked a latent religious emotion in her mother, but this is surmise in a matter where fact cannot be proved.

Lee's advent to the Shaw household was less pleasing to the Shaw children than it was to their parents, and especially to their mother, who liked his money and his music. His sense of humour was elementary, and he had a habit, repulsive to children, of treating them as animated toys. His idea of a joke was to 'decorate' G.B.S.'s 'face with moustaches and whiskers in burnt cork in spite of the most furious resistance' he 'could put up'. Lucy, who derived the greatest benefit from his residence in Hatch Street, because he took great trouble with her voice and developed it into one of considerable beauty, detested Lee, who had fallen in love with her and was ardent in his attentions, all of which, except for his singing lessons, she disliked.

He was unattractive to women, and especially to girls, for he was lame, wore his hair in a way which made it look like a wig, was limited in his outlook on life, and was very vain. His smile was a smirk, a slight disarrangement of the long, hard line of his mouth; his chin was deep and graceless; and his black whiskers curled round his cheeks like a well-starched collar with points as sharp as bayonets. But he had alert, bright eyes that glanced about in a quick, enquiring, gipsy fashion; and he dominated his friends and associates. No one now knows what was his origin, but his looks and his surname suggest that he may have come from gipsy stock.

G.B.S., in his own opinion, had greater cause for complaint against Lee than his elder sister had; for it was Lee who suggested that he should be sent to the Central Model School in Marlborough Street. He had not only left the Wesley Connexional School because his uncle, the curate of St Bride's, said he was learning nothing and forgetting all he had known, but had also left 'a very private school in Glasthule, between Kingstown and Dalkey, kept by a family named Halpin.' This school, however, was attended only during holidays at Torca Cottage.

Lee's suggestion that he should be sent to the Central Model School was never forgotten or forgiven. To understand why, it is essential to remember that there are only two substantial sectarian differences in Ireland, and that they are complicated by social, political and economic differences. In Ireland a person is either a Protestant or a Roman Catholic: all else is largely irrelevant. G.B.S. was nominally a member of the Episcopal Church of Ireland, though no one in his home attended a place of worship; but this fact did not prevent him from attending a school where all the teachers were either Methodist ministers or ordinands. The Shaws, being Episcopalians, were members of the Ascendancy, and considered themselves to be members of the aristocracy, despite their enforced residence in a shabby-genteel street in Dublin. Their musical meetings, at which Protestants and Papists mingled amiably, did not dissipate their sense of superiority to Roman Catholics, and it was sufficiently strong for their son to feel humiliated when he was sent to the Central

Model School, which, though nominally non-sectarian, was, in fact, Roman Catholic, since the majority of its pupils belonged to that denomination. How mortified he felt by his incarceration in this school, for incarceration is what he believed it to be, will be plain to those who read his reference to it in *Sixteen Self-Sketches*.

It is the only school he attended which is not mentioned in any other autobiographical fragments he wrote, and he seems not to have made a single friend in it, or even to have remembered anyone connected with it.

There can be little hope of making people who have not lived in Ireland realise the poignancy of the boy's plight when he discovered what sort of a school the Central Model was. Tell a high-caste Indian that it is absurd to throw away his food because it has been contaminated by the shadow of an Untouchable, and you will receive the look of scorn and contempt that you would have received from Sonny Shaw had you told him that he was a snob for behaving as he did. An Etonian does not feel as far removed from a Borstal Boy, though the difference between them is not always perceptible, as a boy of G.B.S.'s class and creed felt at being a pupil in the Central Model School, mixing on terms of equality with Micks!

His antipathy to the school was so great that after he had attended it for about seven months, he refused to return, and was removed to the Dublin English Scientific and Commercial Day School, at the corner of Aungier and Whitefriars Street, an institution with a curriculum which was less imposing than its title; and here he remained until, in his fifteenth year, he became a clerk in an estate agents' office.

II

In reading G.B.S.'s diatribes against his schools and teachers, it is well to bear in mind that they were written in his middle manhood and old age, and may have been derived more from his theories about education than from his experience of it. He refers habitually to schools as if they were concentration camps or penitentiaries, and to masters as if they were brutal warders or sadistic commandants. In his account of his schools in *Sixteen Self-Sketches*, he says, 'At the Wesleyan I had never dreamt of learning my lessons, nor of telling the truth to that common enemy and executioner, the schoolmaster.'

This fantastic tosh reads like the remark of a man so far removed from his boyhood by age and ideas that have long ceased to have any relevance to known facts that even his reminiscences have become romantic figments. To say this is not to deny that G.B.S. disliked formal education or what was considered to be formal education. It is merely to remind the reader that he probably attributed to Sonny Shaw, the nervous and sensitive boy who was starved of affection at home, the horror of schools which he had developed long after he had left them, which was, indeed, the result of his rebellion against society in general and the views he formed in the Fabian Society, though these were not views that the Webbs, for example, could ever have shared.

The reader, too, must be on guard against a belief that G.B.S. was unhappy in the Wesley School because he was a shy, reclusive child. He seemed quiet to adults at his mother's musical parties, but what else could a boy who liked to listen to music have been? His grievance against the Central Model School was social in its origin. If the majority of the pupils who attended it had been as Protestant as the boys at the Wesley School, would he have made bitter complaint against it? His readers are given no cause to think that he would. He had little, if any, unhappiness at his last school, though it was no better, if no worse, than Wesley. We may believe that he exaggerated his hatred of his schools and schoolmasters, and that his discontent in them, when it was free from the taint of snobbery, was no more than the resentment many active-minded lads feel against authority, discipline and instruction. His quietness was not a sign of inanimation. 'I was rampant, voluble, impudent,' he told Dr Archibald Henderson, 'and I cannot remember ever being physically tired as a boy', an assertion which suggests that his diet must have been more nourishing than his account of it leads the reader to believe, though he was probably referring to the Lee period when he was better fed than he had been in Synge Street. As he was a day boy at all these schools, he did not suffer from the bullying by elder boys which has made many nervous youngsters dread their dormitories. There is no hint in his reminiscences that he suffered from bullying. He was not the sort of boy who would have tolerated bullying.

12

An account of his life at the Aungier Street School was written by one of his contemporaries there, and a version of it appeared in *The Candid Friend*, a short-lived magazine edited by Frank Harris, on July 6, 1901, under the title of *George Bernard Shaw as a Boy*. Its author was Matthew Edward McNulty who died in his eighty-seventh year in the delusion that an ampler, but unfinished and often inaccurate account of his friendship with Shaw was worth a large sum of money. The script, which is in the possession of Mr Ivo L. Currall, bears the endorsement that it is to be sold after its author's death for £8,000 for the benefit of his children! Among Mr Currall's numerous volumes of Shaviana is a copy of *The Candid Friend* article, bearing notes made by G.B.S., who controverts many of its statements. McNulty's memory was full of faults, but so was G.B.S.'s, and it is hard for the reader to decide where accuracy is to be found.

They were about the same age, thirteen, when they met for the first time. Their friendship, strong at first, naturally weakened after Shaw had left Dublin, but it lasted for most of their lives. McNulty, who became a bank manager, wrote several novels and plays. The former are reported to be worthy, but the latter are crude, almost farcical, comedies. Two of them, *The Lord Mayor* and *The Courting of Mary Doyle*, were performed at the Abbey Theatre, Dublin, with great popular success.

When he was an impressionable young man, McNulty spent several holidays with the Shaws in London, and fell in love with Lucy. She refused him because she was his senior by five years. When he was forty-five, still active and brisk, she would be a white-haired old lady of fifty! . . . G.B.S. put words similar to hers into the mouth of Candida 'when she rejected Marchbanks. But Lucy retained more tenderness for McNulty than for any of her admirers, including her husband. 'To the day of her death,' McNulty says, 'she remained my best friend, next to her brother, writing to me on an average once a week. She left me her Bechstein piano in her will.' He burnt all her letters when she died, and probably destroyed a good deal of material that would now be invaluable to G.B.S.'s biographer.

McNulty's reminiscences were not amplified until he was an old man with a failing memory, but he was a man in middle age when his shorter reminiscences appeared in *The Candid Friend*. Both versions are written with so much detail which seems to be exact as well as intimate, that the separation of fact from fiction is impossible, except where irrefutable evidence of their inaccuracy is to be found elsewhere. McNulty begins his article in *The Candid Friend*, for example, with the statement that G.B.S., on the day they first met, was wearing 'an Eton jacket, knickerbockers, long stockings and laced-up boots', a statement which G.B.S. denies. The detail, superficially read, seems convincing, but doubt soon gets the better of belief, for what man or woman of forty-six can recall the clothes worn by a schoolfriend thirty-three years earlier, unless the clothes were of a very remarkable sort? Can many people remember how they themselves were dressed on the day they first appeared at a particular school? McNulty is too precise in his detail: he even remembered that G.B.S. wore laced-up boots. But what was so rare in laced-up boots that he should have remembered them in middle-age?

There is another fact to be kept in mind. G.B.S. seems to have hated any attempt to record his childhood by those who were his companions then. His memory of it was too bitter for him to wish to have it known by anyone but himself; and he habitually discouraged his friends of that time from recording their memories. McNulty was requested to destroy the letters G.B.S. had written to him in their youth, and McNulty foolishly did so. Lady Hanson, too, was discouraged. He seemed eager to obliterate other people's recollections of his childhood and youth, though he preserved his own, and he was unwilling to renew old acquaintance in Dublin. Even the premium apprentices in Townshend's estate office disappeared from his knowledge, though he was happy in their company, and friendly enough to be photographed with two of them shortly before he removed from Dublin to London. There is a depth of bitter feeling here that we cannot hope to plumb.

The last school G.B.S. attended in Dublin no longer exists. It was a large building, originally the town house of Lord Aungier, and had broad staircases and large rooms with ceilings that had been ornamented with stucco designs by Italian artists. The mantelpieces were made of oak in the best Georgian manner. One of the junior masters in this school was called David Anderson. His name was used for the minister in *The Devil's Disciple*. The school, despite its pretentious title, Dublin English Scientific and Commercial Day School, founded by the Incorporated Society for Promoting Protestant Schools in Ireland, had a competent staff under its headmaster, James de Glanville, who was a mathematical scholar of Trinity College, and G.B.S. seems to have learnt more in it than he learnt elsewhere, more, too, than he was accustomed to admit he had ever learnt in any school. He loitered no longer at the bottom of the class, as he had done at Wesley, but was always either at the top or second from the top.

13

The two boys were soon to leave school to work for a living. G.B.S., indeed, when he was between thirteen and fourteen, sought employment with a firm of cloth merchants, Scott, Spain and Rooney with a warehouse on one of the Dublin quays, to whom he had been given a letter of introduction by a friend of his family. Scott had almost engaged him when Rooney, an older man, entered the room and, either through compunction or because he though that the boy was unfitted for the job, declined to confirm Scott's decision, and dissuaded G.B.S. from leaving school, as he had intended to do.

But the respite was short. Events were combining to break up the home in Hatch Street and divide the Shaws; and the most influential of them was the decision of Lee to leave Dublin and settle in England.

Mr Shaw, by this time, had been frightened into sobriety. On a Sunday afternoon, he had collapsed in a fit on the doorstep, and was told by his doctor that if he did not reform, he would die. Sobriety, however, did not enliven him or make him a more efficient miller. He remained what he had always been, insignificant and incompetent, a man almost damned in a fair wife, rendered more insignificant than nature had made him by the domineering and fierce-chinned young woman he had married.

She had made a cipher of him; he was almost obliterated by Lee, who was possessive and dictatorial, and had a right to be possessive in Hatch Street, for, without his means, the Shaws could not have kept the house. He had provided them with Torca Cottage; a fact which should have made G.B.S. grateful to him for ever. 'I still remember the moment when my mother told me that we were going to live there as the happiest of my life. The joy of it has remained with me all my life.' And he had made many improvements in their way of living which lightened the life of the quick-witted boy who had hitherto had little cause to rejoice in his home.

Lee was a rebel of the sort that is called an iconoclast. He challenged established beliefs and refused to conform to convention merely because it was generally accepted. He was not a man of wide culture. Outside the realm of music, he was lost. But he had a habit which was superior to culture, the habit of using his head. It was almost enough to tell him that everybody did this or that, for him to do exactly the opposite. Everybody ate white bread. He ate brown bread. Everybody kept the windows tightly shut, and feared the maleficent effect of the night air. He flung every window open, and inhaled night air with vigour and delight. Everybody said that Johann Bernard Logier, who had been Lucinda Elizabeth's first music master, was the greatest authority on thoroughbass in Dublin. Lee said the Logier was wrong and was ruining his unfortunate pupils. Everybody swore by the routine teachers, but Lee said they were fools who not only misinformed their pupils, but did them positive physical injury, ruining their throats in the pretence that they were developing their vocal chords.

He filled the Hatch Street house with music, and stimulated its conversation. The small boy, who had satisfied his imagination in Synge Street, by wild dreams of his own prowess, was enormously provoked by the lame iconoclast who laid down the law on every subject from the larynx to the Four Last Things.

'He had no faith in doctors, and when my mother had a serious illness took her case in hand unhesitatingly and at the end of a week or so gave my trembling father leave to call in a leading Dublin doctor, who simply said "My work is done" and took his hat. As to the apothecary and his squills, he could not exist in Lee's atmosphere; and I was never attended by a doctor again until I caught the smallpox in the epidemic of 1881.'

G.B.S. seems not to have wondered how much of his improved health was due to improved diet. The apothecary was abolished, we may believe, not by brown bread, open windows, and Lee's improvised medicine; but by better food and ampler meals.

G.B.S.'s natural disposition to overthrow idols was encouraged by the conversations he overheard in Hatch Street, especially when his Uncle Walter was present. This florid and full-faced man of robust appetites, uttered irreverent and improper remarks with the calm and dignity of a bishop addressing nervous ordinands on deviation from ceremonial customs. The extraordinary fact about Uncle Walter's Rabelaisian conversation was that it did not in the slightest degree corrupt his nephew's mind: it may be said to have made him more fastidious in his speech. G.B.S. was conspicuous among his fellows for the purity of his conversation, in which even mild expletives were so rare that to hear him say *damn* was remarkable. His tongue was as chaste as that of an enclosed nun. There are words in James Joyce's *Ulysses* which, he said, he could not even write, so deeply did they shock his spinsterly mind.

But to listen to Uncle Walter and Vandaleur Lee and his father discussing religion and the Holy Scripture was an invaluable experience for a lad whose attitude towards the world was rapidly changing from one of unquestioned acceptance to one of criticism and rejection. When he heard his father admonishing him for some flippancy he had uttered about the Bible, he was overwhelmed when the old man, after telling him that 'the Bible was universally recognised as a literary and historical masterpiece . . . would cap his eulogy by assuring me, with an air of perfect frankness, that even the worst enemy of religion could say no worse of the Bible than that it was the damnedest parcel of lies ever written. He would then rub his eyes and chuckle for quite a long time. It became an unacknowledged game between us that I should provoke him to exhibitions of this kind.'

McNulty asserts that G.B.S. hated his father, and it is probable that there was a period of his life when this statement was almost true. It would have been difficult for his children to retain respect for him when their infancy was full of fear that he would return from the mill, muzzy with drink; but even if they could have overcome these apprehensions, accepting his intoxication as one of his humourous idiosyncrasies, they must have been profoundly impressed by their mother's contempt for him, by his manifest inefficiency in almost everything he did, and, at last, by the ease with which Lee, when he and the Shaws joined forces, 'supplanted' him 'as the dominant factor in the household, and appropriated all the activity and interest of my mother.'

Lucy, long after his death, was accustomed to imitate the way her father laughed: a mirthless giggle that was little more than blowing through his teeth. Yet Mr Shaw seems to have left marks on his son's mind that were never eliminated or forgotten; and the reader of G.B.S.'s various reminiscences is struck by the frequency with which he remembers, not what his mother said, but what was said by his father. 'When I was told in childhood that a Mr Haughton who paid us a visit was a Unitarian, I asked my father what a Unitarian was. He replied humourously that the Unitarians believed that Jesus was not crucified, but was seen running away down the other side of the Hill of Calvary. I believed this for nearly thirty years'; and, indeed, it is not far removed from the belief of many Modernists who explain the appearances of Christ after the Crucifixion by asserting that he did not die on the Cross, but fainted and was smuggled away by Joseph of Arimathea to a convent of Essenes where he lived for many years. This belief has a long history, and has inspired many remarkably diverse books, including *The Fair Haven* by Samuel Butler, and George Moore's *The Brook Kerith*.

This was very different discourse from what Sonny had heard in his Sunday School at the Molyneux Church in Upper Leeson Street. When Mr Shaw and Lee and Uncle Walter debated about the resurrection of Lazarus from the dead, and the boy heard his father uphold the story told in the New Testament, while Lee declared it to be impossible, and Uncle Walter asserted that the whole thing was a put-up job between Lazarus and Jesus, who had asked Lazarus either as a friend or for a consideration to pretend to be dead and then, at the dramatic moment, arise from the grave, he sat entranced by the strange and disturbing talk to which he was listening. His world was being changed even while it was being built. G.B.S. frequently remembers walks he had had with his father, but refers to none, if there were any, with his mother. I have a letter from him, dated

26th July, 1949
— 93 today —

in which he says:

'My first experience of addressing a public assembly occurred when I was still so small that when my father took me for a walk, he had to carry me in his arms when I tired. One evening we were caught in a heavy shower on the quay. We made a rush for the portico; and all the passers-by did the same. I was carried. The building with the portico had been plastered over with advertisements by the bill stickers. Seated on my father's shoulder, I began to read the advertisements aloud. The sensation I created was immense. The Southern proletariat mostly could neither read nor write; and to see and hear an infinitesimal child read print, hard words and all, was miraculous. But I was not shewing off. It seemed to me that when I was confronted with print I was expected and bound to read it aloud like a lesson.

'I remember also being puzzled by my father's habit, when we took a side car home, never to tell the jarvey to drive to 33 Synge St. He always said, "Drive in the direction of the Three Rock Mountain" (much as if, wanting to be driven to Putney, one told the taximan to drive in the direction of Portsmouth). But it was not so silly as it sounded; for all the jarvies knew the road to the 3 Rock. It passed the end of Synge St., which they did not all know. I tell you these senile anecdotes because you seem to imagine that I issued from my mother's womb a fully fledged G.B.S. But I have not much else to tell you. I am again unable to walk far. I am as I was under the portico; and there is nobody now to carry me. I have survived my second childhood and got my second wind. My routine of sleeping and working never varies; and the months pass like minutes. . . .'

On his ninety-third anniversary, he remembered his father, but seemed to have forgotten his mother.

If Lucinda Elizabeth's marriage to this elderly 'downstart' was hard on her, who was young and imperious and unhappy at home, it was equally hard on him who never received, and did not, perhaps, deserve any respect from his wife or his children or his relatives or his associates in business or social life, and was suffered in what was nominally his own house only because no one thought him worth the trouble of expulsion. He had little pleasure in his marriage, and there is every reason to think that when, at last, his home was broken up and his wife and children left him, he found happiness for the first time.

His son, indeed, became convinced that Mr Shaw was delighted to be shut of the lot of them.

He blossomed after their departure and became welcome to many people in Dublin who found his gently humourous conversation very pleasant. He took particular pleasure in the company of his cousin Emily, the widow of the Rev. W. G. Carroll, who had offended Lucinda Elizabeth mortally one morning when, hearing that someone had called and on being told that this was Lucinda Elizabeth, exclaimed, so that she was overheard, 'Oh, that bitch!' He would probably have felt appalled if his family had returned to him! . . .

14

The home was broken up. Lee was the prime cause of its collapse. In 1869, he published a book, entitled *The Voice: Its Artistic Production,*

Development and Preservation,[1] in which he set forth his opinions of voice production in general. G.B.S. asserts that he was incapable of writing a handbill of any worth, and that he hired 'a scamp of a derelict doctor' to write the book, who may have been the Dr Smyly to whom he refers in the preface. Whoever the scribe was, Lee would have done better to dispense with his services and to write in his own fashion, however crude it may have been; for the derelict doctor was addicted to a literary style which may best be described as the sort of debased Burke which continued to be popular in Ireland until recent times. Its last exponent of any note in Ireland was John Redmond, though there are numerous Irish-Americans who still bore audiences with it.

The first part opens with a high-falutin' history of the 'metaphysical influences of music', followed by a chapter on 'historical incidents relating to the origin, development, and cultivation of music', and concluding with an 'apostrophe to music', in which the author indulges himself in a bout of vapouring words that are almost empty of meaning. 'Wonderful power! beautiful and strong! How unfathomable are thy ways! No nature is proof against thy magic spell.' And so on and so forth. The derelict doctor manifestly 'mugged up' his introductory chapters in the nearest reference library, and disguised his shallow thoughts under a veil of nebulous phrases which were calculated to make emotional women feel uplifted.

The second part of the book in which the hand of Lee first appears, is a long essay on physiology, with particular reference to the Larynx or Sound Box. Lee divided theorists on voice-production into three classes: those who compared it to a reed or a pipe; and those who, like himself, compared it to a flute. The first two, Lee contended, were hopelessly in the wrong, and were doing infinite harm not only to the voice, but the the general health of the vocalist. *His* system was the right one, and it was on this system that he trained Lucinda Eizabeth and her daughter Lucy.

The third and last part of the book is entitled Practical, and purports to tell the reader how to manage the voice so that it shall last in purity, as Lucinda Elizabeth's did, into old age. But his instructions are rendered futile by his frequent injunctions that the reader shall consult a skilled teacher before taking action; and it is evident that Lee had no intention of enabling anyone to produce a voice without a master's aid. The reader was told enough to persuade him to take a course of training from the author.

[1] Lee does not appear to have used the name of Vandaleur in Dublin, and G.B.S. asserts that he began to use it only in the pretentious times in Park Lane. The book was published in Dublin by M'Glashan and Gill, and in London by Simpkin, Marshall & Co. I am indebted to my friend, Harold F. Rubinstein, for information about Lee, both about this book and about his death.

The book, which was first published by subscription in Dublin, was heartily praised in the Dublin press, and won so much success there that a second edition was issued in England; and it was the foundation on which, nearly twenty years later, a musical critic, Corno di Bassetto, built numerous articles on the singing voice in a new London evening paper, called *The Star*. Its reception encouraged Lee to believe that a great career awaited him in England, and he caused consternation in Hatch Street by announcing his intention of emigrating.

The consternation was not, perhaps, shared by G.B.S., for it was during the time that *The Voice* was being written that Lee was responsible for his incarceration in the Central Model School. Nevertheless, the boy's life was profoundly affected by Lee's decision, and his nature suffered a change from which it never quite recovered. The Shaws could not possibly maintain the Hatch Street house without Lee's financial support, and they could no longer live rent free in Torca Cottage. Mr Shaw's mill was tottering, though it did not collapse until he died, and none of his children was earning wages. The second girl, Agnes, was unlikely to earn any, nor did she. She would have to be maintained for the rest of her short life. If Lee left Dublin, the hope that Lucy would become a prima donna might fade and die. The Shaws were beset.

In 1872, Lee departed, going first to Shropshire where 'he had been invited to conduct some private performances', and then to London, where he rented a flat in Park Lane, and confidently expected to make his fortune. Torca Cottage was sold, the tenancy of the house in Hatch Street terminated, so far as Lee was concerned, and the Shaws were left to deal with the remains as best they could.

His departure was more than a migration: it was a transformation. He changed for the worse. He had been Mr G. J. Lee in Dublin. He became Mr Vandaleur Lee in London. The great pains he had taken to develop voices in Ireland were no longer practised in a country where proud mothers expected their daughters to be transformed into Pattis after twelve lessons. The Irish had the whole of time before them: the English had only three months. Lee ceased to be the man of genius Lucinda Elizabeth had acclaimed him to be. He turned into a charlatan. He was, as charlatans often are, immensely successful at first. Mammas, who wanted their culture in haste, were willing to pay promptly and even lavishly to have their daughters enabled to sing genteel ballads to refined audiences with all the trills and high sustained notes that were thought to prove a well-trained voice; and Lee, no longer the austere preacher of brown bread and open windows and the need for a well-managed Larynx, yielded to the temptation to take easy money while it was obtainable.

39

15

The Shaws were troubled. A return to Synge Street would be little better than a descent into hell. The pleasant musical parties would cease. Felicity would end. There was much fruitless confabulation, in which Mr Shaw was a broken reed. His advice, when he gave any, was useless and disregarded. Like Mr Micawber, he hoped that something would turn up, but, unlike Mr Micawber, had little expectation that his hope would be fulfilled. One decisive act was performed. Sonny was withdrawn from school and put to work. His ambition at this time—he was not yet fifteen—was to become a painter, though there were times when he thought that he might become an opera singer: two occupations for which he had no qualification whatsoever.

His mother settled his immediate career in 1871, while Lee was still in Dublin. Her brother-in-law, Richard Frederick Shaw, was an important official in the Irish Valuation Office, and influential, therefore, with estate agents. He was able to secure a post for Sonny as a junior clerk with one of the best-known agencies in Ireland, the firm of Charles Uniacke and Thomas Courtney Townshend, of 15, Molesworth Street, at a salary of eighteen shillings a month, which was then, and for many years afterwards, the regulation pay of a boy beginning work in an Irish office. It was not the lurid career that G.B.S. had intended to follow, but it was as good as any that he was then likely to obtain.

McNulty, who had been withdrawn from Aungier Street at the same time as G.B.S., became a clerk in the Bank of Ireland and was posted to the branch in Newry, where he was solitary and bored. He grew morbid, and imagined that he could feel the rotation of the earth, and he feared to lie on a sofa, lest he should roll off it. This condition developed into what he called double consciousness: he believed that he could see the sap circulating in plants and trees. He even saw himself sitting on a pillow, gazing at his body stretched on the bed. The pangs of adolescence had seized him very painfully. In his correspondence with G.B.S., he described this state of double consciousness, and was disconcerted to receive a flippant reply to the effect that G.B.S. had often dualised himself, and was divisible *ad. lib!*

This seemingly callous attitude to other people's distress was a common characteristic throughout his life, and it often caused undiscerning and over-sensitive people to regard him as cruel when it was intended to divert the sufferer's attention from his troubles and to cheer him up by treating his distress as negligible. McNulty benefited from G.B.S.'s derision considerably during this period of adolescent morbidity, and his gratitude is plain in his reminiscences.

McNulty asserts that G.B.S. disliked Uniacke Townshend because he spelt his surname with an aspirate in the middle. This was, he seemed to think, a sign of suburban snobbery, though it was only a sign of G.B.S.'s juvenile insularity, for the spelling is common enough, and there is no evidence that Mr Uniacke Townshend was responsible for it. In any case, a man is not to be condemned for idiosyncracy, even if it is exercised only in the way he chooses to spell his name. Who was more idiosyncratic than G.B.S.? The aspirate in the middle of her surname did not prevent him from marrying Mr Townshend's kinswoman, Miss Charlotte Frances Payne-Townshend, twenty-seven years later, though she, or her parents, had added to the enormity of this offence by using a hyphen.

But G.B.S. was then at the prig stage of life, a stage through which all intelligent people have to pass. Mr Hesketh Pearson makes the curious remark that Townshend's office was 'intensely snobbish'. The word *snobbish* is now used by incontinent undergraduates as a term of abuse for anything or anybody not definitely proletarian or even for people whom they happen to dislike. Mr Pearson does not enrich his statement with a modicum of proof, and it is contradicted by the known facts. He also makes the surprising assertion that G.B.S. endured misery in the land agent's office because one of his most unpleasant jobs was to collect weekly rents from impoverished tenants, compared with which a voluntary visit to Mountjoy prison was a jolly experience.'

The evidence is that G.B.S. was happier in Townshend's office than he had been for a large part of his childhood or was to be for a large part of his early manhood. The fact that he was uncommonly able and successful in his employment is sufficient in itself to refute Mr Pearson's statement; for no man works well in employment which he loathes. All we know of this period of his life proves beyond doubt that G.B.S., in so far as he was able to enjoy office work at all, was happy in the land agency, and that the company of the 'intensely snobbish' premium apprentices gave him pleasure. His unhappiness at this time had no relation to his employment: it sprang from his domestic situation.

Lee's decision to migrate from Ireland to England was not instantly acted on. G.B.S. had been in Uniacke Townshend's office for some months when at last Lee departed, and had already proved himself to be an efficient clerk, doing his work so skilfully that within a year of his entry to the office, his salary had been increased to nearly five times its original figure, and he was occupying a position of considerable responsibility, as we shall see in the following section.

The Shaws, bereft of Lee's share of the upkeep of the Hatch Street house, and in peril of bankruptcy through the declining fortunes of the mill at Dolphin's Barn, were in a parlous plight. Mrs Shaw, who now made all the family decisions, solved their urgent problem abruptly and drastically. She broke up her home and virtually deserted her husband and son. Since her opportunities of finding employment as a teacher of music, as well as her elder daughter's prospects as a professional singer, depended on Lee, she would follow him to London, where his influence as well as his teaching would be invaluable to her and Lucy. Mr Shaw, tied to his deteriorating mill, must remain in Dublin, and so must Sonny, who was doing so well in the land agency office.

Her decision, naturally enough, caused some people to believe that Lee was her lover; but G.B.S., when he heard of this myth, scoffed it into disrepute. He had difficulty in convincing Frank Harris that Lucinda Elizabeth was not Lee's mistress, mainly because Harris believed that adultery was the normal recreation of all able-bodied men and women. Even Dr Archibald Henderson was deeply suspicious.

None of these people perceived the simple fact that G.B.S.'s mother, although she had borne three children, was not only a cold-blooded woman who was describable in the words of the Thirty Nine Articles, as having neither body, parts nor passions, but was also the wife of a man for whom she now felt nothing but contempt. The whole business of sex had become repellent to her. Her son, after her death, informed Harris that Henderson, who wrote the first full-length biography of G.B.S., 'could not divest himself of the idea that Lee was a scoundrel who had seduced my mother', and his comment on this belief was that 'a man who could have done that could have seduced the wooden Virgin at Nuremburg. My mother could have boarded and lodged the three musketeers and D'Artagnan for twenty years without discovering their sex; and they would no more have obtruded it on her than they would have ventured to smoke in her drawing-room.' He might have added that Lee took little interest in sexual relations. The larynx was his love.

16

In 1872, then, Lucinda Elizabeth, having sold her home in Dublin and put the proceeds in her purse, although they properly belonged to her husband, who owned the furniture, departed for London. She was her father's daughter. He had assumed that her money was his: she now assumed that her husband's property was hers. Mr Shaw, however, made no complaint. He was accustomed to being overlooked. The two girls went with their mother. Agnes was manifestly doomed, and Mrs Shaw sent her, in Lucy's care, to Ventnor, in the Isle of Wight, while she settled herself in a large house in a *cul de sac* off the Fulham Road in the south west of London. This was Victoria (now Netherton) Grove. She never lived in Ireland again, and only once did she see her husband when, seven or eight years after she had left Dublin, he paid her a short visit, lasting for a week.

If she wrote to her son during the five years which elapsed between her departure from Ireland and his arrival in London, or showed the slightest interest in him who was at the most difficult period of adolescence, no record of her letters or interest survives. When Professor Henderson wrote to her to ask her if she had any photograph of her son in his infancy and childhood or any letters he had written to her, she made the amazing reply, 'I never had a photo of my son as a boy or child. . . . Nor have I a single letter.'[1] Her explanation of this singular fact is that 'until he married we always lived in the same house, and there was no necessity to write. Since then, postcards suffice.' But there were the five years of his life in Dublin lodgings when she was in London, and he had never once in that period seen her or his sisters, the younger of whom, Agnes, he never saw again.

Mr Shaw, who magnanimously made his wife an allowance of a pound a week, a substantial part of a declining income, until he died, although she was notably failing to perform the functions of a wife, and was, in addition to her earnings as a teacher of music, enjoying small private means and drawing on her grandfather's bequest as it became legally available,[2] removed himself and his son to lodgings at 61 Harcourt Street, close to Hatch Street, where G.B.S. 'made a most valuable acquaintance' who greatly widened his intellectual outlook. This was Chichester Bell, a cousin of Graham Bell, the inventor of the telephone, consequently a nephew of Melville Bell, the inventor of the phonetic script known as Visible Speech.

'His father was Alexander Bell, author of the *Standard Elocutionist*, and by far the most majestic and imposing man that ever lived on this or any other planet. He had been elocution professor in my old school, the Wesleyan Connexional, now Wesley College. Chichester Bell, was a qualified physician who had gone to Germany and devoted himself to chemistry and physics in the school of Helmholtz. My intercourse with him was of great use to me. We studied Italian together; and

[1] *Bernard Shaw: Playboy and Prophet*, by Archibald Henderson, pp. 181–2.

[2] Her income, apart from what she earned as a teacher of singing, included the interest, amounting to £40 a year, on a mortgage on property in Cork, the interest on the £4,000 left from her grandfather's bequest to her children, and the pound a week she received from her husband. Her income cannot have been less than £300 a year, and may have been more.

though I did not learn Italian, I learned a good deal else, mostly about physics and pathology. I read Tyndall and Trousseau's Clinical Lectures. And it was Bell who made me take Wagner seriously. I had heard nothing of his except the Tannhauser march played by a second-rate military band; and my only comment was that the second theme was a weak imitation of a famous air, made up of a chain of turns, in Weber's Freischutz overture. When I found that Bell regarded Wagner as a great composer, I bought a vocal score of Lohengrin: the only sample to be had at the Dublin music shops. The first few bars completely converted me.'[1]

It is plain that the quick-witted boy, despite his cause for unhappiness, was enjoying an intellectual awakening to a far different life from that which he had hitherto lived. He had lost the music he needed, and his office duties prevented him from haunting the National Gallery as he had been accustomed to do; but he was in continual contact in Townshend's office with the sort of people he liked, young men of ampler education than that possessed by the musicians who had frequented his mother's parties and of an age when they are ready to discuss any subject without restraint.

In his lodgings, he had intercourse with a more mature and better informed mind: Chichester Bell's. His memories of his adolescence indicate that he was not only enjoying the mental stimulus he received from the premium apprentices, but that he was stimulating them to the extent that they allowed him to lead them in choral recitals when they should have been studying the management of estates and the rise and fall of produce prices.

There was a morning when Mr Charles Uniacke Townshend entering his office was astounded to find one of his premium apprentices, C. J. Smyth, directed by G.B.S., perched on a washstand behind a screen pretending to be Manrico singing *Ah, che la morte* from his dreadful dungeon. Mr Townshend was so dazed by this unseemly performance in a respectable estate agency that he crept upstairs to his office, unable to speak or act. The young lad who could influence his office superiors in this fashion cannot be said to have been leading an unendurable existence or to have been suffering anything remotely resembling an inferiority complex in the presence of young gentlemen whose parents had paid large sums to have them trained in the collection of rent.

Writing to me on his ninety-third birthday, he told me that he had formed a strong dislike to Parnell who had 'made himself purposely disagreeable to the estate office where I was cashier; so I started with a prejudice against him which I never quite got over without reasoning myself out of it.' Here we have proof of his feeling of loyalty to his

[1] *Sixteen Self-Sketches*, pp. 33–34.

employment which could not have been displayed had he felt miserable in it and totally antipathetic to the Townshends. His prejudice against Parnell was such that when he was talking to me about a book I had written on the Irish leader, he wondered whether Parnell was really a great man, and would not agree when I maintained that he was.

G.B.S., in *Sixteen Self-Sketches*, admits that he had 'some fun and the society of university men', and leaves the reader to infer that, although he disliked his work and his position in the office, he found the company very congenial. His casual references to the debates he held with the premium apprentices makes this fact abundantly clear. It was Smyth, the passionate singer of *Ah, che la morte*, who gave him a severe shock by remarking one morning 'that every boy thinks he is going to be a great man'. G.B.S. had imagined that he alone had that idea. Another apprentice, Humphrey Lloyd, shattered him in debate by exclaiming, 'What is the use of arguing when you don't know what a syllogism is?' and sent him to the dictionary to discover its meaning.

In *The Pictorial Record of the Life and Work of Bernard Shaw* by Dr F. E. Loewenstein, there are two photographs of G.B.S., one with John Thomas Gibbings, and the other with Robert Moore Fishbourne, both of them premium apprentices, which were taken in March, 1876, about a month before G.B.S. left Dublin to join his mother and sister in London. A man does not go to the trouble and expense of being photographed with 'intensely snobbish' persons who treat him as a social inferior. G.B.S. had no cause for complaint against the premium apprentices in Townshend's office: he had ample cause to feel grateful for the fact that he, taken so soon from school, mixed freely and familiarly with young men fresh from Trinity College, sharpening his wits on theirs and learning how to hold his own in civilised discourse.

His position in Townshend's office was far from being negligible or subordinate. His quick wits and his intelligence enabled him to do his work uncommonly well: so well, indeed, that when the middle-aged cashier was detected in petty peculation, Townshend temporarily appointed G.B.S. to his post, and then, finding him exceptionally efficient, confirmed him in it.

G.B.S. received this promotion about a year after he had entered the office, when, that is to say, he was sixteen. He became 'chief cashier, head cashier, sole cashier, equal to any of the staff, and the most active and responsible member of it', at an age when the majority of middle-class boys in offices at that time were licking stamps, copying letters and addressing envelopes.

His duties were not only responsible, but highly diversified. He had to collect rents from tenants of a dozen slum houses in Dodd's

Row, a task he detested; 'receive and pay rents, charges, insurances, private debts, etc., on many estates', work which obliged him to make occasional trips into the country: and supervise his employers' private banking business. It was necessary for him to be told confidential matters about the agency's clients. As he himself stated, 'I became accustomed to handling large sums of money, meeting men of all conditions, and getting glimpses of country house life behind the scenes.'

This was a sufficiently varied experience for any man: it was unique experience for a lad of sixteen; and the surprising fact is that he fulfilled his office without the smallest mishap. His salary was doubled, rising to £48 a year, which was an unusually large salary for a junior clerk in a provincial city to receive not only then, but for a quarter of a century thereafter.

It is impossible to believe that a boy of his age was unhappy in an office where he did important work at a substantial salary and enjoyed constant association with congenial companions. The fact that he did not care for this employment is immaterial to our argument. There was no better employment available to him, and little that was as good. His ambition to become a painter or an opera singer could not be fulfilled, even if he were fit for such employment, which he certainly was not: and what he learnt in Townshend's office was one day to be valuable to him. He could not have written *Widower's Houses* if he had not spent five years in that office.

But his intellectual resources were not limited to the estate agency. There was Chichester Bell in his Harcourt Street lodgings, and there was Edward McNulty in Newry. Note has already been made of his voluminous correspondence with the latter, in which he purged his bosom of much perilous stuff in what was, no doubt, highly priggish language, mostly polysyllabic; but we have now to note that this outlet for his intellectual activities was so attractive to him that he spent a holiday with McNulty in Newry, which lies at the foot of Carlingford Lough between the Mourne Mountains and the mountains of Louth. They were then about seventeen, and they celebrated their re-union by getting themselves photographed. It was taken in 1874, and is the earliest photograph of G.B.S. now obtainable.[1]

During the day, McNulty was, of course, obliged to go to the Bank of Ireland, but their evenings were spent in vehement debates about literature and in a vain effort to compile a work to be called *The Newry Nights' Entertainment*, which perished soon after it was begun. They drew up a declaration of eternal friendship. They would share each other's prosperity or adversity, and would speak

[1] It is reproduced in *Bernard Shaw Through the Camera* and *The Pictorial Record of Bernard Shaw*, both by Dr F. E. Loewenstein.

and write frankly to each other and never become offended by abusive or outrageous language. If there was any life after death, the first to die would appear to the survivor. They signed this declaration with blood drawn from their arms! . . . They also made a pact that they would confide their troubles to each other; a pact which was kept by G.B.S. until he was in his thirties.

It was during this holiday that G.B.S., wandering about Newry while McNulty was toiling at ledgers, found a secondhand bookshop kept be a man called Fitzmaurice: a small, thin, hard-faced fellow with close cropped hair and a short beard, who was almost illiterate, and fanatical in his beliefs. He was meat and drink to an argumentative youth who knew no rules of debate, and would not have kept them if he had. Fitzmaurice could not endure dissent from his opinions, and when G.B.S. refused to accept without question some assertion he had made, Fitzmaurice, in a violent rage, ordered him out of the shop.

It was characteristic of G.B.S. then, as it was throughout his life, that he could not understand anyone taking offence over differences of belief. To him, argument was entertainment, no more than a fencing match between friends, each eager to deprive the other of his foil. The idea that a man should fall into a violent rage about opinions and break a friendship, was incomprehensible to him. He was shocked and upset by this breach with Fitzmaurice, and became eager to avenge himself by a comic plot to frighten the wits out of the ferocious little fellow. McNulty must tell Fitzmaurice that G.B.S. was a Dublin detective, hunting out secondhand booksellers who dealt in immoral literature! . . . He was annoyed when McNulty, who had not worked in the Bank of Ireland without learning something, refused to take part in this ludicrous plot. Neither of them entered Fitzmaurice's shop again.

17

But although G.B.S. had a fairly full intellectual life in the five years after his mother had deserted his father, he had little or no social life; a deprivation of which he became exceedingly conscious. It was due partly to his own nature. He was not then gregarious. Like Enoch, he walked alone. He was at the age when an intelligent youth, whose head is full of ideas and argument, is less interested in women than he is at any other period of his life.

He had a brief flurry with a girl in Dublin which he describes in a letter to Mrs Patrick Campbell, dated August 19, 1912: 'Once in my calfish teens, I fell wildly in love with a lady of your complexion; and she, good woman, having a sister to provide for, set to work to marry me to the sister. Whereupon I shot back into the skies from which I

47

had descended, and never saw her again. Nor have I, until this day, ever mentioned that adventure to any mortal; for though dark ladies still fascinated me, they half laughed at me, half didn't understand me, and wholly thought me cracked.'

Since these are times when any youth or man who is not for ever running after women is suspected of sexual perversion, I think it well to add that there was no trace of this complaint in G.B.S.'s lack of interest in girls. His abhorrence of sodomites was profound, though he seldom spoke of it, and despite the fact that he felt antipathetic to Wilde, he was careful not to join in the attacks on him at the time of the trial. He preferred long conversations with argumentative people to amorous chit-chat with maidens who had little to say and nothing that was worth hearing.

Nevertheless, his social solitude became intensified during the five years he spent in lodgings with Mr Shaw. There was now no intercourse whatsoever between the latter and his grand relations at Bushy Park; and the social life which G.B.S. might have enjoyed as a kinsman of a wealthy baronet was denied to the son of the downstart and semi-bankrupt miller of Dolphin's Barn.

He had enjoyed the social life of Synge Street and Hatch Street. McNulty's account of him at the school in Aungier Street does not describe a shy recluse. In his boyhood, therefore, G.B.S. was evidently at ease in his world and able to participate with pleasure in the general life of his class. This ease of manner slowly declined after his mother had departed from Dublin. Life with an impoverished miller, living in cheap lodgings and made melancholy by compulsory abstinence from intoxicating liquor, afforded few opportunities for a sensitive youth approaching manhood, to enjoy the social amenities which a cadet of the Shaws and Gurlys had every right to expect as his inheritance. Lodgings in Dublin are poor, ramshackle things at the best: in Harcourt Street they were not at the best, though they were better than some. 'Cut off from the social drill which puts me at one's ease in private society,' he 'grew up frightfully shy and utterly ignorant of social routine:'

> 'My mother, who had been as carefully brought up as Queen Victoria, was too humane to inflict what she had suffered on any child. . . .'

an attempt to excuse a neglectful parent which will not deceive any discerning reader,

> '. . . besides, I think she imagined that correct behaviour is inborn, and that much of what she had been taught was natural to her. Anyhow, she never taught it to us, leaving us wholly to the promptings of our blood's blueness, with results which may be imagined.'

Finger-bowls were table furniture which especially discomposed him. He had never seen them until his arrival in London, and did not know what their function was until he had the good sense, as he frankly told his friends, to consult an able and well-written work, entitled *Manners and Tone of Good Society, or, Solecisms to be Avoided*, by A Member of the Aristocracy.

It is characteristic of him that he studied the work in the British Museum, and that his gratitude for the help and instruction he received from it forbade him to show any snobbery about acknowledging his debt to its author.

It appears from his reminiscences that G.B.S., as he came up to manhood, felt himself embarrassed by his ignorance of 'the manners and tone' of the class to which he belonged, and that this embarrassment made him more solitary in Dublin than he would normally have been. The lack of a home, as distinct from lodgings, and the lack of association with any kindred, apart from his ineffectual father, drove him into himself and made him feel an Ishmael where he should have been an Isaac. Even the return of McNulty to Dublin from Newry, though it was beneficial to him, did not compensate him for the loss of family environment; and in any case, McNulty did not return until 1874, by which time G.B.S. had had four years of Harcourt Street. He had changed considerably in those four years. McNulty was depressed to learn that he no longer aspired to become a painter: he wished to found a new religion.

But, McNulty objected, there were far too many religions in the world already, and, with tears in his eyes, he begged G.B.S. to change his mind, which G.B.S., being an obliging person, promptly did. At this time there was no thought in his head of becoming a writer, but to please McNulty, he consented to become a literary genius.

Their indoor recreation was music. G.B.S., assisted by McNulty, who was now studying music at the Royal Irish Academy of Music, taught himself to play the piano, but only in a clumsy fashion, and there was much conning of scores. McNulty was the less informed of the two, though his knowledge of music was not slight, and he says that G.B.S.'s favourite opera at this time was Gounod's *Faust*, 'of which he knew every note while yet a boy and before he could play a five-finger exercise on the piano.' This opera seems to have impressed his mind deeply, and McNulty thinks that it influenced his early writing.

On entering Townshend's office, he had begun to keep a diary, irregularly and not in much detail. The first volume is in a small note-book which probably cost twopence. It contains the first of eight records of his weight made between '27th Novr. 1872', when he was fifteen, and '18th August, 1884', when he was twenty-eight. On the first date, he weighed '9 stone 1 lb': on the second, '10 stone 2 lbs.'

This diary reveals him as a careful lad, noting his expenditure with precision. On the 10th of January, 1871, he 'paid J. Martin' who lived off Fishamble Street, Dublin, '18s. for making a suit', a sum which would scarcely cover the cost of the thread to-day. In 1872–3 he bought season tickets for the Dublin Exhibition and the Hibernian Academy. The number and cost of each ticket is neatly set down. He keeps an account of his fees at the Evening Freehand Class at the Royal Dublin Society's School of Art. 'Voucher No. 303, dated 17th Oct. 1870 for session 1 Oct. 1870 to 26 Feb. 1871—6s.'

There is a mysterious entry in this diary, entitled 'The L . . . Episode,' which opens with the cryptic remark, ' "But food for mirth and mockery." But they laugh best who laugh last.' It is followed by three terse statements which denote that the course of calf love was not running smoothly. 'First acquaintance concluded in 1871.' 'Second period', about which he wrote to his sister Agnes in 1875, is described as 'the Calypso infatuation', and the third item, added 'at midnight of Wednesday, Oct. 24, 1877', when he had settled in London, 'The Catastrophe, or the indiscretion of No. 2.' This odd affair, which lasted, on and off, for about six or seven years, has no other history than these obscure notes.

The diary contains a fairly full account of the staff in Townshend's office. It gives no indication of any talent beyond that of an intelligent boy of careful habits. No one, reading this diary, could feel that its keeper had unusual character and was destined to become one of the world's greatest dramatists. There is nothing in it to indicate that he was different in any degree from a thousand lads of his sort in Dublin or anywhere else, or that he would ever spend his life in any occupation other than that of trusted clerk in a land agent's office.

18

It was during this solitary time in Dublin that he began to visit the theatre on his own account. He saw Barry Sullivan and Henry Irving at the Gaiety Theatre, and convinced himself that Irving was 'his man', although the idea of writing plays had not yet occurred to him. What he meant by 'his man' was probably that Irving was the sort of actor he preferred to the sort of player who was then popular. The fact is isolated in this manner because of its significance in his relations with Irving much later in his life.

19

Mr Shaw was becoming increasingly footling. Reformation had not increased his business ability. It had come too late, and was, if anything, a handicap, since an elderly man who depends on stimulants for his ability to work, must flounder terribly when he is deprived of them. His evenings were spent in futile efforts to balance his accounts, and pride prevented him from asking his son to balance them for him, though he must have known that Sonny, so successful with the estate agency's books, could have disposed of his small affairs in an hour or two.

The superiority of women over men in G.B.S.'s work sprang, according to McNulty, from the spectacle of Mr Shaw struggling ineffectually with bills and ledgers. He despised his father's weakness and inefficiency, and began, because, perhaps, the memory of her incompetence had faded, to admire his mother as a masterful woman who knew how to solve her problems and settle her affairs.

It had long been evident that Lucinda Elizabeth would not return to her husband, who, McNulty asserts, was so vexed by her absence that he contemplated suing for a divorce, citing Lee as the co-respondent. He was deterred from doing so by his realisation that no one in Dublin believed for a moment that she was Lee's mistress. There was little or nothing in common between father and son, and their intercourse was slight. They met at meals, but their evenings were spent apart, G.B.S. seeking the society of Bell and McNulty, or fingering his way clumsily through a score on the piano. His discontent with his work increased, and was brought to a decisive conclusion by two incidents. The first related to what he regarded as a matter of conscience, though he was willing to admit that the rights of the matter were with Mr Townshend.

In the spring of 1875, two famous American evangelists, Dwight Lyman Moody and Ira David Sankey, began a mission in Dublin; and G.B.S., whose interest in religion was profound and never declined, attended several of their meetings. Their effect on him was exactly what any person, knowing him then or thereafter, might have expected it to be. They provoked him into writing his second, but first published, letter to the press.

At the age of fifteen, two months before he had entered Townshend's office, he had written a letter to *The Vaudeville Magazine*. It was not printed. The editor, who thus lost whatever hope of immortality he may have had, printed a note in a column of replies to correspondents in the issue for September, 1871, in which he rebuked the boy. 'You should have registered your letter: such a combination of wit and satire ought not to have been conveyed at the ordinary rate of postage. As it was, your arguments were so weighty that we had to pay twopence extra.' The subject of the letter has not transpired.

Four years passed before G.B.S. recovered from this rebuff. On April 3, 1875, there appeared in *Public Opinion* the letter which is printed in the succeeding section. In it, he sounded the aristocratic and anti-democratic note which is to be heard in all his work. Substantially, he was the same person when he died at ninety-four that he had been when, not yet nineteen, he wrote to *Public Opinion*.

20

'Sir,—In reply to your correspondent, "J.R.D.," as to the effect of the "wave of evangelism", I beg to offer the following observations on the late "revival" in Dublin, of which I was a witness.

'As the enormous audiences drawn to the evangelistic services have been referred to as a proof of their efficacy, I will enumerate some of the motives which induce many persons to go. It will be seen that they were not of a religious, but a secular, not to say profane, character.

'Predominant was the curiosity excited by the great reputation of the evangelists, and the stories, widely circulated, of the summary annihilation by epilepsy and otherwise of sceptics who had openly proclaimed their doubts of Mr Moody's divine mission.

'Another motive exhibits a peculiar side of human nature. The service took place in the Exhibition building, the entry to which was connected in the public mind with the expenditure of a certain sum of money. But Messrs Moody and Sankey opened the building "for nothing", and the novelty, combined with the curiosity, made the attraction irresistible.

'I mention these influences particularly as I believe they have hitherto been ignored. The audiences were, as a rule, respectable; and as Mr Moody's orations were characterised by an excess of vehement assertion and a total lack of logic, respectable audiences were precisely those which were least likely to derive any benefit from them.

'It is to the rough, to the outcast of the streets, that such "awakenings" should be addressed; and those members of the aristocracy who by their presence tend to raise the meetings above the sphere of such outcasts, are merely diverting the evangelistic vein into channels where it is wasted, its place being already supplied, and as in the dull routine of hard work, novelty has a special attraction for the poor, I think it would be well for clergymen, who are nothing if not conspicuous, to render themselves so in this instance by their absence.

'The unreasoning mind of the people is too apt to connect a white tie with a dreary church service, capped by a sermon of platitudes, and is more likely to appreciate "the gift of the gab"—the possession of which by Mr Moody nobody will deny—than that of the Apostolic Succession, which he lacks.

'Respecting the effect of the revival on individuals I may mention that it has a tendency to make them highly objectionable members of society and induces their unconverted friends to desire a speedy reaction, which either soon takes place or the revived one relapses slowly into his previous benighted condition as the effect fades, and although many young men have been snatched from careers of dissipation by Mr Moody's exhortations, it remains doubtful whether the change is not merely in the nature of the excitement rather than in the moral natures of the individual. Hoping that these remarks may elucidate further opinions on the subject,

    'I remain, Sir, yours, etc.

S.

DUBLIN'

21

This was a notable letter to have been written by a youth who had seldom been outside the provincial city in which he was born, and had never been outside Ireland, which was then, as now, one of the world's most backward countries. It was not for nothing that he was an Irish Protestant. The letter had a curious effect on those who read it and knew that he was its author, knowledge which they could, of course, have derived only from him. It was regarded as a declaration of atheism, though there is nothing in it that is in the least degree atheistical, and it puts a point that has often been made against revivalists by parish priests and pastors of all denominations, who have complained throughout the ages that they were left to clear up the emotional mess after the revivalists had departed. It seems to have upset G.B.S.'s relatives and to have caused deep discussions among the premium apprentices. These discussions were so frequent and prolonged that Mr Uniacke Townshend, not unreasonably, reminded G.B.S. that his office was not a forum for acrimonious religious argument. The biographer has difficulty in deciding what G.B.S.'s attitude was when he received his employer's just and apparently temperate rebuke. In one place, he agrees that Mr Townshend had reason: in another, he resents interference with his right to debate belief.

The fact is that he was restive in the estate agency. The discontent of adolescence was troubling him unendurably. So was the fact that Mr Townshend had offended him by introducing his nephew into the office and placing him in authority over G.B.S., though he had no experience to support him in that position and G.B.S. was doing his work with uncommon skill. He was unaware of a still deeper cause of discontent: the desire to fulfil himself by authorship. Estate agency had no charms for him. If Mr Townshend had offered him the privileges of a premium apprentice without the payment of a premium, he would not have felt gratified. The itch to write was about to drive him out of Dublin, though he did not realise then that he had the itch.

His supersession by Mr Townshend's nephew was the immediate cause of his resignation, though what he intended to do was not yet clear. On February 29, 1876, he sent the following letter[1] to his employer.

'Dear Sir,—I beg to give you notice that at the end of the month I shall leave your office. My reason is that I object to receive a salary for which I give no adequate value. Not having enough to do, it follows that the little I have done is not well done: when I ceased to act as Cashier I anticipated this, and have since become satisfied that I was right. Under these circumstances I prefer to discontinue my service, and remain,

Very truly yours,
G. B. Shaw'

This was a singular letter of resignation, but it was well in the character of its author, who was manifestly hurt by his supersession, as, indeed, he had every right to be. Mr Townshend had not behaved well to the able young man he employed when he put his inexperienced nephew in his place. G.B.S.'s pride was humiliated, and his humiliation had made him incoherent. But the wound is plainly visible, and Mr Townshend seems to have realised how deep it was, for he begged him to withdraw his resignation and offered him a substantial increase of salary: two facts which must have assuaged the blow G.B.S. had received.

He was not, however, to be appeased, though he seems not to have made any plans for his future. His 'infernal pride', he said, even prevented him from asking for a reference. In 1878, when he had been in London for two years, his father, displaying almost unnatural acumen, asked Townshend for one, and infuriated his son by sending it to him. It was in these terms:

15, Molesworth Street,
Dublin,
9th August, 1878.

'Mr George Shaw served in our office from 1st November, 1871, to 31st March, 1876, when he left at his own desire. He entered as a youth and left us having attained the position of Cashier. He is a young man of great business capacity, strict accuracy, and was thoroughly reliable and trustworthy. Anything given to him to do was always accurately and well done. We parted from him with regrets and shall always be glad to hear of his welfare.

Uniacke Townshend & Co.
Land Agents'

The Townshends had atoned.

[1] This letter was first published in *Adam* in August, 1946, by Dr F. E. Loewenstein, and was reprinted in *Bernard Shaw: a Chronicle* by R. F. Rattray.

What he proposed to do with himself after he had left their service is a matter for speculation; but it is doubtful if even he had any precise or even imprecise opinion on the matter. His chief thought seems to have been one of relief at enlargement. He had escaped from his office. But like the prisoner who runs away from Dartmoor in a mist, his elation must have been overcast by fear of what might have to be suffered in the fog, with the prospect of capture and a return to prison in the end. He might wander about in the murk of Dublin, and find himself at last obliged to take employment less agreeable than that he had abandoned, where the company at least had been congenial.

McNulty asserts that shortly before he left Dublin, G.B.S. had himself examined by a friend who was a doctor. He was told that he was suffering from 'chronic congestion of the brain', a diagnosis which seems, for some reason known only to himself, to have pleased him immensely. He jeered at McNulty for saying that if he had received such an account of his mental state, he would have felt so frightened by it that he would have had to be put into a lunatic asylum. The diagnosis is very loose, but there may have been some connexion between it and the fact that G.B.S. for most of his life suffered severely from headaches. About once a month, he was prostrated by pain and compelled to stay in a darkened room.

He may have had some loitering intention of a musical career, but if he had, his attempt to master the cornet, under the tuition of George Connelly, a member of the Theatre Royal orchestra, cured him of that ambition. A cornet-player, he said, had to have lips of hornlike texture, and the acquirement of such lips was too tedious for him to persevere in the effort.

22

His indecision was ended by the death of his sister Agnes at Balmoral House, Ventnor, in the Isle of Wight, on March 31, 1876: the day on which his employment in Townshend's office ended. Dublin was now repulsive to him; and he resolved to join his mother in London. This decision seems to have been made without much, if any, consultation with anybody. Presumably, he told his father of his intention, but he did not ask for advice, nor is it likely that he would have accepted any that might have been offered. Mr Shaw no longer felt any wish to have his family near him.

McNulty, who visited him twice a week after G.B.S. had left him, found him 'a lonely, sad little man'. He liked to talk about his wife and children at great length, but does not appear to have desired their return. Once every day, just before bedtime, he smoked a clay pipe. When the smoke was ended, he broke the pipe and flung the pieces into the grate. The pipes were bought by the gross. Out walking with a friend, he would suddenly take a run forward, stop suddenly, await his friend's arrival, and resume the conversation as if it had been uninterrupted. This eccentric small man received little from life, but in the mysterious operations of nature, he gave it much: he fathered a genius. His death will be recorded in its proper place in these pages, but he now virtually disappears from our observation.

G.B.S., having made up his mind to leave Dublin, moved swiftly. He had little luggage, apart from clothes, to take with him, so his journey did not involve him in much preparation. He bade goodbye to his friends, and had himself photographed with two of the premium apprentices, twice with John Thomas Gibbings, once with Robert Moore Fishbourne, thus beginning a habit which grew upon him as he became older, of being photographed or painted or sculpted as often as possible. He had scarcely set foot in Ventnor, whither he went with Lucy to visit his younger sister's grave, than he had himself photographed, once with Lucy, once by himself.

To be photographed five times in a month or six weeks indicates not only considerable interest in oneself, but also the possession of some means; and we may believe, therefore, that G.B.S., when he decided to leave Dublin for London, had a fair amount of money, the savings of a frugal young man who, however, was far from being stingy. There is no shabbiness or eccentricity in his clothes in these photographs; and we know that in additon to the conventional lounge suit he was wearing when they were taken, he possessed the formal garments of a well-placed official in a high-class estate agency, namely a morning coat, the appropriate trousers, and a silk hat, together with a suit of evening clothes. His idiosyncracies in dress did not develop until after he had been in London for some time, and many of them were due to poverty.

His farewell made, he carried his carpet bag on to the cross-channel steamer at North Wall, where he started on his journey to Holyhead and London. He had never been out of Ireland before, and his journeys in Ireland itself had been few. He was a remarkably untravelled young man, but he had considerable business ability and experience, and he had a deep knowledge of music and painting, and a fair knowledge of literature and drama. With his brains and energy, the conquest of London should be easy.

As the steamer moved into the middle of the Liffey and Dublin Bay, he little dreamt as he glanced back at the mountains which almost surrounded his native city that nearly thirty years would pass before he saw them again. But even if he had dreamt this, he would not have felt perturbed.

'I did not set foot in Ireland again until 1905, and not then on my own initiative. I went back to please my wife: and a curious reluctance to retrace my steps made me land in the south and enter through the backdoor from Meath rather than return as I came, through the front door on the sea. In 1876, I had had enough of Dublin. James Joyce in his *Ulysses* has described, with a fidelity so ruthless that the book is hardly bearable, the life that Dublin offers to its young men, or, if you prefer to put it the other way, that its young men offer to Dublin. No doubt it is much like the life of young men everywhere in modern urban civilization. A certain flippant futile derision and belittlement that confused the noble and serious with the base and ludicrous seems to me peculiar to Dublin; but I suppose that is because my only per-sonal experience of that phase of youth was a Dublin experience; for when I left my native city I left that phase behind me, and associated no more with men of my age until, after about eight years of solitude in this respect, I was drawn into the Socialist revival of the early eighties, among Englishmen intensely serious and burning with indigna-tion at very real and very fundamental evils that affected all the world; so that the reaction against them bound the finer spirits of all the nations together instead of making them cherish hatred of one another as a national virtue. Thus, when I left Dublin I left (a few private friendships apart) no society that did not disgust me. To this day my sentimental regard for Ireland does not include its capital. I am not enamored of failure, of poverty, of obscurity, and of the ostracism and contempt which these imply: and these were all that Dublin offered to the enormity of my unconscious ambition.'[1]

The vigour and vehemence of his aversion from his native city seem never to have abated. Writing to Mrs Patrick Campbell on April 3, 1913, when he was in his fifty-seventh year, he told her that 'I drove into Dublin today and cursed every separate house as I passed.'

Arrived in London, he drove in a growler to his mother's house off the Fulham Road, where he was received without enthusiasm. Lucinda Elizabeth was earning a moderate income by teaching music; an occupation which distressed her daughter Lucy, whose ideas about gentility were entirely suburban. Ladies in those days, as Lucy thought was right, did not work for a living: they were maintained. Their greatest exertions were to 'do the flowers', drink tea with other delicately-bred women, and take the little dog for a run round the square. Lucy's ambition to become a prima donna was not unladylike, but her mother's passion for teaching girls to sing on the principles laid down by Lee was.

The advent of G.B.S. into the shabby-genteel and ladylike house in Victoria Grove was disturbing both to his mother and sister. A fortnight had passed since Agnes had died, and they were still under

[1] Preface to *Immaturity*, p. xxxiii.

the shadow of their bereavement. Five years had passed since they had last seen Sonny. He was a boy then, but was now a young man, with a serious face and tediously tidy habits, and, according to their metropolitan standards, gawkily provincial. What, they must have wondered, were they to do with him? Their conversation languished. When the routine questions had been asked, there was little left to say. 'My mother and I lived together, but there was hardly a word between us. She was a disillusioned woman! . . .'

Life in that ill-managed house of shabby shifts must have had an extraordinarily depressing effect on the young man, new from Dublin, where he had had some friends and acquaintances, and settling in a London where he had none, apart from his mother and sister and the seemingly successful Lee. He, who had been easy in his manner in Dublin, and had led the premium apprentices in excerpts from opera, and had discussed all there was to discuss with them and Chichester Bell and McNulty, now had no one with whom to discuss anything. His mother was out all day, trying to teach English girls to sing; Lucy was busy with her voice production; and the food was awful, rivalling that of Synge Street in the days when the Shaw children had dined on stewed beef cooked by Dublin sluts.

He became shy and nervous of meeting strangers. G.B.S. had an air of bravado, but it was affected, for he was shivering in his shoes, and he felt inclined to refuse invitations from his mother's friends. When he had mustered enough courage and aplomb to visit the Lawsons in Cheyne Walk, he 'suffered such agonies of shyness that I sometimes walked up and down the Embankment for twenty minutes or more before venturing to knock at the door; indeed I should have funked it altogether, and hurried home asking myself what was the use of torturing myself when it was easy to run away, if I had not been instinctively aware that I must never let myself off in this manner if I meant ever to do anything in the world.'

His shyness could be overcome only by committing an outrage on his own nature, by a pretence of arrogance and self-assurance he was far from feeling. Quaking with apprehension and unbalanced nerves, he forced himself to frequent parties where he seemed to those shallow-minded men and women who judge us all by our appearance, to be conceited and far too assertive: a most obnoxious young man, whether he was silent or garrulous, and distressingly unlike his charming sister Lucy. For the English, having little charm themselves, over-estimate the value of this delusive quality, forgetting that it is the hallmark of the crook who, were he without charm of some sort, could scarcely earn a living.

23

G.B.S. spent his first three months in London in learning his way about the place. He took an extended holiday. There were concert halls and picture galleries and, more than these, the British Museum to be frequented and explored. The theatre, perhaps because it was comparatively expensive, seems not to have been much, if at all, attended. The National Gallery could be visited for nothing, and had greater munificence to display. At the end of his first quarter, however, the problem of employment began to be urgent and oppressive. The money he had brought with him from Dublin, the savings from his salary, was running out. His wardrobe, he perceived, would soon need to be renewed. Boots were a continual problem. They always are to impecunious young men who try to economise on train and bus fares by walking when they should ride. He was hard up! . . .

Lucy, who had never been congenial to him, and was to become less congenial as she grew older, steadily became more and more antagonistic to him, to the extent that she finally besought her mother to turn him out of the house unless he sought a remunerative job. She seemed not to realize that she had lived without earning a farthing for a far longer time that he had, and that the belated support he was now receiving from his mother, in so far as it could be called support, was a trifle in comparison with the support she had been receiving for years. If Lucy could be maintained while she was learning to sing, could not her brother be supported in meagre style while he learnt how to write? Incited by her, 'people wondered at my heartlessness: one young and romantic lady had the courage to remonstrate openly and indignantly with me "for the which" as Pepys said of the shipwright's wife who refused his advances, "I did respect her." '

Lucy seemed to be the successful member of the family. She had a fine voice, carefully cultivated by Lee, and she was expected to have a spectacular career on the operatic stage. Cold and unloving as her mother, but possessing a good deal of the charm her mother could display when she felt in the mood, Lucy was highly attractive to men —'whom everybody loved, and who loved nobody', her brother wrote to her—and she tried to increase her charm by heightening her resemblance to Ellen Terry. There was a period of her life when her imitation of Miss Terry was close enough to deceive the casual glancer.

There can be no doubt of her attraction to men. Both Oscar Wilde and his brother Willie fell in love with her—it was, indeed, through her that G.B.S. met Oscar for the first time at one of Lady Wilde's farcical parties—and there was a remarkable agreement among her friends and acquaintances that she was certain to have immense success in the concert hall and on the stage. She would, undoubtedly, make a brilliant marriage. These prospects proved delusive. She could sing, but she could neither act nor love, and her mind was singularly conventional and commonplace, despite a bitter cynicism she developed in middle-age which profoundly shocked her mother and her brother. It was, perhaps, a natural reaction from the shiftless home her mother maintained which made Lucy feel immense admiration for solid and secure people, who never deviated in the slightest degree from a well-defined way of living.

Her life in Dublin with her inconsiderable, tippling father and her inefficient mother had made her place excessive value on steadfast and secure and competent people. Her deep aversion from Vandaleur Lee, that noisy anarchist in music, convinced her that her single hope of happiness was to be found among those who lived by a well-proved routine and had no wish for anything but substantial and sufficient means, a practical habit of life, and the esteem, based on reasonable envy, of their less well-established neighbours. Chislehurst was Lucy's ambition: anybody could have Chelsea. Like her mother, she had contempt for Clapton, and had never heard of Canning Town. In the world she admired, a woman did not earn her living: she was kept by her parents until she had induced a man to marry her.

It was bad enough that Mamma should earn her living: it was worse that her brother would not earn his. His intention to become a writer seemed absurd. What made him imagine that he, raw from Dublin and with no more knowledge of the great world than a youth can obtain in a shabby-genteel boarding-house and an estate agency, could write? He was industrious enough in his scribbling, but there was no money at the end of his day's work. Mamma must *do* something about Sonny! . . .

She herself was doing a great deal about him. She gave him no peace, and she begged her friends to give him no peace. Why did he not apply for a post in a bank? After all, the Shaws were prominently associated with successful bankers. Had not the Royal Bank of Ireland been founded by a Shaw? All that experience in Townshend's office should be a recommendation to any sensible banker! . . . An interview was arranged with the manager of the local branch of a great bank. It was very diverting, and the manager felt convinced that G.B.S. was exceptionally clever, original and most amusing, but was not, somehow, quite the sort of person to be let loose on ledgers; though, of course, he had handled ledgers very ably in Ireland. But then everybody knew what the Irish were like, and what was considered to be efficient there, might be looked at with disfavour in England. It had been very pleasant to meet Mr Shaw! . . .

Memories of Matt McNulty's existence in Newry, no doubt, discouraged G.B.S. from seeking interviews with any other banker. Lucy listened glumly to his account of his experience, and then said there was always the Civil Service, the first and last refuge of the helpless Irish. It appeared that some men had managed to be both Civil Servants and writers! . . . Well, then!

The suggestion was carefully, but not enthusiastically considered He applied for particulars of the ways of entry into the Civil Service, and discovered that because he was neither a linguist nor a mathematician, he had no hope of a post except in the lower division of the Excise and Inland Revenue. The fact that he had filled a responsible position in a large office in Dublin made no impression on anybody in London; and the only posts that were offered to him were excessively subordinate. His pride was outraged by such offers.

Nevertheless, he decided to enter the Excise, a strange decision to be made by a rigid teetotaller; and early in July 1876, he went to a crammer to be prepared for his entrance examination. His experience in this school gave him the material for a page or two of *Immaturity*. He paid £3 13s. 6d. a month for his tuition, just as Smith did in the novel, but he did not stay the course to the end of the first month. He was the oldest student in the school, almost a man, and keeping school with callow youths galled him. When, therefore, he was invited by Lee to 'ghost' for him as musical critic of an unimportant weekly paper called *The Hornet*, and to do general utility work in the Park Lane academy, he withdrew from the crammer's school, forfeiting the unexpended part of the month's fee. He was to do all the work on *The Hornet* while Lee drew half the pay.

'I wrote exactly what I thought of the concerts I attended as critic. I was soon refused admission on the usual complimentary terms, and the editor mutilated and interpolated my notices horribly.' In addition to this musical 'ghosting', he acted as Lee's press agent, wrote or re-wrote his pamphlets because Lee's literary style was appalling, occasionally played the piano, and 'ghosted' generally. One of the pamphlets was entitled *How to Cure Clergyman's Sore Throat*. It was during this time that he saw Wagner conduct his own music in the Albert Hall, and 'dared', according to R. F. Rattray, 'to write of him as a great composer instead of denouncing him as a cacophonous charlatan.'

The Hornet led a hand-to-mouth existence until, in October, 1877, it died. G.B.S. was again out of work. His life in London at this time differed profoundly from his life in Dublin. There he had risen rapidly in authority, so that he was doing a man's responsible work while he was still under age, but here he seemed unable to secure a position to equal his ability and experience. The Chief Cashier in the Dublin land agent's office was offered employment as a junior clerk in London! . . . In December, he sought work at the East India Docks. 'Not worth anything,' he wrote in his diary.

He seemed to have lost his Dublin industry and to have become idle, inert and shiftless, unable to settle down to regular and routine employment. It was, however, no more than seeming. His industry was as great in Victoria Grove as it had been in Harcourt Street. The difference was that he was now training himself in a new and highly individualistic work which could not, by its nature, be taught by teachers or even by expert crammers at three and a half guineas a month, or bring him the wages a lad fresh from school received while learning the elements of his occupation. He had been paid 4s. 6d. a week when he was fifteen for addressing envelopes and copying letters in Townshend's office, but who would pay him that sum while, at the age of twenty, he taught himself the elements of writing? The man who hires a lad to lick stamps has at least the assurance that the lad has a tongue on which stamps can be licked, but who can foretell that a youth or a maiden who feels called by heaven to write immortal works will ever be capable of writing even a paragraph about an inquest in an evening paper? This was the training G.B.S. now followed with extraordinary persistence in face of grave discouragement from his mother and sister.

24

The change in G.B.S. was not the only remarkable alteration that had taken place as a result of the several migrations from Dublin to London we have here noted. Lee, who had seemed to be an inspired rebel against crass and conventional authorities in Dublin, now showed himself to be no less ready than the most unscrupulous music master to take pay for work he knew to be useless. He, who would have driven proud mammas out of his school in Dublin, had they dared to insult him with demands that their daughters should be converted into prima donnas in three months, was now willing to betray The System which had always been mentioned in Hatch Street with awe and wonder.

Lucinda Elizabeth, scarcely able to believe that so exalted a man would act in so treacherous a manner, cast him off without a pang. She could not have felt more appalled if Jesus Christ had turned Sadducee. So deep was her indignation that she withdrew from all association with him, practising The System herself, and when he died suddenly, she showed no more concern than she would have displayed had she heard that a flood in China had drowned a crowd of coolies. He had deteriorated dreadfully. His successful school had declined until it was little more than an early example of a night club. He had almost disappeared from the knowledge of the Shaws when, on November 28, 1886, he was found dead on the floor of 13 Park Lane, from what, at the inquest, was described as natural angina pectoris. His financial affairs were in a mess. Julian Marshall, Gentleman, of 13, Belsize Avenue, Hampstead, one of his creditors, proved administration on May 18, 1887. The total effects were £607 12s. 1d. In short, George John Vandaleur Lee was bankrupt.

There is a note in G.B.S.'s diary, under the date of November 30, 1886, in which he states that 'Lucy brings news that Lee is dead,' and another note on the following day. 'Called at 13 Park Lane to verify news of Lee's death. Heard from servant that he was found dead of heart disease on Sunday morning. Went back to tell Mother before going to Podmore.' Lucinda Elizabeth, according to her son, received the news with exceptional fortitude: 'it did not disturb her a jot.' Her indifference, for some reason which will escape general understanding, seemed to her son to denote high moral rectitude; but it will appear to many to be no more than a display of the callous character of this singular woman. It was, no doubt, a proof of her high standards that she despised the master who had betrayed The System for easy money, taking the cash and letting the credit go, but she might have spared a pang for the man who, G.B.S. asserts, 'not only made' her 'sing by a method that preserved her voice perfectly until her death at over eighty, but gave her a Cause and a Creed to live for.'

None of the Shaws attended the funeral, which may not have been their fault. It probably took place without their knowledge; but it is doubtful if any of them would have attended it had they known its day and hour. Lee had passed out of their knowledge a long time before his death. Neither G.B.S. nor Lucy had liked him, but both were in his debt. Even if there had not been the undischargeable debt in the matter of music, there was that moment of exaltation in G.B.S.'s boyhood, a felicity that was never forgotten, when his mother told him that they were to live at Torca Cottage, confronted by Killiney Bay and almost encircled by the Dublin and Wicklow Mountains. That high and lasting emotion was entirely due to Lee. It was surely worth the modest tribute of attendance at a solitary bankrupt's burial?

'I never grieve,' G.B.S. later in life remarked, 'but I do not forget.' A little show, not, perhaps, of grief, but of recollection and gratitude would have been seemly when the corpse of Lee was carried, unaccompanied, to its grave, and the only sorrow expressed was that of angry creditors crying over unpaid debts.

25

The better part of two years after his arrival in London had been spent by G.B.S. in desultory jobs and 'devilling' for Lee. The collapse of *The Hornet* had ended the remunerative part of this employment, and he now set himself down to writing novels. The conviction he had formed in Dublin that he was destined to become a great man, made him feel certain that his novel would not only be eagerly accepted by the first publisher to whom it was offered, but would bring him in a handsome revenue.

Every morning, he filled five pages of a penny exercise book with the work entitled *Immaturity*, the first of the five novels he wrote: a work which, he declared many years later, not even the nibbling mice could finish. It was begun in March 1879, and he finished the first draft on September 28. The revision was completed on November 5. This was quick work, for the novel is long, and disposes of the charge that he was an idler. Its fate was hard, nor was it published until it appeared in a pirated edition in America in 1921. Its first authorised publication in Great Britain was in 1930. Meredith, who was then reading scripts for Chapman and Hall in 1879, dismissed it curtly. 'No,' he wrote on it; and later on he was to recommend the rejection of *Cashel Byron's Profession*. He had already dismissed Samuel Butler's *Erewhon* with equal curtness, and had given Thomas Hardy bad advice.

Yet it was not always rejected with such scorn. Four other publishers, Hurst and Blackett, Kegan, Paul and Co., Chatto and Windus, and Bentley and Son, also declined it; but 'Blackwood actually accepted' it, 'and then revoked.' The firm of Macmillan dallied with it for a long while. 'Sir George Macmillan, then a junior, not only sent me a longish and evidently considered report by the firm's reader, John (afterwards Lord) Morley, but suggested to him that I might be of some use to him in his capacity as editor of the *Pall Mall Gazette*.'

Mr Charles Morgan, in *The House of Macmillan, 1843–1943*, says it is 'not sure' that Morley wrote the report, but the probabilities are that he did. Here it is:

'I have given more than usual attention to this MS., for it has a certain quality about it, not exactly of an attractive kind, but still not common. It is the work of a humourist and a realist, crossed, however, by veins of merely literary discussion. There is a piquant oddity about the situations now and then, and the characters are certainly not drawn after the conventional patterns of fiction. It is dry and ironic in flavour. . . . Recognising all these things, I ask myself what it is all about: what is the key, the purpose, the meaning of a long work of this kind without plot or issue. . . . It is undoubtedly clever; but most readers would find it dry, unattractive, and too devoid of any sort of emotion. And then it is very long.'

This is just and shrewd criticism; of a kind, too, that might well encourage a beginner to persevere. The reader did not end his interest in *Immaturity* with his first report. He returned to it in a second report which, however, was decisively against publication. 'On reflecting over the MS. of Mr Shaw,' he wrote, 'I am very doubtful of the expediency of publication,' and the book, 'evidently with regret and misgiving,' Mr Morgan remarks, 'was refused.'

About this time, McNulty had been incited by letters from Lucy to remonstrate with him because of what she called his idleness; and McNulty had urged him to seek some employment which would keep him in food and clothes while he tried to establish himself as a novelist. The advice was not resented, and on October 5, 1879, G.B.S. drafted a letter which seems to have been intended for some one residing in Dublin, though there is no proof that it was ever sent to him. It is a curious and illuminating document,[1] and is reprinted here for that reason.

'In the last two years, I have not filled any post, nor have I been doing anything especially calculated to qualify me for a business one. During the first half of that time, I was unsettled, and much in that active, but unproductive vein, in which an immature man wanders about London at night, plans extravagant social reforms, reads Shelley, talks in a strain of uncompromising virtue, and so forth. I wrote a few articles, but they were not accepted, and did not deserve to be. Then I found it necessary to work. I attempted to learn French, and bought a "method" (Ollendorff), calculated that the method could be mastered in eighty-six days, mastered it in that time exactly, and found myself able to translate by the constant aid of a dictionary—a sufficiently disgusting result. I also studied harmony and counterpoint, and finally I wrote a novel, which I am now revising. It cost me five months' labour, and I have no means of publishing it when it is finished. . . .'

We may interrupt him here to note that the charge of idleness brought against him by Lucy is here refuted.

'Since I came to London, I have called upon three or four men of business, to whom I had introductions, and enjoyed interviews with them of a more or less amusing, but wholly unprofitable character. Desirous to oblige the friends who had introduced me, they offered me junior clerkships, which, to their evident relief, I could not afford to take. One of them, who was very kind in his manner, did not disguise his conviction that I was a lunatic.

[1] It is cited in R. F. Rattray's invaluable *Bernard Shaw: a Chronicle*, pp. 32–3.

'My only reason for asking commercial employment is a pecuniary one. I know how to wait for success in literature, but I do not know how to live on air in the interim; my family is in difficulties. I may be deceived as to my literary capacity, and in any case, it is as well to be independent of fine art if clean work is to be made in it. I would much rather be an author than a banker, for instance, but I would rather be anything than a literary hack.

'Experience of the organization and administration of such an enterprise as yours, which is in some sort (unlike a land agency) a tangible part of civilization, would be worth working for. I have no illusions on the subject of business, and although it is exhilarating to make a clever stroke occasionally, the everyday work is too serious, in my opinion, to be undertaken for the purpose (as in land agency) of enriching an individual at the expense of the community.

'Pray excuse the length of this letter. I understand that you desired to get some idea of my character, and this I could not have given you by confining myself to the facts, which would not distinguish me from the next fifty clerks who might apply to you. However, I should be loth to press you for a place in which I might not be the right man. But if you can give me any hints as to what I might do with myself elsewhere, I shall be well satisfied, for I know you will be well able to understand my position. Hitherto I have disregarded so much advice from well intentioned friends that I am reputed almost as impracticable as another member of the family, with whom you are acquainted.'

This remarkable letter was written when its author was twenty-three. It issued from a mind made up and mature, a clear and dignified mind, in which there was a purpose and a serious intention. We may well wish that we knew to whom this draft was intended to be sent, for the man who could evoke such a letter must himself have been remarkable, and why it was not dispatched.

The presumption is that the only work which the person for whom the letter was originally intended, could have offered G.B.S. was in Dublin, to which he had no wish to return unless he were driven there by necessity. This surmise is strengthened by the fact that G.B.S.'s cousin, Fanny Johnstone, who had married Cashel Hoey, Agent General for Victoria, and was a novelist of some repute in her time, introduced him to Arnold White, manager and secretary of the Edison Telephone Company of London. White offered him an apprenticeship 'to be instructed in the profession of a telephone engineer'. G.B.S. then revised the letter cited above and sent it to White, together with a copy of the testimonial his father had obtained from Uniacke Townshend.

He began his employment in the Telephone Company on November 14, 1879, at a salary of £48 a year, plus commission. 'I was I believe, the only person in the entire establishment who knew the current scientific explanation of telephony,' he says, but his duty was not to expound this theory: it was to persuade reluctant people in the east end of London to let the Company erect posts or derricks on their premises. Work of this sort is uncongenial and even distressing to those who are shy, and G.B.S. was very shy. He would be paid by commission on results, and could do the work at his convenience. It was this fact, presumably, which induced him to take the job, for it seemed to have no other attraction. At the end of six weeks, he resigned it because the commission he had earned was insufficient to keep him. But his work must have satisfied his employers, for they immediately increased the rate of commission, and his resignation was withdrawn. If he could earn enough money to pay his low costs of living, and have leisure in which to write his novels, he would feel content.

It may be well at this point to remark that G.B.S., when he undertook a job, did it to the best of his considerable business ability, no matter how distasteful it might be. The testimony of all who employed him proves that he was skilful, conscientious and industrious. His Irish Protestant pride forbade him to botch any work he undertook. He was never dismissed from any employment. On the contrary, when he resigned a place, his employers sought to retain him by offers of greater responsibility and higher wages. Less than six months after he had joined the Edison Telephone Company, he had been promoted and had his salary raised at least twice. He was manager of the wayleave department with an office to himself when, on June 1, 1880, the Edison and Bell Companies were amalgamated and all the employees were formally dismissed. The duds had to seek work elsewhere, but the skilful members of the staff were immediately offered reinstatement. G.B.S. was one of those who were to be reinstated. But he refused the offer.

His engaging insolence did not deceive his superiors about his ability, nor did it make them dislike him. An earnest and energetic Prussian, Rudolph Krause, his immediate superior, tried to increase the efficiency of the Company's servants by methods which were popular among drill sergeants in Germany. Seeking to hustle G.B.S., he was astonished and baffled when he heard his requests for greater industry answered with the remark, 'I never work!' and his bewilderment was increased by his discovery that this boastful idler had been busy that morning before Krause himself, and had already done a good deal of work before the hustling had begun.

If any man would seem certain to have disliked G.B.S., Krause was the man, yet no one strove harder to dissuade him from refusing the post he had been offered in the amalgamated companies; and when it became plain to the Prussian that there was no hope of making G.B.S. change his mind, he wrote a letter to him which ended in these terms: 'Do not let me lose quite sight of you, and if possible call upon me, will you? We will arrange to spend some afternoon together at Tottenham.'[1]

The time of G.B.S.'s resignation from the Telephone Company was unfortunate, and he would, perhaps, have been wiser had he yielded to the Prussian's pleas. A tremendous slump in trade had hit Great Britain in 1879, one of the worst in its history and not to be surpassed in severity until 1931: and it still prevailed when the two telephone companies were amalgamated. A less resolute man would not have chosen that time of acute trouble to renounce commercial employment of any sort 'as a sin against my nature', so that he might devote himself entirely to writing. Had there been any demand for his novels, it was likely to be less then.

No man, however, was more highly resolved to do what he believed to be right than Bernard Shaw, who, though he was not physically brave, as he himself confessed with shame, was not surpassed by anyone in moral courage; which is the greater and rarer, but less popular, of the two virtues. Rats will fight in corners, and hens will defend their chickens, but only the higher sort of men will let themselves suffer or be persecuted or put to death for their principles. G.B.S.'s decision not to seek employment in a commercial firm exposed him to reproach, largely through his own fault, for the whole of his life. At the time of his death, a journalist in Australia denounced him for 'sponging' on his aged parents instead of earning his living like a man, and the charge was repeated in papers at home. It was the sort of denunciation he frequently had to endure, but he himself, in a juvenile effort to shock the middle-classes, was to blame for it. It had no foundation in fact.

26

The rejection of *Immaturity* was, undoubtedly, a severe blow to him. Why he had chosen to write a novel is not known. His ambition, when he left Dublin, had not consciously included any desire to become an author, though he had, in his childhood, as nearly all children do, scribbled bits and pieces; and he had collaborated, in his youth, with Matt McNulty in writing sensational stories, none of which came to anything worth mentioning. The single explanation attributed to him appears in *Days with Bernard Shaw*, by S. Winsten, where he is reported to have said, 'When I was young, George Eliot was thought to be the greatest writer of the day. I had to go to a

[1] I have taken this information from an article, entitled *Do You Remember, Mr Shaw?* by F. E. Loewenstein, which was published in *Adam*, an international review, in August 1946.

Young Fabian meeting, held in Hampstead Library, and as I came twenty minutes too early, I took down a novel by George Eliot and shall never forget how disappointed I was. I could do that sort of writing, I thought. Until then I had never thought of writing for a living, but what was I to do?'

This conversation seems to have been reported very carelessly. There was no Young Fabian society, if by this description is meant a society of the younger members of the society, when G.B.S. was young, and all his five novels had been written before the Fabian Society itself was founded in 1884, when G.B.S. was twenty-eight. The Fabian Nursery, of which I was a member, was not founded until about the middle of the first decade of the present century. But whatever it was that set his mind on writing, his decision, once taken was followed with great and persistent industry.

Despite discouragement from publishers and the taunts of his sister, he toiled at his daily task of filling five pages of exercise books with words. It was not until his fifth novel had been declined, that he abandoned the sixth he had begun and gave up his attempt to become a novelist. This, clearly, was not the means by which he would make his name. But the fight was bonny. The serving soldier of fortune was a good fighting man who retreated only to take up a better position for attack. He went down in defeat, but he emerged from his advanced post with a sense of style he had not possessed when he entered it. In those hard years, he shed the routine methods of the youth who begins to write, and made his own weapons.

The title of his first novel is the truest part of it. It is not only a book about immaturity, but its author himself was immature. It lacks cohesion, and its form is clumsy. The characters meet casually and without apparent purpose. They have as little relation to each other as the occupants of a railway carriage or an omnibus; and their encounters are unskilfully contrived. This is not to say that chance meetings are inadmissible in fiction or that all actions in novels must be ordained. Accident and chance are common characteristics of human existence, and much in many lives turns on them. Since they occur in life, they are certainly admissible in fiction; and those who seek to ban them are guilty both of arbitrary decision and blindness to fact.

It is absurd to say that *Tess of the D'Urbervilles* fails in majesty because the fate of Tess turns on the accident that a letter thrust under a door, slips under a carpet and is never discovered. Many fates have turned on such mishaps, and a writer is entitled to take them into account.

But it is the business of an author to illuminate life, to make the irrelevant events seem significant, and there is no illumination in

69

Immaturity, nor are the events related to each other in any significant manner. There was less ingenuity and natural aptitude for writing in G.B.S. than there was in Dickens when he wrote his first novel, *Pickwick Papers*, at the age of 'two or three and twenty'. G.B.S. compared with Shakespeare and Dickens, was a manufactured writer, made by himself almost by force. Yet the influence of Dickens on Shaw is plain enough. The character of that strange man, St John Davis, the evangelist who loses his flimsy balance when he falls in love with the cold little Scotswoman, Harriet Russell, and becomes a ballet dancer and a singer in the chorus of the opera, emerges from the Dickens' school.

> The minister kiss'd the farmer's wife,
> An' could na preach for thinkin' o't.

The style is pedestrian for the most part, giving few hints of the wit and vivacity soon to be developed, though a sentence now and then catches attention because it indicates the future G.B.S.: in the third chapter, for example, when an evangelistic meeting in Shepherd's Market is described. 'Then arose a young man, earnest and proud of his oratory, who offered up a long prayer, in the course of which he suggested such modifications of the laws of nature as would bring the arrangements of the universe into conformity with his own tenets,' suggestions such as G.B.S. throughout his life, was accustomed to make, such, indeed, as are made by every great man who modifies the world in some respect.

The unmistakable Shavian note is sounded in that passage, and so, in a later one, is another but less known Shavian note. His principal character, Robert Smith, an adumbration of G.B.S. himself, 'began to crave for a female friend who would encourage him to persevere in the struggle for truth and human perfection, during the moments when its exhilaration gave way to despair. *Happily, he found none such. The power to stand alone is worth acquiring at the expense of much sorrowful solitude.*' This passage, and especially the part in my italics, is one of the clearest revelations of himself and his needs, not only in his young manhood, but throughout his life, that he ever wrote. It accounts for much in his nature and conduct which baffles and even irritates many people; and it explains his correspondence with Ellen Terry and Mrs Patrick Campbell and other women.

His gay courage and his fortitude in adversity have resulted in a widespread belief that he never felt despondent when times were hard and manuscripts unerringly returned; but it is clear from this sketch of himself that he sometimes lost heart and would have been much the better for a stimulating and affectionate woman friend in whom he could confide his hopes and despair. It was his misfortune that he was too poor to be able to cut the figure that every woman likes her companion to cut, and too proud to accept hospitality he could not return. There is no evidence of any love affair or even friendship with a woman in the greater part of the nine lean years he spent in London searching for himself.

The salient fact about *Immaturity* is its revelation of a crude, but clever young man who was unhappy and unwelcome at home, who still bore the marks of his solitary social life in Dublin, and was losing his ability to mingle easily with strangers. He was becoming a lonely-minded man, almost a recluse, and the change, which began when his mother fled with his sisters to London, was fixed as a habit when he found himself unwanted and poor in her ramshackle house.

His misfortune at this time was increased by his use of a form of expression which was unsuitable to his genius, which he could not handle with skill because he lacked the gift of narrative, and was, therefore, not a novelist. He had, supremely, the gift of dialogue, and was, therefore, a dramatist. Even his gift for dialogue was not yet developed, nor had he yet fashioned his prose into the fine and flexible form he was eventually to achieve.

He had modelled himself too closely on what is oddly called the classic manner: the style which is stultified by pomposity. Educated people and members of the upper classes were characterised in literature by a formal speech of the sort that even politicians would not now dare to utter; and the lower orders were denoted by natural speech. But in life, the conversation of the aristocracy, particularly of those who had spent most of their time on their estates, was nearer to the colloquial utterance of the people they employed than it was to the routine politician's, the grammarian's or the pedant's. The lord of the manor understood his grooms and labourers better than he understood the schoolmaster or well-taught townsman: a fact which was plain to Fielding when he created Sophia Western's father and Parson Trulliber: and his grooms and labourers had no difficulty in understanding him.

Men of family or high quality have often been reproached by men of less quality than themselves for speaking with 'an accent', as if every man and woman has not some sort of accent, even if it be only the debased Oxford accent affected by pretentious people of limited intelligence. His contemporaries sneered at Castlereagh because he had an Ulster accent. Third-rate people, who could not cope with Sir Robert Peel in argument, belittled him because there was a Lancashire note in his voice. Lord Curzon of Kedleston had a Yorkshire accent which was thought by foolish persons to be singular in a man of his origin. Yet the slightest acquaintance with the history of their country should have taught them that gentlemen in all ages have spoken with the accent of their native place; as Boswell's father did, as Scots gentlemen did until the craze for a refined English accent came in.

But when a man of birth or, indeed, any educated man was put into a novel, his speech was devitalised by formality. It lost its colloquial character, and became the grammatical and ponderous utterance of one whose mind had been nourished entirely on editorials. We find this foolish tradition surviving in Thomas Hardy. His peasants talk with the natural grace and distinction of uneducated men who have listened to the beautiful liturgy of the Anglican church so attentively that they have acquired it as part of their daily conversation; but his educated people, whatever their class, talk like tedious pedagogues who have never read anything but the first leader in *The Times*.

It was on this outmoded classic tradition that G.B.S. modelled the conversation of his educated characters; and its effect on his novels was ruinous. When he had removed its defects, however, and had, largely as a result of his open air oratory, learnt that long speeches can be made to seem colloquial if they are spoken conversationally and not oracularly, he produced a form of speech for his plays which fits them admirably and is far finer than the dialogue of any dramatist who has written in English in the past two hundred years: dialogue which has the rich tone of an unusual mind and yet is faithful to the nature of the people who speak it. The prose of his prefaces and general writing is acknowledged, even by his detractors, to be extraordinarily well shaped, but the finer shape of his dialogue is less often and less liberally admitted because, no doubt, of its single fault, its occasional prolixity.

The finest example of his ability to write long speeches that are at once classic and colloquial in form is the great speech on heresy spoken by the Inquisitor in *Saint Joan*, a speech which is spoken on a formal and solemn occasion, and might, therefore, justifiably be modelled on the classic style alone. It is written with such skill that it appears to be an impromptu speech, spoken by a man of wide experience and great wisdom. It is not a set oration. The Inquisitor had not prepared it in the knowledge that it would be delivered on a definite date. It is spoken only because it has been provoked by a remark made by Brother Martin Ladvenu, a remark of which the Inquisitor could not have had any prevision. He was accustomed, no doubt, to meet heretical arguments, and had, therefore, useful replies close to his lips; but even a skilled casuist and debater cannot always, on the spur of the moment, produce so fine and cogent an argument as the Inquisitor delivers in reply to Brother Martin.

His prose, when, after much labour, it was made fine, flexible and full of sinewy strength, lacked a quality which it badly needed: it had very little verbal beauty. There were mental beauty and moral grandeur, but no felicitous phrases. His addiction to adjectives was worse than an alcoholic's addiction to drink; and it sometimes made him seem hysterical; as when, in the preface to *John Bull's Other Island*, he soils his style with this shrill denunciation of Englishmen:

> 'Even if Home Rule were as unhealthy as an Englishman's eating, as intemperate as his drinking, as filthy as his smoking, as licentious as his domesticity, as corrupt as his elections, as murderously greedy as his commerce, as cruel as his prisons, and as merciless as his streets, Ireland's claim to self-government would still be as good as England's.'

Miss Fanny Squeers, writing to Mr Ralph Nickleby, informed him that she was so distraught by his nephew's furious assault upon her father that she was screaming out loud as she wrote. It almost appears from this passage that G.B.S., as he wrote it, was also screaming out loud.

A thick anthology of lovely lines can be made from Shakespeare's plays, but a compiler would be hard put to it to make a small volume of lovely lines from G.B.S., though a large anthology of lofty and moving words could be made with ease. His prose is swift and tightly packed, almost too swift, too tightly packed. It outruns the reader, who puffs and pants as he tries to keep pace with it, and is obliged, now and then, to fling himself down and rest so that he may recover his breath and be able to run after the meaning; but it has grandeur and nobility, brilliance and wit, and high, sustained thought. Shakespeare's lines seem to fall from his lips without any effort by him, but Shaw's lines are carefully and deliberately made. There are profuse strains in his work, too profuse at times, but few that are unpremeditated art.

His platform speeches, which were generally delivered with great ease and every appearance of spontaneity, were not easy to report. Sentences were left unfinished, his grammar was often erratic and infirm, and he repeated himself. These are common faults in fluent orators, though some students of rhetoric, with a good deal of warrant, deny that they are faults, asserting that they are invaluable means of obtaining effects on large, varied and emotional audiences; and they remind us that set speeches, whether they are learnt by heart or read from script, seldom stir an audience, even when the audience is closely interested. Only once in my life did I hear G.B.S. read a speech, a close and cogent address on Equality, which lasted for ninety minutes. He read it uncommonly well, and showed no signs of fatigue when it was finished, but it was the least effective speech I ever heard him deliver, though its matter was brilliant. Practised orators know that it is more fatiguing to read aloud for an hour than it is to speak spontaneously for the same time.

The making of his noble prose was the hard labour he performed in the nine years of servitude he endured after his arrival in London; and it was wrought in a loveless home in circumstances of considerable distress. He has described his hardship and poverty in serio-comic terms in the preface to *Immaturity*, where he states that there were two periods in his lean years which were made acute by 'broken boots and carefully hidden raggedness to cuffs whose edges were trimmed by the scissors, and a tall hat so limp with age that I had to wear it back-to-front to enable me to take it off without doubling up the brim.' No one who has suffered hardship can read that gay, courageous passage without a feeling of sympathy, remembering the times when he, too, trimmed his cuffs with scissors and was careful how he handled the brim of his hat.

27

There is a passage in *Immaturity*, describing Smith's discontent with his employment in Figgins and Weaver's carpet shop which is clearly a description of G.B.S.'s discontent with his employment in London and Dublin:

> 'Smith had some ability, and he liked work; but he hated the duties of his clerkship as barren drudgery, which numbed his faculties and wasted his time. Nevertheless, his unjustifiable contempt for Figgins and Weaver, who were, within their scope, useful if prosaic men, induced him to do his work conscientiously lest he should become their debtor for any part of his salary which, through slackness, he should leave unearned. In this point of view the smallness of his emolument as compared with what he could have earned by condescending to the vulgarity of retail trade, was a consolation to him. His employers thought highly of him.'

It is characteristic of his unromantic creed at this time that he gave his chief character the name of Smith and made him a book-keeper in a firm of carpet merchants. There was glamour in an estate agent's office, with the constant companionship of premium apprentices who had passed through Trinity College, but there was no glamour in the carpet shop, no pleasure to be drawn from the company and conversation of Cockney salesmen who scattered their aitches as if they were chaff.

Yet it is obviously the Dublin estate agency, and not the Edison Telephone Company which is in his mind when he is describing

Smith's bitter emotions in his sweeping and absurd denunciation of clerical employment. ' "I wonder," said Smith to himself, as he walked home, "is there any profession in the world so contemptible as that of a clerk." '

He makes Smith recall a defaulting cashier, and in doing so, is drawing on his own distorted recollection of the defaulting cashier whom he succeeded in Townshend's office. Smith despises this delinquent because, having worked faithfully and well for his employers for thirteen years, during which he handled large sums of money, he had 'absconded with twelve pound, two shillings and sixpence.' The smallness of the sum embezzled seems to have appalled G.B.S. If the man must steal, why did he not steal magnificently? To have handled 'about three millions' during his career as cashier, and then forfeit his reputation for honesty and good service for the paltry sum of £12 2s. 6d., seemed to Smith-Shaw a feeble performance. Smith, like G.B.S., leaves his employment in a moment of piqued pride, and resolves that 'only in the most desperate extremity' will he consent to 'work at a ledger'.

In Smith's bitter reflections on clerical employment, there is a passage which reveals the continuity of G.B.S.'s thought. 'I would rather be the meanest handicraftsman than a clerk, except that I would be under the thumb of a trade union.' This was his belief at the end of his life, when, in a letter to Mr Lawrence Langner, of the Theatre Guild of New York, he complained that Britain, immediately after the Second World War, was controlled and directed, not by a Socialist, but by a Trade Union Government.[1]

The beginning of *Immaturity* is abrupt, and the end is inconclusive. Smith is not adequately accounted for. We spend less than two years in his company, and part with him almost as ignorant of his character and circumstances as we were at our first encounter with him. His age at the beginning of the book is eighteen, and he has been employed by Figgins and Weaver for about a year. Before entering their service, he had worked elsewhere for another year. His business life, therefore, in its beginnings, corresponds roughly with his author's. How or where he had lived before *Immaturity* begins, or where he originated, does not transpire. His parents, who seem to have been dead for several years when the story begins, are barely mentioned, nor does their son appear to have any friends or living relations. Mr and Mrs Smith are alleged to have been poor, and there is an assertion on the penultimate page of the novel that they were tiresome to their son.

'I remember,' he tells Mrs Scott, 'how I secretly hated the solemn humbug my parents used to pour forth on me, when they were seized

---

[1] See *The Magic Curtain* by Lawrence Langner, p. 416.

by an attack of duty': an experience, however, which G.B.S. never, apparently suffered, since his father and mother were never attacked by a sense of duty in the whole of their lives.

Smith's speech and manners are those of a lad of education and breeding whose life has been solitary. He dislikes the world in which he lives, and feels antipathetic to, and humiliated by, his employment. His associates, both in the carpet shop and his lodgings, are uncongenial to him, because of their intellectual and social inferiority. He is said to be fairly proficient in French, and he manifestly has culture greater than would be expected in a child of humble and impecunious parents. Why, the reader wonders, is so little said about the first eighteen years of his life? How and where did he live after the death of his parents? A lad of sixteen cannot, as a rule, maintain himself on his salary, though G.B.S. did, and unless Smith was as able as his creator, and as fortunate in his first job, it is difficult to understand how he lived before his eighteenth year.

An author who raises unanswered questions in the minds of his readers is obviously deficient in technical skill. The extraordinary fact about Bernard Shaw is that although he became an uncommonly skilful dramatist, able not only to write a well-made play, as in *Mrs Warren's Profession*, *The Devil's Disciple* and *Fanny's first Play*, but to break all the rules with an audacity that amounted to genius, as in *Getting Married*, *Misalliance*, *Heartbreak House* and *Back to Methuselah*, he was unable to master the craft of the novel, despite his hard apprenticeship and undeniable industry. Nor did he increase his skill by practice. It declined until it fell to pieces in *An Unsocial Socialist*.

28

There is little to be gained by extensive examination of the four successors to *Immaturity*. None of them contributes much, if anything, to our knowledge of their author. Biography is less apparent in them than in the first of the five novels, nor is there any sign of increasing authority, though Robert Louis Stevenson, dying in Samoa, was to be enchanted by *Cashel Byron's Profession*. We make note of a feeble effort to link the novels together by carrying characters from *Immaturity* to some of its successors. The Scotts reappear. So do Isabel Woodward and her husband. But Smith is neither seen nor heard.

The same ruthless determination to shed all sentiment and romance appears in them as in *Immaturity*. It is more impressive in *The Irrational Knot* than it is in *The Unsocial Socialist*. G.B.S. still abhors the pseudo-aesthete who considers himself an artist when he is only a meddler in text-books on art. Mr Halkett Grosvenor, in *Immaturity*, is such a person. 'He had paid almost every distinguished artist in Europe for lessons in all branches of art. At twenty, he had painted a picture of Jacob's ladder; and this work, much faded because of the liberal use he had made of brilliant but unstable pigments, still hung in a drawing-room at Perspective, where it created mirth enough to confer on it a celebrity as wide as the personal reputation of the painter. He had begun many works subsequently; but they remained unfinished; and of late years Mr Grosvenor had ceased to speak even of his intentions with respect to them.'

Scott is another such, except that he does paint something, though its quality is of no consequence. Isabel Woodward, too, dabbles in art, and is a monger of routine opinions, routine even when they are rebellious, about modes and movements: a woman without the slightest element of creative power in her entire composition. She cannot even create a child, being as barren in her womb as she is in her spirit. These aborted artists are to be found in all G.B.S.'s novels, and they excite abhorrence in the genuine artists they meet.

The most notable of these outspoken denouncers of the pseudo-aesthetes is Owen Jack, the musician in *Love Among the Artists*, who makes a habit of rudeness and is said to have been modelled on Beethoven. His contempt for Adrian Herbert, the mediocre artist, is illimitable and absurd: a man of his quality should be less aware of mediocrities and triflers than Jack is of Herbert. The remarkable character in this novel, however, is neither Jack nor Herbert, but Herbert's mother, whose contempt for her son's artistic pretentions is as deep and derisive as Jack's.

Mrs Herbert is one of the most notable figures in the five novels, worthy to stand on the level of the finest figures in the plays: a vivid and veracious woman from tip to toe. She wears the features of a credible human being, and is a very notable and entertaining character. She is probably based on G.B.S.'s mother, created by him in a period when his admiration for her was warmer than usual.

Adrian Herbert's feeling for his mother is one almost of hatred: the hatred which is felt by incompetent people for those who know them to be totally inefficient. Herbert tells Aurelie Szczymplica, an accomplished pianist whom he eventually marries, how little he likes his mother:

'Can you not understand that a mother and son may be so different in their dispositions that neither can sympathise with the other? It is my misfortune to be such a son. I have found sympathetic friendship, encouragement, respect, faith in my abilities, and love . . . from strangers upon whom I had no claim. In my mother, I found none of them: she felt nothing for me but a contemptuous fondness which I did not care to accept. She is a clever woman, impatient of sentiment, and fond of her own way. My father, like myself, was too diffident to push himself arrogantly through the world; and she despised him for it, thinking him a fool. When she saw that I was like him, she concluded that I, too, was a fool, and that she might arrange my life for me in some easy, lucrative, genteel, brainless, conventional way. I hardly ever dared to express the most modest aspiration, or assert the most ordinary claims to respect, for fear of exciting her ridicule. She did not know how much her indifference tortured me, because she had no idea of any keener sensitiveness than her own. Everybody commits folly from youth and want of experience; and I hope most people humour and spare such follies as tenderly as they can. My mother did not even laugh at them. She saw through them and stamped them out with open contempt. She taught me to do without her consideration; and I learned my lesson. My friends will tell you that I am a bad son—never that she is a bad mother, or rather no mother. She has the power of bringing out everything that is hasty and disagreeable in my nature by her presence alone. This is why I wish I were wholly an orphan, and why I ask you, who are more than all the world besides, to judge me by what you see, and not by the reports you may hear of my behaviour towards my own people.'

The voice is the voice of Jacob, though the hand is the hand of Esau. The sudden sincerity in Adrian Herbert in this passage is caused by the fact that his author has abruptly pushed him aside and spoken very passionately and in deep resentment about himself. This is the bitter cry, not of Adrian Herbert, but of Bernard Shaw. It is not Mrs Herbert who is being scourged and scoriated: it is Lucinda Elizabeth.

It is right and proper to warn us not to attribute to an author the sentiments and beliefs he puts into the mouths and minds of his characters: and we must not press too severely the similarity of Adrian Herbert's feeling for his mother to that of G.B.S. for his. Adrian Herbert was a mediocre artist, and his mother's contempt for his work is justified by his author. G.B.S. was not a mediocrity: he was a man of genius, may be said by those who demur to the suggestion that Adrian's cry of pain is really Shaw's. But the reader must remember that when *Love Among the Artists* was written, there was no sign of his genius to be observed. His plight was much worse than Adrian Herbert's, for he, at least, had obtained some recognition. G.B.S. had obtained none. His novels were everywhere rejected, and he himself seemed, both to his mother and his sister, an idle good-for-nothing, who was content to let his hard-working parent keep him.

Is it likely that all his work would resound with complaints of unsympathetic and imperceptive mothers if his own had been gentler, more appreciative, and less cold-hearted? A man does not harp on a grievance unless he has one; and the more he bores us by railing against his wrong, the deeper his grievance is likely to be. Dickens, as G.B.S. remembered, never forgave his mother for her attempt to bind him to the blacking factory. May we not believe with justice that Jesus, whose recorded words to his mother were always harsh, had cause for his reproaches? G.B.S., despite his quixotic admiration for Lucinda Elizabeth's fixed ideas and implacable pursuit of them, and his extraordinary lack of rancorous emotion, never forgot or forgave her empty heart or ceased to feel wounded and bereft because she withheld from him not only love but common kindness. But his generous heart forbade him to vent his lifelong sense of deprivation directly on her, and he rid himself of his resentment in his fictions.

There is a small scene in *Love Among the Artists*, in which he reveals his sense of parental love. It is so rare in his work, for he was almost morbid in his aversion from sentimental revelations, that it must be cited. Mr Brailsford has repudiated his daughter Madge because she has rebelled against his authority and insisted on her right to make her own life and to follow the profession for which she feels fitted: the stage. He is taken to a theatre where she is acting, and is deeply moved not only by her performance but by the mere sight of her, though he maintains to his hostess, Lady Geraldine, that he will not forgive her, will not even speak to her should she enter the box in which he is sitting. The words have hardly left his lips when the door of the box opens, and Madge, who has stolen off the stage, enters. 'She threw off the cloak as soon as the door was closed, and then seized her father and kissed him. He said with difficulty, "My dear child"; sat down; and bent his head overpowered by emotion for the moment.'

G.B.S., who took great trouble throughout his life to pretend that he was superior to common affection and ordinary human feeling, was intensely emotional, full of affection and eager to possess it; and it is in such rare incidents as this scene between Madge Brailsford and her father that his emotional quality is revealed. The flippancy he sometime displayed, to the great distress of his friends, in sad and sorrowful circumstances was only the semi-hysterical effort of a deeply moved man to conceal his anguish. In the First World War, a brother officer of mine saw his close friend blown into the air by a shell. His immediate reaction to his loss was a shout of laughter! . . . It was in distress as deep as that, that G.B.S. sometimes shocked even his intimates with a jest.

Deprived of sympathy at home, subjected instead to continual disapproval and even to contempt, he lost the sociability he had displayed in Dublin, and became a self-conscious outcast whose solitude was increased by his lack of means and his deteriorating clothes. He must have been much tougher in texture than is commonly supposed, for the more he suffered in these respects, the greater became his determination to persevere in his attempt to make himself a writer. Undaunted by the failure of *Immaturity*, he began his second novel *The Irrational Knot*, in the leisure he was allowed from his employment by the Edison Telephone Company; one which William Archer advised him not to reprint.

His mind was beginning to spread. The conventionally artistic people with whom his mother and sister associated had become distasteful to him, chiefly because he perceived how shallow were their pretensions to be thought artistic at all. The most they could do was to repeat stale beliefs about art in general, while their ingenuous efforts to express such feelings as they possessed resulted in nothing more impressive than mild studies of the English landscape and spiritless water-colour sketches of familiar scenes in Italy. Lake Como was painted to death! . . .

G.B.S. no longer went to the parties frequented by Lucinda Elizabeth and her popular and amusing daughter. He sought the society of men and women who had some distinctive character, whose minds were not routine, who were not accustomed, as Mr Pickwick advised Mr Snodgrass, to shout with the largest mob. Some of them were undoubtedly cranks, but their oddity did not distress G.B.S., who was himself an oddity and was about to become a crank: that is to say, he was about to abandon mob beliefs and have a mind of his own. He was not yet a Socialist, but he was on the way to Socialism. He had already perceived what he believed to be disadvantages in a capitalistic society.

One of them was that the sexes, in such a society, were segregated unnaturally into groups by money: that a woman whose natural mate might be a farmer or a fisherman was prevented by his lack of means and fine manners from marrying him, and must either forego a mate or marry a man of her own financial class, whether he was her natural mate or not.

This is one of the few arguments in Socialism which has some validity; but its validity is on the surface and has little or no relation to fundamental facts, natural or contrived.

What is a man's or a woman's natural mate? Are we to believe the preposterous and entirely sentimental argument that there is only one man in the world who is naturally fitted to be the mate of a particular woman: a supposition which must have seemed absurd to the unromantic G.B.S.? If we believe this nonsense, the widow and the widower will rise up to expose our folly; and all polygamous and polyandrous peoples will join in jeers at such sentimental bosh. If, as appears to be the case, the purpose of mating is the perpetuation of the species, all other considerations, such as love and congenial companionship, being subordinate to it, then it is obvious that any man who can fertilise a woman is fit to be her mate, if, as we shall assume, he is a sane and physically healthy man.

Some societies have been governed by that belief.

The plain fact, staring us in the face, is that people who are uncongenial to each other, are as capable of getting fine and healthy children as people who seem to have been created for each other and for nobody else. There is no society that the mind of men can devise in which any person's range of choice in mates will be wide. Money is the least of the barriers between men and women. The rest are not only numerous, but more difficult to overcome. There are the matters of temperament and habit, of race and religion, of interests and general outlook on life, and those imponderable differences which cannot be defined even by those who feel them, but are, perhaps for that reason, profounder than all the others.

The members of a socialist state will be even more severely restricted by the limitations of time and place than the members of a free state, who can at least move about the country at their will, even if their movements be no more than the wanderings of a tramp or gipsy. But a bureaucratically-controlled community will impose regulations on the governed which will be no better, and may be much worse than those that were imposed in the Middle Ages and included the Statute of Labourers. When people are not permitted to change their occupation, or to migrate from one part of their country to another without a permit from the Government, or are removed from here to there whether they will or no, their hope of any enlargement of their choice of mates will be considerably less than it is now. The likelihood that liberty will be far more strictly limited in a Socialist society than it is in a modern capitalistic society is not denied by socialists: it is admitted and desired.

It appears that none of the social systems on which mankind has so far lived has restricted the choice in marriage of men and women to the extent to which G.B.S., in *The Irrational Knot*, argues that it has been restricted by capitalism. But neither does there appear to be any enlargement of the range of choice in a socialistic or semi-socialistic society, such as he suggests is certain; for the range of any person's choice, whatever his fortune or class may be is bound, because of the general limitations of human interest, to be small. None of us is capable of forming more than a restricted number of friends and acquaintances, and many of these will be uncongenial or of slight value.

What man cannot confirm from his own knowledge, the experience of Dickens who, having loved dearly in his youth a girl who inspired the character of Dora in *David Copperfield*, and been rejected by her because his prospects were poor and he had no fortune at his back, dropped on his knees when, many years later, he met her again, fat, foolish and forty-four, and thanked God that she had declined him. He had suffered severely from her refusal, feeling, indeed, that he would never recover from the blow; but one look at her, when, eager to meet her again, he saw her enter the room, was sufficient to make the remains of his boyish love fall stone dead, to be replaced only by derision that made him recreate her in fiction, not now as Dora, but as Flora Finching in *Great Expectations*.

Marian Lind, in *The Irrational Knot*, marries Edward Connolly because she knows in her bones and blood that he has quality and distinction far beyond those of her own relatives and the people she commonly meets. If he had been a workman, as he snobbishly and stupidly persists in calling himself, whose electrical engineering amounted to no more than repairing fuses and wiring walls for lamps, she would not, for a single second, have considered him as a husband; and she would have been right. There were enough nonentities in her own world from whom to choose, without looking for one in the proletariat.

Connolly is not a common man: he is an uncommon man, and, therefore, in the Shavian line of natural aristocrats when he declares that he has married beneath him in making Marian Lind his wife. She is his intellectual inferior.

He tells Elinor McQuinch, whom he would have done better to marry, that he is a worker. 'I belonged and belong to the class that keeps up the world by its millions of serviceable hands and serviceable brains. All the pride of caste in me settles on that point. I admit no loafer as my equal. The man who is working at the bench is my equal, whether he can do my day's work or not, provided he is doing the best he can. But the man who does not work anyhow, and the class that does not work, is a class below mine. . . .'

He bursts into a ridiculous tirade about Marian when, wounded by his indifference to her, she bolts to America with Douglas.

> 'When I married Marian I was false to my class. I had a sort of idea that my early training had accustomed me to a degree of artistic culture that I could not easily find in a working-class girl, and that would be natural to Marian. I soon found that she had the keenest sense of what was lady-like, and no sense of what was beautiful at all. A drawing, or an engraving framed without a white mount round it to spoil it, pained her as much as my wrists without cuffs on them. No mill girl could have been less in sympathy with me on the very points for which I had preferred her to the mill girls. The end of it was that love had made me do a thoroughly vulgar thing—I had married beneath me.'

The fact which ought to have stared Connolly in the face was that he would never have married a mill girl unless she had been a woman of such exceptional quality and character that the words mill girl would have had no meaning when applied to her; and that if he had had to choose between Marian Lind and the mill girl of fact and not of Fabian fancy, no matter how commonplace and conventional Marian might be, he would, without the slightest hesitation, have chosen Marian. Had he been sincere, he would, after Marian had bolted with Douglas, have sought his ideal mill girl and have married her, thus renewing his allegiance to the class he considered himself to have betrayed; but there is no hint in the novel that such an intention ever entered his mind.

The final chapters are absurdly implausible. They have little relation to reality, and are far from being funny, though there are passages throughout the book which excite the intelligent reader's interest in their author and fill him with a conviction that the young man, though he knows so little, will one day write with great authority. The characters are clearly drawn, even when they are over-drawn, and the dialogue is easier and more natural than that in *Immaturity*, though some of Connolly's remarks, such as the priggish complaint about walking arm in arm with a lady in the street, might have been uttered by a wooden idol worked by an apprentice priest. They make the utterances of Nicholas Nickleby and Little Nell seem faultless in their fidelity to fact.

The novel is remarkable for a scene which G.B.S. repeated in one of his last plays, *The Apple Cart*: a scene which provokes speculation which can now never become decisive. The Rev. George Lind, one of the people carried forward from *Immaturity*, where he is slight and ineffective, becomes fairly important in *The Irrational Knot*. He is a ritualist, more interested in the symbol than the spirit symbolised, but he has his moments of sincerity and force. Perturbed by the fact that Connolly's sister, Susanna, and Marmaduke Lind are living in sin at West Kensington, and have begotten a bastard, he pays her a visit in the hope of reforming her. (Marmaduke seems to be a direct descendant of Lord H. in Richardson's *Pamela*.) At the end of an unavailing interview, he looks at his watch and tells Lalage Virtue, as Susanna calls herself on the stage, that he must go. Then follows this scene:

' "Nonsense," she said, rising also, and slipping her hand through his arm to detain him. "Wait and have some luncheon. Why, Doctor, I really think you are afraid of me. *Do* stay."
' "Impossible! I have much business which I am bound—Pray, let me go," pleaded the clergyman piteously, ineffectually struggling with Susanna, who had now got his arm against her breast. "You must be

83

mad!" he cried, drops of sweat breaking out on his brow as he felt himself being pulled helplessly towards the ottoman. She got her knee on it at last; and he made a desperate effort to free himself.

' "Oh, how rough you are!" she exclaimed in her softest voice, adroitly tumbling into the seat as if he had thrown her down, and clinging to his arms; so that it was as much as he could do to keep his feet as he stooped over, striving to get upright. At which supreme moment the door was opened by Marmaduke who halted on the threshold to survey the two reproachfully for a moment. Then he said, "George I'm astonished at you. I have not much opinion of parsons as a rule; but I really did think *you* were to be depended on." '

Here is a pretty problem in the mystery of authorship. Those who have seen or read *The Apple Cart*, will remember that a scene remarkably like this one occurs in the second act, when King Magnus is tumbled on the floor by his mistress, Orinthia, who resents his habit of being punctual for all his appointments with his Queen, and seeks to make him late for one. There is no reason why G.B.S. should not have borrowed from himself. All authors do. Did not Shelley borrow the beginning of *Queen Mab* and use it, slightly altered, to open *The Daemon of the World*?

But the history of the scene in *The Irrational Knot* involves a peculiar problem when we learn, as G.B.S. himself told me when I lunched with him and Sir Edward Elgar immediately before the first performance of *The Apple Cart* at Malvern, that the incident occurred in Mrs Patrick Campbell's house when she, riled by his determination to keep an appointment with Charlotte, seized hold of him, and, in their struggle, capsized him on the floor, where they were both discovered floundering by a member of the household. It is conceivable that Mrs Campbell had read *The Irrational Knot* and, in a moment of that impish misbehaviour which made her too often infantile, resolved to make G.B.S.'s fiction become her fact. The singular part of this story is that G.B.S., when he talked to me about the incident, did not appear to remember that it had first been used in *The Irrational Knot*. Like Molière and Wilde, G.B.S. borrowed what he needed from whom he could. *Pygmalion* owes something to *Peregrine Pickle*. Wilde's debts were so numerous that he would have bankrupted himself had he tried to discharge them.

The Irrational Knot ends inconclusively, leaving the reader in total ignorance of the fate of the principal characters at the most important period of their lives. What happens to Smith in *Immaturity* is less significant than what, we feel certain, must have happened to him after the novel ends; and the reader of *The Irrational Knot* feels cheated when he perceives that he is to hear no more of the Connollys after Marian informs her husband that she is pregnant by Douglas. He tells her that he must divorce her, but that she will become, for the first time in her life, a free woman, owner of her child and under obligation to nobody: a monstrous piece of nonsensical perfidy, since no one is free from obligation to someone, and no one is entirely free.

Marian will require an income, and as she has no capacity whatever for earning one, she must accept it from her father or her ex-lover or her ex-husband . . . or anyone who will provide it. She thus becomes more of a slave than she was before she was fertilised by Douglas, and may justifiably complain that if she had failed Connolly, Connolly had more terribly failed her. It seems not to have occurred to Connolly that there must have been some fault or defect in him that Douglas could make a mother of her, but he could not. Marian is undoubtedly a fool, but at no moment of her life was she such an irredeemable fool as her husband.

29

The Irrational Knot was written in 1880, the year which saw the end of G.B.S.'s intellectual isolation in London, and the beginning of his more adventurous and adult career. The society commonly frequented by his mother and sister displeased him, partly because he was still shy and nervous and, therefore, awkward in drawing-rooms; but more because the kind of chatter he heard in the drawing-rooms bored him. He was not interested in artistic tittle-tattle by dilletantes, amateur artists, and loungers on the fringes of the artistic world, so he began to seek more congenial society elsewhere. His poverty compelled him to take his entertainment mainly in walking about the streets of London: an entertainment which is the chief resource in that city of all who are lonely and poor, one, too, which is far more formative of their minds than they imagine while they are enjoying it.

But there were, he discovered, other means of enlarging his outlook on life that were not less profitable. He was now in his twenty-fourth year, and, apparently, a total failure, disregarded by his mother, despised by his sister, and ignored by their friends and acquaintances. He was tall, over six feet in height, and pale with the pallor of people with red hair, though his was not notably red, nothing like so red as that of his sister Agnes, whose mane had been like a burning bush. It was worn flat on his head, divided in the middle, and was matched on his chin by a thin, scrubby beard which was slow in its growth. The ears and nose, especially the latter, were large, the nose, indeed, being a big, beaky Shaw nose, almost cancelling the short upper lip, but not detracting from the firm mouth the lips enclosed. It was not a sensual nor was it a cruel mouth, but it was resolute, a determined mouth that could not be dissuaded from the mind's intent.

His eyes were his most notable feature, far more notable than the long, slightly twisted nose which seemed at first sight to prevail over the whole face, or the tightly-drawn lips or the large projecting ears. The eyebrows had not yet achieved the Mephistophelian shape which their owner so carefully cultivated later in life, but they revealed already the strange dissimilarity between the two sides of his face, a dissimilarity which became more easily discernible in his middle and last years. One side was genial, almost benign and full of fun and laughter: the other side had a brooding look that was to become almost tormented in his old age, making him, in some aspects, resemble Tolstoy, but a Tolstoy who had a sense of humour. Few faces are so dissimilar in their halves as G.B.S.'s was. The bewildered prophet, the suffering sage is balanced by the wit who is liable at any moment to turn Pan, kick up his heels and play impish pranks.

The fun is less evident in his twenty-fourth year than it was to become. He had few occasions for fun, then. There is a buttoned-up look about him which is not the less constricted because it is most plainly observable in the way he wears his clothes. These are still the remains of his Dublin glory when he was the trusted and accomplished cashier in Townshend's estate office. But they are showing signs of wear, though no signs of tear, and are not yet beginning to look green. He wears the features of a sober young man, over-earnest, perhaps, about the state of the world and eager to deliver messages, though unable yet to find an audience which will listen for more than a minute or two; but he shows in his laughing eye as well as in the eye that is sombre, and in the resolute lips, that he will one day make the casual and disinterested passers-by stand and look and listen.

In the winter of 1879–80, he became acquainted with James Lecky, a notable authority on music and musical instruments, who was also deeply interested in the study of phonetics. He wrote an article on Temperament, defined as 'Systems of tuning keyed instruments', for the first edition of Grove's *Dictionary of Music and Musicians;* and he was a man of great versatility of mind, exercising a considerable influence on all who came into contact with him. Through Lecky, G.B.S. became acquainted with Henry Sweet, a don at Oxford, and Alexander Ellis, both of whom were students of phonetics.

It may be said that if Shaw had not met these three men, the character of Drinkwater, in *Captain Brassbound's Conversion*, would not have been created or that his pronunciation of English would have been recorded in a more elementary manner than it is in the dialogue of that play: a deprivation for which, perhaps, the reader of the book and the actors who perform the part would feel grateful. *Pygmalion* would almost certainly not have been written at all. G.B.S.'s interest in phonetics was not only profound but was almost lifelong. He continued in this friendship with Lecky and Sweet and Ellis, the friendship and interest he had begun with Chichester Bell when he was a lad in Dublin lodgings. For nearly eighty years, from his youth until his extreme old age, he had studied and tried to promote the science of phonetics and was eager for the reformation of alphabets, forgetful, as all devoted students of that science are, that there cannot ever be a fixing of any language, since language, like those who use it, lives and moves from generation to generation. Chaucer within a century of his death was incomprehensible to the majority of his countrymen.

It was Lecky who took him to a debating society, called the Zetetical Society—the word zetetical means *seeking:* for the truth, presumably—and it was at one of its meetings, in the last weeks of 1879, that G.B.S. made his first public speech. The Society was founded in imitation of a more famous one, the Dialectical Society, which spent a great deal of time and energy in discussing John Stuart Mill's essay, *On Liberty.* For those were the days when men were neither afraid to mention freedom, nor less eager for it than they were for security. The members of both societies were what is called 'advanced' persons, and some of them were cranks, but they were cranks that made revolutions. The Zetetical Society's meeting place was in the rooms of The Women's Protective and Provident League in Great Queen Street, Long Acre, London; and G.B.S., although he was not yet formally a member, felt impelled to make a speech. He seemed to be entirely at ease, but was, in fact, trembling.

His sense of shame at his nervous pusillanimity forced him to join the Society with the intention of speaking as often as possible, even if he were totally ignorant of the subject of discussion, so that he might overcome his diffidence about speaking at all. 'I suffered agonies that no one suspected,' he told Professor Archibald Henderson many years later. 'During the speech of the debate I resolved to follow, my heart used to beat as painfully as a recruit's going under fire for the first time. I could not use notes; when I looked at the paper in my hand I could not collect myself enough to decipher a word. And of the four or five wretched points that were my pretext for this ghastly practice of mine, I invariably forgot three—the best three.'

When he was asked to take the chair at the third meeting of the Society which he attended, his hand trembled so much that he could scarcely sign the minutes. These nervous apprehensions were eventually overcome, but not easily, nor was he ever free from them. Yet he had that delusive air of complete confidence in himself and of feeling entirely at his ease that is one of the most remarkable characteristics of all highly nervous people who take part in any sort of public life. G.B.S. was not more nervous before a public meeting than Henry Irving was on a first night, as Suzanne Lenglen was before she entered a tennis court in a tournament, as a racehorse is on Derby Day. But the nervous temperament is an important element in the brilliance. No person is less nervous or more phlegmatic than the dull dog who has little to say and does not know how to say it.

Among the members of Zetetical Society was a young man, named Sidney James Webb, who was almost exactly three years younger than G.B.S. He was a clerk in the Colonial Office, where his colleagues included Sydney Olivier, also about three years Shaw's junior. These three were destined to become close friends and to have a considerable influence on the world and a profound influence on British affairs. The singular fact about Webb and Olivier, both of whom became peers, is that they were unsuccessful in parliament, where the impression they made was slight and their influence was negligible. Webb, who was superb in committee, was entirely ineffective, chiefly because of his thin, slightly lisping voice[1] and his small stature and peculiar personal appearance. Olivier, in spite of his great success as Governor of Jamaica, was himself indecisive in debate, over-inclined to split hairs, and unable to express his mind clearly. Olivier was not a member of the Zetetical Society, but he met Shaw through the latter's friendship with Webb.

30

The contrast between Webb and Shaw, mentally, physically and spiritually, was startling and deep. Gilbert and Sullivan were not more dissimilar in almost every respect than these two: yet both couples worked harmoniously enough, though they seemed to have nothing in common. G.B.S. was tall and lithe: Webb was so small that he was nicknamed The Gnome by his wife's relations, and he looked ungainly, though he was not. The temptation to regard Shaw and Webb as Don Quixote and Sancho Panza was strong; but, apt to G.B.S., it was entirely inapt to Webb whose remoteness from any

---

[1] But his voice was not always thin and inaudible, as E. R. Pease, in *The History of the Fabian Society*, and R. C. K. Ensor, in his impressive chapter in *The Webbs and Their Work*, edited by Margaret Cole, maintain. Ensor asserts that when Webb spoke at meetings in Oxford, his voice was robust and that he held the close attention of his audiences. My own recollection is of a later date when his voice was beginning to fade, but it was still clear enough for him to be heard distinctly in a large hall, and he continued, outside Parliament, to command attention. The acoustics of Westminster, may have overcome him, for he certainly failed to impress either the Commons or the Lords by his speeches. What was the cause of this fading of his voice is not known.

man of Sancho Panza's class was such that he scarcely knew what to say to a working man, when, through some mischance, he met one.

Each had a peculiarly shaped head. G.B.S.'s was long, almost flat at the back, and as straight as a leadline: Webb's was large and bulbous, and totally disproportionate to his height. He seemed to have more head than body. His hands, like G.B.S.'s, were beautiful, and he had the smallest feet I have ever seen on a man. They might have been bound in his childhood, so small were they.

G.B.S. was witty, but a little lacking in a sense of humour, though he had an immense feeling for fun and larks and was occasionally inclined to rollick in the manner of a low comedian, not vulgarly, but crudely. Webb had little or no wit, but he had a surprisingly large sense of humour, and he delighted in what are called characteristic remarks and actions, Webbisms, which he would let off on dull reporters from the portentous papers, so that they might live for the rest of the year on a tale beginning, 'Do you know what I heard Sidney Webb say. . . ?'

He had a deep loathing of physical exercise. G.B.S., like Dickens, could never have enough of it. Had it not been for Mrs Webb's determination that her husband should move his muscles at least once a day, he would probably never have taken any exercise at all.

G.B.S. was impulsive and extravagant in assertion, though he was often able, because of an uncommonly good memory, to confound opponents with apt quotations and instances. His fault was that he could not resist the temptation to utter a good remark which upset those who heard it, and he would sometimes go out of his way to wound an audience in its dearest beliefs by a remark which was too tersely made to win agreement.

Webb's method was entirely different. He was methodical, exact, and full of facts and figures. He seldom caused laughter or evoked cheers, but he generally gained attention and never failed to win respect. Each, in his way, was a good debater, but Webb was better in committee than in assembly, whereas G.B.S., though he was a very good committee man when he refrained from antics, was extraordinarily effective with a large audience, even when he had started off by shocking it. When he talked at length on the Reform of the Poor Law to a large audience in London, during the Webbs' campaign to popularise Mrs Webb's Minority Report in connexion with the Royal Commission on the Poor Law—Webb wrote the Report: Mrs Webb was one of the Commissioners—he almost shattered those present by remarking at the beginning of the speech that he wondered what would be said and done by the manager of one of the Labour Exchanges the Webbs had proposed when a woman walked up to the counter and said she was an unemployed prostitute! . . .

Both Webb and G.B.S. had unusual self-control in difficult situations, though Webb was a plethoric man. Their industry was amazing, Webb being the more industrious of the two, for G.B.S. occasionally slackened and went slow. Webb was never idle. He could write a report at any moment of the day or night. He seemed as automatic as it is possible for a human being to be. Yet he surprised even his intimates by displays of ordinary human qualities such as G.B.S. did not possess. G.B.S. respected Webb more than Webb respected him. Webb, indeed, sometimes spoke slightingly of G.B.S., who never spoke of him except with the greatest admiration.

Webb read voluminously, and had the rare ability of being able to read a page at a glance. He could size the contents of a long and difficult book in less time than most people take to read a short story, whereas G.B.S. was a slow reader, and had to brood over a book before he felt that he had mastered it. When a thick sociological book was shown to Beatrice, she would say with warrant, 'Oh, Sidney'll soon get through that!' E. R. Pease, in his chapter in *The Webbs and Their Work*, says that Webb once read through the whole of the *Encyclopaedia Britannica*, and adds that 'when we were going to America, he took from the steamer's library a big volume of a history of the United States, and read one volume a day: each of them would have taken me weeks. It is said that when he and Shaw took a holiday in Germany, Shaw had a book which lasted him throughout the tour: Webb read it while Shaw was writing a letter.'

Webb read a great many novels, which he described as picturesque sociology, but Shaw seldom read any, and read them with reluctance. Vehemently adverse to Walter Scott in his early years, he became devoted to him later in life. His passion for Dickens is apparent in all his work. Wells was another novelist he always read. His reading was omnivorous and surprising, for he read books that would cause the majority of intelligent persons to shudder at the thought of boredom beyond belief. He enjoyed reading plays, and would rather read several mediocre dramas than a single novel of quality; yet he would pick up a popular magazine in a hotel lounge and absorb himself in a paltry tale.

G.B.S., despite his disdain of art for art's sake, was deeply interested in the arts, though he sought always to chain them to social science and to make a propagandist of the artist. The function of the artist according to G.B.S., was not with life, but with reform.

The Webbs took notice of art from time to time, but they thought it insignificant and unimportant in comparison with the tables of mortality and statistics in general. Sidney could read poetry, and was fond of Wordsworth, but Beatrice confessed in her diaries that, just as some people are colour blind, so she was poetry blind. She was reputed to have great contempt for poetry, but this belief is, I think, false. She was, in my knowledge of her, full of regret for her obliquity. There is a widely-known story, alleged to be a legend, repeated by Kingsley Martin in *The Webbs and Their Work*, that Sidney and Beatrice were once seen at a performance of *Parsifal* at Covent Garden, and that when he was asked afterwards how they had enjoyed it, he replied, 'Oh, very much, indeed. Our seats were immediately behind Herbert Samuel's, and during an interval we had a very interesting discussion on the incidence of sickness during pregnancy.' The tale, however, is recorded in Beatrice's Diary[1] where she states that:

> 'We have resumed relations with two of the Liberal Ministers—Lloyd George and Herbert Samuel. At a performance of *Parsifal* Sidney and I ran up against them during the long interval in the outer hall and presently found ourselves heatedly discussing, surrounded by an ever-widening circle of amused and interested listeners, the excessive sickness of married women under the Insurance Act owing to the humourously ignorant omission by the Government actuaries of the "risk" of pregnancy. As we hurried back to the gloriously dramatised religious service, Lloyd George appealed to us to help him to get out of the financial hole. The result was a breakfast at 11, Downing Street, with Montagu (Financial Secretary to the Treasury) and Dr Addison as fellow guest; and a dinner at Grosvenor Road to enable Lloyd George to meet Margaret Bondfield and Mary MacArthur.'

This entry in the Diary was made within a few days of the encounter at Covent Garden, and is obviously the true account. Music was the one art that Beatrice enjoyed. It was her custom throughout her long life to walk from Grosvenor Road to St Paul's Cathedral several times a week when she was in London to listen to the music and the service at evensong in St Paul's Cathedral. The discussion with Lloyd George and Herbert Samuel was, no doubt, more interesting to Sidney than Wagner's music or the search for the Holy Grail.

Webb was remarkably conservative in his habits, but G.B.S. was ready to make experiments of all sorts, despite the rigidity with which he held to his fundamental faith. Webb disdained all mechanical aids, preferring a pen to a typewriter. He would not use a fountain pen because, he declared, it always leaked when he used it. There were times when one felt that he would have preferred quill pens to those with steel nibs, if only he could have mastered the method of sharpening them. G.B.S. had a passion for the latest gadget. His interest could be excited immediately by showing him a new machine. He was among the first people in England to ride a motor-bicycle, and he got himself a motor-car as soon as he could, learning to drive it

---

[1] See *Beatrice Webb's Diaries*, 1912–17, edited by Margaret I. Cole, page 22.

himself. Webb, who managed to ride a push bicycle, never attempted to drive a motor-car.

How conservative Webb was appears from two remarks he made to me when I was dining with him and Beatrice in Grosvenor Road. There had been an agitation for the removal of some of the statues in London, and Webb remarked that he would allow any statue to remain in place which had been erect for, I think, twenty years—some such period. It would then have earned the right to remain on view. His second remark was akin to the first. John A. Hobson, the economist, who was also dining with them that night, wondered what would become of the stately homes of England if, as seemed certain, their owners could no longer maintain them. Webb said that he would nationalise the mansions and put their owners in as permanent caretakers, a notable remark when one remembers that the National Trust now follows that policy to a large extent.

The only fad Webb had about food concerned roots. 'I never eat roots,' he told me. For the rest, he ate whatever there was and he took his drop of whisky like a Tory and a man. Both he and Beatrice smoked cigarettes, Beatrice more heavily than her husband. G.B.S. and Charlotte loathed the smell of tobacco, though they provided cigarettes for their guests.

The most remarkable difference between Webb and G.B.S. was spiritual. Shaw was profoundly religious, as nearly Christian as it is possible for a man who repudiates the greater part of Christian doctrine, to be. Webb was totally uninterested in religion, even statistically, a singular lack in one who was happiest when he was tabulating people and arranging them in neat columns of figures, which had been worked out to the last decimal point.

Religion, whatever we may feel about it, is neither negligible nor uninteresting. It is the supreme factor in mundane affairs; and its influence, for good or bad, has been profound throughout human history. Indifference to it denotes serious lack of judgment and understanding; and a man who professes to be expert in devising systems of society and ways of managing communal affairs would seem to be unfit for such enterprises when he cannot take the slightest interest in humanity's supreme interest and need. Webb's indifference is the more remarkable because Mrs Webb had a mystical belief in prayer, which she found both stimulating and soothing, though too often, perhaps, she spoke to the Almighty as if He were a Higher Grade Civil Servant whose interest in the Minority Report on the Poor Law she hoped to elicit. Her antipathy to G.B.S. seems to have been due in some part to her inability to make head or tail of him: he was unaccountable and irregular and could not be nearly defined. Any person wishing to make a report on him for a neat pigeon hole must be defeated—a fact which irritated Beatrice, whose needs and desires were fully satisfied by Sidney. His movements and reactions could be calculated with ease and safety. On June 30, he would be doing exactly what he had been doing on December 30.

The difference between her and Charlotte Shaw was not less than the difference between G.B.S. and Webb. Beatrice had either gipsy or Jewish blood in her veins—possibly both—and she was liable at times to become highly emotional and to demonstrate her love of her husband, which was unbounded, by wild embraces even in the presence of her guests. He never rumpled her: she frequently rumpled him; and the sight of the little, unmoved man enduring her ferocious raptures with fortitude was highly impressive. Her embraces sometimes seemed more like assaults than endearments. He would sit in his chair, with a statistical abstract in one hand and a White Paper in the other, while she balanced on his lap like an entranced houri!

Charlotte Shaw was embarrassed by any demonstration of affection, and seldom or never displayed any. She was as shocked by such demonstrations as that morbid moraliser, Miss Harriet Byron in Samuel Richardson's *The History of Sir Charles Grandison*, when Sir Charles, a fortnight after he and she had become engaged to be married, kissed her on the lips for the first time. He was, she thought, too free.

31

It was his irritation and disgust with his shyness and nervous apprehension which started G.B.S. on the long, tedious and exhausting process of public argument on portable platforms at street corners and in municipal parks, and on fixed platforms in workmen's clubs and select assembly halls. At one moment he was haranguing amused or apathetic proletarians from the plinth of Nelson's Column in Trafalgar Square, and at the next he was striding at great speed to the East End to address derisive dockers in Victoria Park.

Nine years after he had risen timidly to make some incoherent remarks to the Zetetical Society, so nervous that he could scarcely open his lips without hearing his teeth chatter, he was able, with complete aplomb, to address the British Association on economics at Bath in 1888, unabashed by the wrath of Professor Henry Sidgwick who, when he heard Shaw advocating the nationalisation of land, shouted that he would not listen to such economic heresy lest he should be thought by his silence to be condoning a criminal offence. He fled the scene, banging the door behind him as he fled. Was G.B.S., who, a year later, spoke on the Workers' Political Programme in the open air at Trafford Bridge for an hour and three quarters one Sunday morning, to be put out of his stride by an infuriated don? The title of his paper, which was afterwards published as the fifth chapter of *Fabian Essays*, was *The Transition to Social Democracy*.

His fertility and invention were as great as his variety and application. From 1885, when he was twenty-nine, until 1926, when he was seventy, his tally of great and diversified employment, which included the writing of thirty-six plays, most of them major works,[1] as well as a vast amount of journalism, public speaking and general service to the community, was unsurpassed and not easily equalled. His public service was given without price. He never accepted payment for any lecture he gave; and in his early life, when money was scarce with him, he refused to accept his travelling expenses, unless their amount was more than his pocket could stand, in which case he accepted a third-class return railway ticket.

His chief fault was that he became almost exclusively a propagandist, concerned to promote a cause more than to elicit the philosophic fact and the unshakeable truth. To say this is not to say that he preferred party to principle. It is simply to say that having formed a belief and adhered to a party, he refused to admit that either could be wrong. A philosopher might remark with reason that this denotes extreme egotism and may finally be described as an assertion that G.B.S. himself could not be wrong, but who shall escape punishment if that charge is made against mankind? It is, undeniably, true that he held fast to opinions that were unreasonable and even demonstrably false, and that he was inclined, especially in his later years, to shout down opposition. This rigid adherence to partisan opinions made his judgments seem wilful and erratic. It caused him to hail *Hard Times* as one of the best, if not actually the best, of the novels of Dickens, though it is a poor, ramshackle thing with very little of the essential Dickensian quality in it, the sort of novel that is written by a tired man who has just finished one masterpiece, *Bleak House*, and is preparing to write another, *Little Dorrit*.

It also caused him to hail Eugene Brieux in extravagant terms. 'After the death of Ibsen,' he wrote in his long preface to *Three Plays by Brieux*, which was published in 1911, 'Brieux confronted Europe as the most important dramatist west of Europe.' This was a sufficiently extravagant assertion in itself, but G.B.S. was always ready to be hanged for a sheep rather than a lamb, and he went on to say, 'In that kind of comedy which is so true to life that we have to call it tragi-comedy, and which is not only an entertainment but a history

---

[1] At the time of his death, the number of his plays, large and small, was almost fifty. He left the scenario of an unfinished piece, *Why She Would Not*, which was to have been in six scenes. Five of them were outlined and in galley proof when he died.

and a criticism of contemporary morals, he is incomparably the greatest writer'—*writer*, let it be noted, not *dramatist*—'France has produced since Molière.' Assertions such as these made G.B.S.'s friends hold their breath, and it was only by their agreeing to say that he was a fanatic about his faith, that they could cover up his lamentable *gaffe*.

His mind, despite its appearance of volatility, was constant and generally fixed. He changed it less often and less capriciously than H. G. Wells changed his. The belief in economic equality, for example, was formed while he was still a young man, not yet attached to any political party; and the single clause of this belief which has some root in reason and reality, namely, that economic inequality dangerously restricts choice in marriage, is set out, by implication, in *Immaturity*, and, by direct assertion, in *The Irrational Knot*.

Much of the reaction against him in his last years was the result of his partisan behaviour, and if his work loses popularity, a loss, however, of which there is very little sign, it will be because his party bias has made him suspect. In his old age, returning from a nine days' visit to Russia, where he was carefully guided and directed by able and astute conductors, he proclaimed the Soviet Union to be the nearest place in this world to the earthly paradise. His reaction to any question about Russia was almost automatic. The glib phrase of adulation leapt from his lips before the question was completed. He had never at any time in his life admired democracy, and he believed firmly in government by men of quality and determination, even when he was confusing his followers by asserting that there were no great men.

But he was not careful to discriminate between the leader who has a high conception of human society and the leader who is no more than a gangster. It was this failure in discrimination which caused him to give rousing cheers for Hitler, Mussolini and Stalin. Any dictator was better than no dictator, because he could impose his will upon the population without the vexing delays of parliamentary procedure or the lamentable necessity of having to convince doubters that one is right. There were times when one felt that even Al Capone would have met with his approval! . . . .

The fact that wrong decisions can be reached as quickly as right ones was entirely ignored, as was the fact that a policy which has been well considered, well expounded, well argued and well criticised, is more likely to be serviceable than one which has been inflicted on people against their will and without their understanding. Having adopted a belief, he preached it with vigour and vivacity, reinforced by a good memory and wide reading, so that he was able to point his arguments with illustrations that were apt and appeared to be

95

convincing. His charm and equable temper and his total lack of rancour made him a dangerous opponent to challenge; and the swiftness of his wit frightened those who tried to prevail against him. He discomposed people by quick answers that were often evasions of the point under discussion.

I remember vividly the first time I heard him lecture. He had then almost reached the peak of his world-wide renown, and large audiences everywhere thronged to listen to him. This lecture, which caused a rumpus, was delivered to the members of a Christian Socialist society and their friends: the Guild of St Matthew, which had been founded by a Fabian, the Rev. Stewart D. Headlam. In the audience was, I subsequently read, Gilbert Chesterton, who asked a question; but oddly enough I have no recollection of seeing or hearing him.

But I remember very distinctly a question asked by a small-voiced and demure woman which shook my faith in G.B.S.'s argument to some extent. The title of the lecture was *Some Necessary Repairs to Religion*, one which was sufficiently exciting in itself to stimulate curiosity; and the place of the meeting was the Essex Hall, owned by Unitarians, in Essex Street, off the Strand.

During question time, the lady enquired in a voice that was almost inaudible, whether Mr Shaw believed in the doctrine of the Immaculate Conception. The words had scarcely left her lips than she received this answer. 'Yes, I believe that all conceptions are immaculate!' which was neither a reply to her enquiry nor in accordance with his own plea for better births and the production of a finer race than we possess. The Catholic believes that all conceptions are not immaculate, that only two conceptions in the whole history of mankind were immaculate: our Lord's and our Lady's. The questioner was so overcome by G.B.S.'s reply that she sat down without uttering another word; but my own reaction was sharp, and if I had not been terrified of public utterance on such an occasion, I should have reminded him that he was not only wrong theologically, but wrong biologically and socially.

Nevertheless, I came out of the Essex Hall with my beliefs in disarray. As I walked along the Thames Embankment, I wondered whether I should ever be able to assemble my faith again. Such was his effect on audiences. People left a meeting which he had addressed, not always agreeing with him, but with their minds responsibly provoked.

32

In January, 1881, Mrs Shaw removed herself from Victoria Grove to 37, Fitzroy Street, which was more conveniently placed for her purposes as a teacher of music, and here G.B.S. wrote *Love Among the Artists*, a work which is technically superior to any of his novels. *The Irrational Knot* was more promptly rejected than *Immaturity* had been. He was a little humbler when he sent it out on its futile rounds that he had been over *Immaturity*. The marks of immaturity were still plain upon him. What was less clear was the fact that he was not a novelist.

He himself, in the introduction to the American edition of *Love Among the Artists*, sorrowfully confessed himself a bungling amateur as a novelist. 'I have given up novel-writing these many years,' he said, writing in 1899, 'during which I have lost the impudence of the apprentice without gaining the skill of the master.' There is no more to be said, except that 'the novels of my nonage' collapsed in *An Unsocial Socialist*, which is a work so futile and incoherent that the reader almost believes that G.B.S. was suffering severely from neurosis when he wrote it. Nine years of failure and poverty and malnutrition had taken a heavy toll, leaving him intellectually limp. Sidney Trefusis, the wealthy socialist of this novel, talks and behaves like a lunatic who is very nearly a criminal lunatic. There is a scene in the ninth chapter, when Trefusis enters the room where his young wife, Henrietta, is lying dead: it defies credence. The man acts and speaks as if he were out of his mind, but not from grief. The moment, he seems to think, is ripe for a piece of flatulent political oration. He is almost ready to deliver a ranting lecture at the girl's grave on surplus value, with special reference to Karl Marx's theory of dialectical materialism! . . .

The remarkable fact about G.B.S. at this critical period of his life is that he did not perceive the direction in which his genius lay, nor did he perceive it until it was pointed out to him by William Archer. There was still a large tract of wilderness to be travelled before he reached the land not only of promise but of fulfilment. In the meantime, much trouble had to be endured. He had become a vegetarian in January, 1881, a conversion which was thought to have been caused by Shelley, whose influence on him at this time was profound, but it was also due to his hope that a vegetable diet would end the severe headaches from which he suffered once a month. It was not due, he was careful to state, to compassion for slaughtered animals, though he foresaw a day when his corpse would be followed to the grave by herds of grateful cattle: it was due to his deep dislike of burying dead bodies in one that was alive. We may surmise, however, that the main factors in this conversion were the ill-cooked and unpalatable food he was given at home, and the fact that there was a sudden spread of vegetarian restaurants in London at that time, where he could obtain meals that were edible and cheap.

In the last days of May 1881, he fell ill of the smallpox and was confined to his room for three weeks. G.B.S. was not reticent about his illnesses, as a rule, but he was remarkably silent about this one. He liked to maintain that he was healthier than carnivorous people, and that he recovered from illness more quickly than they did: neither of which statements was true; but beyond a bare reference to the smallpox as the cause of his opposition to vaccination, he made little allusion to it, though he once remarked that the defects of *The Unsocial Socialist*, though he did not begin to write it until 1883, must have been due to the general feeling of debility with which it left him.

It is obvious, however, that an infectious and foul and greatly dreaded disease—about fifty per cent of its victims died—which was very painful and almost certain to leave disfiguring marks on the sufferer's body, and especially on his face, was sure to disrupt the life of every person in the victim's home. It is not certain whether Lucy was living with her mother at this time, but Lucinda Elizabeth, who earned a substantial part of her income from teaching music either at home or at the North London Collegiate School under Miss Buss and, subsequently, Dr Sophie Bryant, must have been isolated as strictly as her son. How the family fared at this time is not now known. Apart from denouncing Edward Jenner in terms that could hardly have been harsher had they been applied to Herod for his slaughter of infants, and condemning cow lymph as if it were actively immoral, G.B.S. made no mention of his illness.

When he had recovered sufficiently to be removable, he went to Leyton in June, to stay with his doctor uncle Walter who was in practice there, and, under his influence, no doubt, ceased to be graminivorous; nor did he become a vegetarian again until the following October. Thereafer, he was steadfast except on occasions when, because an adequate vegetable meal was unobtainable, he ate fish. While he was convalescing with his uncle, he worked on *Love Among the Artists* which he had begun shortly before his illness began, and pondered over the problem of his future. He dallied with the idea that he might find better employment in America than he had been able to obtain in England; and we may well wonder what his fate would have been had he emigrated. He tried to obtain work with the National Telephone Company, and answered advertisements, but in each instance, without success.

Lucy had now left home. She had joined the Carl Rosa Opera Company and was on tour. Her absence and, perhaps, the fact that G.B.S. had contracted smallpox in Fitzroy Street, made Lucinda Elizabeth decide to remove to 36, Osnaburgh Street, which she did on April 28, 1882. *Love Among the Artists* was finished, and G.B.S. was now working on *Cashel Byron's Profession*. The routine of their lives had been resumed. They remained at Osnaburgh Street until the spring of 1887, when they removed to 29, Fitzroy Square, the lease of which, when G.B.S. began to prosper, he bought for his mother. Later on, when the lease expired, he bought another lease, that of 8, Park Village West, and here she lived until she died.

33

It will be well, at this point, to contest the belief, for which he himself was chiefly responsible, that he sponged on his mother during the nine years of hardship. His family, it must first be stated, showed no interest in his ambition or his work. His mother, who, so far as he knew, had never read a line of his novels, accepted his 'idleness' with what fortitude she could muster. Every family had its good-for-nothing: he was hers. But Lucy, flushed with her appearance of popularity and impending success, and scornful of her socially awkward brother and his futile efforts to become a novelist, nattered and nagged about his sponging on his mother to all who would listen.

It seemed never to have occurred to her that she had enjoyed advantages of the sort that she desired, her training as a singer, for example, which had been denied to her brother. Heaven, she thought, had intended him to be the confidential clerk in a large, flourishing and highly respectable estate office, but he had flouted heaven's manifest will and sought to make himself what it was plain he could never become, a writer! Such stuff and nonsense! No publisher would look at his work! What was the Civil Service for if it was not to provide comfortable and secure posts for the likes of him?

His own account of this distressing period of his life is entirely fantastic, the sort of stuff a man writes when he is indulging in the juvenile pastime of intellectuals who think it is great fun to shock the respectable middle-classes. The French decadent poet, Rimbaud, is reputed to have opened a conversation in a café with the remark, made in a loud voice, 'When I murdered my mother! . . .' He did not shock the Parisian bourgeoisie more than G.B.S. shocked his English readers when he asserted:

'I was an ablebodied and ableminded young man in the full strength of my youth; and my family, then heavily embarrassed, needed my help urgently. That I should have chosen to be a burden to them instead was, according to all the conventions of the peasant lad fiction, monstrous. Well, without a blush I embraced the monstrosity. I did not throw myself into the struggle for my life: I threw my mother into it. I was not a staff to my father's old age: I clung to his coat tails. . . .

'Callous as Comus to moral babble, I steadily wrote my five pages a day and made a man of myself (at my mother's expense) instead of a slave. And I protest that I will not suffer James Huneker or any romanticist to pass me off as a peasant boy qualifying for a chapter in Smiles' *Self Help*, or a good son supporting a helpless mother, instead of a stupendously selfish artist leaning with the full weight of his hungry body on an energertic and capable woman. . . .

'My mother worked for my living instead of preaching to me my duty to work for hers. . . .'

We may doubt if Rimbaud, if it were he, shocked anybody when, having first glanced carefully around to see how many shockable persons were present, he accused himself very loudly of matricide. Those who overheard him probably concluded that he was either drunk or daft or talking for foolish effect.

But no one, wishing to defame himself, could have achieved his purpose so successfully as G.B.S. did when he published these extracts from his preface to *The Irrational Knot*. There is scarcely a word of truth in the whole fantastic tale, and G.B.S., endeavouring to make everybody's flesh creep, was less convincing than the Fat Boy in *The Pickwick Papers*. His head was full of romantic nonsense about ruthless artists who refused to let themselves be diverted from their purpose by conventional opinions on morals or public duty or common humanity; and he delighted to horrify those who prefer that poor boys who achieve success should always have been examples to everybody, incessantly leading the life of an earnest Boy Scout prowling round the town, doing daily good deeds.

He may have felt an academic admiration for the heartless genius who cannot be dissuaded from his purpose, no matter what suffering he may cause to other people, but he certainly did not behave like one. It is not a fact that he exploited his aged parents without pity or compunction. Neither of them was aged when he began his nine years of hardship and bitter effort to become a writer. If anybody in the Shaw family was a sponger, it was Lucinda Elizabeth who took a pound a week from her hardpressed husband whom she had virtually deserted, though she was better off than he was. G.B.S. received no help of any sort from his father after he had settled in London, nor had he received any from him for nearly four years before he left Dublin. The weekly allowance would still have been made to Lucinda Elizabeth had G.B.S. been drowned on the voyage from North Wall to Holyhead or had never been born.

It is inconceivable that his entire nature could have changed as a result of crossing the Irish Sea and that the moment he set his feet in London, he ceased to be able and industrious, becoming instead an incorrigible loafer and sponger.

There was, in fact, no decline in his industry. There was only a change in its display. Had his novels been published, no one could have complained of his 'idleness'. The fact that he was slow in achieving success, does not alter the supreme fact that he was preparing himself in hardship for the position he was eventually to win, and that those who were supposed, quite wrongly, to have suffered through his persistence in his difficult task, profited handsomely by it when he had won his way.

Apart from the fact that he had engaged in several occupations for three out of the nine years of distress, and in each of them had displayed the skill and industry he had shown in Townshend's estate agency, obtaining promotion and high responsibility quickly, and being urged to remain in the service of his employers in still higher positions and with larger salaries, and that for a portion of the time that he was 'unemployed' he was, as we have noted, ill with smallpox, there are four points to be kept in mind in considering this period of his life.

The first is that during the time when boys of his class would have been at school or at a university, he was working in Townshend's office so skilfully that he was practically earning the whole cost of his living when he was sixteen.

Oscar Wilde was still at Portora School in Enniskillen when G.B.S. went to work, nor did he got to Trinity College in Dublin until he was seventeen. Three years later, he went from T.C.D. to Oxford, where he remained for four years. At the age of twenty-one, he had squandered his inheritance of £4,000 from his father and was borrowing money from his mother, Lady Wilde, whose means were small. Yet no one accused him, as any one might well have done, of exploiting his aged parents while he luxuriated in idleness. G.B.S. had earned his own living for five years when Wilde was preparing to enter Magdalen.

John Galsworthy went from Harrow to Oxford, and then, after being called to the Bar, where he never practised, made a long tour round the world, nor did he earn a farthing by writing or any other work until he was thirty-seven. But no censorious people called him a sponger.

Robert Browning is said by Mrs Betty Miller, in her brilliant 'portrait', to have lived on his parents until he was thirty-four. His father was an unimportant clerk in the Bank of England, earning £275 a year after forty-nine years' service, an income which was not much more than Mr Shaw derived from his corn mill. Browning insisted that his father and mother should keep him while he made himself a poet, and he disdained the reproaches of the few people, such as Jane Welsh Carlyle, who disliked him because he lacked 'seven or eight hours a day of occupation'.

When he married Elizabeth Barrett, he had no money to pay for their honeymoon trip to Italy, and when he discovered that his bride, who had an income of £300 or £400 a year in her own right, could not transfer any of it to him without revealing her intention to marry him, he had to borrow £10 from his straitened father. A man of thirty-four who had never attempted to earn a living, but was content to live on the allowance his ill-paid father made him, who lived without a twinge of conscience on his wife's money, and was so idle that he wrote only one poem, *The Guardian Angel,* in the first three years of his marriage, would seem to be a suitable subject for scorn; but, apart from Mrs Proctor and Mrs Thomas Carlyle, nobody said that Browning was guilty of any fault in dedicating himself to poetry at the expense of his parents.

Every man who puts his son into a profession, church, law or medicine, expects to have to maintain him during the long period of his training and for several years after he has qualified. Who supports the young barrister while he is waiting for briefs or the young doctor while he is acquiring a practice? No one thinks it is shameful of a daughter to let her parents keep her while she trains to become an actress or a singer or a secretary.

During the years between his fifteenth and his thirtieth birthday, G.B.S. supported himself for at least eight: the remainder were no more than the time any middle-class parent expects to have to maintain his son or his daughter at a public school and a university and while training for, and becoming established in, a profession. Until lately, any father who put his son in the Army or the Navy, had to make him a substantial allowance for several years after he had been commissioned. Yet no one dreamt of calling these subsidised children spongers.

The second point is that G.B.S.'s residence with his mother in London involved her in considerably less expense than she had incurred in maintaining her second daughter, Agnes, who had never earned any income because of her illness. Lucinda Elizabeth, in addition to renting a large unwieldy house in Victoria Grove, supported Agnes in rooms at Ventnor until her death. Measured in money, the cost of maintaining G.B.S. was trivial in comparison with the cost of maintaining his sister. His room was there; and it involved his mother in no more expense than it would have cost her had it been empty. The sketchy and unpalatable meals he was given may have cost her two or three shillings a day. They certainly could not have cost her more.

The third point is that G.B.S. was far from idling while he was out of remunerative employment, any more than a young barrister is idling while waiting for briefs or a young doctor while waiting for patients; he was employing himself with exceptional industry and determination to the task of making himself a writer, a task which he eventually performed with great success, despite every sort of discouragement. If every apprentice to a craft or profession were to work as hard as he did in acquiring skill, we should have little cause for complaint.

The fourth and final point is the least known and, perhaps, the most important. Lucinda Elizabeth's children, in fact, did not cost her a penny for their maintenance. They were of considerable financial benefit to her.

Note has already been made of the bequest they received from their great-grandfather, John Whitcroft, a sum of £5,000, of which £1,000 had been misappropriated by Lucinda Elizabeth's father, who should have been imprisoned for his crime. By her power of appointment under Whitcroft's will, she was able, with her children's consent, to make use of each child's share as he or she came to the age of twenty-one. Apart from any interest that may have accumulated during the children's minority, on what was left of the capital sum after Gurly's fraudulent misappropriation, each child's share amounted to more than £1,300.

It is obvious, therefore, that between 1874, when Lucy was twenty-one, and 1877, when G.B.S. reached that age, Lucinda Elizabeth's income, with her children's consent, was substantially increased. Lucy's share was, presumably, spent, partly to maintain her and partly to pay for her musical education. Her mother and her sister Agnes benefited incidentally. The younger girl's inheritance may be said to have been pure profit to her mother, for Agnes died within a week or two of her twenty-first birthday.

G.B.S. had been in London for a year when his share of the bequest fell due. It, too, was used by his mother, and he was surely entitled to think that in consenting to yield it to her, he was paying for his board and lodging in the hard years of his apprenticeship? He could have lived more comfortably and been far better fed in lodgings for twenty-five shillings a week or even less than he was in his mother's house.

A dish of tepid eggs dumped on his desk by a casual char at midday was unlikely to cause any financial embarrassment to his mother at a time when eggs were plentiful and cheap—about a halfpenny each—and his share of his great-grandfather's bequest would have kept him in comfort for the whole of the nine years of his hard apprenticeship to letters, even if he had not earned any wages during that time.

The legend of a callous and selfish young man, sponging without scruple on his aged and impoverished parents is seen to be fantastic stuff invented by G.B.S. himself. He was uncommonly generous to his relatives, even to remote cousins whom he scarcely knew, and especially to his mother and his sister Lucy, neither of whom had shown him much grace of spirit when grace would have been consoling and kind. He lived in acute discomfort with his mother until he married. For the greater part of the time, he provided the means which kept her house together when the Whitcroft bequest was spent, and he rewarded her handsomely for the little she did for him. In addition to the leasehold he bought for her, he made her an allowance of £400 a year when that was a substantial sum. It was also a substantial part of his earnings.

34

Cashel Byron's Profession was written in Osnaburgh Street, but a more important event of that year, 1882, from his point of view was the chance that led him on September 5 into the Memorial Hall, built on the site where the famous Fleet Prison had formerly stood, in Farringdon Street. He went into the hall to listen to Henry George, the author of *Progress and Poverty*, describing how poverty could be abolished or greatly reduced by the taxation of land values: a method which was to be tried nearly thirty years later when another George achieved the remarkable result, not of abolishing or reducing poverty by taxing land values, but of adding to the number of the impoverished by completing the ruin of estate owners which had been started when governments decided to favour industry at the expense of agriculture.

As he left the hall, he bought a copy of George's book for sixpence—years later, recalling the incident, he wondered how he had come into possession of a spare sixpence—so that he might examine its theory at length and leisure. Little did he dream that a day would come when crowds even larger than those that had thronged to hear Henry George, would thrust their way into the Memorial Hall to hear *him*.

This persuasive American, whose good temper and charming manners in all circumstances, won respect that amounted almost to affection, was making a deep impression on the British people. Miss Mary Gladstone, arguing with him at Professor Stuart's house in Cambridge, records that 'we tried our very utmost to convert him, but, alas, he far more nearly converted us. He deeply impressed me with his earnestness, conviction and singleness and height of aim. I don't think we made the slightest impression on him, and he was very clear and quick in argument.'

J. L. Garvin records the effect made by *Progress and Poverty* when it appeared in 1883. Its influence on Radical working-men was as powerful as that of Tom Paine's *The Rights of Man* in 1791, and George, by the force of his impressive and pleasing personality and the cogency with which he put his argument, had prepared a great public for the book when it appeared, by lectures up and down the land, such as G.B.S. heard in the Memorial Hall. 'Amongst' the Radical working-men, Garvin writes, 'that passionate and ingenious work, *Progress and Poverty*, went like wildfire. Chamberlain read it electrified; the effect on Morley was the same.'[1]

George, by his clear and brilliant exposition of his theme, and also by his courage and courtesy in debate, won admirers even among those who were unwilling to accept his proposals. His fault was one that G.B.S. was to display in his turn: inflexible faith that his doctrine was not only good, but perfect, and that any person who failed to perceive its perfection must be mentally dense or spiritually destitute. He was too logical, as G.B.S. often was, and logic, according to Lecky in his *History of European Morals*, 'is greatly studied and prized in most ages of intellectual poverty.'[2] Had Henry George been less rigid in his belief that the solution of all economic, social and political problems would be found in the Single Tax, his influence in Britain would have been greater. As it is, he still has fervent followers who advocate his policy with skill and devotion.

G.B.S. may be said to have modelled his literary style to some extent on George's. There are passages in *Progress and Poverty*, especially in the early pages, which he might have written in his early and middle periods; but G.B.S. wisely loosened his style, though he continued throughout his life to pack his sentences too tightly. Compared with Henry George, however, G.B.S. was loose. George's pages are so closely crammed with words and thoughts that the reader quickly tires of reading them, and abandons the book because it is intellectually exhausting. His hold on Shaw, firm though it was at first, was soon relaxed, for G.B.S., after reading a French translation of Karl Marx's *Das Kapital* in the British Museum, abandoned his belief in the Single Tax as a remedy for our economic ills, and accepted instead the belief that all forms of capital should be nationalised. He retained this belief to the end of his life, despite his experience of the disastrous policy of the Labour Government which came to power after the end of the Second World War. Nevertheless, Henry George played an important and decisive part in the formation of his mind.

35

His breach with his mother and sister's friends was now complete. Lucy was a frequent visitor to Lady Wilde's comic receptions; but G.B.S., except on a few occasions, did not often accompany her there,

[1] *The Life of Joseph Chamberlain*, Vol. I, p. 385.
[2] See Vol. i, chapter 2, *The Pagan Empire*.

though Lady Wilde, he testified, treated him with consideration and kindness. There was never any likelihood that he and Oscar Wilde could be more than cool acquaintances. The texture of their minds was utterly dissimilar, and in any case, the very thought of sodomy was repulsive to G.B.S., who was essentially a lover of women. His clothes alone were sufficient to make Wilde, who was in his man of fashion period when they met, averse from his company, while G.B.S. probably regarded him as a fop to whom epigrams were more important than main drains and uncontaminated homes.

His abstentions, too, made intercourse with the generality of people, and especially with men and women of fashion, difficult if not impossible. Like the prophet Daniel, in argument with Malzar, he held that those who ate pulse and drank water appeared fairer and fatter in flesh, and were abler to decipher signs and wonders than were all the children that ate of the king's meat; and he was a living refutal of St Paul's assertion that those who are weak, eat herbs.

It was not his vegetarianism alone which made association with carnivorous people difficult. A man who does not drink distilled, brewed or fermented liquors, who abstains from tea, coffee and tobacco, and abjures all but farinaceous food, fruit and vegetables, automatically excludes himself from a large part of the general life of the community, and is compelled to lead a less gregarious existence than he might desire. A man with his regimen of diet is a nuisance at dinner parties, even when his conversation is stimulating in its audacious wit and thought. He was accommodating about food, and an intelligent hostess could easily discover what to offer him that would at once satisfy him and cause no complaints in the kitchen; but those who were unfamiliar with his domestic life felt frightened by the thought of feeding him adequately and pleasingly, with the result that contacts with people other than his immediate friends were fewer than they might have been. He was not often found at public dinners, but when he went to one, he generally dined at home and turned up at the function after the food had been eaten. Yet he was the least exacting of men at a table, and would eat whatever there was that conformed to his culinary creed.

He was assiduous in exercising his body, taking long walks, and rising early to swim in the pool at the Royal Automobile Club every morning when he was in London. He took an impish delight in walking men much younger than himself off their feet, he seemingly as fresh at the end of a long expedition as he had been at the beginning, they limp and exhausted.

He would invite an abounding youth to join him in climbing the Malvern Hills, and enjoy the spectacle of the bedraggled and no longer abounding youth crawling home footsore and sad while he was ready, it seemed, to repeat the expedition at once. All this energy, he would assert, was derived from Brussells sprouts and runner beans: and he would remind people that the elephant and the horse are vegetarians, but say nothing about the lion and the tiger, which are not. In his old age, however, he would confess that men and women less abstemious than himself, thrived at least as well. Ibsen, he admitted sadly, was addicted to drink, but he lived to be seventy-eight, never had a headache that anyone had heard of, and, apart from many poems, wrote about twenty plays that profoundly changed the character of drama throughout the world.

His energy was, indubitably, great, but it was almost entirely nervous, and his appearance of immense vitality on platforms was not sustained when the speechifying was over and the platforms were deserted. All his movements were quick and animated. His stride was long and swift, and he moved through the streets at a pace that would have caused many people to run if they had tried to keep up with him. But, unless he was in an impish mood, he deferred to other people's limitations and adapted his pace to theirs.

He was happiest in debate after a meeting of the Fabian Society in Essex Hall. His wit and his wisdom were more often heard then than on more elaborate occasions, though his elaborate orations, especially when he had built them up by practice, were highly stimulating to hear and left ineradicable marks on the minds of all who heard them.

But his readiness in retort and rejoinder was acquired slowly and with great labour, and it was acquired in despite of his nature. He forced himself to become a speaker when his single desire was to run away and blush for himself in private. Parnell was not more determined to cure his stammering tongue than G.B.S. was to overcome his nervous fear of any public utterance. Accounts of his extraordinary persistence must appal the reader with a sense of wasted energy.

In a letter, dated March 1, 1895, to Charles Charrington, he describes what appears to have been a fairly representative week of his life at that time:

'I could not answer your letter before, because I have had to work until I became sick—positively and literally sick—this week. I have replied to Clement Scott's article on Pigott last Monday. . . . Also I have written an elaborate article on the County Council election. Further, I have gone all over the stage business and dialogue of *The Philanderer*, corrected numerous and fearful errors in the prompt copy, and sent it off in time to catch Thursday's boat at Queenstown for New York, where it is to be produced by Mansfield on Easter

107

Monday. . . . Having achieved these feats since Monday, I went and delivered speeches at the Humanitarian Conference; partook of a dinner with the Humanitarians; made another speech, went home with Olivier and a violent headache; got sick as aforesaid; and crawled off this morning to apply my favourite remedy, the excavation of another tooth. . . .'

Was there any need for him to dissipate his physical and nervous strength in haranguing labouring men in Victoria Park? He would have said 'Yes' without hesitation.

The confidence he gained on platforms was less important than the confidence he gained in himself. He acquired a deep knowledge of people, and was no longer oppressed by a feeling of frustration that his shyness and the failure of his novels to find a publisher seemed certain to make permanent. Nor can the case be confounded by statements that his output of literary work would have been greater had he refrained from oratorical bouts in the East End of London; for his tally of books and plays and general writing refutes that argument which is no more sensible than his own assertion that if our alphabet were reformed, men of genius could write more works of genius. Just what an American does with the time he saves by omitting the *w* from *slow* is not apparent to him or anybody else.

It may, perhaps, be said that the quality of his plays might have been better if he had not squandered so much mind and energy at street corners; but can such an assertion be maintained with any sort of conviction? His output was immense, and its quality, even in his old age, was remarkably high. An author who could write *Saint Joan* in his seventieth year cannot be said to have exhausted himself either physically or intellectually by youthful indiscretions. His journalism was supremely good, as vigorous and vivacious as that of Dickens, and it is still good reading, though the matters with which most of it is concerned were passing events which occurred a long time ago.

In all his journalism, he was more than topical: he related the momentary matter to his fundamental faith and, so far as he was able, to matters that he believed to be permanent.

Shakespeare did not harangue the rabble, which he despised, but he died when he was fifty-two, and his output of work, great though it was, is nothing like so large as G.B.S.'s when he was fifty-two. If we say that he wrote more great plays than Shaw did, we shall find many to dispute our statement with some show of authority. *Widowers' Houses* is not a notable play, but neither is *Love's Labour's Lost*. As first plays go, G.B.S.'s is superior to Shakespeare's, which is a tedious imitation of the dull stuff turned out by the university wits. *The Philanderer* is bad enough, a too-clever-by-half piece, but it is not so bad as *Two Gentlemen of Verona*, which is one of the worst plays any man of genius has written, far inferior to many plays that have been written by men of mediocre talent. It is true that *Widowers' Houses* was written when its author was older than Shakespeare was when he wrote *Love's Labour's Lost;* but if we compare the first writing Shaw did with the first writing done by Shakespeare, *Immaturity* with *Venus and Adonis*, we shall have difficulty in deciding which is the better work. Shakespeare was twenty-nine when he wrote his poem. *Immaturity* was written when Shaw was twenty-three.

The number of Shakespeare's plays that have remained untarnished by time is less than we are accustomed to believe. Can we feel certain that it is greater than the number of G.B.S.'s plays that will still be performed three centuries after *his* death? All authors, including Shakespeare, pass under a cloud at some period of their lives, and some of them, though their genius is indisputable, remain under it for ever. How many readers has Edmund Spenser to-day? Is Milton widely read? Richardson's *History of Clarissa Harlowe* has been acclaimed as the greatest novel that has been written in English, but few people to-day have read it, and multitudes of Richardson's countrymen do not know that he ever existed or that he wrote three novels which were highly praised, and are still highly praised, by critics and writers of distinction. Dr Johnson, whose literary judgments were often sad stuff, asserted that 'there is more knowledge of the heart in one letter of Richardson's than in all *Tom Jones*,' as foolish a statement as any man of quality ever made; yet there are nearly two columns of quotations from Fielding in the *Oxford Dictionary of Quotations*, but not a single quotation from Richardson!

Each of us has to make the world fit for his habitation, and G.B.S. began his task in every circumstance of discouragement. He knew that he would have to fight for his life, and he fought for it with courage and gaiety and immense skill and pertinacity. The legend, for which he is partly responsible, that he was recognised in Germany long before his quality was acknowledged in England, is untrue, as his translator, Siegfried Trebitsch, makes plain in his autobiography. Eminent editors derided Trebitsch for his ardent advocacy of 'that crazy Irishman', and one of them with heavy German humour, pretended to believe that G.B.S. was invented by his translator; and that there was no such person.[1]

Man and Superman has never been popular in Germany; *Caesar and Cleopatra* was only moderately successful when it was first performed in Berlin, under the direction of Max Reinhardt; and *The Doctor's Dilemma*, under the same direction, was 'an out and out failure'. Paul Goldman, the correspondent of the *Neue Freie Presse*, rushed out of

[1] See *Chronicle of a Life*, by Siegfried Trebitsch, pp. 167–171–405.

the Deutsche Theater, shouting at Mrs Trebitsch as he rushed, 'Your husband really might have spared us this disgusting stuff,' discouraging the poor lady so profoundly that, on their way home, she said to her husband, '*Do* drop this Irish friend of yours now! People simply don't want him, and you can't force them to share your taste.' *Major Barbara*, too, was a failure at the Burgtheater in Vienna.

The single play by Shaw at this time that was undoubtedly successful in Germany was *Mrs Warren's Profession* which had been banned in England. It was not, indeed, until *Pygmalion* was performed for the first time anywhere in the world at the Burgtheater in Vienna that G.B.S. became a popular dramatist in German-speaking countries. 'The reception the play received in Berlin was no less enthusiastic than in Vienna, and initiated, financially interested circles suddenly discovered that this English dramatist whom they had avoided so nervously could write sensationally successful plays as well as anyone.'

Long before *Pygmalion* had been produced in Vienna, G.B.S.'s genius had been widely recognised in England, and his plays, after the famous performances at the Royal Court Theatre in London, became popular throughout Great Britain, though they were subjected, as was right and proper, to considerable and sometimes acute criticism. An author who is deliberately provocative and polemical, cannot reasonably complain if those whom he provokes, retaliate in robust terms. That is what he should wish them to do.

The single European monarch who commanded a performance of a Shaw play was Edward VII, though His Majesty thought that the man was mad.[1] Arthur Balfour not only attended his plays, but besought his colleagues and opponents to do the same. G.B.S. was never gentle with his adopted country, and was often grossly unjust to it; but the inescapable fact is that he lived in it for seventy-four years, that most of his friends were English—he had few that were Irish—and that his remains were mingled with English earth.

To please his wife, who had the extraordinary sentimentality about Eire that is felt by many English people, he became a registered citizen of the Irish Republic in his old age, only to feel appalled by the fear that he might lose his British nationality as a result of this act. In his alarm, he wrote a letter to *The Times* in which he suggested that Eireans should be permitted to become honorary Britons. The thought of having to settle in Dublin, a city he detested, and spend the rest of his life listening to its tedious wits and insufferably garrulous intellectuals endlessly repeating themselves was his idea of hell upon earth! . . .

[1] But the ex-Kaiser, Wilhelm II, praised *The Apple Cart:* 'a great play by the greatest of living satirists. What genius and what humour.'

The most significant fact, in this respect, is to be found in a clause, 43, at the end of his will, where he states that:

> Having been born a British subject in Ireland, subsequently registered as a citizen of Eire, *and finally privileged to remain a British subject*,'[1]

he declares that his *domicile of choice is English*. Charlotte had wished to have her ashes scattered on the Three Rock Mountain in Eire, but G.B.S. had them mingled with his own and scattered in England.

36

His last novel, *An Unsocial Socialist*, was begun on July 9, 1883. It was finished on November 1. The first title was *The Heartless Man*, which, though not good, was better than that finally chosen: one which was sufficient in itself to secure its rejection. The publishers unanimously declined it. One of them, indeed, refused to read it. Many years later, G.B.S., in a letter which accompanied the gift of the manuscripts of his novels to Dublin, wrote that he 'did not know that' he 'was being ostracised on social and political grounds instead of,' as he thought, 'declined on my literary merits, which, as is now clear, were never in question.' This is nonsense. Publishers seldom, if ever, reject scripts 'on social and political grounds.' There have been instances when publishers have declined to publish a book because they disapproved of the principles advocated in it, but no one will consider them deserving of condemnation on that acount.

A publisher is as much entitled as any other man to possess a conscience, even if it be one which, in time, seems to have been narrow or wrong. The title of the novel was sufficiently deterrent to the generality of readers to make the publication of the novel a certain loss to its publisher; and publishers are not philanthropists, though they sometimes behave as if they were. By the time the novel was finished, however, G.B.S. had become accustomed to having his scripts returned, and he seems not to have minded the failure of *An Unsocial Socialist* very much. Other matters were absorbing his interest.

He had listened to a discussion in the Social Democratic Federation, a society which was founded by a well-to-do Ulsterman, Henry Mayer Hyndman, who was a disciple of Karl Marx, though he was personally disliked by that surly and graceless German. After he had spoken in the debate, a subsequent speaker told him that no one had

[1] The italics are mine.

any right to discuss Socialism unless he had read *Das Kapital*, which, at that date, had not yet been translated into English.

The remark rankled, and G.B.S., who was uncommonly conscientious about these matters, went off to the British Museum to read Marx's masterpiece in French; and was observed there, studying it and the score of Wagner's *Tristan und Isolde* simultaneously, by a young Scot, William Archer, who was Shaw's junior by two months. This was in the winter of 1882–3.

The encounter was of immense importance to G.B.S., though the two young men did not become acquainted until, some months later, they met at a party and became fast friends. In the meantime, G.B.S. completed his study of *Das Kapital* and was converted to Communism. He returned to the Social Democratic Federation only to discover that he, who had felt humiliated when he was told that he was unfit to discuss Socialism because he had not read Marx, was the only person in the group who had! It is one of the extraordinary facts about Marx that he has more followers who have never read a line he wrote than any other revolutionary in the whole history of social change.

Among the societies G.B.S. now frequented was the Land Reform Union, whose members included James Leigh Joynes, formerly a master at Eton, a school which has a remarkable record of rebels, cranks and highly articulate individualists, both among its teachers and its pupils. Another of these revolutionary Eton masters was Henry Salt, who thought, very oddly, that life at Eton was too luxurious, and, having married the sister of J. L. Joynes, thus doubling his capacity for unconventional behaviour, decided, when he had accumulated enough private capital, to lead a life of cultured simplicity, on his unearned income, in a labourer's cottage. Its carefully arranged simplicity seemed somehow to make Eton appear bleak with austerity, and it caused dismay among Salt's neighbours, who feared that if this cult of simplicity were to spread they might themselves be obliged to join it: a prospect that gave them no pleasure at all.

A third member of the Land Reform Union was Henry Hyde Champion, one of Henry George's numerous converts, who had been educated at Marlborough and 'the shop' at Woolwich, from which he emerged as an artillery officer: a brilliant, restless man who could not continue faithful to a scheme long enough to obtain any result from it. He was 'so extraordinarily ready with a practicable plan in every emergency,' Shaw said of him, 'that if the plan could only have remained the same for half an hour he would have been the greatest general of his age.' It was he who, during unemployment trouble in 1886–7, told a meeting that 'if the whole propertied class had but one throat he would cut it without a second thought, if by doing so he could redress the injustice of our social system,' a method of reform which ought to have troubled the mind of Henry Salt, who was living in such careful culture on rent and interest.

Champion's life was an incoherent romance. It made him at one moment assistant editor of *The Nineteenth Century* and, at the next, of *The Labour Elector*. He started Labour movements which were immediately disowned by his fellow Socialists. He was a guerilla fighter, with a single thought in his head, that Henry Hyde Champion should be the leader of all who were willing to be led, and that the whole enterprise of raising a row was good fun for Harry. He emigrated from England to Australia, where he soon made himself a public nuisance, enjoying himself enormously in the process, but his health, which had begun to deteriorate in England, now steadily declined, and in the end he petered out and died, the dampest squib that ever spluttered and failed to explode effectively.

These men, with Sidney Webb and Sidney Olivier, were now G.B.S.'s constant companions, though they were not a group that mingled easily. Webb's mind could not have been more remote from that of any Archbishop of Canterbury than it was from the mind of Henry Hyde Champion. He had no desire to live in an agricultural labourer's cottage with Henry Salt. The single wish Webb had about country cottages was that they should be demolished and replaced by well-built and sanitary Council houses. He did not deceive himself with the belief that a picturesque hovel, adorned with roses round the door, was an object worth preserving; and he certainly did not think it was romantic to have to fetch every drop of water one required from a well that might be a quarter of a mile away. Olivier's mind was too fastidious to make him eager to frequent the society of a fire eater like Henry Hyde Champion, whose dearest ambition was to sever a million throats. It is the measure of G.B.S.'s extraordinary power of easy association that he could consort comfortably and familiarly with people so diverse as these five and with others equally dissimilar.

Oscar Wilde, in one of his silliest epigrams, said that Bernard Shaw had no enemies, but that all his friends disliked him. The jape was puerile, for G.B.S., like all men of highly distinctive character, had many enemies, some of whom were deeply embittered and never reconciled, and numerous friends who were devoted to him. These enemies included people who shared his political beliefs. One of the first Fabians, William Clarke, could scarcely speak civilly to him. He had many admirers who abhorred his political opinions.

A man whose friends, in addition to those already named, included Graham Wallas, Mrs Annie Besant William Morris A. B.

Walkley, Ellen Terry, H. W. Massingham, Lillah McCarthy, Gilbert Murray, Lady Astor, Sybil Thorndike, G. K. Chesterton, Harley Granville-Barker, Lady Gregory, Sir Horace Plunkett, Sir Edward Elgar, Mrs Partick Campbell, Sir Barry Jackson, the Masaryks, father and son, Dean Inge, T. E. Lawrence, Gene Tunney and the Abbess of Stanbrook, together with a great diversity of Labour and other politicians, such as Will Crooks and Arthur James Balfour, must have had unusual qualities of charm and personality. Sir Arthur Pinero, who had been almost savaged by him in *The Saturday Review*, was one of his friends, and so was Sir James Barrie. Henry Arthur Jones, until they had a ferocious quarrel late in their lives, a quarrel which proved that one person is enough to make a row, had been a close friend, a friendship which was continued by some of Jones's children after their father had broken with him. Henry Irving's son, Laurence, was almost a familiar of G.B.S. when G.B.S. and Sir Henry were open enemies.

This gift for general and varied friendship was one of G.B.S.'s most engaging qualities. It was characteristic of him for the whole of his life. He had no intimates in whom he confided, but he had a host of affectionate friends whose deep regard for him could not be diminished even by himself. There were times when he put a great strain on their affection, when he seemed to be wilfully wounding in his behaviour, expecially in relation to Great Britain, but the friendship did not collapse under the strain, and the feeling for the man, apart from his opinions, never faltered.

He was now well furnished with friends of the sort he liked. The trivial aesthetes, with their little bits and pieces of polite culture, who were frequented by his mother and sister, saw him no more. He knew men and women whose knowledge of life was drawn, not from arty and crafty books, but from experience; and in their company he flourished and developed. He still had to solve his problem of finding a place in which he could reveal his genius, but the lean years were ending, the fat years were about to begin.

37

But before they began, he fell vehemently in love for the first time in his life. Among his mother's pupils was a beautiful girl, a hospital nurse, called Alice Lockett. G.B.S., who was always impetuous and importunate in love, was instantly overcome by her. Exactly when they met is not now discoverable, but he wrote some lines of verse to her in March, 1882, in which he made artful play with her surname, which he changed to Sprockett.

Love lifted to his lips a chalice,
    And said, 'My power, though many mock it,
Hath triumphed through the charms of Alice,
    Here's to the health of Alice Sprockett!'

A youth, o'er hearing this, grew jealous.
    'Sure as thou hast a head I'll knock it,'
Said he, 'for speaking thus of Alice,
    For daring to admire Miss Sprockett.'

Love answered, with a smile of malice,
    Wretch, hadst thou money in thy pocket,
How wouldst thou show thy love for Alice?
    What wouldst thou do for Alice Sprockett?'

The youth replied, 'I'd build a palace
    And with all rich and rare things stock it,
To live for ever there with Alice,
    To fill my heart with Alice Sprockett.'

Said Love, 'She knows thou are not zealous,
    And that thy life's light in its socket,
Wasting, makes thee unworthy Alice—
    Thou art despised by Alice Sprockett.'

The youth was shamed; but Love was callous
    Took wing, and vanished like a rocket,
Leaving the swain to mourn for Alice,
    To sigh in vain for Alice Sprockett.

The letters begin with one written on Sunday, September 9, 1883. Miss Lockett had visited Osnaburgh Street either for a lesson or entertainment, and G.B.S. had escorted her to Liverpool Street, where she was to catch a train. What happened on the platform is not clear. Did he discompose her by making ardent and abrupt love to her? Young men in those days wooed young ladies in a more restrained manner than G.B.S. was likely to display. They would probably have asked her parents' permission to pay their addresses before showing any ardour in her presence. She felt perturbed, and allowed him to see that she was; and he was full of remorse, for he wrote to her:

'Forgive me. I dont know why, on my honor; but in playing on my own thoughts for the entertainment of the most charming of companions last night, I unskilfully struck a note that pained her—unless she greatly deceived me. I have felt remorseful ever since, and she has been reproaching herself all day for wilfully missing a train. Heavens! to regret having dared at last to be frank and kind!

'Did you not see at that moment a set of leading strings fall from you and hang themselves on me in the form of golden chains? The heart of any other man would have stopped during those seconds after you had slowly turned your back upon the barrier and yet were still in doubt. Mine is a machine and did not stop; but it did something strange. It put me in *suspense*, which is the essence of woman's power over man, and which you had never made me feel before—and I was always certain of what you would do until that question of the train arose. And I repaid you by paining you. I did not intend to do so any more than you intended to please me, so forgive forgive forgive forgive me.

'I cannot (or perhaps will not) resist the impulse to write to you. Believe nothing that I say—and I have a wicked tongue, a deadly pen, and a cold heart—I shall be angry with myself tomorrow for sending you this, and yet, when I meet you, I shall plunge headlong into fresh cause for anger.

'Farewell, dear A. . . . There! is it not outrageous? Burn it. Do not read it. Alas! it is too late: you *have* read it.

G.B.S.'

The letter is incoherent, as a love letter ought to be, for what man can be coherent in a passion for a girl, but it is also curiously calculating. Its writer knows how to make an apprehensive young woman, accustomed only to formal addresses, feel that informality in wooing is delightful, even if it is alarming. She replied, but we do not know what, for although she kept his letters, a sign that he had stirred her feelings, he did not keep hers; but she must have written to him on Monday, for his long letter in reply—more than a thousand words of it—is dated the 11th September. 'Come!' he cries, without any superscription, 'if you meant all you said, you would not have written to me at all. When you are with me, you have flashes of generosity. You strive to keep it down, you have tried to prove that it does not exist by a wicked letter, and yet the letter—most ungenerous of letters—owes its very existence to that generosity. Was it not weak to write to me? Not at all. It was strong! . . .' And then he starts a game of giving her a double personality: a Miss Lockett character who pretends to be strong, but is really weak, and an A. . . . character who pretends to be weak, but is full of strength. (For some obscure reason the second and lovable character is always A. . . ., never Alice.) He plays the game entertainingly. A. . . . is warned to beware of that dragon, Miss Lockett, 'I hate her with a mortal hatred.' He goes on, flashing his wit around the bewildered girl's head until she must have felt herself to be in a maze from which there was no way out. He denounces Miss L. because she claims respect to which, he says, she has no right. 'Respectability is a quality, not a right. The lily does not claim whiteness—it *is* white. A. . . . will not claim respectability —she *is* respectable.'

But the love affair does not prosper. Miss Lockett is still deeply puzzled by this wild Irishman who whirls dangerously attractive words round her. She complains that he is not serious: he complains that he pleases her even less when he is serious. 'But has anyone been more serious with you than I? If you have made me feel, have I not made you think?'

The novel he was writing in 1883 was *An Unsocial Socialist*, and he tells Miss Lockett that her 'dual entity (if you understand that) makes the foundation of the most sentimental part of my new book.' Was she the original of Henrietta Jansenius? The original of Agatha Wylie, he said, he did not know. 'At the British Museum I saw a young lady. Her expression interested me, and I instantly conceived the character and wrote the description of Agatha Wylie;' but this account of Agatha's beginnings does not preclude the possibility that there was a good deal of Miss Lockett in her. The divided nature of Henrietta, however, seems more akin to her.

The affair gradually petered out, after a long and occasionally tempestuous correspondence; but it did not end, so far as she was concerned, for a considerable period after it had ceased to have any interest for G.B.S. As she grew older, and even after her marriage, she retained sentimental feelings about him; but there was no intellectual sympathy between them. Her habits and outlook on life were essentially suburban, and although G.B.S. fascinated her, he seems also to have frightened her.

The fact that his income was small and uncertain, coupled with the dismaying fact that no publisher would accept his novels, must have disconcerted a girl whose conception of life was founded on the sober and substantial middle-class beliefs. His hope that he had found a woman who had beauty and would be a good companion to him proved delusive. Never in this world could her mind and his have been attuned. She stirred no sentimental emotion in him, when, after her marriage, they met again, not even the modicum of interest that Maria Beadnell stirred in Dickens. It was fortunate for both of them that their love affair ended when it did, abruptly and unrenewably. She married a doctor, Salisbury Sharpe, by whom she had several children.

Her failure to return his affection did not close her relations with his family. She continued to take lessons from Lucinda Elizabeth, whom she also visited socially; and once, in May 1887, according to an entry in her diary, he met her unexpectedly as she was leaving the house, and walked with her to the hospital where she was nursing, and 'we got on the old terms in less than 5 minutes.' But it was a brief recovery of a fading affection. Alice, like many women, was strongly attracted to him, but she was not his woman, nor was he her man. She rightly married her doctor. They met occasionally, mostly by chance, and he sometimes wrote to her, but only as a friend. When G.B.S. finished an affair, it was finished, and there could be no revival. Friendship remained, but love had gone.

How deep her concern for him became is shown by the fact that on a Sunday in February 1894, she suddenly arrived at his mother's house, accompanied by her husband, and insisted that G.B.S., who, she felt certain, was suffering from tuberculosis, should let himself be thoroughly examined. Dr Sharpe 'could find nothing but a spot which he said might be a "consolidation" and might be nothing but an artery a little out of its normal position.' Alice Lockett was the first and, perhaps, the only wildly *romantic* love of his life, and the survival value of wildly romantic love is slight. Can we believe that Romeo, had he and Juliet survived that night in the Capulets' tomb, would have been as ardent about her in middle age as he had been in adolescence? Perhaps, but, more probably, perhaps not.

> Think you, if Laura had been Petrarch's wife,
> He would have written sonnets all his life?

38

In the long, lean period, now ending, G.B.S.'s total earnings by writing amounted to £6: fifteen shillings for an article on Christian names in *One and All*, a weekly paper, edited by a popular journalist and melodramatist, George R. Sims, which had a short career; five pounds for an advertisement of a patent medicine; and five shillings for a verse to fit an old block, one of a number which an enterprising publisher had bought with the intention of using them for a school-book prize.

This reward compares sadly with the earnings of one of G.B.S.'s younger contemporaries, H. G. Wells, whose dearest belief was that he had suffered great hardship in his childhood and youth: a belief which had scarcely any foundation in fact. According to *Experiment in Autobiography*, Wells, in the first four years of his serious authorship, beginning when he was twenty-seven, earned the following sums which denote popularity almost as swift and substantial as that of Dickens:

			£	s.	d.
1893	-	-	380	13	7
1894	-	-	583	17	7
1895	-	-	792	2	5
1896	-	-	1,065	7	8

These earning, which were nearly trebled in three years, were considerable for a young, uninfluential man with, as he falsely believed, everything, upbringing, health, appearance and education, against him; especially when it is remembered that a sovereign then was worth, not seven, but twenty shillings, and that income tax was only a few pence in the pound. Wells's earnings, when he was twenty-seven, would have seemed wealth to G.B.S. when he was that age.

There had, of course, been other earnings in these hard nine years, including a small sum for acting as polling clerk during an election, but £6 was the sum of his pay from writing. By the time that he was in the toils of Alice Lockett, however, he was beginning to make a small but erratic income, mainly from propaganda journals and magazines. *To Day*, which was edited and published monthly by the former artillery officer, Henry Hyde Champion, assisted, uneasily for the most part, by Ernest Belfort Bax, a Socialist philosopher with a deep bias against women in politics, and James Leigh Joynes, the ex-Etonian master, decided to serialise G.B.S.'s novels. The first of them to appear in this form was *An Unsocial Socialist* which ran from January to December, 1884.

Unluckily, *To Day* was one of those magazines which live precariously on free contributions from authors. G.B.S.'s fortune, therefore, was not improved by the serialisation of his last novel; but his circle of friends was. William Morris, poet and craftsman, had read each instalment of the story with pleasure, and sought its author's acquaintance. It was also read by the author's father, who however, made no comment upon it. Then the publishing house of Swan, Sonnenschien, Lowry & Co. decided to publish it in a scarlet bound volume which was handsomely reviewed by the critics, though the general public and the libraries abstained from it with remarkable unanimity.

In an article in *The Novel Review* for February, 1892, G.B.S. boasted that this edition had been a startling success: his royalties had increased between 1889 and 1891 by 170 per cent. 'I doubt,' he wrote, 'if any other living novelist can show such a record. In fact, 170% is an understatement; for the exact figures were two and tenpence for 1889 and seven and tenpence for 1891.' This statement is an excellent example of the skill with which he would put up a pretence of boasting and conceit, only to deflate himself in the final sentence.

That was a notable year in his history. An Aberdonian Scot, Thomas Davidson, who had lived for fifteen years in Canada and the United States, returned to Great Britain in 1881 and founded an uplifting society, called The Fellowship of the New Life, in his rooms at Chelsea. Here earnest-minded men and women assembled to discuss all that was discussable and much that was not. Their desire was to lead a simple, strenuous, intellectual life, communistically, if possible, on a basis of what was vaguely called 'natural religion'. Presumably someone enquired what natural religion might be, and where it was followed, but if anyone did, no report of the enquiry or its result was published.

Davidson, who had had a brilliant career at Aberdeen University, from which he never recovered, aspired to found a group of high-minded and ostentatiously noble men and women who would set a good example to the rest of the world. They were to withdraw themselves from general society and live very uncomfortably in harmonious communion with each other, showing baser people how they, too, might lead the higher life if only they would make an effort. Their intention was to form a colony either in a village easily accessible from Euston or Charing Cross or, if that were too drastic because of distance or, more probably, the inherent contempt felt by villagers for earnest people who wish to return to nature, in some terrace or square in town where the members could live in adjacent houses.

The scheme was too transcendental to last, and Davidson became discouraged. He returned to the United States where, it seems, the supply of high-minded people is higher than it is in the United Kingdom or the number of primitive people is so large that any addition to it is unlikely to be noticed, and little more was heard of him.

But he left a small band of disciples, including Havelock Ellis, who were willing to be as noble and high-minded as the facts of life would allow them to be.

The time was one of considerable commotion, intellectual and physical, and earnest people were greatly worried about the state of the world. Where could they find a refuge from a society which was steadily becoming more and more materialistic and mechanised? William Morris was seeking to halt the march to a machine-made world by encouraging medievalism, the manufacture of magnificently florid wallpaper, and a revival of handicrafts.

Trouble of every sort, from war and assassination to spiritual turbulence, abounded. Ireland was conducting its monthly rebellion. There was large scale unemployment in Britain. Cities were foul with slums in which masses of men and women and children festered from birth to death. Epidemic disease was rife. It became clear to some of Davidson's disciples that transcendentalism was not enough, and that the starry-eyed people must mingle their remote mysticism with a little practical politics. The sickness of society could not be cured by solemn assemblies sitting in splendid isolation and thinking noble thoughts. Somebody would have to do something to clear up the mess, somebody who had unending patience, courage and resolution, and was not easily made despondent by general indifference and frequent failure. Davidson had hardly landed in New York before the seeds of division were sown among his English disciples.

39

It will be well at this point to note two supremely important facts. On March 14, 1883, Karl Marx died in London, where he had lived for about thirty years without making any English friends, and was buried in Highgate cemetery. No one realised that this surly fellow, whose coffin was followed only by a few persons, was one of the world's supreme revolutionaries, or was able to foresee that because he had written a long, dull book, full of fallacies, kings and emperors many years after his death would be tumbled off their thrones and great nations would be totally or extensively changed.

Morose, vindictive, unscrupulous and immensely egotistical, he was almost unknown to his neighbours, except as one who was continually hard up and ready to sponge on anybody who would allow himself to be victimised; he liked few people, and was himself heartily disliked by nearly all the men in the Labour Movement of that time; but he had the devotion of his wife, who was his social superior, his children, and his German domestic servant, who was half starved and seldom paid; and he was revered by his compatriot, Friederich Engels, who, out of meagre means, almost maintained him. The world is now divided into multitudes who regard Marx as the saviour of society, and multitudes who regard him as the enslaver and destroyer of civilised men and women. In whatever way he is regarded, there is the indisputable fact that he changed the mind of the world, though there was no one on March 14, 1883, who could foresee his influence. Even in the small group of Socialists or incipient Socialists which he sometimes frequented, Henry George was considered the more important man.

About a year before his death, another revolutionary who changed the mind of the world died in the village of Down in Kent on April 19, 1882. This was Charles Darwin. These two men, who never met, though the distance that separated them was slight, one of whom, indeed, Darwin, was unaware of the existence of the other, profoundly influenced the outlook on life of masses of men and women who never read a word they wrote. There is no one alive to-day, whether he agrees or disagrees with the doctrine contained in them, whose existence has not, in some measure, been affected by *The Origin of Species* and *Das Kapital*.

Darwin's authority was more potent in 1883 than Marx's was to be for another fifty years. He had shaken the religious world as it had not been shaken since Luther nailed his Ninety Five Theses on the door of the castle church at Wittenburg; and the effect of his shaking was far profounder than Luther's, since it shook, not an insignificant, if socially distressing practice of the Church of Rome, but the entire fabric on which Christianity was based. If *The Origin of Species* were right, then the *Book of Genesis* was wrong.

Little more than two centuries before *The Origin of Species* was published, James Usher or Ussher, Archbishop of Armagh, a man of vast learning, published a work, entitled *Annales Veteris et Novi Testamenti*, in which he proved that God created the world at six p.m. on October 23, 4004 B.C. Other erudite men, as Professor Arnold Toynbee tells the readers of his *Study of History* (Vol. 7, pp. 298–9), were equally precise. The Jews were convinced that the date of creation was October 7, 3761 B.C., and the Eastern Orthodox Christians were as firmly convinced that it was September 1, 5509 B.C. Their calculations were based on the knowledge that was available at the time; and he would have been a daring man who had challenged the beliefs of these intellectuals, though they now seem to us absurd.

If the theory that the world was created almost instantaneously were true, then the creation must have occurred at some moment of time, and it was no more absurd of Archbishop Ussher to believe what he did than it is for us to believe that the earth has existed for some four thousand million years, and has supported human lives for perhaps a million. The Archbishop started off with the belief that the Bible was an exact record of creation, inspired by God Himself; and he had, on that belief, a better ground for his calculation than any of the fanciful guesses about the duration of the world which are held by learned men to-day; guesses which may seem to our descendants no more than the babbling of babies.

The theory that man was the result of a special act of creation was still widely held when Darwin published his book; and so was the theory that this creature, made by the breath of God blown through the nostrils of a clay figure, had been perfect, but had fallen through disobedience into a state of great sin. When, therefore, Darwin suggested that man was not a perfect creature who had fallen from grace, but an imperfect creature who was striving to rise up to grace, struggling out of primeval slime and climbing painfully up the dark crags of the world he scarcely understood, to some undiscerned peak on which he would understand much, if not all, and that this long and arduous struggle had taken ages so numerous that 4004 B.C. was, in comparison, but yesterday, the disturbance men underwent was almost unimaginable.

The members of The Fellowship of the New Life had grown up during this turmoil; and while they were bewildered by the wind that Darwin had blown upon them, they were tossed and battered by the whirlwind that was already blowing from Marx. Their religious principles had been torn to pieces: their social and economic principles were about to be torn to pieces.

It is a singular fact that G.B.S., who was twenty-six when Marx died, and was a frequenter of conventicles where Marx might sometimes have been seen, never once set eyes on him, not even in the British Museum which they both haunted daily. None of the first Fabians ever saw Marx, though several of them, including G.B.S. and Pease, had read the French translation of *Das Kapital*. One would have thought that, having suffered, through reading this work, a conversion to Communism as swift as any in the whole history of apocalyptics, G.B.S. would have had enough curiosity to wish to see and, if possible, hear its author, whose daughter, Eleanor, he was to know well a year or two later. It seems that Marx while he lived and Engels, whom G.B.S. met only by chance during a Labour demonstration in Hyde Park long after Marx's death, remained incurably alien in England, though Engels knew people in Manchester, where his business was, and was not so isolated that he failed to find a mistress in a young Ulster girl he met there. It was the death of this girl, to whom Engels was devoted, which nearly broke the friendship between him and Marx. Marx, when he heard of the girl's death, wrote a perfunctory note of regret, and then filled sheets with wails about his need of money: an illuminating example of his appalling and shameless egotism.

40

Davidson's deserted disciples assembled in the rooms of Edward Reynolds Pease, a member of a famous North Country family of industrialists who belonged to the Society of Friends. These rooms were at 17, Osnaburgh Street, the street in which G.B.S. and his mother lived. The first of their fortnightly meetings was held there on October 24, 1883, when they formed themselves officially into The Fellowship of the New Life. Soon after its foundation, however, division of opinion, already noted, developed among the members. The leader of the materialists was Hubert Bland, a Tory Democrat from Blackheath, who sported fashionable clothes, wore a monocle, and maintained simultaneously three wives, all of whom bore him children. Two of the wives lived in the same house. The legitimate one was E. Nesbit, a renowned and popular writer of charming books for boys and girls, who had a disconcerting habit of making scenes at meetings of The Fellowship and fainting in the middle of them.

The breach between the transcendentalists and the mundane

members widened, and when a proposal was made by the former that the entire society should emigrate to Brazil and lead a nobler life there than was possible in Central London, the split was complete and The Fabian Society was born. One section, which included Havelock Ellis, Edward Carpenter, Henry Salt and, a little later, a young Highlander, called James Ramsay MacDonald, who could never make up his mind whether he was starry-eyed or opportunist, and tried hard to be both, continued to uphold The Fellowship of the New Life. They published a manifesto, *Vita Nuova*, which they were simple enough to think would catch and hold the attention of the proletariat, despite their pre-occupation with the urgent and daily problem of finding food for a family.

The purpose of The Fellowship was 'the cultivation of a perfect character in each and all,' an achievement which has so far baffled and defeated the Almighty, but seemed to offer no difficulties to The Fellowship, whose principle was 'the subordination of material things to spiritual'. They were to hold numerous meetings 'for intimate social intercourse, as a step towards the establishment of a community among the members', who still hankered for isolation from the mob, though they had soon abandoned the desire to settle in Brazil. They continued to meet, without any perceptible increase in their own or anybody else's nobility, for fifteen years, when, quietly and without remark, they formally ceased to exist.

The second group, who, according to Professor Archibald Henderson, were animated 'by a passion for social, rather than individual, betterment', met in Pease's rooms on Friday, January 4, 1884. About fourteen persons were present, and these dissenters from exclusive attention to transcendentalism, founded The Fabian Society that evening in a very tentative mood. At the end of the evening, 'a collection was made to provide funds for past expenses: the sum collected amounting to 13s. 9d.' The leader of this group, Frank Podmore, who was to become fairly well known as an investigator in Psychical Research, originated the Society's name, which was based on the belief, never verified, that Fabius Cunctator was the author of the military injunction, 'For the right moment you must wait, as Fabius did most patiently, when warring against Hannibal, though many censured his delays; but when the time comes, you must strike hard, as Fabius did, or your waiting will be in vain and fruitless.'

The Fabians, as this group shall henceforth be named, believed, as a greater and simpler man than any of them, William Booth, the Founder of The Salvation Army, had discovered while they were still mewling and puking in their nurses' arms, that it is useless to offer an uplifting tract to a homeless and starving labourer. They proposed, therefore, that the hungry should first be fed and then offered suggestions about the reconstruction of the globe.

The Fabian Society, whose history was written by one of its founders,[1] E. R. Pease, who was also, for many years, its overworked and underpaid Secretary, has receded from authority almost to impotence; but it was formerly influential, not only in British politics, but in social politics in Europe and America. Its time of greatest authority was when its membership was small. The modern Labour Party is largely, if not entirely, its product, but its chief value to the world in general lies in its reasoned opposition to the economic dogmas laid down by Marx.

G.B.S. was accustomed to say that the Fabians had relieved people of the necessity to read *Das Kapital*, and this remark is substantially true. It will seem strange, however, to those who remember that he had been converted to Communism by reading the book before he had joined The Fabian Society, and that he remained a Communist for the rest of his life. It is said, indeed, that he was largely responsible for converting Sidney and Beatrice Webb, who were highly antipathetic to Soviet Russia, to something, certainly in the case of Beatrice, like fanatical faith in it. Having damned it thoroughly, they went to Russia for a few months, inspired by G.B.S.'s enthusiasm for it after he had spent nine days there, and when they returned to England, they wrote their massive work, *Soviet Communism: a New Civilisation?* though, with characteristic caution, they put a note of interrogation after the title. Their devotion did not blind them to the defects of the system, which are set out with notable candour, but they seem to have reconciled themselves to the brutalities committed by the Bolshevists by regarding them as part of the mess which all fundamental changes in social structures involve at the outset. Whether they would have been as ready to condone outrage and murder in a rising individualistic society is dubious.

There is no need to set out the history of the Fabian Society in this book: it has been published many times, and Pease's *History* is authoritative in regard to its period of power. The causes of its decline have yet to be stated. They are several. One is the fact that it did its work so well that it became unnecessary: the fate which all good societies of a reformatory character should aspire to meet. It had permeated the Liberal Party so thoroughly that the Liberals, after a sensational parliamentary victory in 1906, fell to pieces before the advancing Labour Party and are now virtually extinct.

The Society began to decline after it had yielded to the mindless

[1] *The History of The Fabian Society.* See also *Webb and the Fabian Society*, by the same author, in a symposium, entitled *The Webbs and Their Work*, edited by Margaret Cole. Pease, who was the last of 'the Old Gang,' died on January 6, 1955. His age was ninety-seven.

importunities of H. G. Wells that it should abandon its useful function as a research station and become a swollen body of strict adherents to Socialism. It was to add to its numbers as extensively as possible. But the Labour Party could not then, nor for a long while afterwards, do effectively what The Fabian Society did: assemble the facts about any problem in the best and most effective order. The Fabians had never sought a large membership. They had, indeed, done their utmost to discourage candidates for election by putting obstacles in their way, such as no other society places or has ever placed.

A person seeking to become a Fabian had first to provide two guarantors that he was known to them to be in general agreement with the Society's objects. He had also to attend several meetings before he was allowed to become a candidate; and he had to promise that he would do serious work for the Society of the sort that it was accustomed to do. He was then placed on probation for a year, at the end of which time, if he satisfied the Executive of his ability and devotion, he was admitted to full membership. People who thought it would be pleasant to spend a Friday evening once a fortnight listening to Bernard Shaw and other dreadfully clever people discussing this, that and the other, were repelled from the Society as if they were poisonous. There were other societies at whose meetings the seeker after entertainment could obtain it with little effort and at small cost.

When *Fabian Essays* was published with extraordinary and entirely unexpected success in 1889, there were only about 150 members in the Society.[1] The Secretary was in receipt of a salary of one pound a week. In 1891, the membership was 361, and the 'subscription list— thanks in part to several large donations—' had risen 'from £126 to £520'. In 1894, the members numbered 681. In 1909, the total membership was 2,462, of whom 1,227 lived in London. There were about 500 members of the provincial societies who were not also members of the London society. Associates, unwilling to sign the Fabian Basis and proclaim themselves Socialists, numbered 217. What greater tribute could we have to it than this, that it should have imposed the Newcastle Programme on the Liberal Party in 1891 when its total membership was 361? It is probably true that its most active workers then were Bernard Shaw, Sidney Webb and E. R. Pease, and that the total number of vitally active members was under twenty. We may doubt if there had ever been a society so few in members and so poor financially that was so powerful and influential in the political life of the British people.

[1] *History of the Fabian Society*, by E. R. Pease, p. 88.

41

The outbreak of the War in 1914, and the fact that the founders and first members of the Society were ageing men and women, and that the younger members who had flocked into Essex Hall when Wells won part of his way, and admission to membership was made easy, had less ability than their seniors, were potent factors in the Society's decline; but the chief factor was the rise to power, political and intellectual, of Transport House in the Labour Party. Able young men and women who would formerly have joined the Fabian Society, now sought employment in the Euston Road, where they obtained a close view of the whole Labour Movement which they could not have obtained in the company of the Fabians. It is sometimes suggested that the decline was due to the middle-class origin and intellectuality of the Fabians who were ill at ease with working men; and it is probably true that the average Conservative, especially in rural areas, felt more at home with labourers than any of the Fabians, many of whom were higher grade Civil Servants and incapable of associating or hobnobbing easily with anybody. They did not hobnob easily with each other. In the whole of a long and intimate friendship with G.B.S., I met a Fabian only once at his table. This was Olivier. If Pease ever went to the flat in Adelphi Terrace or in Whitehall Court, I never met him there, nor did I ever hear of his visit. The Webbs exchanged formal visits with the Shaws—indeed, the last time I saw Beatrice was when she was on her way to Whitehall Court—but they were about as genial as the visit of an Asiatic prince to Buckingham Palace. Sidney, who was easily bored, had few friends, as his wife deplores in *Our Partnership*, and there were not many people whom he liked.

The Fabians were as remote from jollification and lively social intercourse as were the Liberal intellectuals of their period, many of whom were Fabians masquerading as Liberals. The saddest evening G. K. Chesterton and Hilaire Belloc ever spent was at a dinner party with the Webbs. Their spirits were low for a long time thereafter. They might, it was alleged, have got along with Sidney, but Beatrice was too much for them. The Trade Union leaders of the 'eighties distrusted the Webbs for many years, and were never congenial with them. Beatrice, in her diaries, displays a dislike for them which is almost pathological, but her inability to like people was as great as Sidney's. Nevertheless, the authority of The Fabian Society in its prime is indisputable; and the chief factors in its authority were the Webbs whose house was frequented by politicians as diverse as Asquith, Arthur Balfour, Haldane, Lloyd George and Winston Churchill. A young Fabian, if he were asked to dine at Grosvenor

Road, was more likely to meet a prominent Liberal or Tory there than any Trade Unionist or Labour leader.

Both the Webbs, in their later life, disliked Ramsay MacDonald, whose dislike of them was deep, and Beatrice loathed J. H. Thomas, who, she said, deliberately dropped his aitches, partly to curry favour with the proletariat, and partly because he believed that disrespect for aspirates was democratic; but oddly enough, considering how little he liked either of them, she had great respect and admiration for John Burns, who might, she thought, have won the highest position in Labour politics, and have deserved to win it, had he not been eaten up with egotism and suspicion and envy of his colleagues, and unable to conceal his bitter hatred of some of them, such as Keir Hardie.

If there was any intercourse between the Webbs and the Philip Snowdens it was as cold as the Arctic regions. They are not even mentioned in *My Apprenticeship* or *Our Partnership*, and nearly all the references to him in *Beatrice Webb's Diaries*, 1912–1924, are casual and perfunctory or bitter and deprecatory. The single occasion, so far as mention in her published works is concerned, on which Snowden entered her house and ate a meal there, was when the first Labour Government was formed. She was a snob, both intellectual and social, despite her disclaimers of any class feeling, and, apart from her short experience of slumming before her marriage, kept as far away from the proletariat as she could. Sidney, who regarded the human race as raw material for statistical surveys, cared as little for the hopes and desires of the working-class as he cared for those of any other class. His and her purpose in the world was to get everybody neatly and tidily catalogued. A. G. Gardiner, a brilliant editor of the *Daily News* before it became the *News Chronicle*, described them as two typewriters with but a single thought.

42

The first publication of The Fabian Society was a pamphlet, entitled *Why Are the Many Poor?* which is said to have been drafted by the only working-man among the Fabians, W. L. Phillips, a housepainter, who did not long continue to be a member. By chance, a copy of this leaflet was given to G.B.S., who, some years later, revised it. 'The happy and clearly educated name Fabian suggested that this might be the society Webb and myself were looking for.'[1]

He made enquiries about it, and, on September 5, 1884, was elected a member. A fortnight after his election, he wrote the second pamphlet: *A Manifesto*. It has never been reprinted, but is reproduced in Pease's *History*, and bears all the stigmata of G.B.S.'s style and

[1] See G.B.S.'s chapter in *The Webbs and Their Work*, p. 7.

thought. Wealth, under existing circumstances, he contended, could not be enjoyed without dishonour or foregone without misery. Society was now divided into two hostile classes, those with large appetites and no dinners at one extreme, and those with large dinners and no appetites at the other. The State should compete with private individuals—especially with parents—in providing happy homes for children, so that every child should have a refuge from the tyranny or neglect of it natural custodians. Since Men no longer need special political privileges to protect them against Women, the sexes should henceforth enjoy equal political rights. The established Government had no more right to call itself the State than the smoke of London had to call itself the weather. . . . The pamphlet concluded with the assertion 'that we had rather face a Civil War than such another century of suffering as the present one has been.'

It was not until May 1, 1885, that Sidney Webb, who had read a paper to the Society on March 20, was elected a member. Sydney Olivier was elected at the same time. In April, Mrs Annie Besant was elected, and so, in the following February, 1886, was William Clarke. Then, in April, Graham Wallas joined the Society, and the seven authors of *Fabian Essays* were assembled.

It was in this remarkable group of able, if socially difficult men and women, that G.B.S. began to mature. He was himself an influential, industrious and devoted member, though his authority was of a different sort from Webb's. He was ostensibly a platform Fabian, though he did far more of the drudgery of the Society than is generally known, whereas Webb was the forerunner of those who are now called 'the backroom boys'. G.B.S. was not a thinker in the sense that Webb was. He had not that antlike devotion to a task that was characteristic of both the Webbs, but he had, supremely, the flashing thought, the moment of vision, the significant intuition, and he could, in a single sentence, illuminate a problem as the Webbs, who were plodders and often uncommonly dull and even obtuse, never could do.

The work he did for The Fabian Society, especially in its early years, was immense in its variety, and all of it was brilliant. It was also unpaid, though G.B.S. was poverty-stricken in comparison with his colleagues. Mrs Webb, who, of course, did not know him or Webb at this period, uses a vivid phrase about him as he was when, about 1893, she became acquainted with him. She describes him as 'a fellow with a crank for not making money, except he can make it exactly as he chooses.'[1] This is the strict fact about him. His chief

[1] *Our Parternership*. By Beatrice Webb, p. 38. Mrs Webb's statement is supported by Gilbert Murray, who in an article, entitled 'The Early G.B.S.', which appeared in *The New Statesman* on August 16, 1947, said 'Shaw did not want much. Neither the World nor the Flesh made much appeal to him, and such attractions as the Devil may have presented were only of a literary and inexpensive sort.'

extravagance in his prosperous period were his numerous and private benefactions.

He was still in the nine lean years when he joined The Fabian Society, though his Irish Protestant pride forbade him to mention his poverty even to his intimates, such as Webb, and he must often have been hard put to it to share their activities when such matters as railway fares had to be settled. Webb and Olivier were resident clerks in the Colonial Office, in receipt of adequate salaries. Wallas had a teaching job which rewarded him well enough. Mrs Besant had emerged from her period of severe poverty, after she had separated from her husband, and was earning good money by journalism and lecturing. Pease had private means. All of them were able to work for The Fabian Society without payment because they could support themselves in other ways.

But G.B.S. had no occupation, and the work he did for The Fabian without payment was done in considerable hardship: a fact of which only Mrs Besant seemed to be aware.

Mrs Webb, whose judgments of people were erratic and often wrong—she thought Asquith was coarse-grained and unimaginative merely because he did not appreciate her and Sidney as much as she thought he ought to have done, and she admired Haldane because he admired them both—could not understand him, and she never at any time appreciated his genius, chiefly because she was almost destitute of a sense of humour, had no wit and little appreciation of any art, except music, and was morbidly puritanical. She felt far more admiration for Graham Wallas than G.B.S., yet it was G.B.S. who supported Sidney from start to finish of their friendship, and Wallas who tried to thwart his educational scheme for London; and it was G.B.S. who was mainly responsible for getting them both buried in Westminster Abbey.

Mrs Webb, when she first knew him, was 'inclined to think he' had 'a slight personality'. That, perhaps, is the measure of her ability to judge anybody. She was, of course, upset because she could not subdue him to her intentions. He persisted in using his mind in his own way and not in hers, and he was too rebellious to be liked by a woman whose ideal man was a rule-ridden Civil Servant. Then, too, he was mixed up with the arts, and Beatrice distrusted artists, none of whom was amenable to laws other than those of the craft he followed. Plato, compared with her, was positively fond of poets. . . .

Mrs Besant, perhaps because she, too, had been poor and had suffered hardship and misrepresentation, was the first among the Fabians to realise that G.B.S. needed money, and she contrived to put some in his way without offending his pride or even allowing him to know that the sums she paid him for serialising two of his novels in her monthly magazine, *Our Corner*, were advanced from her private purse. When he discovered this fact, he refused to accept any further payment, demanding his right to be one of her unpaid contributors.

43

She began by disliking him for a cause that was natural enough. This extraordinary woman, who combined great personal beauty with a strong will and unusual oratorical power, had led a tempestuous career, and, about the time that she and G.B.S. became acquainted, had been deprived of the custody of her daughter by her husband, a deprivation which was upheld by the law. In one of his debating societies, G.B.S. surprised and shocked the members by supporting the legal decision. Quoting William Morris's remark that parents are the worst possible guardians of any child, he said that he strongly approved of the decision which had deprived Shelley of the custody of his children.

G.B.S. was a profound admirer of the poet, and had been deeply influenced by his work; but these facts did not prevent him from thinking that Shelley was about the last man on this earth who should have been allowed to govern any child's life. The haphazard existence of the whole Shelley household, with its excitements and disruptions and its incessant state of overwrought emotions, male and female, seemed to him to be the worst environment any child could endure. Mrs Besant's life, spent largely in travelling from town to town to lecture on atheism and in being reviled by pious ladies and gentlemen in terms that made the language of bargees seem, by comparison, chaste and civil, must, he contended, create an unwholesome atmosphere in which to bring up a young and sensitive child. The fact that she was more often away than at home, and that her daughter, therefore, must be left in the care of servants was sufficient condemnation of her house as a nursery.

The reader of this book will have no difficulty in understanding what was the experience that brought him to that conclusion.

Mrs Besant, on hearing what he had said, was deeply offended, and when they met at some meeting, her dislike of him, as a result of what she had heard, was increased when he rose up during the discussion and announced that he was a loafer. Mrs Besant, like Mrs Webb, accepted almost every statement literally. But her dislike was short lived. She was told that G.B.S. was extremely poor, that he refused to take work which his conscience forbade him to take, and that he gave a great deal of unpaid service to the causes he upheld. She went to a meeting he was to address, filling him with fear that she, an accomplished platform speaker, would destroy him, and amazed him by upholding his point of view. Thereafter their friendship was firm. It is certain that she was in love with him. She is said, indeed, to have drawn up a contract of 'free marriage' with him which frightened him so much that he was in dread of meeting her except in a large assembly.

Annie Besant's life was so remarkable in several respects that she is now a legendary figure. Almost entirely Irish in origin, with only enough English blood in her veins to preserve her sanity, she had a mixed ancestry. Most of her relatives were Protestants, but some were Roman Catholics, and this variety of influences in her family resulted in such a volatile medley of febrile emotions and drastic changes of belief in her mind that the wonder is she survived to the age of eighty-six. Her father, William Burton Persse Wood, despite or, perhaps, because of the great piety of his Roman Catholic mother and sister, was a sceptic about all religion, ancient or modern, and sometimes sent his wife, Emily Morris, flying from the room because she could not endure his derisive remarks. On both sides of the family Mrs Besant was related to well-to-do members of the upper middle class who were affiliated to peers and eminent politicians.

Her life, in her childhood, seemed certain to be one of comfortable culture among highly-placed people; but this hope was dispelled by her father's sudden death. Mr Wood, who had graduated in medicine from Trinity College, Dublin, had decided not to practise as a doctor, but to go into the City of London, where he quickly established himself in what appeared to be solid prosperity. But the appearance was delusive. His daughter was five years old when he died. Mrs Wood's distress was increased by the frightening discovery that she was left less well off than she had every right to expect to be: she had only a few hundred pounds on which to maintain herself and three young children, one of whom, Alfred, solved his problem by dying in his infancy. The stricken mother received offers of help from her kindred which were, she thought, remarkably meagre.

One of them, Sir William Wood, afterwards Lord Hatherley, became Lord Chancellor in Mr Gladstone's first ministry in 1868: and he proposed that her remaining son, Henry, should be sent to a sound, but undistinguished school in London, where he would receive a commercial training which would fit him for a clerkship in a City office, to which Sir William would nominate him. This offer shocked her, though why is obscure. She declined the proposal indignantly, insisting that her son should receive the education of a gentleman in a public school and an ancient university. Her presumption offended her relatives, some of whom were never reconciled to her, but she had more spirit and resource than any of her relatives imagined, and she made a surprising and successful effort to fulfil her ambition, which suffered from one grave defect, so far as her daughter was concerned; that it took account only of the boy. The girl's education was regarded as unimportant.

The young and determined widow rented a house in Harrow because she had discovered that boys who lived in the town were admitted to the school at lower fees than were charged for boys from other parts of the country. She wisely consulted the headmaster, Dr Vaughan, who helped her more than any member of her family. She told him that she proposed to start a school house for Harrovians, a plan of which Dr Vaughan approved, and she hoped that he would recommend her to parents, which he did. The venture became so successful that she was able not only to send her son through Harrow and Cambridge and start him on a successful career, but to save enough money to buy a house on the South Coast and provide herself with investments on which she could live comfortably in retirement. Unluckily, she was less discerning about people than she was about school houses, and her hope of a serene and secure old age perished when her lawyer misappropriated her means at a time which was critical not only for her, but for her daughter. The shock of this loss brought about her death when Annie had most need of her.

Such was the stock from which Mrs Besant descended. She was a romantically minded and almost morbidly imaginative girl, full of unsatisfied longings which she felt certain were religious and mystical, but were, she would have been horrified to learn, largely physical. She was serious in her thoughts, very beautiful, exceptionally spirited, brave and determined, entirely tactless, and suffering from a severe feeling of wrong. All the opportunities of education and advancement had been given to her brother because he was male: they had been denied to her, because she was female and would probably marry. In those days, an ill-educated woman was considered highly suitable to be a mother.

She had even been deprived of her life with Mrs Wood, to whom she was devoted, and sent to live with a pious and well-to-do spinster who had a craze for forming the minds of young and impoverished girls of the upper-classes on narrow evangelical principles. This was Miss Marryat, a sister of Captain Marryat, a naval officer famous for his novels and superb books for boys. Annie's semi-adoption by Miss Marryat was financially helpful to Mrs Wood, but was resented by her daughter, who felt the loss of her home and her mother very deeply. Nevertheless, she developed great affection for Miss Marryat, as was right, for that singular lady was uncommonly kind to her, giving her opportunities of developing her mind and tastes, mainly through foreign travel, that she could not otherwise have received, that were, indeed, unenjoyed by Henry.

The young girl, whose beauty, considerable in her childhood, increased as she grew older and was still great when she was an old woman, was docile, and she conformed easily to her mother's and Miss Marryat's religious injunctions, though she had an inner life of which they were ignorant. Had she been a Roman Catholic, it is almost certain that she would have become a nun, a probability she herself acknowledges in her incoherent autobiography, where she states that 'the Roman Catholic Church, had it captured me, as it nearly did, would have sent me on some mission of danger and sacrifice and utilised me as a martyr: the Church established by law transformed me into an unbeliever and an antagonist,' a statement so extravagant, especially in its last clause, that it has no relevance to reality. But it is true that evangelicalism, with its cold ceremonies and its austere distaste for any beauty in its ritual, left her deeply dissatisfied. It was inevitable, therefore, that the revival of ritual in the Church of England, as a result of the Oxford Movement, should attract her to High Anglican services. 'She shut herself in her room to spend hours on her knees before a lighted shrine.'[1] She read avidly in the works of the Fathers, knowing more about Polycarp, Ignatius, Chrysostom, and Saint Augustine than was known by many venerable ministers. 'She imitated the most extreme observations; denied herself water, food and sleep on fast days, and flagellated herself to see if she could bear pain.'

44

It was while this beautiful and romantically-pious girl was staying with her maternal grandparents in Clapham, a suburb of London which was then almost a rural retreat, that she met a young curate of the local high church. He was Frank Besant, a younger brother of Sir Walter Besant, an able and deservedly popular novelist in the Victorian era. The younger brother had none of his elder's ability. He had a long, dull face that became dreary in old age. He was a commonplace clergyman, whose piety was uninspired, the sort of man who would one day be made a rural dean and perhaps a prebendary through sheer length of life. His theological training had left him unaware of any difficulty in reconciling one Gospel with another. He believed what he was told to believe by the people in authority, and deeply disapproved of any person, male or female,

---

[1] See *The Passionate Pilgrim* by Gertrude M. Williams. See also *Annie Besant: an Autobiography*. The latter, however, deals only with about half her life. The first work was published before Mrs Besant's death.

who did not follow his example. It may be said of him, not unfairly, that he became a clergyman, a profession his elder brother had narrowly escaped, because it was genteel and, in those days, comparatively well-paid, one in which a man of mediocre ability could do tolerably well. He had no intention of acting or speaking in any way that could be called disturbing.

His vicar was a disciple of Dr Pusey, but Besant, though he found ornate ritual agreeable and pretty and, at all events among women, popular, was not so eager for copes and chasubles and candles that he was willing to undergo any distress of mind or social relations for them. Far less was he willing to trouble his thoughts about discrepancies in the Scriptures. There was, no doubt, a sufficient explanation of all these difficult matters somewhere. He would read the Lessons Appointed for the Day, and leave the closer study of the Testaments to those who liked to bother themselves. It would be enough for him to tell his congregation to be good and shun dissent.

He cast an approving eye on Miss Wood. With this lovely girl as his wife, he could feel certain of a comfortable living in a pleasant parish; for she had influential relatives. A residential canonry in a cathedral in one of the more pleasing counties might come his way. Cathedral closes were sometimes soothing places, despite what was written about them in Mr Anthony Trollope's upsetting novels. The fact that the girl he was proposing to marry was intensely religious seemed to have eluded his notice. He was ignorant of the fierce fires that burned in her mind and heart, and would have quenched them had he known. He was not perceptive enough to observe that Miss Wood, despite her quiet and subdued demeanour, had a strong and resolute will and was capable of making herself a martyr, if that should be necessary. He discouraged her from discussing theological subjects, partly, perhaps, because he was soon out of his depths in such matters, and so their conversation gradually became a succession of disjointed remarks on trivialities. The girl felt deeply disappointed, but was not yet sufficiently in possession of herself to be more assertive.

She had lately made a parallel account of the Passion and the Crucifixion, drawn from the four Gospels, with a column for each Gospel, and was surprised and deeply disturbed to find so much difference in the accounts. Her attempt to discuss the discrepancies was heavily rebuked, and she was made to feel that she had almost committed blasphemy in mentioning the discrepancies at all. Anyhow, Mr Frank Besant could not explain them, and he preferred to talk about some rather nice people who had lately come to live in the parish! . . .

Like the majority of able women, Annie preferred the company of men to that of women, though she seems to have been unaware of the fact at the time that she and Mr Besant were taking an interest in each other. She thought that her mind was entirely concerned with theology: she did not realise that it was also concerned with the way of a man. The conversation of her own sex bored her beyond belief, but the conversation even of this commonplace curate was full of interest. When, very cautiously and in the stilted phrases used by his sort of man, he proposed to her, she accepted him gladly. Perhaps he would talk better and more freely when they were married! . . . Her mother, who realised that Besant and her daughter were uncongenial characters, opposed the engagement, but, finding Annie determined, consented to it. There was a brief period during which the young girl herself doubted if Besant was the mate she needed; but she found her mother as opposed to a breach of the engagement as she had been to the engagement itself. In a mystical sense, it *was* marriage, and in an earlier age and more primitive community would have been consummated the moment the contract was concluded. A broken engagement, in Mrs Wood's belief, was as bad as a broken marriage. She, therefore, insisted that Annie, having made her engagement, should keep it.

The bride was twenty, and as innocent as a child. It is not easy now to believe that a young woman of her age could go to her bridal bed in total ignorance of what would happen to her there; and, indeed, the legend of the ignorant Victorian girl has been grossly over-stated. But there were girls then, and there may be girls now, to whom the facts of life, as we euphemistically call them, were unknown or were known only in a sentimental and entirely false way. The consummation of Annie's marriage frightened and appalled her, and its horror was increased by the peculiar clumsiness of her unimaginative husband who was almost as ignorant as she was.

In due course, she recovered from the shock of her bridal night, for she was an ardent woman, full of physical as well as moral passion; and she bore two children, a son and a daughter, quickly enough. But she never recovered from the shock of finding that her husband's mind was dull and lethargic, that his habits and thoughts were so routine that they could never be altered or even stimulated. W. T. Stead, many years later, said of this extraordinary woman's silly marriage, that 'she could not be the bride of Heaven, and therefore became the bride of Mr Frank Besant, who was hardly an adequate substitute.' They began their married life in Cheltenham, where Besant taught for a time in a school, and then went on to a living in Sibsey, a small parish in Lincolnshire, to which Besant was nominated by his wife's kinsman, Lord Hatherley.

Besant was one of those men who, when they feel bewildered or unable to meet or sustain an argument, lose their temper. He could not understand why his beautiful young wife, the mother of two charming children, should bother her head with disputatious points of doctrine. Why could she not do what he did, accept the beliefs of nice people and leave the whole troublesome business of eschatology to those whose occupation it was? *She was a woman,* and ought, therefore, as St Paul had said, to submit herself to her husband, whose orders at that moment were that she should attend strictly to her household affairs and cultivate the society of those of her neighbours whom he considered to be suitable persons for her to know.

He became less and less capable of understanding or sympathising with his impulsive young wife, who was, in every respect his intellectual superior, and he met her increasing enquiries at first with impatient and inadequate replies and afterwards with angry denunciations. She sought counsel in books, and then, made despondent by their futility, consulted clergymen whose minds were better furnished than her husband's. She even went to Oxford to ask for guidance from Dr Pusey, who turned out to be worse than useless, for he filled her with a suspicious fear that he had the mind of a fanatical inquisitor at the court of Spain. Benign and gentle to those who were obedient to his will, he was harsh and tyrannical to those who were not.

'It is not your duty to ascertain the truth,' he thundered at her. 'It is your duty to accept and believe the truth as it is laid down by the Church.' When she replied that she must try to find out what was true, he charged her with intellectual pride, and told her that she had 'no right to make terms with God as to what you will believe or what you will not believe.' His final remark was characteristic of this futile person. She had apologised to him for wasting his time, and had said she would go home and face her difficulties by openly leaving the Church and taking the consequences. 'I forbid you to speak of your disbelief,' he cried like the would-be Torquemada he was. 'I forbid you to lead into your own lost state the souls for whom Christ died.'

It appeared that Christ had died so that Dr Pusey should be fulfilled. In another age than theirs, this vehement old gentleman would have rushed the bewildered girl into the market place of Oxford and would there have had her roasted alive. Yet she felt no resentment against him, and when, nine years later, he died, she remembered him with greater kindness and generosity that he had shown her.

She went home to report her decision to her husband. She would, she said, continue to attend the services in his church, but she would no longer partake of the sacrament. Surprisingly, he consented to this arrangement, although her elaborate and, surely, unnecessary withdrawal from her pew when the Communion Service began, caused disturbing comment in the parish; but when a relative told him that his prospects of advancement in the Church were likely to be harmed as a result of his wife's eccentric behaviour, he retracted his approval, and ordered her to receive the Sacrament or leave the Vicarage.

She left the Vicarage, to the deep distress of her mother.

45

But before she went, she made a discovery about herself, that she possessed a power of which she had not previously been aware: she had a powerful and moving voice and a remarkable flow of rhetorical words. She had gone into her husband's church one afternoon, to play on the organ, and as she was about to leave, she took a whim to enter the pulpit from which the vicar droned his dreary sermons. Suddenly, she heard herself declaiming to the empty pews, and was astounded not only by the facility of her speech, but by its eloquence. This was a Pentecost, indeed.

There is nothing remarkable in the fact that a person discoursing in an empty church or hall, feels that he has received the gift of tongues. Many people have so deceived themselves. But the surprising fact about the revelation made to young Mrs Besant that afternoon is that she *had*, amazingly, been given the power of great emotional oratory. It is a gift which many very dissimilar women have possessed.

I will not attempt to judge between Mrs Besant and Mrs Pankhurst in this respect. The first was entirely different in her habit of public speech from the second, but both of them were moving and powerful and extraordinarily effective in their control of an audience. I heard Mrs Besant address the Fabian Society in her old age, when, clad entirely in white and looking very lovely, she uttered a flaming fire of eloquent words that seemed as if they must consume every man and woman who heard her. I came out of the Essex Hall almost stunned by what she had said, and was glad to feel the cool air of the Thames blowing up the street. My amazement at the speech Mrs Besant had delivered was slight however, in comparison with my surprise, as I stood in that dark street off the Strand and realised that I could not recall a single sentence she had spoken. I could recall only a sense of having been so beaten by burning words that my mind and body felt scorched.

It was this power over audiences that she discovered in herself in Sibsey Church that afternoon when she was in deep distress about her future life.

She had a hard time after she left Sibsey. Her husband made her a small allowance which was insufficient for the maintenance of herself and her mother, now ruined by her defaulting lawyer, and her daughter; so she sought employment from a benevolent society which offered work to ladies in reduced circumstances. By stitching for a week, she was able to earn 4s 6d, a sum which was insufficient for the needs even of a lady who had become accustomed to being reduced and had no one but herself to support. A firm in Birmingham was willing, in return for a small fee, to put here in the way of adding usefully and easily to her income. She sent the small fee, receiving in return a pencil case. By hawking similar pencil cases among her friends, together with other articles such as silver-plated cruets, there was no telling what sums she could earn! . . .

Amelia Sedley, in *Vanity Fair*, was not more baffled by her genteel inefficiency after she had become a widow, than was Annie Besant at that moment. Their ladylike education had not equipped them with enough knowledge to enable them to earn six shillings a week. There were times during this period when the young outcast from Sibsey forwent a meal because she could not afford to buy meat for three. The thought that she might earn a living by her eloquence had not yet occurred to her.

It was while she was suffering this distress, that she first met Charles Bradlaugh, an amazingly influential orator of working-class origin, who was then engaged in a crusade against Christianity in particular and the idea of divinity in general. He was to make a wide and deep change in her general condition and outlook on life.

There have been few orators of Bradlaugh's stature anywhere or in any time. His authority over an audience, and especially of a working-class audience, was immense and unique. Yet he lived in an age of eloquent men, including Gladstone and Disraeli. How far he was entitled to be called an atheist is disputable. He said little or nothing that is not now familiar stuff in sermons or exegetical works by clergymen of all denominations. But he belonged to a time when the Bible was still believed by the vast majority of men and women of all classes to be the 'impregnable rock' which Mr Gladstone had called it. Disraeli was not derided when, at a Meeting of the Society for Increasing the Endowments of Small Livings, he said that if the choice were between apes and angels, he was on the side of the angels.

That was the choice that almost everyone in the civilised world, despite Darwin, was then willing to make. The idea that there was something heroic in the spectacle of an ape struggling to become an angel, had not occurred to them. They preferred to admire inadequate angels who fell at the first temptation! . . .

Bradlaugh was a sincere and upright man, who had had the misfortune to marry a dipsomaniac, and it is conceivable that his almost incessant lecturing was an effort to escape from the horrors of his home. He suffered as much for his opinions, short of the supreme suffering of cruel death, as any man or woman in the whole hagiology; and he had some of the characteristics of a saint. He is remembered now, when he is remembered at all, mainly because of what he had to endure when, elected to the House of Commons for Northampton, he was thrown into Palace Yard because he refused to take the oath 'in the name of God'. The procedure with regard to the oath was altered eventually, and Bradlaugh was able to take his seat in peace. He was a highly significant figure in his time, too significant, indeed, to be remembered beyond his time. Victory was, in a sense, his undoing. That won, there was nothing left for him to do but to repeat himself, and no one is so soon forgotten as the man who converts his opponents into supporters.

His meeting with Annie Besant was casual. She chanced to buy a copy of his paper, *The National Reformer*, and noticed an advertisement of a body called the National Secular Society. She then wrote for information about it, and, eventually, attended one of its meetings in the Hall of Science, which was addressed by Bradlaugh. She spoke to him at the end of the meeting and began a friendship which was to last for the rest of his life and was to be profoundly influential on her affairs. The first upshot of this encounter was that she shed any remains of her Christianity that were left. Her association with the National Secular Society became as close as Bradlaugh's, and since she was almost as eloquent as he was, and had great personal beauty, her popularity on platforms very nearly equalled his.

She was now, and forever, separated from the cheerless curate whose chief interest was paleography, mitigated by a smaller interest in mathematics. When a tree had to be felled, he would estimate the length of its fall, and then place himself at the point where he thought its tip would land. If the branch hit him, he would murmur 'slight miscalculation', and go back to his study and get galled about it. The contrast between Bradlaugh and Besant was too striking for Besant to have any hope of ever recovering his wife.

Her activities in the National Secular Society were, naturally, distressing to the Vicar of Sibsey. It was unpleasant for an ordained minister of the Church of England to hear and read reports of his wife's public profession of what he and most people called atheism. Like Bradlaugh, she was sometimes assailed at meetings, and once, when she was twenty-seven, she was severely kicked as she came out of the hall where she had been speaking.

Mr Besant was infuriated by the reports he received, and rushed up to London to rage at her. It is asserted that he struck her in these bouts of anger, but we must, if we believe that he did, make a large allowance for his situation. He, too, had rights, and it was uncommonly hard on him that his wife should now be rampaging up and down the country, trying to undermine and destroy the religion in which he believed, of which he was a professional servant.

Mr Besant does not cut a pretty figure in the history of his wife's career, but he could, with considerable justification, plead that she did not cut a pretty figure in his. The injury she did him was greater than the injury he did her. He could not help being a stupid man with a routine mind. There was no necessity, except, no doubt, some inner and inexplicable compulsion, for her to tear up beliefs very roughly by the roots, when she had nothing to put in their place except the bleak denials and empty despair of the Hall of Science.

At the end of their interviews, a formal separation was arranged. She was to receive an allowance of £110 a year, and to have the custody of her daughter, Mabel, the boy remaining with his father. The arrangement did not last for long.

Soon after it was made, Bradlaugh and Mrs Besant became interested in birth control. They had convinced themselves that any hope of improvement in the material and intellectual state of the proletariat was impossible so long as poverty was accentuated by prolific births. They, therefore, began to advocate the restriction of of families by the use of contraceptives, causing a deep division among the Secularists, some of whom, including one of the most important of them, George Jacob Holyoake, were opposed to mixing contraception with secularism. The row in the National Secular Society, however, was nothing in comparison with the row throughout the country, and Bradlaugh and Mrs Besant had to bear the brunt of it, not only in their public, but in their private lives.

About half a century before their campaign began, a pamphlet, entitled *Fruits of Philosophy, or The Private Companion of Young Married People*, was published by a respectable doctor, Charles Knowlton, in Massachusetts. He was prosecuted for doing so, with the result that the pamphlet quickly ran through nine editions in seven years. This small and insignificant work was issued in England by one James Watson and, on his death, by Charles Watts, another eminent Secularist, who founded the publishing house which still bears his name. It had been sold in Great Britain for about forty-two years when a bookseller in Bristol inserted some indecent pictures in the copies he was offering for sale, and the result of his peculiar enterprise was that not only was he arrested, but so was Watts, though he knew nothing of the bookseller's arts, and would have disapproved of them if he had.

The entire situation was serious, not only for Watts, but for the National Secular Society, which was now riven with bitter dissension.

Watts had married a second time, and his young, pretty and frivolous-minded wife was displeased by the prospect of her husband's imprisonment just when she was beginning to enjoy marital felicity. Bradlaugh himself, though willing to be imprisoned for a point of principle, was not ready to risk the ruin of his entire organisation and undergo imprisonment as well, for the free and open sale of contraceptives. The quarrel became acute, and old friends became enemies. But Mrs Besant, because, perhaps, she was a woman and knew the misery that numerous births, slightly spaced, brought to her sex, would not be deterred by quarrels and splits from spreading knowledge among those who were most in need of it; and when Watts and his wife withdrew from the whole affair, Bradlaugh and she continued the publication of *Fruits of Philosophy*.

They were arrested and brought before the magistrates at the Guildhall in London, and were tried eventually before the Lord Chief Justice, who summed up in their favour, but was mortified by the jury's refusal to follow his advice. The verdict was that Bradlaugh and Mrs Besant were guilty of publishing a work 'calculated to deprave public morals', but they were exonerated from the charge of corruption in publishing it. Bradlaugh appealed, and he and Mrs Mrs Besant were released on bail; and in the end, the indictment was quashed. The defendents had won a great moral victory.

They were at once the recipients of immense gratitude from a vast number of women whose lives had been made wretched by numerous pregnancies, many of which had ended in miscarriages or the birth of unhealthy infants whose lives were brief; but they were also the recipients of gross abuse from their opponents. A Town Councillor in Brighton publicly hoped that 'such an animal as Mrs Besant would not be allowed to use the Town Hall' for one of her meetings. She was described as foul, and a newspaper in Essex complained that 'that bestial man and woman' went 'about earning a livelihood by corrupting the young of England.'

The Vicar of Sibsey was horrified, not unreasonably, by what he read in the press. His wife's advocacy of atheism and her public association with the notorious infidel, Bradlaugh, had been bad enough, but that she should become an advocate of what he believed to be immorality was more than he could stomach. The wife of a clergyman of the Established Church was openly and unashamedly telling young women how to prevent the conception of children! . . . Before long, men and women, married or unmarried, would be carnally concurring all over the country, and the last state of the world would be worse than the first.

The thought that his daughter, Mabel, was in the care and control of this immoral mother, who must, he feared, have gone out of her mind, appalled him, and he began an action to deprive her of the child's custody. The case was heard before the Master of the Rolls, Sir George Jessel, whose prejudice against Mrs Besant was plainly revealed every time he opened his mouth, and judgment was given against her. Public opinion, however, was sharply divided on the matter, and Mrs Besant's sympathisers were numerous and able, both in the press and among the general public: and working-men subscribed £2,000 to defray the costs of the case.

The child, who was suffering from scarlet fever, was taken, screaming and struggling, from her mother's house and conveyed to her father's, where the mother was denied all access to her. Besant also ceased to pay his wife's allowance. Fearing that she might take action against him on both counts, he obtained an order from the Master of the Rolls, the same Jessel who had treated her with so much discourtesy, restraining her from taking any action against him. He was, it appeared, entitled to do this under the deed of separation which was held to deprive a wife of the right to take action against her husband 'while the clauses giving' her 'the custody of the child were set aside.' It was this peculiar technicality which caused her to lose her suit for divorce, a suit in which she described six separate occasions on which the infuriated incumbent of Sibsey had used her with considerable cruelty. Besant denied the charges, adding, however, that if there had been any violence, it was committed in the heat of the moment.

That was the end of their association. They never met again.

These two totally unsympathetic characters were unfortunate in their strange marriage, which brought neither of them any happiness. Besant lived at Sibsey, more or less a recluse, until 1917. His time was spent in studying parish records and attempts to solve mathematical problems. The vicarage was neglected and the garden rampant with weeds. Gates and doors leaned away from their hinges or fell flat. The walls of the house were still covered with the gloomy paper that had been stuck on them when he took his young wife to Sibsey for the first time. The place, like its occupant, was steadily falling to pieces.

On a morning in 1917, his housekeeper went to waken him and found the room empty and the bed unused. She descended to the study and found him lying dead on the floor where he had collapsed during the previous night. He was a poor creature, but he was unfortunate enough to mate with a woman far beyond his understanding or his powers of endurance; and we may spare him a little pity. He was not built for greatness or association with it. His life would have been admirable and without cause for complaint or blame if he had married a submissive young woman from the Bible

Class who could read the two Testaments from end to end without observing the slightest discrepancy in either of them. If his wife's fate was hard, so was his. A man should not marry intellectually above him. She survived him by sixteen years. On the 20th of September, 1933, she died. Her age was eighty-five.

46

It was this tempestuous petticoat whom G.B.S. encountered as his nine lean years approached their end; and it was she who tried to put money in his purse when he was sorely in need of it. Like Bradlaugh, she was not a Socialist, but an individualist so determined on self-expression that she was practically an anarchist; but she was in process of becoming a Socialist, a feat Bradlaugh never performed. When she joined the Fabians, she was easily the most renowned member of their society, with an extraordinarily national reputation and the beginnings of one that was international.

How far the Fabians were pleased with her accession is difficult to say. Webb was not the sort of man to feel enthusiastic about a petrel who went about looking for storms. G.B.S. was probably the single prominent Fabian who delighted in her sudden decision to become a Socialist.

All her decisions were sudden. She was capable of repudiating every article in the Socialistic creed at one moment, and of demanding the nationalisation of almost everything at the next. She ceased to be a Socialist as suddenly as she had ceased to be an Individualist. But while she was a Socialist and in love with G.B.S., she was a vivid and exceedingly picturesque figure in the revolutionary movement. Her contribution to *Fabian Essays* is the least impressive in the book. Despite her facility in writing, which was almost as great as her facility in speech, she wrote poor, sentimental and shallow stuff. Her publicity value was considerable: her political and economic value was slight; and it is very certain that the bureaucratic Socialists, such as Webb, were impatient with her.

Webb probably found her difficult to talk to. Wallas almost certainly despised her mystical maunderings, for Wallas, being the son of a parson, had endured all the piety and mysticism he could stand, and wanted no more of it. The mind revolts at the thought of Hubert Bland endeavouring to be companionable with her. Sydney Olivier could have sat in her presence for hours without being aware of it. But she was meat and drink to G.B.S., whose liking for oddities was unlimited.

Her generosity to him over the serialisation of his novels in her magazine, had made him her debtor for life, though he declined to take another penny when he discovered her kindly plot. He was not in the least in love with her, though his admiration for her was immense; and he would have found her curious way of life, especially in her last years when she became a Theosophist, unendurable. He was, it must be stressed, a regular man: that is to say, he liked a regular life with a regular woman in a regular house. The upheaval and disorder of a bohemian house were utterly repellent to him, but he was also repelled by a house in which every member was engaged in some uplifting enterprise, rushing here and rushing there and rushing back only to start rushing somewhere else. He had suffered much from a ramshackle house already, and was to suffer a good deal more until Charlotte came and snatched him out of it and set him down in an orderly home and gave him the regularity he needed.

To live in a house full of ecstatic Theosophists or roaring orators who were always arriving from railway stations or about to depart to them, would have been unbearable for him: though he was himself, at this time, continually tearing round the town to meetings or catching trains to conferences and congresses and the rest of the wasteful jamborees on which public persons expend their energies and minds. It is one thing, however, to tear about oneself, and another thing to live in a house where everybody is tearing about.

Moreover, G.B.S., who had begun to realise how attractive he was to woman, and was also beginning to be able to meet them on fair terms and conditions so far as money was concerned, had just taken a toss from Miss Lockett and was now landed with another and much more alluring lady who had caught him when he was most sore from the wounds inflicted on him by his first love. Among his mother's pupils was a Mrs Jenny Patterson, a woman with a fiercely passionate nature and an ungovernable temper, who became the model for Blanche Sartorious in *Widowers' Houses* and Julia Craven in *The Philanderer*.

Mrs Patterson was thought by those who knew her to have been fifteen or even more years older than G.B.S.[1] She was the widow of a well-to-do country gentleman from whom she had inherited substantial means. She had a house in London and another in the country. Meredith's description of Diana of the Crossways might, except in one particular, have been a description of Jenny. 'She has a straight nose, red lips, raven hair, black eyes, rich complexion, a remarkably fine bust, and she walks well, and has an agreeable voice; likewise delicate complexion.'

[1] According to her Death Certificate, her age was eighty, but as the information was given to the Registrar by a servant in the house in which she was staying at the time of her death, the certificate cannot be accepted as accurate. She died on September 15, 1924, which makes her his senior by twelve years, but she told G.B.S. that she was fifteen years older than he was.

Jenny's hair was dark brown.

Later in the novel, Meredith makes a character say of Diana, 'what is more, the beautiful creature can talk.' Her voice, whether in speech or in song, was lovely to hear, says one who knew her well, and she was intelligent. Her supreme defect was her violent temper, which was made more distressing by her delight in making scenes. Peace-loving and sensitive people yielded to her importunities and demands rather than endure the distress of the trouble she created when she was thwarted or denied.

She was uncommonly attractive in several ways, and especially in the ways that were pleasing to G.B.S., and, despite her ferocious temper, she was likeable and generous-minded. She was gay and clever, and, except for her fury which distressed him who was highly sensitive, the companion he needed, She herself asserted that she had been badly educated because, in her childhood, she threw things at her governesses and all who tried to control her. Nevertheless, she was a fairly accomplished woman, well-bred, travelled, and a good linguist. It is a point in her favour that her temper was most easily provoked by cruelty to animals and children. Her warm and glowing nature, her abundant physical beauty, and the ardour of her rich and unrestrained desire made her sexually attractive to a young man in whose life women had hitherto played scarcely any part. She was entirely feminine, and she did not conceal her delight in men or her eagerness to enjoy them. Her charm for women was almost as great as her charm for men. Lucinda Elizabeth and Lucy liked and admired her, and they probably hoped that G.B.S. would marry her. His life, economically at least, would be secure with so wealthy a wife. Their friendship was continued after G.B.S. had broken with her, and was discontinued only because her jealous fury, which compelled her to abuse him to his mother almost incessantly, made friendship impossible. There is no doubt that she loved him devotedly, but he never loved her, although he found her physically satisfying.

47

G.B.S., at the date of their first encounter, was in a state which can best be described as sexual starvation. He was continent to a degree that was almost unique in a man of his age, but continent only because the circumstances of his life forbade him to have much, if any, contact with women, innocent or otherwise. Too fastidious to purchase them off the pavement, even if he had been able to pay their price, he was unable, because of his poverty and his increasing shyness during the nine years of his bondage to letters, to make many women friends. His abortive love affair with Alice Lockett offered little hope of consummation, and, in any case, she was not the sort of woman who was likely to hold his affection long. Compared with Jenny Patterson, Alice Lockett was mindless. At the age of twenty-nine, therefore, G.B.S. was still a virgin, leading a monastic life without the physical and moral support of an institution and a satisfying ritual.

This unusual abstinence was the cause of his extraordinary pursuit of women when, at last, he was earning enough money by writing to enable him to enjoy social relationships. His pent up emotions burst their banks and spread a flood around him in which he seemed likely to founder. How he managed to do his work and maintain his surprising relations with women is a matter for marvel. His energy was abundant, but even his animation must have caused a decline in health had he persisted in the exhausting activities which were consuming his strength in the last decade of the nineteenth century. These activities can be described with accuracy because he kept a diary, 'the first of this kind I have kept,' from January 5, 1885, until October 12, 1897. The entries for the year 1892 are missing: an unfortunate loss since much was happening to him at this time that was important. That was the year in which the Webbs married.

The diary is scrappily written, and many of the people mentioned in it can no longer be identified because they are indicated only by initials. The nine years of penury were ending, and G.B.S., although he was not yet making much money, was at least maintaining himself in moderate comfort: though he was still likely on occasions to find himself short of enough pence to pay for his mid-day meal. A fairly common entry in the Diary informs the reader that he suddenly discovered himself unable to go to the Wheatsheaf for his vegetarian dinner because he was literally penniless. So he stayed at home and ate 'some bread and apples'. There was even an occasion when, about to pay for a seat at a theatre, he found he was a penny short of the sum required, and had to go away, though we may believe that the ticket-seller would have overlooked the penny had he been told it was short. G.B.S., however, has not accustomed to mention his lack of means, even to his friends.

His range of friends, male and female, was extensive, and they were frequently visited. His sociability was returning to him, although he was never able to rid himself of the shyness which had been developed in the hard times. His employment was mainly in desultory journalism. His guardian angel, Archer, had obtained a post for him as musical critic of *The Dramatic Review*, and his first article appeared in the second number, on February 8, 1885.

At first, he wrote only signed articles, but afterwards he contributed unsigned paragraphs 'every week for the musical column'.

The magazine ceased to pay its contributors in the autumn, but G.B.S. continued to write unpaid notes for it. Archer, by that time, had obtained another job for him, on the reviewing staff of *The Pall Mall Gazette*, whose editor was W. T. Stead. His first contribution appeared on the 16th of May. This post was obtained for him in a manner highly characteristic of Archer, who told Stead that he was much too busy to review a particular book, and that he had handed it to Shaw, whose criticism of it was so well written that he was allowed to choose as many books as he liked to review. The payment he received was two guineas for a thousand words. He reviewed books of every sort, including two novels by Marie Corelli, *A Romance of Two Worlds* and *Thelma*, and one by Hall Caine, *Son of Hagar*, as well as general works, such as *The Good Queen's Reign*, a life of Darwin by Grant Allen, and *From Cornwall to Cairo* and *Physiognomy*. *Thelma* gave him great trouble. 'Began my review . . . but did not get on very well with it.' He finished it 'with difficulty' on the following day.

In addition to these reviews, he did odds and ends of journalism, writing articles 'pretty regularly' for *The Magazine of Music* during the latter part of 1885, and including 'a scrap of fiction', entitled *The Serenade*, which he had written four years earlier. He also wrote notes for Mrs Besant's magazine, *Our Corner*, and edited Laurence Gronlund's *The Co-operative Commonwealth: Its Outlines: and Exposition of Modern Socialism*, which was published in America in 1884, and became, in England, the second volume in The International Library of Social Science; and he made an index, which is obscurely mentioned as 'the Lodge Index', but is not otherwise described.

There was a good deal of drudgery in this life, but not much money. His income in 1885 was £117. The money, however, might have been larger if he had not spent so much of his time in unremunerated employment for the causes he had at heart. He was delivering lectures in obscure halls to small audiences not only in London but outside it; and a good deal of time was wasted by inefficient secretaries who muddled his dates with other people's. The diary makes fairly frequent mention of his arrival at a hall to deliver a lecture, only to discover that some other person had been engaged for the same evening. These muddles were generally settled by G.B.S. taking the chair for his innocent rival. There are several entries which record the fact that there was no audience. The secretary of the society had either made a mess of the date or the members were not eager to hear about the earthly paradise which G.B.S., on behalf of the Socialists, was prepared to promise them.

In the month of January, 1885, he delivered three lectures, and would have delivered four had he found an audience 'at St John's Coffee House, Hoxton'. In addition to these exacting engagements,

G. Bernard Shaw

*An early photograph of mother (left),
and father (right), with George
John Vandeleur Lee in the middle*

Lucy (sister) and G.B.S. (1876)

*Birthplace,
33 Synge Street, Dublin*

Jenny Patterson

Annie Besant

Beatrice Webb

Sidney Webb

An early portrait of Mrs. Bernard Shaw

Barrie, Galsworthy, G.B.S. and Granville-Barker

G.B.S. and H. G. Wells

Pastel portrait of Charlotte by Sartorio

G.B.S. in his forties

G.B.S. and Mrs. St. John Ervine at Torquay, about to start for one of his long walks

Helen Keller, G.B.S. and Lady Astor

Mrs. Patrick Campbell

Ellen Terry

G.B.S. and Ellen Pollock's son (1934)

G.B.S. at work in his garden hut

G.B.S. in his garden on his 90th birthday

he attended a Conference on Industrial Remuneration, which lasted for three days, and made his first appearance as an amateur actor. In February, he lectured at six meetings. One of these was delivered 'to 21 people'. Its subject was The Iron Law of Wages. These lectures were in addition to attendance at meetings where he took part in debates. 'Went to South Place and made a disagreeable but somewhat forceful speech.' He had begun to learn German in this month, but as he was almost constitutionally incapable of linguistics, he made little progress in it. The diary contains several references to attempts to learn foreign tongues, including Danish, but all of them were failures.

The entries in respect of January and February, 1885, are characteristic of those for the rest of the period, except that the number of lectures increased. Many of the entries in this diary are in shorthand, and they reveal the extraordinary tidiness of his mind, and display the particularity he had shown in the diary he had kept as a boy in Dublin. His expenditure is carefully noted. On January 7, 1885, for instance, he spent 11d on his dinner, which would to-day be called lunch, 1½d on stamps, 'advanced a shilling to Mrs Whitcomb on a/c of Furnivall's Ms., Borax 1d, Ammonia 1d, train to Moorgate 3d;' and there is an entry on a later date, recording a penny he gave to a child in Bedford Square. His dinner at this time was eaten at the Wheatsheaf Vegetarian Restaurant in Rathbone Place, and it seldom cost more than a shilling and was usually 9d or 10d.

This scrupulosity about details was strangely extended to matters which called for no scruples. Among his papers, I found short notes and letters from people long since dead and no longer remembered, inviting him to, say, a musical party in Bedford Park. Each envelope was neatly slit across the top, and the invitation, when read and recorded, was replaced. Almost anybody else, when the occasion was over, would have destroyed it. But G.B.S. kept bundles of such notes, many of them fifty years old.

His austere engagements did not prevent him from taking part in more frivolous occupations, such as amuse intellectuals. There was an occasion when, discussing the character of God, who was then still regarded as the irascible and capricious deity of the Old Testament, he jeered at the widely spread belief that the Almighty, if dared to strike a person dead, would instantly do so. Pulling out his watch, he proposed to ask God to strike him dead within a couple of minutes; and was cynically amused to find that even the agnostics and atheists in the company pleaded with him to abandon his proposal.

He had the customary interest in psychical experiences, increased in his case by his friendship with Frank Podmore of the Psychical

Research Society, who suggested to him that he should join a daring band who were willing to sleep at Ivy House, Grove Rd., St Anne's Hill, Wandsworth, which was reputed to be haunted.

> 'I agreed, hurried home and sent off my copy, and stayed very late. Went by train to S. Kensington and walked the rest of the way. Found Leonard, Goodman and Fountain at the house. Slept there. Terrific nightmare.' This was on October 29, 1885. The entry for the following day reads, 'Walked in from Wandsworth to Charing Cross with Goodman, very tired from want of sleep and fatigue. Made a speech at the Browning Institute in the evening.'

At a later date, he 'went to Croydon by the 7.17 p.m. train to meet Massingham at Bax's. After some singing, we began spirit rapping and table turning, and in the excitement of it I forgot the last train:

> 'I cheated from the first, and as soon as Massingham detected me, he became my accomplice and we caused the spirits to rap out long stories, lift the table into the air, and finally drink tumblers of whisky and water, to the complete bewilderment of Bax. I lay down on a sofa in the drawing-room to sleep—in a blanket—at 3 in the morning, and slept with a break or two, until 9. I have not laughed so much for years.'

In the next entry, he says, 'At breakfast, we explained to Bax how we had deceived him last night. At noon we went off for a walk and did not get back until past 6. I had just time to swallow a couple of eggs and catch the 7.7 train at W. Croydon. I was very tired. It was close on nine when I got to the lecture for the Paddington Branch of the S.D.F. on The Programme of Social Democracy, but I lectured rather well. Had a dish of rice when I got home.'

What feats of endurance he performed on a couple of eggs and a mess of starch!

There is a poignant note in the diary. As a result of his father's death in April, 1885, the weekly allowance made to Lucinda Elizabeth abruptly ended. It had been a pound a week, but G.B.S. refers to it as 30s., which may have been a slip or have denoted that the allowance had been increased. Another result of Mr Shaw's death was that his widow came into the possession of a little less than £100, the sum of an insurance policy he had effected. After the payment of some law bills in Dublin, there was enough money left to discharge her debts. The poignant passage appears in the entry in the diary for the 17th June. 'Ordered clothes at Jaegar's—the first new garments I have had for years. These will be paid out of the insurance on my father's life.'

G.B.S.'s extraordinary equanimity of temper seems at this time to have been temporarily lost; and there are notes in the diary describing bouts of depression. The entry for the 23rd June, opens with 'Out of sorts in the morning. . . . Did nothing much, depressed all day. Tried on clothes at Jaeger's.' This suit of clothes must have meant much to him, for he mentions it several times. It was not the only suit he bought then, for on the 30th June, he describes its delivery and how he immediately 'put it on and went to a Women's Meeting at Exeter Hall.' Then, scrupulous as ever about details, he adds, 'All wool suit, £5. 15s., Black Coat and Vest, £4. 4s. Collars 4s. Cravat 2s. Pants 16s. Total £11. 1s.'

The diary, apart from its detailed information about his relations with Jenny Patterson and his women friends, is interesting, too, because it reveals his pleasure in recreations which has not hitherto been known. He played card games, euchre, baccarat, poker, bezique, whist and patience, with his mother, and played them well; and he and she were adept at chess. There is a note of a wet afternoon when he and Sidney Webb passed the time in playing Beggar My Neighbour and Patience! He frequented boxing matches, a pleasure he loved as long as he lived, and once, when spending the day with the Blands, put on the gloves and sparred a few rounds with Hubert, who was a boxer of considerable strength and skill. He even played golf. Sir Barry Jackson tells a story of him during the rehearsals of *Back to Methuselah* at the Birmingham Repertory Theatre, when he was found to be missing. Charlotte became troubled about his long absence, for he was then approaching his seventieth year, and there was some agitation in the theatre. In the middle of the turmoil, G.B.S. walked in, entirely unperturbed. On his way to the theatre in the morning, he had seen an advertisement of a boxing match, and had gone off to see it, enjoying it, apparently, more than the rehearsal.

There was one sporting event for which he had a peculiar and unexpected liking. This was the Boat Race which he witnessed, year after year, for the whole period covered by the Diary. Cricket bored him because he preferred quick games and was impatient with leisurely proceedings. These likes are mentioned chiefly because there is a general belief that he detested games of any sort, a belief which is largely due to his statement in *Who's Who* that his recreations were 'anything except sport'.

48

The beginnings of his long period of prosperity put an end to his deprivation in regard to the company of women; and he now discovered, greatly to his surprise, that he, who had begun to think of himself as an unlikeable Ishmael, was singularly attractive to them: an attraction which he retained into his old age. 'I used to think,' he told my wife, 'that when I reached seventy, women would no longer bother about me. But it gets worse!' He was now not only making a living, though it was still bare, but was making, much more importantly, many substantial friends. He was intimate enough with Webb to receive his confidence over a disappointment in love. Webb had met a most attractive and good-looking girl in Cornwall, by whom he was fascinated. She, however, did not return his passion, and he was overwhelmed. It was said that the entire Western Circuit was in love with her, and she married a young barrister, Corrie Grant, who became a Liberal M.P. When, many years later, their daughter Margaret, now Lady Slesser, joined the Fabian Society, Webb, still mindful of her mother, always treated her with exceptional kindness and consideration.

The first reference in the diary to Jenny Patterson appears under the date of February 10, 1885, but it indicates that G.B.S. had known her for several months and that she was an intimate of Lucy and Lucinda Elizabeth. Her love for him was not yet declared, but must have been evident to his mother and sister, if not to him. There is nothing in the early part of the diary to show that he felt much interest in her, apart from that which any man of quality feels in a vivacious, intelligent and good-looking woman. He was much more interested in Mrs Besant who was now, apparently, sufficiently conscious of him to feel embarrassed in his presence. In the first week of March, 1885, he went with John M. Robertson 'to meet Mrs B. and Horatio Bottomley coming back from Northampton. Saw them into a cab. Mrs B. and I did not speak or bow. She did not know how we stood with one another.' The fact that Bottomley was Mrs Besant's companion will seem odd to a generation which knows him only as the founder and editor of *John Bull* and as a shady speculator and gaol-bird; but it will seem less inexplicable to those who remember that he was generally reputed to be Charles Bradlaugh's bastard.

Mrs Patterson's name occurs many times in the diary, but the entries usually indicate that the relationship displeased G.B.S., even when he was physically satisfied by it. On the 20th of April, he found her with his mother: his comment is, 'wasted all the evening'. But on the following Monday, he 'went to Richter concert, and instead of waiting for the symphony, went on to Mrs Patterson. Found her alone and stayed until midnight. Dinner 1s. 1d. Concert 2s. 6d.' Their meetings continued in this intermittent manner until the 4th of July, when he called at her house 'at 8.20. She was out.' He was not in love with her, but he felt some urgent need of her, although their relations were not yet intimate. Turning away from her house that evening, he met some friends whom he had not seen 'for years' and he spent an hour or so in their company, returning to Mrs Patterson's house where he 'stayed until 1. Vein of conversation distinctly gallant.' A week later, he 'found Mrs Patterson' in his mother's house, and 'walked to her house by way of the park. Supper, music and curious conversation, and a declaration of passion. Left at 3. Virgo intacta still.' The last words suggest that the passion was declared by the lady who appears in the Diary always as 'Mrs Patterson' or 'J.P.,' and never as Jenny: a significant fact in itself; indeed, the small introduction which he made to the earlier books of the diary ends with the statement that 'on the 26th July, my 29th birthday, begins an intimacy with a lady of our acquaintance. I was an absolute novice. I did not take the initiative in the matter.'

The affair, remarkably long drawn and one-sided, evidently bewildered G.B.S. He was not yet willing to yield himself to the voluptuous widow, despite her importunities, and his delight at finding himself outside her house at 3 a.m., still unseduced, is manifest.

The 23rd, 24th and 25th of July were of particular importance to him. On the first day, he met May Morris and escorted her 'to Ludgate Hill station where she had some coffee.' On the following day, he wrote at length to Mrs Besant. On the 25th, he visited Mrs Patterson in the afternoon, and found her in conversation with his mother. That night, at eleven, he returned 'to Brompton Square, where' he 'met her and his mother' again.

Lucinda Elizabeth and Jenny had had a long session together, and we may believe that the subject of discussion was G.B.S., who escorted his mother to a bus, but returned to Brompton Square 'and stayed there until 3 o'clock on my 29th birthday, which I celebrated by a new experience.' Jenny, after a long siege, had received his submission. She had at last seduced him. When he left her and was dallying on the doorstep, making his farewell, he 'was watched by an old woman next door, whose evil interpretation of the lateness of my departure, greatly alarmed us.' She seems to have harangued them for waking her up at that hour of the morning with their unrestrained conversation; but her interpretation 'of the lateness of his departure', though it may have been evil, was surely correct?

By this time, Mrs Hubert Bland had also revealed emotion for him, but, despite his liking for her and her enchanting conversation, she made no headway with him. Her husband was his friend, and G.B.S. did not carry on affairs with his friends' wives.

The reaction to his adventure with Mrs Patterson was one of self-mortification. On the 3rd of August, he wrote a full account of his seduction to McNulty. It was in the evening of this day that he heard Sidney Webb mourning for his lost love in Cornwall. After leaving Webb, he went home and 'wrote a rather fierce letter to J.P.' Her reply must have been delivered by hand on the following morning, for he wrote to her again 'in reply to her answer to yesterday's explosion'. On the following day, Alice Lockett came to see him, and that night he went to J.P. to eat and make love until 1.20.' Their encounters were now numerous, not, indeed, daily, but almost so. In the middle of these amorous meetings, Webb and he began to read the second volume of the German edition of *Das Kapital*. 'Sat rather late talking with him and drank some lemonade that resulted in a nightmare.' From this time onwards, his relations with Jenny were at once ardent and tempestuous, becoming increasingly ardent on her part, plainly ceasing to be ardent, except physically, on his. The pattern is the familiar one where the woman is a middle-aged widow and the lover is still a young man.

He sought diversion. On Monday, the 7th of August, 'a Miss Consuelo called, wanting to be taught a part in a burlesque at the Gaiety Theatre before next Monday. Mother being out of town, she asked me to help her, and I consented. Went to her in the afternoon.' He gave her lessons on the 9th and 10th, though what ability he had to teach her is not stated, nor is there any account of the lessons she received. On the 11th, he went to the first performance of the burlesque, 'and wrote' Miss Consuelo 'a note about it'. She sent him 'a box of silk handkerchiefs' which he returned. She then disappeared from his history.

But Mrs Patterson remained.

49

In October, she was writing him 'angry and plaintive' letters, but in November 'she gave me a pair of slippers she had worked for me.' She began to haunt his mother's house, and was prompt in making scenes. In the meantime his relations with Mrs Besant were becoming more cordial, but also more alarming. The preface to the 1886 volume contains the following paragraph:

> 'During this year my work at the Fabian brought me much into contact with Mrs Besant, and towards the end of the year, this intimacy became a very close and personal sort, without, however, going further than a friendship.'

The preface to the 1887 volume is full of self-disgust:

> 'The intimacy with Mrs Besant alluded to last year reached a point in January at which it threatened to become a vulgar intrigue, chiefly through my fault. But I roused myself in time and avoided this. I however frequently went to her house on Monday evenings and played pianoforte duets (mostly Haydn's Symphonies) with her. At Xmas, I returned her all my letters and she mine. Reading over her letters before destroying them rather disgusted me with the trifling of the last 2 years with women.'

But before he had reached this point, there was much encounter, some of it gravely disturbing, between him and J.P. On January 9, 1886, he paid a visit to her which is described with the single word, 'Revulsion'. Three days later he visits her again, and finds a man with her who 'was bent on seduction, and we tried which should outstay the other. Eventually he had to go for a train. To bed late.'

During February, his sister Lucy, while staying with Mrs Patterson, sickened of pleurisy and remained in Brompton Square until she was well. Jenny was in a retributive mood then. She 'had to go out', and 'refused to allow me to go with her and I put her into a cab at the corner of her square and left her.' On the following Sunday, she went to listen to a lecture he gave on Socialism and Scoundrelism. On Saturday, he visited her again and did not go 'home until 2 a.m.' On the 13th of March, she took Lucy to Broadstairs to convalesce, and he did not see her until the recovery was complete.

On her return from Broadstairs, Jenny became more demanding. There was a 'violent scene at the Square. Wrote to J.P. on my return that our future intercourse must be platonic.' That was on Sunday. On Thursday, she 'called here this morning, distracted about my letter. There was a scene and much pathetic kissing and petting, after which she went away comparatively happy.' The very wording of this entry denotes how little Mrs Patterson now meant to him: a flippancy that no man who felt any love for a woman could use. On Sunday, there was a 'slight scene in consequence of my refusing to budge from our new platonic relations.' But it was easier to form a relationship of this sort, especially with a passionate and devoted woman, than it was to break it off. Jenny, perhaps, realised that scenes were unlikely to improve their relations, and for a few weeks she restrained herself. They seemed to have settled into a quiet period, seeing each other two or three times a week, and then only in conditions of peace. If her jealousy of other women still possessed her, she did not display it.

The tiresome woman now was Mrs Bland who demanded his company on long, pointless expeditions suddenly desired, and seemed devoid of any consideration for anyone but herself. This accomplished woman had a childlike simplicity of mind which enabled her to write stories for children which held their attention. She made a world that children understood because it was the world in which she still lived. If she suddenly took it into her head that G.B.S., after a long and tiring meeting, should travel to Blackheath with her and walk about the roads in the vicinity of her home, this was the right and proper thing for him to do; and the fact that he missed the last train to London and had to walk home, arriving there at 3.30 a.m., after a weary tramp lasting for $2\frac{1}{4}$ hours, caused her no contrition. The number of times he missed the last train to London and had to walk the whole way from Blackheath to Osnaburgh Street was extraordinary; and the reader of the diary wonders in vain why he wasted his energy in such profitless activity. About two months after this tedious experience, he had another experience of the same sort, arriving home after his long walk at 2.30 a.m., and correcting proofs until 3. One such tramp should surely have been enough.

During this period, Mrs Patterson was comparatively quiet, content, seemingly, with what had almost become a domestic habit, of humdrum visits at intervals that were gradually becoming longer. She went off to Broadstairs unmurmuringly, and was met on her return. 'Found myself much indisposed for her society.' Three weeks later, he 'walked with her as far as her door and then home. Much out of humour with her and things in general.' The platonic arrangement was collapsing into one of impatience or total indifference. In comparison with the exacting Mrs Bland, however, she seemed subdued. On a wet day in September, this childlike lady decided that she must go out to Enfield and walk in the rain, and that G.B.S. must also splash about in it. 'When we got to Enfield it was very wet. I got her some hot whisky to prevent her from catching cold.' It was 1 a.m. before he got home.

In the middle of November, Jenny became ill. He did not see her again for a week, during which she continued to be ill, but was very affectionate nevertheless. The singular quiet in which Mrs Patterson seemed to have settled herself continued until the middle of December, when he met her and his mother after a visit they had made together to the Princess's Theatre, and he saw her home. 'We finished at 1 o'clock with a quarrel.' A week later, she visited Osnaburgh Street. 'She was out of temper, so I went out and walked round Haverstock Hill and back by Fitzjohn's Avenue, returning at 11 p.m.' So ended 1886. The year 1887 opened with the decision to finish his entanglement with Mrs Besant, which was neither one thing nor the other. Between the 19th and the 26th of January, he had written to her five times, apart from meeting her several times; and he was tired of the business, which was then concluded. Thereafter, they went their ways amicably, and met without reproach.

The affair with Jenny, however, revived, though not, so far as he was concerned, with the old fervour. It was during this period that Alice Lockett, on one day, and Mrs Bland on the next, began to reassert themselves again. Alice called on the family, and G.B.S. 'went back with her to the hospital' where she was nursing, and they 'got on the old terms in less than 5 minutes.' Mrs Bland, after taking tea with him, 'insisted'—she was always insisting on something—'on coming to Fitzroy Square', to which the Shaws had now removed from Osnaburgh Street. 'My mother was out, and she went away after a very unpleasant scene caused by my telling her I wished her to go, as I was afraid that a visit to me alone would compromise her.'

About a week later, he quarrelled with Mrs Besant, who wished to give him an umbrella which he declined to receive. His encounters with Mrs Bland now practically ended; those with Mrs Besant were almost entirely in public; he saw less of Jenny than formerly, though he saw more of her than of any other woman. He was done with his philandering, he thought, and must make a plan of work for himself. He would attempt again to learn German and would study algebra! . . .

50

In 1888, he met a charming girl, called Grace Gilchrist who was a member of the Fabian Society and a friend of Miss Emma Brooke, another Fabian woman, who was a novelist of some repute. Miss Brooke, the daughter of a wealthy landlord, was aware of G.B.S.'s reputation as a philanderer, and as she considered herself to be in some degree Grace Gilchrist's guardian, she spoke her mind to him on the subject of his attentions, though these were innocent and open. On Easter Sunday, which fell that year on All Fool's Day, she called on him 'about Grace Gilchrist and heaped abuse on me. Wrote to G.G. in consequence. J.P. called in the afternoon.' The result of these encounters was that he 'delivered an incoherent lecture at Battersea about nothing in particular.' He then visited 'J.P.' and 'got to bed at 2 a.m.' Miss Brooke was determined to end his acquaintance with Grace Gilchrist. He wrote to her, and she wrote a letter which crossed his. It was answered after she had heard a lecture by Belfort Bax on the Deification of Woman. 'Most of the day' of the 12th of April was 'occupied by my interview with Miss Brooke in the hall of the British Museum to talk over the Gilchrist affair.' During these wrangles with her, he 'made the acquaintance of a pretty girl, named Geraldine Spooner', and 'saw her', at the end of their first meeting, 'to her train at Blackfriars'. He now had six affairs on his hands, three of them languishing, two of them beginning, and one seeming to go passionately on and on and on. No wonder Sidney Webb remarked 'My! You do warm both hands at the fire of life!'

The odd fact is that Jenny seems never to have known of this innocent affair with Grace Gilchrist nor of the more serious, though equally innocent, affair with Geraldine Spooner, though the first of these affairs was causing great gossip in The Fabian Society which, in the matter of gossip, was not surpassed by a sewing party at the

157

vicarage. Miss Brooke was busy. 'Went to the Museum after dinner and wrote a letter to Miss Brooke about the Gilchrist affair which took up all the afternoon. Went to J.P. in the evening.' It was characteristic of him that when he had finished with any matter, it ceased almost instantly to concern him. Names which occur frequently in the diary, suddenly disappear from it, nor is there any explanation of the disappearance. Grace Gilchrist is mentioned many times for a few weeks, and then ceases to be mentioned at all. The last reference to her is a statement that G.B.S. while crossing Hampstead Heath saw her, but that is all. He does not appear to have spoken to her. He could clear his mind of matter that was of no further interest to him. Ladies came suddenly and went suddenly. Their lives afterwards were of no consequence.

The affair with Grace Gilchrist, which was never more than a mild and almost publicly conducted flirtation, would have petered out sooner than it did if the officious Miss Brooke had minded her own business. The deeper regard he felt for Geraldine Spooner would have wiped it out of his memory. But Miss Brooke could not leave the little affair alone, and she pestered and pried and made mountains out of molehills. Long after Grace Gilchrist had disappeared from the diary, this austere lady maintained a cool attitude to G.B.S. Once, after a Fabian meeting, when he and Webb and other prominent members of the Society were on their way home, she treated him in public almost with discourtesy. 'As we passed [Piccadilly] Circus, I saw Miss Brooke waiting there alone and offered to wait with her, but retired, snubbed.' Piccadilly Circus was not a place where an unaccompanied woman could loiter at night without drawing undesirable attention to herself; but Miss Brooke, majestic in her virtue, presumably regarded herself as immune from misunderstanding in any circumstances. She became reconciled to him eventually, though she took a long time to realise that his easy manners and mildly flirtatious habits were mainly affability and genial disposition.

He was not a seducer: he was, indeed, in the major affairs of his iite at this time, the seduced. Grace Gilchrist and Geraldine Spooner, were as safe with him as they might have been supposed, perhaps erroneously, to have been with the Superintendent of a Sunday School. . . . Had he been the man Miss Brooke imagined him to be, he would have had little difficulty in obtaining willing accomplices among the numerous women he knew and liked at this time. His difficulty was not to draw them to him, but to drive them away. Of the six women with whom he was more or less emotionally entangled when Miss Brooke needlessly engaged in Rescue Work, only two were carnally known to him, and he was not the first lover of either of them.

Geraldine Spooner need not detain us much longer than Grace Gilchrist. G.B.S. was, undoubtedly, attracted by her, far more attracted than he had been by her predecessor. She was a gallant girl, fine in spirit as she was good in looks, and she won G.B.S.'s admiration as well as his affection by her courage and her disregard of herself in any cause she embraced. There was nothing overbearing or bossy about her. She did not behave as if her business were the only business in the world, nor did she assume that a thing was right because she did it or that her desire should instantly be satisfied because it was her desire. He and she were on far friendlier terms than Grace Gilchrist and he had ever been. There is an entry in the diary, under the date of April 21, 1890, about two years after he had first met her which runs 'Rather in love with Geraldine.' But his earnings in that year amounted to £250 13 2d, a substantial increase on the earnings of the previous year, and so Geraldine, whom he might have married, but would not commit to a life financially uncertain, faded out of the diary as abruptly as Grace had done, though she took a much longer time to go.

The lapse from Fabian austerity was ended. He had had his bout of sex appeal later than the majority of men, but it was over, and he could now resume the serious business of life. There were the *Fabian Essays* to edit. There were lectures to be delivered. There were committee meetings to be attended. There were grave men and plain, serious women to be met in social conferences! . . . There was also a play which he had agreed to write in collaboration with Archer. Part of it, indeed, was done and the manuscript was lying about somewhere, but he had not looked at it lately. He must try his hand at it again. He glanced through it—it was not yet named *Widowers' Houses*—and thought it promised well, so he wrote some more of it, and then went round to Archer's to read it to him and Mrs Archer. Archer received it 'with contempt', so it was put away again and would remain in neglect for some time. There were too many distractions in his busy life. There had been all those women, and now there were all these lectures and committees and what not! . . .

In the middle of October, Jenny, who had been ominously silent for some time, resumed her sudden moods. 'J.P. here when I returned. Went home with her. Tedious quarrel about Mrs Besant.' Their relationships were not improved when, in his absence, she entered his workroom and found Mrs Besant's letters, 'which I had incautiously left on my table', and took some of them away. On Christmas morning, he 'was wakened by J.P. knocking at my door. She came about the letters. I at last got those she had taken and destroyed them.' Once, coming away from a Fabian meeting with Mrs Besant and her—she would have joined the Primrose League if he had been a member of it—he left her in Piccadilly to go home, while he escorted Mrs Besant up Bond Street to a bus halt. 'Then I found J.P. had been following us. Saw her to her door.' The thing was becoming a scullery-maid's scrimmage. . . .

Until he met Jenny Patterson, his acquaintance with women, and especially with passionate and possessive women, was derived, in so far as he had any acquaintance at all, from paper. He had read about women, had even, and especially in his youth, dreamt of magnificent females who swooped upon a man with imagination bolder than his behaviour, and carried him off to their beds and made a hero of him, lifting him up to the heavens and bidding him pluck the stars from their orbits.

But he had never met any.

Miss Lockett could not inspire a man to more than careful deposits in the Post Office Savings Bank, but Jenny Patterson, a most possessive and demanding woman, could stir the pulses of a man in the deepest lethargy and bring him in a blaze of love to her bed.

The end of the affair was wrathful and absurd. G.B.S. had become acquainted with an intellectual actress.

51

She was Florence Farr, whom he had met at Morris's house in Hammersmith, where she was working on embroidery for May. She was the daughter of Dr William Farr, who had a substantial reputation as a sanitary reformer in the middle of the nineteenth century. He 'survived his wits', according to G.B.S., and lost his fortune in 'senile speculation', though he retained enough of it to enable his daughter to live in fair comfort without working. This was probably the ruin of her, for she remained an amateur actress for the greater part of her life. If she had had to earn her living, she might have become considerably accomplished. As it was, she frittered her ability away, too intelligent to be a good actress, too much entranced by the stage to be able to put her mind seriously to anything else.

She was, in some respects, like G.B.S.'s eldest sister, Lucy, one of those clever women who disappoint their friends and admirers by not fulfilling their promise. She even resembled Lucy in that she married an actor, called Emery, who could not live with her and was sensible enough to disappear. She meddled in the arts, and was inclined on little or no provocation to chant poetry in a rasping manner while she plucked a stringed instrument whose single merit was that it had only one string which was easily broken. This chanting was called 'cantilating', and was a melancholy noise. I remember a night when she persuaded W. B. Yeats, into whose affection she passed when

G.B.S. had done with her, to lift up his voice in a depressing howl while she plucked her strings to pieces. Yeats, who loathed and detested music, became so pleased with his singing that his friends had difficulty in preventing him from 'cantilating' every time they spent an evening in his dark rooms in Woburn Buildings, behind the Euston Road.

It was she who, in conjunction with Miss Horniman, ran the celebrated season at the Avenue Theatre in London in 1894 when *Arms and the Man* was performed and G.B.S. received his first production in the regular traffic of the stage; but she had been associated with him before this when she took the part of Blanche Sartorious in the first performance of *Widowers' Houses* at the Royalty Theatre in 1892. She probably felt great pleasure in portraying Jenny Patterson, from whom she had at last detached G.B.S. But Mrs Patterson was the larger woman.

This was his first experience of high passion. He was more deeply in love than he had ever been before, than he was ever again to be, even with Mrs Campbell. The affair with Alice Lockett appeared now as what it was: calf love. Jenny Patterson had ceased to be a physical convenience and was an intolerable nuisance. Florence Farr had abolished Alice and Jenny and Grace and Geraldine as completely as a gale blows away pretty pieces of paper.

He had begun his brilliant career as musical critic of *The Star*, and this fact, joined to her love of music, enabled him to take her to concerts where her comments stimulated his critical faculty. Jenny Patterson had been particularly tiresome, and Miss Farr resumed her acquaintance with him at a time when he was ready for some relief from that stormy woman, who could not keep out of his mother's house and was now making a habit of invading his room and reading his letters. She was getting on his nerves, which were already strained by over-work. He was becoming dilatory about his reviews of books for the *Pall Mall Gazette*, and Stead had had to write to him for one. 'J.P. here made it hard to work. After dinner, played Haydn to steady my nerves.' 'J.P. in the house all day.' The contrast between Jenny and the dashing and gallant Geraldine Spooner became more and more striking, especially after Jenny had stayed in Fitzroy Square for nearly a fortnight. She interrupted his work. The fact that his mother was out for most of the day, teaching music, meant that she had almost uninterrupted access to him. She would dash into his room in the middle of his work and indulge in what was almost a paroxysm of jealous fury. One afternoon, 'J.P. came, raged, wept, flung a book at my head etc.' *Etc* is good: it denotes some regularity. On another occasion, 'J.P. was here, and though I made a beginning with my article, I could not get on, as I felt very tired and good for nothing.'

It was a relief when Alice Lockett came to spend the following day. 'Spent the afternoon at the New Gallery where I seemed to know everybody. When I got home, I sang some of the old Figaro bits with Alice, who presently went home, overcome, I think, by old associations. I went with her to the hospital. . . .'

The single relief he had from this omnipresence was his work for *The Star* which, by taking him to concerts and operas freed him not only from her prevailing company, but gave him this freedom without reproach from her. It was about this time that he met Janet Achurch, his second intellectual actress, at a Sunday night dinner to celebrate the production of *A Doll's House* at the Novelty Theatre. Miss Achurch played the part of Nora. She is described in the diary as an 'interesting young woman', who, however, could safely display her quality to him, since she was the wife of Charles Charrington. These two were to be considerably mixed up in his theatre beginnings. Janet, indeed, became almost a burden to him because his loyalty to her and her husband made him insist that she should play the part of Candida at a time when her reputation as an actress was not wide enough to permit her to take leading parts in the ordinary traffic of the theatre. The Charringtons were a happy-go-lucky couple, often in financial difficulties because neither of them had any sense of money. Their friends had to do a good deal of rescue work for them.

At the time of this meeting, on June 16, 1889, however, Janet Achurch had only begun her stage career and, except in a very limited circle, was totally unknown. Even G.B.S. was unaware of her existence, though his acquaintance with the intelligent unknown, was extensive. On the following day, he sent her *Cashel Byron's Profession* and *An Unsocial Socialist*, and wrote 'her a letter' which 'kept me up until 2'. He talked about her to his friends, as many years later, he was to talk about Mrs Patrick Campbell, until they tired of the sound of her name. He upset Mrs Archer by his ding-dong on the subject, and had to explain himself on the following day to her husband because of 'some unlucky offence I have given Mrs Archer by going on about Miss Achurch'. He was over-inclined to 'go on' about his women friends. Luckily, the Charringtons had undertaken a tour in Australia, and about three weeks after he had met Miss Achurch for the first time, G.B.S. went to Charing Cross to see her and her husband off on their journey. One result of his 'offence' to Mrs Archer was *The Philanderer*, which had its origin in this quarrel, though much more came into it than Mrs Archer was ever likely to have put there.

52

The pressure under which he was working can best be illustrated by an excerpt from the diary which illustrates not only this pressure, but the ease with which he could work in any circumstances and in total disregard of his surroundings. While he was in the office of *The Star*, he was asked to write an article in great haste. He had just completed one. But he 'could not get on' with the second article, 'so I went out and wrote it in the street, finishing it on a coping of the Embankment near Blackfriars Bridge.' Some of his articles, and not the least successful ones, were written while standing under a lamp-post. He could write almost anywhere, on the top of a bus or in a railway train and even in the Reading Room of the British Museum. 'When I got home,' the entry continues, 'I hurried off to Walworth, a letter from Radford having led me to remember that I was to lecture there; but when, after a long tram drive from Wandsworth Rd. station, I got down at the Town Hall, I found that Radford had mistaken the date. I then took train at Wandsworth station on the Waterloo line; but got into the wrong one and was carried to Mortlake before I found my mistake and changed into an up train. On my way from Waterloo, I called on Webb; but he was out, so I wrote a message for him on the slate and gave it to Ada Webb. When I got home, I ate something and wrote part of a dialogue for the projected play.'

Manifestly, he was making trouble for himself, by these wasteful labours, apart from the exactions of his legitimate work and the unlimited demands made by his emotional adventures. The reader's amazement at such expenditure of strength as this extract indicates will be increased by the knowledge that much of the work he did brought him no payment, caused him, indeed, some expense. The article hastily written on the Embankment—not for *The Star*, but for a paper edited by a member of *The Star's* staff whom G.B.S. was obliging by writing for it once a week—was unpaid.

It was immediately after this exploit that he went to see Jenny and found that she had gone to a concert at the Albert Hall. As he had an article to write for *The Star*, he 'wandered about the neighbourhood, scribbling and moving about, as it was foggy and chilly. J.P.... came up as I was writing under a lamppost!...' In the last weeks of November, 1889, while toiling in these conditions, he met Samuel Butler, the author of *Erewhon*, for the first time, and also met George Moore. 'Wrote letters until 4,' he notes in the first week of December. 'Then was about to go out to dinner when I found that I had no money; and as Mother was out, I had to dine off bread and butter and apples.'

His total earnings for that year of exacting toil were £197 6s 10d.

53

In May, 1890, he 'went to J.P. in the evening, but found her so fractious that I presently shook the dust off my feet and went away.' A fortnight later, she called at his mother's and 'we had a long talk. It looks like a breaking off.' A week later, she was again making scenes, causing him to forget an appointment to speak on the following day. Two days later, he wrote to her, apparently ending their relations; and on the following day, she came 'whilst I was at breakfast in childish distress, as usual, about my letter. She did not go away until 1.' The breach seems to have been repaired, but it was only a brief repair. The end was coming fast. It would have come sooner had he not paid a visit to Germany and been so heavily engaged in work that there was little time for meetings. In the middle of all these trials and travels, he found himself lecturing to an audience of 50 or 60 people in Kendal on the subject of the Evolution of Socialism; and was astonished to discover that his audience 'had never heard of Socialism and were greatly puzzled by my discourse'. They resembled the Christians at Ephesus who surprised St Paul by telling him that they had never so much as heard of the Holy Ghost.

On October 4, 1890, he 'had a long talk with Florence Emery at the private view of Arts and Crafts.' This is her first appearance in the diary. Their friendship ripened fast. A week later, he took her to a concert at the Crystal Palace, and soon afterwards was having a row with Jenny about her. 'Was much upset by having to interfere in an altercation between a young couple and a private watchman who was apparently trying to blackmail them. I brought them off victorious; but the incident spoiled the evening, as I got rather angry in bullying the watchman. J.P. was angry and jealous about F.E., so the day ended unpleasantly.' So his life went on until at last he writes in his diary, 'Am driving myself too hard.' He suffers from neuralgia and toothache, and incessant emotional agitation. In the middle of November, he visits 'Florence Emery', as cool in her passion as Jenny was hot, and they have their 'first really intimate conversation'. Thereafter, Jenny and she are seldom out of his company. The fight is increasing in its intensity, though the two women seem never to meet. He tries to distract himself by working on *Widowers' Houses*. On December 30, 1890, he 'went over to F.E. in the evening—a happy evening.' On the following night, he 'went to see J.P.—just back from Broadstairs.'

The issue was now sharply joined. Jenny decided to go to the East for the rest of the winter on January 9, thereby committing a grave tactical error: she left the ground free for F.E., who met him continually, though they, too, had bouts of disagreement. 'In the evening, I went to F.E., but we were both in a most horrid frame of mind.' They were meeting two or three times a week, but not, apparently, without Jenny's knowledge, for on her return from the East late in April, he was assailed with great vehemence for his infidelity. 'Fearful scene about F.E. this being our first meeting since her return from the East. Did not get home until about 3 a.m.'

The row was resumed on the following day. While he was writing a short article on the Eight Hours Day for *The Labour World*, 'J.P. came before I had got far with it, and the scene of last night was resumed until [his Uncle] Walter happened to come in.' It was immediately after these rows, that he wrote a rapturous letter 'in the train' on May 1, 1891, to Florence Farr, in which he declared that he had reached breaking point with 'that other' relation:

> 'At this moment I am in a contemptuous fury and vehemently assert that your Christmas estimate of it was the right one. Not for forty thousand such relations will I forego one forty thousandth part of my relation with you. Every grain of cement she shakes from it falls like a block of granite on her own flimsy castle in the air, the work of my own imagination. The silly triumph with which she takes, with the air of a conqueror, that which I have torn out of my entrails for her, almost brings the lightning down upon her. Imagine being told—but I cannot write it. Damnation! triple damnation. You must give me back my peace. If you are disengaged tomorrow afternoon, will you come to Prince's Hall (*not* St James's, mind) on the enclosed ticket. The hart pants for cooling streams.'[1]

It was characteristic of him that even in this tempestuous note, in which the fact that he had never for a moment loved Jenny Patterson is plainly revealed, he remembers, in a parenthesis, to tell Florence not to go to the wrong hall. She was probably the sort of woman who would otherwise unfailingly have done so.

Less than a fortnight later, there was another row. 'J.P. came in the evening and made a scene about F.E. I was just beginning my *World* article. Don Giovanni at Covent Garden rather spoiled in consequence. When I got back after midnight, I found her wandering about the Square. Took her back in a hansom. Walked back and did not get to bed, very tired, until after 3.' On his next visit to F.E., he stayed so long that he missed his last train—he was always missing last trains—and during his walk home, he 'Picked up a drunken old woman who was in the Goldhawk Rd and was delayed $\frac{1}{2}$ an hour putting her in the way to get home. Out of sorts, revolted by everything. Not in bed until past 2.'

[1] See *Letters to Florence Farr from Bernard Shaw and W. B. Yeats*. Edited by Clifford Bax, p. 3.

It was during this exhausting experience that he was invited to contest East Bradford as a Labour candidate for parliament. 'Advised them to choose a working man.'

There was an evening when he spent the first half of it with F.E. and the second half with Jenny! On the following Sunday, Jenny 'came here, and made a terrific scene', but, presumably, he was consoled by F.E. on the next afternoon! F.E. herself was beginning to be tiresome. An evening with her is described in one word: disillusion; but on the following day, he was composing verses about her, 'being more deeply moved than I could have imagined'. While he was composing them Jenny came to tea. He had tea with her on the next day, and 'she followed me' to a concert. She was at another concert two days later, having heard, no doubt, that he was accustomed to take F.E. to them. So he swayed about for weeks, interrupted by a pleasant visit to Italy, which was forgotten immediately after his return because he was greeted by a visit from Jenny. 'Could get no work done as J.P. came in the morning and made terrible scenes all day. I went out before dinner to the Museum and to Archer to avoid her, but she was there when I returned.' Four days later, 'another desperate day finishing the paper amid intercourse and scenes with J.P. Very tempestuous whilst I was at tea. At last pretended to throw her out of the window. Went into Regent's Park, hoping that she would not be there when I came back. Read paper on "The Difficulties of Anarchism at the Fabian".' He could speak with authority on his subject.

There was a brief interlude when Jenny went to Ireland, but its peace ended when she returned. 'Writing Mozart article. In the afternoon, J.P. came. She came into this room and made a scene. I got out of the room by main force, and went to the Museum, telegraphing on my way to Mother to get the house clear before I came back. Wrote at the Museum until closing time, and then went back. Found the coast clear, and finished the article, getting pretty late to bed. The scene upset me.'

54

The diary for 1891, ends with a statement of his income. He had earned £281 16s 10d in that year. Unfortunately, the diary for 1892 has disappeared. How events developed cannot, therefore, be told, but on February 4, 1893, the end came. 'In the evening,' according to the diary, 'I went to F.E., and J.P. burst in on us very late in the evening. There was a most shocking scene, J.P. being violent and using atrocious language. At last, I sent F.E. out of the room, having to restrain J.P. by force from attacking her. I was two hours getting her out of the house, and I did not get her home to Brompton Square until near 1, nor could I get away myself until 3. I was horribly tired and upset, but I kept my patience, and did not behave badly nor ungently. Did not get to bed until 4, and had a disturbed night. I made J.P. write a letter to me expressing her regret and promising not to annoy her again. This was sent to F.E. to reassure her.' That was virtually the end. There were a few letters and one or two meetings, but the dreadful business was concluded.

References to her in the diary after the scene in Florence Emery's room are few. One dated August 15, 1893, reads: 'My mother was not here; she is staying with J.P. at Pangbourne.' He had a letter, 'notably . . . from J.P.' on the 6th of October, but no comment on it is made: and there is another entry, made on the 25th that 'as J.P. was coming here, I had to keep out of the way all evening.' On the 26th of November, 'in the forenoon, J.P. called ostensibly to cheer up Mother, who is still in bed with influenza. I went out to avoid her, and called on Archer and on the Carrs; but they were both out. So I came back and spent the evening, beginning a new play—a romantic one—for F.E.' But he does not appear to have encountered F.E.'s defeated rival.

His affair with Florence Farr did not last as long as his violent relation with Mrs Patterson. Her passion was too precise to last, and his too importunate to keep her in thrall. Her relations with Yeats were even shorter, and ended, according to Yeats's widow, because she was bored by them. But she retained the friendship of her lovers, who continued to admire her even when she had ceased to love them and they had ceased to love her. She had parted from Yeats many years when I met her in his rooms and listened, with much impatience, to her 'cantilating', but they were still good friends though the 'old passion' had ended long ago. G.B.S., too, remained her friend until she died.

In 1912, she left England to settle in what Mr Clifford Bax calls 'a Vedantist seminary' in Ceylon, and there she died of cancer on April 29, 1917. In the note she sent to Mr Bax, committing her letters to his charge, she stated that G.B.S. 'has been a most faithful friend to me', a statement that everyone who had the honour of knowing him, could repeat.

It is remarkable that all the women who fell in love with G.B.S., and they were many, were either beautiful or exceptionally intelligent, and were usually both.

55

There was, however, one love affair which was unique among the rest, and might, had his financial circumstances been happier, have ended in marriage. This was with May Morris.

This very beautiful woman, daughter of a beautiful mother and a handsome father, for William Morris had the masculine beauty which many poets have possessed, did not disguise her deep love for G.B.S. In a charming essay, *William Morris as I Knew Him*, a work which appears to have been published separately only in America,[1] G.B.S. describes his curious and innocent relations with her.

Morris and he, despite the disparity in their ages—Morris was his senior by twenty-two years—had become close friends; and G.B.S., after having lectured a few times in the hall which Morris had made out of his coach-house at Kelmscott House in Hammersmith Mall, soon became a familiar of the family. Morris is not much read to-day, even in Socialist circles, where, indeed, the only book he wrote that was ever widely read was *News from Nowhere;* but he was a poet of distinction whose communism belonged, not to the age of Karl Marx, but to the ages of the Icelandic sagas. His influence on the general life of his country was wide and diverse. The Mid-Victorian abominations in furniture and decoration were largely abolished by Morris, whose passion for fine houses and fine furniture and highly civilised living was intense. There was scarcely anything in the normal surroundings of well-to-do people which was not drastically changed by him. Even the wallpaper was radically reformed. He persuaded the middle-classes to cover their walls with brilliantly coloured patterns, too brilliant, perhaps, for the fashion did not last, and walls which, under his direction, had been adorned with exotic birds and tropical flowers, became plain, unpatterned and even bare. Dull browns and whitewash replaced the splendour of the tropics. Nevertheless, the Mid-Victorian era was never the same after Morris had done with it.

His house at Hammersmith, like his country house, Kelmscott Manor, in Gloucestershire, was one of the most civilised houses in England. He was, perhaps, less aware of the need for good drainage than he was of the need for colour, but he taught the rich merchants of his day to shake off their tedious pomposity and their dull-witted delight in accumulating vast sums of money. Himself wealthy, he was able to indulge his desire for a well-bred existence to the top of his bent. His interests were many and varied. Uncommonly skilful with his hands, he liked to make things himself, and wished, in the machine-made age, to persuade people to share his delight in making things. In his last days, he said to G.B.S., 'I have always wanted to make fiddles!' and had he lived, he would, undoubtedly have made them.

The man himself was magnificent, with a large, leonine head, full of rich quality. No one, seeing him in his blue serge suit and carefully

---

[1] It forms the Introduction to Vol. 2 of *William Morris, Artist, Writer, Socialist*, by May Morris (1936).

hand-dyed blue shirt, could fail to realise that he was a man of unusual character. His wife, Jane, was very beautiful: a remote, aloof lady who was 'the silentest woman' that G.B.S. 'had ever met.' Her clothes, like herself, were lovely, and she habitually lay about on sofas looking elegantly ill, though her health was excellent. Her movements were full of grace, and when her Rossetti face was first observed, men stared at her as if she were a bright being from another and more beautiful world. She was the chief ornament in Kelmscott House, a fact of which she was well aware, and she tried, rightly, to live up to her own beauty.

She did not care much for G.B.S., who was to her only one more of the tiresome people who orated on economics and infantile mortality and the need for extended local government in what had once been her coach-house. He was badly dressed, and his ugly clothes were as affected, in her judgment, as his ugly meals. The Morrises like fine food, well cooked and well served, and it is almost certain that Jane Morris was prejudiced against G.B.S., less for his eccentric garments and his dreary Socialism than she was for his vegetarianism. 'When I found myself dining at Kelmscott House,' he says in the essay already mentioned, 'My position was positively painful: for the Morris meals were works of art almost as much as the furniture. To refuse Morris's wine or Mrs Morris's viands was like walking on the great carpet with muddy boots:

> 'Now, as it happened, I practise the occidental form of Yoga: I am a vegetarian and a teetotaller. Morris did not demur to the vegetarianism: he maintained that a hunk of bread and an onion was a meal for any man; but he insisted on a bottle of wine to wash it down. Mrs Morris did not care whether I drank wine or water; but abstinence from meat she regarded as a suicidal fad. Between host and hostess I was cornered; and Mrs Morris did not conceal her contempt for my folly. At last pudding time came; and as the pudding was a particularly nice one, my abstinence vanished and I showed signs of a healthy appetite. Mrs Morris pressed a second helping on me, which I consumed to her entire satisfaction. Then she said, "That will do you good: there is suet in it." And that is the only remark, as far as I can remember, that was ever addressed to me by this beautiful and stately woman, whom the Brotherhood and Rossetti had succeeded in consecrating.'

Mrs Morris was almost as prominent as her husband in the reaction against Mid-Victorian ugliness and the general appearance of respectable dowdiness which the Queen, herself spectacularly dowdy, encouraged. Windsor Castle had been turned into a mausoleum in which a widow, swathed in crape, incessantly moped and mourned. Jane Morris was in open but delicate rebellion against this cult of uncomeliness, and, like all irregular soldiers, she went beyond reason in her rebellion. Her husband's absurd preoccupation with grubby proletarians displeased her. She never realised that his vision of working men was far different from the reality; and that his dream was of a day when agricultural labourers would look as if they had stepped out of a drawing by Walter Crane. She had no wish to see her drawing-room infested with unkempt sons of toil, and it was abhorrent to her that her coach-house should have been converted into an assembly hall for wage slaves and heralds of the revolution.

G.B.S. did not inspire her with any feeling of rapture. He was now firmly fixed in the sartorial eccentricity which had begun in his nine lean years, mostly, if not entirely, because he was poor. Had she known that he had tried lining his trousers with brown paper to keep himself warm, she might, though this is not certain, have felt less antipathetic to him. But what had been imposed upon him by poverty was now embraced as a cardinal point in his advanced creed. Sydney Olivier had been upset by one of his crank suits which, caught in a heavy shower, shrank almost visibly and, when it was dry, developed a rattle like the sound of loose wires. If they were to walk together, Olivier, usually imperturbable, cried in wrath, G.B.S. must doff his tinkling suit . . . !

It was this odd fellow, with a scraggy beard, so unlike the bold and buccaneering beard of her husband, and clad in a suit which would have made a tramp feel self-conscious, who now began to haunt her house.

56

But if Jane Morris was obstinately silent in his presence, her daughter May was not. May was 'then in the flower of her youth. You can see her in Burne-Jones's picture coming down *The Golden Stair*, the central figure.' G.B.S., naturally, fell in love with her at once, though he was well aware that, in the state of his purse at that time, he could have little or no hope of marrying her, even if she were willing to marry him, which she most certainly was.

'One Sunday evening after lecturing and supping, I was on the threshold of the Hammersmith house when I turned to make my farewell, and at this moment she came from the dining room into the hall. I looked at her, rejoicing in the lovely dress and lovely self; and she looked at me very carefully and quite deliberately made a gesture of assent with her eyes. I was immediately conscious that a Mystic Betrothal was registered in heaven, to be fulfilled when all the material obstacles should melt away, and my own position rescued from the squalors of my poverty and unsuccess; for subconsciously I had no doubt of my rank as a man of genius. . . . I did not think it necessary to say anything. . . . It did not occur to me even that fidelity to the Mystical Betrothal need interfere with the ordinary course of my relations with other women. I made no sign at all: I had no doubt that the thing was written on the skies for both of us.'

Here we have a notable example of the singular obtusity which sometimes dumbfounded his most ardent admirers. The supreme fact about him was that he never became intimate enough with anybody to understand him or her as thoroughly as any human being can be understood. He was too interested in himself and his own expression, a charge which he brought, fairly enough, against Sir Henry Irving without, however, perceiving that it could have been brought with equal fairness against himself, to be able to understand anybody intimately: and his inhuman lack of rancour and his total inability to sustain a quarrel or to bear malice, added to his acceptance of any fault or misdemeanour in other people as a humorous idiosyncracy, deprived him of all power of full appreciation of any person's character. He is the only man I have ever known who never, so far as I could discover, felt jealous of other people's success. This may have been a virtue in him: it may also have been a vice.

His realisation not only of his own love for May Morris, but of her love for him must seem singularly lacking in human quality when we read that strange quotation from *William Morris as I Knew Him*. A full man would have taken her in his arms there and then and would have printed his love on her lips. But he never spoke his love: he remembered only his poverty, as if that would have mattered to her who had enough money for both of them.

The complacency with which he accepted his Mystical Betrothal, as if it were no more than a promise to take a vegetarian lunch at the Wheatsheaf, received a severe shock when Miss Morris announced her engagement to an odd little insignificant fellow who hung about the fringes of adventurous and artistic societies, hoping that some day somebody would take notice of him. This was H. Halliday Sparling, the slightest looking man one could meet, seeming as if he were Uriah Heap's grandson.

'Suddenly, to my utter stupefaction, and, I suspect, that of Morris also,' he says, 'the beautiful daughter married one of the comrades. This was perfectly natural, and entirely my own fault for taking the Mystical Betrothal for granted; but I regarded it, and still regard it in spite of all reason, as the most monstrous breach of faith in the history of romance. The comrade was even less eligible than I was; for he was no better off financially; and, though he could not be expected to know this, his possibilities of future eminence were more limited.'

Miss Morris obviously was tired of being taken for granted, and, as sometimes happens with women of great beauty and distinction of mind, she turned from the lover she desired to a little ragbag of a fellow who was totally unsuited to be her mate.

The conclusion was almost comic. G.B.S., attempting to explain his own stupidity and her defection, says that he was suffering severely from nervous strain as a result of overwork and irregular habits and, he might justly have added, inadequate meals. He suffered a collapse and 'needed rest and change very pressingly,' but 'holidays of the usual sort were beyond my means'. 'The young couple thereupon invited me to stay with them for a while. I accepted and so found myself most blessedly resting and content in their house, which had the Morris charm; for she had inherited her father's sense of beauty and also his literary faculty in a form curiously Miltonic as well as Morrisian:

'Everything went well for a time in that *ménage à trois*. She was glad to have me in the house; and he was glad to have me because I kept her in good humour and produced a cuisine that no mere husband could elicit. It was probably the happiest passage in our three lives.

'But the violated Betrothal was avenging itself. It made me from the first the centre of the household; and when I had quite recovered and there was no longer my excuse for staying unless I proposed to do so permanently and parasitically, her legal marriage had dissolved as all illusions do. I had to consummate it or vanish.'

So he vanished. Once again, he failed May Morris. He had taken her for granted, the worst insult a woman can endure, and then, when he could no longer do this, he bolted. 'But when it became evident,' he says in excuse, 'that the Betrothal would not suffer this to be an innocent arrangement the case became complicated.'

'To begin with, the legal husband was a friend whose conduct towards me had always been irreproachable. To be welcomed in his house and then steal his wife was revolting to my sense of honour and socially inexcusable; for though I was as extreme a freethinker on sexual and religious questions as any sane human being could be, I was not the dupe of the Bohemian Anarchism that is very common in socialist and literary circles. I knew that a scandal would damage both of us and damage the Cause as well. . . . The more I reasoned about the situation the worse it was doomed to appear. So I did not argue about it. I vanished.'

And now the comic element came into this tragi-farce. Sparling also disappeared. He fled to the Continent and allowed himself to be divorced. He then married another and, one may hope, more suitable lady. And May Morris was left mateless and unfulfilled. Her beauty did not become ashes, as one young man knew when, for the only time in his life, he met her, and perceived in her elder years the magnificent remains of loveliness; but the hopes she had of fulfilment proved to be delusive. Like Pegeen Mike in Synge's play, she had lost her only playboy of the western world. The conduct of a school for elegant embroidery was little consolation for that loss, especially when she discovered that one of her pupils, Florence Farr, was enjoying the happiness of which she had been deprived.

Sparling, later in life, accused G.B.S. of preventing May from cherishing him. But this was essentially a false charge. Sparling failed, could not, indeed, have done otherwise than fail to inspire the slightest passion in Miss Morris. The man tried to rise above himself, and fell flat on his face.

57

Time has been overshot in some respects, and we must return on our tracks for a year or two. It was during this distracting time that G.B.S. had the great good fortune to meet William Archer, as we have casually noted in the previous pages. It was the most momentous meeting of G.B.S.'s life. Archer, a tall, handsome Scot, serious, but not sombre in expression and manner, had observed him with interest and curiosity as he studied *Das Kapital* in French and the score of *Tristan und Isolde* simultaneously in the Reading Room of the British Museum. No two men differed more in character and habit and mind than these two did, nor have many friends been more differently brought up. Yet their friendship was almost instant, unshakable and deep, even although Archer often regarded G.B.S. with bewilderment and disapproval, and even, throughout his life, disbelieved him to be what he called a dramatist. Archer's ideal playwrights were Scribe and Sardou and Pinero, highly accomplished craftsmen who followed well defined rules in the construction of plays. In comparison with them, G.B.S. was an anarchist, was not, indeed, a dramatist at all.

These two men, so dissimilar in character and mind, apart from a singular and unexpected strain of puritanism in G.B.S., and a more singular and unexpected strain of light heartedness in Archer, were such intimate friends that no separation in time or in place could make them feel they needed a spell in which to renew their friendship. They took it up exactly where they had left it, the moment they met. How little alike they were in their experience is evident from the fact that Archer, when he first saw *Widowers' Houses* performed, could not understand the violence of Blanche Sartorius. He had never met a woman like her, and was disinclined to believe that she could ever have existed except in G.B.S.'s impish and disorderly mind.

But G.B.S. had felt the full fury of Jenny Patterson's wrath about the time that he and Archer were making each other's acquaintance, and he knew that Blanche Sartorius, by comparison with Jenny, was mild as milk. There was no suspicion in Archer's mind when he and G.B.S. met in friendship that the shy, nervous man with the worn clothes and scrubby red beard was in conflict with a tornado who bitterly resented his attraction to a polar passion.

58

Archer, who was born in Perth on September 23, 1856, and was, therefore, two months younger than G.B.S., was a man of exceptionally fine and upright character: the Scot at his magnificent best. There is a tendency among some of G.B.S.'s biographers, and even on the part of Professor Archibald Henderson, who might, more than most people be expected to appreciate Archer, to dismiss him as a glum and dour Scotsman who joked with great difficulty and was accustomed to think that any author less serious than Ibsen was beneath notice. There never was a graver misunderstanding of a man than this, unless it be the common error that G.B.S. was an irresponsible sprite who never took anything seriously in his long life. If there was any base metal in Archer's nature, none of his friends ever saw a sign of it. There was so little in his character that could be called mean or ungenerous that he could tell a man to his face how little he liked his work without hurting his feelings or incurring his contempt. Of the three men to whom G.B.S. was most attached, Sidney Webb, Gilbert Chesterton and William Archer, who had nothing in common except G.B.S.'s affection for them, Archer was the one he loved best.

Like many Scots, the Archers had old and close associations, both business and personal, with Scandinavia. William's grandfather, after whom he was named, emigrated from Scotland, taking his wife, Julia, and their family to the town of Larvik, in Southern Norway, where he engaged profitably in trade.

Thomas Archer, the sixth son of this William, who was born in Glasgow, led a roving life for many years, first in Australia, as a shepherd, squatter, explorer and drover, and, second, in California, fighting Indians and prospecting for gold. When he had made a modest accumulation of gold dust, he returned to Scotland, where he disconcerted everybody by falling suddenly and vehemently in love with Grace Lindsay Morison, the second daughter of James Morison, post-master of Perth, who was also a bookseller, stationer and publisher.

The Morisons were said to be of Norwegian descent, though they had inhabited Perth for two hundred years. James Morison was a man of many agreeable parts: a lover of literature who was also an important member of a severe religious sect, the Glassites or Sandemanians, and yet had a large sense of humour, told stories uncommonly well, and did not disdain the theatre. He kept the Sabbath as strictly as any Wee Free in Scotland, and was addicted to the savage habit of reading long passages from the Bible to his children, who heard them with reluctance, developing in his grandson, William, a gift which was to be most useful to him later in life: the gift of being able to sleep bolt upright and apparently attentive to what was being said. It was this gift from his grandfather which, Archer always averred, had saved his reason and physical health through many years of dramatic criticism. When a play bored him, he let sleep overcome him without exposing himself to those around him.

William Archer was the eldest son of the roving Thomas and the young Sandemanian girl, who had a family of five sons and four daughters. His circumstances were entirely different from those of G.B.S. He was essentially middle-class, almost lower middle-class, whereas G.B.S. was upper middle-class on one side and landed gentry on the other; but he was far more fortunate in his upbringing. His formal education was better, and his knowledge of the world was wider and deeper. By the time he first met G.B.S., he had travelled extensively, knew several languages, and was intimately informed about European literature, whereas G.B.S., who had never been out of Ireland until he was twenty, and had never moved about his own country more than a hundred miles from Dublin, had made no longer journey in his life than that from Dublin to London, and was unable to speak any language but his own. Archer's infancy and childhood, until he was fourteen, were spent in moving from one house or town to another; for Thomas Archer was a restless man and was inclined to think that his expensive failures in farming could be put right merely by changing farms.

Because of this movement from place to place, William's mind was never centred on any home in Scotland: the one permanent home he knew in his childhood and youth was his grandfather Archer's house, Tolderodden, in Larvik: 'the first place I can remember,' he wrote many years later in his life, 'and the last that I shall forget.' He lived so long in Larvik, when he was four, that he forgot all the English he knew and spoke only Norwegian; but he quickly recovered his native tongue when his parents returned to Scotland.

This roving life, which included a spell, after Larvik, in Lymington on Solent, deprived William of an accent. No one who heard him speak in his fine, grave and distinguished voice could have told that he was a Scot. It would have been hard for anyone to guess his nationality, beyond, perhaps, a surmise that he was a middle-class Englishman who had spent a large part of his life abroad and in several countries. Yet he was educated in Edinburgh and was a graduate of Edinburgh University. It was while he was still a student that his father suddenly shifted the rest of his family to Australia, where he settled in Queensland. This withdrawal had a profound effect on William's life; for he was now largely independent of kindred. Old William Archer, his grandfather, was dead, but his widow, despite her Scottish ancestry, lived on in Larvik. There were Morisons in Perth. But these, in the matter of access, were the nearest relatives he had. He stood on his own feet in Edinburgh, making his own life. He experienced home life only when he paid his annual visit to his Norwegian kindred, who regarded him as an oddity: a tall, big-boned youth with a frank and engaging countenance, a quiet and peaceable manner, and a temper so equable that no one could easily ruffle it. He could talk well when he wished to talk, but he was not communicative nor was he garrulous, though he had plenty of self-confidence and a gently ironic wit. It was evident that he had great intelligence, but he seemed not to have much, if any, ambition. He could win prizes, but was not in the least eager to win them.

It was while he was staying at Larvik that Archer became aware of Ibsen's work:

> 'I used to see in the Norwegian shopwindows books by one Henrik Ibsen, but my interest in him was not excited until one day I chanced to hear a lady express the opinion that *Love's Comedy* was *glimrende vittig*—brilliantly witty. "Hullo," thought I, "if there is anything brilliantly witty in Norwegian I must read it", and I bought the paper-covered book little thinking how much that series of paper-covered books was to mean to me. From *Love's Comedy*, I went on to *The League of Youth, Brand, Peer Gynt, The Vikings, The Pretenders*—all that the poet had yet published.'

Emperor and Galilean, he says later, 'was then his latest work. When the "World-Historia drama" came into my hands, I remember locking myself up in a bare little hutch of a bathing-house by the fiord, in order to devour its ten acts in the luxury of unbroken solitude. By the connivance of my grandmother's housekeeper (an old ally of mine), I laid in provisions to enable me, if necessary, to stand a siege. Even in those early days, you see, Ibsenite and Ishmaelite meant much the same thing. But how I should have stared had I foreseen that such a word as Ibsenite would ever be added to the English language.'[1]

By the time he had graduated in 1876, the year in which G.B.S. left Dublin for London, Archer could be called not only widely read, but widely travelled. He had also begun a career in journalism by

---

[1] I have taken this passage and all the information in this section from *William Archer*, by his brother, Lt-Colonel Charles Archer. See also chapter on Archer, in *Pen Portraits and Reviews*, by Bernard Shaw.

writing a daily editorial for the Edinburgh *Evening News*. He was familiar in Norway, acquainted with Sweden and Denmark, and had visited Berlin, Dresden, Prague and Vienna before he was eighteen. In 1875, he went to Paris where he saw Sarah Bernhardt for the first time. In June 1876, he sailed for Australia to join his family, remaining there until April 1877, when he set off on the return journey to Scotland. This trip took him to New Zealand, Honolulu, San Francisco, Salt Lake City, Chicago, New York, Philadelphia, Boston and, at last, Glasgow, where he landed towards the end of June 1877. His age was twenty-one.

It was not until September 1878, that he settled in London, where, in November, he entered the Middle Temple with the intention of going to the Bar. He also resumed his journalism and began to write articles about the theatre. In 1880, his father, having been made Agent General in London for Queensland, brought his family back to Britain, but although Archer was again united to them, he was less happy with them than he had formerly been because his religious opinions had altered radically. He had become a Rationalist, mainly through the influence of his friend, John M. Robertson, an able man who tried to join a career as a writer with that of a politician, and failed in both, despite great labour and learning. He wrote *A History of Freethought in the Nineteenth Century*, which is still regarded as a considerable work, and wrote with authority on Shakespeare and the Elizabethans. He was given a small office in a Ministry, but his talent which seemed certain to become distinguished, somehow missed its mark. He was, perhaps, too serious a man, unable to relax and mingle with the mob.

Archer's health at this time was poor, and he was over-working himself. Hoping to recover his vigour, he went to Italy in 1881, and there, in November, he met Ibsen for the first time, and found that grim old gentleman with the tightly buttoned lips, fairly friendly, but less impressive, at first sight, than Archer had expected him to be. The friendship increased, and Ibsen's authority and power became more apparent with the growth. It would have been hard for anyone to resist the charm of Archer's serene and generous nature. Certainly, Miss Frances Elizabeth Trickett, who was spending the winter in Rome with her parents, found him irresistible. He frequented her society with as much ardour as a Scot is capable of displaying, and when her family left Rome to go north to Tuscany, he contrived to be in Florence, Venice, on the shores of Lake Como, and, in the summer, Switzerland when she was there. When he went on to Munich in the middle of May, preparatory to returning to England in September, he and she were virtually engaged to be married, though the contract was not ratified for five years because he had not established himself in any employment by which he could earn enough to support a wife.

In March 1887, he felt sufficiently secure to become formally engaged to Miss Trickett, and on the following 23rd of October, they were married. They lived in felicity for the rest of their lives, begetting a charming and remarkable boy, who called himself Tomarcher, and was to become the close and devoted friend of G.B.S.

Archer's engagement reminded him of his obligation to earn his living: a reminder which was reinforced by the fact that his father, owing to a change in the government of Queensland, had lost his office as Agent General. These censorious people who cannot contain their contempt for G.B.S. because he was not clerking incessantly during his nine years of servitude to letters, will do well to note that Archer, a man of extraordinary probity of character, seems to have felt no compunction about dependence on his parents at this period of his life. He had earned some money, but nothing like as much as G.B.S. had earned in Townshend's estate office or his various employments in London.

He had been maintained at Edinburgh University and during his study of law in London. It was his father who kept him while he was roaming about Italy, France, Switzerland and Germany, seeking health and knowledge of life and drama. The cost of his transport to Australia and back again to Scotland was certainly not paid by himself. Yet Archer and his father would have been astonished and indignant if anyone had accused him of sponging on his aged parents who were not well off. The law seemed unlikely to suit his talents and temperament, and he suggested to his father that it was hardly worth his while to spend a further £100 in getting himself called to the Bar; but his father insisted that he should, and in November 1883, he was. That was as far as he went in the law.

His history has been set out at this length, not only because he was the most important influence in G.B.S.'s life during this period, but because of the striking contrast between his education and Shaw's. In comparison with Archer, G.B.S. was an ignoramus who had never been anywhere and had been given a sketchy sort of education. Archer had a fairly intimate knowledge of a large part of the world: G.B.S. knew only a backward provincial city well and a capital city locally. Their whole education and outlook on life were different, though there were points at which they met and were in union. Sidney Webb was not more different from Shaw than Shaw was from Archer, who would not have been able to make much of Webb if he had met him then. Yet Archer, more than any living soul, was responsible for starting G.B.S. on the career he was to follow with extraordinary skill and success; and G.B.S. was always more at ease and happier with Archer than he was with Webb.

The meeting in the Reading Room of the British Museum did not directly result in the friendship. Archer's own account of their meeting is vague. 'How we first made acquaintance I have forgotten, but one did not need to meet him twice to be sure that George Bernard Shaw was a personality to be noted and studied. . . . At any rate, we became fast friends.' Archer was then beginning to be known as a writer on the general affairs of the theatre. It was, indeed, his book on *English Dramatists of To-Day* which secured his first employment as a dramatic critic for him. He had offered an article on Ibsen to Edmund Yates, the editor of *The World*. Yates declined the article, but offered Archer the job of dramatic critic at a weekly salary of three guineas: a sum which would scarcely pay for a contemporary critic's 'bus fares.

'My dear Sir,' he wrote, 'Ibsen won't do, but—if I am addressing the author of *English Dramatists of To-Day*—you will.'

That is editing—a lost occupation in these times of Little Men in Large Places. Archer was taken on trial for three months, not because his predecessor, Dutton Cook, was incompetent, for Yates thought him the best dramatic critic of his kind then in London, but because he thought that *The World* critic should have a light and even flippant touch. Anyone less light or flippant than Archer can scarcely be imagined, and he himself, as he accepted Yates's offer, felt certain that his survival on the paper would be for less than the trial three months; but he was able and dexterous enough to last on it for about twenty-one years.

In addition to criticising plays on *The World*, he was also reviewing books for *The Pall Mall Gazette* and contributing articles to various magazines. His apparently imprudent marriage was justified by his success in journalism: a success which was not diminished in the least by his habit of writing unpopular articles, for which he received no payment, in unpopular papers.

He had another habit which is important to be noted here. When an editor offered him employment, he was accustomed to say that he was unfit to accept it because he was entirely ignorant of the subject on which he was expected to write with authority or because he was too pressed with other work to undertake so exacting a post as he was now being offered. *But*, and the *but* is important, he had a friend, a red-haired and red-bearded and peculiar Irishman who was just the man for the job: a devilishly clever chap, full of wit and odd ideas, who could write brilliantly about anything. The less he knew about a subject, the better he wrote about it! . . .

Archer tries, but fails, to pay G.B.S.

He had already foxed the editor of *The Pall Mall Gazette* into giving G.B.S. a job as a reviewer of books. It was not long before Archer foxed Yates in much the same way. Yates needed an art critic, and proposed that Archer should do the work. Archer protested that he knew nothing whatever about pictures, and was horrified to hear this was his best qualification for the post. Reluctantly, he yielded to Yates, but he persuaded G.B.S. to go with him to exhibitions, partly to keep him awake, partly to tell him what to write about the pictures. When he repeated to G.B.S. what Yates had said about ignorance of an art being the best qualification for criticising it, G.B.S. shocked him by endorsing his editor's opinion.

'You will learn all you need to know by looking at pictures,' he said, which was exactly what he himself had done in the National Gallery of Ireland.

This singular collaboration lasted for several weeks, causing Archer increasing discomfort. He had tried to make G.B.S. accept at least half the pay he received for his articles, but G.B.S. refused the offer.[1] That was in December, 1885. Archer sent him a cheque: G.B.S. returned it. Archer sent it again.

G.B.S. wrote:

'I re-return the cheque, and if you re-re-return it, I will re-re-re-return it again ("again" being here, as you justly observe, tautological). . . . The idea of one man sucking another man's brains is a depraved individualistic idea. No man has a right of property in the ideas of which he is the mouthpiece. The law does not permit a man to patent a discovery, but only an invention concreted in a machine. The ideas of your criticism are mere natural raw material which neither of us is entitled to monopolize. . . . If I am to be paid for what I suggested to you, for example, the painters must be paid for what they suggested to me. The devil has presented you with a depraved conception disguised as conscientiousness. . . .'

The letter, a long one, is cited in Colonel Archer's *Life*, and is characteristic of G.B.S., both in his manner and in his generous nature, and it is highly creditable to him and to Archer.

But Archer was obstinate, too, and he had not finished with G.B.S. over this business. He went to Yates and told him that he could not continue to do work for which he was totally unfit. He then dismissed himself, and Yates sent for Shaw, who was engaged, at fivepence a line, to be *The World's* Art critic. The single mistake Archer made in this matter was his assumption that G.B.S. knew no

[1] The note in G.B.S.'s diary under the date 12th December is 'Archer sent me a cheque for £1 6s. 8d. for my share of his picture criticism in *The World*. Returned it.' On the 14th, he notes that 'Archer's cheque' has come 'back again. Again returned it. Took tea at Archer's.'

more about pictures than he did. G.B.S. could not have known less than Archer on that subject, for Archer knew nothing at all, but there were few critics in London then who knew as much about art as did G.B.S. He had not toiled through the National Gallery in Dublin for nothing.

G.B.S. seemed to be inert about his own advantage. Either he was well aware of his destiny and determined that it should fulfil itself, or he had, almost without his knowledge, become convinced that there was no hope of employment for him in London. His novels had been rejected by every publisher to whom they had been offered. Even American publishers, who might have been expected to be more adventurous than their English colleagues, had disdained them, though they were soon to make up for this disdain by publishing them almost lavishly, without, however, remembering to reward their author.

No one seemed to want G.B.S. in the one job he now felt certain he could do: the job of writing. His earnings in the nine years from writing had been so small that they were comic. The last sum he had received was the five shillings paid to him for the verses he wrote for the children's school prize. He had written them in a spirit of jest, and had been stupified with astonishment when they were accepted and he was rewarded with a crown. Stirred by this success, he wrote some more verses, this time in a serious mood, and was no less stupified to learn that they were regarded as a joke in bad taste. How often was he to suffer a similar experience in the future?

It was then that Archer rendered Shaw his greatest service. It will seem strange to those who know his history as a dramatist, that the idea of writing plays had not occurred to him until Archer suggested that they should collaborate in one. Archer confessed that, although he could construct a plot for a play, he could not write dialogue with any life in it: G.B.S. confessed that although he could write reams of flashing dialogue, he could not construct a plot. It seemed, then, that heaven had intended them to join their talents together, Archer bringing his plot to be embellished by G.B.S.'s dialogue. The collaboration failed, chiefly because G.B.S. was obviously incapable of collaborating with anybody. As well might the Falls of Niagara seek to collaborate with a barge as Shaw seek to collaborate with Archer. The history of the attempt is familiar and has been told by G.B.S. better than it can ever be told by anybody.

Archer, working on the principles laid down by Scribe and Sardou, had manufactured a neat and rigid plot for what would, had it been done as he wished it to be done, have turned out to be a tidy piece of melodrama. It was not original in any way, for Archer had boldly lifted it, as was a common practice of the time, from a French play by Emile Augier, entitled *Ceinture Dorée*, and given it a setting in a hotel garden overlooking the Rhine. The setting, used only in the first act, was all that was left after G.B.S. had finished with it. He was not wasting his mind on the sweepings of the French theatre.

Archer was dazed when G.B.S. informed him that he had used up all his plot, and asked for more. He complained, naturally enough, that the plot of a play is an organic whole which would be ruined by addition. But G.B.S., who never took much interest in plots, persisted in his demand, and so Archer, irritated and bewildered, scraped up a few fragments from the French factory and sent them to him. But these were not enough. A demand was made for more plot. This was too much for Archer, who withdrew from the collaboration, but not from the friendship, which seemed, indeed, to be increased by their failure to work together.

60

Archer had directed his mind to the drama, but the collapse of their collaboration momentarily dismayed G.B.S. He had had ample cause for feeling a failure in the matter of novels. Now, it seemed that he was a failure, too, as a dramatist; and there were moments when he wondered if he would ever be able to assemble his mind sufficiently to be able to do something of the sort he wanted to do. Archer had undoubtedly been an angel of the Lord to him at this critical period in his career. There was no encouragement at home; there was flat failure outside it; and there was remarkably little kindness or encouragement anywhere.

The script of the abortive play was put aside, and G.B.S., now becoming busier in general journalism, abandoned temporarily his hope of storming the stage. If he despaired of himself as a great writer, he showed no sign that he did, though the fact that he had been a failure as a novelist and now showed signs of failure as a dramatist must have oppressed him. But he had well and truly laid the foundations of the life he wished to lead. His friends were numerous, and they were the sort of people he liked: intelligent, free from superstition, social, economic or religious, and eager to find out the facts and to form a faith which should have some relation to reality. Truth was no jesting matter to them, as Bacon alleged, without the slightest warrant, it was to Pontius Pilate; and they sought for it assiduously, trying to remember as they sought, that they, too, had defects of mind and nature, and that their search, though it might bring them an inch or two nearer the truth, must, in the event, be lopsided and full of fault. They did not forget the ancient adage that the road to hell is paved with good intentions, though they must sometimes have wondered whether there were not a good many bad intentions among the paving stones.

In the company of these people, men and women, G.B.S., despite his deep disappointments in himself as a writer, marched forward, making a vivid impression on all whom he met. E. Nesbit, according to her biographer, Doris Langley Moore, described him as he was in 1885:

> 'G.B.S. has a fund of dry Irish humour that is simply irresistible. He is a very clever writer and speaker—is the grossest flatterer (of men, women and children impartially) I ever met, is horribly untrustworthy as he repeats everything he hears, and does not always stick to the truth, and is *very plain* . . . and yet is one of the most fascinating men I ever met. Everyone rather affects to despise him. "Oh, it's only Shaw". That sort of thing, you know, but everyone admires him all the same. Miss H—— pretends to hate him, but my own impression is that she is over head and ears in love with him.'

So, indeed, was E. Nesbit, who wrote several sonnets which, though they were not addressed to him, were, her friends believed, intended for him. One of them, entitled *The Depths of the Sea*, and inspired by a Burne Jones picture, concludes with the following passage:

> Her lithe cold arms and chill wet bosom's beat
> Vowed him her beauty's unillumined shrine:
> So I—seeing you above me—turn and tire,
> Sick with an empty ache of long desire
> To drag you down—to hold you—make you mine.

The poet's biographer asserts that this passionate appeal 'elicited from its object nothing but a heartlessness which he knew how to make amusing, and it was soon transmuted into a gay and untroubled friendship.'

E. Nesbit may mislead the reader with her description of G.B.S. as 'untrustworthy' and a liar. He did, indeed, delight to tell stories about his friends, sometimes with less discretion than was desirable, but they were intended to be entertaining tales, not malicious revelations, and his extravagant variations of fact were made only to improve the quality of his stories. William Archer was often his victim in this respect, and no one enjoyed G.B.S.'s accounts of Archer's alleged wild adventures more than Archer himself.

One of his stories was that Archer, while fast asleep at a performance of Shelley's *The Cenci*, 'fell forward flat on his nose with a tremendous noise, leaving a dent on the floor of the theatre which may still be seen by curious visitors,' to which Archer, according to Professor Henderson, retorted that if the incident occurred during 'the third act of *The Cenci*, nothing but slumber was refuge from it.'

He professed pride in the dent he was alleged to have made. But a funnier story about Archer, which made him wriggle in helpless laughter, was one which described him during a performance of *Paul Pry*. 'One of the characters, holding a revolver, falls asleep; someone touches him on the shoulder, he gives a convulsive start and the pistol goes off with a roar. Archer, suddenly aroused from his slumber, starts wildly to his feet with a scream, automatically burying his clenched hands in the hair of the lady just in front of him. To Archer's consternation and horror, the lady's hair came off, and Archer was left standing there, holding the wig in his hands.'[1]

G.B.S. laughed with his whole body, His laughter would start in his feet, which seemed to dance, and ran up his long legs, shaking them thoroughly as it ran, and then it caught hold of his shoulders and almost shook them off. Then he would fling up his arms, smiting his hands together as if they were cymbals, and his legs would begin to be riotous. Chesterton's laughter was a bubble and squeak in comparison with G.B.S.'s. He would chuckle like a child, but his body, being too fat, could not heave itself about as G.B.S.'s did. G.B.S. spread an infection of laughter all round him, and could make Charlotte cry with laughing.

61

In 1885, entirely through Archer, he was able to maintain himself on his earnings which then amounted to £117. Soon after that time, however, the desultory employment on *The Pall Mall Gazette* was lost in circumstances characteristic of the scrupulous way in which he did his work. Had he been less conscientious he would not have lost it. The editor had asked him to review a philosophic work by Professor Henry Sidgwick. A year later, the review had not yet been written, and the publishers complained to the editor who, therefore, ceased to send G.B.S. any more books.

The cause of the delay was extraordinary. Feeling that he was not competent to criticise Sidgwick's work until he had read about a dozen volumes, ranging from 'Thales to George Henry Lewes', he set about reading them so that he might qualify himself to write a short review for an evening paper! This was straining conscience out of all reason, and it is not surprising that the story, when it became known, was received with incredulity. Fleet Street was not used to people like Bernard Shaw. The loss of this employment was serious for a man whose total earnings were just over two pounds a week, but it did not distress G.B.S., who still did a great deal of unpaid labour for the Fabian Society, as Archer did for the Secularists. It is

[1] *Bernard Shaw: Playboy and Prophet.* By Archibald Henderson, pp. 258-9.

impressive to note that Archer, although he was a Scot, was indifferent to money for the whole of his life, and that he never hesitated to do arduous and unpaid work for any cause he adopted. He was able, as a good Scot should be, to make a living, but he never had more than he needed until, late in life, he had great fortune with an excellent melodrama, *The Green Goddess*.

G.B.S. was still addressing the proletariat at street corners and in public parks, but he was coming more and more into demand for important meetings: at one of which, a young student at the Royal College of Science listened for the first time 'to a lean young Shaw with a thin, flame-colour beard beneath his white illuminated face'. The name of the young student was Herbert George Wells, and he and G.B.S. were to meet again, and often, in strenuous and, on the part of Wells, but never on the part of Shaw, acrimonious debate.

Although the year was full of work and increasing friendships, nothing of note occurred in it, apart from the death, on the 19th of April, of Mr Shaw. His age was seventy-one. He died, presumably in lodgings, at 21, Leeson Park Avenue, of congestion of the lungs. It is significant of this odd man that he died only a short distance from the house to which he had taken his disillusioned bride, the house in which his children were born, and that he seems never to have moved very far from it.

He must often have wondered what unkindly chance had made him the husband of Lucinda Elizabeth. Like the father of Napoleon Bonaparte, he was denied the comfort of knowing that he had begotten a genius. In his son's philosophy, he had been used for a purpose that was not his own, and the world was the gainer by his employment; but what did *he* gain? If we are thinking reeds, have we not cause to complain that we are used as reeds and not as thinkers? When George Carr Shaw was called to his account, might he not with justice have thought that his Maker should have been called instead? With a more congenial mate, one who was less intent on herself, kindlier and more tolerant of a man's little habit of taking a drop too much now and then, his life might have been very agreeable, for he demanded little and he got less.

Drink, was, no doubt, very comforting to an insignificant man who knew that his wife, like David's, looked upon and despised him in her heart. Unfortunately for him, George Carr Shaw could not, as David did, care less than one hoot for his wife's opinion and contempt. So he went, almost unattended, to his grave, and faded out of the knowledge of all his immediate kin, remembered only by a few old and remote relatives who had found him pleasant company. It was from him, however, that G.B.S. inherited his wit and sardonic humour: Lucinda Elizabeth had none to leave.

62

By the time he was thirty-one, G.B.S. had established a reputation for brilliance of wit and style in a narrow circle of intelligent admirers; but that was all he had established. He still had not found himself, had not even found his way to his proper starting place. *Cashel Byron's Profession* had been published in book form in 1886 at a shilling, but although a few discerning people, such as Robert Louis Stevenson, praised it, its sale was slight.

In 1887, Swann Sonnenschien had published *An Unsocial Socialist* unprofitably for them and for Shaw, but were not sorry that they had. It must have been comforting to G.B.S. to receive a letter dated December 30, 1887, from a member of the firm, in which he proclaimed his impenitence at having published what he believed to be 'as clever a novel as we have brought out'. This letter is remarkable not only for its generous encouragement of an author in sore need of encouragement, but also because it included a suggestion that G.B.S. should write plays, 'which are even more suited to you in my opinion' than novels. It ended with the remark, 'I certainly don't regret the small sum of money we probably have in "U.S." still; and shall not do so unless you drop your pen, or die, or do something else foolish.'[1]

It was not until the beginning of 1888, that G.B.S. obtained regular and comparatively profitable employment. On Tuesday, January 17, the first issue of an evening paper, edited by T. P. O'Connor, an Irish Nationalist member of parliament, and entitled *The Star*, appeared. The assistant editor was a very able young journalist and Fabian, H. W. Massingham, who was, many years later, to become the editor of one of the most brilliant weekly reviews ever published in this country, *The Nation*. Massingham informed O'Connor that he would be doing himself a grave disservice if he did not instantly engage Shaw to be a leader writer, and O'Connor, who had never heard of his countryman—what Irishman has ever heard of any other Irishman?—thereupon engaged G.B.S., who started to work on the paper on the second day of its existence. His salary was £2 10s a week. Among his colleagues were two young men, little less brilliant than himself: A. B. Walkley, a clerk in the General Post Office, who was employed as dramatic critic, and Joseph Pennell, who became art critic, and owed his employment to G.B.S. It is almost incredible that any newspaper could have had five men so brilliant as O'Connor, Massingham, G.B.S., Walkley and Pennell on

[1] This letter is quoted by F. E. Loewenstein in *The History of a Famous Novel*, and is also cited in *Bernard Shaw: a Chronicle* by R. F. Rattray.

its staff simultaneously. Even *The Manchester Guardian*, in its great days, did not surpass that record.

But G.B.S. soon gave O'Connor cause for complaint. *The Star* was a Radical newspaper, but the new leader-writer treated it as if it were the official organ of *The Fabian Society*. His articles were full of socialistic propaganda. Venerable statesmen, such as John Morley, opening the paper in the expectation of seeing themselves applauded as the saviours of their country, were shocked to read that they were almost its ruin. Morley remonstrated with O'Connor who remonstrated with his indisciplined contributor. The upshot was that on February 9, about three weeks after he had joined the staff of *The Star*, G.B.S. resigned. He wrote a long letter to O'Connor in which, very amiably, he told that dulcet-voiced politician that he had no policy and that 'the fourteen million wage workers with their halfpence and their school-board education are a cypher to you.' He implored O'Connor to rouse himself from his sleep and make himself as hated as W. T. Stead was: a prospect which was repulsive to O'Connor, who liked a quiet life and was eager to be friendly with everybody. G.B.S. was highly explicit:

> 'I may as well mention some reasons why we cannot pull together on an editorial staff. Ten years ago it would have been true that I am no journalist, because I will write on subjects that I have thought about. But to-day the journalist-in-chief must be above all things an apostle, a man of convictions, illusions, fanaticisms, everything that made a man impossible in the days when *The Star* was impossible. From these two points of view I appear a greenhorn to you, and you appear a dreamer to me. . . . I shall come down in the morning as usual in case there should be any press of work; but next week I must retire into the privacy which best befits an unassuming man. Let not your unfortunate good nature prevent you from taking me at my word. The magnitude of my personal vanity, reflected from the magnitude of my cause, places me above literary huffiness. . . .'

This was all very well, and O'Connor probably enjoyed it, but an apostle and man of convictions has no right to expect the editor of a newspaper to let him loose with political advocacies which are fundamentally different from those which his paper was formed to advocate. A grocer does not rejoice in an assistant who advises all his customers to deal with his rival across the road.

But T.P. was tolerant of rebellious young men, and he was unwilling to part with G.B.S., whose letter of resignation contained a notable forecast about Joseph Chamberlain. 'Tell John Morley roundly in private that the latest principles from Voltaire and Bentham will not do for Stonecutter St, and that your *Star* must cross his sooner or later if he persists in his 18th century Rip-van-Winkleism.

Alas, that the people instinctively mistrust a close shaven man. Nevertheless, in spite of razors, Chamberlain's loss of ground is only temporary; and so far from being extinct, he is certain to have a very big, if not a very longlived boom yet. And you attack him, and are tender with Broadhurst.'

When, on the following morning, G.B.S. appeared in Stonecutter St to clear up any work that needed to be cleared up, T.P. talked to him. G.B.S. suggested that, instead of being leader-writer, he should become musical critic at two guineas a week, which was eight shillings less than he was paid for writing leaders. O'Connor was delighted by the proposal, and G.B.S. now began to spread himself more lavishly among the radical and proletarian readers of the brightest evening paper in Great Britain.

Critics in those days were anonymous, but G.B.S. never had any use for anonymity. He was not allowed to sign his articles with his name, so he invented a pseudonym, Corno di Bassetto. This was the name of an instrument better known, in English, as the basset horn, which had gone out of use in the time of Mozart, and has now been replaced by the bass clarinet. G.B.S. knew its name, but that was all he knew about it. It had a 'peculiar watery melancholy' and 'a total absence of any richness or passion in its tone. If I had heard a note of it by 1888, I should not have selected its name for a character I intended to be sparkling. I took care that Corno di Bassetto should always be amusing and, by using knowledge, to provide a solid substratum of genuine criticism.'

It was about this time that G.B.S. met a long, lean, remote-looking young man who seemed to have mislaid himself. This was W. B. Yeats, who was then twenty-three and had lately arrived from Dublin, trailing clouds of Celtic Twilight. Yeats, in a letter to Katharine Tynan, dated February 12, 1888, tells her that 'last night at Morris's I met Bernard Shaw, who is certainly very witty. But, like most people who have wit rather than humour, his mind is maybe somewhat lacking in depth. However, his stories are good, they say.' What Yeats meant by the last sentence is hard to tell, and as he had neither wit nor humour, his remarks are as shallow as one might justifiably expect them to be, considering his youth and inexperience. G.B.S. seems to have been less impressed by Yeats than Yeats was by him. The entry in his diary, made on Sunday, February 12, 1888, is that he had supper at William Morris's, where he 'met an Irishman named Yeats'. That is all.

Yeats, despite his poetic genius, was a dull correspondent. His letters are bare and graceless and more concerned with money than with transcendental thought. He was the rapt poet of commonplace imagination in 1888, a being so lofty that mundane matters eluded his notice. Vague, except about money, and so short of common sense that in his youth his father believed him to be 'wanting', as Irish people say about those who are astray in the head, he could not cope with the most familiar facts of normal life. He began letters, but forgot to finish them. If they were finished, they were folded in wrong envelopes. A letter would lie on his desk for several days because he had no stamps, and seemed not to know where they could be bought. If he went out to post a letter, he was more likely to put it in his pocket than the pillar-box, and it would lie there for days. This vagueness, and his air of not knowing where he was, and his mournful Irish voice, which he used with great effect, made romantic maidens regard him with awe and wonder, and caused them to dress themselves in trailing garments as if they were the daughters of Deirdre or Dervorgilla and had not an earthly thought in their heads.

Gilbert and Sullivan had produced *Patience* in 1881, and the figure of Reginald Bunthorne was said to have been based on Oscar Wilde. But G.B.S. denied that this could be true. Wilde, he said, except for a brief period, did not affect arty-and-crafty clothes. He was a man of fashion, careful about his cravats and always clad in elegant frock-coats and toppers. By the time that *Patience* had been performed often enough for it to have become familiar and influential, there walked into London, said G.B.S., William Butler Yeats who might have modelled himself on Bunthorne. He wore flowing dark garments and had a general air of artistic disarray and transcendental abstraction that went, according to Surbiton, with the writing of poetry: and he was a living proof of Wilde's assertion that nature copies art. Gilbert, alleged to have worked on Wilde, had anticipated Yeats.

When, about forty years after they were first published, G.B.S.'s muscial criticisms in *The Star* and *The World* were collected and published in four volumes, musicians and critics were astonished and even astounded, not by their wit and humour, which were to be expected, but by the knowledge of music they displayed and, more, by the veracity of his forecasts on the survival of musical reputations. Apart from a niggling review in *The Times Literary Supplement*, the critics were surprised by the lasting quality of the articles.

G.B.S., being mortal, had defects. He was less than fair to Brahms and inclined to over-praise Wagner, not so much for the music as for the political allegory which he fancied he detected in *Das Rheingold*, where Wagner is said to be pleading for the nationalisation of the means of production, distribution and exchange! He was muddle-headed about Schubert, but quick to praise Verdi, nor could he be deterred from telling his readers what a genius Mozart was. He loved

Mozart a little more than Beethoven. He was not the first to appreciate Elgar, but he was among the first, and his praise was resounding.

'Although I am rather a conceited man,' he told an audience at Malvern in 1929, 'I am quite sincerely and genuinely humble in the presence of Sir Edward Elgar. I recognize a greater art than my own, and a greater man than I can ever hope to be.'

Ernest Newman, who had no idea, when he was a young man in the provinces, that G.B.S. was writing in *The Star* and afterwards in *The World* the best musical criticism then being published, criticism that was not to be diminished in value by later critics, including Newman himself, read the three volumes of *Music in London, 1890–94*, in amazement that he could have been unaware for a moment that such brilliant work was being done. Reviewing the volumes in *The Sunday Times*, he accused himself of deplorable ignorance. Because of this ignorance, every line in *Music in London* is 'completely new to me. I do not know how these articles struck people at the time; but to-day they strike me as being far the most brilliant things that musical journalism has ever produced in this country, or is ever likely to produce.'

Such praise from a critic of Newman's distinction, a critic, moreover, who had often, and very skilfully, crossed swords with Shaw, was praise any man might be proud to receive.

Both Newman and the editor of *The Musical Times* remarked that G.B.S. was fortunate in his time of musical and dramatic *causerie*. People in the nineties were either less sensitive to criticism or more reluctant to issue writs for libel than people are to-day. It is a sad and disturbing fact that criticism so fiercely frank as G.B.S.'s would probably not now be published. The courts of law would be crowded with plaintiffs if it were. What would be done by the Luton Girls Choir if a contemporary critic were to write about their performances as G.B.S. wrote about the Bach Choir? 'Nothing can be more ruinous to the spirited action of the individual parts in Bach's music, or to the sublime march of his polyphony, than the dragging, tentative, unintelligent, half bewildered operations of a choir still in the stage of feeling its way from interval to interval and counting one, two, three, four, for dear life.' On another occasion, the Choir were informed that they 'were not within fifty rehearsals of any sort of real proficiency—in short, they were making an execrable noise under the impression that they were singing a Bach motet.' When they deserved his praise, they received it, but they seem very seldom to have deserved it.

Signor Randegger cannot have felt pleased when he was told that his conducting of *Don Giovanni* at Covent Garden was the most 'scandalously slovenly, slapdash and unintelligent performance of the orchestral part of a great work' that was ever heard in a leading European opera-house. Paderewski's feelings must have been mixed when he read that he, 'a man of various moods . . . was alert, humorous, delightful at his first recital: sensational, empty, vulgar, and violent at his second; and dignified, intelligent, almost sympathetic, at his third.' On the whole, however, he could take comfort from the criticism. The final quotation reveals the principles on which G.B.S. worked. Referring to complaints that his notices were full of personal feeling, he remarks that a criticism written without personal feeling is not worth reading; and follows this statement with a vivid example of the skill with which he turned complaints against him into tributes:

> 'It is the capacity for making good or bad art a personal matter that makes a man a critic. The artist who accounts for my disparagement by alleging personal animosity on my part is quite right: when people do less than their best, and do that less at once badly and self-complacently, I hate them, loathe them, detest them, long to tear them limb from limb and strew them in gobbets about the stage or platform. (At the Opera, the temptation to go out and ask one of the sentinels for the loan of his Martini, with a round or two of ammunition, that I might rid the earth of an incompetent conductor or a conceited and careless artist, has come upon me so strongly that I have been withheld only by my fear that, being no marksman, I might hit the wrong person and incur the guilt of slaying a meritorious singer.) In the same way, really fine artists inspire me with the warmest personal regard, which I gratify in writing my notices without the smallest reference to such monstrous conceits as justice, impartiality, and the rest of the ideals. When my critical mood is at its height, personal feeling is not the word: it is passion: the passion for artistic perfection—for the noblest beauty of sound, sight, and action—that rages in me. Let all young artists look to it, and pay no heed to the idiots who declare that criticism should be free from personal feeling. The true critic, I repeat, is the man who becomes your personal enemy on the sole provocation of a bad performance, and will only be appeased by a good performance. . . .'

The arts have flourished best in all ages of great criticism. When the critics are mealy-mouthed and unctuous and eager to keep in with prominent people, then, indeed, the arts decay. But the critic who conforms to G.B.S.'s creed, cannot hope to be popular with the criticised, and must reconcile himself to being at once the Ishmael of the arts and their finest friend, cursed and calumniated and excluded from agreeable company because he has been faithful to his cause.

63

There is a familiar story of 'Tay-Pay's'[1] only instruction to G.B.S. on his appointment to be *The Star's* musical critic. He could write what he liked, but 'for God's sake don't tell us anything about Bach's Mass in B Minor!' G.B.S. promised not to use any jargon, a promise that was easy to make, for he detested the stuff, but his impish temperament made him open his first article with the words: 'The number of empty seats at the performance of Bach's Mass in B Minor at St James's Hall on Saturday afternoon did little credit to the artistic culture of which the West End is supposed to be the universal centre.'[2]

But although he eschewed jargon, he did not disdain the use of technical terms when they were essential to his purpose; and he taught his readers to understand them. O'Connor did not complain of these technical terms because it soon became evident that the articles were widely read and, except among those who were derided in them, immensely popular. They probably increased the young paper's circulation.

There is a legend that G.B.S. wrote less about music than about politics in his articles in *The Star* and, later, in *The World*, and that he was liable to write about municipal trading when he should have been writing about roulades. This legend is not supported by the articles in collection. There is very little political propaganda in them, and none that is not apposite to the point in music he is making. When, for example, he was accused by 'young genius' of being 'flippant and unenlightened' because he did not 'tear around and proclaim the working man as the true knower and seer in Art', he retorted on his accusers with this piece of sociology which could, perhaps, be called political propaganda, but was strictly relevant to his argument and pertinent to the case for an increased audience for music:

'Take a laborer's son; let him do his boarding-school mostly on an empty stomach; bring him up in a rookery tenement; take him away from school at thirteen; offer him the alternative of starvation or 12 or 16 hours work a day at jerry building, adulterated manufactures, coupling railway waggons, collecting tramway fares, field labor, or what not, in return for food and lodging which no "animated clothes-peg" would offer to his hunter; teach him by every word and look that

---

[1] This nickname, which, according to the English, was the way in which O'Connor pronounced his initials, was detested by him. The surest way of incurring his contempt and wrath was to call him Tay Pay.

[2] It appeared on May 14, 1888. A selection of *The Star* articles was published in 1937 in the Collected Edition under the title of *London Music in 1888–1889 as Heard by Corno di Bassetto (Later Known as Bernard Shaw) With Some Further Autobiographical Particulars*.

he is not wanted among respectable people, and that his children are not fit to be spoken to by their children. This is a pretty receipt for making an appreciator of Beethoven.'

It is, indeed. But the feat has been accomplished, even by children who had not the good fortune G.B.S. had to be brought up in a home full of music. A love of music is not confined to any class. Many people who have the resources of all the musical academies and concert halls at their disposal if they choose to use them, have no more music in them than enables them to listen to a musical comedy and chant their way through Yip-i-addy-i-ay-i-ay. Gilbert Chesterton had no ear for music, though he was brought up in more comfortable circumstances than G.B.S. was. W. B. Yeats, whose upbringing was in a home so full of culture and aesthetics that normal people would have felt stifled in it, detested music. So did Dean Inge, who complained of vain repetitions of *amen* in anthems, and asserted that he could not tell the difference between God Save the Weasel and Pop goes the King.

Yet, in its substance, G.B.S.'s argument is sound, in relation to the time in which it was uttered. It is not sound now. The labourer's child has opportunities to-day that were not easily available to middle-class children in 1888. For that change in social conditions, G.B.S. and his political associates are partly responsible. But other people of a different political persuasion, are entitled to credit, too. G.B.S., better than most people, knew that the most determined opponents of proposals to raise the school age and abolish half-time employment of children in mills and factories were the working-people themselves. The Labour Party had to watch its step in Lancashire and Yorkshire when the raising of the school age was suggested. It can, of course, be argued in favour of G.B.S.'s mythical labourer's son that only 'the exceptional child of the working-class develops the ability which makes him a man of culture; but the same is true of a child of any class.

The two great services G.B.S. did to music were to smash the stale conventions of the age, and make its discussion interesting to people who would ordinarily have been discouraged from reading about it because of the tedious style in which the critics were accustomed to write. His articles appealed at once to the host of men and women who knew little about music and to the minority who loved it and were familiar with its technicalities. The skilled and the unskilled alike enjoyed G.B.S., and not only because he was uncommonly entertaining, but because he put his points explicitly.

He did not restrict himself to the West End of London. He was as ready to listen to a concert in a girls' school in the south suburbs of London or to visit a performance in the East End as he was to listen to concerts in the Albert Hall or operas in Covent Garden. All his sentences were fresh. 'Mr Docker', he told his readers, 'must cure his singers of the notion that choral singing is merely a habit caught in church, and that it is profane and indecorous to sing Handel's music as if it meant anything.' He praised skill whenever he found it, astounding people by telling them how excellent were the performances of Salvation Army brass bands at a time when the very thought of such a band was abhorrent to the cultured inhabitants of Holland Park. Discussing the cornet, he wrote that two cornet performances had left an abiding memory with him. One was *The Pilgrim of Love*, played by an itinerant artist outside a public house in Clipstone Street, Portland Place. (Observe how careful he is to report the details):

> 'The man played with great taste and pathos; but, to my surprise, he had no knowledge of musical etiquette, for when, on holding out his hat to me for a donation, I explained that I was a member of the press, he still seemed to expect me to pay for my entertainment: a shocking instance of popular ignorance.'

The end of the quotation is, of course, only his fun. We may be sure he gave the man as much as he could afford.

His praise was as graceful as his dispraise was damning. He scarified Madame Patti because of her spoilt *prima donna* manners; but he paid a compliment to an old clarionettist, Mr Lazarus, at St James's Hall, that must have warmed the old man's blood and sent him to his retirement with a thankful heart:

> 'Listening to the septet, it was impossible to avoid indulging in some stray speculations as to the age of Mr Lazarus. Fifty or sixty years ago, when the great clarionettist was beginning to rank as a veteran, the subject might have been a delicate one. To-day it is difficult to know how to treat him critically; for it would be absurd to encourage him as if he were a promising young player; and yet there is no use in declaring that he "played with his usual ability", because his ability is still, unfortunately for us, as far as ever from being usual. The usual clarionet player is stolid, mechanical, undistinguished, correct at best, vulgar at worst. A phrase played by Mr Lazarus always came, even from the unnoticed ranks of the wood wind at the opera, with a distinction and fine artistic feeling that roused a longing for an orchestra of such players. And his phrases come just that way still.'

A paragraph or two later, he delivers a body blow on the coughers who were so impatient to hear Mr Santley ballad-mongering that they made Madame Hass's playing of Beethoven's op. 110 sound like the accompaniment to hacking noises in a sanatorium. 'But when every possible excuse is made for the people who coughed, it remains a matter for regret that the attendants did not remove them to

Piccadilly, and treat their ailment there by gently passing a warm steam-roller over their chests.'

He was less considerate of the feelings of 'some vulgar and dis-respectful ruffian in the stalls last night', who announced each entrant in a loud, familiar voice. 'If this should meet the eye of that man, I ask him, as a personal favour to myself, to commit suicide. Nothing in life can become him like the leaving it.' He flayed a pretentious pianist. 'M. Vladimir de Pachmann gave his well-known pantomimic performance, with accompaniments by Chopin, a composer whose music I could listen to M. de Pachmann playing for ever if the works were first carefully removed from the pianoforte.'

But how generous he was with his help and praise when he found someone who deserved them. He had been invited to a party in celebration of a production of *A Doll's House*. Among the guests 'was a very quiet lady of forty or thereabouts, with some indescribable sort of refinement about her that made her seem to have lost her way and found herself in a very questionable circle. Nobody was taking any notice of her; so I charitably introduced myself (she pretended to know who I was) and tried to make her feel more at home.' Later in the evening when the after dinner entertainment was about to peter out because the resources of the company seemed to have been exhausted, 'our hosts had to play their last card. Could anybody play the Helmer piano and oblige us with a tune?

'There was general shaking of heads until it appeared that the quiet lady, neglected and unknown, could play some pieces. As she went to the piano we prepared ourselves for the worst and stopped talking, more or less. To encourage the poor lady, I went to the piano and sat beside her to turn over for her, expecting The Maiden's Prayer or an oldfashioned set of variations on The Carnival of Venice. I felt I was being good to her. After the first two bars I sat up. At the end of the piece (one of her own composition) I said, 'Has anyone ever told you that you are one of the greatest pianists in Europe?" Evidently a good many people had; for without turning a hair she said "It is my profession. But this is a bad instrument. Perhaps you will hear me at the Philharmonic. I am to play Beethoven's E Flat Concerto there." Her name is Agatha Ursula Backer-Grondhal. She played upon Helmer's pianoforte as it was never played upon before, and perhaps never will be again. A great artist—a serious artist—a beautiful, incomparable unique artist! She morally regenerated us all; and we remained at our highest level until we were dragged down by the shrieks and groans of two Italian waiters who started quarrelling among the knives in the saloon. . . . Later on it was felt that the evening would be incomplete without a song from me; and after some pressing I reluc-tantly consented. The guests then left precipitately; and the scene, a historic one in the annals of the theatre, closed.'

64

The finest service G.B.S. rendered his uninformed readers was to make them realise that music is much more than a melodious noise, that a composer is not merely a man bombinating in the void, but a man trying to express himself and state his vision of life, that a piece of music is an attempt to describe in sound something felt or seen or believed.

His success on *The Star* now made publishers who had rejected his novels, eager for his work. Fisher Unwin suggested in November 1888, that he should write another novel, but 'no, thank you: no more novels for me,' was his reply. 'Five failures are enough to satisfy my appetite for enterprise in fiction:

'I have no intention of lowering myself to the level of Bruce's spider. The success of future attempts must be guaranteed by a cheque for £500 for seven years' copyright. Otherwise the attempt will not be made.

'Seriously, I have no longer either time or inclination for tom-fooling over novels. And your repudiation of *Cashel Byron* is a positive relief to me; for I hate the book from my soul.

'I have just had a pretty novel running through *Our Corner* which you ought to read if you ever come across the volumes of that moribund magazine; but it would be of no use to you professionally. *Love Among the Artists* is the name. When you are tired of saleable novels, and want to read something really dainty, you will find it the very thing for you.'

But it was not the very thing for Mr Fisher Unwin, who, however, continued, but unsuccessfully, to tempt G.B.S. on to his lists.

65

He stayed on the staff of *The Star* for two years, during which time his reputation, but not his wages, steadily increased. On February 5, 1890, he resigned. 'Reviewing is hell,' he wrote to O'Connor, 'I had enough of it on *The Pall Mall Gazette*. I can do the best literary causerie in London (not a word about books in it); but nothing short of twelve guineas a week would tempt me to begin it. I hate literature. If I tumble to the ground I will avail myself of this soft place which you made for me so as to avert the painful spectacle of Corno di Bassetto left sitting on his bottom, but I think I shall pull through without a larger dose of adversity than I need to shake me out of my present groove. Nothing is as fatal to an artist as a regular income. . . .' Is it not incredible that the man who was writing these extraordinarily vivacious articles and helping very substantially to build up the circulation of his paper, was paid only two guineas a week?

It was during this service that, on September 7, 1889, he and William Archer went to Greenwich to see *Dorothy*, one of the most popular musical comedies ever produced on the English stage: the piece in which Marie Tempest, then almost unknown, instantly became a star. The libretto was written by B. C. Stephenson, and the music was composed by Alfred Cellier. The play had been performed nearly a thousand times in the West End, and the touring company, when Archer and G.B.S. saw it, had appeared in it 788 times. They liked it so little that they 'only stayed out 2 acts'.

G.B.S. fell into the common error of imagining that actors and actresses must be bored to death by repeating the same performance a great many times. But an actor's mind, if he is to be effective, must be alert all the time he is acting. If it is not, his performance falls flat. Moreover, and this is a factor of enormous importance, though it is generally disregarded, the audience changes every night. This change is more drastic for a touring company than it is for a company in the West End. Players performing in Torquay in one week and in Widnes in the next, find themselves contending with audiences so dissimilar that unless the acting is skilful and quick in response to the change of mood, the entire performance will be ruined. There is no room, therefore, for boredom in the performance of a play many times. Every performance is a fresh fight to be won, each audience is a new foe that must be reduced to submission.

G.B.S., writing of 'young persons doomed to spend the flower of their years in mechanically repeating the silliest libretto in modern theatrical literature, set to music which, pretty as it is, must pall somewhat on the seven hundred and eighty-eighth performance', was writing in total ignorance of acting as a craft. If he found 'a settled weariness of life, an utter perfunctoriness, an unfathomable inanity' pervading 'the very souls' of the company he saw at Greenwich, the inference any informed person would draw from this desolation would be that they were incompetent or idle. One smartly-conducted rehearsal would have put an end to their slackness.

But why, the reader enquires, are we treated to this digression on a suburban performance of an ancient musical comedy? The cause will presently appear. First, we must read what G.B.S. had to say about the leading lady:

'The ladies fared best. The female of the human species has not yet developed a conscience; she will apparently spend her life in artistic self-murder by induced Dorothitis without a pang of remorse, provided she be praised and paid regularly. Dorothy herself, a beauteous young lady of distinguished mien, with an immense variety of accents ranging from the finest Tunbridge Wells English (for genteel comedy) to the broadest Irish (for repartee and low comedy), sang without the slightest effort and without the slightest point, and was all the more desperately vapid because she suggested artistic gifts wasting in complacent abeyance.'

The actress who performed the part of Dorothy was G.B.S.'s elder sister, Lucy. The tenor was her husband, who is thus described by his brother-in-law: 'The tenor, originally, I have no doubt, a fine young man, but now cherubically adipose, was evidently counting the days until death should release him from the part of Wilder. . . .'

There was no nepotism in *The Star's* musical criticism.

Lucy, who had fled her mother's home the moment she was financially able to do so, had unaccountably married 'a little dumpling of an ex-insurance clerk whose pretty face seemed to be carved on a bladder of lard'. His name was Charles Butterfield, and he was entirely insignificant, no match in any way for Lucy. But like mother, like daughter. Lucinda had married an insignificant man, and so had Lucy. Lucinda Elizabeth had deserted her husband: Lucy told hers to depart, which he did without the slightest reluctance. The extraordinary fact is that they became good friends after their separation and eventual divorce. He would spend the evening with her in complete amity. When he died, his brother, Douglas, a blameless and successful business man, succeeded to his place, which he filled almost every evening until she died.

Lucy was a singular figure of a woman. She had talent which she could not use. Lively off the stage, she was wooden on it. She was unable to live in any comfort with her mother, but she became devoted to her bedridden mother-in-law, Mrs Butterfield, and was greatly esteemed by her and her family. Attractive to men, Lucy could have married well, as the phrase goes, but she married badly. She had a great deal of personal vivacity, and her friends were warmly attached to her, yet she seemed indifferent to them, and she failed to hold the love of her relatives. She was too like her mother to be able to live in comfort with her, and she enjoyed the society of her husband's conventionally suburban relatives more than she had ever enjoyed that of her own.

Mrs Butterfield, who had the discerning eye of the chronic invalid, saw that Lucy craved for security and regular life and the certainty that there would be enough money at the end of the month to meet the bills, and that the spurious bohemianism which delighted her son Charles would never satisfy her daughter-in-law. So she brought her into her house and family circle and gave her the kind of comfort she needed. The drunkard's child becomes a rigid teetotaller; the miser's son ends in the bankruptcy court; the children of the atheist become devout Roman Catholics or Theosophists; and the child of the roistering bohemian seeks a placid and uneventful life in the most conventional and demure suburb he can find.

For a long time, Lucy, rejoicing in the regularity of her new life, saw little or nothing of her mother and brother. She had become, mentally and spiritually, one of the Butterfields, and was no longer a Shaw. Later in her life, when the invalid was dead, she returned to her own family, but in so dull a state of mind that her brother found himself silent in her society. She became a figure of fun to her mother. Yet she shocked them both by publishing two small books of bitter essays in the form of letters of advice to a young girl. They were entitled *Five Letters of the House of Kildonnel* and *The Last of the Kildonnel Letters*, written ostensibly by the Lady Theodosia Alexandra Kildonnel to her infant god-daughter, The Honourable Theodosia Carmelita Kildonnel from Kildonnel Castle, Ballymoira, Co. Kerry.

The ideas expressed in the letters are obviously derived from her brother, but have none of his intensely religious feeling about life in general and social relations in particular. They are cynical, the bitter beliefs of a deeply disillusioned woman. She had been the star of her family, destined, in her mother's mind, to become not only a great singer, but the exponent of the superb system invented by George John Vandaleur Lee; and she had been a failure. The ugly duckling of the family, Sonny, who was shy and nervous and socially awkward, had risen, after a period when he seemed to be entirely detrimental, to a great height, and was still rising. Lucy had friends, especially in Dublin, who were devoted to her. There was enough of the family charm in her to make her attractive to women as well as to men; but she was a snob without a sense of style, and her mind was essentially commonplace. The fact that the *Letters* she published were supposed to have been written by The Lady Theodosia Alexandra Kildonnel to her god-daughter The Honourable Theodosia Carmelita Kildonnel, denoted Lucy's outlook on life. The rank of the correspondents had no relation whatsoever to the points made in the *Letters* which would have been as good or as bad if they had been addressed by Mrs Muldoon to Biddy Flanagan. But Lucy's thoughts were full of the lost glories of the bedraggled and down at heel county family that once were the Gurlys. It must have embittered her to learn that her spiritual home was with the Butterfields at Denmark Hill in the south suburbs of London.

The *Letters* are not ill-written, but they are sour. In the third of the second volume, she tells her god-daughter that self-sacrifice is 'a vice that leads of a surety to the destruction not only of your own well-being, but of that of everyone who comes within range of its blighting effects; it is a depravity that is always blatantly and aggressively obvious to those who piously practise it, and is calculated to drive the wholesomely sane who have the moral courage to be healthily and normally selfish into hopeless lunacy and even suicidal extinction.'

> 'This may seem an extravagant and outrageous contention to those who hold that the highest of which one is capable is the laying down of one's life for a friend. But if you stop for a moment to consider, Theodosia, it should not be a sentimental question of giving up your life for your friend, but a tremendous ethical problem of which life were the better worth preserving.'

The volume in which this *Letter* appears was published in 1908. *The Doctor's Dilemma* was performed for the first time in 1906. One sees, therefore, from whence Lucy drew her thoughts, despite the shock they gave to her brother.

But the book is not entirely derivative. Lucy was aware of failure. She had been carefully prepared for a great career in music. She could have married one of several able and brilliant men. But she had achieved no more than a tour in a popular musical comedy, and she had petered out as a singer. Her acting had no life in it. She had married an insignificant little fellow who was shoddy in every respect and destitute of the virtues of his decent suburban family. She had sought beauty, and been given ashes, and ashes are bitter when beauty is sought.

Lucy must have remembered *Major Barbara* when she caused The Lady Theodosia to advise The Honourable Theodosia to 'spread the Gospel of Wealth; denounce the vice of indigence, and remember the wisdom of the Preacher, "Money answereth all things".'[1] But perhaps she remembered, too, the shabby shifts of Synge Street and Victoria Grove, and thanked whatever god she had for the comfort and certainty of Denmark Hill.

66

His independence of mind had caused G.B.S. to resign his post as art critic of *The World* in 1889. The paper was owned by a woman who requested him to write favourable reports on pictures painted by her friends. She would allow him to publish equally favourable reports on the pictures painted by *his* friends. She went so far as to interpolate 'ecstatic little raptures' in his articles 'about minor Academy pictures by painters who invited her to tea in their studios', and was deeply pained when he remonstrated with her about her

[1] *Ecclesiastes* x. 19.

amiable and, she thought, harmless habit. He failed to convince her that she had no right to put her opinions over his signature, and so, in May 1889, he dismissed himself from her service. The man who had written so bluntly about his sister's performance in *Dorothy* was not likely to tolerate any nonsense from the proprietress of *The World*.

But he soon returned, though in a different capacity, to *The World's* staff. In 1890, the music critic, Louis Engel, had to leave the country in great haste. Archer promptly told Yates that G.B.S. was the only person in London who was fit to take Engel's place; and Yates offered him the post at a salary of five guineas, which was wealth to him. He left *The Star*, amid wails from O'Connor, who had been paying him two guineas. T.P. was less lavish with money than a sentimental Englishman, having heard his soothing and dulcet tones, would have expected him to be. He did not deliberately grind the face of the poor, but if a face should get in the way of his feet, well, well, and glory be to God, wasn't it a pity, but why do people not keep their faces out of the way of feet? The payment of salaries on *The Star* was on the low side, and there was no rule about the payment of expenses, except that the payment should be irregular and deferred for as long as the contributor's pocket could stand the strain.

On February 28, 1890, G.B.S., who was not a man to hurry over his dues from other people, though he was quick in paying his debts, wrote to H. W. Massingham, saying, 'I have been driven by destitution to make up my *Star* accounts; and I find that the paper owes me no less than £7 0s 1d since the 30th March, 1889, for expenses. . . . This does not, by the bye, include the expenses of the premiere at Amsterdam or Bayreuth or Bristol or anything outside London. . . . I find it is impossible for me to continue as I have been doing lately. This week I have had to attend five concerts; have advanced fourteen shillings from my exhausted exchequer; and have written the Bassetto column, all for two guineas. It cannot be done at the rate. If the column is to cover all the concerts, it is worth five guineas. If not, I must send in a notice nearly every morning and get decently paid for it. . . .'

Nevertheless, O'Connor howled like a distracted banshee when G.B.S., having given him fair warning, left him for *The World* and five guineas.

67

And now began the brilliant series of articles on music in *The World*, which have since been collected in three volumes, entitled *Music in London, 1890–1894*. The first article appeared on May 28, 1890, and it began with the following statement:

'Something had better be done about his Royal Italian Opera. I have heard Gounod's *Faust* not less than ninety times within the last ten or fifteen years; and I have had enough of it. Here is *Tristan und Isolde*, which we can no longer afford to do without, now that all the errand boys in New York can whistle it from end to end: yet to hear it I have to go to Germany—to cross that unquiet North Sea, the very thought of which sets my entrails aquake. *Tristan* is more than thirty years old: and as the composer died in 1883, at the age of seventy, I am sanguine as to the possibility of driving Mr Harris to produce it presently as "Wagner's new opera".'

Harris became in music to G.B.S. what Sir Henry Irving was later on to become in drama. The unfortunate impresario was belaboured until he must have felt intellectually black and blue, but the belabouring was not pointless abuse. It was conducted on two principles: one, that the proper way to conduct a fight was to look around for the strongest man on the field and go for him good and hard; and the other, that Wagner's operas ought to be performed in London even if Gounod's *Faust* was less often produced. These were sound principles.

The first was derived from the English working-class which had drawn it from the Bible: the principle that a game little chap, naked and with no weapon but a sling, such as David, deserved encouragement more than a great, hulking and uncircumcised giant, enclosed in armour plate, such as Goliath. The proletarian principle was strengthened by G.B.S.'s belief, one that is held by every good fighting man, that the way to train oneself in authority is to fight a man who is more than your match. This is the principle on which clever young politicians generally work: Joseph Chamberlain looked around for a bigger man than himself and found Gladstone; Lloyd George, in his turn, set about Chamberlain; Winston Churchill set about all the big men there were, in total disregard of whether they were on his side or not; and Mr Aneurin Bevan sets about Sir Winston without, however, doing Sir Winston any harm or himself much good.

It was on this principle, that G.B.S. fought so fiercely with Henry Irving. When he wished to lay about him in music, he looked around for a de Reszke or a Paderewski: he did not bother himself with the small fry, unless they looked like growing into great fish. Wagner, in point of popularity, was at this time a David in comparison with Gounod, the Goliath. G.B.S. was now immensely busy. The number of concerts he attended was remarkable, for he was conscientious in his attendance and would have starved rather than follow the custom practised by a modern dramatic critic, of criticising and condemning a play he had not seen.

But his musical pilgrimages, though they were strenuous, were not the total of his activities. He was still hard at work for The Fabian Society, and immediately before Christmas, 1889, the first edition of *Fabian Essays*, which he edited, to which he contributed two brilliant chapters, was published. It had a frontispiece by Walter Crane, in which a romantic-looking agricultural labourer belied the declaration of the Essayists that all labourers, urban and rural, were in an advanced state of malnutrition. The Society was its own publisher, and 1,000 copies of the *Essays* were issued: a number which was judged to be enough, since none of the seven, except Mrs Besant, was known to more than a small number of people, and Mrs Besant's renown was not then likely to send the generality of men and women running to the book-shops to buy her works. The Fabians themselves numbered only 150. The young people who governed the Society must have felt themselves audacious in issuing over 1,000 copies of their work. They were amazed when they found that the whole edition was sold out within a month.

> 'The subject of their volume', Pease writes, 'was far less understood by the public than is Syndicalism at the present day. And yet a six-shilling book, published at a private dwelling-house and not advertised in the press, or taken round by travellers to the trade, sold almost as rapidly as if the authors had been Cabinet Ministers.'[1]

A second edition of 1,000 copies was issued in March, 1890; and in the following September, arrangements were made with Walter Scott, the publisher, to issue a paper-back edition at a shilling. Before the edition appeared, 5,000 copies had been sold in advance, 'and some 20,000 more within the year'. In 1908, Scott published a six-penny edition, with a new preface by G.B.S. and 10,000 copies were sold in a few months. The circulation of this remarkable work in England alone was more than 46,000; and the number of copies of translations is unknown, but must have been large.

Time has 'dated' the book, and it is now more or less obsolete, except as an historical and literary document. The Essayists under-estimated the growth of Trade Unionism which has landed us all in the grip of the most powerful form of social, economic and political dictation that mankind has yet witnessed: a form of dictation which has not yet reached its peak of power.

The formidable fault in the Essays is the ignorance, almost total, of industrial conditions outside London displayed by the Essayists. The North was foreign territory to the seven. They were speculating in the dark, but, luckily, they knew that they were. They did not imagine that they were laying down the law once and for all. They

---

[1] *The History of the Fabian Society*, p. 88.

were laying it down only for the period of approach to the society they desired. Their *Essays* would, they realised, sooner or later fall out of date. Nevertheless, they were remarkable, far superior to the volume of *New Fabian Essays* published by their successors in 1952; and they made a profound change in the political thought of the time in which they were published.

The Fabians, moreover, were only at the beginning of their activities. There was a vast amount of research and study still to be done before they could reach the point towards which they were struggling. The Webbs had not yet met to form that extraordinary partnership which, more than any other individual activity, was to result in the Welfare State. Beatrice Potter was still a Herbert Spencerian individualist, though she was less amenable to her master's tuition than he wished her to be. Just as G.B.S. had to make his world in the theatre, creating not only an audience which could understand and appreciate his plays, but also creating actors and actresses who could understand and act them, so the Fabians had to create a body of opinion which would enable them to found the community they had imagined.

The Labour Party, as a separate political group, did not exist, nor was it until 1892 that Keir Hardie was elected to the House of Commons for West Ham. He was the only Labour man standing at the election that year, who was; and he caused aged men in clubs almost to swoon because he entered St Stephen's wearing a cloth cap instead of a glossy silk hat. They could hear in their minds the tumbrils rattling over the stony streets as they nattered to each other about this frightful outrage of a working-man wearing the headgear of his class as he walked into the Commons.

The two principal political parties were the Conservatives and the Liberals. There were also the Irish Nationalists who had only nuisance value. In 1885, Lord Salisbury took office as Prime Minister, and, except for Mr Gladstone's third and fourth ministries, both of which were brief, and Lord Rosebury's, which was also brief, the Conservatives were in power for about twenty years. How could the Fabians, when they published their *Essays*, foresee the enormous increase in power of the Trade Unions, the swift rise of the Labour Party, the decline and virtual elimination of the Liberals, and the disappearance of the Irish Nationalists, not only from Westminster, but from Ireland, where they were followed by the Sinn Feiners? It was surprising that the *Essays* were as impressive as they were.

Their publication involved G.B.S. in a great deal of unpaid labour. He had not only edited the volume, but had written two of its most brilliant chapters. Editing, for him, implied much more than merely inviting people to contribute to the work, and seeing the book through the press: it included frequent consultations with the other contributors and, in some instances, collaboration in writing chapters. The book was a joint effort of the seven. Each essay was carefully read and criticised by all the Essayists, Shaw, adding, with the consent of the author, passages which he thought would improve it. Throughout his life, he read Webb's scripts, as Beatrice testifies in her Diaries, putting vivacity into those parts of Webb's prose which were beginning to fall flat.

The fact that he received no payment for what he wrote, despite his need of money, did not deter him from doing the work as well as he was able. He sometimes neglected work for which he would be paid, so that he might do unpaid work for the Fabian Society, work, indeed, which left him out of pocket.

68

One result of the publication of *Fabian Essays* was important, though unforeseeable. Miss Beatrice Potter read them, and was more deeply impressed by Sidney Webb's contribution than by any of the others.

She was one of the nine daughters of Richard Potter,[1] a railway magnate of handsome appearance and forceful character, whose father, a Yorkshire man, had accumulated substantial means by his ability, his energy and his enterprise: qualities which the old man's grand-daughter did not sufficiently appreciate and was to do her utmost, by her deplorable propaganda, to render nugatory or, at least, difficult. Springing from what is often called humble stock, though what is humble in it is hard to perceive, he added business to business, a general provision shop to a farm, and cotton to both.

Both these Potters were Richard. The elder, who was a Radical and a Unitarian in times when it was discreditable to be either, entered the House of Commons as a member for Wigan in 1832, and there became an intimate friend of Richard Cobden and John Bright. The younger Richard graduated at London University, of which his father was a founder, and was called to the Bar without, however, having any intention of practising at it.

His good looks, his intelligence, and his amiable nature made him careless and neglectful of his ability, and he meant to spend his life in leisurely culture, travelling in comfort to the more civilised parts of the earth, and enjoying himself, when he was tired of travel, in a pleasant seat in one of the Home Counties.

In Rome, he met Laurencina Hayworth, an austere girl with gentle eyes which had a gleam of humour in them, and instantly fell

[1] There was a son who died when he was three years old.

in love with her. She came of the same sort of North Country stock as himself. Her father belonged to the section of the working-class who were known in those days as 'domestic manufacturers', that is to say, people who did their work at home instead of in a factory or mill. They were weavers and spinners. Lawrence Heyworth, the father of Laurencina who presumably, derived her ugly Christian name from her father, followed the hideous fashion of giving daughters faked masculine names. It did not deter Richard Potter from wooing and winning its owner.

They married and settled themselves 'as mere *rentiers*', according to their daughter's opinion, on an estate in Hertfordshire; where, after several years of happy life, misfortune befell them. The Famine of the Forties had begun in Ireland. There was widespread poverty in Great Britain and, especially, in Scotland. A financial crisis in 1847–8, by which time the Famine in Ireland had devastated the population, swept away a large part of Mr Potter's fortune. The Irish were fleeing from their country in great numbers, and times were troubled and turbulent: 1848 was nicknamed 'the Year of Revolutions', for not only did Louis Philippe abdicate from the throne of France, but Louis Napoleon became President of a French Republic, in preparation for another empire that was to crash ignominiously; and there were revolutions in Austria, Germany, Hungary, Italy, Poland and Spain. To lose the greater part of one's fortune at such a time seemed certain to bring poverty on the loser for the rest of his life.

But Richard Potter came of good energetic stock, and so did his wife. While she was busy upsetting the balance of the sexes, by producing nine daughters to one son, he set about recovering his prosperity. He was fortunate in his father-in-law—his own father had died several years earlier—who had taken a lead in promoting railways. Mr Heyworth made his son-in-law, whose gift for friendship stood him in great stead at this time, a director of the Great Western Railway. One of his schoolfellows, W. E. Price, who remained his friend for life, offered him a partnership in his timber-yard in Gloucester. In a short while, Potter, by his personal ability, improved upon his gifts from heaven, and became a very distinguished man of business: chairman of the Great Western Railway, President of the Grand Trunk Railway of Canada, and director or promoter of numerous other enterprises. He was a peculiar mixture of motives and beliefs. He liked good living, and he retained a childlike faith in the divine government of the universe in the terms in which it had been taught to him when he was a child. His daughter remarks of him that, incredible as it may seem, he still, in his middle and old age, repeated the prayer 'taught to him at his mother's lap: Gentle Jesus, meek and mild, look upon a little child.'

This remarkable man who read Dante in the original and was a lover of Shakespeare and Plato, reading Jane Austen and Thackeray with equal affection, and admiring Edmund Burke, Thomas Carlyle and John Henry Newman without the slightest sensation of intellectual discomfort at such a singular combination of affections, treated his daughters as if they were his equals in experience and knowledge, discussing with them 'not only his business affairs, but also religion, politics and problems of sex', recommending Beatrice, when she was thirteen, to read Fielding's *Tom Jones*, which was then reputed to be very strong meat even for men, a reputation it still had at the turn of the century when Mrs Pearl Mary Theresa Craigie, who was widely known and popular as John Oliver Hobbes, a novelist, created a perturbed discussion in the press by going further than Mr Potter. He had advocated *Tom Jones* only as reading for girls. It was perilous stuff for boys.

But John Oliver Hobbes recommended it as suitable reading for girls *and* boys; and there was great agitation and anxiety in many homes in consequence. One boy read it without perceiving any offence in it, though he felt great contempt for Tom on two counts: first, that he was a great gawk, and, second, that he never had the idea of earning his living when he set out on his peculiar adventures.

Potter adored his austere wife, who was a very bossy woman, and, therefore, obviously her daughter Beatrice's mother, and was, his daughters thought, 'far too long suffering of Mother's arbitrary moods', but as *she* thought that he was too submissive to his horde of daughters, honours were easy. Nevertheless, he was the man in authority over his house.

69

Beatrice Potter was more her father's than her mother's child, because, perhaps, she was more like her mother than her father. Laurencina was almost forty before Beatrice 'became aware of her existence', and she seems to have had a poor opinion of her singular daughter. 'Beatrice', she wrote in her diary, 'is the only one of my children who is below the average in intelligence'. Highly educated, intelligent within the degree of her melancholy temperament, determined to have her own way, disturbed in her soul by her inability to reconcile the facts of life with her faith, and continually harassed by her failure to find any firm footing for her spirit in a belief that would allow her to face the contradictions of existence with fortitude, Mrs Potter was less happy than she might have been, despite the deep devotion of her husband, the security of her fortunate circumstances, and the variety of character and temperament in her daughters which should have made them perpetually interesting to her.

It was in this remarkable home, well found and filled with extraordinary people, that Beatrice Potter grew up.

Two other important factors in her making must be mentioned: the first that Herbert Spencer was a close friend of her father and of her: the second, that there was a strain in the Potter blood which accounted for the oddity of most of the family. Beatrice's paternal grandfather had married 'a tall, dark woman of Jewish type who read Hebrew and loved music'. This unhappy lady developed a desire to lead the Jews back to Jerusalem, a desire not usually supposed to be demented, and got as far as Paris, 'alone and without her fancied following'. She had to be confined in a lunatic asylum. Her strain was powerful in its effect on the Potters.

Beatrice, who was a handsome woman with a love of colour and clothes which she could not always control, had a look about her that was either gipsy or Jewish. Her love of finery, which shamed her, would suddenly run riot, and she would adorn herself very recklessly, but becomingly in clothes that would have seemed garish on other women.

But her sense of style was defective. She was never well dressed, though she was often dressed attractively, Dining with her and Sidney one night, and seeing her stretched on the floor of their drawing-room in Grosvenor Road in her favourite position, close to the fire, with her hand outstretched to the coals as if, as was probably true, she was perpetually cold—Sir William Nicholson's portrait of her, now hanging in the London School of Economics, catches this characteristic habit—I saw that one of her stockings was in ropes round her leg. There was always a stocking in ropes round everything she did. She lacked the last touch of grace and distinction that is the crown of femininity.

Her childhood was less happy than it ought to have been in a comfortable home, full of lively people. Her father had a nature so rich and buoyant that his children might have been expected to find in him alone ample cause for happiness. His financial misfortune had increased his quality, proving that he was a resourceful man, who, having taken a toss, did not lie down and whine, but got up and stood on his feet and began his life again: a man full of character and resource and determination, with the gift, rare in men of his sort, of enlivening his home and enriching it with his abundant personality.

Her mother was of a different sort: an intellectual prig, inclined to be morbid and moody, devoted to her husband as she had been to her father, shocked by the loss of her husband's fortune, and deeply disappointed because she had produced a long brood of daughters and only one son, who had died young. The regiment of women she had conceived troubled her. 'Her daughters were not the sort of women she admired or approved. She had been brought up "a scholar and a gentlewoman": her daughters refused to be educated and defied caste conventions. For the most part they were unmistakably Potters. . . .'

So her daughter, Beatrice, whom she liked least of her children, writes in *My Apprenticeship*. 'But besides these untoward circumstances my mother was cursed with a divided personality; she was not at peace with herself.

> 'The discords in her nature were reflected in her physiognomy. In profile, she was, if not ugly, lacking grace: a prominent nose, with an aggressive bridge, a long straight upper lip, a thin-lipped and compressed mouth, a powerful chin and jaw, altogether a hard outline, not redeemed by a well-shaped but large head. Looked at thus, she was obviously a managing woman, unrelenting, probably domineering, possibly fanatical.[1] But her full face showed any such interpretation of her character to be a ludicrous libel. Here the central feature, the soul of the personality, were the eyes, soft hazel brown, large but deep set, veiled by overhanging lids and long eyelashes set off by delicately curved and pencilled eyebrows: eyes uniting in their light and shade the caress of sympathy with the quest of knowledge. To this outstanding beauty were added fine glossy hair, an easily flushed fair skin, small flashing teeth, a low musical voice, pretty gestures, and long delicate hands: clearly a woman to charm, perhaps inspire.'

When, in 1884, Beatrice met John Bright at a political demonstration in Birmingham, three years after her mother's death, and she said to him, 'I think you knew my grandfather, Lawrence Heyworth,' Bright replied, 'Then you are the daughter of Laurencina Heyworth —one of the two or three women a man remembers to the end of life as beautiful in expression and form.'

This singular woman seems not to have liked her daughter Beatrice, who disliked her. The 'absence of affection between us was all the more pitiful because, as we eventually discovered, we had the same tastes, we were puzzling over the same problems; and she had harboured, deep down in her heart, right up to middle life, the very ambition that I was secretly developing, the ambition to become a publicist.' Like Lucy Carr Shaw, Beatrice Potter resembled her mother too closely to be able to live with her in comfort and happiness. But, unlike Lucy, Beatrice discovered her mother's quality later in life. Mrs Potter disliked women. So did her daughter. If she was a managing and domineering woman, 'possibly fanatical', so was

[1] This description of her mother's face in profile is not supported by the portrait of Mrs Potter which is reproduced in *My Apprenticeship*, where the face is certainly not ugly in any degree.

Beatrice, who owed far more of her character and disposition to her mother than she owed to her father, a man of such charm and distinction that he captivated Herbert Spencer, a man not easily captivated, as George Eliot discovered.

Beatrice, in her early youth, entered the period of neurotic religious fervour which many able women experience in their girlhood, as Florence Nightingale and Annie Besant did, and she never entirely withdrew from it. In this, too, she derived from her mother. Her solitude in her childhood created a need for companionship that sent her down to the kitchen, where she found it among the domestic servants, 'to whom as a class I have an undying gratitude.' Sickly and solitary, bored by her surroundings, her unhappiness and ill-health and her inability to sleep, an inability from which she suffered throughout her life, she found a warmth of feeling in the servants' hall which relaxed her hardening heart and gave her relief from her morbid emotions. 'I have a vivid memory of stealing and secreting a small bottle of chloroform from the family medicine chest as a vaguely imaginative alternative to the pains of living and the ennui of living; and of my consternation when one day I found the stopper loose and the contents evaporated.'

When she was ten years old she committed her thoughts on the education of women to paper. She found great fault with it. At fourteen her religious faith began to slip away from her. 'Christ seems to have been separated from me by a huge mass of worldliness and vanity . . . I am very wicked. I feel as if Christ can never listen to me again. Vanity, all is vanity. I feel that I have transgressed deeply, that I have trifled with the Lord. I feel that if I continue thus, I shall become a frivolous, silly, unbelieving woman, and yet every morning when I wake, I have the same giddy confident feeling and every night I am miserable.

'The only thing is to give up any pleasure rather than to go into society; it may be hard, in fact I know it will, but it must be done, else I shall lose all my remaining sparks of faith, and with those all the chances of becoming a good and useful woman in this world, and a companion of our Lord in the next. December 23, 1872, Beatrice Potter. May God help me to keep my resolution.'

She now went through the period of juvenile disturbance when she toyed with the thought of becoming a Roman Catholic: the period of despair when the young abandon hope and are ready to sacrifice their minds to their emotions and give up all effort to understand anything. She was in Rome then, in 1880. She was reading philosophical and 'serious' works with great assiduity, and her brain was tired. But not so tired that she could surrender to Rome. 'It is impossible', she wrote in her diary about this time, 'for a woman to live in agnosticism', but she found it equally impossible to live in servile submission to celibate priests. Ornate and beautiful ceremonies were not enough. The pretty lights on the altar were insufficient for her needs. In 1876, she had 'shaken off the chains of the beautiful old faith', and now hoped that she might rise to a higher one.

'This rejection of all traditional religion . . . was made easier for me because it was during the autumn of 1876 that I thought I had reached a resting-place for the soul of man, from which he could direct his life according to the dictates of pure reason, without denying the impulse to reverence the Power that controlled the Universe. This resting-place was then termed, by its youngest and most uncomprising adherents, the Religion of Science. The God was the Unknowable: the prophet was Herbert Spencer,' a philosopher now so discredited that he is not even mentioned by Bertrand Russell in his *History of Western Philosophy*. 'Prayer might have to go,' Beatrice confided to herself, 'but worship would remain.' But it was prayer that remained for her.

She was eighteen when she repudiated traditional religion and put her trust in a god made in the image of T. H. Huxley and John Stuart Mill. But when she was an old woman, she trudged along the Embankment to St Paul's Cathedral to find in evensong and private prayer the consolation she had failed to find elsewhere.

70

Her sister Kate, after an apprenticeship under Miss Octavia Hill, had become a rent-collector in Whitechapel. This was not a means of earning a livelihood: it was a means of learning how the poor lived. Young women, and even young men, of wealthy families in the Victorian era, periodically had a fit of remorse for their affluence and comfortable lives which sent them slumming. There was the Kyrle Society which humbugged its members with the belief that if the poor were supplied with reproductions of great works of art, they would not only be greatly uplifted, but would no longer feel that poverty was unendurable. There was indiscriminate charity, which benefited chiefly the hypocrites and rascals, leaving unhelped those who were genuinely in need. And there were the scientific investigators, the least pleasing of the lot, who went about with little notebooks observing the queer habits of the strange animals who lived in overcrowded areas and were almost chronically underfed. Kate was one of these. She made entries in her little notebook, but what was the result of her entries is unknown.

Beatrice first became aware of the poverty of the poor while she was staying with her sister. She does not state how this knowledge was acquired, but presumably she helped Kate to collect her rents: a method of informing oneself about poverty which is likely to be misleading, for those who are most vocal about their inability to pay their rent are seldom short of the means to pay it, and are more inclined to spend it elsewhere.

Whatever it was she learnt about poverty then seems not to have made much impression on her mind. She was too much preoccupied by her household affairs, for, following the death of her mother, she had become her father's housekeeper, she being the elder of his two unmarried daughters. She was also his business associate. Her responsibilities had the effect that Florence Nightingale's release from the trivialities that delighted her silly mother and sillier sister had on her. 'From being an anaemic girl, always paying for spells of dissipation or study by periods of nervous exhaustion, often of positive illness, I became an exceptionally energetic woman, carrying on, persistently and methodically, several separate and, in some ways, conflicting phases of life—undergoing, in fact, much of the strain and stress of a multiple personality.'

She was still educating herself, but she had not yet come to any conclusion about her purpose in life. She knew quite well what she did not wish to do, to make 'a good marriage' or to be a domesticated daughter, giving to her father what ought to be given to a husband of notable employment; but she still did not know what she did desire. She read Goethe intensively, and she solved algebraic problems until the gipsy in her made her throw her books aside and plunge into what she called dissipation: that is to say, a dance or two or a dinner party or an outing on a river. Her married sisters, wise in their connubial experience, reasoned with her and rebuked her. What was the sense of all this intellectuality she was pursuing so tirelessly, so greatly to the detriment of her health? She was just showing off! . . .

They invaded her room to tear her away from Euclid; and were dismayed when she rounded on them and ordered them out. Nevertheless, they had reason on their side. A young woman who rose at five in the morning to read deep works, and spent the rest of the day organising and supervising a household was clearly seeking trouble. Such earnest women can only be convicted of folly by a nervous breakdown. But Beatrice, so she says, found that her early morning studies were preserving her health.

Three hours before breakfast with Herbert Spencer's *Principles of Psychology* were meat and drink to her. 'These quiet three hours of study are the happiest ones of the day. Only one trouble continually arises—the stimulus a congenial study gives to my ambition, which is continually mortified by a gleam of self-knowledge; meeting with the most ordinarily clever person forces me to appreciate my own inferiority. And yet, fool that I am, I can't help feeling that could I only devote myself to one subject, I could do something. . . . If I could rid myself of that mischievous desire to achieve, I could defend the few hours I devote to study, by the truly satisfactory effect it has on my physical nature. It does keep me in health—whether through its direct influence on my circulation or through the indirect effect of a certain self-satisfaction it induces. Dissipation doesn't suit me, morally or physically; and I don't see why I shouldn't be true to my own nature and resist it.' A year later, however, she made this record in her diary: 'In this whirl of town society life the superficial part of my small intellect and the animal part of my nature are alike stimulated.'

It was not until the autumn of 1883 that she began seriously to follow the way of life she was to pursue for the rest of her existence. She had joined the Charity Organisation Society, of which she was to become a dangerous opponent in later life, acting as one of its visitors in the slums of Soho; but she very sensibly realised that the down and outs, the drunkards and the wastrels 'could not more be regarded as a fair sample of the wage-earning class than the "sporting set" of London could be considered representative, either in conduct or intelligence, of the landed aristocracy and business and professional class'. She determined, therefore, to make herself familiar with the decent working-class whose pride and self-respect is as strong and fierce as that of any other class in the country.

Among the servants in her father's house, she discovered, was a poor relation, Martha Mills, her nurse. Martha was one of her mother's kindred, belonging to a family of weavers in Bacup, and she had spent all but the first eighteen years of her life as Mrs Potter's companion and, eventually, nurse to her children: a woman greatly loved by those whom she served. Martha was known to the Potter children as 'Dada' or 'Da', and it was through her that Beatrice became for a time a member of a working-class family in the North: her own kindred, though they did not at first know this fact.

'Da' had told her of some working-class relations of the Potters who still lived in Bacup, people called Aked, and the result of this revelation was 'a pious fraud', as Beatrice calls it. 'Da' and she would pay a long visit to her kindred, but Beatrice would be known as Miss Jones, a farmer's daughter from Monmouth.

This was the beginning of a sort of innocent duplicity which was to characterise the work of the Webbs in their social enquiries. It was, I maintain, innocent and intended only to conciliate those who might have been offended and distrustful of the Webbs' intentions; but I have known Fabians who deeply disapproved of it and were inclined to consider it a sign of their lack of scruples, a charge which was also brought against them by many people in political and social life who were far from being Fabians. It was commonly made, without justice, in my belief, during the time that the Royal Commission of the Reform of the Poor Law was making its enquiries. The Webbs were short of grace in some respects, but their conduct in their social investigations was selfless, animated only by a social idealism which can best be described as religious.

The beginning of this innocent duplicity was made in the chapel-keeper's cottage in Bacup. At no time of her life did Beatrice forget that there is an aristocracy and a middle-class of working men and women with a code of honour as fine and sensitive as that of any other group of people; and that the fairly common conception of the working-people as mainly, if not entirely, composed of graceless and greedy men and women, living without an honourable thought in their heads in conditions that are often squalid, is so far from the fact that it may be denounced as shamefully false. The great tradition of self-respect and pride in which the majority of working-class people were bred is in grave danger in these days when men and women are encouraged to sponge on the community; but it is not a sentimental delusion to believe that when the Welfare State has steadied itself, our people will prove themselves to be what they have always been, an upright and proud and valiant race.

71

The visit, inevitably, was a short one, but it was repeated twice, in 1886 and 1889, nor was her identity revealed to her relations until the last day of her second visit. 'I told my gentle cousins who I was. I feared they would be offended: on the contrary, they were delighted, and glad I had not told them before they got to know me.'

The deepest impression Beatrice received during these visits to her relatives was of profound piety. Men become what they believe, and these upright mechanics and millhands of the eighteen-eighties, a period when, as Beatrice was often to say during her campaign to reform the Poor Law, most of the working-class were living in the 'moress' of destitution—she invariable turned long *a*'s into short *e*'s— maintained a way of life which was incompatible with any suggestion of squalor and malnutrition.

We can detect in her account of her experience with her poor relations in Bacup the impulse which resulted in the singular woman who became the wife of Sidney Webb. We can see, too, how valuable was this experience to her later on when she became a freelance bureaucrat and was inclined, as all bureaucrats are, to treat people

214

as if they were no more than names on card indexes, carefully filed away from all human understanding. In the middle of her desire for more and more regimentation, there was a recollection of the upright mechanics and millhands of Bacup who kept the faith their Lord had died in anguish and great pain to create.

Beatrice herself perceived the value of her expeditions to Bacup in the shaping of her mental outlook on life. She had decided to become an investigator of social conditions.

72

Her mind was detached to a remarkable degree. Charity was not the motive power which sent her into the East End to make enquiries into destitution. That was the impulse which drove her sister Kate to collect rents, so that she might learn who were in need and who were not. Beatrice, in her study of science, had acquired some of the cool and detached manner which scientists, quite untruthfully, are said to possess. 'I had never been moved by "hard cases",' she says, because they 'make bad law. What impelled me to concentrate on the condition of the people as the immediate question for investigation was the state of mind in the most vital centres of business enterprise, of political agitation and of academic reasoning.'

The time was full of divided beliefs about the condition of the people. Rule-of-thumb opinions were becoming more and more discredited. There was a clearer perception of the fact that the industrial system had reached a point in its development at which a workman's ability to govern his affairs in disregard of other workmen was not only declining, but must soon disappear. Artisans throughout the industrial North were learning to cooperate not only in their relations with their employers, but in their domestic relations. Robert Owen, that fool of genius, had taught them a lesson in cooperation that they were never to forget, even if they had no liking for the extremities of life in common which he commended.

The workman was not greatly interested in, was not much aware of, the controversy which raged among the thinkers of the age. Was the poverty of the many a necessary condition of the wealth of the nation, which seemed to be considered as something abstract and separate from working-class life, and of its progress in civilisation? How far was it safe to let uneducated or insufficiently educated people participate in the government of the country? Ought Trade Unions to be tolerated? These were not academic questions, as they seemed, perhaps, to be when they were first mooted, as we to-day, when we are governed by Trade Unions, have cause to realise. What was poverty? Could it be abolished? Was the world to be ruled by a small group of very able people or by an uninformed and disinterested mob with a short memory and little or no capacity for sustained thought?

These were the problems that troubled thinkers in 1884. They were still troubling the generation of thinkers who were on their heels. H. G. Wells was asking such questions in *The New Machiavelli* nearly thirty years later. Seventy years later, Professor Gilbert Murray despaired of democracy which, he declared, did no more than prepare the path for corrupt dictators. The proletariat, he said, could not govern. It would not be the proletariat if it could. The questions continue to be asked by a bewildered and dismayed generation which has discovered with mingled fear and disgust that the proletariat can be as indifferent to the general comfort of the community in a Welfare State as the landed gentry and the industrial lords were to the well-being of working people in the eighteenth century and the first half of the nineteenth. The lightning strikers who deliberately withhold their labour at the moment when it will cause the greatest inconvenience and hardship to the generality of people, and mostly to other members of their own class, are little removed from the state of mind of Mr Bounderby and Mr Gradgrind in *Hard Times*.

Beatrice was better situated for hearing such discussions than the majority of men and women. Her brothers-in-law alone were an informative group of very able men. They included Alfred Cripps, afterwards Lord Parmoor, the father of Sir Stafford Cripps: Leonard, afterwards Lord, Courtney of Penwith, who was at that time Financial Secretary to the Treasury in Gladstone's second Administration; Henry Hobhouse, a country gentleman of great distinction; and, later on, Robert Durning Holt, a member of a famous firm of Liverpool shipowners; Daniel Meinertzhagen, a great banker; and Arthur Playne. The most important of her relations, however, was Charles Booth, who had married her cousin Mary Macaulay.

Booth, a wealthy shipowner and merchant, is celebrated in the history of sociology for his great work, *Life and Labour in London*, to which Beatrice was allowed to contribute chapters. Booth's book, in the nature of such works, is now out of date. The conditions it reports no longer exist. But it was an essential item in the reconstruction of English life, and its influence was wide and deep. Booth was an individualist who had little or no sympathy with Beatrice Potter's socialism and would have abhorred her subsequent communism; but she was still an individualist when she worked for him, and he found her a useful assistant, despite her periodical flights of morbid emotion. He belonged to the remarkable hierarchy of great business men and merchants who were as far removed from the anarchy of the early industrialists as they were from the raucous revolutionaries who asserted, though they seldom believed, that the unskilled labourer was fit to rule the world.

The part these men played in the prevention of poverty has never been adequately acknowledged. Booth, in his famous work, and Seebohm Rowntree, in his similar work on a smaller scale, *Poverty: a Study of Town Life*, the setting for which was the cathedral city of York, provided the facts on which the new merchant adventurers, greater and more daring than their Elizabethan predecessors, founded their schemes. Such men as the Rowntrees, the Cadburys, the Leverhulmes, the Frys, the Willses, and many other wealthy business men, were as influential in making the vast social changes that have occurred in our time as any other group of people, especially in the matter of housing estates. Nor were these the only men outside the ranks of politicians who greatly helped to make the change. A man of meagre means, Ebenezer Howard, who began the housing estate at Letchworth, and Canon and Mrs Barnett, of Toynbee Hall, who were active in the East End of London, and, eventually, in the creation of the Hampstead Garden Suburb, were not less active in the reforms that have altered the face of our country profoundly in my lifetime.

The first Fabians were more akin to such men as I have named than they were to the spouting demagogues and maudlin visionaries who were crowding into the Labour world. Such people, and especially the woolly-witted dreamers, were repulsive to G.B.S., who denounced one of them in terms that ought to have taken his hide off. In three pages of his fine, clear handwriting, he told this man what he thought of him.

'You twaddle about your principles and your ideals and your purity to an extent that would nauseate a chaplain to a girls' school. . . . By God, Johnson, I blush for you—I am ashamed of Manchester—I apologise to the British nation for associating Socialism with men who set about making the millennium as children set about making a mud-pie.'

G.B.S. and the Webbs and the Fabians would have found Charles Booth and Seebohm Rowntree and even that bold buccaneer, the first Lord Leverhulme, more congenial to them than the emotional rag tag and bobtail of the Independent Labour Party, who thought they had solved a problem when they had merely shed tears over it.

73

Her first close experience of working-people had been with its finest representatives, the devout and self-respecting millhands of Bacup. Now, she was to come into close contact with 'the submerged tenth', as they were then called, in the East End. She began, in the time she could snatch from the management of her father's household, by collecting rents in tenement buildings, making enquiries and investigations for the Charity Organization Society, and collecting facts for Booth. She spent about four years in this work, distracted in the middle of it by the sudden paralysis of her father in 1885. The rent collecting and the special investigations had to be abandoned, so that she might look after him and his house and affairs.

In 1886, however, he was induced to give his son-in-law, Daniel Meinertzhagen, a general power of attorney which relieved Beatrice of a labour which she could not efficiently or easily cope with. Her married sisters arranged to take four-month turns in caring for their father. Gradually, therefore, she was able to resume some of her tasks, and she spent a good deal of time in observing dock labourers in their daily scramble for work.

The contrast between her early morning labours in the East End and some of her evening entertainments was striking. The young woman who stood outside the dock gates watching the casual labourers fight for a day's employment or turning away in despair because they had failed to catch the foreman's eye, would dine in the evening with a company which included John Morley, Arthur Balfour, and a surprising person, a manufacturer of nails, from Birmingham, Joseph Chamberlain, who had incurred the Queen's enmity because he was reputed to be a Republican.

She was becoming known for her peculiar researches, and her reputation was enhanced when, in *The Nineteenth Century* for October 1887, she published her first essay as a recognised social investigator. It was an article on *Dock Life in East London*. She was modest about it, calling it scamped work because of lack of time, and treating it as superficial; but its publication stimulated her to her first big piece of enquiry. Sir James Knowles, the editor of the magazine, invited her to lunch, and not only agreed to accept the article she proposed to write on Sweated Labour, but incited her to write one on Co-operation.

The article on Sweating became four articles, all of which appeared in *The Nineteenth Century*, between October 1887, and October 1888. Two of them were republished in Booth's first volume, together with one on *The Jewish Community of East London*. It was remarkable enough that a young woman of twenty-nine, brought up in a cultivated and wealthy home, should have written these articles, but the way in which her knowledge was acquired was still more remarkable. She had herself trained as a trousers-presser, and then went to work in a sweat-shop in Stepney. It was this episode in her life which G.B.S., nearly sixty years later, included in *The Millionairess*, in a scene entirely irrelevant to the rest of the play.

74

Her experience in the East End of London, so different not only from her own conditions of life, but from those of her poor relations in Bacup gave Beatrice Potter a severe shock. She was still a Liberal with Tory tendencies, still essentially opposed to any kind of collectivism. She had ventured into queer assemblies, such as The Hall of Science, and had been repelled by Mrs Besant's 'rabid Socialism, embittered by personal suffering against the morality and the creed of Christendom', and she had had a chance encounter in the British Museum with Eleanor Marx, the neurotic daughter of Karl, in the spring of 1883, but was not much impressed by her. Of Karl Marx himself she seems to have known very little. He is described in her diary as a 'socialist writer and refugee'. Outwardly, she was the same woman that she had been before she went to work in Stepney, but inwardly her mind and spirit were in a ferment.

> 'The contrast between the sweated workers of East London and the Lancashire textile operatives made me realise how the very concentration of wage-earners in the factory, the iron-works and the mine had made possible, in their case, what the sweater's workshop, the independent craftsman's forge and the out-worker's home had evaded, namely, a collective regulation of the conditions of employment, which, in the Factory Acts and Mines Regulation Acts, and in the standard rates of wages and the normal working day of the Trades Unions on the other, had, during the latter part of the nineteenth century, wrought so great an improvement in the status of this regulated section of the World of Labour.'

The incipient bureaucrat in her rejoiced.

The vast difference between the regulated factory workers in Bacup and the unregulated workers in the East End made her eager to investigate more closely the great Co-Operative Movement in the North of England and the Lowlands of Scotland, a movement which was still feebly feeling its way in London and the South. The task was not easy to perform. Booth wished her to do a difficult job of investigation into the general conditions of women's work: a subject which attracted her. Moreover, he doubted if she was qualified to make an enquiry into the Co-Operative Movement that would be of much value. This doubt she, too, felt, but her pride was roused by Booth's depreciation.

She received another check when, during a visit to the Mandell Creightons at Cambridge[1] she met Professor Alfred Marshall, to

[1] Mandell Creighton, a man of great charm, learning and wit, subsequently became Bishop of London. He and his wife were close friends of Beatrice.

whom she confided her ambition. Did he, she enquired, think she could achieve it. Yes, he thought she could, but it was unusual—not the task to which he thought her best suited. 'There is one thing that *you* and only you can do—an enquiry into the unknown field of female labour. You have, unlike most women, a fairly trained intellect, and the courage and capacity for original work; and you have a woman's insight into a woman's life! There is no man in England who could undertake with any prospect of success an enquiry into female labour. There are any number of men who could write a history of Co-Operation. . . . If you devote yourself to the study of your own sex as an industrial factor, your name will be a household word for two hundred years hence: if you write a history of Co-Operation it will be superseded and ignored in a year or two. . . . A book by you on the Co-Operative Movement I may get my wife to read to me in the evening, but I shan't pay any attention to it.'

Despite this grave discouragement, reinforcing Booth's, she persisted in her intention; and she produced a book, *The Co-Operative Movement of Great Britain*, which justified her faith in herself, though Marshall, many years later, was to describe it as a 'pernicious book'. It was, indeed, superseded, as Marshall had foretold, but only by *The Consumer's Co-Operative Movement*, which she and Sidney Webb published in 1921; and in the meantime it had been widely circulated in Great Britain as well as translated into a dozen languages. She was now a recognised social investigator with an increasing renown.

It was while she was making her investigations into Co-Operative societies that she made a mistake which she was to regret deeply for many years, a mistake which arose out of the contempt which able women often feel for their own sex, one, too, which she tried to cancel at a later date. Mrs Humphry Ward, a well-known novelist in her day—*Robert Elsmere* is still a very readable and impressive book—composed a manifesto against women's suffrage which was signed by a number of eminent women, of whom Beatrice was one!

75

While the enquiry was being made, her father was lying helpless and, towards the end of his life, semi-conscious. On January 1, 1892, he died.

76

But before his death, Beatrice had made a new acquaintance, with whom her friendship quickly developed and deepened. This was Sidney James Webb. Their meeting, which took place at the beginning of January, 1890, was casual. A woman journalist, to whom she had mentioned her need of reliable information about the Co-Operative Movement, replied, 'Sidney Webb, one of the Fabian Essayists, is your man. He knows everything: when you got out for a walk with him he literally pours out information.' She made an appointment to meet him, and he promptly supplied her needs.

A few days later, he sent her a copy of his new Fabian Tract on the Rate of Interest, which may be described as the first love letter he wrote her. This epistolary encounter almost supports H. G. Wells's assertion about the Baileys in *The New Machiavelli*, that they 'met, so to speak, in the pages of *The Contemporary Review*'. A marriage such as theirs would have seemed certain to be grubby: but it was as emotional as a serial story in *Home Chat*.

Her diary now begins to be full of 'the Other One', as she named him, when she was not calling him 'My Boy', after their marriage. There is a note, made on February 14, 1890, following one made on the first of that month, in which she says, 'At last I am a socialist!'

> 'Sidney Webb, the socialist, dined here (Devonshire House Hotel) to meet the Booths. A remarkable little man, with a huge head and a tiny body, a breadth of forehead quite sufficient to account for the encyclopaedic character of his knowledge. A Jewish nose, prominent eyes and mouth, black hair, somewhat unkempt, spectacles and a most bourgeois black coat shiny with wear. But I like the man. There is a directness of speech, an open-mindedness, an imaginative warm-heartedness which will carry him far. He has the self-assurance of one who is always thinking faster than his neighbours; who is untroubled by doubts, and to whom the acquisition of facts is as easy as the grasping of things; but he has no vanity and is totally un-selfconscious. Hence his absence of consciousness as to treading on his neighbours' corns. Above all, he is utterly disinterested, and is, I believe, genuine in his faith that collective control and collective administration will diminish, if not abolish poverty.'

Her sharp eye for detail is evident in this description of Webb. It was her clear and swift power of observation, more, perhaps, than her ability to draw conclusions, which made her effective. Once she had convinced herself that collective effort was preferable to individual direction, she swept her mind clear of any faith she ever had in unsocialised societies. In April, 1890, she moralises in a way that seems as harsh as it is surprisingly shallow:

> 'Every day my social views take a more decidedly socialist turn, every hour reveals fresh instances of the curse of gain without labour: the endless perplexities of the rich, the never-failing miseries of the poor. In this household there are ten persons living on the fat of the land in order to minister to the supposed comfort of one poor old man.

All this faculty expended to satisfy the assumed desires of a being wellnigh bereft of desire. The whole thing is a vicious circle as irrational as it is sorrowful. We feed our servants well, keep them in luxurious slavery, because we hate to see discomfort around us. But they and we are consuming the labour of others and giving nothing in return, except useless service to a dying life past serving. Here are thirteen dependents consuming riches and making none, and no one the better for it.'

Had these servants been employed in a chocolate factory, wrapping candies in silver paper, they would have been less beneficially employed than they were in domestic service. The characteristics of a civilised society include the division of labour in the way that is most convenient to the community, with each member, so far as can be arranged, doing the work he or she is best suited to do. Such a community is distinguished from a primitive society, in which only the bare necessities of life are found, by the number of adornments and decorations that are available. The more numerous and widely these adornments and decorations are enjoyed, the more civilised is the community. The Puritan who frowns on amenities is a reactionary, turning back to the kraal, the igloo, the mud hovel, and the shanty.

Beatrice Webb too frequently looked back to the bare walls of the windowless hut as if she were looking forward to the earthly paradise. She was a singular mixture of gipsy girl, in love with gay colours and dancing, and frowning puritan, to whom beauty is bestial. Accustomed to hurl herself amorously on Sidney, even in the presence of their friends, she showed signs of horror on seeing that young girls in Russia, where spartan severity was such that the Roundheads, by comparison, were positively loose, were beginning to prink themselves in pretty clothes and even to adorn their faces with paint and cosmetics. 'There is no spooning in the Parks of Culture and Rest,' she remarked with smug satisfaction.

Sidney, while still suffering from the effects of his stay in Russia, was upset by the shocking spectacle of a husband kissing his wife on the platform of an English railway station. Had the man behaved like that in Russia, he would have been fined with, apparently, Webb's approval. These puritanical prohibitions are common enough. They are still made in Eire, where the sexes, including married couples, in towns such as Clones, are segregated in cinemas by command of celibate priests. They were enforced by the Pilgrim Fathers in the United States, and are enforced to-day by Roman Catholic priests in Spain.

At Whitsuntide, 1890, Webb and Beatrice, now noticeably aware of each other, travelled in the same third-class carriage to Glasgow to attend a Co-Operative Congress in that city. It was clear to the discerning that romance was mixing itself in co-operative matter.

'In the evening, S.W. and I wandered through the Glasgow streets. A critical twenty-four hours, followed by another long walk by glorious sunset through the crowded streets, knocking up against drunken Scots. With glory in the sky and hideous bestiality on the earth, two socialists, came to a working compact.'

So Beatrice writes in her diary. One almost expects to read that she asked what was the first item on the agenda, and that he replied, 'A proposal of marriage. I move that the question be now put! . . .'

But although they came to a working compact, whatever that may mean, she warned him 'that the chances are a hundred to one that nothing follows but friendship.' She belonged to a wealthy family, the aristocracy of business: all of its members being opposed to socialism: Webb was lower-middle-class, a minor Civil Servant, and unattractive to look at. Even Beatrice did not expect to be able to overcome the objections her relatives would raise to their marriage. But they were indubitably in love, and their love was steadily increasing in strength, though they saw little of each other, partly because she was in close attendance on her dying father, partly because, in her off time from this mournful duty, she was staying in provincial cities, studying co-operation. They corresponded, however, and she had a hard job to restrain his impatience to be married. 'I am a piece of steel,' she told him, and he replied, 'One and one placed close together, in a sufficiently integrated relationship, make not two but eleven.'

In the summer, they became secretly engaged, 'my father's state making disclosure, even to my own family, undesirable'. But they met oftener, and, more and more, they developed into collaborators. 'We are both of us second-rate minds; but we are curiously combined, I am the investigator, and he the executant; between us we have a wide and varied experience of men and affairs. We have also an unearned salary. These are unique circumstances. A considerable work should be the result if we use our combined talents with a deliberate and persistent purpose.' His uncommonly good health enabled him to do much work for her when she was exhausted by fatigue or illness. 'Without his help I doubt whether I could get through this bulk of material; I have too little staying power for the bigness of my aims.'

77

'On the first of January, 1892, my father died; and six months later we were married.' The family was dismayed. Webb's origin in the lower-middle-class was not considered a fault. Two generations earlier the Potters themselves had been in the same class. But he had a Jewish look which disconcerted some of Richard Potter's sons-in-law, though why it should have done so is not understandable, seeing that there was Jewish blood in their wives and that Beatrice herself could easily have been taken for a handsome Jewess. In *Our Partnership*, she tries to give him a long East Anglian ancestry, but the information on which it is based is too scrappy to be trusted.

Webb's appearance was peculiar. It was not English in any degree. Beatrice herself had observed that the large nose was Hebraic, and it is a fact that, in my youth, none of the young Fabians with whom I associated doubted that Webb was a Jew. H. G. Wells, in *The New Machiavelli*, describes Oscar Bailey, for whom Webb was the prototype, as having a Mongolian look, and, indeed, he might easily have passed for one of the Georgians who cluttered round Lenin and Stalin. But Pease, the Secretary of the Fabian Society, denied that he was a Jew, though his denial had no other authority than Beatrice's unconvincing genealogy.

Webb had never been poor in the way that Shaw had been. His home, though it was graceless, was comfortable, and he was well fed. His mother 'was a woman of character and capacity', according to Beatrice; 'a clever shopkeeper and excellent housekeeper, giving her children good fare, open windows and cold baths, and training them in good habits. . . . It was she who, after consulting with a friendly customer, sent' her two sons, 'at a considerable sacrifice of income, first to a Swiss school to learn French and then into the family of a German pastor at Wiemar to learn German—an accomplishment which indirectly led to Sidney getting into the first division of the Civil Service.' He was a good linguist, a fact which, added to his personal appearance, caused him to be thought a foreigner by people who did not know that he was English. He was, indeed, thought, on the Continent, to be a Frenchman, and was once abused by a German in that belief.

The Potters and their husbands, not unnaturally, suspected that Webb had been impressed by Beatrice's income, which was £1,000 a year. In this suspicion, they did him grave injustice. He was far less acquisitive than G.B.S., though G.B.S., who was among the most generous of men, did not so much seek money as attract it. Webb spent very little on himself. He was earning enough money by journalism, apart from his income from the Civil Service, to keep him in considerable comfort. He had, in fact, resigned his post in Whitehall before his marriage, and was now engaged in organising the Progressive Party in the London County Council, to which he was elected in March, 1892.

But although he was indifferent to money in relation to himself, he was not indifferent to it as an essential aid in the life that he and

Beatrice intended to lead. Her money would be useful to them as social investigators, for their work was likely to cost more than it earned, as, indeed, it did for several years after their marriage. In that sense, and only in that sense, was Webb a fortune hunter. But what was wrong with that? Gentiles are not averse from living on their wives' money. If it was right for the Earl of Rosebery to marry a Rothschild, why was it almost a criminal offence for Webb, assuming him to have been a Jew, to marry a Potter who was herself partly a Jewess?

The family, however, had a graver cause for complaint against their marriage. All the Potter girls, except Beatrice, had married well: eminent men of means and conspicuous ability; and they felt that she was letting them down by not marrying at least as well as her sisters had done. Webb was not her first suitor. Joseph Chamberlain had proposed to her and been refused. Whatever one might think of his opinions, he was, undoubtedly, an able man and certain to be in the next Conservative Cabinet, with prospects, too, of becoming Prime Minister. To refuse him, a fine figure of a man, with a good income, and accept a penniless runt like Webb! . . . The man, of course, was clever in a small and insignificant way, though John Morley could not see anything in him. *How* clever Webb was, the family could not imagine. How much of his assurance was due to knowledge, how much to sheer bumptiousness? Was he any more than an able and adroit secretary, the sort of man who knows where everything is and can, at a moment's notice, provide the facts or the apt quotation his employer requires? The Gnome stuck in the family's gizzard. Beatrice had always been odd, but this marriage was easily the oddest thing she had ever done.

The family was confounded, for the marriage was spectacularly happy. Each was the exact complement of the other. Their purpose in life was the same, and what she lacked, he had. Their devotion to their common intention was only equalled by their devotion to each other. They were unhappy apart. Nor did Sidney fall short of his brothers-in-law in eminence. He surpassed them. His future, of course, was not discernible at the time of his marriage, and so the family were displeased. Their displeasure, however, was unavailing. Beatrice was thirty-four, and if a woman does not know her own mind at that age, she never will know it. They were stultified, moreover, by the fact that Webb was totally indifferent to their feelings; he had not married *them;* he had married *her.* He was a man with few friends, nor did he desire many. His closest friend was G.B.S., and, next to him, but far behind, Haldane. Women, except for his wife, generally bored him, especially if they were temperamental or intellectually pretentious. He detested Mrs Patrick Campbell, and could not understand what G.B.S. saw in her to admire so much, a disability which other people shared. Webb was a lover of blue books and white papers, and he took a delirious delight in statistics.

He had no recreations, apart from reading, yet he was obviously a happy man, doing with immense zest the work he wished to do. His pleasures were few and easily satisfied, and they did not distract him from his employment. His health, despite his aversion from physical exercise, was exceptionally good, and he was not known to have suffered from any illness until he had a stroke in his old age, which disabled him from work for the rest of his life. Beatrice was his colleague as well as his wife, and her death was an irremediable deprivation. They were childless, but the books they wrote served them as offspring. He realised that he was not a platform man, as G.B.S. so superbly was, and had no power to move great audiences by his eloquence. But he knew also that he was a very good committee man; that he had the power to impress people he wished to impress, that he could give useful and acceptable counsel, and draft documents and parliamentary bills and draw up memoranda and find solutions for problems of procedure which seemed insoluble to his colleagues. He was Grey Eminence to Prime Ministers and members of the Cabinet, whatever their party might be, consulted as freely by Lloyd George as by Arthur Balfour. And he was content. What greater happiness can any man have than to do the work he wishes to do, and to do it well? Like the good Fabian he was, he did not care who got the credit for the work, so long as the work was done.

78

Before her marriage, Beatrice had formed the habit of inviting young, unmarried Fabians to her home in Gloucestershire. The only Fabian who refused her invitations was G.B.S., who, in an impish mood, asserted that they were asked for inspection so that she might make up her mind which of them she would marry. As she was already engaged to Webb, this was only his nonsense. Nevertheless, he never went to Gloucester, which, for him, would have been a penitential pilgrimage to Canossa. He disliked bossy women, and Beatrice was very bossy; and he knew that she had little liking for him. 'As to his character,' she wrote in her diary, 'I do not understand it. He has been for twelve years, a devoted propagandist—hammering away at the ordinary routine of Fabian executive work with as much persistence as Wallas or Sidney. He is an excellent friend, at least to men ... but beyond this I know nothing. I am inclined to think he has a slight personality; agile, graceful, and even virile; but lacking in weight. Adored by many women, he is a born philanderer. ... Vain is he? A month ago I should have said that vanity was the bane of his nature. Now I am not so sure that the vanity itself is not part of the *mise en scène*, whether, in fact, it is not part of the character he imagines himself to be playing in the world's comedy.'

Her judgments of people were seldom sound. She thought more highly of Graham Wallas than she did of G.B.S., and, very surprisingly, she thought that John Burns was a potentially great man: an opinion which she changed when, after he had been made head of the Local Government Board by Sir Henry Campbell-Bannerman, he displayed an antipathy to her and Sidney which was almost pathological. It was shrewd of her to realise that G.B.S.'s vanity was a façade, the sort of façade erected by a shy man to conceal his shyness, but how shallow, how lacking in discernment she was when she found Shaw 'a slight personality . . . lacking in weight'. She was to make many misjudgments such as that in the course of her life, chiefly because her mind was essentially dreary and she was destitute of a sense of humour, one of those deplorably earnest women who feel sure that any person who can crack a joke must be trifling on the verge of calamity. She had enough sense, however, to realise, or perhaps Sidney told her, that G.B.S., whom 'some people would call a cynic', was 'really an idealist of the purest water'.

There was an idea in her head about marriage for able young Fabians who had no private means and were, therefore, compelled to give a large part of their energy to work that provided them with a livelihood, but diverted them from their 'real' employment. She had delivered Sidney from this bondage. Why should she not deliver his comrades in the Fabian Society by marrying them to solemn young women with ample means? It was for this purpose that she had invited some of them to Gloucester, and it was for the same purpose, after she and Sidney were married, that she invited them to meet eligible girls at the country houses or rectories which she rented every summer. These well-endowed young women were to maintain the clever Fabians in that state of comfort and security to which heaven had carelessly neglected to call them. The fact that she was denying her new principles seems not to have occurred to her, nor did she notice that the difference between her scheme and the idea of a leisured class was slight. The single rebel against her attempt to guide and direct the Fabians in all their ways was G.B.S., who was antipathetic to her as she was to him, though he never failed to show her the courtesy which she frequently failed to render him.

He was not amenable to bossy women, and it was her habit to find great fault in men who were rebellious. G.B.S., despite his tendency to moralise, was an artist, and artists are indisposed to be ordered about. She was too busy with her statistics and her study of

The Co-Operative Movement and her little plots to regiment people, to have any time to spare for such fripperies as art, literature and drama. Life was real, life was earnest; and it was to be found in committee meetings in Runcorn and Rochdale, reading minutes kept by the secretaries of the local Co-ops. She disliked those who were not amenable to any authority but that of their art or craft, and felt certain that we should all be much better off if we would allow ourselves to be controlled by superior persons of the governing 'cless', such as Sidney and herself. 'Her job', G.B.S. said, 'was the discovery of the common rules by which men bind themselves to co-operate for social ends. She had no use for exceptional people: degrees of ability and efficiency she could deal with, but the complications introduced by artists, Irishmen, and the eccentric and anarchic individuals who infest revolutionary movements and have to be shot when the revolution succeeds were, from her point of view of social definition and classification, simply nuisances.'

It galled her when some elaborate scheme for the better ordering about of people was kicked to pieces by insubordinate persons who persisted in having minds of their own and flatly refused to believe that a clerk in Whitehall knew better than they did. In her impatience with G.B.S., she called him a sprite, and imagined vainly that she had disposed of him. But the sprite had his uses. He could speak uncommonly well, and he could control an audience as Sidney would never, in this or any other world, be able to control one; and he had a brilliantly flashing wit, shot through with uncommon sense that sometimes turned into high moral fervour and became genius.

Nor was there any denying that he was industrious, working as hard as Sidney at dull tasks, and that he could manipulate Sidney's flat prose and hers, which was flatter, so skilfully that a passage which would otherwise have been skipped, was read with pleasure. There is a good deal of Shaw buried in the Webb's work. He read and revised their proofs, sometimes altering them extensively, and always for the better. He could, Beatrice felt, be very irritating because there was no knowing what he would say or do next; and it was important to Beatrice to know what people would do or say next. She would have fallen in admiration at the feet of that French Minister of Education who boasted that all the schoolchildren in France at any given moment would be reading the same lesson! . . .

79

The Webbs spent their honeymoon partly in Dublin, investigating ramshackle trade societies, and Belfast, interviewing what she calls 'hard-fisted employers and groups of closely-organised skilled craftsmen,' and partly in attendance at the Trade Union Congress at Glasgow: an exhilarating way of consummating their love. When these intense raptures were ended, they settled down in 'a hard little house', as H. G. Wells called it in *The New Machiavelli*, 41 Grosvenor Road, where their next-door neighbour was Mrs J. R. Green, the widow of the historian; and here they spent the next forty years of their lives. They began to write an excellent book, entitled *The History of Trade Unionism*, which was followed by a bigger and better one, *Industrial Democracy*. Sidney was also working hard on the London County Council, where his smooth, or, as some people called them, slippery ways of getting what he wanted, were deeply distrusted by members who, normally, would have been on his side.

They went to Wales in September, where Graham Wallas 'severly criticised the form of' their first chapter, which they revised drastically. Then Bernard Shaw arrived and spent the whole of his holiday working on their book. 'The form of the first chapter' of *The History of Trade Unionism*, which had been rewritten after Wallas had condemned it, 'satisfied him, and he altered only words and sentences. The second chapter he took more in hand, and the third he has to a large extent remodelled. Sidney certainly has devoted friends. But then it is a common understanding with all these men that they use each other up when necessary. That is the basis of the influence of The Fabian Society on contemporary political thought: the little group of leaders are practical communists in all the fruits of their labours.'

The Webbs now perceived the need for a Labour Party. The old alliance between Labour and Liberalism obviously could not continue much longer. It was absurd, as G.B.S. had said, that the Trade Union Secretaries should struggle with employers over wages and hours of work and, at the same time, support them on political platforms during elections. Working men must send their own representatives into parliament. The days of the Lib-Labs were ending. The doubt Beatrice had felt about trade unions when she had listened to her father and her brothers-in-law and Herbert Spencer and their friends discussing the potentialities and perils of trade unions was now dispelled.

Her elders had fears of the future in which trade unions would prevail. Working-men, naturally, thought strictly in terms of wages, hours of labour and regular employment. Their minds ceased to operate beyond these points. They were distrustful of inventions and new ways of working. They had learnt this distrust from their fathers and grandfathers, some of whom had helped the Luddites to smash the new machines, which meant that some workers would become, in a word not yet part of the jargon of economists, redundant. How were men to maintain their families if machines displaced them?

The fear that haunted Herbert Spencer's mind, of a great tyranny of ochlocrats, voting in vast numbers for politicians who offered them the largest bribes, no longer troubled the mind of Beatrice, who was now convinced that Sidney's bureaucracy would deal with the proletarian tyrants effectively. Time, so far from dispelling the fears that Spencer and his associates felt, has intensified them. They are no longer theoretical: they are facts; and G.B.S., in his old age, was to complain with some bitterness that the Fabians, who had intended to create a Socialist society, had only established government by trade unions.

80

While the Webbs were busy with their books and schemes, G.B.S. seemed to be marking time. But this was only seeming, for he was not only busy with Fabian affairs, but busier with his musical criticism in *The World*, and any other sort of criticism that came his way. Fisher Unwin continued to badger him for books, which he was foolish enough to decline when he received them. In January, 1891, he wrote again, but G.B.S. did not answer his letter until the beginning of March, and then he tried to divert attention from himself to Graham Wallas by proposing that Wallas should be commissioned to write a history of England from the time of the industrial revolution 'to the present time'. This was characteristic of his lifelong habit, contracted from Archer, of trying to persuade publishers and managers to employ his friends. Wallas, he told Unwin, 'is now delivering a series of University Extension lectures on this very subject. . . . At the present moment he probably knows more about it than anyone else in the world of his age. From now to 1900 he will be in the very flower of his energy, not too young and not too old . . . and he has the capacity for taking infinite pains which produces permanent work in literature.'

But Fisher Unwin was not interested in this proposal. Had not G.B.S. himself a work he could publish? Well, yes, there was *Love Among the Artists*, but G.B.S. could not consent to let him have anything of his so long as he persisted in having his books printed by non-union printers. He would greatly like to make a book out of his musical criticism in *The Star* 'and to issue Shaw's Tales from Ibsen, uniform with Lamb's Tales from Shakespeare,' but Walter Scott wanted to publish that. A fortnight later, he writes again to Unwin, sending him 'the three volumes of *Our Corner* containing *Love Among the Artists:*

'I thought it best not to send it to the city, as you are never there and probably do nothing—after the city fashion—when you *are* there.

'Archer most strenuously advises me to let these early novels of mine die. So that is one adverse critical opinion to begin with.

'I looked over a few of the Corno di Bassetto columns the other day. Such sickening, vulgar, slovenly slosh never blasted my sight before. I cannot believe that there is enough good stuff sunk in this mud to be worth diving for.

'I have actually attacked the Ibsen essay—put in 14 hours work on it last Monday. When ready for the press it will contain at least 25,000 words. Scott is immensely on to it: I have just received a postcard from him to say that a formal proposal will come to-morrow for its publication. It seems to me that as he has so much capital invested in Ibsen the book must be worth more to him than to you. I suppose you are not particularly sweet on it. If you are, send me by return a cheque for £5,000 with an agreement securing me a 66⅔ per cent royalty, not to commence until the sixteenth copy.   G.B.S.

This essay, *The Quintessence of Ibsenism*, it must be borne in mind, was written as a lecture to The Fabian Society: that is to say, G.B.S. spent a good deal of time and energy and thought in composing a long paper, for which he would not receive any payment. It was delivered to a very large audience at St James's Restaurant on July 18, 1890, and made a deep impression on all who heard it. G.B.S.'s attitude towards Ibsen was entirely different from Archer's. Archer thought little of Ibsen as a philosopher and much of him as a poet. G.B.S. seemed less interested in his artistry than he was in his propaganda.

The lecture was extended in its scope and published in 1891. It also appeared in America in that year, and, in another edition, in 1894. In 1913, a fresh edition, brought up to the time of Ibsen's death, was published. In this book, which is described by Henderson as 'Shaw's masterpiece in the field of literary criticism', G.B.S. expounded Ibsen with a profundity that had not previously been shown in examination of his work by any writer in English. The book, being by G.B.S., is, as Henderson states, 'thoroughly one-sided', a statement of what Ibsen would have thought had he been Bernard Shaw, but it is nonetheless impressive on that account. A book by Confucius on Mahomet or by each of them on Christ could not fail to be deeply tinged by its author's opinions; but it would be valuable despite the fact, would, indeed, be more interesting because of it, than would a severely detached work. The attitude of one great man to another teaches us much about both. G.B.S. was a Socialist who was to become a Communist; but Ibsen was an Individualist who would have felt appalled by contemporary Russia. He had no doubt about his belief. Towards the end of January, 1882, in a letter to a friend which is cited in William Archer's introduction to *Ghosts*,[1] Ibsen asserts his Individualism. 'I, of course foresaw that my new play would call forth a howl from the camp of the stagnationists; and for this I care no more than for the barking of a pack of chained dogs. . . . I myself am responsible for what I write, I and no one else. I cannot possibly embarrass any party, for to no party do I belong. I stand like a solitary franc-tireur at the outposts, and fight for my own hand.' G.B.S. could, substantially, have said the same, despite his party attachment; for his party represented him: he did not represent it.

The Irishman was attracted by the Norwegian because he was one of the people who change men's minds. No one who read his plays or saw them in performance was quite the same person that he had been before he read or saw them. He might feel antagonistic to Ibsen, but he could not be indifferent to him, and his attachment to his own belief would be more vehement because of what Ibsen had told him. If he accepted Ibsen as a guide, he abandoned his previous beliefs. When Graham Wallas read *The Wild Duck*, he felt that the bottom had fallen out of the universe.

The extraordinary fact about Ibsen and Shaw is that Shaw was a resolute supporter of what used to be called women's rights, but that Ibsen, though he was acclaimed as the liberator of women, was not much interested in their political rights, was, if anything, opposed to them. It was not the right to make a mark on a ballot paper that excited Ibsen's interest: it was the right of every human being to possess a free mind, untrammelled by the prejudices of other people, and to be delivered from the tyranny of mobs and arbitrary men in office. He would have set the Russian serf free from oppression by the Tsar and the Orthodox Church, but he would also, and with greater joy, have delivered the Russian slave from oppression by the Communist clique in the Kremlin. The nature of a domineering priest is not changed when you disrobe him and put him in plain clothes and call him a Commissar. St Paul was not, in his essence, altered by the vision on the road to Damascus. He had been a fanatical rabbi, brutally misusing the followers of Christ: he was now a fanatical Christian, only deterred from brutally misusing pagan people by the fact that he was in a minority and could not depend on the law and the mob for support.

The difference between the Orthodox Church and the Politbureau would have seemed slight and indistinguishable to Ibsen, who would have been horrified by G.B.S.'s admiration for the latter. Both men, after their fashion, carried their creed to ridiculous extremes, but Ibsen's extremity was preferable to G.B.S.'s. We cannot live without each other, but neither can we live if we are

[1] See *The Collected Works of Henrik Ibsen*, Vol. VII, published by Heinemann.

continually huddled together. Dr Stockmann, in *An Enemy of the People*, becomes absurd, after having been superb, when he states that 'the strongest man in the world is he who stands most alone.' Robinson Crusoe was uninteresting until he met Man Friday. Sam Weller made a man of Mr Pickwick.

Neither the majority nor the minority is always right or wrong. But, unfortunately, the majority, especially if it is led by ruthless leaders, can foully use and almost eliminate the minority, though it will probably ruin itself if it does. There is, however, more enduring power in minorities than there is in majorities. The Jews have suffered every sort of wrong in their long and painful history, and their extermination ages ago would have seemed certain. Yet there are more of them in the world to-day than ever there were; and they are more numerous in New York than they were in Israel in the time of Christ.

81

G.B.S. was not deceived by the illusion of progress, but he sometimes talked and wrote as if he were. He thought, or at all events said, that a republic was superior to a kingdom, an error which he shared with H. G. Wells. But a world which has seen the number of European thrones reduced to seven in less than half a century, is now disinclined to believe that there has been any progress whatever in the change from kingdoms to republics, and is more inclined, especially in the case of Russia, to believe that a republic is a relapse to barbarism. The arts flourished under the Tsars as they have failed to flourish under the Communists; and the general condition of life in the unwieldy Russian Empire, many of whose inhabitants were, as they remain, semi-savages, was slowly improving. A Russian had more liberty of mind under the last Tsars, as Tolstoy, Turgenev, Doestoevsky, Chekhov and Maxim Gorki could testify if they were alive, than any Russian, outside the governing gang, has enjoyed since the Revolution; and even members of the gang are liable to be liquidated when 'the boss' is annoyed with them. We imagine ourselves to be making improvements when we are merely making changes; and man's long and heartbreaking search for a system of society which will be suitable for civilised men and women to inhabit, seems no nearer to success than it was in the time of Socrates. Dare we believe that the age which allowed Hitler and Mussolini to rise to power was superior to the age of Charlemagne? Was Stalin less of a cruel autocrat than Peter the Great?

And here we come to the point at which men so dissimilar in belief as Henrik Ibsen and Bernard Shaw could meet in amity and agreement. The democratic heresy is the faith in numbers. But a million men are not more important than one man, nor are they wiser or less arbitrary or more generous in their beliefs.

All progress, whatever its nature, depends on individuals and minorities. The mass of men are unwilling to change their condition, and reluctant to go forward, especially in the dark. They prefer to follow established habit and to stay where they are. They bear the troubles of other people with Christian fortitude, and they are deeply distrustful of uncommon people. They prefer familiar things to things which are unfamiliar, shrinking from any alteration in the state of things as they exist, and they are irresponsible. They feel antagonistic to foreigners whose names and speech and behaviour seem to them absurd. Their tendency when they meet an alien is, at best, to poke fun at him, at worst, to assault him.

If the deliverance of the Hebrews from Egyptian bondage had depended on the Hebrew helots themselves, they would still be making bricks and providing their own straw in the delta of the Nile. Their march to the Promised Land depended on one inspired and determined man who, though he belonged to their race, was brought up, not as a Hebrew, but as an Egyptian. They hampered him in every way they could while they were on the road to freedom, plotting sometimes to murder him, and they were always ready, on the slightest excuse, to bolt back to the fleshpots of Egypt. The moment his back was turned, they reverted to their idolatries, led by that commonplace curate, Aaron, and it was not until Moses took them into the wilderness and kept them there for forty years, to breed out the servile host and raise up one born free, that he was able to go forward and conquer his enemies.

And just as the Hebrews, not yet known as Jews, had to be led against their will to freedom and independence, so the general mass of mankind must be led by the lonely and often misunderstood adventurers of the mind and spirit who are deeply resentful of all oppression and dependence.

'The inventions and organizations that have produced the peculiar opportunities and dangers of the modern world have been the work so far of a few hundred thousand exceptionally clever and enterprising people. The rest of mankind has just been carried along by them, and has remained practically what it was a thousand years ago. Upon an understanding and competent minority, which may not exceed a million or so in all the world, depends the whole progress and stability of the collective human enterprise at the present time.'[1]

Depressed by the indurated stupidity of the mob, the rare and uncommon man, on whom depends all our growth and development

[1] *The Science of Life.* By H. G. Wells, Julian Huxley and G. P. Wells. p. 875.

and progress, may well wonder if Aristotle was wrong when he said that servitude was essential to a well-governed community. The natural state of a large part of the population in any community is one of subordination, and we run severe risks when we commit our lives and the welfare of our community to their charge. The tyranny of one million men is worse than the tyranny of one man, for he can be deposed or put to death easily enough, but who can depose or put to death a million men in arbitrary power? The proletariat can dictate only its own enslavement, for knowing itself to be incapable of government, because of its impatience and irresponsibility, its lack of knowledge, ability, and mental resilience, it soon abandons control to bureaucratic gangs, and the last state of man is worse than the first.

That was the society the Webbs sought to found. It is the society the Labour Party has partially created. It is the society which G.B.S., most surprisingly, and because he was bemused by Webb, sought to impose upon people, although he was himself a rebellious man who, had he been a Russian in Stalin's Empire, would almost certainly have been hanged.

82

G.B.S. and Ibsen, despite the profound difference between their beliefs about society, were essentially in agreement about the value of the rebel against authority. G.B.S. was more interested in the community than he was in the individual, a fact which, perhaps, reduces his stature as a creative artist and dynamic thinker. Ibsen, on the contrary, was less interested in society than he was in persons, and rightly so, for he realised the essential fact that a community is what individuals make it. Neither believed in the absolute rightness of any law. Law for each of them was a social convenience, desirable for the time, but not a divine ordinance which must never be cancelled or even questioned. The generality of people accept the law as if it were indisputable and always right.

But rare and uncommon men perceive clearly that any law is a social convenience only so long as it is suitable to the circumstances of the time; and that a law which is valid in one place may not, and need not, be valid in another. The rule of the road is devised for the general good. Without it, traffic would be impossible. But the English would be foolish if they supposed for a moment that their rule, that vehicles shall keep to the left, is the only good rule, inspired by heaven and not to be violated or changed except at the peril of immortal souls; and that Americans and other foreigners whose rule is to keep to the right are guilty of blasphemy or very bad taste.

235

To G.B.S., romance was the enemy of the real; to Ibsen, the enemy was the idealist. The romantic and the idealist deceived themselves by their faith in a world which did not exist, and their indifference to the world that did. 'Brand', G.B.S. declares in his analysis of Ibsen's great poetic drama of that name, 'dies a saint, having caused more intense suffering by his saintliness than the most talented sinner could possibly have done with twice his opportunities.' He contrasts Brand with Peer Gynt. 'Brand would force his ideal on all men and women; Peer Gynt keeps his ideal for himself alone: it is indeed implicit in the ideal itself that it should be unique—that he alone should have the force to realize it.'

It was part of G.B.S.'s argument in his illustration of Ibsen's belief, that men can change themselves by their own will, and that all attempts to change them against it must fail. The theory should have made him apprehensive of the Webbs and their cohorts of officials who seek to impose their opinions on the rest of the community as laws which must neither be broken nor abrogated; but inexplicably it failed to do so.

There are two impressive passages in *The Quintessence of Ibsenism* in which he shows that it is the 'literate and cultured' and not 'the ignorant and stupid' who maintain error, though he fails to perceive that the argument implicit in them wrecks a large part of his faith:

'The man who has risen above the danger and the fear that his acquisitiveness will lead him to theft, his temper to murder, and his affections to debauchery: this is he who is denounced as an arch-scoundrel and libertine, and thus confounded with the lowest because he is the highest. And it is not the ignorant and stupid who maintain this error, but the literate and the cultured. When the true prophet speaks, he is proved to be both rascal and idiot, not by those who have never read of how foolishly such learned demonstrations have come off in the past, but by those who have themselves written volumes on the crucifixions, the burning, the stonings, the headings and hangings, the Siberia transportations, the calumny and ostracism which have been the lot of the pioneer as well as of the camp follower. It is from men of established literary reputation that we learn that William Blake was mad, that Shelley was spoiled by living in a low set, that Robert Owen was a man who did not know the world, that Ruskin was incapable of comprehending political economy, that Zola was a mere blackguard, and that Ibsen was "a Zola with a wooden leg". The great musician, accepted by the unskilled listener, is vilified by his fellow-musicians: it was the musical culture of Europe that pronounced Wagner the inferior of Mendelssohn and Meyerbeer. The great artist finds his foes among the painters, and not among the men in the street: it was the Royal Academy which placed forgotten nobodies above Burne Jones.'

Here, he overlooked the fact that the man in the street was guiltless of these faults because he was unaware of the works which caused them in his betters. He is not, in fact, any readier than the most rule-ridden civil servant to greet the pioneer and the new belief with a rousing cheer; and he is always among the first to throw stones when the pioneer arrives. But this fact does not invalidate G.B.S.'s argument against the conventional cultured classes, nor does it destroy his argument in the second passage; in which he asserts that Ibsen, had he concerned himself with Darwin's theory of Natural Selection, would probably have attacked it.

'. . . but his genius pushed him past it and left it to be demolished philosophically by Butler, and practically by the mere march of the working class, which, by its freedom from the economic bias of the middle classes, has escaped their characteristic illusions, and solved many of the enigmas they found insoluble because they did not wish to have them solved. For instance, according to the theory of Natural Selection, progress can only take place through an increase in the severity of the material conditions of existence; and as the working classes were quite determined that progress should consist of just the opposite, they had no difficulty in seeing that it generally does occur in that way, whereas the middle class wished, on the contrary, to be convinced that the poverty of the working classes and all the hideous evils attending it were inevitable conditions of progress, and that every penny in the pound on the rates spent in social amelioration, and every attempt on the part of the workers to raise their wages by Trade Unionism or otherwise, were vain defiances of biologic and economic science.'

The effect of this small book is still powerful more than sixty years after it was first published, although Ibsen has become a classic and ceased to trouble anyone's mind. Its effect when a summary of it was delivered as a lecture was, according to those who heard it, explosive, as, indeed, it well might be, for it contains much that was highly challenging to the thought and belief of the time. The lecture altered the point of view about G.B.S. which had been held until then, even by people who admired him. If they agreed with Beatrice Webb that he was a slight personality before they heard the lecture, they held that opinion no longer or held it less firmly; and the book confirmed them in their change of mind. They expected wit from him, but here was a depth of thought with which he had not previously been credited.

There are impressive passages in it, such as that in which he wonders why the detestable people created by Dickens, such as Sairey Gamp, escape censure because they are comic, whereas the well-intentioned and even nobly-minded characters created by Ibsen, incur censure because they are earnest. Why is Malvolio, who has many admirable qualities, despised, when that sot and sponger, Sir Toby Belch, who has none, is admired?

The final section of the book contains a superb passage which must have shaken the thoughts of conventionally pious people severely, and at the same time have stirred some feeling in their perturbed minds that G.B.S. was right.

> 'The larger truth of the matter is that modern European literature and music now form a Bible far surpassing in importance to us the ancient Hebrew Bible that has served us so long. The notion that inspiration is something that happened thousands of years ago, and was then finished and done with, never to occur again: in other words, the theory that God retired from business at that period and has not been heard from since, is as silly as it is blasphemous. He who does not believe that revelation is continuous does not believe in revelation at all, however familiar his parrot's tongue and pew sleepy ear may be with the word.'

Just as *ideal* meant to Ibsen a word of illusion and deception, so *romance* meant to G.B.S. humbug and pretence: an infantile effort to cast a glamour over relationships that were muddy and false. But these definitions manifestly are far from the whole matter. Neither an ideal nor a romance is a self-deception in itself, and no one is willing to believe that it is better to make the worst than the best of any human fact. Ibsen had his ideal: G.B.S. had his romance. Dr Stockmann's passion for blurting out the truth though the heavens fall was as silly as the deception against which he protested. There was surely some reasonable ground between him and 'the damned compact Liberal majority'. It was not an incurable desire for the drab which sent G.B.S. careering from Trafalgar Square to Victoria Park to preach his doctrine to reluctant listeners, but an ideal of betterment and decency.

Ibsen leaves the Doll-woman, Nora, in the air. The play ends, but she does not, when she bangs the street door behind her. Dramatic attitudes are no doubt exciting, but they fail to satisfy the hungry and homeless. Nora, soon after she leaves her husband's house, will need a meal and a bed. Is there any proof in the play that she is capable of of providing one or the other? Galsworthy, in *The Fugitive*, made a diversion on Ibsen's theme; and a melancholy business it proved to be, for Clare Dedmond is so hopeless and incapable of fending for herself that when she leaves her husband, she lands herself in the street. She must become a prostitute or destroy herself. Of these alternatives, she chooses the second. Just what is the benefit Nora gains, the benefit gained by Clare Dedmond, in rejecting the gloss or glamour or ideal or romance or whatever one calls it and accepting without thought the bare fact, the stark naked truth?

Neither Ibsen's Nora nor Galsworth's Clare is intuitively intelligent or mentally acute. Nora has faults far exceeding her qualities. She is a liar, she is greedy, she believes that all things which are convenient to her, even if they are inconvenient to other people, are essentially good; and she is so irresponsible that she instantly abandons her children, her husband and her home when she finds her folly is not appreciated as the finest nobility. Galsworthy's Clare marries for money a man she does not love, and then bilks him of the physical satisfaction for which he has paid. She is less admirable than a common whore who does at least try to give value for her wages.

Neither of these women truly demonstrates a tragic situation, such as that of a woman who feels compelled to live with a man she despises because she and her children are economically dependent upon him. When women are financially free, as many of them now are, the whole fabric of marriage will change, as, indeed, it is being changed under our eyes, and the relations of men and women, together with the propagation of children, will be revolutionised.

It is highly probable that monogamous marriage will be general in the world, and that many couples will remain faithful and devoted to each other throughout their lives; but it is inconceivable that women, in a world where they are economically independent and occupying positions of importance, will remain content to be loverless and barren merely because they are unmarried. It is absurd to suppose that an able woman, holding a high and responsible post, will abdicate her right to hold it because she has married a husband and intends to conceive children. It is even more absurd to suppose that society will remains content with a system which denies maternity to a woman of ability in other spheres than the home because, having spent a large part of her life in attaining a high position, she has foregone ordinary marriage. She may, as many such women do, have a lover, but if she conceives a child by him, she will lose her position.

Yet she is probably capable of producing the sort of children her country needs and desires. We are not well enough informed about biology to be certain what men and women are fit to beget offspring, and probably we shall always have to take a chance with parents; but we know enough about it to realise that we do the state disservice when we sterilise able women because we will not let them hold the responsible positions they are fit to hold if they conceive children either in or out of wedlock. This is a state of affairs which obviously will not last in a society where all women are financially free.

G.B.S. was writing brilliantly about music, and he was working hard for The Fabian Society; but he had not yet produced any work that could distinguish him from other brilliant journalists. Had he died in 1892, when he was thirty-six, his output would have been five novels which had failed to find a public; a substantial number of notable articles in newspapers; an unfinished play; two chapters in *Fabian Essays;* several Fabian tracts; and *The Quintessence of Ibsenism:* a production which could scarcely have kept his name alive for more than a month after his interment. This is not to say that he was idle. He was, on the contrary, much too busy. But he was busy about ephemeral things. Events, however, were preparing a way for him.

It was not until 1891 that Ibsen became in England what he had already been in Scandinavia for most of his life and was to continue to be for the rest of it: the centre of fierce and frequent storms of foul abuse. In January of that year, *A Doll's House* was revived—it has been performed in Great Britain more often than any other Ibsen play—and in February, on the suggestion of G.B.S., Florence Farr produced *Rosmersholm*, with herself in the part of Rebecca West. This production according to Archer's brother, Charles, was ill-made and ill-acted, and the play itself received what was now almost routine denunciation from the dramatic critics. *A Doll's House* had been abused as an attempt to break up family life. The mildest of the epithets used against *Rosmersholm* was 'cancerous'. In March, a Dutch Jew, Jacob Thomas Grein, a tea merchant in Mincing Lane who was also Consul, first, for the Congo and, second, for Liberia, but was much more interested in the advanced drama than he was in tea or Consulates, completed the plans he had been laying for a year to found a play-producing society on the principles which guided Antoine when, in 1887, he founded the Thèâtre Libre in Paris.

This was The Independent Theatre, and it was the first of a series of similar societies Grein started: a form of entertainment in which he indulged, without profit to himself, for the rest of his life. He hired a grubby and depressing hall in Tottenham Court Road, and boldly announced the impending production of a translation of *Genganere*, which is called *Ghosts* in English. The place seemed admirably suited for the play; but an immediate result of its announcement was such a demand for tickets of admission that Grein had to abandon the hall in Tottenham Court Road and hire the Royalty Theatre in Dean Street, Soho.

He was a brave and audacious man, but it is conceivable that if he had foreseen the fury with which he would be insulted and assailed because of *Ghosts*, he would have devoted himself more assiduously to tea and his consular duties than he did to the drama; but, luckily, for the English theatre, he had no such fearful prevision.

On Friday, March 13, 1891, Grein, having, it seemed, no superstitions about dates, produced the play, and was instantly denounced and traduced by almost the entire press. If he had been Jack the Ripper, he could not have been more bitterly abused. The shocked drunkards and libidinous club loungers who were among them, were genuinely horrified by *Ghosts*. It made revelations which, they thought, should never have been mentioned except in the strictest seclusion and only to men; and the possibility that women might hear about such matters appalled them. Some of them may have felt that *Ghosts* came too close to their own lives to be tolerated. Scott screamed like a demented banshee. 'Ibsen's positively abominable play, entitled *Ghosts*', was, he proclaimed, 'an open drain; a loathsome sore unbandaged; a dirty act done publicly; a lazar-house with all its doors and windows wide open ... absolutely loathsome and fetid ... gross, almost putrid in decorum ... literally carrion ... crapulous stuff,' and his editor was almost as vituperative. He wondered what the police were doing that such a play should be performed. They would have been stupified had they foreseen the day when young girls would know well what was unknown to their grandmothers, that there are disastrous venereal diseases. The pioneer of one age is the reactionary of the next; and the man who was stoned by one generation is commemorated in statues by its successor.

Archer and Walkley and G.B.S. fought well and intelligently to counteract the reckless and incoherent stuff that Clement Scott and those who shared his opinion were writing in the public press. Walkley, with more courage than he was to display later in life, informed the readers of *The Star*—he was its dramatic critic, Spectator—that, 'yesterday I received an invitation, innocent enough on the face of it, yet possibly to be valuable one of these days as an epoch-making document in connection with the history of the English stage'. This was a request to witness the first performance of *Ghosts* in London. His prophecy was amply fulfilled: the English theatre was changed and improved by the production of *Ghosts*. Pinero became more daring than he had hitherto been, and a vast amount of rubbish was swept out of the way of Wilde and Shaw. But for this production we might never have had the brilliant band of dramatists who made the Vedrenne-Barker seasons at the Court Theatre memorable in our theatrical history.

Ghosts is not a cheerful piece, and there are doubts now of its validity in terms of medicine. Its end, the general collapse, through inherited disease, of Oswald Alving is irrelevant to the main theme of the play, which is that Mrs Alving, Oswald's mother, was guilty of futile idealism as well as infidelity to fact when she remained faithful to her scallywag and drunken husband instead of eloping with the idealistic Pastor Manders. The conclusion is that those who betray their purpose, acting on routine rules of conduct rather than the compulsion of their inmost needs and aspirations, betray not only themselves and others, but are as guilty of sin as those whom they loudly denounce. None of this meaning was apparent to the majority of the critics. *The Sporting and Dramatic News* informed its austere and virtuous readers that 'ninety-seven per cent of the people who go to see *Ghosts* are nasty-minded people who find the discussion of nasty subjects to their taste in exact proportion to their nastiness', while *Truth* howled like a hungry hyena in denunciation of Ibsen, the play and those who thought well of it. 'The sexless . . . unwomanly women, the unsexed females, the whole army of unprepossessing cranks in petticoats . . . educated and muck-ferretting dogs . . . effeminate men and male women' alone were likely to hold Ibsen and his works in esteem'. Among the 'male women' thus denounced were George Meredith and Thomas Hardy. Ibsen, it added, was 'a crazy, cranky being . . . not only consistently dirty, but deplorably dull'. *The Gentlewoman*, forgetting its gentility, invited its readers to believe that Ibsen was 'a gloomy sort of ghoul, bent on groping for horrors by night, and blinking like a stupid old owl when the warm sunlight of the best of life danced into his wrinkled eyes'.

The abuse was grossly overdone,[1] and reaction was, therefore, certain to follow; but it did not follow quickly. One of the worst results of the reaction was that the devotees of Ibsen began to treat him as if he were solemn, portentous and didactic. They forgot his humour and poetry and wit, and insisted that his plays should be performed as if they were part of a penitential service conducted by a sour-minded priest in a gloomy and ill-lit chapel. This unfortunate attitude is still maintained, with the result that Ibsen's genius is less discernible to-day than it was when Clement Scott howled at him like a village virago. Nevertheless, the still, but not small voices of Archer, Walkley and G.B.S. were eventually heard, and reason began to prevail.

But Grein suffered a good deal of opprobrium. According to his biographer,[2] it took about ten years for him to get rid of the odium he incurred. He was a foreigner and a Jew, so he was fair game for anybody with a spite to indulge. A Mr William Champion, of *The Topical Times*, having heard that Grein was to be present at a meeting

---

[1] A long list of extracts from it appears in G.B.S.'s *The Quintessence of Ibsenism.*
[2] J. T. Grein *The Story of a Pioneer*, 1862–1935. By his wife, Michael Orme.

of journalists in connexion with the opening of Olympia, rose up in a moral fury and declared that if the man who produced *Ghosts* were to be present, he, William Champion, of *The Topical Times*, most certainly would not. But *Ghosts* to-day is almost a conventional piece. Perhaps the most impressive way of proving this assertion is to be found in the fact that more than twenty-three years after the performance at the Royalty Theatre in 1891, *Ghosts*, with the full approval and connivance of the British Government began a long and unrestricted run at the Haymarket Theatre on July 14, 1914, mainly for the benefit of the British troops.

84

How far G.B.S. was stimulated by the shameful exhibition the London dramatic critics had made of themselves over *Ghosts*, is difficult to say; but he was not yet stimulated to the writing of plays, though his interest in the theatre, which had always been keen, was revealing itself in his musical criticism: setting out to write about a concert, he sometimes found himself writing about a play. He was still politically propaganding, was, indeed, becoming better known in politics than he was in literature or criticism.

He wrote a tract for The Fabian Society in 1892, in which he implored the proletariat to create a party of its own instead of hanging on to the coat tails of Radicals and Liberals. It was not the only Fabian tract he published in that year, but it was the most important. 'A subscription of only three halfpence a year from every male worker in the Kingdom would bring in a parliamentary fund of £50,000 a year.' He foresaw the fact; now clearly perceived, that organised labour is not only numerically, but financially the most powerful party in the state. The Conservatives cannot amass the large sums of money for electioneering and propaganda purposes that can easily be collected in small sums by the Trade Unionists. The Liberals, now in their last throes, cannot amass either money or members. When the ageing remnant of what was once a great, but is now a decrepit party is abolished by discouragement or death, there will be two powerful parties, Conservatives and Socialists, with, perhaps, a noisy and mischievous group of Communists with nuisance value for Russia.

G.B.S. demanded a new Reform Bill, providing for payment of members of parliament and their election expenses out of public funds, demands which had been made fifty-five years earlier by the Chartists and were to be satisfied by the Labour Party twenty-eight years after G.B.S.'s pamphlet was published. The salary of a member of parliament not in office or Leader of the Opposition was to be

£400 a year, together with free travelling facilities to and from his constituency. It is now £1,000 a year, but is said, with justification, to be inadequate to cover the expenses of a member who has no private means or occupation, apart from parliament, from which he can draw an income.

Herbert Samuel described G.B.S. at this period of his life accurately and vivaciously. 'Shaw, bearded, amiable, emphatic, quizzical . . . a lovable character, always considerate in his personal relations with other people. . . . His intellectual arrogance and frank self-advertisement were nothing but a pose,' which was a shrewder remark than Beatrice Webb's to the same effect. It was about this time that Samuel said to Graham Wallas that if there were a revolution Shaw would not be at the barricades, to which Wallas replied, 'There you are quite wrong. That is just where he would be, but explaining to everybody within earshot how preposterous the whole proceeding was!'

Seven months after G.B.S.'s Labour Manifesto was issued and widely distributed, the Independent Labour Party was formed. Its first party programme was drafted by him and Keir Hardie, as oddly dissimilar a pair of collaborators as ever existed, though Hardie had a grace of mind and manner which caused G.B.S. to say to me that he was the only gentleman in the House of Commons.

85

Soon after the uproar about *Ghosts* had subsided, J. T. Grein, who had announced his ardent desire to produce a play of quality by a British dramatist, went for a long walk with G.B.S. which started in the Hammersmith Road round about midnight and ended they knew not where in the early hours of the morning. Grein complained with sorrow that he had not received a single play of any worth in response to his appeal. G.B.S. suggested that he should announce that his next production would be a play by him, and Grein, almost greedily, accepted the suggestion.

The unfinished piece he had tried to write in collaboration with Archer was then disinterred. Two acts were complete. He added a third, named the play *Widowers' Houses*, and dispatched the script to Grein.

On Friday, December 9, 1892, it was performed at the Royalty Theatre. Florence Farr acted the part of Blanche Sartorius with considerable satisfaction to herself, since Jenny Patterson was in the audience. Casting the part of Lickcheese had given Grein and the producer, Herbert de Lange, and G.B.S. great trouble and anxiety, and they had not yet found a suitable actor for it when, one day, during a rehearsal at the Bedford Hotel in Maiden Lane, 'a diminutive young man, with an old face, and short, crispy red hair, popped his head in at the door.' He had come there by mistake, but his appearance was such that he was drawn into the room, handed the book of Lickcheese's part, and invited to read it, which he did so well that he was immediately given the part. His name was James Welch, a brilliant comedian, who was then unknown, and he was immensely successful as the slum-lord's rent-collector.

Widowers' Houses, which was described as 'An Original Didactic Realistic Play', a description sufficiently deterrent to the vast majority of playgoers at that time, as it would be to audiences to-day, was performed twice: a fact which would seem certain to prevent it from receiving much attention in the public press. It received a great deal, some of it abusive, but none so hysterically vituperative as that evoked by *Ghosts*. Two daily papers published editorial articles on it, together with long reviews by their dramatic critics, and the argument lasted for a week: for those were days when men could stretch their legs under the table and have their argument out, as Dr Johnson said. Several of the critics attacked it as a piece of Ibsenism, although the first two acts had been written before G.B.S. had either seen or read an Ibsen play. But to mention rackrent and slums on the stage was, it seems, almost as great a breach of good taste as it was to mention the wages of sin. The excitement in the papers was equalled by the excitement in the theatre. While the Socialists in the pit and gallery lustily cheered G.B.S.'s debating points, the Conservatives in the stalls and dress circle lustily booed.

Widowers' Houses suffers severely from the fact that its third act was written in haste seven years after the first and second, both of which are well and carefully composed. The third act almost collapses at its conclusion. The mood of the writing, moreover, is notably different at the end of the play from what it was at the beginning. The mind of a man of thirty-six is not what it was when he was twenty-nine. The play, therefore, is inconsistent with itself. Moving with vigour through two acts, it stumbles to a lame conclusion in the third. The characters, except for Trench, are where they were at the start, and Trench is a disillusioned and despondent man, willing to live on means he despises, and certain, sooner or later, to be discarded by Blanche when her lust is sated.

Those who have seen or read *Widowers' Houses* can easily understand why Archer withdrew from the collaboration when they remember his account of the plot he had contrived from Augier's *Ceinture Dorée*. There was nothing of Archer or Augier in it: it was pure and unabashed G.B.S., except for two characters, Sartorius and Lickcheese, both of whom are derived, not only in nature and relationship, but

245

in actual situation, from Casby, the owner of Bleeding Heart Yard in *Little Dorrit*, and Pancks, his rent collector.[1]

But Archer's inability to appreciate the quality of the dramatist who had now appeared in the theatre for the first time, is surprising. There is here no taint of envy that G.B.S. had succeeded in doing what Archer had hitherto failed to do, write a play. The writer will not have done his duty if he has failed to make his readers realise the rectitude and incorruptible integrity of William Archer, who could not lie or palter with friend or foe, but treated the one as he treated the other, with transparent sincerity. His affection for G.B.S. was profound, and it did not weaken even when, as sometimes happened, G.B.S. disappointed or angered him. The noble generosity which he showed him when help was needed should be sufficient in itself to reveal the greatness of his character. He may have been, indeed, he was obtuse at times, but he was never for a second of his life insincere, envious or spiteful. His inability to perceive value in G.B.S. as a writer of plays was entirely due to the short view he took of the nature of plays: a view which, oddly enough, was at variance with an opinion he expressed in a letter, dated September 28, 1890,[2] to the famous American dramatic critic, Brander Matthews; 'The great dramatist will make his own technique, will study the conditions of life for himself, and, by gradually dominating his public, modify his conditions to suit his own needs of utterance,' all of which is precisely with G.B.S. did. To say this is not entirely to agree with Archer. Dramatists do not fail to be great because they submit to certain conditions in regard to the theme or the form of their plays; as the Greek dramatists, as Shakespeare largely did. But Archer's argument is sufficiently sound to justify its use almost as an irrefragable law of the drama's growth; and it makes his inability to detect the genius in G.B.S. all the harder to understand.

As he listened to the mingled cheers and boos with which the author was received at the end of the first performance of *Widowers' Houses*, and observed how completely G.B.S. subdued the audience by an entertaining speech lasting for three minutes, he might have been expected to realise that here was a dramatist who, though his work was antipathetic to him, was nevertheless a man of remarkable and, perhaps, great parts. But no such recognition was made. The play bewildered and disconcerted Archer. It was deplorably unlike the work of Pinero. Why had G.B.S. made Blanche an ill-conditioned termagant who half-throttled her maid when she was in a violent

---

[1] The reader who is curious about the matter, may entertain himself by comparing the scene in Act Two, where Sartorius dismisses Lickcheese from his service, with that in chapter 32 of the second book of *Little Dorrit*. G.B.S. had a deep love of Dickens's work.

[2] *William Archer*, By Charles Archer, p. 190.

rage? What was the point of this irrelevant digression? He might as well have wondered why Hamlet, when the Players came to Elsinore, thought it necessary to treat them to a dissertation on acting, why Ibsen made Nora in *A Doll's House* so greedy for chocolate creams.

The explanation of Blanche, both as a woman and as a brutal mistress of a maid, is plainly given in the play. Her father is a man of sudden and ungovernable rage, a greedy man who will not allow any duty or obligation to stand between him and his desire. Like father, like daughter. G.B.S. was writing about people he had observed in his intimate social relationships or seen in the street, and not about people who had been manufactured in Scribe's factory. There was a night when, walking down Mandeville Place, he had seen a virago seize her cowering and devoted companion by the hair and almost haul her head off, and the memory of that spectacle had furnished him with material for the second act of *Widowers' Houses*. And had he not intimate knowledge of Jenny Patterson? How idle it is to enquire why a dramatist makes a character do this or that! He may not know. Why should we expect an author to understand why his creatures behave as they do when parents are bewildered by the acts of their children? If the people in a play have any life in them, they take possession of themselves and disobey their author when the fit seizes them; and an author realises that his people have come to life only when he feels them tugging at his reins in their efforts to gain release from his control. G.B.S., in fact, does account for Blanche, but even if he had not done so, he could do no other than let her rage and storm when she was thwarted.

Archer, despite his deep and unquenchable affection for G.B.S., was to feel puzzled for the whole of his life by the cuckoo he had hatched. In his bewilderment at *Widowers' Houses*, he charged him with total ignorance of rack-rented slums, exposing his critical chin in doing so as mortal man has seldom done; for G.B.S. wrote him an affectionate postcard in which he wondered at Archer's reckless assertion. 'Here am I, who have collected slum rents weekly with these hands, and for $4\frac{1}{2}$ years been behind the scenes of the middle-class landowner— who have philandered with women of all sorts and sizes—and I am told gravely to go to nature and give up a-priorising about such matters by you, you sentimental Sweet Lavendery recluse.' Dickens, when he exposed Dotheboys Hall in *Nickolas Nickleby*, knew less about the hell holes that were called schools in Yorkshire than G.B.S. knew about slums in London and Dublin, yet no one accused him of total ignorance of Squeers and his dreadful family and the miserable little boys he starved.

But Archer was to make a bigger gaffe even than these two when the play was published in the Independent Theatre series edited by

Grein, in 1893. Reviewing the book, to which he, as well as Grein and G.B.S., had contributed a preface, he solemnly assured his readers that:

'It is a pity that Mr Shaw should labour under a delusion as to the true bent of his talent, and, mistaking an amusing *jeu d'esprit* for a work of creative art, should perhaps be tempted to devote further time and energy to a form of production for which he has no special ability and some constitutional disabilities. A man of his power of mind can do nothing that is altogether contemptible. We may be sure that if he took palette and "commenced painter" or set to work to manipulate a lump of clay, he would produce a picture or a statue that would bear the impress of a keen intelligence, and would be well worth looking at. This is precisely the case with *Widowers' Houses*. It is a curious example of what can be done in art by sheer brain-power, apart from natural aptitude. For it does not appear that Mr Shaw has any more specific talent for the drama than he has for painting or sculpture.'[1]

This is singular stuff. No man, however powerful his mind may be, can work in any other form than his own in such a manner as to reveal his keen intelligence to the casual beholder. A poem or a symphony by Darwin would be a strange performance, more likely to excite derision than respect; and we may doubt if a statue carved by Beethoven or Milton or Cervantes would cause anybody to do more than scribble on it offensive or indecent remarks. G.B.S., despite his boyhood ambition to become a painter, had no talent whatever as an artist, was devoid even of the small talent H. G. Wells had for drawing comic caricatures. That Archer should have described a sociological work, full of moral passion, as *jeu d'esprit*, is absurd; but that he, with the evidence of a definitely dramatic genius before his eyes, should have been capable of asserting that Shaw had no 'more specific talent for the drama than he' had 'for painting or sculpture', defeats all understanding.

Archer must have forgotten, if he ever knew, that many great dramatists, like many great artists of all sorts, have been solemnly told by 'experts' to give up hope of ever succeeding in the art they have chosen to follow. Had he forgotten that Keats was ordered back to his gallipots on the ground that he 'had no specific talent' for poetry, and that Ruskin, the Pope of painting, accused Whistler of flinging a pot of paint in the public's face? He must, one would have thought, have known that Ibsen was told by the leading dramatic critic of Copenhagen that he 'had no specific talent for' writing plays and would be better employed doling out ipecacuanha in that apothecary's shop in Grimstad from which he had come to change the drama of the world. He would probably have agreed with the

[1] Cited by Archibald Henderson in *Bernard Shaw: Playboy and Prophet*, p. 458.

248

theatre manager in Moscow, who, with kindly intent, told Chekhov that he, too, 'had no specific talent' for writing plays and would be wise to return to his pills and potions. Had not the dramatic critics in St Petersburg driven Chekhov to the verge of suicide by their taunts and derision? Did not the dying Greene, whose plays were unpopular in his lifetime and have faded out of the memory of men, deride and denounce the upstart Shakespeare who had the audacity to write plays and challenge him, Greene, who had forgotten more about the drama than the clown from Stratford was ever likely to know? Archer should have remembered these things. Amazingly, he forgot them, though he was, and very soon, to eat his words when *Mrs Warren's Profession* appeared.

Despite its faults, *Widowers' Houses* has immense vitality, and it still seizes the attention of audiences wherever it is produced, although the world it describes scarcely exists, and, where it does exist, lives only because the good will of the world has been temporarily thwarted by the evil effects of two World Wars. Sir Toby Belch and Maria are more likely to be met in the common encounters of life than Lickcheese and Blanche, but this fact does not destroy the verisimilitude of G.B.S.'s people who continue to exist, but in a less elementary and uncouth condition. Vehement women with violent and uncontrollable tempers have not vanished off the face of the earth, and Lickcheese, though he is now sprucer and more prosperous than his prototype is still to be seen about. Squeers and Fagin have tidied themselve up, and their speech is trimmer than it was when Dickens drew them, but they remain essentially the same. The three card trick and the pea and the thimble still seduce simpletons, who will continue to be plentiful as long as life lasts.

If Archer had complained of the scramble that was the third act of the play, he would have displayed critical faculty and have rendered G.B.S. another service. But he was too busy wondering why Blanche nearly choked her maid to notice that Lickcheese, four months after he has been dismissed by Sartorius, suddenly turns up in evening dress and furred coat splendour, rich and ready to be richer, though the explanation of his prosperity would not impose upon a child of twelve. The play was a propagandist piece, written in a passion for social reform, but it was more than that: it was a Morality Play with veritable men and women for its characters, a piece written strictly in the mood, though superior in the writing, of the Morality Plays of the Middle Ages, to enforce the faith that the Church had been failing to enforce for several centuries.

All the moral fervour that was G.B.S. is transparent in *Widowers' Houses*. This lightweight and flippant person, who flashed his wit everywhere and was pursued by women, was a man with a profound belief about life, a preacher not less determined than Savonarola to call sinners to repentance. To him, slums and poverty and hunger and malnutrition and avoidable disease were evils that stank before high heaven.

86

The itch to write plays had taken a long time to develop, but now that it had developed, he wrote them rapidly. His second piece, like the second play of many dramatists, was a poor thing, in which he set out to guy the Ibsenites. In every camp of pioneers there are hangers-on, tedious people who are always on the prowl for something new or rampant with desire to do what everybody does. It was inevitable that *A Doll's House* should start silly women from Surbiton banging doors behind them, as Nora had done in Ibsen's play: and G.B.S., who had no more illusions about advanced women than he had about those that were retrograde, wrote *The Philanderer* to deride them. There is a moment in the life of every pioneering man when he feels the need to round on some of his followers.

The most devoted of G.B.S.'s admirers have difficulty in liking *The Philanderer*. Its chief value is that it enabled him to get Jenny Patterson out of his system. When he created Julia Craven, he destroyed Jenny. So far as G.B.S. is concerned, she disappears from knowledge. Little is known of her life after the breach was made. But she played a notable part in his history. She taught him the way of a woman with a man, and gave him knowledge of her sex that he had never had until he met her. If she could have controlled her moods of violence, she would have had a greater influence in his life and would have given him revelations of femininity that he still required.

She was a gifted woman, with a swift sense of humour that enabled her to recoil from her own wrath and turn it into laughter. One night, while still in friendship with Lucinda Elizabeth, she was walking through a country lane at night with Lucinda's step-niece, Judy Gillmore. They were both startled by the figure of a man lurking in a hedge, and Jenny, who had plenty of spirit, caught hold of her dog with one hand and went forward with her stick in the other. The lurking man turned out to be a youth who had crept into the hedge because he felt abashed by meeting two women. When Jenny angrily demanded, 'Why the devil didn't you speak, boy?' he replied, 'I ain't got nothin' to say!' a remark so wise and unexpected that Jenny dissolved her rage in laughter and gave him half a crown.

The Philanderer was written in haste, and it is singularly lacking in vivacity and wit. Leonard Charteris, the philanderer, is obviously

G.B.S. himself, and an inept figure, called Joseph Cuthbertson, is admitted by him to have been modelled on Clement Scott who, however, must have had far more *to* him than appears in Cuthbertson. There is a scene in the first act, in which Julia Craven invades Grace Tranfield's home and rails at her like a shrew: it is based on the encounter between Jenny Patterson and Florence Farr which has already been described. The third and fourth acts are superior in quality to the first and second, an unusual characteristic of plays by beginners, many of whom can write a tolerably good first act, but fall to pieces over the last. The good scenes in the play are those in which Dr Paramore is horrified by discovering that his great cure for liver complaints has been exposed by other doctors as totally ineffective.

This is the first of his attacks on doctors, and especially on those of them who profess to be scientists when they discover that a dog, after it has been vivisected, suffers some disability. But the scene is not sufficient to save the play from dullness and triviality.

It was offered to The Independent Theatre, but G.B.S. decided that it needed a delicacy of acting and a longer period of rehearsal than Grein's slightly-financed society could afford. It was, therefore, put aside, and was not publicly performed until 1905, twelve years after it was written. But its revivals have been few and unfavourably received. Its author came to dislike it as much as the public did. In a letter to Ellen Terry, he belittles it in extravagant language. While staying with the Webbs, to whom he read plays in the evening—he read them extremely well—he had 'to fall back on my Opus 2, a comedy called *The Philanderer*, now some years old. It turned out to be a combination of mechanical farce with realistic filth which quite disgusted me: and I felt that if my plays get stale at this rate, I cannot afford to postpone their production longer than I can help.' What he means here by 'realistic filth' is beyond conjecture, but there is nothing in the play to deserve that description in the common understanding of it.

The next play G.B.S. wrote was as serious and as moral in its purpose as *Ghosts*, and it would almost certainly have met with the same reception had it been publicly performed. The Lord Chamberlain, however, banned its production because, like Shelley's *The Cenci* which was also banned, it had a hint of incest in it. The rules governing the production of plays in England were fixed early in the eighteenth century at the behest of a corrupt politician, Walpole, who feared the effect of Fielding's satire when expressed on the stage.

Corrupt politicians always start their persecutions by professing high moral standards; and Walpole unctuously followed the fashion.

Several subjects were forbidden to be treated in plays. Sacred figures, such as God and Jesus, must not be exhibited, although their exhibition was common in the Medieval Morality Plays. God might be heard, as he is in *Everyman*, but must not be seen. Walpole's true purpose appeared in another rule, which forbade actors and actresses to portray living people on the stage. They might be cartooned and caricatured in the press, but not in the theatre. Members of the Royal Family, even if they had been dead for a century, were not to be dramatised, though their biographies, favourable or unfavourable, might be written. Laurence Housman's play, *Pains and Penalties*, which is concerned with the marriage relations of George IV and Queen Caroline, was banned, though they had both been dead about a hundred years. Our forefathers were less squeamish. Shakespeare wrote a play, dealing frankly with the matrimonial misadventures of Henry VIII, and it was publicly performed in the reign of his daughter. Housman, who seemed to have a passion for prying into the lives of royalties, wrote another play, outlining the life of Queen Victoria, which was also banned; but, because of the good sense of the Royal House, the ban on both his plays was lifted.

Walpole was far less interested in the protection of his sovereign than he was in his own. He was determined to prevent any stage satire of himself and his gang of devious ministers; and he inserted a clause in his Bill to prevent dramatists from including any living person or any person in a particular class in the list of his characters. This gross violation of the people's rights to utter opinions about important persons continues to be the law, though it has been greatly modified and the conditions of play production, so far as the Lord Chamberlain is concerned, substantially improved, chiefly as a result of the wise administration of the late Earl of Cromer, who showed great discretion during his term of office.

Among the matters which were not to be mentioned in plays was incest. Our minds have changed considerably on this subject in recent years, and there are biologists who say that where the stock is sound, incest has no deleterious effect on the stamina of the race. There are, of course, other grounds of objection to incest than its effect on the stock, and we need not, therefore, much concern ourselves with what the biologists say. But it is plain that to ban incest as a matter of dramatic interest is absurd, especially when any novelist may make it the central theme of his work, and the dramatist, indeed, may publish his play, though he may not have it performed. This cause of ban has now been removed, but it was in force when *Mrs Warren's Profession* was written, and it is impressive to learn that the sole cause of the ban was the incidental reference to the possibility that Vivie Warren and Frank Gardner might be half-brother and sister.[1] Had the few short speeches in which this possibility was mentioned been removed, the play could have been publicly performed, despite the peculiarity of Mrs Warren's profession.

But G.B.S. was determined to put the whole of his argument, and would not agree to have any part of it suppressed.

Let it be made plain at the start, that *Mrs Warren's Profession* is an entirely moral play, written with no other intent than to expose a grave social evil. It could be endorsed with the approval of the Archbishop of Canterbury, the Cardinal Archbishop of Westminster, the Moderator of the General Assembly, the Chairman of the Congregational Union, and, with more authority perhaps than any of the others, the General of The Salvation Army. There may be some force in the argument that the stage is not the proper place in which to conduct reformations, though this is a highly debatable argument, but it is clear that if subjects which are considered unpleasant by polite people, deeply averse from anything that is not insipid and undisturbing, are to be banned on the stage, then the right of the dramatist to express himself is profoundly restricted, and in a way that would not be tolerated by any other person.

Had there been a censorship of plays in Great Britain in Shakespeare's time, similar to that which resulted in the banning of *Mrs Warren's Profession*, a large number of his plays would not have been performed and would probably not have been written. *Hamlet* is concerned with the incestuous marriage, as Hamlet calls it, of his mother and uncle. In *Pericles, Prince of Tyre*, a scene is laid in a brothel in which Marina is immured, and we see her in danger of losing her virginity when the Bawd attempts to sell her to one of his customers, Lysimachus. Such a scene would almost certainly not have been licenced in the work of any modern dramatist in the Victorian era, though, by some singular logic, plays which had been written and performed before the Walpole Act came into force, were left unbanned, and so there was no interference with Shakespeare's work.

Mrs Warren, who, like her sister came out of a slum to become a prostitute, has, again like her sister, prospered exceedingly. It was part of G.B.S.'s offence that he did not bring his prostitutes to a bad end, financially as well as morally. The sister, who does not appear in the play, saves so much money that she is able to retire to a Cathedral city, where she lives in the odour of sanctity and is highly respected by all the inhabitants of the Close, who, of course, are unaware of her history. Mrs Warren becomes the managing director of a chain of hotel brothels scattered about Europe,

[1] A similar situation, much more elaborately described and more important in the general scheme of the play, occurs in *A Confidential Clerk* by Mr T. S. Eliot, without, however, causing the Lord Chamberlain to turn a hair. It is a pleasing thought that G.B.S. prepared the way for Mr Eliot.

and one of her directors is a country gentleman, Sir George Crofts.

Some remnant of proletarian pride and sense of shame has made Mrs Warren conceal her occupation from her daughter, Vivie, who has been educated in good schools and at Cambridge. How she contrived to keep her daughter ignorant of the source of her income is not explained, but it is impressive to compare G.B.S.'s treatment of such a situation as this with Oscar Wilde's in *A Woman of No Importance*. Wilde ignores the probabilities in his play, letting Mrs Arbuthnot's noodle of a son grow to manhood without ever once having wondered why he had no paternal relatives and had never seen a portrait of his father. Wilde was intellectually incapable of conceiving such characters as Vivie and her mother, and could not have composed the dialogue that follows Mrs Warren's tearful enquiry: 'Have I no rights over you as your mother?'

> Vivie: Are you my mother?
> Mrs Warren (*appalled*): Am I your mother? Oh, Vivie!
> Vivie: Then where are our relatives—my father—our family friends? You claim the rights of a mother: the right to call me fool and child; to speak to me as no woman in authority over me at college dare speak to me; to dictate my way of life; and to force on me the acquaintance of a brute whom anyone can see to be the most vicious sort of London man about town. Before I give myself the trouble to resist such claims, I may as well find out whether they have any real existence.
> Mrs Warren (*distracted, throwing herself on her knees*): Oh, no, no. Stop, stop. I am your mother: I swear it. Oh, you can't mean to turn on me—my own child: it's not natural. You believe me, don't you? Say you believe me.
> Vivie: Who was my father?
> Mrs Warren: You don't know what you're asking. I can't tell you.
> Vivie (*determinedly*): Oh, yes you can, if you like. I have a right to know; and you know very well that I have that right. You can refuse to tell me if you please; but if you do, you will see the last of me tomorrow morning.
> Mrs Warren: Oh, it's too horrible to hear you talk like that. You wouldn't—couldn't leave me.
> Vivie (*ruthlessly*): Yes, without a moment's hesitation, if you trifle with me about this. (*Shivering with disgust*) How can I feel sure that I may not have the contaminated blood of that brutal waster in my veins.

Her mother assures Vivie that, whoever her father may have been, she is positive that he is not Sir George Crofts.

This passage of dialogue still sounds shocking; but we are a more sophisticated people than our grandparents were in 1893, and we can listen with little more than mild discomfort to words and sentiments that would have shattered them. The world, even that part of it which was tough-minded and held advanced views, was not yet ready for G.B.S. *Mrs Warren's Profession*, which is a well-made play, as skilfully devised as any piece by Sardou or Pinero, marches convincingly from revelation to revelation with ease and assurance. The culmination comes at the conventional right moment, when Vivie and Frank are told by Crofts that Frank's father, the vicar of the parish, who seems to have been a scallywag in his youth, begot Vivie. She and Frank are, therefore, half-sister and brother. But the play concludes with a hint that he is not her father, though he could have been. Mrs Warren herself obviously does not know who begot her daughter.

It is doubtful, indeed, if G.B.S. knew. Writing to Janet Achurch on September 4, 1893, he tells here that:

> 'the play progresses bravely; but it has left the original lines. I have made the daughter the heroine, and the mother a most deplorable old rip (saving your presence). The great scene will be the crushing of the mother by the daughter. I retain the old *roué*, but keep him restrained by a continual doubt as to whether the heroine may not be his own daughter. The young lover's father, an outrageous clergyman, is in the same perplexity, he also being an old flame of the mother's. The lover is an agreeable young spark, wholly good-for-nothing. The girl is quite an original character. The mother, uncertain who the girl's father is, keeps all the old men at bay by telling each one that he is the parent. The second act is half finished and wholly planned.'

Mrs Warren's Profession is the first play in which the modern, independent-minded woman appears. Vivie is entirely unromantic, and would, in life, be remarkably unattractive to the mass of men: a woman almost certain to live in perpetual virginity; the sort of woman G.B.S. professed to admire, though none of the women with whom he philandered was in the least like her.

It was Beatrice Webb who demanded that he should write a play 'about a real, modern, unromantic, hardworking woman', resembling, presumably, Beatrice Webb; and as neither he nor she liked each other, the effort to create a sympathetic character in her image was certain to result in a very displeasing woman. Why Beatrice should have imagined that a romantic and idle woman, full of sex, is unreal, is hard to understand. Jenny Patterson was as real as she was and, in certain respects, much more pleasant to live with. But G.B.S., when he wrote this play, was in full reformatory mood, very indignant about almost everything, and deliberately challenging all the conventions of his age. He wished to create a character who would be in complete, if not violent, contrast to the popular heroine, the sort of soft, yielding girl who can best be described as the Rector's only daughter, a girl who has no opinions of her own, and will, on the slightest provocation, rise up and recite *The Collier's Dying Child* in the Parish Room, amid rounds of applause from sycophantic old women.

But unpleasing though Vivie is, she was, undoubtedly, a sign and a portent to those who had discerning eyes in 1893. A generation of girls who were in their cradles then, would, in a couple of decades or so, reveal her characteristics. They would soon be demanding votes, and, after the demand was made and many of them had been imprisoned and forcibly fed, be put into uniform and packed off to the battle fields of France and elsewhere. In a later war, *their* daughters would be conscripted: a fact which, strangely, revolted G.B.S. What experience was it that made Vivie round on her mother when she began to snivel about being the victim of her environment? 'People are always blaming their circumstances for what they are,' Vivie exclaims in contempt and disgust. 'I don't believe in circumstances. The people who get on in this world are the people who get up and look for the circumstances they want, and, if they can't find them, make them.' She may be forgiven much for that valiant remark.

Mrs Warren's Profession is a hard, almost bitter, play, but it is as moral as Savonarola. It goes to its end without a deviation. The impish and digressive Shaw is here held strictly in leash. This is no play for nonsense.

Praed is the single character in the play who is not accounted for. How did be become acquainted with Mrs Warren? What bond, if any, was between them? He reminds Crofts that he has never had anything to do with 'that side of Mrs Warren's life', but as it is the only side of life she had shown the world since her flight from the factory in the East End of London, where, as a young, nubile girl, she was employed, it is hard to understand how he came to know her, apart altogether from working with her in a considerable degree of intimacy. These, however, are minor faults, both of which could easily have been removed. But as the play had been banned, a possibility of which G.B.S. could not have been oblivious, there was, we may suppose, no point in their removal, since, so far as he could discern, there was no likelihood of the ban ever being lifted. Thirty-two years after it was written, it was publicly performed for the first time in London at the Regent Theatre on September 28, 1925,[1] but it then seemed to be dated and remarkably mild. The crowd had not only caught up with the pioneer, but had passed him.

[1] It had, however, been privately performed by the Stage Society, after great trouble in obtaining a theatre, at the New Lyric Club in Coventry Street, on January 5 and 6, 1902. See Rattray's *Bernard Shaw: a Chronicle*, p. 151. There was another performance given a decade later by the Pioneer Players under the direction of Miss Edith Craig, Ellen Terry's daughter.

256

87

His chief associates in the theatre at this time were Janet Achurch and her husband, Charles Charrington (Martin), to whom he wrote many letters.[1] One of them, written to Charrington, and dated March 1, 1895, in addition to a scarifying account of his activities in a single week, contains an impressive statement of his artistic creed. It is too long to quote in its entirety, but the following excerpts give the gist:

'I have not often formulated the lessons of my apprenticeship as a writer; but I did once write down in a notebook something like this: YOU CANNOT BE AN ARTIST UNTIL YOU HAVE CON-TRACTED YOURSELF WITHIN THE LIMITS OF YOUR ART. Now, the effect the artist produces on others is that of unlimitedness; and it is this great mystery and infinitude which attracts us all to art at first in these days. but when you get to practice an art, you find that the unlimited length before you is of exactly the same nature as the unlimited length before a horse in a circus. . . .

'I have my feeling for the exquisitely cultivated sense of beauty— an almost devotional sense—and the great pains and skill of execution which produces work of one kind, and for the bold ideas, the daring unscrupulous handling, the imaginative illusions that produce another kind. And I have a leaning towards the former that you dont sympathise with, although some bit of work resulting from it may here and there captivate you. I prefer a woman knitting to Ajax fighting the sheep, because I know that although very little will come of the knitting, nothing will come of the fighting. . . .'

a statement which can be denied reasonably and historically.

'. . . So do you, in acting, because you know all about the histrionic Ajax; but in literature you still have a notion that there is a future for Ajax, and that I am opposing my limitations to his infinity.

I assure you he cant get out of the ring any more that I can: and as to your crowds, they are very fine things; and in *William Tell* and *Rienzi* you have very stirring dramas of the crowd: Hauptmann's *Weavers* also suggests good business in that direction; but when you see a man like me, trying to do in counterpoint in even so few as three real parts, as in *Candida*, or in seven, as in the finale of *The Philanderer*, never tell him he ought to go and write choruses instead. I grant you the work is not so skilful as if I had been more years at it; but there is no more worthy sort of work to try for. It is as good as I can get it at my present stage. . . .

'You are rather like Hedda Gabler in respect of your having discovered so much of what was shoved down your throat as a virtue to

[1] I am indebted to Mr Ashley Dukes, one of my oldest friends in London, for copies of the letters to the Charringtons.

be a fraud, that you idealise the repudiation of the seven deadly virtues. Now, in art this does not do. You must plod away diligently in the station of life to which your vocation has called you, making the work always as good as you can, turning methodically from the fine sentence of which you have corrected the grammar to the punctuation of the next, like the ant or the bee or the good boy, or any other disgusting character in books for the edification of youth. . . .

'I got nothing for nothing; had to slave and plod for bare life to make myself at all current; and the result is the brilliant red-bearded creature you now see. Nature gave Janet a success half ready made, and enabled her to do things with impunity for which I should, so to speak, have been pelted from the stage and sacked next morning.

'I want a revival of the art of beautiful acting; and I know it to be impossible without tremendous practice and constant aiming at beauty of execution, not through a mechanical study of poses and pronunciations (though every actor should be a plastic and phonetic expert), but through a cultivation of delicate feeling and absolute renunciation of all the coarser elements of popularity. And I must lay my plays out for that

'You have no idea, I believe, of the limitations under which I write, and constant search for the right sort of distinction, whether of style or thought or humor or vulgarity—how very nicely I have to ascertain the truth in order that I may find the true error with such precision as to make it appear that it was the first thing that came into the head of the character into whose mouth I put it. Of course, that is no more than my business; and you are quite right to take it for granted, and proceed to grumble at what I have *not* done; but it is none the less indispensable. . . .

'You may depend on it, I will get my plays performed all I can, whatever I may say to Wyndham in another connexion. Also, I will let emotion and passion have all the play I can in my characters. But you must recollect that there is distinction even in emotion and passion; and that the finer kinds will not run through the well worn channels of speech. They make new intellectual speech channels; and for some time these will necessarily appear so strange and artificial that it will be supposed that they are incapable of conveying emotion. They said for many years, remember, that Wagner's endless melody was nothing but discord.'

88

He had now written three plays, one of which had been performed, and that only for two times in semi-privacy. He had not earned a penny piece by any of them. There had been a lively argument in the press about *Widowers' Houses*, some of it full of admiration, some of it very acrimonious, but all of it stimulating. That, however, was all. Neither the play nor the discussion in the newspapers had any effect on theatre managers, who, probably, had not so much as heard of the production or read the press debates, and would not have paid much attention to either if they had. If the managers were indifferent or ignorant, so was the general playgoing public who took no notice of any reports they may have seen in the press of a new star ascending the theatrical heaven. There was always a star rising or shooting somewhere. One more luminary in a universe resplendent with stars was neither here nor there. It was impossible to keep count of the stars, even if keeping count were worth the trouble.

Widowers' Houses subsided into silence after its two performances before selected and rarified audiences. *The Philanderer* had not been performed at all. *Mrs Warren's Profession* had been banned. Grein, who was deeply shocked by it, a curious fact when we remember that he had produced *Ghosts* almost in an evangelistic mood, could not have produced it for the Independent Theatre, if he had wished to do so, because the theatre owners were fearful that if they allowed a banned play to be performed even in semi-privacy in any theatre belonging to them, the Lord Chamberlain might visit his displeasure on them by opposing the renewal of their licences.

As a beginning to a career in the theatre, this record could not be called encouraging. The plays, like the novels, had fallen by the wayside, and seemed certain to die ungerminated. The outlook for G.B.S. in the theatre was bleak. But there were bright passages in his life, and as long as he could earn his keep, while doing the job of socialist propaganda which he liked, he did not greatly care how his pocket flourished.

The Fabian Society kept him busy, and he had lately begun in a casual manner a charming correspondence with Ellen Terry. The letters they exchanged are among the most pleasing examples of epistolary writing that have ever been published:[1] as charming and witty and wise on Ellen Terry's part as on G.B.S.'s. When, after her death, the letters were collected and published, aged women in Kensington hotels professed to feel shocked by them, and could not be convinced that the correspondants had not lived in sin; despite the clear statement in the book that they had not met until after the correspondence had virtually ended. They had exchanged a few words in the vestibule of a theatre at the end of a performance, but she was unaware of the identity of the stranger who offered her some courtesy, nor did she know of their encounter until it was casually mentioned by G.B.S. in one of his letters.

The correspondence was entirely platonic, a delightful exhibition of paper passion, carried on by two brilliant people who wrote to each other purely for pleasure, and quite deliberately did not meet lest

[1] *Ellen Terry and Bernard Shaw. A Correspondence.* Edited by Christopher St John.

their romance should be spoilt by reality. When there was a suggestion that she might produce *Candida*—she never did—he refused to let her have it to read because the recurrent trouble she had with her eyes was bothering her again. He would read it to her, 'if I have to do it through the keyhole. But I, too, fear to break the spell: remorses, presentiments, all sorts of tendernesses wring my heart at the thought of materialising this beautiful friendship of ours by a meeting.'

In October, 1896, he wrote, 'Mind, I am not to be your lover, nor your friend: for a day of reckoning comes for both love and friendship. You would soon feel like the Wandering Jew: you would know that you *must* get up and move on. You must enter into an inexorably interested relation with me. My love, my friendship are worth nothing. Nothing for nothing.

> 'I must be used, built into the solid fabric of your life as far as there is any usable brick in me, and thrown aside when I am used up. It is only when I am being used that I can feel my own existence, enjoy my own life. All my love affairs end tragically because the women can't *use* me. They lie low and let me imagine things about them; but in the end a frightful unhappiness, an unspeakable weariness comes; and the Wandering Jew must go on in search of someone who can use him to the utmost of his capacity. Everything real in life is based on *need;* just so far as you need me I have you tightly in my arms; beyond that I am only a luxury, and, for luxuries, love and hate are the same passion.'

But this is nonsense, as he himself in the following sentence, confesses. He makes a list of his women friends in a later passage of the same letter, mentioning 'my Irish lady with the light green eyes and the million of money', who was Charlotte and destined to marry him. Finally, 'There is Ellen, to whom I vow that I will try hard not to spoil my high regard, my worthy respect, my deep tenderness, by any of those philandering follies which make me so ridiculous, so troublesome, so vulgar with women. I swear it. Only, so as you have hitherto done with so wise an instinct: keep out of my reach.'

Ellen Terry was his senior by eight years, and she had married G. F. Watts before she was sixteen. She left him to live with Edward William Godwin, the architect, by whom she had two children, Edward Gordon Craig, who was twenty when the correspondence with G.B.S. began, and his sister Edith. Ellen was now the wife o Charles Wardell, to whom she was married in 1876, the year in which G.B.S. arrived in London. It was soon after his arrival that he saw her on the stage for the first time, in T. W. Robertson's comedy, *Ours*, during the Bancrofts' seasons at their little theatre in Tottenham Court Road. He was less struck by her performance than he had expected to be, but when, towards the end of 1876, he saw her in *New Men and Old Acres*, he was enchanted by her.

Her knowledge of his appearance was confined to a few glimpses of him taken in November, 1896, through the peep-hole of the curtain in the Lyceum Theatre:[1] the means by which players can look at an audience without themselves being seen.

The letters illuminate the character of each of the correspondents very vividly, and those written by G.B.S. contain scraps of autobiography that are invaluable. They are full of wit and wisdom and brilliant argument about acting and production of plays, but are more impressive than anything else that has been written because of their account of G.B.S.'s antagonism to Henry Irving. The reader sometimes suspects that G.B.S., at one period of the correspondence, is using Ellen as a means of gaining access to Irving, but if such was his intention, his efforts were unavailing, for Irving would have no truck with him. The quarrel was profound and could not be composed by polite patchings.

The cause of the quarrel is usually misstated. It sprang from a fundamental difference in the nature of the two men. Irving was a romantic egotist: Shaw was a realistic egotist. Irving saw the play, the stage, the cast as means by which he could realise his vision of himself. Shaw saw them as instruments for the reform of the social and economic system he advocated. There was, therefore, little likelihood that they would have any sympathetic understanding of each other. But they could, in certain circumstances, have worked together. Had Irving been more aware of the changing values of his world and of his own ability to make use of the new values that were coming into currency, and if G.B.S. had been less brash and more considerate of the feelings of the great actor whose genius he recognised, the story of their relations and of the LyceumTheatre might have been a very different and much happier one than it was.

It is not true that G.B.S. disesteemed Irving, though he sometimes expressed himself with harsh vehemence about him when he was irritated by what seemed to him crass stupidity. One could make a substantial list of highly appreciatory references he made to Irving throughout his critical career. What galled G.B.S., was that he used the theatre as an instrument on which to perform himself. The fact that the performance was sometimes superb did not reconcile him to its misuse. He complained that Irving degraded authors, notably Shakespeare, and other players, especially Ellen Terry, for his own glorification.

But never did he seriously underestimate Irving's genius. He complained, and rightly complained, that the great actor laid

[1] *Ellen Terry and Bernard Shaw*, Letter LXVIII, p. 105. 'I've seen you at last. You *are* a boy! And a Duck!'

irreverent hands on Shakespeare's plays, mutilating them shamelessly not only in their form but in the very nature of their characters.
'He had really only one part; and that was the part of Irving. His
Hamlet was not Shakespeare's Hamlet, nor his Lear Shakespeare's
Lear: they were both avatars of the imaginary Irving in whom he
was so absorbingly interested.' It is indisputable that Irving's
Shylock was not 'the Jew that Shakespeare drew', but it is equally
indisputable that the Jew Irving did draw was a figure of immense
power and quality. G.B.S., indeed, goes so far as to say that 'The
Merchant of Venice became the Martyrdom of Irving, which was, it
must be confessed, far finer than the Tricking of Shylock.'

It was a cardinal point in his complaint against Irving that he not
only committed sacrilege when he produced a play by Shakespeare, in
that he thought he knew better than its author how it should have
been written, but that he wasted both his own talent and that of
Ellen Terry 'on obsolete reactionary or' mutilated 'Shakespearean
drama'. He never produced a play by Shakespeare in which the
principal part is a woman's; and G.B.S. found it hard to forgive him
for not letting Ellen Terry perform Rosalind in *As You Like It*, 'which
she would certainly have insisted on playing if she had cared as much
for her own professional renown as for helping Irving.' It may be said
that Irving could hardly be expected to produce a play in which
there was no part, except the comparatively small one of the melancholy Jaques, for him; and he could have added the strong financial
objection that a production from which he was absent had an
unfortunate effect on the receipts.

G.B.S. overstated his case in this respect. It was not true, as he
himself admits, that Irving never produced a play in which Ellen
Terry performed the principal part. *Madame Sans-Gêne* is a play in
point. She took the chief woman's part in all the productions in
which they both appeared, and it is debatable who is more important,
Shylock or Portia, in *The Merchant of Venice*. Beatrice, in *Much Ado
About Nothing*, is not less than Rosalind. In any case, Irving was not
to blame for the fact that women figure less prominently than men
in the majority of the Shakespearean plays. There were no actresses
on the stage in the Elizabethan age. The women's parts were performed by boys and effeminate young men, and, therefore, Shakespeare was largely prevented from drawing women characters on as
large a scale as he drew men. It is one of the signs of genius that,
despite his disabilities in this respect, he created so many superb and
important women's parts.

The most substantial grievance G.B.S. had against Irving was his
neglect of modern drama; and the magnitude of this complaint is not
reduced because one of the modern dramatists almost ostentatiously

neglected was G.B.S. himself. But in making this complaint Shaw overlooked Irving's limitations. His ability to appreciate Ibsen was due to his nature, for which he was not responsible. A romantic cannot be denounced because he fails to appreciate realism. He would not be a romantic if he could. It is incredible and almost criminal that Irving did not produce *The Pretenders* and *John Gabriel Borkman*. The part of Bishop Nicholas in the first, and of Borkman in the second might have been written for him. But neither of these plays, despite their grandeur, have been profitable to those who produced them; and it was, surely, asking a great deal of a romantic actor that he should accept the certainty of heavy loss in work that he himself did not appreciate.

His failure to perceive the genius of Ibsen convinced G.B.S. that Irving was the protagonist of a dying dramatic tradition who wilfully refused to become the protagonist of a new and vigorous tradition. His refusal to produce *The Man of Destiny* and *Captain Brassbound's Conversion* was confirmation, if G.B.S. needed any, that Irving's day was done, and that there was no hope that he could rise from his ashes. Irving had forgotten what G.B.S. always remembered, that he was a comedian as well as a tragedian; and that the man who could make so much fun out of Jingle could be trusted to make as much out of Brassbound; and his sense of dignity, caused him to suspect that Shaw was trying to make him look ridiculous. He once, indeed, complained that G.B.S. had no respect for great people, which was not true, though it might easily have seemed to be true. A phrenologist, indeed, supported Irving's opinion. Feeling G.B.S.'s bumps, he complained that where there should have been a mound of reverence, there was a deep depression! The misunderstanding was total and could not be removed; and so the Lyceum was deprived of the spectacle of Irving, a brilliant comedian, and Ellen Terry, an equally brilliant comedienne, in two superb parts, Brassbound and Lady Cicely Wayneflete.

The substantial fact is that although G.B.S. often and sometimes absurdly denounced Irving, he never lost his great respect for him. In the preface to the Letters to Ellen Terry, he describes how in his youth, he saw Irving playing the part of Digby Grant in *The Two Roses*, a play which made an impression in the second half of the nineteenth century, but seems to those who read it to-day a tawdry piece of crude and pointless sentimentality. Still under the spell of a famous Irish actor, Barry Sullivan, whose description suggests that he must have been mentally deranged in some of his performances, G.B.S. saw in Irving more than a complete contrast to Sullivan:

'I instinctively felt that a new drama inhered in this man, though I had then no conscious notion that I was destined to write it; and I perceive now that I never forgave him for baffling the plans I made for him (always, be it remembered, unconsciously). . . . He was utterly unlike anyone else; he could give importance and a noble melancholy to any sort of drivel that was put into his mouth; and it was this melancholy, bound up with an impish humour, which forced the spectator to single him out as a leading figure with an inevitability that I never saw again in any other actor until it rose from Irving's grave in the person of a nameless cinema actor who afterwards became famous as Charlie Chaplin.'

What a theatre the Lyceum might have become had Irving and Ellen Terry and Shaw worked in it together, as Shaw worked with Granville-Barker at the Royal Court Theatre many years later. Irving might have been spared the last desolate years of his life when, like an old trooper, he went wandering in the wilderness, trying to live on his reputation.

89

Arms and the Man, which was originally called *Alps and Balkans*, G.B.S.'s fourth play, was produced at the Avenue Theatre, after-wards the Playhouse, in Northumberland Avenue on April 21, 1894. It was the first of his plays to be performed in the regular traffic of the West End theatre; and it owed its production to the bounty of a remarkable woman, Miss Annie Elizabeth Frederica Horniman, a member of a well-known and wealthy family of Friends, or, as they are sometimes disagreeably called, Quakers. Her father was a wealthy tea-merchant, and she had inherited a substantial sum from her grandfather in 1893, with which she financed enterprises that excite little or no enthusiasm in rich men who prefer to squander their substance on hospitals and orphanages, and would consider them-selves eccentric or otherwise disreputable if they were to spend a pound or two on any of the arts. Part of her history may be read in Mr Rex Pogson's *Miss Horniman and the Gaiety Theatre, Manchester*, and it proves how influential a woman, whose means, though ample, are not munificent, can be when she makes up her mind to do only what she believes to be worth doing.

She was the first person to finance a play by Bernard Shaw for public performance. She also produced one by W. B. Yeats, though his plays, except for the short piece called *Kathleen ni Houlihan*, were of no consequence. Yeats was a poet without any sense of drama. His plays are full of men and women who were never alive. The Abbey Theatre is thought by those who are ignorant of the facts to have been founded and largely maintained by Lady Gregory, that monumental widow who went about swathed in weeds and crape as if she were

Queen Victoria's understudy. It would not exist but for the substantial sums, amounting, in the aggregate, to £20,000, which Miss Horniman bestowed upon it. Those who are familiar with Eireans will not be surprised to learn that she was treated with ingratitude. When, in accounts of the Abbey Theatre, she is mentioned at all, she is made to seem vastly inferior to the Widow Gregory, who is now reputed to have practically ruined herself to found and support the theatre when, in fact, she never gave a farthing to it, but, quite legitimately, took many pounds from it.

Florence Farr had enlisted Miss Horniman's interest in a season of uncommercial plays she intended to produce at the Avenue Theatre. The first was to be *The Comedy of Sighs* by Dr John Todhunter, and it was to be supported by a short piece, entitled *The Land of Heart's Desire* by Yeats. Miss Horniman agreed to finance Miss Farr's season on one condition, that her association with it should not be made known. She had no wish to be involved in puritanical squabbles with her family because she was financing sinks of iniquity and hobnobbing with the sons and daughters of Belial. Todhunter's play was a total failure, and Florence Farr asked G.B.S. to let her revive *Widowers' Houses*, but he preferred to have a new play produced rather than an old one revived. He finished *Arms and the Man* at great speed, and it was immediately put into rehearsal. The cast, which contained some names that were afterwards to become notable in the theatre or elsewhere, was James Welch, who had already made a brilliant appearance in a Shaw play, Bernard Gould, who, as Bernard Partridge, was to become widely known as one of the finest black and white artists on the staff of *Punch*; Yorke Stephens; A. E. W. Mason, afterwards immensely popular as a writer of brilliant novels of adventure; Orlando Barnett; Mrs Charles Calvert; Alma Murray; and Florence Farr.

The first performance was boisterous. The author took a curtain call, and was received with cheers. When they had subsided, and before G.B.S. could utter a syllable, a solitary hiss was heard in the gallery. It was made by R. Goulding Bright, who was afterwards a very successful literary agent, and it was made, as he told me, under a misapprehension. He thought that G.B.S., in his satire on florid Balkan soldiers, was reflecting on the British Army. G.B.S. bowed to him, and remarked, 'I quite agree with you, sir, but what can two do against so many?' This retort is now part of the lore of first nights, and is often ruined in the telling. The scene, the time and the details of the incident have frequently been changed.

A reporter alleged that G.B.S., while addressing an open-air meeting in Northampton in 1938—G.B.S. was then eighty-two and had ceased to speak at public meetings—was interrupted by a man in his audience who shouted 'Boo'. G.B.S. then made his famous reply.[1] But Dr C. E. M. Joad, who was not a bigot about truth, garnished his version of the story with rich and glowing details. He transferred the incident from the first performance of *Arms and the Man* to that of *Fanny's First Play* in 1911, some seventeen years later, and was audacious to declare that he heard the hiss and the retort. But by 1911, G.B.S. had ceased to take curtain calls. No one booed. G.B.S. did not utter any remarks from the stage for the good and sufficient reason that he was not on it. Joad could not have claimed to be present when the retort *was* made because he was under three years of age in 1894. There have been other variations, and there will probably be many more. A time will come when the retort will be attributed to a dramatist or, more probably, a politician who, at this time of writing, has not yet been born.

The play, although it was a disastrous failure in London, was the beginning of G.B.S.'s fortune in the theatre. It ran at the Avenue for eleven weeks, from April 21 to July 7, and the average receipts for each performance amounted to £23 2s 5d. The cost of the season was about £4,000, the total receipts being £1,777. Yet the play may be called a success, considering how different it was from the generality of plays, how discordant it was with the popular taste. Intelligent critics praised it highly. A. B. Walkley, who was then writing for *The Speaker*, was full of enthusiasm, and so, in *The World*, was William Archer, now almost abjectly penitent for his imperception when *Widowers' Houses* was performed. 'There is not the least doubt', he wrote, 'that *Arms and the Man* is one of the most amazing entertainments at present before the public. It is quite as funny as *Charley's Aunt* or *The New Boy;* we laughed at it wildly, hysterically; and I exhort the reader to go and do likewise,' good advice which the reader signally failed to take.

There were some austere Radicals who felt aggrieved by the play, which, they gloomily remarked, would injure the cause of liberation in the Balkans by mentioning that Bulgarians were not addicted to daily baths or even washing their hands and faces every day; and indeed, some years later, when the comedy was produced in a Balkan theatre, the sort of mischievous undergraduates who are always creating trouble somewhere, made a scene during the performance.

King Edward VII went to see it at a revival at the Savoy and, although he enjoyed its wit, was offended by its satire on sentimental soldiers. He left the theatre, muttering 'of course, the fellow is a damned crank!' His Majesty, gazing indignantly at the Swiss mercenary who carried chocolates in his bandolier in preference to bullets, had, perhaps, forgotten that his revered mother had justified G.B.S. when,

[1] See *Northampton Independent*, July 26, 1946.

several years after his play was written, she presented every British soldier in South Africa during the last Boer War with a box of chocolates. It is odd to reflect that *Arms and the Man*, which was received with so little interest during its first run, was immensely popular at the end of the First World War with ex-Servicemen, who were openly derisive of the flamboyant heroics of the battle scenes in Rostand's *Cyrano de Bergerac*. A popular light opera, entitled *The Chocolate Soldier*,[1] with music by Oscar Strauss, was based on the play, which is now a favourite production in English schools.

Arms and the Man would seem to have been a failure. Miss Horniman lost money over it, and G.B.S. gained very little: a hundred and some pounds, perhaps. But for the demon which was driving him to fulfil his intention about himself, he might reasonably have abandoned hope of overcoming the stage. Literature was certainly a hard mistress to this devoted lover. Yet *Arms and the Man* was to bring him the first substantial sum he ever earned; and the actor who was to be the agent of this happy issue from his financial afflictions was already in London and had seen the play.

His name was Richard Mansfield, and he was a popular actor in the United States. The part of Bluntschli tempted him, as it has tempted many actors, but he was worried about the fact that the Swiss mercenary, who may be called the hero of the play, though hero is a word that seems irreconcilable with any play by Shaw, scarcely appears in the second act: that which is the most important part of any three act comedy. But Mrs Mansfield, who was delighted with it, persuaded him to buy the American rights.

The absence of Bluntschli from almost the entire second act is another demonstration of G.B.S.'s indifference to the form of a play. It caused many people, not unreasonably, to think that he was ignorant of the elementary laws of stage-craft, when, in fact, he was creating a new craft. He believed that a play should fashion itself, and that events in it should occur as the play demanded they should occur, and not as stage carpenters said they should. The stage carpenters insisted that the principal figures should be seen often and prominently throughout the play's course, but G.B.S. insisted that this was an artificial and even a false arrangement of the facts of life. In life, it seldom happens that one or two persons are always visible at the centre of all events. G.B.S. was striving to present life as it is in reality and not as it is contrived on the theatre, and he saw no reason why the regular course of events should be disorganised merely to

[1] R. F. Rattray is in error when, in a footnote to *Bernard Shaw: a Chronicle*, he states that *Arms and the Man* 'was shamelessly plagiarised' in *The Chocolate Soldier*. Plagarism connotes some intention to conceal the source of the work in which the plagarism occurs; but there was no disguise of the source of *The Chocolate Soldier*. The librettists, indeed, sought G.B.S.'s : › e tto their work. It was not given, but the librettists did without it.

give the principal players ampler opportunities of disporting themselves. He felt that he had as much right to keep Bluntschli off the scene for most of the second act as Euripides had to let Pylades wander through the *Electra* without uttering a single word.

The playgoing public, like the critics, had not yet perceived that G.B.S. was an implacable revolutionary, determined to change the stage and, if he were able, the entire community. They were accustomed to heroes who feared no foe in shining armour and never suffered from physical necessities. The soldier in routine plays was always performing gallant deeds, routing superior forces, and declaiming noble sentiments. He felt no fatigue nor apprehension. At any moment, even if he had not tasted bite or sup for several days, he was ready, with only a broken sabre in his hand, to charge and scatter a large host of enemies, uttering exalted eloquence as he hacked and slew, and, when the fight was won, treating the wounded with tender care while he dropped a tear for the dead.

G.B.S. was impatient with this outworn romance. 'I am quite aware', he says in the preface to Vol. II of *Plays, Pleasant and Unpleasant*, 'that the much criticised Swiss officer in *Arms and the Man* is not a conventional stage soldier. He suffers from want of food and sleep: his nerves go to pieces after three days under fire, ending in the horrors of a rout and pursuit; he has found by experience that it is more important to have a few bits of chocolate to eat in the field than cartridges for his revolver. . . .' A page later, he remarks that 'idealism, which is only a flattering name for romance in politics and morals, is as obnoxious to me as romance in ethics or religion. In spite of a Liberal Revolution or two, I can no longer be satisfied with fictitious morals and fictitious good conduct, shedding fictitious glory on robbery, starvation, disease, crime, drink, war, cruelty, cupidity, and all the other commonplaces of civilization which drive men to the theatre to make foolish pretences that such things are progress, science, morals, religion, patriotism, imperial supremacy, national greatness and all the other names the newspapers call them:

'On the other hand, I see plenty of good in the world working itself out as fast as the idealists will allow it; and if they would only let it alone and learn to respect reality . . . we should all get along much better and much faster. At all events, I do not see moral chaos and anarchy as the alternative to romantic convention; and I am not going to pretend I do merely to please the people who are convinced that the world is only held together by the force of unanimous, strenuous, eloquent, trumpet-tongued lying. To me the tragedy and comedy of life lie in the consequences, sometimes terrible, sometimes ludicrous, of our persistent attempts to found our institutions on the ideals suggested to our imaginations by our half-satisfied passions, instead of on a genuinely scientific natural history.'

The play is full of lines in which the characters explode romantic elusions and blunt the edge of speeches intended to wound. When Louka says 'You have the soul of a servant, Nikola', Nikola, instead of using the stale rhetoric of the traditional servant, replies complacently, 'Yes: that's the secret of success in service.' Sergius, inclined to a little philandering with Louka, asks her if she knows what the higher love is, to which she replies in astonishment, 'No, sir', and is informed that it is a 'very fatiguing thing to keep up for any length of time. One feels the need of some relief after it.'

Sergius, who is the death or glory kind of soldier, the roaring, shouting, sabre-flourishing cavalry man that the Foot Guards detest because he is the sort of blundering ass who causes the virtual elimination of a Light Brigade at Balaclava, tells Bluntschli that 'I' could no more fight with you than I could make love to an ugly woman. You've no magnetism: you're not a man, you're a machine,' to which Bluntschli, not in the least disconcerted or hurt, replies, 'Quite true, quite true'. There was nothing of Sir Richard Grenville in Bluntschli, who was based on Sidney Webb, and would, we feel convinced, have turned the Revenge into a well-managed ferry boat. G.B.S. never appreciated the value of full-blown valour, nor understood its heartening effect on dispirited men. It has its worth in the world, and is not less useful in stimulating us to overcome our sloth and inertia, our craven fears and deep dejection when the heart is sick and the body seems as if it can bear no more. Neat lists of things, and tidy plans for improvement fail to stir a pulse in the day of disaster when a single shout, 'Fight on, fight on!' and a reckless dash against a massed array will rouse the weary and uplift the dejected and snatch victory from defeat.

Mansfield produced *Arms and the Man* in America without much effort to display it, and it remained part of his repertoire for several years. The days of the big productions and long runs had not yet arrived, but they were well on their way. In the meantime, the small returns from Mansfield's periodical performances were welcome.

90

On May 19, 1894, Edmund Yates, the editor of *The World*, died, and G.B.S. immediately resigned from the post of music critic which he had held for about four years, but was besought by the new editor to remain in office until the end of the season lest his resignation might seem to reflect on him. G.B.S., therefore, continued to be music critic until the beginning of the winter.

In September, Frank Harris, a strange adventurer in Fleet Street, bought *The Saturday Review* and invited him to become its dramatic critic at a salary of £6 a week. He accepted the offer, and his first article appeared on January 5, 1895, The play reviewed was *Slaves of the Ring* by Sidney Grundy. G.B.S. found some resemblance between the theme of Wagner's *Tristan und Isolde* and Grundy's play, which differed, he said, from Wagner's 'in this very essential respect, that whereas *Tristan* is the greatest work of its kind of the century, *Slaves of the Ring* is not sufficiently typical or classical to deserve being cited as the worst. It is not a work of art at all: it is a mere contrivance for filling a theatre bill, and not, I am bound to say, a very apt contrivance even at that.'

A week later, he saw Henry James's ill-made and roughly-conceived *Guy Domville* at St James's Theatre and Oscar Wilde's *An Ideal Husband* at the Haymarket. He was not the only new dramatic critic who attended the first performance of *Guy Domville*. Two others were present. One was Arnold Bennett, who had made himself general critic, under the name of Cécile, for the paper, *Woman*, he then edited: the other was H. G. Wells, who had donned a dress shirt that night for the first time in his life, so that he might adequately represent *The Pall Mall Gazette*.

G.B.S. was far kinder to *Guy Domville* than he ought to have been, but his generosity was not, as one might suspect, due to the chivalry which made him run to the side of those who are rudely and ignorantly assailed, nor even to his contempt for a world in which the judgments of the mob are accepted as the final authority on everything. He was, in fact, antipathetic to the work of Henry James and writers of his sort: work 'in which passion is subordinate to intellect and fastidious artistic taste'. But he maintained that if the life Henry James depicted were real to him, it must be real to others; and he saw no reason why these others should not have their drama 'instead of being banished from the theatre (to the theatre's great loss) by the monotony and vulgarity of drama in which passion is everything, intellect nothing, and art only brought in by the incidental outrages upon it.'

> 'As it happens, I am not myself in Mr James's camp: in all the life that has energy enough to be interesting to me, subjective volition, passion, will, make intellect the merest tool. But there is in the centre of that cyclone a certain calm spot where cultivated ladies and gentlemen live on independent incomes or by pleasant artistic occupations. It is there that Mr James's art touches life, selecting whatever is graceful, exquisite, or dignified in its serenity.'

He goes on to describe the virtues of the play. 'First among the qualities, a rare charm of speech. Line after line comes with such a delicate turn and fall that I unhesitatingly challenge any of our popular dramatists to write a scene in verse with half the beauty of

Mr James's prose.' The second virtue he found in the play, surprising in him who despised plots, was 'a story, and not a mere situation hung out on a gallows of a plot. And it is a story of fine sentiment and delicate manners, with an entirely worthy and touching ending.' The third virtue was that the play relied 'on the performers, not for the brute force of their personalities and popularities, but for their finest accomplishments in grace of manner, delicacy of diction, and dignity of style.' He then deals with the play's demerits shrewdly, but kindly. His criticism must have been comforting to James, who was deeply wounded by the severity with which *Guy Domville* and himself were received on the first night and, subsequently, in the press.

The criticism is cited at this length because it is highly character-istic not only of Shaw's work, but of his mind and spirit. His plea for a place in the theatre for 'these others' who subordinate passion to intellect and delicate manners is inadmissible, since 'these others' are not numerous enough to be able to support a play for more than a night or two. We can agree with him that we are under no obligation to believe that the judgment of unmannerly and mindless people is to be preferred to that of well-bred and intelligent men and women on the general ground that 'the drama's laws the drama's patrons give'. 'Pray which of its patrons?—the cultivated majority who, like myself and all the ablest of my colleagues, applauded Mr James on Saturday, or the handful of rowdies who brawled at him? It is the business of the dramatic critics to educate these dunces, not to echo them.'

Wilde's rubbishy play, *An Ideal Husband*, which deserved the boos that were given to *Guy Domville*, was treated more gently by G.B.S. than it ought to have been. He felt, perhaps, that his situation was awkward and delicate. He, too, was a Dublin dramatist, but whereas Wilde had been successful from the start, G.B.S. was a manifest failure. Wilde had made more money out of a single week's perfor-mance of his first play, *Lady Windermere's Fan*, than G.B.S. had made out of the four pieces he had then written: only one of which, indeed, had been publicly performed. An attack on *An Ideal Husband* by him might be regarded as an exhibition of petty spite by a disappointed dramatist against a successful rival. 'As far as I can ascertain,' he wrote with the assured wit which was daily becoming more charac-teristic of him, 'I am the only person in London who cannot sit down and write an Oscar Wilde play at all. The fact that his plays, though apparently lucrative, remain unique under these circumstances, says much for the self-denial of our scribes.'

In his haste to praise Wilde, he lets himself use a passage of approval which every act of his own intellectual and social life repudiated. Sir Robert Chiltern, the ideal husband, has won great wealth and powerful position as a Cabinet Minister by means which, had they been detected at the time his offence was committed, would have landed him in prison for a long period and would, if they were now revealed, ruin him socially and politically. He had given information about a Government purpose to a man to whom it was invaluable, and for this information had received a very large sum of money. Yet G.B.S. makes this astounding statement in defence of a shabby crime which G.B.S. himself could not have committed:

> 'The modern note is struck in Sir Robert Chiltern's assertion of individuality and courage of his wrongdoing as against the mechanical idealism of his stupidly good wife, and in his bitter criticism of a love that is only the reward of merit. It is from the philosophy on which this scene is based that the most pregnant epigrams in the play have been condensed. Indeed, this is the only philosophy that ever has produced epigrams.'

There is nothing to be said for the pernicious nonsense that passage contains. Criminal conduct continues to be criminal no matter how modern is the note it strikes; and although 'mechanical idealism' is deplorable, it is better than spontaneous villainy.

The productions seen by G.B.S. in the first weeks of his new position were exceptionally interesting. A critic of the contemporary theatre might support his case against it by citing the plays and acting witnessed by G.B.S. in January and February, 1895. In addition to those already named, they include Henry Irving's production of *King Arthur*, by J. Comyns Carr, at the Lyceum; *The Importance of Being Earnest*, by Wilde, at St James's; and *The Notorious Mrs Ebbsmith*, by A. W. Pinero at the Garrick. He took a poor view of *King Arthur*, which, he suggested, had been written on the strictest archaeological principles; but he gave high praise to Irving's acting.

> 'There is one scene in the play in which Mr Irving rises to the height of his art, and impersonates, with the noblest feeling, and the most sensitive refinement of execution, the King Arthur of all our imaginations in the moment when he learns that his wife loves his friend instead of himself. And all the time, whilst the voice, the gesture, the emotion expressed are those of the hero-king, the talk is the talk of an angry and jealous costermonger, exalted by the abject submission of the other parties to a transport of magnanimity in refraining from reviling his wife and punching her lover's head. I do not suppose Mr Irving said to Mr Comyns Carr in so many words, "Write what trash you like: I'll play the real King Arthur over the head of your stuff": but that was what it came to.'

If Irving was not filled with pride by such praise as this, he was incapable of feeling pride or of understanding great praise when he read it. The praise plainly was not sycophantic. A man who had wished to ingratiate himself with the great actor would not have concluded his article with an attack on him for misusing the genius of Ellen Terry and preferring second and third rate writers to those that were first rate.

'It is pathetic to see Miss Terry snatching at some fleeting touch of nature in her part and playing it, not only to perfection, but often with a parting caress that brings it beyond that for an instant as she relinquishes it, very loth, and passes on to the next length of arid sham-feminine twaddle in blank verse, which she pumps out in little rhythmic strokes in a desperate and all too obvious effort to make music of it. I should prove myself void of the true critic's passion if I could pass with polite commonplaces over what seems to me a heartless waste of an exquisite talent. What a theatre for a woman of genius to be attached to! Obsolete tomfooleries like *Robert Macaire*, schoolgirl charades like *Nance Oldfield*, blank verse by Wills, Comyns Carr, and Calmour, with intervals of hashed Shakespeare; and all the time a stream of splendid women's parts pouring from the Ibsen volcano and minor craters, and being snapped up by the rising generation. Strange, under these circumstances, that it is Mr Irving and not Miss Terry who feels the want of a municipal theatre. He has certainly done his best to make every one else.'

The reader of the last lines of that extract may well believe that Miss Terry was wiser than either Irving or G.B.S. The thought of any one of these three being subject to the control of the Manchester Watch Committee almost curdles the blood.

The Importance of Being Earnest gave G.B.S. little pleasure. He disliked it heartily, a dislike he maintained to the last days of his life; but how he, who had praised the wretched melodrama, *An Ideal Husband*, could fail to appreciate the brilliant farce which was Wilde's last contribution to the stage is impossible to understand, except in the belief that his sense of humour was defective: a defect which is common in Southern Ireland where a man seems to English sentimentalists to be supremely humourous when the poor creature intends to be serious. There was nothing funny to G.B.S. in *The Importance of Being Earnest*. It was a painful reminder of the folly of his countrymen.

His knowledge of Wilde was slight. Irishmen are not fond of each other, as Dr Johnson very well knew when he remarked that the Irish are a fair minded people: 'they never speak well of each other'. Wilde, Shaw, Yeats and George Moore were incompatible. They seldom met, and disliked each other's work. G.B.S.'s contempt for Moore was immense, but it was little less than Yeats's. None of them lived in Ireland any longer than he could help. Wilde revisited his country once after he had left it, and Moore, after a spectacular descent on Dublin during the Boer War, had hardly settled himself there than he made ready to decamp. G.B.S. did not put his feet in the place for nearly thirty years after he had departed from Dublin, and would not have returned then but for the importunities of Charlotte. The single Irishman of any quality in letters who lived in Dublin was the Ulster poet, George Russell ('A. E.') and even he, shortly before he died, could endure it no longer. The one editor for whom G.B.S. felt illimitable contempt was his countryman, T. P. O'Connor.

Wilde and Shaw met, certainly, a dozen times, none of the encounters being designed, all of them being brief. There was a difference of mind and purpose and habit between them which made intimacy impossible. As Wilde was arrested soon after the production of *The Importance of Being Earnest* and, on his release from prison, disappeared from England, any likelihood of more familiar acquaintance ended. But G.B.S. showed him the generosity which was characteristic of him whenever there was an opportunity to do so. In all his references to him he mentioned him with courtesy.

Pinero's play, *The Notorious Mrs Ebbsmith*, was dismissed with contempt. Had it not been for the performance of Mrs Patrick Campbell, the play, G.B.S. asserted, must have died the death. The whole piece, from start to finish, was, he contended, thoroughly shoddy. Pinero had obviously based his play on a sentimental view of Mrs Besant's relations with her husband, the Rev. Frank Besant, and Charles Bradlaugh; and this fact, in itself, may have prejudiced him against the play: for G.B.S. knew Mrs Besant well, whereas Pinero knew only rumour and ill-informed gossip and newspaper reports about her. The characters in the play, he stated, were 'the merest stock figures, convincing us that Mr Pinero either never meets anybody now, or else that he has lost the power of observation:

> 'Many passages in the play, of course, have all the qualities which have gained Mr Pinero his position as a dramatist; but I shall not dwell on them, as, to tell the truth, I disliked the play so much that nothing would induce me to say anything good of it. And here let me warn the reader to carefully discount my opinion in view of the fact that I write plays myself, and that my school is in violent reaction against that of Mr Pinero. But my criticism has, not, I hope, any other fault than the inevitable one of extreme unfairness.'

In March, he saw Lugné-Poë's company, the *L'Œuvre*, in a repertoire, of plays at the Opéra Comique theatre in London, and was greatly moved by their performance in Ibsen's *Rosmersholm*. 'There were drawbacks of course. The shabbiness of the scenery did not trouble me; but the library of Pastor Rosmer got on my nerves a little. What on earth did he want, for instance, with *Sell's World's Press?* That he should have provided himself with a volume of my own dramatic works I thought right and natural enough, though when he took that particular volume down and opened it, I began to speculate rather uneasily on the chances of his presently becoming so absorbed as to forget all about his part. . . .' That entertaining passage is cited, less for its amusing quality, than for its revelation of the close observation with which G.B.S. regarded everything he saw. He had the quick eyes of a bird, and he seemed to observe very quickly all there was to observe. To travel in a car or a train with him was to notice his head continually turning to see all the sights.

Enough has been cited from *Dramatic Opinions and Essays* to show that a new and powerful mind had come to the criticism of the English stage. It proved to be as creative and influential in the English theatre as Lessing's *Hamburgische Dramaturgie* had been in the German. In a few weeks, his initials were known and feared or admired throughout the theatrical world. Archer and A. B. Walkley were critics of great distinction and wider knowledge than G.B.S., but neither of them then or ever had such authority as his during the three and a half years he wrote for *The Saturday Review*. Archer sometimes wrote as if he felt that any person who cracked a joke in his presence was taking a liberty which a gentleman must either ignore or severely rebuke; and his style, though not his personal manners, was that of an earnest Presbyterian minister addressing Writers to the Signet. Somerset Maugham used to say that when he was young, he searched the streets of Paris for a typical Frenchman, such as was once commonly portrayed in *Punch;* but he failed utterly, until, one morning, he saw the typical Frenchman approaching him and looking exactly as if he had strayed out of a *Punch* picture. Filled with elation, he hurried to meet the long-sought figure, and was horrified to discover that he was Walkley.

Shaw, the spritely Irishman of English origin, however, was so much to the intelligent playgoers' taste that even when he wounded their national pride, as he did far too often and sometimes very wantonly, he was still appreciated by most of them! His witty and virile prose naturally attracted readers, but he had also a passionate sincerity and a remarkable diversity of knowledge of the arts and of experience, personal and public, with which to reinforce them. His critical faculty had been sharpened more keenly and in a greater variety of ways than any other critic then in practice or, indeed, any critic since. He had reviewed books, criticised music, pictures and sculpture, and was now criticising plays and performances. He was an adept in public oratory and a prominent exponent of advanced politics. He knew the East End of London, in which Walkley had probably never adventured himself, almost as well as he knew the West End. He had met on terms of familiarity a great diversity of men and women in every walk of life, from carpenters and curates to Cabinet Ministers, and his list of friends was immensely diversified. He was less well-informed about foreign countries and literature than Archer and Walkley, but he was making up this deficiency with great speed. It was fortunate for the English theatre that these three men were critics of acting and the drama simultaneously. Without them, its history in the nineties and for more than a decade thereafter might not have been as impressive as it is.

This section cannot be closed without a quotation from *The Author's Apology* to the collection of the articles in *The Saturday Review*. It was written eight years after the last of them had appeared in that paper: long enough not only for G.B.S. to have reached a position of world renown as a dramatist, but to have acquired a mood of dispassion about the articles themselves:

> 'In justice to many well-known persons who are handled rather recklessly in the following pages, I beg my readers not to mistake my journalistic utterances for the final estimates of their worth and achievements as dramatic artists and authors. It is not so much that the utterances are unjust; for I have never claimed for myself the divine attribute of justice. But some of them are not even reasonably fair: I must therefore warn the reader that what he is about to study is not a series of judgements aiming at impartiality, but a siege laid to the theatre of the XIXth Century by an author who had to cut his own way into it at the point of the pen, and throw some of its defenders into the moat.
>
> 'Pray do not conclude from this that the things hereinafter written were not true, or not the deepest and best things I knew how to say. Only, they must be construed in the light of the fact that all through I was accusing my opponents of failure because they were not doing what I wanted, whereas they were often succeeding very brilliantly in doing what they themselves wanted. I postulated as desirable a certain kind of play in which I was destined ten years later to make my mark as a playwright (as I very well foreknew in the depth of my own unconsciousness); and I brought everybody, authors, actors managers, to the one test: were they coming my way or staying in the old grooves.
>
> 'Sometimes I made allowances for the difference in aim, especially in the case of personal friends. But as a rule I set up my own standard of what the drama should be and how it should be presented; and I used all my art to make every deviation in aiming at this standard, every recalcitrance in approaching it, every refusal to accept it seem ridiculous and old-fashioned.
>
> 'In this, however, I only did what all critics do who are worth their salt. The critics who attacked Ibsen and defended Shakespeare whilst I was defending Ibsen and attacking Shakespeare; or who were acclaiming the reign of Irving at the Lyceum Theatre as the Antonine age of the Shakespearean drama whilst I was battering at it in open

preparation for its subsequent downfall, were no more impartial than I. And when my own turn has come to be criticised, I also was attacked because I wanted to produce what I wanted to produce and not what some of my critics wanted me to produce.'

Here we have an affirmation of faith in a belief about life, from which, except in small points of detail, G.B.S. never departed. His religion, for it was a religion, was much the same when he was ninety as it was when he was nineteen.

91

His fifth play was *Candida*, a charming comedy, almost conventional in its construction. It will be well at this point to state emphatically that the general legend that G.B.S. made a virtue of his incapacity to write a well-made play by treating good construction as if it were not only unimportant but a sign of inferior mind, was false. No man who admired Ibsen could possibly have held the view that ill-made plays were superior to those that were well-made. G.B.S., in fact, could shape a play as well as anybody. Note has already been made of the skill with which *Mrs Warren's Profession* is constructed. *Candida* is equally well built.

Despite its charm and distinction, it was not produced in London for many years, and was performed in the provinces in 1897–8 by the Independent Theatre Company, led by Janet Achurch, long before it reached the West End. Yet it is now one of the most popular of G.B.S.'s plays, though he pretended to despise it in his later years. The curious fact remains, however, that two very dissimilar women, Ellen Terry and Beatrice Webb, did not like it. Mrs Webb thought that Candida was an immoral woman! But G.B.S., in a letter to Ellen Terry, said she was his conception of the Virgin Mother.

Candida has become popular enough for some contemporary critics, following G.B.S.'s absurd example, to despise it. One of them, an American, Joseph Wood Krutch, writing on revivals of *Pygmalion* and *Candida* in the New York weekly review, *The Nation*, said that neither piece was 'among' Shaw's 'best plays'.[1] The latter, he declared, was written in 'a deliberate attempt to win a public', an attempt which, for some singular reason appears to Mr Wood Krutch to be reprehensible, though every author who has ever put pen to paper has done so for exactly the same reason. Why should a writer not keep his thoughts to himself if he has no desire to win a public? Even Mr Wood Krutch communicates his to the press when he might exalt himself by hoarding them in the secret places of his own head.

[1] April 20, 1946.

Candida, he continues, 'is one of Shaw's most factitious comedies, in a sense that it is probably not really very sincere.' On what grounds does Mr Wood Krutch make this statement? And what is the meaning of his loose assertion that *Candida,* 'in a sense', is probably not really very sincere? In what sense?

If G.B.S. was putting his tongue in his cheek when he wrote *Candida* and corrupting his character by writing what he did not believe, he showed himself to be extremely incompetent in deception: for he failed to get his play performed when it was essential to him to win some success. He himself, in an interview, which was published in *The Melbourne Age* on March 23, 1946, stated that English journalists who reproached him for 'ingratitude to their country, to which they attribute all my success and reputation', seemed to have forgotten or never to have known, 'that when I came to England I got nothing for nothing, and very little for a halfpenny: that I was abused, vilified, censored, and suppressed to the limit of possibility until my successes in Germany and America convinced my detractors that there was some money in my evil doctrine.'

This is an extravagant statement, expressed when he was ninety and ought not to be held against him, as it can be, on the ground that it is false to the facts, and that his reception in America and Germany, as has already been noted, was no more pleasing than his reception elsewhere. France, like Italy and other Latin countries, still does not pay much attention to his work. He forgets that he was a natural rebel against authority, who must have behaved in any country as he had behaved in England, and that his reception in America would have been rougher than it was in England, had he emigrated to New York instead of London. Americans might complain as bitterly about his treatment of them and their country as the British journalists complained of his ingratitude to England.

He was right when he said that he had given the world good value for its money, but he was wrong when he complained that he 'got nothing for nothing and very little for a halfpenny'. Why should he have got anything for nothing? What right had he to expect more for a halfpenny than a halfpenny can buy? Were the English under an obligation to buy goods they did not desire? Has any man the right to complain because the wares he offers for sale are not to the taste of buyers? Either he must make wares that are or keep his stock until tastes and the times change and what was once disdained is now desired. That, in fact, is what he did do, and it was exclusively in English journalism that he found the work that kept him until his plays became acceptable. The bitter memories of a lonely nonagenarian ought not to be taken too seriously; but it is a fact, which the most devout Shavian cannot deny, that G.B.S. abstained with remarkable restraint from praising the country in which he had chosen to live for the greatest part of his life, and that he sometimes seemed over-ready to dispraise it, especially when it was in trouble.

He had the long Irish memory for grievances, and the short Irish memory for benefits. But the fact remains that even when he was doing his adopted country grave injury during the World Wars, the English did not interfere with his activities as they might reasonably have done, nor did they treat him as he would certainly have been treated in his native Eire. They allowed him to take liberties that would have brought him, had he taken them in Russia, to the salt mines in Siberia or have ended in his liquidation in an Arctic Circle labour camp.

Would any Eirean, any Russian, any German have striven so hard to find congenial employment for him as William Archer strove? Was not H. W. Massingham a good friend to him when *The Star* was founded? Had not Miss Horniman, English to the heart's core, spent her money to give him his first public performance? Honours of all sorts were offered to him by English Universities and British Governments, but were declined. At least one Prime Minister, Ramsay MacDonald, despite the fact that he had never cared for the Fabians, offered to submit his name to the Sovereign for admission to the Order of Merit, an offer which he refused. But no university in Ireland offered him honour, nor did the Eirean Government recognise him in the slightest degree. Three of his plays were banned in England on grounds that he knew when he wrote the plays would cause them to be banned; and the ban on all of them was subsequently lifted; but several of his books were not only banned in the republic of Eire which had not been banned in Ireland when it was still part of the British Empire, but remain banned to this day.

If he had had to depend for his livelihood on his Irish earnings as a writer, he would long ago have died of hunger. Had he written vehemently against the policies of Cosgrave, Costello and De Valera in time of comparative peace as he wrote against the policy of Sir Edward Grey in time of war and grave danger to the country in which he lived, he would soon have found himself serving an indeterminate sentence in Kilmainham Prison, if, indeed, he had not been summarily shot as Erskine Childers was.

If Mr Wood Krutch had any reason for his singular judgment on *Candida*, and G.B.S., in writing it, was no more than a common hack seeking to make money by hawking his mind and soul in the public market, ready to take a good price for them from any buyer, he signally failed, as we have noted, to fulfil his intention. *Pygmalion* was not the sort of play, as we shall presently note, that was likely to please the generality of theatre managers. It is costly to produce and its subject would seem to the majority of minds unlikely to interest many playgoers. Yet it was produced by Beerbohm Tree, a leading actor-manager, at His Majesty's Theatre, which was one of London's most important playhouses; and it was received with favour, although it contained a line which was a matter of anxiety to Tree and was thought likely then to cause resentment that might ruin the production. G.B.S. never wrote anything insincerely. He was often extravagant and sometimes perverse, and there were times when he presumed on the good nature of the people among whom he lived; but never in his life was he insincere.

Candida was a comedy as unusual at the time it was written as Tom Robertson's *Caste* was in 1867. That was why its author had the same difficulty in obtaining a production for it as Robertson had in obtaining one for his equally charming comedy, as Somerset Maugham had in getting *Lady Frederick* staged in 1907. If it had contained the slightest trace of insincerity, it would long ago have died of neglect. Who that has heard the superb scene at the end of the X third act, in which Candida gently but firmly corrects her husband when he talks of supporting her with his strength, his honesty of purpose, his ability and his industry, and tells him the solemn fact about himself, that he has all his life been pampered and petted and protected by his women folk—who that has heard this scene can feel for a moment that its author was insincere, a man blarneying play-goers for money? He himself saw that he had turned the tables on Ibsen by showing that it was the man, not the woman, who was the Doll in the house. Candida incites Eugene to look at her husband, 'spoiled from the cradle', and then, 'with deepening gravity', says:

> 'Ask James's mother and his three sisters what it cost to save James the trouble of doing anything but be strong and clever and happy. Ask me what it costs to be James's mother and three sisters and wife and mother to his children all in one. Ask Prossy and Maria how troublesome the house is even when we have no visitors to help us to slice the onions. Ask the tradesmen who want to worry James and spoil his beautiful sermons who it is that puts them off. When there is money to give, he gives it: when there is money to refuse, I refuse it. I build a castle of comfort and indulgence and love for him, and stand sentinel always to keep little vulgar cares out. I make him master here, though he does not know it, and could not tell you a moment ago how it came to be so . . . .'

There is a tendency among some actors to play the part of the Rev. James Mavor Morell, Candida's husband, as if he were the Rev. Dr M'Guffog, in *The Newcomes;* a sad-browed and sour Presbyterian who was known as the Ezekiel of Clackmannan. This is an entire falsification of his character, as it is described by G.B.S. He is not a stupid man: he is an exceedingly able parish priest whose eloquence has made him widely known. A clergyman who was a member of the Guild of St Matthew and the Christian Social Union in 1894 was far from being an imperceptive and stodgy minister who droned his congregation to sleep.

Morell's supreme fault is one which is typical of all eloquent people, whether they be politicians or priests. Such men as Gladstone, William Bryan, Bishop Boyd Carpenter, Spurgeon, Dr Talmage, Father Bernard Vaughan, Lloyd George and, in our own age, Mr Aneurin Bevan deceive not only emotional audiences, but, what is worse, themselves, because they vainly imagine that eloquence and mind are identical. There comes a moment in the life of all orators when they begin to feel for the cheers of their audience, sacrificing sense for applause, and, when they gain the cheers for which they have a drunkard's craving, convincing themselves that they have displayed statesmanship or sanctity. Unpopularity is death to such people, and they will modify their minds to win the esteem of a half-illiterate and wholly sentimental mob.

Morell is a good and sensible man, who has allowed himself to become infected with the disease of eloquence. That this was G.B.S.'s view of him is apparent from the stage directions at the beginning of the first act, in which Morell is carefully described; and it is a plain misinterpretation of the part to play it as is now the custom, just as it is a plain misinterpretation of Ibsen's intention if Gregers Werle in *The Wild Duck* is played as a tragic character when he is essentially comic, in the Meredithian sense of comedy.

The unconvincing figure in *Candida* is Burgess, Candida's father, 'a vulgar, ignorant, guzzling man', who seems incredible as the parent of such a daughter. The man's speech is a low form of Cockney, though G.B.S. himself, when I once expostulated with him about Burgess, denied this. 'Burgess', he wrote to me, 'was born in 1840 in Oxfordshire, or possibly of Oxonian parents in Hackney; which then had turnpike gates and pigs running about the road, miles and atmospheres from the sound of Bowbells. To this day, and certainly to the date of *Candida*, even Shoreditch is less completely Cockneyfied than Charing X: cockneyism, being smarty, always went west and not north or east. Burgess, with his emotional rhetorical *h*s, is studied closely from a well known and long deceased Oxford character. He does not utter a sound of modern cockney; and the difficulty I have at rehearsal . . . is that Burgess *will* try cockney. Jo Gargery chalking up HOUT on the forge door is still authentic Essex or Ascot or Chertsey or Hitchin.'

This is very entertaining, but it is stuff, and was probably thought of for the first time when he wrote to me. G.B.S. had a debating trick of trying to establish veracity by citing an array of unverifiable details, but those who knew him were not likely to be led astray by them. Here is a passage of dialogue spoken by Burgess in the first act, after he has been accused by Morell of sweating his labourers:

'Why helse should I do it? What does it lead to but drink and huppishness in workin men? It's hall very well for you, James: it gits you hinto the papers and makes a great man of you; but you never think of the arm you do, puttin money into the pockets of workin men that they dunno ow to spend, and takin it from people that might be makin a good huse on it.'

Despite his absorption in phonetics, G.B.S.'s ear was here at fault. It is almost impossible in ordinary conversation to say 'good huse' instead of 'good use', and the foundation of Cockney speech, which is French, is ease, not distortion. The Cockney is trying to make his speech slip easily from word to word when he sheds his aspirates; an assertion which is supported by the fact that although he still drops aitches, despite more than eighty years of compulsory education, he no longer sounds them where they should not be sounded. It is only old men and women in villages to-day who perform the difficult feat of intruding aitches into words where they have no right to be. The reader need only sound the words 'good huse' to perceive that he must make an effort to say 'huse', though no effort is needed to drop an aitch.

The Cockney, remembering his ancient lineage, seeks to make his conversation flow fluently. So he drops his h's, an act which is no more reprehensible than the country gentleman's habit of dropping his final g's or Sir Anthony Eden's trick of saying *strenth* when he means *strength*. It is no worse to say *untin* than it is to say *huntin*, and much less disagreeable than to obtrude an *r* between two words, one ending, and the other beginning with a vowel: as, for example, *Indiaroffice* or *Lenar Ashwell;* a habit which some B.B.C. announcers have, one, too, which is sometimes characteristic of Etonians. There is some excuse for this obtruded *r*. The conjunction of a word ending in a vowel and a word beginning with one, is often ungainly, and the obtruded *r* is an attempt, usually made subconsciously, to lighten the strain and make the two words run easily together.

G.B.S. was inconsistent, too, when he made Burgess pronounce *and* with its final consonant intact, but allowed him to drop the *g* from words ending in *ing*. Burgess is out of place in *Candida*. He has no veracity in mind, speech or habit as Candida's father.

92

The year 1895, which, judging by its immediate predecessors, might have seemed likely to be misfortunate for G.B.S., considering how little success as a novelist and a dramatist he had enjoyed, turned out to be the beginning of his fat years. He was now definitely a dramatist, despite his total failure to obtain serious production in the West End theatre. The financial collapse of *Arms and the Man* would have discouraged a less determined man, and might have discouraged him had he allowed his seeming failure as a dramatist, coming on top of certain failure as a novelist, to depress his spirits. He had begun, but had failed to finish, a sixth novel. There was, he perceived, no hope for him as a novelist, and so he threw the script of his unfinished novel aside, and had so little remembrance of it that when it was recovered, he had difficulty in believing that he had written it. In a letter to Mr Maurice Holmes, written on March 15, 1932, he says, 'My secretary [Miss Patch] has just unearthed a beginning of a novel' written 'in 1888, which, were it not for my own handwriting against me, I would swear I never wrote, saw, conceived nor heard of in my life.'[1]

But although his future in the theatre seemed as dark as his past in the novel, he *knew* that he was a dramatist, though he had never known that he was a novelist; and there was now no power on earth which could discourage him from writing plays. He began to write a long piece in one act about Napoleon, entitled *The Man of Destiny*, with one eye on Richard Mansfield, and the other eye on Ellen Terry. Neither of them acted in it, nor was it performed until 1897, when it was produced on July 1 at the Grand Theatre, Croydon.

Mansfield declined the play. 'I was much hurt by your contemptuous refusal of *A Man of Destiny*,' G.B.S. wrote to him in 1897, 'not because I think it is one of my masterpieces, but because Napoleon is nobody else but Richard Mansfield himself. I studied the character from you and then read up Napoleon and found I had got him exactly right.' If he had imagined that this statement would please Mansfield, he was sadly in error: it infuriated him; but Mansfield, being an actor, was not a man of deep intelligence, and he saw only the surface of the character Shaw had created: the man who wolfed his meals greedily and was careless about his behaviour. Mansfield ought to have known that there was more to Napoleon than untidy table habits.

The play is an awkward length—too long to be a curtain-raiser, too short to fill an evening's bill; and it has seldom been acted. But it is an entertaining piece, though it infuriates Frenchmen, including G.B.S.'s translator, Augustin Hamon, who said that G.B.S. had read all the wrong books about the Emperor. *The Man of Destiny* is

---

[1] But there is a note in his diary on Christmas Eve, 1890, in which he states that he had 'turned up the beginning of an old novel, and was rather pleased with it.' But not pleased enough to finish the book.

important mainly because it brought G.B.S. into direct contact with Henry Irving for the first time without reconciling the actor to the author.

Irving, who had suffered great hardship in his first attempts to take possession of the stage, and had been so discouraged by open antipathy from audiences and derisive remarks from dramatic critics, that he had almost made up his mind to leave the theatre and submit to his mother's puritanical ambition that he should become a respectable clerk instead of a disreputable actor, was now the leader of the English theatre, a powerful influence in the theatre of America, and one of the most prominent players in the world. He had a position of authority in Britain, such as no other player possessed, and was treated by men of great intellect and power as few actors in the whole history of the drama have been treated: on terms of equality.

He was eighteen years older than G.B.S., a fact of importance in judging their relations with each other. It is unreasonable to expect that a man who had overcome so many obstacles in his rise to the highest place in his profession and a distinguished place in the general republic of eminent people, should defer to a man so much his junior, especially when that man had failed utterly to establish himself either in the world of the novel or the world of the theatre. *The Saturday Review* was an unimportant weekly paper with a very small circulation. Could any sensible man or woman expect Irving, a man of such eminence and great renown that he was almost out of Shaw's sight, to pay heed to a scribbling fellow who had been a dramatic critic for about six weeks and was not only destitute of any practical experience of the theatre, but was trying to make a breach between Irving and his leading lady by flattering her almost fulsomely in the public prints and telling her that she was being sacrificed to Irving's illimitable egotism?

Such were probably Irving's feelings, and they were natural feelings. He might, perhaps, have remembered that if Shaw's record as a writer at this time was one of almost uninterrupted failure and deep disappointment, which had been borne with heroic fortitude, so had been his own record as an actor when he was the age Shaw then was. Irving, indeed, had suffered severer hardship and deeper discouragement than G.B.S., both publicly and privately. His mother, a woman of forceful character, had the mindless antipathy to the stage which was common among dull pietists of her time; nor was she ever reconciled to his career. This fact, in itself, was wounding to him who loved her dearly. He had to endure taunts and derision about his bodily peculiarities and his utterance for the whole of his life, as if there had ever been an actor at any period of history who had not had peculiarities of gait and speech of some sort. He had been hissed in Edinburgh, and half starved in Liverpool; and his first appearance in London was a fiasco, from which he had to fly back to drudgery in the provinces.

But he had fought his way to the head of his profession with a courage equal to G.B.S.'s.

Irving was now a man supremely in power, and G.B.S. was a man aspiring to power without, it seemed, much prospect of obtaining it. The discerning might have seen that Irving's day was dying, that G.B.S.'s was very slowly beginning, but the discerning were not numerous, nor had they any authority. What was seen by the majority of people was an impudent Jack throwing stones at a Giant; and few of them cared for the sight. No one realised that G.B.S., who had begun by regarding Irving as the man to lead the modern movement, was infuriated by Irving's failure to rise out of the worn and crumbling rut of the past. He had flattered and then abused him in the desire to provoke him into giving the new drama the vast aid of his immense authority in the theatre.

But Irving remained impervious to Shaw's beguilements, though he was sometimes infuriated by his taunts and derision. The extraordinary fact about this singular and distressing row is that although Irving professed or genuinely felt no interest in G.B.S., his sons, H.B. and Laurence, and especially the latter, were friendly with him. It was Laurence who told G.B.S. that 'All my people think you the most appalling Yahoo!' When at last, *Captain Brassbound's Conversion* was performed by the Stage Society, Laurence Irving played the part his father had scorned.

The correspondence with Ellen Terry was started not by a letter to G.B.S., but by one she wrote to Edmund Yates, the editor of The World.[1] The reader is reminded that at this time G.B.S. was a musical critic. Apart from a few interjectory remarks in his articles on music, he had written very little about the theatre, though these interjections make it plain that he was a theatregoer when he had time for the play. If Ellen Terry had any knowledge of him when her letter to Yates was written, it was not because of anything he had said about the drama. In her letter, she enquired what hopes of success there were for a young 'composer-friend of mine' in London. This was Elvira Gambogi, who failed to win the renown she was expected to win, so she became a teacher of music: an excellent example of

[1] Ellen Terry, in *The Story of My Life*, makes slips about this letter. She says it was written to G.B.S., who was then, she says, 'musical critic of *The Saturday Review*'. It was, however, written to Yates, and was passed on by him to Shaw, who did not join the staff of *The Saturday Review* until 1895, nearly three years after the letter was written. Nor was he musical critic of *The Saturday Review*. That post was held by John F. Runciman. G.B.S. was the dramatic critic.

G.B.S.'s epigram, that those who can, do: those that can't, teach. Yates passed the letter on to G.B.S., who seems to have been in some doubt about the way in which to answer it. He could not adopt the familiar manner used by breezy young men in the B.B.C., who are on Christian-name terms five minutes after they meet the people whom they have to announce.

To begin with, it was unlikely that Ellen Terry knew of his existence. Nothing in his life so far had brought him to her knowledge. On the other hand, she was Ellen Terry, and one does not write to a great woman as if she were nobody.

His incurable shyness settled his problem. He wrote her a cold, informative letter in which there was not a scrap of his personality, and it almost closed their correspondence. 'I didnt like you when you first wrote to me,' she told him in her second letter. 'I thought you unkind and exceedingly stiff and prim. Now I beg your pardon most heartily.' G.B.S. had acted characteristically, taking great trouble, as he generally did, to be of service to Elvira. On June 24, 1892, he went to the Lyric Club to listen to her singing, and the letter he wrote on the following day was a long and useful report on her performance. Miss Terry herself had taken part in the concert, and G.B.S. skilfully contrasts her performance with Elvira's. He describes his emotion on hearing her recite a poem, *The Captive*, by Monk Lewis, which he disliked, and asserts that she moved him, not because of her personal attractions, but 'because you have made yourself one of the six best actresses in the fourteen thousand millions of people in the world'. He was stirred, not by the poem, but because she had spoken it beautifully.

'My whole claim to be a critic of art is that I can be touched in this way. Now Miss Gambogi did not touch me in the least. I liked her at once: she is very amiable, very clever, and very goodlooking. But—and now the murder is coming out—she is not interesting as an artist. She sang the bolero from The Sicilian Vespers prettily and fluently, just as she would, I dare say, repeat one of Ophelia's speeches if you taught it to her. What is more, she sang it intelligently. You know, however, that this is not enough.

'The quality of execution that makes apparently trivial passages interesting, the intense grip of one's work that rouses all the attention of an audience: these she has not got to anything like a sufficient degree to make a career for her; and what is more she will never acquire them in drawingrooms or in the Lyric Club. What she does is not convincing to me: it is only a development of that facility to music which clever children acquire when they are brought up in a musical atmosphere.

'You must know how children who grow up amid theatrical surroundings catch up a certain familiarity with stage ways which inexperienced people easily mistake for genuine artistic talent. Bedford Park is full of such imps, who will nevertheless be hopelessly beaten in the long run by comparatively unpromising youngsters.

'Now singing is to Miss Gambogi partly what acting is to the imps: more a picked up habit than an art. She has got to turn the habit into an art—to put purpose into it—to make it the means of realizing herself, concentrating herself, throwing herself completely and exhaustively into action—I cannot express; but you will perhaps recognize what I mean.

'I therefore think she ought to work on the stage if she can obtain an opening. All her drawingroom beauty will vanish at once behind the footlights; and she will have to remake herself, build herself up from the foundation, instead of taking herself down from a peg as she was hung up by Nature, and wearing herself at the Lyric Club before audiences more or less packed.'

The letter goes on in this frank and discerning manner. 'My verdict briefly is that as a drawing-room singer Miss Gambogi is no better than many others: and I would not walk a hundred yards to hear her sing again. But if she takes good care of herself and her voice, ten years work on the stage may make something of her.'

But her destiny was to be a teacher, and a teacher she became.

Thereafter, with breaks of varying length, some of them due to her tours with Irving in America, their correspondence continued for twenty-six years, each, fortunately, keeping it almost entirely intact. They were now beginning to be elderly people, and the days of glory for her were drawing to a close. The great partnership with Irving was shortly to end. The Lyceum would pass from his hands. Other stars, such as Beerbohm Tree, were rising. Irving, conscious that Ellen Terry could no longer play youthful parts convincingly, but loth to say so or to break their long partnership by a refusal to renew her contract, tried a less frank and manly way of severing their connexion. He broke off all relations with her outside the theatre.

'Ah, I feel so certain Henry hates me,' she wrote to G.B.S. on November 7, 1900, when she was in Liverpool. 'I can only *guess* at it, for he is exactly the same sweet-mannered person he was when "I felt so certain" Henry loved me! We have not met for many years now, except before other people, where my conduct exactly matches his of course. All my own fault. It is *I* am changed, not he. It's all right, but it has squeezed me up dreadfully, and after the long pause of illness, I went back last night, weak and nervous, but looking well and acting well, thank the Lord. Only for the first time not glad to go back to my dear work.'

Two years later, the break was made, and young Cissie Loftus, to be more sedately known as Cecilia, was engaged, on Ellen's suggestion, to play the part of Marguerite in the revival of *Faust*. There would be gorgeous reminders of the glory, when, for example, Tree produced *The Merry Wives of Windsor* at His Majesty's Theatre, with himself as Falstaff and Ellen Terry and Madge Kendal as the Wives, a production which no one who saw it will ever forget. At the end of the first four years, the correspondence became desultory and less intimate and vivacious. It was even said that G.B.S. was deeply disappointed in her when at last they met, and that he 'could not bear her'. And some kindly person told her this. It was untrue.

I saw what must have been one of their last meetings, if it was not actually the last. The occasion was a lecture he gave in London, and Ellen Terry, now old and almost blind, was present to hear him. While he and I were talking, she came feeling her way to him, and I shall always remember the look of great and tender kindness that came into his eyes when he saw the old lady, one of the darlingest women that ever adorned a stage.

93

G.B.S.'s efforts to persuade Irving to produce *The Man of Destiny* were slow, highly difficult, and, in the end, abortive. The critic must not only be incorruptible, but be seen to be incorruptible. I find myself in some difficulty in writing about these matters, for I was dramatic critic of *The Observer* for a long period, and my experience tempts me to believe that either the critics of my time were all honest and incorruptible men and women or that managers thought that none of us was worth bribing. Not once in my career as a critic did any manager or player make an attempt to offer me a bribe of any sort, nor had I the slightest cause to believe that any of my colleagues in the Critics' Circle were capable even of being offered a bribe; and I should be surprised if I were told that any of the contemporary critics are corrupt. But it seems that there were some men in the eighties and nineties whose praise could be purchased. I doubt if they were numerous.

Irving was reputed to follow the managerial custom of buying plays from dramatic critics without having any intention of staging them; and G.B.S. seems to have believed that the legend was true. He was terrified of being thought the sort of man who would sell his good opinion, and it is evident that he feared he might be regarded as seeking a bribe when he sent *The Man of Destiny* to the Lyceum. It is immaterial to the argument whether Irving was or was not in the habit of bribing critics. The essential point is that G.B.S. knew that some men were suspected of accepting bribes, and that he believed bribery to be part of the common practice of managers, including Irving. He made it plain, therefore, at the outset that he did not desire a payment on account of royalties, that what he desired was a production at the Lyceum Theatre of *The Man of Destiny*, with Irving as Napoleon and Ellen Terry as The Lady. If he had added that his great hope was that Irving would one day act in a longer play of his, their relations might have been pleasanter.

Irving could make nothing out of Shaw or his work. *The Man of Destiny* is not a great play. It is a small piece of quality, but no more than that. Its quality, however, eluded Irving, whose mind was set rigidly on romantic and spectacular plays. He complained once that Shaw had no respect for great and distinguished people; and it must have seemed to him that the portrait of Napoleon in *The Man of Destiny* was nearly blasphemous. Richard Mansfield had felt something of the sort when he read the play. Napoleon, even to his enemies, had become a legendary figure, who must always be presented in a romantic manner. The same is true of Nelson. A dramatist who had written a play about the hero of Trafalgar which showed him as the queer mixture of ignominy and nobility that he was, would probably have failed to obtain production for it. Had it reached the stage, it would almost certainly, at any time prior to the First World War, have been hissed off again. The uproar which occurred when a play entitled *Nelson's Enchantress* was announced for performance was remarkable. The hero-worship, in Nelson's case, had reached a point at which anyone who had said that Nelson had made mistakes, had, on occasions, been defeated in battle, would have been mobbed. The vast majority of the British people were unaware that Nelson had a Neapolitan naval officer, Francesco Caracciolo, hanged in circumstances which are described in the *Encyclopaedia Britannica* as 'indecent'. There is a suspicion that his behaviour on this occasion was due to the fact that Caracciolo had aspired to Lady Hamilton's love.

The Napoleon legend was almost as firmly fixed in sentimental romance as Nelson's; and Irving, who was highly susceptible to romantic myths about eminent people, could scarcely believe his eyes when he read *The Man of Destiny* and saw how the Emperor was treated by its irreverent author. His emotions were such that he felt certain there was some ulterior intention in Shaw's mind, and that this intention was not so much to mock and deride Napoleon as it was to mock and deride Henry Irving.

The fact that G.B.S. would not accept an advance on account of royalties was in itself disturbing. Why should Shaw not do what all dramatists did? G.B.S. could not tell him that his refusal was due to his reluctance to rouse the slightest suspicion in any person's mind that he was being bribed. Irving would have denied indignantly that he had ever attempted to bribe anybody, and would almost certainly have felt increased aversion from G.B.S. for so much as hinting at such a thing.

The negotiations for the play's production moved very slowly. Irving disliked it, and disliked even more its author. He was sincere in finding no merit in the play or, indeed, in any of Shaw's work. This impudent Irishman was a new sort of man in his experience, and he could not make head or tail of the fellow or his work. Yet there were men and women of intelligence who thought highly of him. So Irving dithered and dallied over *The Man of Destiny*, asserting always that his difficulty was to fit so long a short play into the Lyceum programme: an excuse which had reason in it. There was a period when a production seemed certain, for Irving had accepted a play adapted by Sidney Grundy from a German piece which was of a length that allowed room for *The Man of Destiny*, and G.B.S. was invited to meet him in his office at the Lyceum on August 26, 1896.

It was an uneasy encounter. That very day there had appeared in *The Saturday Review* a savage criticism of *Cymbeline* which had received its first performance on the previous Tuesday. Not only was the play dismissed as 'stagey trash of the lowest melodramatic order, in parts abominably written, throughout intellectually vulgar, and judged in point of thought by modern intellectual standards, vulgar, foolish, offensive, indecent and exasperating beyond all tolerance', but Irving, both as a manager and producer, was hewn into bloody gobbets. That was not the morning a man would deliberately choose to meet an actor-manager whom he wished to produce one of his plays. 'In a true republic of art, Sir Henry Irving would ere this have expiated his acting versions on the scaffold. He does not merely cut plays: he disembowels them. In *Cymbeline* he has quite surpassed himself by extirpating the antiphonal third verse of the famous dirge. A man who would do that would do anything—cut the coda out of the first movement of Beethoven's Ninth Symphony, or shorten one of Velasquez's Phillips into a kitcat to make it fit over his drawing-room mantelpiece. . . .'

Irving, had he been willing to admit that he had read G.B.S.'s article, which he most certainly had, might well have enquired when they met, why he was willing to have *The Man of Destiny* produced and acted by a man who was 'incapable of acting another man's play'. But if he winced under some of G.B.S.'s stinging sentences he could console himself with others. These, for example:

> 'Now I have already described Shakespeare's Iachimo as little better than any of the lay figures in *Cymbeline*— a mere *diabolus ex machina*. But Irving's Iachimo is a very different affair. It is a new and independent creation. I knew Shakespeare's play inside and out before last Tuesday; but this Iachimo was quite fresh and novel to me. I witnessed it with unqualified delight; it was no vulgar bagful of "points", but a true impersonation, unbroken in its life-current from

end to end, varied on the surface with the finest comedy, and without a single lapse in the sustained beauty of its execution. It is only after such work that an artist can with perfect naturalness and dignity address himself to his audience as "their faithful and loving servant".'

The elder man, reading this tribute from the younger, might feel compensated for the harshness of the opening passages. Irving undoubtedly had an extraordinary fascination for Shaw, whose incontinent wrath was no more than the Chinaman's anger against his disappointing god. He confesses this fascination in a letter to Ellen which was written on the day previous to the interview with Irving. 'Unfortunately, he will have the satisfaction of getting the better of me in personal intercourse. In correspondence I can always maintain an iron consistency. In conversation I shall get interested in *him*, and forget all about the importance of my rubbishy little play. What with the article and the interview combined, it is I, not he, who will need to be taken to Richmond to be petted.'

What happened at this interview has never been reported. Ellen had intended to be present at it, but her courage failed her at the last moment. 'I was also there that morning,' she wrote to G.B.S. 'I intended coming straight into the office, but got no further than the doormat. Heard your voice and then skedaddled home again full tilt, and, oh I was laughing. I *couldnt* come in. All of a sudden it came to me that under the funny circumstances I should not be responsible for my impulses. When I saw you, I *might* have thrown my arms round your neck and hugged you. I *might* have been struck shy. The Lord knows what I might or might not have done, and I think H.I. might not have seen the joke!'

The Shaw-Terry letters contain the history of Henry Irving's relations with G.B.S. over *The Man of Destiny*, and since the history was written while it was happening, we may regard it as conclusive in general, though we could wish for more details. The first fact to be borne in mind is that although the play was written for Richard Mansfield, who declined it, the part of The Strange Lady was written for Ellen Terry, and it may be assumed, therefore, that G.B.S. had in his mind a possible production at the Lyceum, with Irving as the Emperor. He had no illusions about the play. 'This', he wrote to Ellen, 'is not one of my great plays, you must know: it is only a display of my knowledge of stage tricks—a commercial traveller's sample. You would like my *Candida* much better; but I never let people read that: I always read it to them. They can be heard sobbing three streets off.' Ellen Terry, not Irving, therefore, was the principal moving spirit in the play, and it was she who made Irving aware of it, and urged him to perform it.

The fear G.B.S. felt that Irving was less eager to buy the play than he was to buy its author's good opinion, was intensified at their interview. 'The negotiations concerning *The Man of Destiny* did not get very far,' he wrote to Ellen Terry:[1]

'I proposed conditions to Sir H.I. Sir H.I. declined the mental effort of bothering about my conditions, and proposed exactly what I barred, namely, to treat me handsomely, by making me a present of a £50 note every Christmas on condition that nobody else got the play, with an understanding that it should be produced at some date unspecified, when the tyrannical public would graciously permit the poor manager to indulge it. To this I replied by proposing three alternatives.
1. My original conditions (virtually).
2. That you should have the play to amuse yourself with until you were tired of it, without any conditions at all.
3. That he should have a present of it on condition of his instantly producing works by Ibsen. The effect of this on his mind was such that I have not heard from him since. Only the other day there suddenly flashed on me something that we have been forgetting all along— *Madame Sans Gêne*. If you are really bent on playing that ridiculous washerwoman, there is an end of *The Man of Destiny*, since H.I. cannot play two Napoleons, mine and Sardou's, on top of one another. Why on earth did we not think of this before? I see the hopelessness of dissuading you from the washtub. You will certainly be the very worst laundress that ever burnt holes in the drama; but that is just what attracts you: you like to play at your profession on the stage, and to exercise your real power in actual life.'

On August 28, 1896, still writing from Stratford St Andrew Rectory at Saxmundham, he mentions his future wife to her:

'. . . we have been joined by an Irish millionairess who has had cleverness and character enough to decline the station in life—"great catch for somebody"—to which it pleased God to call her, and whom we have incorporated into our Fabian family with great success. I am going to refresh my heart by falling in love with her. I love falling in love—but, mind, only with her, not with the million; so somebody else must marry her if she can stand him after me.'

94

On October 2, 1896, William Morris, for whom G.B.S. felt affection only equalled by his regard for William Archer, Sidney Webb and G. K. Chesterton, died. His authority is less now than it was at the time of his death, but his influence, profound then, is still operating on our lives.

He began his revolution when he married. His home must be

---

[1] *Ellen Terry and Bernard Shaw. A Correspondence.* Letter XVII, p. 32.

entirely different from the routine home of his time. He designed furniture for it. He made pots and pans for it. He fashioned and dyed curtains, and made gay and extravagant wallpaper. His revolution was not restricted to the home: he invaded the churches, the factories and the printing presses. The firm he founded would design anything, from china to church ornaments, from metal-work to stained glass, from books to tapestry and carpets. In 1877, after the restoration of Burford Church, he founded the Society for the Protection of Ancient Buildings because he was terrified by the prospect of what 'practical' people might do when they started to restore Tewkesbury Abbey. The whole traffic of typography was drastically changed by him; and when he founded the Kelmscott Press, from which he issued a remarkable variety of beautifully designed and printed books, culminating in the lovely edition of Chaucer's works which had occupied his thoughts for five years and took two years to print, he had completed his great task. The fashion in this respect has changed and Morris's editions, especially the Chaucer, are no longer admired as they once were, but this change does not diminish the value of what Morris did; and the fashion may swing back to him.

He was a romantic communist, setting forth his ideal of life in *News from Nowhere*, that charming utopia where it is always summer. But his utopia, like all the utopias, is a world inhabited exclusively by men and women remarkably like its author, a world in which all the men and women are handsome and well-made, and there is no illness, no war, no envy, malice or any uncharitableness, where every mind is noble; and the only crime committed comes from a lovers' quarrel.

News from Nowhere is an enchanting work to read; and if we put it down with a sigh because it seems remote from any life we know, we feel that the fault is ours. No man ever felt less at home in political life than William Morris. Economics were beyond his understanding. The sordid Soviet Republics, inhabited by carefully graded slaves, would horrify him if he were alive to-day. There is a sense in which Morris can be called an unpractical man, a dreamer whose feeling for facts was slight; yet it is such men as he who change our world. Looking like the captain of a ship in full sail, the sort of man who is found on the bridge of the *Cutty Sark* rather than in a workshop, testing dyes, or a study, writing poems about the Middle Ages, he spread an emotion about human society which altered and enriched our lives. The fact that G.B.S. could unite William Morris and Sidney Webb in his mind and faith is one of the signs of his extraordinary universality.

The death of Morris was the first great personal loss G.B.S. felt. The death of his father had not discomposed him much, but the death of William Morris gave him deep distress. 'You can lose a man like that by your own death,' he wrote of him in *The Saturday Review*, 'but not by his'.

95

G.B.S., in his efforts to dispel any suspicion of corrupt practice because Irving was thinking of producing *The Man of Destiny*, had become sharper in his criticism of Lyceum policy and productions. About a week after the revival of *Richard III*, his criticism of it appeared in *The Saturday Review*. It was unfortunate not only in its phrasing, but in its time of publication. Irving was a temperate man. He could not have led the exacting and responsible life of an actor-manager in control of a large and expensive theatre if he had been a tippler. First nights are nervously disturbing to all who are intimately concerned in the performance; and many fine players are at their worst then. Henry Ainley told me that he was sometimes sick with nervous excitement before curtain rise on a first night. Irving was never as good on a first night as he was thereafter, a fact of which all who knew him were well aware. Allowance, therefore, was made for mishaps in his performance on these occasions. He had now to contend not only with first-night nerves, but with a production from which Ellen Terry was absent and the knowledge that the Lyceum's bank account was heavily overdrawn.

During the performance, he made slips of speech and behaviour which were ignored by the audience, who knew quite well what was their cause. But G.B.S. seems not to have known, nor to have been sufficiently imaginative to realise why they were made: a singular lack of discernment is one who was himself highly nervous. In his *Saturday Review* article, he commented on the slips so clumsily that Irving and his associates instantly concluded that he was accusing him of having been drunk on the stage. He mentioned the fact that Irving had said 'you' when he ought to have said 'I', a slip which a more experienced critic would have ignored. Complaint was made because a remark, not part of the play, was made by Irving to Miss Maud Milton. He told her 'to get further up the stage', which is the sort of undertone remark actors often make during a performance. But Irving made it loudly enough for it to be heard in the auditorium.

Had G.B.S. been more familiar with the stage and less addicted to the society of 'intellectual' actresses, he would have known that players commonly carry on private conversations during a play. It is recorded that Irving, while playing Othello and engaged in throttling Desdemona, asked the actress who took her part what they were having for supper that night, for he lodged with her mother, and as she breathed her last groan, she told him. G.B.S. was being a Dublin smartie when he made these trivial complaints; but he was being stupid when he wrote his criticism of *Richard III;* and an accident made him seem more stupid than he was.

Irving, already fatigued by the strain of the first performance, was strained still more by a supper party in the Garrick Club, followed by a long conversation with Professor James Dewar in the latter's rooms at the Royal Institute in Albemarle Street. When he left the Institute, Dewar walked with him to his rooms in Grafton Street, where their conversation was continued until dawn. Then, when Dewar had departed, Irving, following his custom, prepared to take a bath. As he climbed the stairs to the bathroom, he struck his knee against a chest, but managed, despite the pain he was in, to get to bed. The pain became worse, and he was unable to move his leg when his servant came to him in the morning. He had ruptured the ligaments of his knee cap and would be unable to act for several weeks.

This was a great disaster in every respect. A new production, made at great expense, must be suspended after the first performance. Without Irving in the cast, the audiences would dwindle to a few scattered people in the pit. The theatre was closed for a week. Ellen Terry could not return from Germany until the end of January, so a stop-gap revival of *Cymbeline* was made, which was a financial failure. The theatre was again closed, this time for three weeks, at the end of which time, Ellen Terry having returned to London, *Cymbeline* was again revived, but with little more success than it had previously had. *Olivia* was revived, and kept the theatre going, with a small loss, until the end of February. Irving lost £10,000 on that disastrous season.[1]

It was at the beginning of this grave misfortune, in the week after Irving had ruptured the ligaments of his knee cap, that G.B.S.'s article appeared in *The Saturday Review*. It could not have been more untimely. A man who chooses the wrong time to be right is wrong; and G.B.S. was more often wrong in this respect than one would have expected a man of his quick and sensitive wits to be. He failed in courtesy to a distinguished man who was much older than himself, and it is difficult to defend him. But he was not being deliberately spiteful: he was being surprisingly thick.

His article contained the following passage:

'As to Sir Henry Irving's own performance, I am not prepared to judge it, in point of execution, by what he did on the first night. He was best in the Court scenes; in the heavy single-handed scenes which Cibber loved, he was not, it seemed to me, answering his helm very satisfactorily; and he was occasionally a little out of temper with his

[1] I have taken these details from *Henry Irving*, by Laurence Irving.

own nervous condition. . . . In the tent and battle scenes his exhaustion was too genuine to be quite acceptable as part of the play. . . . The attempt to make a stage combat look as imposing as Hazlitt's description of the death of Edmund Kean's Richard reads, is hopeless. If Kean were to return to life and do the combat for us, we should very likely find it as absurd as his habit of lying down on a sofa when he was too tired or too drunk to keep his feet during the final scene.'

No one who reads the article can believe for a moment that G.B.S. thought and was telling his readers that Irving was drunk during the first performance of Richard III; but it was almost inevitable that Irving himself and his immediate associates, all anxious and distressed because of the disaster of his accident, should conclude that such was his intention. Those unfortunate words about Edmund Kean made them feel certain that the charge of drunkenness was intended to be made. Irving's biographer and grandson is charitable enough to believe that G.B.S. had no such intention as was attributed to him; and G.B.S. was stating the bare fact when, writing to Irving on April 29, 1897, he said: 'They tell me that you consider that my criticism of *Richard III* implied about you what it said about Kean. I reply flatly that it didn't: if I had thought so, I'd have said so bluntly or else said nothing at all.'

Irving's reply to G.B.S. was the conventional and stale reply of the actor to the critic. He had not had the pleasure of reading 'your criticism—as you call it—of Richard. I never read a criticism of yours in my life. I have read lots of your droll, amusing, irrelevant and sometimes impertinent pages, but criticism containing judgment and sympathy I have never seen by your pen.'

This was the sort of sarcasm that is greatly esteemed by players, who generally take up an attitude of lofty indifference and disdain to critics and pretend never to have read a word they have written— only to reveal in the course of their conversation that they have read every word with close and sometimes furious attention. It is inconceivable, though his grandson seems to find it likely, that Irving did not read an article which was causing so much passionate argument in his theatre. How could he remain indifferent to it when Bram Stoker and L. F. Austin were assuring him that G.B.S. had stated in print that he was drunk on the first night of *Richard III* and unable to remember his lines? The Almighty would not have left it unread, and Henry Irving was not the Almighty, but a mortal man with partialities and resentments, a human love of applause and a deep dislike of condemnation.

Greater men than Irving have been as sensitive to blame as he was: poets and novelists, painters and sculptors, composers and musicians, all creative artists have been infuriated by dispraise and have spat venom on those who fell short in approval. Of course he read it and of course he was infuriated, as, indeed, with Austin and Stoker influencing his thoughts, he had every right to be.

96

The quarrel was now complete. There could never now be any reconciliation between these two foes who should have been friends and allies. Irving was more to blame than G.B.S., though G.B.S. invited enmity, for Irving was much the older and more powerful man and could have afforded to be magnanimous. Ellen Terry, who had not seen the *Richard III* article, because she was in Germany when it appeared, was deeply distressed by the collapse of her plan to reconcile these difficult men of genius to each other. 'Oh, dear, oh dear, My Dear, this vexes me very much,' she wrote to G.B.S. 'My friends to fight! And I love both of them, and want each to win.' That moan of unhappiness and despair was her response to G.B.S.'s furious declaration of war on Irving.

'Dearest Ellen, Look out for squalls. I have just received from Stoker a cool official intimation that Sir H. has changed his mind about producing *The Man of Destiny*. My answer goes by the same post as this card. I am in ecstasies. I have been spoiling for a row; and now I have Mansfield to fight with one hand and H.I. with the other. Hooray! Kiss me good speed; and I'll toss them all about the stage as Cinquevalli tosses oranges and dinner plates! . . .'

He was whistling to keep up his courage, but he would have done better to confess his fault and make atonement for it. His performance was not pretty: it was unpardonable.

This was not the only blow he received then. Exactly a week after he had received Stoker's letter, Cyril Maude and he agreed that *You Never Can Tell*, which had been in rehearsal at the Haymarket for a fortnight, should be withdrawn without public performance. The rehearsals had not been happy. Two members of the cast had thrown up their parts after hearing the play read once. It had 'no laughs and no exits', one of them said as he departed into oblivion. 'Exits', for him, meant lines in which the actor could strike an attitude as he prepared to leave the stage and utter a sentence which would hit the gallery between wind and water. In Shaw's play, people left the stage as people leave a room every day of their lives, without attitudinising and declaiming.

Any other man must have been flattened out by such an experience as this, but, like the good soldier of fortune he was, G.B.S. took the blows with gay courage and high fortitude. Ellen Terry wrote him one of her short, wise letters before the decision about *You*

Never Can Tell was made. 'Don't let anything stop that comedy at the Haymarket,' she said. 'You have written a crowd of splendid plays. Now let some of 'em *be acted*. . . . Do NOT let anything put that play off for I'm your loving old friend and I KNOW it will hurt your success.'

And, indeed, it did, for eight years passed before, in 1905, the Vedrenne-Barker season was started at the Court Theatre, and G.B.S. at last came to power. That was the year in which Henry Irving died. It may be that Irving and Shaw were incompatible, and could never have worked together, as some people assert, but perhaps it is nearer the truth to say that G.B.S. belonged to a theatre which was struggling to be born, whereas Irving belonged to a theatre which was tottering to the grave. Is it not significant that when G.B.S. began to triumph in Sloan Square, Henry Irving, old, poor and spent, was dragging his tired body round the provinces, still the humble and obedient servant of a public which was no longer eager for his service, and that he staggered out of the playhouse in Bradford to die in the lounge of his hotel, unable to live any longer? The flame of his life went out as the flame of G.B.S.'s life burst into brilliant fire.

The old enmity seemed to revive even in the hour of Irving's death; for G.B.S. was asked to write an obituary article on him for the Viennese paper, *Die Neue Freie Presse*. Here was another example of his singular obtuseness in such matters, his inability to realise that to be right at the wrong time is to be wrong. The article was translated from G.B.S.'s original into German, and was given a malicious twist by the translator. A correspondent of a London newspaper made a translation from the German into English that was even more malicious than its source. The result was that G.B.S. appeared to be throwing stones at Irving's coffin. There is no doubt that the article, as G.B.S. had written it, was fair criticism, even if we feel that that moment was not the time for its publication or, rather, that he was not the man who should have made it. He had copies of his original article printed and sent them to all the leading newspapers, 'placing it at their disposal as a free contribution'.

> 'Unfortunately, in newspaperland a slander is interesting news always welcomed by news-editors. An explanation that it is baseless is disappointing and goes into the wastepaper basket: hence by the way the excellent French law that if a newspaper disparages a citizen it must willy-nilly publish his reply at equal length. No such law existing in Britain, only one newspaper, and that not a London one, inserted my authentic version.'

Here, perhaps, his remarkable instinct for obtaining publicity was at fault. Had he sent a *letter* to each of the newspapers, repudiating the mistranslations and explaining what he *had* written, the letter would have been published. If he felt that he must send the article, he could have done so, mentioning it in his letter and adding that the article was sent so that the editor could judge for himself between it and the mistranslations; but he was, perhaps, in too great a hurry to consider the matter as carefully as he ought to have done.[1] The episode was unfortunate. It detracted little or nothing from Irving: it detracted much from G.B.S.

Ellen Terry, naturally distressed by it, wrote to G.B.S. 'You never wrote the words they say you wrote, except when Henry was well, was at work and fighting. Then it was all right enough—fair. You never said it I am sure when all his friends were sore and smarting. *You* don't add hyssop to the wounds. That would be *un*fair. I never knew you to do an unkind action, but heaps of lovely ones. *He* was prematurely old from constantly doing practical little goodnesses. Did he have faults? Yes! But of course *we* have none! I'm far away in the North and have only just heard that you were unkind. I don't believe that. I suppose time will bring me printed matter. When it comes I shall have no eyes to read with. I couldn't *cry* and something seemed to fix my eyes open and strain them. I feel badly. I'm sorry because I didn't do enough whilst I could, just a little longer. Of course I am glad for him, and I believe no one appreciated him much more than *you* did! I'm sure of it. My love to Charlotte, and you, for you wrote that a long while ago I'm sure. Tell me so!'

His reply to this poignant letter cited one of his original sentences, the mistranslation into German, and the mistranslation back into English. What he had written was: 'The truth is, Irving was interested in nothing but himself; and the self in which he was interested was an imaginary self in an imaginary world. He lived in a dream.' The German into which this passage was rendered ran as follows: 'Nur eine imaginäre Person in einer imaginären Pose'. The English into which this German was translated was, 'He was a narrow-minded egoist, devoid of culture, and living on the dream of his own greatness'. But even if this were the entire truth, which it was not, might it not also have been written of G.B.S. himself or of any other man of genius? Ellen Terry's final comment on the matter was the most sensible that was made. 'Well, it was just stupid of you, that's all— and that's enough I should say for *you*. I can't understand how one without gross food in him, who takes no wine to fuddle his wits, can have been so indelicate. Nothing is expected of *me*, or of most of us, but of you I expect everything . . . I can't help wanting to burn you, but all my impulse is bad and wrong. I've no head and my heart is rotten.'

[1] See the *Shaw-Terry Letters*, Letter CCLXX, p. 338.

We have run too far ahead of order, and must return to the year 1897, which, in its first half, had treated G.B.S. very roughly. To have two plays accepted, one of them actually in rehearsal, and then to have them refused performance was small encouragement to continue writing plays. But fortune was walking towards him, and would soon begin to run. Even in May of that year, despite his decision not to produce *The Man of Destiny*, Irving talked about it to Ellen Terry,[1] suggesting that it might fit in with a play he thought of producing. She, too, still hoped that it would be done at the Lyceum. There was rumour that Forbes Robertson and Mrs Patrick Campbell were thinking of performing it, but Ellen was confident that Forbes Robertson would 'not get half out of it that Henry would', though she thought that Mrs Pat 'would do the Lady *well enough*. (But it is Nap. who is the play.) Dont be a dear Idiot, and let anyone do that part but Henry.'

G.B.S. might have retorted to her that it was not he who was preventing Henry from playing the part, but Henry himself. Nevertheless, her advice and reproof were good and sound, and G.B.S. would have done well to be guided by her. She reminded him that he knew nothing about the theatre as a place of business enterprise. 'Sometimes, in the *Saturday*, you speak just like an amateur on the subject of the conduction of a theatre (Forgive me darling) . . . Henry always blunders in the same manner when he *will* talk of the "Art of Music"—or of Painting, and I can't explain to him, but at least I often *stop* him. At least I know I dont know, but then I know he doesnt know. Oh, heavens! You'll read me no more. You'll love me no more. I disgrace myself when I *will* write. When H. read me his letter to you last evening I screamed with laughter when he came to "callous to the feelings of others", and "lost the consciousness of vulgarity". Remember those paragraphs were none of his. This, of course, you understand since you are not a born fool. Now let Henry do the play when he can. The time will come, *I* think, sooner than he reckons for.'

But she was wrong in her prophecy, though she was right in her belief that 'your interests and his are wrapped together, and he knows quite well that is best for himself'. G.B.S., however, would not hearken to her sage counsel. The rejection of the play had hurt him, though he could hardly have expected it to be accepted and produced after that stupid business over *Richard III*. He was resolved, he told Ellen, to have nothing more to do with Irving, and he even desponded of a

[1] See *Shaw-Terry Letters*, Letter CXX, p. 160.

future for himself in the theatre. 'There is no use in wasting the play: J.F.R. and Mrs Pat may as well do it as anybody; but I shall trouble myself no more about the theatre. I don't care, and never did care who plays Napoleon (it was written for Mansfield); but I should have liked you to play the Strange Lady; and since your infant has put a stop to that, it may be played by Mrs Pat's dresser for all I care.'

Ellen's statement that Irving was not the author of the sentences which had made her scream with laughter, was a reminder, which G.B.S. scarcely needed, that Austin drafted most of Irving's letters and that the phrases which excited her derision expressed his mind not Irving's. Irving, having had little schooling himself, was bemused by education and thought more highly of men of formal instruction than a man of his genius had any right to think. A succession of pompous polysyllables in a letter pleased him, and when Austin produced one full of such monstrosities, Irving signed it with delight. But his own letters, simply phrased, were superior to Austin's pedantic rubbish.

Time was to convince Ellen that Irving would never produce a play by Shaw. She had shown him G.B.S.'s latest play, *Caesar and Cleopatra*, and felt certain that 'he could have done *wonders* with that Play if he had done it', but 'Henry will never produce a play by you'. If Irving was stiff-necked, so, now, was G.B.S., and his reply to her remarks was 'It may be that H.I. will never play anything of mine. It is quite certain that, except through you, he will never get the chance.' Nor did he. Disaster was now impending for him. His day as sole owner of the Lyceum was ending. It would soon become the property of a limited company, and its greatness would dwindle and presently decay. A time would come when it would be no better than the Elephant and Castle Theatre; a place of proletarian trash; and the great house which had seen Irving and Ellen Terry in *The Merchant of Venice*, would see much lesser people in *The Worst Woman in London*. It was bombed by the Germans in the Second World War, but was rebuilt and is now a popular dancehall.

There was some danger that G.B.S. might, at this period of his life, have allowed himself to be discouraged from drama by Irving's antipathy to him. His letters to Ellen Terry, more than anything else, reveal the hurt he had sustained. He is full of fury, writing screeds of recrimination to her against Irving, provoking her into telling him that he was 'quite stupid after all, and *not* so unlike other people. You should have given in and said, "Take the play and do it when you can. You'll do it better than anyone else, and *nurse* it better than anyone else." Don't pity H. He thinks he has quite got the best of it in the recent altercation. The fact is he dont think the whole thing matters much. I do, and I'm angry with you. I keep out of the affair as you tell me to.—What I cared for more than for you or H.—or the parts, WAS THE PLAY—and NOW—wellgoyourways—Oh my darling you are the horridest old—'

There were signs in the sky that he now wondered whether his career was not really in political life. He could earn a living by journalism which would support him in parliament. The Webbs were always at his side, nudging it, and trying to fill him with contempt for all this Art that he was constantly talking about. What was a play or a symphony or a picture in comparison with a neat system of drainage. Poetry! . . . How Beatrice's nostrils sometimes drew up when verse was mentioned. Read that stuff and nonsense when there was an excellent White Paper on Grants in Aid to be studied! She and Sidney were thinking hard about Local Government. Why could not G.B.S. think about it, too? He did, and, amazingly, got himself co-opted as a member of St Pancras Vestry. That was in 1897 when he had taken the terrible toss over *The Man of Destiny* and *You Never Can Tell*. And more amazing than his co-option was the fact that he turned out to be a very good Vestryman, attentive to the affairs of St Pancras, skilful in committee, and devoid of any fantastic airs.

98

Luckily for the theatre, he had become acquainted, through Mrs Webb, with a remarkable woman, whom Beatrice had designed to be the wife of Graham Wallas. Charlotte Frances Payne-Townshend, was a woman of wealth. Her father, Horace Payne-Townshend, was an Irish barrister and a member of the family of estate agents by whom G.B.S. had been employed in Dublin; and her mother was Mary Susannah Kirby, a wealthy Englishwoman from Worcestershire.

She was born at Derry, Rosscarberry, Co. Cork, on January 20, 1857, almost exactly six months after the birth of G.B.S. in Dublin; and was a woman of great character and firmness of will, dissimilar in almost every respect from G.B.S. She had a hatred of publicity which was almost morbid. It was as difficult to get her to pose for a photographer as it was to keep him away from cameras. She seldom appeared in public, and if she ever made a speech in her life, no one, not even herself seems to have heard it. How she came to know the Webbs is not known, but she probably sought them out, for she was discontent with her life as an idle, rich woman, and was eager to find some employment or purpose which would occupy and interest her and enable her to be generally useful.

The Webbs had met her in the autumn of 1895, and, learning

that she was wealthy—they had a keen scent for wealth—and in romantic rebellion against her family and class, sought to enlist her interest in the London School of Economics which Sidney had founded in the previous spring with the £10,000 left to him for some such public purpose by Henry Hutchinson. Its principal was Professor W. A. S. Hewins, who was afterwards prominently associated with Joseph Chamberlain in his campaign for Tariff Reform. The School was started at 9, John Street, in the Adelphi, but soon had to remove to larger premises at 10, Adelphi Terrace. Charlotte, as I shall call her for the rest of this book, not only gave £1,000 to the School Library and founded a woman's scholarship, but took the two top floors of the house at £300 a year for rent and service. She was then about thirty-eight: an attractive woman who dressed well and, despite a general appearance of plainness, occasionally looked beautiful, especially when she wore flowing white evening clothes. 'By temperament, she is an anarchist', Beatrice says of her in *Our Partnership*,[1] 'feeling any regulation or rule intolerable, a tendency which has been exaggerated by her irresponsible wealth.

'She is romantic, but thinks herself cynical. She is a Socialist and a Radical, not because she understands the collectivist standpoint, but because she is by nature a rebel. She has no snobbishness and no convention; she has "swallowed all formulas", but has not worked out principles of her own. She is fond of men and impatient of most women; bitterly resents her enforced celibacy, but thinks she could not tolerate the matter-of-fact side of marriage. Sweet-tempered, sympathetic, and genuinely anxious to increase the world's enjoyment and diminish the world's pain.]. . To me, she seemed at that time, a pleasant, well-dressed, well-intentioned woman; I thought she would do very well for Graham Wallas! Now she turns out to be an "original", with considerable personal charm and certain volcanic tendencies. Graham Wallas bored her with his morality and learning! In a few days she and Bernard Shaw were constant companions. . . .'

This description, characteristically slapdash and shallow, was set down in Beatrice's diary in September, 1896, at the time when G.B.S. met Charlotte for the first time. She had invited him, as an eminent Fabian, to an At Home at the School in February, 1896, but, as he tersely states, in a diary he was keeping then, he 'did not go'. They seem not to have met until the beginning of August of that year, when he was invited to spend six weeks with the Webbs in the rectory of Stratford St Andrew, near Saxmundham, in Suffolk. It was the habit of the Webbs to rent a house, usually a rectory, every summer, but this time the tenancy was joint with Charlotte, who had joined the Fabian Society that year. G.B.S. was then in several toils. He had

[1] Page 90.

extricated himself, with great difficulty, from his entanglement with Jenny Patterson, and the fervour of his passion for Florence Farr was beginning to abate, but he was more importantly entangled with Henry Irving in regard to *The Man of Destiny*. It was, indeed, during his stay at the Rectory that he went up to London to discuss the play with Irving. He was becoming more and more engrossed in his correspondence with Ellen Terry. And he was busy with a new play, *You Never Can Tell*.

His renown was spreading rapidly, and he was better off, economically, than he had ever been before. His total earnings in 1895 were £573 1s., which included royalties, amounting to £270, from *Arms and the Man* and *Widowers' Houses*. His income almost doubled in 1896: £1,089 4s., of which sum, £123 11s. 9d came from the production of *Arms and the Man* by Richard Mansfield in America, and £674 8s. 3d from the same actor's unexpectedly successful production of *The Devil's Disciple*. For the first time in his life, he was able to spend money without anxiety. If ever a man could feel fairly certain that he was unlikely to fall in love for some time, G.B.S., at the outset of his holiday at Saxmundham, was the man. The happiness and high spirits which are plain and infectious in *You Never Can Tell* may, without extravagance or sentimentality, be attributed to the delight he felt in Charlotte's company. It was surprising to those who knew her and him superficially that they should instantly feel attracted to each other. He was not at that moment in the mood of love-making. He was, if anything, tired of women. He had had his enough of them, as the Irish say, and required only a long rest from their importunities.

Charlotte was an entirely new kind of woman in his experience. 'She had none of the feminine traits that I had expected, and all the human qualities I had only hoped for,' he said of her. Despite her disposition to what Beatrice Webb called 'volcanic tendencies', she was conventional and highly fastidious in all her social relations. Her membership of The Fabian Society lay lightly on her. G.B.S. was regular in his attendance at its meetings, but Charlotte, though she never missed a Committee, rarely attended the public meetings. She went only to those at which her husband or one of her friends, such as the Webbs or Sydney Olivier, lectured or when a row was impending and votes were important. In this respect, however, she resembled Beatrice Webb, who was even less regular in her attendance.

Charlotte had the hatred of poverty and pain which any sensitive person must feel, but she did not think that her profession of democratic principles obliged her to hobnob with *hoi polloi*. She retained the right to choose her company. She was almost totally uninterested in politics, though she had what may be called a committee mind and was eager to promote the welfare of such organisations as the London School of Economics. But she was not one of those maudlin men and women who talk and behave as if the proletariat had a monopoly of virtue. She was convinced that hearts just as rare beat in Mayfair as in the lowly air of Seven Dials; and she was inclined to think that, on the whole, the hearts in Mayfair were superior to those in Seven Dials. She did not disguise her liking for well-bred and intelligent people, especially if they belonged to the landed gentry and were of ancient lineage; but she did not deceive herself with the delusion that all well-bred men and women were noble and personally disinterested in their public acts. There were aristocratic and plebeian blackguards. Of these two evils, she would have preferred to choose neither, but if she had been compelled to choose between a blackguard with pleasant manners and conversation, and one without either, she would undoubtedly have chosen the former; and in this choice she would have had the support of almost the entire population.

There is a sense in which she could have been called a snob, but so, in the same sense, could G.B.S. and Beatrice Webb and the majority of the Executive Committee of The Fabian Society, who kept themselves severely aloof from the Independent Labour Party and were strongly disinclined to associate with the Social Democrats. The chief, if not the only member of The Fabian Society who could not be called a snob in this sense was Sidney Webb, who had so little regard for people as individuals, regarding them solely as subjects for enquiry and enumeration, that the idea of treating a duke differently from a dustman never entered his head. One does not snub or flatter sheep: one numbers and classifies them.

The word *snob* has become debased in vulgar usage, and is now a reproach to any person who does not delight in habitual association with coal heavers and clerks in co-operative societies. Charlotte was a snob only in the sense that she insisted on choosing her company in accordance with her own desires and not in accordance with rules and regulations laid down by organised bodies. Like all Conservatives, she had the courage of the Liberals' convictions, and it was immaterial to her who or what a person was so long as she liked him. But she did not pretend to prefer people who could not talk her language to people who could. If she had to choose between those who were intelligent and those who were not, she would unhesitatingly choose the first, because they surveyed the world with serenity even when they wished to change it. She was less gregarious than G.B.S., though she loved travel more than he did. She had, indeed, a passion for travel which increased as she grew older, so that when she disembarked from a ship on which she had gone round the world she was ready to embark on another to take the same trip. G.B.S. loathed travel, especially in anticipation, for he enjoyed it well enough for a period while he was undergoing it. When she took him to Greece, he howled to Ellen Terry in distress:

'Good God, Ellen, the Grecian Archipelago! Can't you see it in your mind's eye, a group of exquisite islands in a turquoise setting? Ugh! Cold, storm, sleety grey, pitching and rolling, misery, headaches, horrors of universal belchings! A moment's respite in the Dardanelles enables me to write to you: soon we shall be in the Sea of Marmora, reputed, as I learn for the first time, the coldest and windiest in the world. However, I am at least quit of Athens, with its stupid classic Acropolis and smashed pillars. Charlotte, who *will* cultivate French acting and thinks the Comédie Française the most perfect thing on earth, insisted on my going to hear that bellowing donkey, Mounet Sully, as Othello. Good Lord! The 4th act ended at 12.30; the fifth began punctually at one. Poor Moony Silly grinned like a fairy queen in a fifth rate pantomime and howled like a newsboy. Shakespear won the third act triumphantly; and Moony got the credit of it. A horrible experience. At Athens the best thing was your letter. . . .'

All of which means only that the weather was bad at Athens, just as it is sometimes bad elsewhere; that G.B.S. was uncomfortable on ships because he suffered severely from sea-sickness; and, more than all, that he was eager to go home and get on with his work. The singular fact about these two is that Charlotte, despite her passion for globe-trotting, hated sight-seeing, whereas G.B.S., who would never have left London if he could have had his way, delighted in seeing things and places. She would travel through a country without leaving the car unless she was obliged to do so; but he could hardly wait for it to stop so that he might see all there was to see. Once, at Olivet, Charlotte remained in their car while G.B.S. went off to climb the Mount and take photographs. In a short time, he returned, saying 'Charlotte, you must see this place. It's where Jesus took off for the Ascension!' She complained to me once, after a journey in Germany, that when they arrived in a town, she would go to her room in a hotel to rest, but G.B.S. would instantly set off sight-seeing. On his return, he would exclaim, 'We'd better move on now, Charlotte, I've seen this place!'

Part of his discomfort in travel was due to his inability to learn foreign languages. He had striven for a long time to learn German, but had failed, though he knew enough to be able, with the help of a German-English dictionary, to make rough translations. He could read French moderately well, but could not speak it, except very brokenly, and was unable to understand it when he heard it. Archibald Henderson, having heard that he was sitting to Rodin who could not speak English, asked the sculptor if G.B.S. could speak French well. 'Ah, non,' Rodin replied. 'Monsieur Shaw ne parle pas Français. Mais de manière ou d'autre, par la violence même de son air et de ses gestes, il réussit à vous imposer sa pensée.' When Anatole France visited London and gave an address to The Fabian Society, at which G.B.S. took the chair, Charlotte had to whisper explanations to her husband as the address was delivered. She was an accomplished linguist. It was at this lecture that Anatole France embarrassed G.B.S. by kissing him on both cheeks. He blushed like a shy schoolgirl.

Writing to Mrs Patrick Campbell in 1912, he tells her that he 'is the most deplorable of linguists', and that he would 'rather write three plays than ask my way anywhere' in a foreign country. 'On such occasions, I miss Charlotte, who, when in the smallest difficulty, demands information and assistance from every bystander (giving them copious and detailed information as to every relevant or irrelevant event of the last three months) and generally gets them, too. The things of this world bruise my soul.'

Charlotte's own company was congenial to her, but this statement does not mean that she was morose or ill at ease in society. She was kind and amiable and generous, and she had the power to make people feel welcome, but she was not given to casual visiting, and she seldom dropped in on people. She was an ardent reader, and was happiest when she and G.B.S. were alone together in the evening, he reading to her while she knitted: a comfortable suburban couple, deeply attached to each other and not in the least eager to have their solitude invaded. As she grew older, her interest in religion, which had been slight in her girlhood and middle age, became intense, and she spent most of her evenings in reading books on what are called fancy religions, without, however, finding the consolation she sought, which could have been found round the corner at the nearest Christian church. In 1914, she published a small book, written in stiff, unwieldy prose, entitled *Knowledge in the Door: a Forerunner*. It described the religious belief of an organisation *The Fellowship of the Way*, which was founded by Dr J. Paster Mills, whose most important work appears to have been *From Existence to Life: the Science of Self-Consciousness*. The Secretary of the Society was the distinguished actress, Lena Ashwell (Lady Simson), one of Charlotte's closest friends. The book is transcendental in style and consists mainly of a series of unproved assertions.

She was not musical, as G.B.S. was, nor was she greatly interested in the theatre. Actors and actresses soon exhausted her interest in them. But her deepest aversion was the horde of hero-worshippers who beset G.B.S. wherever he went. They were accustomed, when they succeeded in entering her house, to treat he almost as if she were an intruder. They had come, especially if they were gushing women, to commune with her husband, and they had no wish to hear her interrupting their profound conversation! . . . Her discomfort was increased by the fact that G.B.S. expected her to rescue him from these importunate people. This, however, is part of the hardship suffered by the wives of great men.

Charlotte was, in many respects, the converse of G.B.S. Her horror of publicity was intense. I have seen her withdraw from a group of people about to be photographed because she realised that the picture would appear in the press; and she told me once in tones that left no doubt of her sincerity that she greatly loathed being gaped at wherever she and G.B.S. went. There is no question of merit or demerit in this like or dislike of publicity: it is entirely a matter of personal temper. G.B.S., whose face was exceptionally photogenic, liked to be photographed and to be gaped at, though even he had had enough of it after his world tour; but Charlotte hated the one and the other. Once, with that witty understatement that was characteristic of her, she remarked to me, 'St John, I think G.B.S. rather likes publicity!' Even in the matter of statement, they were at opposite poles: for he over-stated almost everything.

She was highly critical of her husband's work, and amazed me once by telling me how much she disliked *Heartbreak House*, which is thought by many people to be his best play. I heard her exclaim, after G.B.S. had described a piece he wanted to write, 'Well, I hope it'll be better than the thing you're writing now!'

Their conversation was often banter, at which G.B.S. was superb in the sense that not only was he uncommonly funny, but that he managed to tease his subjects without ever wounding their feelings; but it never led those who listened to it into the delusion that they were not deeply devoted to each other. They had achieved what seemed to be perfect comradeship, in which each subserves the other and still retains his or her individuality. How dearly she loved him is shown in a remark G.B.S. made to me. 'If Charlotte were on her death bed, I know an infallible way of restoring her health. I'd simply go to bed and say I was dying!'

99

Charlotte, who had had a ruined romance with Axel Munthe, the author of *The Story of San Michele*, seems to have recovered from her misadventure in love immediately she met G.B.S., who was not the sort of man, so far as his clothes and general appearance are concerned, that she would have been expected to admire instantly. The conventional woman in her must have been repelled by his eccentricities of dress and his faddiness about food. He was now in full revolt against the conventional code in such matters. He was not only a vegetarian, but a dress reformer. She shared his hatred of tobacco, but this, apparently, was the only feeling they had in common. It is doubtful if G.B.S. ever at any time of his life smoked or drank alcoholic liquors. There is no evidence that he was addicted to either while he was employed in Dublin, and he was too poor in his nine years of servitude to letters to be able to afford indulgence.

By the time Charlotte and he had met for the first time, his abstentions were numerous and ingrained. He no longer slept in sheets, though what complaint he could bring against linen is hard to understand. His clothes, purchased at Jaegers, were austerely hygienic. There was even a period when he paraded Bond Street in sandals. He disdained top hats and bowlers, and affected a broad-brimmed soft hat or Trilby, as it used to be called. He declined to wear evening dress on the ground that stiff white collars and shirt fronts took all the colour out of a man's face and made him appear a ghastly sight, which is true; but he was, I fancy, conscious of the fact that evening dress deprived him, more than most men, of his look of distinction.

Some of these 'fads' are now the common habit of the majority of people: the crank once more has proved himself a pioneer; and the sort of hat G.B.S. wore in 1896, a hat held in contempt as headgear that no one but an anarchist would wear, is now in general use: it is the man in a bowler hat who is eccentric to-day. Silk hats are seen only at weddings, state functions and royal garden parties. The population of Great Britain may be divided into two groups: those who wear hats and those who do not; and Bond Street, that sacred grove into which, formerly, few men and women had the courage to intrude unfashionably clad, is to-day full of hatless people of both sexes. If G.B.S. were alive and were to appear in public in the clothes he used to wear in the nineties, he would not be noticed: he would be one of a large crowd. Such is the fate of the pioneer: he becomes in the course of time old-fashioned and even reactionary.

His eccentricities did not repel Charlotte. As she listened to his audacious opinions and witty conversation, she forgot his queer clothes and his faddiness about food; and her delight was to join him in bicycle rides through the Suffolk lanes. Axel Munthe was forgotten as she and G.B.S. discussed the play, *You Never Can Tell*, he was then writing and was to finish in the autumn. When the holiday was ended, the friendship was firmly fixed. G.B.S. frequently found his way to 10, Adelphi Terrace, to spend the evening in her flat, and in a little while she was helping him by doing his secretarial work. She learnt shorthand and typing so that she might be of greater assistance to him. Affection clearly was deepening, but there was not yet any question of marriage. His letters to Ellen Terry are now full of references to his 'green-eyed Irish millionairess'. 'Well, shall I marry my Irish millionairess? She, like Edy (Ellen's daughter) believes in freedom, and not in marriage; but I think I could prevail on her; and then I should have ever so many hundreds a month for nothing. Would you ever in your secret soul forgive me, even though I am really fond of her and she of me? No: you wouldn't.' He ends the letter by saying that 'I think I'll treat her to a stall' at the Lyceum, 'can't very well take a millionairess to the pit'.

A little later, when his wooing seems to have gone a little askew, he writes to Ellen again:

> 'She doesn't come back until Tuesday. And she doesn't really *love* me. The truth is, she is a clever woman. She knows the value of her unencumbered independence, having suffered a good deal from family bonds and conventionality before the death of her mother and the marriage of her sister left her free. The idea of tying herself up again by a marriage before she knows anything—before she has exploited her freedom and money power to the utmost—seems to her intellect unbearably foolish. Her theory is that she won't do it. She picked up a broken heart somewhere a few years ago, and made the most of it (she is very sentimental) until she happened to read *The Quintessence of Ibsenism*, in which she found, as she thought, gospel, salvation, freedom, emancipation, self-respect and so on. Later on she met the author, who is, as you know, able to make himself tolerable as a correspondent. He is also a bearable companion on bicycle rides, especially in a country house where there is nobody else to pair with. She got fond of me and did not coquet or pretend that she wasn't. I got fond of her, because she was a comfort to me down there. You kept my heart so warm that I get fond of everybody; and she was the nearest and best. That's the situation. What does your loving wisdom say to it?'

Ellen would not tolerate this nonsense. 'Plainly and bluntly,' she wrote in reply, 'you are a great silly. . . . If *she* does not dote upon the quintessence of *you*, she'd better marry the book. . . . But somehow I think she'll love you quick enough. I *think* so, but it's what's in herself I can tell her, not what is in you. How very silly you clever people are. Fancy not knowing! Do *you* know you love her? 'Cos if so, that would be safe enough to marry on. For if it came to the last second and she didn't love *you*, she couldn't kiss you, and then you'd know quick enough. I'm supposing she's a woman, not a — a — (I don't know what to call the thing I mean)—a female that never knows! Those are often married things, and they have children, and there are many such, but I pity their husbands. It is borne in upon me that if she is your lover and you hers, I ought not to write to you quite as I do. She might not understand. I should understand it if I were the SHE, but it's because I'm not clever. I never was, and sometimes, looking at you all, I hope I never shall be. One thing I am clever enough to know (TO KNOW, mind. I know a few things, but I know what I know). It is this. You'd be all bad, and no good in you, if you marry anyone unless you know you love her. A woman may *not* love before marriage and really love afterwards (if she has never loved before). We all love more after union (women I mean, and surely, oh surely, men too). *But a man should know.*' That, indeed, was Ellen's loving wisdom.

A fortnight later, he told her that he had been to Paris where Charlotte was. 'I swooped on Paris, and swooped back like a whirlwind; and now, dear Ellen, she is a free woman, and it has not cost her half a farthing, and she has fancied herself in love, and known secretly that she was only taking a prescription, and been relieved to find the lover at last laughing at her and reading her thoughts and confessing himself a mere bottle of nerve medicine, and riding gaily off. What else can I be to any woman, except to a wise Ellen, who can cope with me in insight, and who knows how to clothe herself in that most blessed of all things—unsatisfied desire?'

This stuff does not deceive Ellen. 'Oh, I see you, you two, walking in the damp and lovely mist, a trail of light from your footsteps, and —I don't think it's envy, but I know my eyes are quite wet, and I long to be one of you, and I don't care which. . . . Why you dear precious thing, if you are not as happy as she, you *are* wasting your time. But you *are* happy, aren't you? Tell me.'

It was immediately after she had written this note to him that she saw him for the first time, through the peep-hole in the Lyceum's curtain. In December, she asks him to bring Charlotte to her dressing-room after they have seen *Cymbeline*, but he says No. This matter of a meeting between Miss Payne-Townshend and Ellen went on for several letters. He was determined that the two women should meet in the ordinary course of life, and not in the emotional atmosphere of a dressing-room after a performance. 'My real feeling', Ellen wrote, 'was a somewhat earnest desire to hear the voice of the lady beloved of my friend. The attitude of my heart towards her, perhaps you do not understand, dear clever one. My heart is on its knees to her. . . .'

But he insists that the two women shall meet, not as the great actress and the awed playgoer, but as women in the normal course of life, and on terms of equality. 'She shan't be brought round to your dressing-room as an appendage of mine, to be exhibited as my latest fancy. Will you never understand what I mean when I say that I can respect people's humanity as well as love their individuality. I should feel nice standing there between you. Of course she is greatly interested in you, as everybody else is; and she is quite capable of understanding your feeling. But you must manage it for yourself if you want to see her. Her address is Miss Payne Townshend, 10, Adelphi Terrace, W.C. She has delightful rooms overlooking the river, over the London School of Economics (door round the corner, opposite the Caledonian Hotel). On Saturday night, hearing that Janet [Achurch], between the matinée and evening performance, had no refuge but the Solferino, she promptly went to that haunt, yanked Janet (who was half dead) out of it, took her to Adelphi Terrace, put her to bed, and delivered her punctually in magnificent condition for the performance.'

Ellen seemed to be hurt by this letter, for she wrote, a little tartly, 'I'm afraid you took my last words to you as a further urging to bring Miss T. within my close range. You mistake. But that is done with, and you (and she) may rest quietly in the certain knowledge that I shall not even look through the curtain at you (or her).'

That brought him to his feet. 'If you don't look at her, I will never forgive you. Oh, I can't explain; and you understand perfectly well. I want you to meet one another without any reference to me: I hate these contrived occasions. Well, never mind, wait until you can do something for her, or she for you: I can always wait: that's my secret—even wait for Thursday night. Only, *do* look at her; and yet how can you? F18 and 19 is six rows off.'

But what Ellen thought of Charlotte is not known. If she wrote her thoughts, the letter has disappeared. There was talk in March, 1897, of Ellen visiting a house in Woking which Charlotte and Beatrice Webb had taken; but nothing came of it, nor is there any evidence that Charlotte ever saw Ellen off the stage. Then the Webbs wished her to go with them on a tour round the world which was to start in March, 1898, but Charlotte seems not to have travelled further than Rome. In April of that year, G.B.S., who had been gravely over-working for a very long time, broke down badly. A trivial injury to his foot, caused by a tightly-laced shoe, developed into necrosis of the bone and required two operations. He was on crutches for eighteen months. 'I'm afraid about that foot,' Ellen wrote to him in April. 'Do tell Miss P.T. to come back and look after it.'

Charlotte required no bidding. She returned to London when she received the news, and visited G.B.S. in Fitzroy Square. His room appalled her, and she bade him prepare at once to go to her house in the country where she would see that he was properly tended. But G.B.S. was careful of her reputation. If he was to go to her house, she must go to the registrar and give notice of their marriage, which she did; and on June 1, 1898, he hobbled on crutches into the Register Office in the District of the Strand in the County of London, and there, in the presence of Graham Wallas and Henry Salt, was joined with her in legal matrimony by the Registrar. The bride was forty-one, and the bridegroom was forty-two.

100

Why, it may be wondered, were they so long in making up their minds to marry? Their affection for each other was transparent, and it increased and deepened as they grew older. The delay had several causes, only one of which was of major importance. G.B.S. was acutely conscious of Charlotte's wealth and the likelihood that he would be charged with fortune-hunting if he married her. His jokes about her money, his habit of calling her his green-eyed Irish millionairess, these were the signs in him of uneasiness: for he was never more serious than when he was apparently flippant and unseasonably jocular. His intimates knew that he was most deeply distressed when he uttered a jest that made him seem to be insensitive and heartless.

The fact that he was not a man who needed much money, since his necessities were few and soon satisfied, has some bearing on the matter, and at the time of his marriage he was earning more money than he required, and could have earned much more if he had not dissipated his energies in propaganda meetings and a vast amount of unpaid work for The Fabian and other societies. He was now, indeed, earning enough money to be able to support one or two spongers, a burden which became heavier and heavier as he grew older and wealthier. Shiftless Irishmen, such as Tim Haffigan in *John Bull's Other Island*, largely engaged in making political or industrial trouble, soon smelt him out and came to him, cadging; and he, despite the contempt he felt for them, gave them money when he had better have directed them to the nearest incinerator with a request that they should enter it.

There was no doubt now in G.B.S.'s mind that he could keep himelf and his mother in as much comfort and security as they desired. He had never seriously doubted his own genius, and was convinced that his time would come, though he feared occasionally that it would be longer in coming than he wished. He had numerous and diverse friends to whom he was attached, and he led the life he liked to lead. He had disciplined himself to bear success with as much fortitude as he had formerly borne failure. His costs of living were small: a vegetarian meal at the Wheatsheaf which might cost him tenpence or, if he were in an extravagant or greedy mood, one shilling and twopence, and a cup of cocoa and a couple of poached eggs in the evening.

His friends frequently invited him to meals, and were perturbed unduly by the spareness of his appetite; unduly because he long out-lived all of them except Pease. They feared that he was suffering from malnutrition. He himself seemed to have suspected that his lungs might be infected, and he spent a large part of every morning singing at the top of his voice in the belief that this exercise would strengthen them. He went for long walks, either alone or with William Archer or Graham Wallas or Sydney Olivier, and he continued this habit for 'health's sake' until he was too old to walk any longer. During the Second World War, he frightened motorists at Ayot St Lawrence by looming out of the dark in a long white coat; and some of them, in their distress, appealed to his housekeeper to make him stay at home at night. But he persisted in walking, even when his legs, which were always tottery, let him down and he fell on the road.[1]

Ivo Currall, commenting on this passage, says, 'During the last [Second World] war, when I cycled to Ayot, G.B.S. looked in amazement at the lamp on my bicycle and said that in that village no cyclist used a lamp and, consequently, when he went for a walk after dark, it was he who carried a light. During the blackout years, there was always a battery storm lamp in the porch at Ayot.'

None of his habits, however, involved him in much expense; and his income, when he met Charlotte, was more than enough for his needs. It is true that he dreaded poverty. His experience of it had not been pleasant. That is why there is so much insistence in his work on the need for money and security. In one of his letters to Ellen Terry, written immediately after he had finished *The Devil's Disciple*, he says, 'I shall try to earn a little supplemental money—not that I really want it; but I have always been so poor as to coin that nothing can persuade me that I am not on the verge of bankruptcy.'[2] That, indeed, was his last delusion when, met with vast demands from the Inland Revenue, for income tax, he suddenly panicked and felt certain he was ruined.

His financial position when he met Charlotte was good and becoming better, but it was, like the financial position of all authors and persons dependent for their income on public taste, uncertain. His long illness as a result of the injury to his foot must have increased his anxiety about his financial future. If he had not been thrifty and had not been fortunate enough to earn a fairly substantial sum from journalism and American performances of his plays in the two years

[1] *Shaw-Terry Letters*, Letter LXX, p. 107.
[2] Ibid.

in which his illness occurred, he would have been in a very grave plight; for Lucinda Elizabeth's earnings were small, and she was becoming more and more dependent on him. If his time were long in coming or if, when it came, its duration were short, he would expose himself to contempt and derision, no matter how little they were deserved, if he married a woman with a fortune of a hundred thousand pounds. 'That's your Socialist for you!' Despite his jokes about Charlotte's wealth, he was uneasy. The Puritan in him was a man of firmer will than those who, like Beatrice Webb, thought him an irresponsible sprite, ever imagined. And he was more than a Puritan: he was a proud Irish Protestant, unwilling to be beholden to anybody but himself. An uncertain income, even although it was about £2,000 a year when he married, looked meagre beside the safe income enjoyed by a woman with more than £100,000 well invested. G.B.S., in this matter, was beset.

But there was a much graver cause of the delay in their marriage. Charlotte had a horror of sexual relations which was paramount over all her emotions and principles. The unhappy ending of her love affair with Axel Munthe may have been due to her determination that any marriage she made should never be consummated. She had no wish to become a mother, and she expressed her aversion in a way that made her seem to shallow-minded people to hate babies and very young children. This was not the fact. But she had no wish to bear any. G.B.S., on the contrary, was a man who delighted in women and enjoyed carnal concurrence with them. There is a legend, entirely false, that he, too, disliked children, just as there is a legend, equally false, that he disliked animals. No one who ever saw him in the company of children and perceived how quickly they became friends with him, or saw him 'talking' to dogs, could believe this pernicious nonsense which is spouted only by those who did not know him or had some animus against him. In his old age, he expressed regret that his marriage had been fruitless, and thought that he ought to have been firmer with Charlotte about sexual relations. But Charlotte's will was as firm as his, and it is improbable that she would have married him on any other condition than that the marriage should not be consummated.

The cause of her deep and morbid aversion from the sexual act in marriage or out of it, may have been partly psychological or due in part to some experience which settled her mind on the subject for ever, but whatever it was, it was strong enough to make her determined that although she wished to be married, and to be married to G.B.S., she was prepared to sacrifice all hope of a home with a husband unless her demand was granted. A wife who refuses to consummate her marriage, cannot complain if her husband seeks satisfaction elsewhere, but Charlotte was sometimes ferociously jealous of G.B.S.'s philanderings, none of which, so far as anybody but his women friends can know, ever went beyond extravagant expressions of paper passion. She was especially angry about G.B.S.'s relations with Mrs Patrick Campbell. This singular fact in a woman to whom the very thought of copulation was abominable, suggests that G.B.S. might have overcome her objection to the consummation of her marriage had he been, as he said, 'firmer' with her.

But he was a peculiarly tender man, very delicate in his behaviour to those he liked or loved, and he was incapable of forcing himself on a woman in that way. There must be consent on both sides, so far as he was concerned. It is almost certain that the delay in their marriage was due to Charlotte's condition that there should not be consummation. G.B.S. loved her, and she loved him. Their profound affection for each other was beautiful, and it delighted their friends who were fully conscious of it, although neither of them was publicly demonstrative. His consideration for her was unlimited. Her wishes came first with him, and any promise he made her, however trivial it might be, was kept and kept promptly. How ferocious her love of him could make her is proved by the fact that when she saw a caricature of him—she hated caricatures—by Max Beerbohm, she tore it to pieces in Beerbohm's presence.

A man had to think not only twice but many times before he committed himself to marriage with a vestal virgin who took her virginity very seriously. Had it not been for that visit to Fitzroy Square, when Charlotte felt appalled by the spectacle of a crippled man living in conditions which seemed to her, though not to his mother or to him, utterly squalid, and had insisted on removing him to her own house at Haslemere, they might never have married. She would have lived in her flat in Adelphi Terrace, typing his plays and letters, and he would have continued to live in discomfort with his mother in Fitzroy Square or somewhere else, enduring the discomfort as he endured everything that was disagreeable, with the feeling that none of these things mattered, so long as he was consumed by a vehement purpose which used up his energy and made him conscious that he was an important part of a great intention.

He would have spent his free evenings with her, talking to her about the play he was writing or was about to write, reading to her, making her laugh with his comic fables about William Archer; and sometimes taking her to the theatre. Every summer they would have spent a month or six weeks with the Webbs in a rented rectory, where there would be a great deal of conversation that Charlotte would say was 'very interesting', even when it was beyond her understanding: talk about the iron law of wages and the need for an independent labour party and the reform of the poor law and the necessity for municipal trading; two middle-aged people with cooling emotions and a deep and abiding affection for each other, all passion nearly spent, desirous only of quiet communion and unexciting social intercourse. But the spectacle of G.B.S. crippled and very tired after his long and hard expenditure of nervous energy in causes, stirred that impulsive quality in Charlotte which disconcerted her friends who had not yet realised her possession of it, and made her resolved to remove him at once from Lucinda Elizabeth's 'throughother' house and settle him in country air in the comfort he now sorely needed.

It will seem to the majority of people that marriages of this sort, in which the major purpose is deliberately avoided, are certain to collapse; but medical psychologists know that they are sometimes highly successful and that a deep and abiding love, like that of a sister for a brother, can develop between a husband and wife who have not consummated their union and have abandoned any intention of doing so. The vagaries of human nature are innumerable, and there is room in the world for eccentrics in love. In 1930, writing to Frank Harris, he said, 'Not until I was past 40 did I earn enough to marry without seeming to marry for money, nor my wife at the same age without suspicion of being driven by sex starvation. As man and wife we found a new relation in which sex had no part. It ended the old gallantries, flirtations, and philanderings for both of us. Even of these it was the ones that were never consummated that left the longest and kindliest memories.'[1] The last sentence seems to suggest that Charlotte had philanderings that *were* consummated, but we must read it as applying exclusively to G.B.S. I have not the slightest doubt that he was faithful to Charlotte throughout their marriage, though I think it is likely that he might have yielded to Mrs Patrick Campbell: a matter which will be discussed in its proper place later in this book. 'How splendid!' Ellen Terry wrote to him on the morning of their marriage. 'What intrepidity to make such a courageous bid for happiness. Into it you both go! Eyes wide open! An example to the world, and may all the gods have you in their keeping.'

Charlotte took him into the country to restore him to health, and it was from their rented house at Blen-Cathra, Hindhead, in Surrey, that he wrote his first letter to Mrs Patrick Campbell on April 12, 1899. There had been talk of her and Forbes Robertson producing *Caesar and Cleopatra*, but the negotiations had hung fire. The play would be very expensive to perform, and G.B.S. was not known as Pinero then was. He suggested that the first act should be performed 'as a curtain raiser', but this suggestion, luckily, was not accepted. He goes on to tell her how well in health he now is. 'The vegetables

[1] See *Sixteen Self Sketches*, p. 115.

have triumphed over their traducers. I was told that my diet was so poor that I could not repair the bones that were broken and operated on. So I have just had an Xradiograph taken; and lo! perfectly mended solid bone so beautifully white that I have left instructions that, if I die, a glove stretcher is to be made out of them and sent to you as a souvenir.' His personal acquaintance with her was then so slight that he addressed her as 'dear Mrs Patrick Campbell'.

101

The marriage disconcerted Charlotte's family. Her sister was seriously upset, to such an extent that relations were disrupted. Mrs Mary Stewart (afterwards Lady) Cholmondeley, the wife of a distinguished soldier, knew nothing about G.B.S., except that he was an eccentric Socialist. That knowledge, however, seemed to her more than enough: the man obviously could not be a gentleman; and Mrs Cholmondeley felt certain that her sister, herself somewhat eccentric, had been trapped into marriage by a common fortune-hunter who spent his time spouting sedition at street corners and inflaming the working-class with envy and malice towards their social superiors. It would not be this Irishman's fault if the proletariat did not try to steal the property of respectable people after they had first taken the trouble to cut their throats.

In these times of absurd tolerance—we have almost forgotten that there are things which ought not to be tolerated—such opinions as Mrs Cholmondeley's must seem ridiculous; but they were common enough in 1898. Lucinda Elizabeth, who shared none of her son's political shibboleths, was walking with him in Bond Street one morning, when Cunningham Grahame, a great dandy, passed by and saluted them with a magnificent sweep of his silk hat. 'Who is that man?' she demanded. G.B.S. told her. 'But he can't be,' Lucinda Elizabeth exclaimed. 'Cunningham Grahame's a Socialist, and that man's a gentleman!' It was an odd remark for a mother to make to her son, who, in spite of being a Socialist, was a gentleman, not only by nature, but by birth and descent.

There was a rift between Charlotte and her sister Mary for some time, but a reconciliation was made by a stratagem. Charlotte, knowing how charming and engaging G.B.S. could be, took him with her when she went to visit a friend in whose house Mrs Cholmondeley also was to be a guest. She contrived that Mary and G.B.S. should be left alone, without her knowing who he was. On her return, she found them in animated conversation, Mrs Cholmondeley being delighted with her companion, though she was momentarily dazed when she was told that he was her brother-in-law. Their friendship

318

never faltered. It was she who asked him to write a book explaining Socialism to women who knew very little about it, and knew that little wrong, and when *The Intelligent Woman's Guide to Socialism and Capitalism* was published, it was dedicated to her.

The whole circumstances of G.B.S.'s life were now entirely changed. He went to the flat in 10, Adelphi Terrace, and there he and Charlotte lived for more than thirty years.

There are so many legends about his residence in Adelphi Terrace, that it is well to make pointed note of the fact that it was Charlotte's home, not his, and that the inscription over the fire place in their drawing-room—*Thay say. Quhat say thay? Lat Thame say*—was placed there before Charlotte rented the place. For the first time in his forty-two years, G.B.S. had a satisfying home, and was properly and regularly fed. Charlotte was not a domesticated woman, but she was uncommonly good at securing efficient servants whom she supervised with tact and skill and good judgment. They stayed with her a long time, leaving usually to get married or because they wished to retire. She had the gift of winning the affection of those who worked for her. The result was a home life that was highly agreeable to G.B.S., who had hitherto lived in ramshackle conditions, where there was neither comfort nor regularity, and such servants as there were, were incompetent and shiftless. Charlotte's relations with Lucinda Elizabeth and her daughter, Lucy, were cold. The sight of G.B.S., crippled and on crutches, in Fitzroy Square, and the knowledge she had gained of his life in the first nine years he spent in London, made her feel less warm to his mother than she might otherwise have been; and she positively disliked Lucy.

Lucy is not a reliable witness in this case. Writing to her friend in Dublin, Constance Shaw, whom she had nicknamed the Barnacle, she complained first, that Charlotte 'hates her own sex and children', a statement which is false, and second, that 'she is the drop of gall in our cup, all the more bitter that she is externally so charming and agreeable. She pays duty visits to the Square, but we never dream of going near her. She is inexpressibly good to * * * * * * * * * who, with her mother, lives with Mama, sends her boxes of the most beautiful clothes, and pays for luxurious holidays at swagger sanatoriums, and has her on week-end visits, all these things go to make her impossibilities so much the harder to bear.'

It is easy to detect the signs of envy in this complaint. Lucy seems not to have wondered why Charlotte bestowed benefits and favours on * * * * * * * * * which were not bestowed on her, nor does it seem ever to have occurred to her that Charlotte disliked and despised her. The knowledge that Lucy, who had enjoyed all the advantages that Lucinda Elizabeth could confer on her, had urged her mother to

319

turn G.B.S. out of her house, must have sunk very deeply into Charlotte's mind and made her feel intensely averse from this harsh sister who had withheld her sympathy and affection from her brother when he was struggling with his genius, but was full of admiration and applause when his genius was recognised. G.B.S. had as little affection for Lucy as was shown by Charlotte. He maintained her after she had divorced her husband, and he was punctilious in visiting her in her house on Denmark Hill; but he was bored by her, and any feeling of affection he may ever have felt for her had died long ago.

Her mind became sour. Her published writing was cynical, but less cynical than her personal correspondence. Writing to 'my dearest Con' in 1898, she concludes her letter with a spate of bitter words. 'I don't think you will ever go to live with your mother, and it certainly is not advisable that you should. You would never feel happy under restraint, at least not that kind of restraint. . . . God, what could one not hazard with £200 a year and your fingers snapped in the face of the world. But you are weak in one point, and that is your affection. It is a halter round your neck, and whoever handles the rope end at the moment, can lead you anywhere, provided you are fond enough of them. LOVE, my Con, is dead sea fruit, whether it is parental, fraternal or marital, and anyone who sacrifices their all on its altar plays a game that is lost before it is begun. . . . Anyway, it's a damnable world, though we have made life worth living since we have done away with the immortality of that function we call "soul".'

This despondent note was written when Lucy was ill, and it concludes surprisingly with the words 'My undying love to all, Ever, darling Con, affectionately Lucy', who was living then with her mother and G.B.S. in Fitzroy Square, about the time when Mansfield was proposing to produce *Candida*, with Janet Achurch in the name part. Janet was to be paid £50 a week, with an advance of £100 for her preliminary expenses, most of which she promptly spent on new clothes, with the result that 'George has had to bolster her up with another hundred'. George was now bolstering up a lot of people. A servant called Harris, who had been employed by Lucinda Elizabeth for a long time, failed in health. G.B.S. 'started her in a lodging house in Reading where she comes from'.

Lucinda Elizabeth resumed her tedious consultations with spirits, and a ouija-board was now a prominent piece of furniture in the flat. An Indian rajah was particularly informative about things past, present and to come, and he gave Lucinda Elizabeth a great deal of spurious comfort. The circumstances of the house, almost entirely through G.B.S., became easier. Lucy had lived in Germany with a family named Schneider, and a daughter, Eva Maria, known as Katie, became nurse-companion-housekeeper to Lucy in London, living with her until Lucy's death in 1920 'We are flat-hunting at present,' Lucy wrote to Barnacle. 'George's increasing business, not to say prosperity, makes it absolutely necessary that we should have more room; but flat-rents are frightful, and I don't think we shall do better than another house-top.' Here, however, she was attributing to G.B.S.'s needs, her own desire for grandeur. When Katie became an invalid, G.B.S. helped her, and he left her an annuity 'in remembrance of her devoted service to my sister'.

Long after Lucy's letter of complaint about Charlotte was written, after, indeed, Lucy's death, G.B.S. commented on this relationship. 'There was no love lost between them. Charlotte dreaded and disliked my very unconventional family; and I took care not to force them on her. When a woman marries at 40, she is confronted with a crowd of friends and relatives who know her husband ten times as well as she does. They made her a stranger in her own house. So I kept them off until we had been married long enough for her to know me better than any of them, and invited only my political acquaintances who were also hers. As my family took no particular interest in her and had plenty of friends of their own, they let her go her own way without worrying themselves or me about it, with the result that after the first few civilities to put us on speaking terms, neither Lucy nor my mother ever crossed the threshold of our dwelling. There was no bad blood; but it happened so quite naturally.'

Here, he is putting a gloss on the relationship and not stating the facts accurately. Lucy's letter to Constance Shaw makes clear the feeling *she* had about Charlotte's coldness to her. Moreover, Lucy crossed the threshold of his house many times. This was only one more example of the common fact that a man is likely to lose all his friends when he marries, and that these friends may sometimes include close relatives. The deep intimacy between G.B.S. and Archer, Graham Wallas, Olivier and others was not maintained as closely and deeply after his marriage as it had been before it; but the life of a bachelor, and especially of a bachelor who feels uncongenial at home, is very different from that of a husband, and it is inevitable as people grow older and more occupied with business of all sorts that their communications with each other shall dwindle. This dwindling does not denote a decrease of friendliness: it denotes only that the general conditions of life are no longer what they were. In any case, it is absurd to think that a man or a woman must feel as much affection for a wife's or a husband's friends and relatives as they feel for each other.

The tide of adversity which had seemed at first to be set unalterably against G.B.S., threatening to submerge if not to drown him, but had lately turned and was bearing him comfortably along with it, now seemed to be a tide entirely under his command. He was working on *You Never Can Tell* when he first met Charlotte at Saxmundham Rectory; and commentators on this play have seen in it, as they have seen in all his work, signs of origin in living people. 'Mrs Clandon', says R. F. Rattray, 'is said to have been founded on Mrs Besant, but surely there are traces in her of Shaw's mother?' Mrs Besant is the obvious model to be chosen for Mrs Clandon, but there are considerably more than traces of Lucinda Elizabeth in the character. The truth probably is that G.B.S., as was often his habit, used several models, taking a trait from one and a trait from another; but we can detect more resemblance between Mr and Mrs George Carr Shaw in Mrs Clandon and her husband than we can detect between Mrs Besant and the dreary curate she married.

Mrs Clandon is separated from her husband. So was Lucinda Elizabeth. Mrs Clandon has a son and two daughters. So had Mrs Shaw. There are substantial differences between the real and the fictive woman, the differences that must appear in any work of imagination, but these are apparent only to those who know the facts of G.B.S.'s family life. Mrs Clandon, like Mrs Besant, left her husband deliberately, but Mrs Shaw left hers, so to speak, accidentally. Mr Shaw was left in Dublin to look after his decrepit mill while his wife went off to London to start a musical career for her elder daughter and herself; and she failed to return. Lucinda Elizabeth felt no love for her husband, and it is plain from the play that Mrs Clandon felt no love for hers. It is doubtful if Mrs Shaw or Mrs Clandon felt any love for anybody. Like Mrs Jellyby, in *Bleak House*, they were addicted to causes, especially if they were remote, but remained obtuse about their neglected children. G.B.S. regarded his mother at best with amusement and reluctant admiration, exactly as Mrs Clandon is regarded by her twins.

It is in the stage directions of *You Never Can Tell*, more than in the dialogue, that we discover in Mrs Clandon the lack of love that was a dismaying characteristic of Lucinda Elizabeth. All displays of affection by her children are distasteful to Mrs Clandon. At the beginning of the second act, Gloria, who, perhaps, owes a few touches to Lucy, 'suddenly throws her arms round her mother and embraces her almost passionately', but Mrs Clandon is displeased by this demonstration. 'Smiling, but embarrassed,' she exclaims, 'My dear, you are getting quite sentimental', and her daughter, eager for affection, recoils abashed.

Soon after the third act opens, Mrs Clandon has a conversation with Valentine, the impoverished dentist, about his love for Gloria. 'I am going to speak', she says, 'of a subject of which I know very little—perhaps nothing. I mean love.' She then describes her marriage in terms which are exactly applicable to Mrs Shaw's, and applauds herself for admiring causes more than persons. This is, undoubtedly, Mrs Jellyby, raised to the nth power. Mrs Clandon is one of those women who, when they take to public life, collect committees as if they were trinkets. She loves mankind in the abstract so much that when she contemplates it in the concrete, she loses her temper. She is fond of people who live a great distance away, but she hates the sight of her next door neighbours. Her husband, when he meets her again after a long separation, remarks with deep and justifiable bitterness, 'She did me a great wrong in marrying me without really caring for me'.

G.B.S.'s resentment against the loveless and inefficient homes in which he spent his childhood, youth and early manhood is apparent throughout the comedy, though he makes the conditions of Mrs Clandon's home different from those in which he was brought up. The twins, Philip and Dolly, treat their pretentiously intellectual mother with tolerant contempt, and listen to her talk about being an advanced woman with high and noble ideals as if it were the merest poppycock. They are much readier to respect their father when they discover him, and here I remind the reader that G.B.S., despite his father's seeming insignificance and inability to assert himself, writes more appreciatively of him than he writes of his mother, and cites his opinions and casual remarks as if they had impressed him, but seldom cites her. When he refers to his childhood, it is usually to relate some anecdote or remark about Mr Shaw: it is seldom or never to mention Mrs Shaw.

The fate of the play at the Haymarket has already been described. Who could have dreamt on that depressing day during the play's rehearsal by a sullen and bewildered cast when the decision was taken to withdraw it without a single performance, that it would eventually be performed thousands of times amid general applause, all over the world?

But although the tide had turned, a person observing G.B.S.'s situation immediately before his marriage, might well have wondered if it had not increased in strength against him. The long illness, arising from what seemed a trivial cause, and the necessity to move about on crutches would, in itself, have been sufficient to make him feel moody and despondent if he had been the sort of man who allows himself to despair. He displayed his spirit to Ellen Terry in a letter dated January 27, 1897, when she complained that he had not written to her for some time. He was then crawling around on crutches. 'No, I really can't write to you whenever I want to—how should I earn my living . . .? No, my knee isn't really bad: only it won't work properly. The bit of cartilage will presently get absorbed, or tumble out of the way, and then I shall be all right.

'In this world you must know *all* the points of view, and take one, and stick to it. In taking your side, don't trouble about its being the right side—north is no righter or wronger than South—but be sure that it is really yours, and then back it for all you are worth. And never stagnate. Life is a constant becoming: all stages lead to the beginning of others. The Lyceum business, on its present plane, cannot be carried any further than it has been carried, consequently we have now reached a beginning. H.I. may think he is free to abandon the drama to Wilson Barrett or Marie Corelli; but he isn't. The theatre is my battering ram as much as the platform or the press: that is why I want to drag it to the front. My capers are part of a bigger design than you think: Shakespear (*sic*), for instance, is to me one of the towers of the Bastille, and down he must come. Never mind your young families: omelettes are not made without breaking eggs; and I *hate* families.

'Did you ever read Morris's *Sigurd the Volsung*? If so, do you remember Regan the dwarf, who taught the people all the arts and lived on and on, the new generations not knowing that he had taught anything and ascribing all his work to Bragi and the rest of the gods. Well, what I say to-day, everybody will say to-morrow, though they will not remember who put it into their heads. Indeed, they will be right; for I never remember who puts the things into my head—it is the Zeitgeist. So I will give H.I. a bronze bracelet with this inscription:

> It is not for your silver bright
> But for your leading lady.

'Your reproaches are undeserved. I have not been unfaithful to you. But I am like the madman in *Peer Gynt* who thought himself a pen and wanted someone to write with him. That was wise of you. But the green-eyed one was also wise in her way—the way that was your way when you were at her stage of the journey. She used me too, and so far widened my life. I am not for all hands to wield; so I do not throw away my chances. You say you do not compete: well, you need not. *I* do not compete with all the men you love (more or less—I am convinced that with you a human relation is love or nothing; there I am, not possibly to be confused with any of them, and ten times better realised because of the knowledge you have gained from them than if you knew nobody but me. . . .'

The thought here is confused. No one, unless he be a criminal or a lunatic, adopts a point of view unless he believes it to be the right one, and G.B.S. was surely nonsensical when he begged Ellen to take a side without bothering about its rightness. How does a man make sure that a side is really his, and, having done so, back it for all he is worth? Either he convinces himself that it is the side that will be most profitable to him and supports it ruthlessly for that reason, in which case he is a scoundrel who ought to be serving an indeterminate sentence in a concentration camp, or he convinces himself that it is morally right, and is ready to die for it, in which case he is a hero with a strong likelihood of becoming a saint and a martyr.

And is it true that one tower must come down because someone wants to build another tower? Are there not many mansions in My Father's house? Must St Paul's be demolished because its architecture is different from that of the Abbey? Are we to believe that Shakespeare must be forgotten so that Shaw may be remembered? The argument is full of fallacies, and may be disregarded. But what is important is the revelation of a determined character, tireless and tameless and proud. We see here what it was that supported G.B.S. throughout the long period of adversity and deep discouragement: his unquenchable conviction that he was of value to the world, and his inflexible resolve that he should not be wasted.

He declined to be cast down by continual disappointment; nor did he permit himself to feel depressed by his long illness. When Ellen Terry was unhappy and in pain, he advised her to do what he did. 'Now, shall I tell you how to get a rest at the theatre, drive all worry from your brain, and be perfectly light of heart and happy, though in bodily agony. Sprain your ankle. I did it again on Monday —for the third time—frightfully—the bad foot: and I can guarantee the effect. I have been immoveable ever since. The pain has stopped now; but the foot looks perfectly AWFUL.' All his life he had tumbled and fallen and hurt himself. It was a fall that killed him in the end. His nervous energy was such that he would hurry unnecessarily to places, or attempt tasks beyond his strength. A quick, misplaced step—and he was down on the ground. That eighteen months on crutches must have exhausted his patience many times, and one's surprise is not that he sprained his ankle thrice, but that it was ever unsprained.

While he was suffering from the trouble with his leg, he came to an important decision about his work. Since no manager would produce the plays, he would publish them. It had better be noted here and now that G.B.S., although he was not quite the acute business man he believed himself to be, was, nevertheless, abler at business than the majority of authors are willing to be. He never suffered from the folly which makes apprentice authors disdain any knowledge of how contracts should be drawn; and he had a profound contempt for the fool who says, 'I'm not interested in the money: I'm interested only in the glory!' A large part of the time of the Society of Authors is spent in trying to extricate these ninnies from contracts made in the death-or-glory mood.

Nor was G.B.S. ever tamely submissive to editors. He defended his rights with skill and pertinacity when T. P. O'Connor and Edmund Yates attempted to interfere with them, and was much readier to offer his resignation than a frightened contributor was ever likely to be. When Horace Voules, for whom he worked on *Truth* for a short period, requested him to praise some painter Voules admired, G.B.S. finding argument useless, advised him to get another and more amenable critic. Any editor who, having asked for contributions, dillied and dallied about publishing them, got the rough edge of G.B.S.'s tongue, and was generally wise enough to take it sensibly. One editor who was foolish enough to withhold an article from publication, could never induce him, despite frequent demands, to write for his magazine again. It was one of Frank Harris's few virtues that he did not interfere with G.B.S.'s articles in *The Saturday Review*, even when he dissented, as he sometimes did, from the point of view expressed in them. An editor is entitled to defend himself from contributors who may cause actions for libel; and can justifiably request that sentences which are excessively severe shall be modified or omitted. But that is as far as he should go with a responsible contributor, unless he feels that his policy and the contributor's cannot be pursued in the same paper; in which event, he should dismiss the contributor and appoint in his place one who is more in sympathy with him.

For the greater part of his life, G.B.S. was his own publisher: that is to say, he bore the cost of issuing all his works, employing a publisher merely for office and mechanical purposes, such as distribution of books and the general convenience of a staff trained in the details of publication and sale. He chose his printers, and he was highly particular about the type used in setting up the pages and in the style and colour of the binding. He imagined himself to be expert in detecting the difference between type set by hand and type set by machine, but he was sometimes caught out in this matter. The green covers in which his books were first issued in Great Britain were less satisfactory than he had hoped they would be: the colour faded easily; and he therefore used an entirely different format when his works were collected. He insisted that emphasis should be denoted by spaced letters and not by italics, and he was equally insistent on the abolition of apostrophes from contracted words: using *dont* instead of *don't*. His fussiness in these respects was not, surprisingly, displayed in connexion with his publications in America, which seem to have been left entirely to the discretion of the publishers. Argument across the Atlantic, because of the distance, was likely to last longer than argument in London. He was less fortunate in some of his American publishers than he was with his publishers in England. I lunched with him about the time that the house of Brentano, by whom his plays were published in New York, suddenly crashed; and I remarked how surprised I had been that Brentano's had bankrupted. 'I thought they were like the Rock of Ages!' 'Yes,' he retorted angrily, 'rocking for ages.' He regarded such mishaps as a reflection on himself. A man as astute as G.B.S. should not have allowed himself to suffer such reverses.

But, despite these misadventures, his affairs were conducted with considerable skill. As his renown and popularity increased, his works grew in demand in foreign countries. The management of the mere business of translation, publication and production of plays all over the world and in many languages was a heavy job. There was a period of his life when at least one of his plays was being performed some-where every night; and it is probable that a fairly large number of them were in production simultaneously. The collection of fees from amateur dramatic societies was a business in itself. This increasing work was first done by him alone; but it soon became impossible for him to cope with it and, at the same time, write new plays.

Luckily, he was able to engage secretaries who were highly efficient. His first secretary was Charlotte, who, however, could not give her entire time to his business, so he engaged his half-cousin, Judy Gilmore, afterwards Mrs Musters, who descended from his grandfather, Gurly, by his second wife; and she remained with him until her marriage five years later to a naval officer. Her successor was Ann Elder, now Mrs Jackson, who left him eight years later when she married. His fourth and last secretary was Blanche Patch.

Judy Musters and Ann Elder had a deep affection for him because of his courtesy and gentle manner, and both of them were greatly liked by Charlotte. Miss Patch, who was highly efficient, stayed with him for thirty years, until his death. She published a book in which, unwittingly, she gave the impression that he was mean. His generosity to her included a bequest of £500 a year.

103

In the spring of 1898, he published two volumes of plays: pleasant and unpleasant. There were four plays in the first book: *Arms and the Man*, *Candida*, *The Man of Destiny*, and *You Never Can Tell*, and three in the second: *Widowers' Houses*, *The Philanderer*, and *Mrs Warren's Profession*. The publisher was Grant Richards. The volumes

were unusual in every respect. The public had lost the habit of reading modern plays, partly because the majority of them were not worth
reading, but chiefly because those that were published appeared in
what were called prompt copies. These paper-backed books, badly
printed on inferior paper, soon torn and yellowed, were intended for
the use of amateur dramatic societies, which were not then numerous;
and they were full of technical instructions about movements on the
stage which, though valuable to the producers of the plays, rendered
the books unreadable to the general public. Pinero had issued his
plays in a library edition, but their sale was so small that William
Heinemann was discouraged for a long time from publishing any
more.

G.B.S. was a pioneer in this matter as he was in several others.
He realised that no one would read a prompt copy of a play unless he
had to. The technical jargon, expressed chiefly in capital letters, such
as *L.C.* for *left centre*, repelled the general reader who took it for
granted that play-reading was none of his business. *Plays, Pleasant
and Unpleasant* were, therefore, issued in a form which was a mixture
of novel and play. Instead of the abrupt stage directions of the
prompt copies, the reader was given long descriptions of the scene
and accounts of the persons in the play. The emotions of the characters at a particular point were described. A woman would blush
with embarrassment or a man would appear to be temporarily
abashed. Dull people imagined that G.B.S., in writing these accounts,
was naively revealing his inability to write plays at all. How could
an actress blush to order? Apart from the fact that some actresses,
Duse, for example, could, there was the more important fact that
make-up—Duse did not use it—would prevent the blush, if it were
generally commandable, from being seen.

But G.B.S. was not the innocent abroad that his intellectual
inferiors supposed him to be. He knew and appreciated these facts
better than they did. His stage directions were not stage directions in
the common sense of that term: they were accounts of character and
statement of feeling, such as a novelist would write, and were intended,
so far as players were concerned, to enlighten them on the state of
mind of the characters. When an actress reads in her script that the
character she has to interpret blushes at a certain moment, she
realises, if she has any intelligence at all, that she is not expected to
display mantling cheeks, but to express the emotion of mantling
cheeks.

This was not the only innovation G.B.S. made. He published a
long preface to each volume in which he expounded views which were
sometimes irrelevant to the plays, and at the same time indulged in
autobiography. How grateful we should feel if Shakespeare had been

as careful in the publication of his plays as Ben Jonson and G.B.S. were. How useful it would be to have his account of himself and his purpose in writing at all. The whole traffic of play production in book form was revolutionised by G.B.S., and the fact that publishers' lists now commonly include plays is entirely due to him.

The reception of the volumes was impressive and surprising. They were widely and gravely reviewed; for G.B.S., although he was still almost unknown to the generality of people, even in the theatre, was well known to the makers of opinion. One of the longest and severest reviews was written by William Archer in *The Daily Chronicle*: it appeared in two parts, one for each volume, and it almost maltreated G.B.S.

Archer seems all his life to have been as bewildered by Shaw as a hen is by the brood of ducklings she has hatched. He could not fit him into any of the categories he knew, and was often exasperated by him. Their friendship at this time was intimate and close. They met several times a week, taking long walks together, and frequenting each other's home. G.B.S. must have eaten almost as many meals with the Archers as he ate with his mother. When Archer was unable to attend a first night, G.B.S. deputised for him. Archer's extraordinarily attractive son was especially G.B.S.'s friend. This was an intimacy of home and friends that G.B.S. had not known since his own childhood, and it was, in almost every respect, superior to that intimacy.

It may have been their dissimilarity of nature which attracted them to each other; but whatever it was, it lasted as long as Archer lived, deep and steadfast and irreducible even by the separations, sometimes long, which inevitably occur when men's work takes them apart and their home ties become more binding. No one could see G.B.S. and Archer together without perceiving their deep affection for each other.

Archer's first article opens with ominous words:

'I have never approached a more difficult task than that which now confronts me. How am I to make clear to myself—to say nothing of other people—the tangle of emotions with which I lay down these two volumes of Mr George Bernard Shaw's plays!

'He calls them *Plays: Pleasant and Unpleasant*, but that is a mere catch phrase. Almost any other pair of antithetical adjectives would have been more applicable. With one exception the plays are all unpleasant; and even the exception is dubious. If Mr Shaw had wanted a really descriptive title for his dramatic works, he should have called them *Plays, Wise and Silly*, or *Intelligent and Unintelligent* or *Admirable and Despicable*. But no such mechanical antithesis would meet the case.

'Two of the seven plays are works of genius for which even Mr Shaw's modesty could not possibly find an adequate epithet; while one of the remaining five is an outrage upon art and decency, for which even my indignation cannot find a printable term of contumely. To express my sense of the beauty of *Candida* and the baseness of *The Philanderer*, I should have to borrow Mr Swinburne's vocabulary of praise and scorn—which is (perhaps fortunately) as inalienable as his gift of song.

'An hour ago I was reading *Candida* for the third time with bursts of uncontrollable laughter not unmingled with tears. The thing is as true a poem as ever was written in prose, and my whole soul went out in admiration and gratitude to the man who had created it. Then I re-read an act of *The Philanderer*, and I wanted to cut him in the street. Both feelings, no doubt, were exaggerated, hysterical. Perhaps the second, no less than the first, was a compliment to Mr Shaw—at any rate I am sure he will take it as such.

I record these emotions, not as a criticism, but simply to show the dynamic quality of the book. Good or bad, it is certainly not indifferent. Its appearance is an event, literary or theatrical, of the first magnitude. From the theatrical point of view—the point of view, that is to say, of those enthusiasts who long and hope to see a worthy dramatic literature of the English stage—it is not an entirely encouraging event.

'One has a sense of a great force going more or less to waste from sheer wilfulness. That the man who wrote *Candida* should have written *The Philanderer* and should proceed to write *You Never Can Tell* is a bewildering and saddening phenomenon. It is scarcely less bewildering that he should care to print a piece of crude 'prentice work like *Widowers' Houses* cheek by jowl with a masterpiece—yes, with all reservation, a masterpiece—like *Mrs Warren's Profession*.

'But the main fact is that we have among us, and still in the full vigour of his faculties, the man who wrote *Mrs Warren's Profession* and *Candida*. While there is life there is hope; and who knows but that, sometime in the coming century, Mr Shaw may arrive at years of discretion.'

He then discusses the plays in detail, citing passages of dialogue at a length which makes a contemporary critic feel incurably envious at the space which was allowed to writers in newspapers in the Victorian Age.

This was rough usage, even from so good a friend as Archer, and it caused lesser men to follow his lead. *The Echo* described *The Philanderer* as 'a very clever, but a very vulgar, very ignoble, and a very tedious piece of work, worthy only of Marcel Prevost or Catulle Mendès,' and *The Star* critic felt an overwhelming desire 'to rush out' and have 'a talk with some entirely commonplace, unintelligent, inarticulate person, some mere automaton or creature of instinct— one of the porters at the railway station or the old apple woman round the corner,' which, of course, was only his nonsense. The craving for communication with mindless people is felt only in print. G.B.S. can hardly have been gratified by the reception the plays had been given.

There is much with which we can agree in Archer's criticism, but there is more from which we must dissent. We cannot forget that if G.B.S. had been less certain of himself, and had accepted Archer's extraordinary advice to him, after the first performance of *Widowers' Houses*, to abandon hope of success on the stage since he had no talent for writing plays, we should have lost one of the world's greatest dramatists. Archer's severity about *Widowers' Houses* is absurd, and may, though he probably was unaware of the possibility, have sprung from a secret resentment of the fact that G.B.S. had made such havoc of the plot he had proposed as the original basis of the play. The surprising feature of Archer's articles is his bitter attack on *You Never Can Tell* which is condemned almost as if G.B.S. had committed a felony in writing it. *Mrs Warren's Profession*, one of the two plays in the volumes which are praised by Archer, has faded considerably since it was written, had, indeed, faded by the time it was licenced for public performance; and it occupies a minor place in the canon of Shavian drama. The extraordinary fact is that Archer, who, when he read it, proclaimed it to be a masterpiece, was horrified by it when he saw it performed. But *You Never Can Tell* has retained its popularity, and is still widely performed.

But even this charming comedy could come under a cloud, though one would have thought it as certain to last uncondemned as *As You Like It*. When it was revived in New York in 1948, it was denounced by the dramatic critics as dull and dated, a trivial piece of little or no merit. One waits with impatience but little hope for these loftily censorious critics to write anything half as entertaining.

Archer, like G.B.S., was my senior by twenty-seven years, and I may, therefore, be regarded as a representative of the generation which succeeded theirs. I first saw *You Never Can Tell* performed in 1905, and I have seen several performances since that year, in addition to having read it more than once. It gave me immense pleasure at my first sight of it, and has never failed to please me, either in perusal or performance. I cannot understand why Cyril Maude allowed it to be withdrawn from the Haymarket during its rehearsals there; and I feel dazed by the ineptitude of the players who threw up their parts because there 'was not a laugh in it'. It is easy to say that one generation's meat is another generation's poison, but the difference between a man of twenty-two and a man of forty-nine is not so great that it was possible for me at the former age to feel highly entertained by *You Never Can Tell* when William Archer, at the latter age, was made desolate by it, finding it in perusal, a 'formless and empty farce', which, he declared, 'would seem very tedious on the stage.'

The vagaries of taste are unaccountable and often puerile, and it may well be that the generation which is on my heels, as my contemporaries were on the heels of Archer's generation, will feel less interest in *You Never Can Tell* than we did, though no one can convince me that this charming comedy will ever fail to find admirers. The substantial fact, however, is that G.B.S., in respect of this play, as he was in respect of much else, was at least a generation ahead of his own, and that he knew better than Archer did, what would one day be in almost universal demand.

I am jumping ahead in what I am about to write. The single occasion in G.B.S.'s life when he showed signs of mortification and wound was when Ellen Terry, for whom he had written *Captain Brassbound's Conversion*, announced her dislike of it, failed to see that the part of Lady Cicely Wayneflete was essentially *her* part, and was bored by the supremely comic part of Drinkwater. 'I dont think that play of yours will do for me at all,' she writes in one letter, and, in the next, she says, 'I dont like the play one bit. Only *one* woman in it. How *ugly* it will look, and there will not be a penny in it.' The play, which was originally named *The Witch of Atlas*, seems to have thoroughly irritated Ellen. 'No one but Shaw', she writes to G.B.S., 'could have written' it, 'but it's not the play for me, in the least . . . I couldnt do this one, and I believe it would never do for the stage.' She thought that Mrs Brown Potter might play the part of Lady Cicely, but that Mrs Patrick Campbell would be better. The one actress who would be useless in it was herself.

Several times she tells him that although it reads well, it will not act well, will not act at all, that it is a closet piece, and that it will be a financial failure. I find his answer to all these foolish remarks, very moving. In a letter, dated August 4, 1899, he writes:

'Alas, dear Ellen, is it really so? Then I can do nothing for you. I honestly thought that Lady Cicely would fit you like a glove, that I had sacrificed everything to make the play go effectively from second to second, even that Drinkwater was a tragi-comic figure worthy of Robson. And now you tell me it is a play for the closet, and that Lady Cicely would suit Mrs P.C.—all of which proves that either I am mad, or you are mad, or else there is an impassable gulf between my drama and your drama. I wont suggest it to Mrs Pat because I am now quite convinced that she would consider herself born to play it, just as you want to play Cleopatra. No: it is clear that I have nothing to do with the theatre of to-day: I must educate a new generation with my pen from childhood up—audience, actors and all, and leave them my plays to be murdered after I am cremated. Captain B. shall not be profaned by the stage: I will publish it presently . . .'

as he did, in 1901, when it appeared with *Caesar and Cleopatra* and *The Devil's Disciple*.

Caesar and Cleopatra, which was intended for Forbes Robertson and Mrs Patrick Campbell, was written in 1898, but was not performed in London until 1907, when Robertson and his beautiful wife, Gertrude Elliott, played the principal parts. It was the first play written by G.B.S. on the grand scale. In his previous works, he had dealt mainly in characters who were animated and moved by ideas, the creatures rather than the creators of circumstances. But in this play he deals with a man who is the master of his mind, the conceiver of ideas which he manipulates for his own purposes. John Tanner, in *Man and Superman*, is subdued, unwillingly, indeed, but nevertheless subdued by the Life Force, and compelled to perform its purpose; but Julius Caesar has a purpose of his own, though Shaw might have denied that, and he makes his ideas his servants. They work for him: he does not work for them. This is made plain in a short and passionate scene between Caesar and Theodotus in the second act when the philosopher pleads with the Emperor to save the Library of Alexandria from the flames which are destroying it.

Caesar refuses. Theodotus, with all the passion of the pedant, repeats his plea. 'Caesar,' he says on his bended knees, 'once in ten generations of men, the world gains an immortal book,' but inflexible Caesar replies, 'If it did not flatter mankind, the common executioner would burn it,' an answer which is not, perhaps, as profound as Caesar seems to think. Then Theodotus, appalled by this Philistine reply, exclaims, 'Without history, death will lay you beside your meanest soldier,' but Caesar is undismayed. 'Death will do that in any case,' he says. 'I ask no better grave.' Theodotus, now nearly in despair, makes another effort. 'What is burning there', he cries, 'is the memory of mankind,' but Caesar remains unmoved. 'A shameful memory,' he says. 'Let it burn.'

That finishes Theodotus, who, horrified and disgusted, demands, 'will you destroy the past?' 'Ay,' Caesar replies, 'and build the future with its ruins.'

This is a very different man from John Tanner in *Man and Superman* and the dentist in *You Never Can Tell*, each of whom squirms in the grip of the Life Force, squealing because Ann Whitefield and Gloria Clandon mean to make fathers of them. Caesar is the sort of man Dick Dudgeon in *The Devil's Disciple* seemed likely to become, the sort of man who is superior to common humanity, the stoic who bears the blows and burdens of mortality without complaint while seeking steadfastly to lighten the load. How far we share Caesar's opinion of the past is another matter. It is part of the present, which is the shortest period of time, and the future, and we can neither ignore it or get rid of it by refusing to remember it. But, whether we share his opinion or not, here, we must admit, is a man of decision, a man who has made up his mind, a maker, and not the victim, of his environment; and it is immaterial that some people, H. G. Wells, for example, vehemently dissented from G.B.S.'s appreciation of Caesar.

In his Outline *History of the World*, Wells describes the Emperor as 'a bald middle-aged man, past the graces and hot impulses of youthful love', who 'spent the better part of a year in amorous pleasantries with the Egyptian queen, Cleopatra. . . . Such complications with a woman mark the elderly sensualist or sentimentalist—he was fifty-four at the commencement of the affair—rather than the master ruler of man.' The single comment that need be made on this passage is that Wells seems to have forgotten all he ever knew about master men when he wrote it. He concludes the Julius Caesar 'had the megalomania of a common man,' and asserts that 'his vulgar scheming for the tawdriest mockeries of personal worship is a silly and shameful record; it is incompatible with the idea that he was a wise and wonderful statesman, setting the world to rights.' Here, surprisingly, is an entirely different Caesar from G.B.S.'s.

I am not enough of an historian to say whether Wells or Shaw is right, though Shaw has Mommsen on his side; but it does not appear to me to matter much whether Shaw's emperor was the Caesar of history, any more than it matters which is the truest portrait of Shaw himself, Augustus John's, William Rothenstein's or John Collier's. Shakespeare's Joan of Arc is a paltry figure beside Shaw's, but is true to the information Shakespeare had. If he had known as much about the Maid as we know, he would have drawn her very differently. What does matter is that the Caesar of this remarkable play is Shaw's conception of a great man. Having seen and read Shakespeare's *Julius Caesar*, G.B.S. felt profoundly dissatisfied with the portrait he found there, and decided to make another Caesar in his own image. X He drew the picture of a genius as he conceived a genius to be, and for the purpose of convenience, called it a portrait of Julius Caesar. But it could as justly have been called a portrait of Robert E. Lee. We shall fail in understanding if we do not perceive the fact that in this play we have G.B.S.'s conception of greatness rather than a faithful portrait of an historical character.

Caesar is a stuffed shirt in Shakespeare's tragedy. Although it bears his name, he is a minor character in it, a lay figure at that, dispatched by assassins soon after the play begins. Mark Antony, Cassius and even that eloquent and pompous prig, Brutus, who over-ruled the wiser, if more envious and meaner-minded Cassius, and was, on each over-ruling, hopelessly wrong, are much more important characters. Shakespeare's Caesar might have been a successful X importer of bananas: Shaw's is a genius whose every speech has the sound of genius. Is it not a great man who, in the fourth act, con-

334

demns the murder of Pothinus? How superb is his denunciation of vengeance when the followers of Pothinus come knocking on the gate. He turns in anger and mortification on the quailing queen who has had Pothinus murdered, and cries in reproach:

> 'You have slain their leader, and it is right that they shall slay you. And then in the name of that right shall I not slay them for murdering their queen, and be slain in my turn by their countrymen as the invader of their fatherland? Can Rome do less than slay these slayers, too, to show the world how Rome avenges her sons and her honour? And so, to the end of history, murder will breed murder, always in the name of right and honour and peace, until the gods are tired of blood and create a race that can understand.'

G.B.S.'s deep aversion from the vulgar belief that a wealth of great engines is positive proof of progress is made clear and plain in his Notes to the published play. Of what avail are great machines if the people who mind them are mean? Man's increased command of Nature is seen to be paltry if it be not accompanied by increase of his command over himself. This, he says, is 'the only sort of command relevant to' the evolution of man 'into a higher being'. In this play, that theme is fully and dramatically developed, a play of a great man in opposition to the mean-minded rabble. Its largeness, in extent of production, makes it difficult to perform: the expense of its casting and production are too great for amateur societies and repertory theatres. It demands a great theatre and large means behind it. Those who had the good fortune to see Forbes Robertson acting in it during his farewell season at Drury Lane Theatre will remember it as a great occasion.

It is a fundamental part of my belief that a man of genius is constantly a man of genius, that his quality does not fluctuate according to the opinion of him held in a particular period, remaining as great in ages when he is unappreciated as it is in ages when he is. The distrust felt by a generation for an original mind is understandable, since the majority of people fear what they cannot instantly perceive; but what is not understandable is the denial of genius by a generation which has done no more than conduct a juvenile rebellion against the opinions and beliefs of its predecessors. What is there about any period which entitles those who live in it to repudiate a talent, not on the permissible plea that tastes change and differ, but on the totally impermissible plea that it is not a talent at all? Is it not possible that the dissenting generation may be trivial or stupid? The fact that the successors to this dissenting generation may, and generally do, react almost violently against the dissenters seems to prove that the suspicion may be truly and firmly founded.

There was a period when Shakespeare was slightly esteemed.

Taine thought that Byron was the greatest poet of his age and one of the greatest poets that have written in English. But was Shakespeare diminished in the slightest degree by the failure of the seventeenth and eighteenth century intellectuals to appreciate his quality—or were they diminished for ever? Were Wordsworth and Keats and Shelley reduced in stature by Taine's absurd infatuation for Byron?

G.B.S. was to experience an amazing reversal of belief about himself. Ellen Terry was the first to change her mind abruptly about *Captain Brassbound's Conversion*. In 1899, when it was still necessary for a dramatist to secure his copyright in his play by giving a performance of it which need be no more than a hurried and unrehearsed reading on a more or less bare stage before an audience of one person who had paid at least a guinea for admission, Ellen obliged G.B.S. by 'copywriting' the play for him at a theatre in Liverpool immediately before her departure with Irving for America. The result of this scratch production was her conversion to belief in the play, which she now 'adored', and to a realisation that the part of Drinkwater is uncommonly entertaining.

But, writing from America in January, 1900, she had to tell him that she could not hope to produce the play for some time because she must first perform in popular pieces, so that she might amass money for her retirement and be able to cope with her extravagant children's demands. 'My head aches too often for me to to consider the chances of my breaking up under the pressure of anxious times, of times of enterprise. If I did break down the younger people would soon make ducks and drakes of the very moderate sum I have got together by close steady work. I rather dread poverty! . . .'

This was a dread which G.B.S. felt. 'Very well, Ellen,' he replied to her, 'we cry off Brassbound. I have always foreseen, and foretold to you, that when it came to the point, you would find it practically impossible to detach yourself from the Lyceum. . . . I have pitched so many dreams out of the window that one more or less makes little difference. In fact, by this time I take a certain Satanic delight in doing it and noting how little it hurts.' But it did hurt, hurt severely.

The time was coming, and fairly soon, when *Captain Brassbound's Conversion* and many other Shaw plays would be performed on the perimeter of the West End theatre, at the Royal Court Theatre in Sloane Square, and the famous Vedrenne-Barker productions[1] would

[1] John E. Vedrenne was the business manager, Harley Granville Barker, who had not yet hyphenated his names, was the brilliant producer of these productions. Their tenancy of the theatre lasted for two and a half years, during which period a remarkable number and diversity of plays were produced. The Vedrenne-Barker policy was to found a repertory theatre in which plays of quality, ancient and modern, should be performed for short runs, so that the players should not be staled by prolonged repetition of one part, and frequent revivals, ensuring the dramatist a more regular income than he would normally

begin the world-wide vogue which G.B.S. was to enjoy for the rest of his long life, a vogue which shows no signs of serious decline, despite the curious detraction of him and his work which is now common in certain shrill quarters.

Mr Arthur (afterwards Earl) Balfour was so deeply impressed by *John Bull's Other Island* that he persuaded eminent politicians, Liberal as well as Conservative, to see it and enlighten themselves on a country about which so many of them were willing not only to pontificate but to legislate on the most meagre knowledge of its people and its needs: and a special performance was given for the convenience of King Edward VII.

G.B.S. had now captured the outworks of the citadel, but had still to capture the citadel itself. He had educated the upper classes and the intelligent young of all classes, but had not yet educated the middle classes and such members of the proletariat as were amenable to education. The business of making an audience for himself was set up, and was establishing itself. Granville Barker had trained the actors and actresses he needed for the proper performance of his plays: and Ellen Terry had handsomely capitulated. She played the part of Lady Cicely Waynflete in *Captain Brassbound's Conversion* for six matinees, beginning on March 20, 1906, and, despite the fact that she now 'adored' the play she had begun by hating, was surprised to find it put into the evening bill on April 16, to be performed for twelve weeks. At a later date, she took the play on tour.

But she was then in her decline. She had given up her right to the play when she was in the plenitude of her power because, 'Dear G.B.S., a financial success is all I want,' and she failed to win what she wanted and took what she needed only when she was too old to

receive. Thirty plays, some of them short pieces, most of them long, were produced. Eleven of them were by G.B.S., who was, beyond a doubt, the most profitable playwright whose work was performed. These were *Candida, John Bull's Other Island, How He Lied to Her Husband, You Never Can Tell, Man and Superman, Captain Brassbound's Conversion, Major Barbara, The Doctor's Dilemma, The Philanderer, Don Juan in Hell,* and *The Man of Destiny.* Three plays by Euripides, translated by Gilbert Murray, were performed: *Hippolytus, The Trojan Women,* and *Electra.* There were two plays by Ibsen: *The Wild Duck* and *Hedda Gabler;* two by St John Hankin: *The Return of the Prodigal* and *The Charity that Began at Home;* and two by Maurice Hewlett: *Pan and the Young Shepherd,* and *The Youngest of the Angels.* Granville Barker himself was responsible for one play, *The Voysey Inheritance,* and partly responsible for another: the charming pierrot play, *Prunella, or Love in a Dutch Garden,* which he and Laurence Housman wrote. The music was composed by Joseph Moorat. John Galsworthy's *The Silver Box;* Gerhart Hauptmann's *The Thieves' Comedy; Votes for Women,* by Elizabeth Robins; Arthur Schnitzler's *In the Hospital;* Robert Vernon Harcourt's *A Question of Age;* and Cyril Harcourt's *The Reformer,* as well as John Masefield's *The Campden Wonder,* Maurice Maeterlinck's *Aglavaine and Selysette,* Frederick Fenn's *The Convict on the Hearth,* and *The Pot of Broth* by W. B. Yeats were also produced. 'No other modern managers have given so many memorable performances in so short a space of time,' says Desmond MacCarthy in *The Court Theatre, 1904–1907,* which is the authoritative work on its subject.

give it her best. Had she failed in *Captain Brassbound's Conversion*, which is inconceivable, she would have failed magnificently. She did not fail entirely, for she was Ellen Terry, and Ellen Terry, even in her old age and decrepitude, was better worth seeing than many other people in their youth and strength. Nor did the play fail. Its exposure of the wrong a man does himself when he surrenders to the base desire for revenge was not what the generality of playgoers, even in 1906, expected to find in a play, but this piece undoubtedly held attention, even when it puzzled. Ellen Terry in herself was sufficient to draw crowds to see it, but G.B.S. had taken great trouble to conceal his pill in excellent jam, as, indeed, he always did.

The scene was picturesque. It had colour and costume, sunshine and bright surroundings, comic characters and a dramatic situation. This was not a grim Ibsenite piece: it was as brilliant in its setting as a musical comedy; and it caught the mind of a large and increasing audience.

104

The years 1897–8 had been years of fortune and misfortune, with fortune prevailing. The necrosis of a bone in his leg would have been a grave misfortune, since it would have prevented him from doing dramatic criticism for *The Saturday Review* and thus have deprived him of his main source of income, but the success of *The Devil's Disciple* in America, where it was brilliantly produced by Richard Mansfield, enabled him not only to maintain himself and, to a large extent, his mother, but to resign from *The Saturday Review*, in May, 1898. His last article was published on May 21, 1898, and was entitled Valedictory.

'As I lie here, helpless and disabled, or at best, nailed by one foot to the floor like a doomed Strasbourg goose, a sense of injury grows on me. For nearly four years . . . I have been the slave of the theatre. . . . These circumstances will not bear thinking of. I have never had time to think of them before; but now I have nothing else to do. . . . I can never justify to myself the spending of four years on dramatic criticism. I have sworn an oath to endure no more of it. Never again will I cross the threshold of a theatre. The subject is exhausted: and so am I.

Still, the gaiety of nations must not be eclipsed. The long string of beautiful ladies who are at present in the square without, awaiting, under the supervision of two gallant policemen, their turn at my bedside, must be reassured when they protest, as they will, that the light of their life will go out if my dramatic articles cease. To each of them I will present the flower left by her predecessor, and assure her that there are as good fish in the sea as ever came out of it.

'The younger generation is knocking at the door; and as I open it there steps spritely in the incomparable Max. For the rest, let Max speak for himself. I am off duty for ever, and I am going to sleep.'

The incomparable Max, a half brother of Beerbohm Tree, and now, still incomparable, Sir Max Beerbohm, took over with grace and distinction; maintaining, but in his own fashion, the great tradition G.B.S. had established.

The Philanderer had failed to find either admiration or acceptance. Mansfield had declined it for America, despite his production of *Arms and the Man*, which, however, was only a moderate success with playgoers. During his autumn tour in 1894, the audience, on the night *Arms and the Man* was performed, was always the smallest of the week; but Mansfield, who had an artistic conscience, believed that it would 'awaken intelligence and advance taste', and he gamely kept it in his repertoire. The American audience, no less than that of Great Britain and Germany, had to be educated by G.B.S., and it was reluctant to be educated.

The situation was worse in London than in New York. When *Candida* was read to Charles Wyndham, its author was told that the public would not be ready for it for a quarter of a century. George Alexander was willing to play the part of Marchbanks if G.B.S. would make him blind! Cyril Maude asked to be shown the script, but G.B.S. preferred to let him see *You Never Can Tell*, with the dire result already described. Mansfield accepted *Candida* for production in America, but abandoned it during rehearsal, although he had brought Janet Achurch from London. When, many years later, Archibald Henderson asked Mansfield why he had not produced the play, he replied, 'because I didn't like it,' which was game enough, but not in the least deceptive. Henderson very rightly asserts that Mansfield was not suited to the part of Marchbanks, and that Janet Achurch, during rehearsals, showed that she would act him off the stage.

On April 14, 1895, Mansfield wrote to G.B.S. from New York announcing his decision not to produce the play. '*Candida*', he said, 'is charming—it is more than charming, it is delightful, and I can well see how you have put into it much that is the best of yourself, but, pardon me, it is not a play. . . . Here are three long acts of talk, talk, talk. . . . There isn't a creature who, seeing the play, would not apply Eugene's observation concerning Morrell's lecturing propensities to the play itself. If you think a bustling, striving, hustling, pushing, stirring American audience will sit out calmly two hours of deliberate talk you are mistaken, and I'm not to be sacrificed to their just vengeance.' I interrupt him here to remark that the capacity of his countrymen to sit out seemingly interminable speeches, especially by politicians, was seriously under-estimated by Mansfield. He goes on to say that the play is 'a mere incident'.

> 'All the world is crying out for deeds, for action. When I step upon the stage, I want to act—I'm willing to talk a little to oblige a man like you, but I must act, and hugging my ankles for three mortal hours won't satisfy me in this regard.'

This is followed by a revelation which Mansfield did not realise he was making, namely, that he was antipathetic to Janet Achurch:

> 'To be frank and to go further, I am not in sympathy with a young, delicate, morbid and altogether exceptional young man who falls in love with a massive, middle-aged lady who peels onions. I couldn't have made love to your Candida [Janet Achurch] if I had taken ether. I never fall in love with fuzzy-haired persons who purr and are business-like and take a drop when they feel disposed and have weak feminine voices. My ideal is something quite different. I detest an aroma of stale tobacco and gin. I detest intrigue and slyness and sham ambitions. I don't like women who sit on the floor or kneel by your side and have designs on your shirt bosom. I don't like women who comb their tawny locks with their fingers and claw their necks and scratch the air with their chins. You'll have to write a play that a man can play and about a woman that heroes fought for and a bit of ribbon that a knight tied to his lance. . . .'

all of which means that Mansfield was a romantic actor in the Lewis Waller style and that he disliked Janet Achurch fiercely, not only because he was antipathetic to her type, but because he foresaw that she would get all the praise. It is conceivable, however, that he was right about her, and that G.B.S., whose fidelity to his friends was sometimes absurdly quixotic, was in danger of sacrificing himself very obstinately to one of his whims. There are few dramatists who can say, as G.B.S. could, that two of his plays, one in London and one in New York, had been abandoned during rehearsal.

So far as the theatre was concerned, then, the year 1897 seemed certain to be disastrous for him.

But Richard Mansfield atoned for his failure to produce *Candida*, by producing *The Devil's Disciple* at Harmanus Bleecker Hall in Albany on October 1 of that year. The 'try out' was so encouraging that he removed the play to Fifth Avenue Theatre in New York three days later. It was an immediate success and was performed sixty-four times. In December, G.B.S. was able to tell Ellen Terry that 'if I invest the author's fees from the New York run in County Council stock I shall have £20 a year for my old age. They run to £850. I roll in gold. I am a man of wealth and consideration. I will take a theatre presently, and engage Henry for eccentric comedy.' By the time the run had ended, he had drawn £2,500 in royalties from it; and this sum was increased by revivals when Mansfield went on tour in a repertoire of plays.

It is bare justice to repeat that G.B.S. first received substantial recognition as a dramatist in America.

Two years were to pass after Mansfield's first performance of *The Devil's Disciple* before, in September 1899, it was performed in London, and even then Mr Murray Carson had to be content with a few weeks' run at Kennington, in the south-eastern suburbs of London.

In September 1900, *The Devil's Disciple* was revived by Forbes Robertson at the Coronet Theatre, Notting Hill, and then taken on tour. But it did not reach the West End until 1907 when it was performed at the Savoy Theatre.

Candida received spasmodic performances in the provinces and the London suburbs, mainly, one charitably supposes, because G.B.S., with that obstinate chivalry which was characteristic of him, insisted that the part should be played by Janet Achurch, and would not consent to any other actress appearing in it. In America, however, despite the defection of Mansfield, the play had a highly successful production, made by Arnold Daly, in 1903. There had been some private performances in Chicago, given by Miss Anna Morgan in her small theatre in the Fine Arts Building,[1] but it was not until Daly, working with Winchell Smith, on the preposterous capital of 350 dollars, produced the play for a trial matinee at the Princess Theatre in New York, that it won popular favour: despite changes of cast and frequent changes of theatre. It was performed 150 times in New York, and then went on a successful tour. It was repeatedly revived. In 1905 Daly produced *You Never Can Tell* at the Garrick Theatre, where it ran for five months. G.B.S. was an established and popular dramatist in New York before London, outside a small circle of intelligent playgoers, had so much as heard of him.

Candida did not reach the West End until 1904, and even then, it reached only the fringe of it. On April 26 of that year, the Vedrenne-Barker management tested its strength by giving six afternoon performances at the Royal Court Theatre, Sloane Square, which, although it is the most easily accessible theatre in London for playgoers—the Underground Railway, running from the extreme East End to the extreme West End and connected with all other underground railways, has a station immediately adjoining the theatre—had fallen out of favour. There is a large residential population, including people of small, middling and large means, in the neigh-

[1] I am indebted to Archibald Henderson for these particulars of Shaw's American productions. See *Bernard Shaw: Playboy and Prophet*.

bourhood; but the playgoer seeks theatrical entertainment in well-lit streets where there are a number of theatres and he can, if he is crowded out of one, obtain admission to another.

Because of its disfavour, the Court, as it is generally called, could be rented at a much smaller cost than a theatre centrally situated; and as the performances to be given by Vedrenne-Barker were to be in the afternoon, players could be persuaded to take part in them at small salaries because they were free to perform in other theatres in the evening. The costs of the productions, therefore, were low, but even in these exceptional conditions they were heavy enough.

Candida's reception was sufficiently encouraging to justify a longer and more ambitious season; and on October 18, a season of twenty-seven performances of five plays was begun with the production of *The Hippolytus* of Euripides in Gilbert Murray's translation. The second production was 'a new and unpublished play', entitled *John Bull's Other Island* by Bernard Shaw. The other plays were *Aglavaine and Selysette* by Maurice Maeterlinck; a revival of *Candida*, which had the longest run of the five; and *Prunella, or Love in a Dutch Garden*, by Laurence Housman and Granville Barker, with music by Joseph Moorat, which had the shortest run, a single performance, not because this very pleasing fantasy was unpopular, but because the season was at its end, and Granville Barker, naturally, was eager that the play he and Housman had written should be seen, even if only once.

This exceptionally highbrow programme of plays, all of which, it must be remembered, were given in the afternoon and could, therefore, be attended only by persons at leisure at that time of the day, apparently convinced Vedrenne, who was a despondent business man with a strong tendency to take the worst view of almost everything, that there were enough intelligent persons among the eight or nine million inhabitants of London to support such a theatre: a hope that had too often proved delusive. It was decided, therefore, to take a longer lease of the Court; and on February 7, 1905, seasons began which lasted until, some two years later, Barker removed to the Savoy Theatre in the Strand, where he produced three plays by Shakespeare, *A Midsummer Night's Dream*, *The Winter's Tale* and *Twelfth Night*.

The conjunction of Vedrenne and Granville Barker is characteristic of the strange partnerships that are made in the theatre more than in any other partnerships, except marriage, where conjunctions seem to be made on grounds that would, if they were applied to stevedoring or the hawking of beetroot, seem certain to end in total ruin. The union in the theatre of a producer of genius, such as Barker, with a pessimistic business man who felt certain he was on the verge of bankruptcy, such as Vedrenne, seems essential if the enterprise is to have any hope even of short life. The producer has no time, even if he had the ability and the will, to deal with monetary affairs; and he must, therefore, associate himself with someone who thinks strictly in terms of pounds, shillings and pence, and, particularly, of pence. It is the task of the latter to cut down all the former's proposals by half. Where Granville Barker asked for a pound, Vedrenne had to say five shillings and refuse more than ten.

Producers have no conscience; and business managers must possess enough of what they call conscience to serve for two. A producer will squander a thousand pounds, especially if they belong to some other person, without a qualm. He is not paid to feel qualms. That is the business of the manager. He is paid to produce plays, and as his costly trade and his highest ambition go together, he demands whatever he thinks he needs without the slightest consideration of its cost. Henry Irving, who was his own producer and manager, was evidence enough for anyone of the havoc which can be caused when both these offices are held by the same person. Irving, the actor and manager, earned vast sums which were promptly squandered by Irving, the producer.

Granville Barker, had there been no Vedrenne to squeal with pain at the expenditure of half a crown more than should have been spent, would have ruined the Vedrenne-Barker management soon after it was formed. As it was, his extravagance at the Savoy was sufficient in itself to bring the great enterprise to an end; though the blame for that disaster is generally placed upon the First World War, which, indeed, must bear some of it.

Barker, who had some Italian blood, but not nearly so much as was supposed, was a curious mixture of poetic and dreary imagination. Like many producers, he could tell other people how to act. This is one of the mysteries of the theatre. I have known many men who, themselves dire as actors, were brilliant in drawing out other men and women's power. Granville Barker was a notable example of a man with this mysterious power. He had equal authority in poetic and in realistic plays, producing Galsworthy's *Justice* with as much fidelity to fact as he had produced Shakespeare's *Twelfth Night* with fidelity to poetic imagination.

His mastery of what seemed insignificant detail was such that when the details were added together they amounted to revelation. This ability was especially evident in his production of *Justice*. In the court scene, during Falder's trial, immense effect was obtained by the lighting of lamps in the court as the evening closed on the final episodes of the trial. The lights, one after the other at intervals, were turned on; and the accumulated result of this illumination was strong enough to be vividly remembered by one enthralled spectator forty-five years after it was witnessed. The production of *Twelfth Night* was the most beautiful production I have ever seen on any stage.

Barker was, indubitably, a man of genius in the staging of plays. He was far less important as a dramatist, despite the acclamations of G.B.S., who was over-generous to writers whom he admired; and he was successful only in collaboration. There was something essentially dreary in his composition, and the signs of it were evident when he was in repose or unaware that he was being observed; and he had the trick which Beatrice Webb also had, of expressing his dreariness by drawing up one nostril. This dreariness appeared in his plays, but not at all in his productions. He was restless, too, and could not long continue in one way. He once told me how he had apportioned his life. For so many years, he would be an actor: for so many years, he would produce plays; for so many years, he would write plays. What he was then to do was not mentioned. His besetting sin was his love of rich and easy life, a fact which G.B.S. was quick to discover. 'Harley always loved luxury,' he said to me when I complained of Barker's desertion of the theatre for a life of cultured elegance in expensive hotels after he had married a wealthy American woman who felt ashamed of his connexion with the stage.

He did not entirely waste his genius, for he wrote a series of important books, under the general title of *Prefaces to Shakespeare*, which have influenced the minds of many of his successors in production. But there are some lovers of the stage who wish that he had spent his energies, not in writing about, but in making, productions. His early death was a misfortune for the theatre, even although he had ceased for some time to take a prominent part in it. When he came out of his cultured retirement in 1921 to put Maeterlinck's *The Betrothal* on the stage of the Gaiety, of all theatres, his hand had not, despite its long misuse, lost its cunning.

Inevitably, no doubt, a legend ran round London that Granville-Barker was G.B.S.'s son, though no mother was ever mentioned. When I first heard it, I suggested to my informant that the strongest refutal of it was G.B.S.'s failure to boast about it, as he certainly would have done, had it been true. Both G.B.S. and Charlotte were greatly attached to Harley, and behaved to him as if he were their adopted child; but their affection diminished when he was divorced from Lillah McCarthy who had been a mainstay of the Vedrenne-Barker productions. (She afterwards married a distinguished scientist, Sir Frederick Keeble). G.B.S., despite his advanced views, hated to hear of divorce among his friends, and it was a blow to him and to Charlotte when Granville-Barker and Lillah parted.

There was an unhappy evening when Granville-Barker lectured

to a distinguished assembly under the chairmanship of Arthur Balfour. G.B.S. was to propose a vote of thanks to the lecturer, and he started off, unfortunately, by announcing that he would now tell The Professor's Love Story: the professor, of course, being Granville-Barker. It was an embarrassing speech, all the more so because Barker's second wife was sitting immediately behind G.B.S., and, as G.B.S., suddenly displaying traces of the superstitions he had acquired from Irish servants in his childhood in Dublin, stoutly maintained, casting evil spells upon him. The narration was too close and intimate to be pleasant, and Balfour had to interrupt G.B.S. and make an end of the matter. Thereafter, the relations between Granville-Barker and G.B.S. were discordant.

There was a day, indeed, when the younger man paid a visit to the elder at Ayot St Lawrence to beg him not to write a preface to Lillah McCarthy's autobiography, a request which was refused, and the parting was inharmonious. But some while after Granville-Barker had departed from the house, he came hurrying back in distress, crying out that he could not part from G.B.S. on those terms! . . .

He did not long survive their last encounter. He had drifted from Paris to New York and then to London and Sidmouth, drifting back again to Paris, where, unexpectedly, he died. His death drew a letter from G.B.S. to *The Times Literary Supplement* which ended with the last two lines of the following passage from Swinburne's *Dolores*:

> Time turns the old days to derision,
>   Our loves into corpses or wives;
> And marriage and death and division
>   Make barren our lives.

That was a sorrowful conclusion to a happy and brilliant association which had been crumbling for some time. Once, while staying with G.B.S. in Torquay, we took him to lunch with Miss Clemence Dane at Axminster. On the way, we passed the entrance to a road which led to Granville-Barker's superbly appointed house at Farway, a house that was more like a museum than a home, one, too, in which the chief piece was Granville-Barker, and as we passed, I said to G.B.S.: 'Harley Granville-Barker lives up that road.' He looked at it in the odd way he had when he was moved, and, almost as if he were indifferent, said, 'Oh, Harley!' But when G.B.S. was as terse as that, he was under deep emotion.

105

Vedrenne and Barker at the end of their first season were still chary of evening performances which would considerably increase their costs of production; and so, when they re-opened the theatre with a revival of *John Bull's Other Island*, they contented themselves with matinees; except on March 11 when Edward VII 'commanded' an evening performance, and laughed so heartily that he is said to have broken his chair. Max Beerbohm, indeed, asserted in an article in *The Saturday Review* on December 9, 1905, that the monarch's delight in the play established G.B.S.'s popularity. The play had pleased a small group of playgoers, but it had not reached the knowledge of the comfortable classes in Chislehurst or Wimbledon.

'But', says Max, 'not long after its production, the play was witnessed by a great lady, who advised an august person to witness it; and this august person persuaded a person yet more august to witness it. It had been withdrawn, meanwhile, so there was "a command performance". All the great ladies, and all the great gentlemen were present; also, several paragraphists. That evening Mr Shaw became a fashionable craze; and within a few days all London knew it.'

Max, who had begun his career as a dramatic critic, in succession to G.B.S., had felt some aversion from the Shavian drama. *Man and Superman* was not a play: it was a series of witty dialogues. But Max, whose candour was equal to G.B.S.'s, grew in appreciation, and he confessed himself a convert whose sins in the past had been dire. He had the courage to tell his readers that when he had read *Man and Superman*, he had denied that it would 'act' well, but that when he saw it performed he had felt ashamed of himself for failing to perceive how actable it is. He had also failed to observe G.B.S.'s high sense of character, insisting that his people were gramophone records of their inventor—as if G.B.S. were not a human character like the rest of us—and was astounded to find, when he saw *Major Barbara* performed, how acute his characterisation was.

'Mr Shaw, it is stated, cannot draw life: he can only distort it. He has no knowledge of human nature: he is but a theorist. All his characters are but so many incarnations of himself. Above all, he cannot write plays. He has no dramatic instinct, no theatrical technique. And these objections are emphatically reiterated (often with much brilliancy and ingenuity) by the superior critics, while all the time the fact is staring them in the face that Mr Shaw has created in *Major Barbara* two characters—Barbara and her father—who live with an intense vitality; a crowd of minor characters that are accurately observed (though some are purposely exaggerated) from life: and one act—the second—which is as cunning and closely-knit a piece of craftsmanship as any conventional playwright could achieve, and a cumulative appeal to emotions which no other living playwright has touched. With all these facts staring them in the face, they still maintain that Mr Shaw is not a playwright.'

He then, very charmingly and frankly, confesses that he, too, had insisted a few years earlier that G.B.S.'s plays 'would be quite impossible on the stage. This simply proved that I had not enough theatrical imagination to see the potentialities of a play through reading it in print.' If Sir Max Beerbohm had done no more than write this fine recantation of heresy, he would have earned our gratitude, he would still have been 'the incomparable Max'.

It was not until May 1, 1905, that Vedrenne's fear of bankruptcy could be overcome. On that date, 'for three weeks only', *John Bull's Other Island* was performed in the evening. The policy was to produce one play at night, with a single matinee, and another play in the afternoon. In the same week, therefore, *You Never Can Tell* was running simultaneously with *John Bull's Other Island*. When the latter play reached the end of its three weeks' run, *Candida* took its place in the evening bill for three weeks, with *Man and Superman* running in the afternoon. Then *You Never Can Tell* was put into the evening bill.

So the great seasons ran.

The total number of performances given at the Court was 988, 701 of which were of plays by G.B.S. He had, at last, arrived. His age was 48 when *Candida* received its first regular performance on the London stage, an age at which any dramatist would, in the normal course of things, be well established. He had had to wait a long time for success, but when it came, it ran at him with both hands effusively held out.

He was now beginning to be as well-known in Germany as he was in London; but it was the American playgoer who saved him from what might have been acute poverty when he was disabled by the trouble in his leg for almost two years and must have given up his main means of support, the post on *The Saturday Review*, because a man on crutches cannot easily do dramatic criticism, though it has been done, and he could, no doubt, have done it. But even in America, he was still made to take a toss or two. On October 27, 1905, Arnold Daly produced *Mrs Warren's Profession* at the Hyperion Theatre, New Haven, Connecticut. The Mayor, John Studley, instructed the police to close the theatre until after Daly's company had departed because, '*from what he had heard*', the play was grossly indecent and an insult to the New Haven public. Such is the behaviour of arbitrary officials, and such is the behaviour that G.B.S., with his demand for general State control, would have inflicted on the world. The New Haven newspapers denounced the play and warmly approved of the Mayor's action. When Daly took it to New York, the Mayor of that city instructed Mr William McAdoo, the police commissioner, to tell him that if he performed it, he and his company would be arrested and the theatre would be indefinitely padlocked.

Daly, with great moral courage, disregarded the Mayor's threat, and he and his company were duly arrested. The *New York Herald* for October 31, 1905, published a criticism of the play which is entitled to a prominent place in the list of scabrous publications. The headlines were numerous and foul: Shaw Play the Limit of Stage Indecency. Mrs Warren's Profession Has Not One Redeeming Feature About It. Morbidly Curious Audience Present. Slight Alterations Made in the Text, but There Is a Superabundance of Foulness Left. Story Is Wholly Immoral. Not One Ray of Sunshine or Cleanliness to Lighten Up the Moral Darkness.

The article began with the statement that "the lid" was lifted by Mr Arnold Daly and "the limit" of stage indecency reached last night in the Garrick Theatre in the performance of one of Mr George Bernard Shaw's "unpleasant comedies" called *Mrs Warren's Profession*. "The limit of indecency" may seem pretty strong words, but they are justified by the fact that the play is morally rotten. . . . The whole story of the play, the atmosphere surrounding it, the incidents, the personalities of the characters are wholly immoral and degenerate. The only way successfully to expurgate *Mrs Warren's Profession* is to cut the whole play out. You cannot have a clean pig stye. The play is an insult to decency because:

> 'It defends immorality.
> 'It glorifies debauchery.
> 'It besmirches the sacredness of a clergyman's calling.
> 'It pictures children and parents living in calm observance of most unholy relations.
> 'And, worst of all, it countenances the most revolting form of degeneracy by flippantly discussing the marriage of brother and sister, father and daughter, and makes the one supposedly moral character of the play, a young girl, declare that choice of shame, instead of poverty is eminently right.'

The man who wrote this pestilential trash could not have lied about the play more successfully if he had hired a band of liars to help him in traducing a work which is so bleakly moral that any work by Tolstoy, in comparison with it, is almost flippant.

An indignant comment on this outrageous diatribe, which is typical of the general New York press criticism of the play, was made by an anonymous writer who told his readers that words equally gross were written about the first performance of Molière's *Tartuffe*, which was prohibited after its first performance in Paris in 1664. 'A week after *Tartuffe* was forbidden, a play called *Scaramouche Ermite* was acted at Court, and the King, as he left the theatre, said to Prince Condé, "I should like to know why people who are so scandalised at Molière's comedy say nothing about Scaramouche!" The Prince answered, "The reason is that Scaramouche laughs at heaven and at religion, about which these gentlemen care nothing, and that Molière's comedy laughs at the men themselves, and this they will not tolerate!" '

William Archer, who was extraordinarily liable to go off at emotional tangents, condoned the action of the Mayor of New York over this production in an article in the *Morning Leader* on November 4, 1905, a condonation all the more surprising because Archer, who was shocked by the play in performance, had declared it to be a work of genius when he read it. This blow from his friend must have wounded G.B.S., who, however, did not display his wound. He replied to Archer's article on November 7 in a letter in which, with courtesy and dignity, he exposed Archer's fallacies. Their friendship was too firmly fixed for G.B.S. to feel permanent offence: he knew how liable Archer was to fly off the wheel when his mind was not working easily.

In New York at this time there was a man called Anthony Comstock, a mixture of Chadband and Stiggins, with a large dose of Pecksniff thrown in, who was Secretary of the Society for the Suppression of Vice. This man had been derided by G.B.S. on a previous occasion, and his methods were exposed as what G.B.S. called 'Comstockery'. The name stuck, and its owner was galled by it. The production of *Mrs Warren's Profession* was, therefore, meat and drink to him. Here was an opportunity to revenge himself. Without having read or seen the play, and after he had refused an invitation to witness a rehearsal of it, he began a protest against the production, with the result that the company, immediately after the first performance, was arrested and the theatre was shut. Its members were eventually brought before the Court of Special Sessions. On July 6, this Court acquitted Daly and his manager, Mr Gumpertz, of violating Section 385 of the Penal Code; and the Judge, Olmsted, relieved the monotony of unrestrained and hysterical denunciation by delivering a reasonable judgment. 'If virtue does not receive its usual reward in this play,' he said, 'vice at least is presented in an odious light and its votaries are punished. The attack on social conditions is one which might result in effecting some needed reforms. The court cannot refrain from suggesting, however, that the reforming influence of the play in this regard is minimised by the method of

349

the attack.' The Bench had, not for the first time, taught the Press how to behave itself.[1] That shameful exhibition of scurrility, however, was unique in American treatment of G.B.S., where his work, though it has sometimes been severely and even unjustly criticised, has, on on the whole, been sensibly received.

106

Here, however, time has again been over-run, and a return to 1895 must be made. In that year, he published *The Sanity of Art: an Exposure of the Current Nonsense about Artists being Degenerate*. The history of this short, but brilliant essay, is odd. In 1893, Dr Max Nordau published a work, entitled *Entartung* or, as it was translated into English, *Degeneration*, in which he advanced the idea that all contemporary artists, whatever form of expression they used, were degenerates. They included Ibsen, Tolstoy, Wagner, Victor Hugo, Nietzsche, Rossetti, Ruskin, Burne-Jones, William Morris and Maeterlinck. For a brief while, the vast body of routine-minded people who are always ready to believe the worst about their intelectual superiors, accepted Nordau's nonsense as if it were a divine revelation; and his book, now almost forgotten, was widely and favourably discussed, though serious consideration of it should have convinced intelligent readers that Nordau knew very little about the subject he was discussing with so much assurance.

In the spring of 1895, Benjamin Tucker, who is described by G.B.S. as 'a philosophic anarchist', was editing an American magazine, entitled *Liberty*. He cabled to G.B.S., inviting him to discover the highest fee that had ever been paid to anybody, including Mr Gladstone, for an article, and he would pay G.B.S. that amount for a review of *Degeneration* in *Liberty*. The review, for which G.B.S. refused to accept payment, became a very long essay, and it filled the whole of one issue of Tucker's magazine. Twelve years later, the essay was republished in book form, and it had a considerable sale. It is now included, in a slightly altered state, in *Major Critical Essays* in the Standard Edition of the Works of Bernard Shaw.

It was the more effective because G.B.S. did not share the belief that artists can do no wrong. It was impossible, he said, 'to deny that the Arts have their criminals and lunatics as well as their sane and honest men . . . and that the gratuitous delusion that the great poet and artist can do no wrong is much more mischievous than the necessary convention that the King can do no wrong and that the Pope is infallible'. Long after the controversy with Nordau had died

---

[1] I have lifted some of the facts in this matter from Professor Henderson's book, pp. 436–7, and am indebted to Mr Currall for a copy of the review in the *New York Herald*.

down, G.B.S. wrote *The Doctor's Dilemma* which turns on this point. 'I know no harder practical question than how much selfishness one ought to stand from a gifted person for the sake of his gifts or on the chance of his being right in the long run. . . . Every step of the "pioneer's" progress must horrify conventional people; and if it were possible for even the most superior man to march ahead all the time, every pioneer of the march towards the Superman would be crucified.'

The essay exemplifies one of G.B.S.'s characteristics, the care with which he wrote even ephemeral articles. He dismisses *The Sanity of Art* as a piece for an occasion, but it was composed as carefully as if intended to be his masterpiece. He wrote little or nothing that was not intimately concerned with his faith about man and society, which is, perhaps, why so much of his seemingly topical pieces remain as fresh and pointed to-day as they were when they were first published. There are passages, too long to be quoted, in this essay which have the quality of great thought; and although it was written as a review of a book which has long since been forgotten, was indeed, struck dead by it, it might be used with little alteration in any age where a new form in art is attacked by those who cannot bear anything that is not old and decrepit.

A single fact about it is sufficient to reveal how careful he was. Nordau had cited Dr Henry Maudsley, who is described by G.B.S. as 'a clever and cultivated specialist in insanity', as a witness in support of his argument. The essay gives evidence that G.B.S. had taken the trouble to read the 'several interesting books' which Maudsley had written before he began his review of Nordau's work. He had lost his employment as a reviewer of books in *The Pall Mall Gazette* because he had thought it necessary to read about a dozen works before he felt fit to review one. The question of money had no bearing on his behaviour in these matters. The payment he received for his *Pall Mall* reviews was fivepence a line: he took no payment at all from Tucker for *The Sanity of Art*, though he must have spent a long time in writing it. Whatever he wrote was written as well as he was able to write, whether he was paid well or ill or not at all.

107

In 1897, G.B.S., through what he himself would certainly have called a piece of political jobbery, became a vestryman of the London district of St Pancras: he was allowed an unopposed election in return for an unopposed election of another candidate. The local government of London, in its larger aspects, was directed by the London County Council which was formed in 1889; but the vestries, which were eventually merged in larger bodies, called boroughs, looked after the business of each district.

G.B.S. surprised his fellow vestrymen by being an uncommonly good committee man. They had expected him to be eccentric and tiresome, uttering untimely paradoxes and always being 'funny' and Irish. But he showed himself to be an adroit business man in public affairs, as, indeed, he was in the conduct of his own; and when, six years after his election to the Vestry, which had become a Council during his terms of office, he retired, he took with him the respect of his fellow-Vestrymen and Councillors. 'He never voted otherwise than on the merits of the business and was, for the most part, a party all to himself, with complete impunity,' writes R. F. Rattray in *Bernard Shaw: a Chronicle:* and he adds:

> 'He served on the Public Health, Parliamentary, Electricity, Housing and Drainage Committees. He fought the slum landlords and brothel-keepers (many of the hotels round the three great railway stations were brothels). He was a pioneer in providing public lavatories for women. It was a difficult campaign. Councillors were shocked when Shaw suggested that some women should be members of the committee concerned.'

For those were the days when there was a widespread conspiracy in Great Britain to pretend that women had no bowels.

It was in November, 1904, that he ceased to be a member of St Pancras Borough Council; but the recollection of his service to the Borough is still remembered. On Saturday, May 19, 1951, Sir Barry Jackson, the founder of The Birmingham Repertory Theatre, unveiled a plaque which was placed on the front wall of 29, Fitzroy Square, where G.B.S. had lived, to commemorate his service on the local authority.

'The sole surviving fellow councillor of Shaw', Rattray writes, 'has testified that his colleagues respected Shaw enormously for his earnestness and industry, were somewhat amused at his constant endeavours to obtain publicity,' because, no doubt, of its value to the purposes he was serving, 'but were not aware that they had a genius among them.' G.B.S.'s own comments on his service can be found in a letter he wrote to Ellen Terry on May 28, 1897, soon after he had become a Vestryman:

> 'Of course it is all right: it is good for me to be worked to the last inch whilst I last; and I love the reality of the Vestry and its dustcarts and H'less orators after the silly visionary fashion-ridden theatres; but the machine, Shaw, is not quite perfect yet. . . .'

It was in this year, too, that he finished *The Devil's Disciple* which he had begun in 1896. It was intended for a popular and handsome actor, William Terriss, the father of an equally popular actress, Ellaline Terriss, who married Seymour Hicks. It is improbable that Terriss, whose mental parts were not notable, would have produced the play, but any hope that he would do so ended when he was murdered outside the stage door of the Adelphi Theatre by one of those ineffective egotists who feel certain that if people who occupy high positions would get out of their way, their own amazing merit would soon be discovered. Terriss was thwarting this person's rise to renown; so he stabbed him to death on December 16, 1897. The man was incurably insane and was sent to Broadmoor.

On October 4, however, the play had been produced at the Fifth Avenue Theatre in New York by Richard Mansfield, and it was an immediate success.

The play turns on G.B.S.'s mystical belief that we are compelled by the Life Force, or, as some would prefer to say, by God acting through the Holy Ghost, to perform good deeds against our will. Why does Dick Dudgeon risk his neck for the minister's sake during the War of Independence? Not because he loves the minister's wife, nor because he feels admiration for the minister, nor even because he and the minister are Americans in rebellion against England. 'I had no motive and I had no interest', he says:

> 'all I can tell you is that when it came to the point whether I could take my head out of the noose and put another man's into it, I could not do it. I don't know why not: I see myself as a fool for my pains: but I could not and I cannot.'

But here, surely, we are dealing with the inexplicable spirit which has animated many men and women, causing them to risk or lose their lives for people who were of no importance to them. It is true, if reason be our argument, that every man who won the V.C. was a fool, but where would men and women be if the world were empty of such folly?

108

In 1900, he wrote his most important political pamphlet, *Fabianism and the Empire*, the first of the Fabian Tracts to be published in book form. It was too long—about 20,000 words in its final form— to be issued as a penny Tract, and a new publisher, Grant Richards, was invited to publish it at a shilling. It was one of the three small volumes he wrote about this time. In 1898, *The Perfect Wagnerite* appeared: a misleading title, since it deals only with *The Ring*, which is shown to be Wagner's way of advocating that the means of production, distribution and exchange shall be nationalised! There is not a single word in it about *Rienzi*, *The Flying Dutchman*, *Tannhauser*, *Lohengrin*, *Tristan and Isolde*, *The Mastersingers* or *Parsifal*. In 1904, after he had been defeated in St Pancras, he published his third small volume: *The Common Sense of Municipal Trading*.

These works, and especially the political ones, have been neglected by the public, and the most important of the three has long been out of print. Even The Fabian Society has only one copy of it. G.B.S., for some reason unknown, has not included it in *Essays in Fabian Socialism* in his Collected Works, although some of its forecasts have proved to be remarkably accurate. This neglect is inexplicable, for they are full of sense as well as wit and style; and his arguments are about important, rather than party, points. Free Trade, for example, is discussed, not in the manner of a passionate Free Trader, to whom the polemical remarks of Bright and Cobden are sacred lore, or of a furious Tariff Reformer whose single remedy for our troubles is to clap a thumping tax on all imported goods, but in the manner of a sensible person seeking a sensible solution of a difficult problem.

Tariffs, he wrote, might be desirable to protect the general standard of life. The doctrine of buying in the cheapest market and selling in the dearest suited the common huckster, but it was not worthy of a serious citizen, who could not ignore the fact that a Japanese, living on a low standard of life, was a dangerous competitor in world and even in home markets for people whose standard was high. We have cause to-day to realise that this is still true.

He was less wise, and more intensely Fabian, in his advocacy of municipal trading, especially as he advocated its adoption only in those trades which had been successfully established by private proprietors, who were to be deprived of their industries because they were flourishing. The prime fact dodged by the Fabians is that a private industrialist has to pay for his mistakes. If he is inefficient he becomes a bankrupt. But the Civil Servant or the municipal officer can cover all losses by an increase in rates or taxes. There is no danger of personal bankruptcy for him if he cannot conduct his business successfully. The public must pay the price of his failures.

109

In *Fabianism and the Empire*, a larger theme was attempted; and its subject was one which, because of the war with the Boers which was then raging, was unsavoury to the majority of Left Wing minds. The reader must remember that many Fabians were advanced Liberals, and that some of them sat in the House of Commons, not as Labourites or Socialists, but as members of the party led by Sir Henry Campbell-Bannerman. Their attitude towards the Empire was that of highly refined persons when they are confronted with something which is glaringly vulgar.

The difference between the British Empire and the Empire in Leicester Square was scarcely perceptible to many Liberals and Radicals. Such men as Asquith, Haldane and Sir Edward Grey were regarded with suspicion by members of their party because they called themselves Liberal Imperialists and were not accustomed to think of Australians, Canadians, New Zealanders and South Africans as if they were drunken undergraduates on Boat Race Night. The Empire, indeed, was not respectable in 1900; and worthy men and women tried to hush it up as if it were a scallywag son who had been sent abroad in the hope that he would drink himself to death where nobody knew anything about him.

Imperialists were considered to be cads who flag-flapped in public-houses and imagined they were being patriotic when they were only being rowdy. The cartoonists in the Liberal and Labour Press always portrayed an Imperialist as a ranting fellow whose mouth was as wide as the Cheddar Gorge: a description which gravely misrepresented the most notable Imperialists of that period, Cecil Rhodes, Alfred Milner and Joseph Chamberlain. No one was less of a rowdy than Milner, whose spiritual home was in the more sedate areas of Balliol. But those were the days when colonial premiers were still thought to be, what, indeed, some of them were, uncouth characters whose minds were on the level of a suburban grocer or the proprietor of a village inn.

Even now few people realise how recently the sense of common-wealth was developed. The American Republic would still be part of the British Commonwealth had the modern feeling for unity prevailed in the eighteenth century. But in those days, colonies, as they were then called, were regarded merely as conveniences for Great Britain, to be exploited for the benefit of the home population; to be denied reciprocity of treatment in trade; to be used as dumps for habitual criminals and persons who, for one reason or another, laudable or otherwise, were disaffected towards the Government; and to be disowned when they seemed likely to become expensive. This was the general attitude of all countries then to colonies.

The War of Independence demonstrated the bankruptcy of British statesmanship, though the American Colonists were themselves in very considerable fault: a fact which is usually overlooked not only by Americans, but by Britons. The war and the subsequent separation ought never to have happened; and a great deal of the world's troubles since 1774, including the two World Wars, are in a great degree due to the fact that it did happen. It increased the deep antipathy to colonies which was common in Great Britain for more than a century. There was, for example, a serious proposal that Canada should be disowned on the ground of its cost to Britain, and Gladstone was willing to exchange the Dominion for the Island of Guadeloupe. Disraeli was no better than Gladstone in respect of the colonies, which were, he said, a millstone round his country's neck.

W. E. H. Lecky, in *Historical and Political Essays*, states that:

'Not many years ago it was a popular doctrine among a large and important class of politicians that these vast dominions were not merely useless but detrimental to the mother-country, and that it should be the end of a wise policy to prepare and facilitate their disruption.

'Bentham, in a pamphlet called *Emancipate your Colonies*, advocated a speedy and complete separation. James Mill, who held a high place among these politicians, wrote an article on Colonies for the *Encyclopaedia Britannica*, which clearly expresses their view. Colonies, he contended, are very little calculated to yield any advantage whatever to the countries that hold them, and their chief influence is to produce and prolong bad government. . . . Goldwin Smith wrote a book, the object of which was to show how desirable it was that this Empire should be gradually but steadily reduced to the sweet simplicity of two islands.

Similar views prevailed very generally in the Manchester school. Cobden frequently expressed them. The question of colonies, he maintained, was mainly a question of pounds, shillings, and pence; and he expressed his confident hope that one of the results of free trade would be "gradually and imperceptibly to loosen the bands which unite our colonies to us". About our Indian Empire he entertained much stronger opinions. He described it as a calamity and a curse to the people of England. He looked on it, in his own words, "with an eye of despair", and declared that it was destroying and demoralising the national character.'

It was not until the advent of Joseph Chamberlain to the Colonial Office that this nonsense was checked, and a far finer understanding of the Empire, which was soon to become the Commonwealth, began to pervade the Conservative Party and even some members of the Liberal Party. It will seem extraordinary that The Fabian Society should have held views about it that were more in harmony with Chamberlain's than with the prevalent Left Wing opinion; but it must be remembered that Sidney Webb and Sydney Olivier had both been highly placed Clerks in the Colonial Office, and that Olivier was to become Governor of Jamaica and could, if report be true, have become Governor of Ceylon had he wished for the office. Shaw, as an Irish Home Ruler, might have been expected to hold views similar to those of the Irish Nationalists, but these were opinions which, except in the matter of self-government, he deeply disliked; and he was more inclined to share the beliefs of Webb and Olivier and even of Chamberlain on this subject than he was to share those of Parnell and John Redmond.

Fabianism and the Empire was described as 'edited by Bernard Shaw', who, in a foreword, attempted unsuccessfully to convince his readers that he was no more than a skilful secretary with a gift for writing vigorous and trenchant prose. It was, substantially, the work of the entire Fabian Society in London, in the sense that it was discussed and debated during several meetings and that its proposals were endorsed by the great majority of the members. But it would be stupid to suppose that G.B.S. was no more than an accomplished draftsman with an unusual gift for vigorous expression. Those who saw him at Fabian meetings or worked with him in committees in his prime do not need to be told that his part in any discussion such as this pamphlet must have involved, was always important and influential. In a letter, dated August 31, 1900, to Grant Richards, he made it clear that *Fabianism and the Empire* was substantially his work:

> 'I have just drafted an Election Manifesto for the Fabian Society. It is still far from complete; yet it runs to 11,600 words—out of the question for a magazine article or a penny tract. It is full of ideas about the Empire, China, etc. Whether the Society will swallow it or not I cannot say; certainly not without a struggle. But if they will not have it, I can still publish it on my own account as a personal election manifesto, I being a party of one. Are you disposed to speculate in this . . .?
>
> 'I am suggesting this on my own responsibility. Even the Executive cannot answer for the Society; but at worst the stuff belongs to me, and can be published as my own. . . .'

These extracts, which have not previously been published, make quite clear that the pamphlet was originally G.B.S.'s unaided work. E. R. Pease, in his *History of The Fabian Society*, describes it as the best, but least widely read of his political pamphlets. He would hardly have written this had its editor been no more than an able amanuensis; and it seems probable, therefore, that, apart from some minor alterations or additions made as a result of the Society's discussions, the small book was entirely G.B.S.'s composition, in its ideas as well as in its style.

110

The problem is stated in the opening sections. It 'is how the world can be ordered by Great Powers of practically international extent, arrived at a degree of internal industrial and political development far beyond the primitive political economy of the founders of the United States and the Anti-Corn Law League. The partition of the greater part of the globe among such powers is, as a matter of fact that must be faced, approvingly or disapprovingly, now only a question of time: and whether England is to be the centre and nucleus of one of those Great Powers of the future, or to be cast off by its colonies, ousted from its provinces, and reduced to its old island status, will depend on the ability with which the Empire is governed as a whole.'

This statement of the problem, though sound enough when it was written, is vitiated by several fundamental faults. One is that G.B.S., more, perhaps, than any other Fabian, was, like Queen Victoria, obsessed by largeness. She liked big things. So did he. He preferred the giant to the giant killer. The thought that the world has gained more from small nations, such as Israel, Greece and the England of the first Elizabeth, than from great empires, such as Babylon and Rome, seems never to have entered his head.

Another defect in the pamphlet is one which, like the first, is more particular to G.B.S. than to the Fabians in general. This is his abject belief in centralised government, especially on the German model, and his inability to perceive or, at least, his reluctance to admit that the rule of a rigid and centralised bureaucracy may be fatal to an empire's existence. It was the over-centralised Germans who lost the First and Second World Wars! . . . A people who are excessively drilled in obedience and dissuaded from argument about, and resistance to, imposed authority so that they may become malleable by the centralised authority, is certain to be destroyed, either by internal disorder or by defeat from a less rigidly ruled enemy.

More important faults in the pamphlet, but not particular to G.B.S., were, first, the fact that the Fabians seem to have had no conception of the way in which the Empire was to be quickly and brilliantly converted into the Commonwealth, though they, or G.B.S. for them, appear to have been the earliest to use the word in its contemporary political and geographical meaning. They thought that the colonies would become so impatient with government from Downing Street that they would shake off imperial control altogether. What they never realised was that both the Home Government and the Colonies would evolve what we now call Dominion status, and that this relationship would bind the Empire or Commonwealth more closely together than it had ever been bound before. Rigid government from London cost us the American Colony, but who now believes that we shall lose a single Colony, Dominion or Republic from the Commonwealth of self-governing nations we have substituted for the rule from Downing Street? The return of the United States and Eire to a loose union of English-speaking countries with a common principle of political faith is more likely than the dissolution of the Empire which the Fabians foresaw.

The second grave fault in *Fabianism and the Empire* is that there is no recognition in it that the Labour Party, which the Fabians founded, would rapidly rise to power and displace the Liberals, and that any disintegration of the Empire that might occur would be due to the reckless haste of the Labour Government to disrupt it. We withdrew, almost precipitately, from India, with the immediate result that large numbers of Hindus and Moslems were slaughtered in the racial and religious riots which ensued. The people of India were wiser in the event than Mr Attlee and his colleagues; for they took care to maintain a flexible form of association with the Commonwealth: a display of wisdom which was not shown by the Government of Eire, though the people of that secluded republic sought and, surprisingly, received rights in Great Britain which are not enjoyed by any other aliens.

III

But these are small matters, to which the Fabians, had it been possible for them to form a Government in 1900, would, no doubt, quickly have adjusted their minds. It was when China came under discussion that their boldness of mind appeared, a boldness which, we may reasonably believe, was aroused by G.B.S. The Chinese maintained an attitude towards the rest of the world which the Fabians found intolerable. They claimed that no alien had any right in their territory, and they refused to give the rest of the world facilities for entering it to trade or to make railways, postal and telegraph routes across it for the general convenience of mankind.

> 'Now the notion that a nation has a right to do what it pleases with its own territory, without reference to the interests of the rest of the world, is no more tenable from the Internationalist Socialist point of view—that is, the point of view of the twentieth century—than the notion that a landlord has a right to do what he likes with his estate without reference to the interests of his neighbours.'

This, it may be added, is a situation no less untenable from the national individualistic point of view.

> 'Nearly half a century ago we made war on China and forced her to admit our ships and give us a footing in certain ports. In concert with the Powers, we have just had to send an armed expedition to the Chinese capital to force them to tolerate the presence and the commercial and political activity of Europeans. Here we are asserting and enforcing international rights of travel and trade.
> 'But the right to trade is a very comprehensive one: it involves a right to insist upon a settled government which can keep the peace

and enforce agreements. When a native government of this order is impossible, the foreign trading power must set one up. This is a common historical origin of colonies and annexations; and it may, for practical purposes, be regarded as an irresistible natural force, which will lead sooner or later to the imposition by the Powers of commercial civilization on all countries which are still refractory to it.... The State which obstructs international civilization will have to go, be it big or little. That which advances it should be defended by all the Western Powers. Thus huge China and little Monaco may share the same fate, little Switzerland and the vast United States the same fortune....

Still, there remain our international rights of travel and trade, with the right to settled government which they involve. With these the present institutions of the Chinese Empire are incompatible; and these institutions, accordingly, must go. If the Chinese themselves cannot establish order in our sense, the Powers must establish it for them.'

This is bold, almost brazen doctrine: and its implications are numerous and even dismaying. The Liberals in The Fabian Society were shocked by it, since it justified in almost every particular the Boer War which was then being fought amid disapproval and denunciation from a large part of the Left Wing population. Who was the more progressive-minded man, Cecil Rhodes or Paul Kruger? G.B.S. and those who shared his faith would have replied, with some reservations, Cecil Rhodes. The Fabians of his way of thinking had as little use for Kruger politically as they had theologically. From their point of view, he was a greedy peasant with unpleasant personal habits and a view of God's will which was only slightly removed from that of Abraham, and was entirely repulsive.

A political belief of this sort fully justified the British in their claim to govern Ireland, since it has immense strategic value to their enemies. The efforts of the French to subdue the English to their obedience were always based on the belief that Ireland must first be invaded before assault on Britain was made, not only because the Irish were antipathetic to their political masters and could, therefore, be persuaded to regard the French as their saviours, but because an attack on the larger island could be launched more advantageously from Ireland than from anywhere else. A nation will not expose itself to grave danger through the independence of a small neighbour, nor are the rights of little nations scrupulously respected in war.

Nevertheless, there is substance in the Fabian argument that no groups of people have the right to squat on minerals, oils or other universal necessities because they will not produce these themselves or allow anybody else to do so. The community will not permit one of its members to make a nuisance in his backyard or to put up an outhouse which blocks the light of his neighbours or to defile a place of beauty with unsightly cottages or to spoil the appearance of a handsome street by building an incongruous shop; and it insists that an obstacle to the improvement of a road must be removed.

G.B.S. was exceptionally antipathetic to simple savagery, and a large part of his feeling about the last Italian War on Abyssinia was due to his revulsion against the extensive remains of primitive life in the empire of the Negus. He was especially disgusted by the habit the Abyssinian warriors had, of detaching the genital organs of their defeated enemies and presenting them to their women as proof of their valour: the organs of one white man being esteemed as equal to those of four black men. Why this one of the noble savage's habits should have infuriated him more than all the others is difficult to understand, but it rendered him almost speechless with rage.

The release of the animal in men and women horrified him, except when his political principles were engaged. The Abyssinians must not mutilate their dead enemies to please their women, but Hitler might thrust Jews into gaschambers and furnaces, and Stalin might exterminate his opponents or send them to the saltmines in Siberia, and Mussolini might have dissentient Italians murdered by thugs. A dictator could do no wrong: an amorous Abyssinian could do no right.

Yet it is true, so mixed are the emotions of men, that physical cruelty was abhorrent to G.B.S., though mental cruelty, which is sometimes worse, seemed not to move him at all. He felt wounded by physical cruelty even more when its object was a helpless creature or a corpse. When Lord Kitchener ordered the body of the Mahdi to be dug up and desecrated, G.B.S. had a greater sense of outrage than he would have felt had the Mahdi been alive and Kitchener had crucified him. Desmond MacCarthy somewhere states that once, when lunching with G.B.S., he observed a building nearby and enquired what it was. The reply, made with emotion, was, 'It's a place where they torture animals. I can't look at it without shuddering!'

112

After their marriage, G.B.S. and Charlotte spent several years in searching for a country house where they could live in seclusion and yet be convenient to London. They lived, first, in Haslemere, moving from there to Hindhead. After a spell in Ruan Minor in Cornwall, they returned to Haslemere, and then removed to St Katherines, close to Guildford. They next went in succession to Maybury Knoll, near Woking; to a house near Welwyn; and then to the house in Ayot St Lawrence where they stayed for the rest of their lives, though their intention was to occupy it only for so long as it took them to find the house they wanted. They were, presumably, tired of shifting from place to place in search of the home that seemed not to exist; and so, though they both disliked the New Rectory at Ayot St Lawrence, they remained there.

A great deal of nonsense has been written about this house, mainly by niggling people whose ignorance of the facts caused them to write as if G.B.S. had had the place built for him. The fact that he had it renamed Shaw's Corner seemed to infuriate these people, who found in this designation another proof of its owner's colossal conceit. Obviously, the New Rectory was likely to mislead people who were looking for the Rector of Ayot St Lawrence; and what name could more easily enlighten G.B.S.'s visitors to this singularly inaccessible village than Shaw's Corner? G.B.S. had a practical mind, and he saw no sense in putting more obstacles in the way of enlightenment of any sort than already exist, all of which, indeed, he would have removed. It was not vanity that caused him to give the house the name it now bears; any more than it was vanity which caused peers of the realm to give their territorial titles to their town houses.

The furniture at Shaw's Corner was Charlotte's choice. G.B.S., who had the ascetic's indifference to his environment, left all domestic arrangements to her; and as she hated housekeeping and liked to live in hotels, the result was an insignificant house in which there was comfort, but no distinction. G.B.S., too, disliked removals as much as he disliked travel. But Charlotte enjoyed them. She told me more than once how deeply G.B.S. disliked the house at Ayot St Lawrence, how bored he was with the road from the village to London, and how much he wished to go somewhere else. But they had both by then acquired the inertia of old people who are unwilling to change even habits they hate; and this, added to his indifference to his surroundings, caused them to remain at Ayot St Lawrence when their desire was to leave it.

G.B.S., later in his life, was accustomed to tell his friends that he and Charlotte had settled in Ayot St Lawrence because of an inscription they had read on a tombstone in the churchyard. The stone recorded the fact that Mary South had died when she was 70, with the added comment that 'her time was short'. This statement convinced him, he said, that Ayot St Lawrence was the proper place for him.

They were tenants of the house until the landlord, just after the outbreak of the First World War, told them that he wished to sell it, and that they must either buy it or leave it. When Charlotte told me about this, I thought, Now, after all these years, they will move, and was amazed to hear that they had bought it. Habit makes us put up with what sometimes seems unendurable, and G.B.S., who was the complete rebel in his mind, was remarkably conservative in his general behaviour. He could kick over traces as abruptly as any man of quality is accustomed to do, but he was unusually systematic in his habits, and he kept to his routine more closely than the majority of people. He tried to do his regular daily jobs always in the same way so that he might have more leisure for the hard work which could not be done in a ritual fashion. It was convenient to find pens and ink and paper in the same place every morning, but no pleas of convenience could enable him or any other person always to have ideas in the same order from one day to another.

Few people are so generous as G.B.S. was. He would do more for his friends than they would do for themselves, and he was one of those uncommon men and women who offer help before it is demanded. Most of us can be grateful for a month or a year, but G.B.S. had the rare virtue of being grateful all his life for kindness shown to him when he needed it. It was this unending gratitude which made him help Frank Harris, who had given him employment in his days of poverty, even when Harris was busy blackguarding him.

Examples of his prompt and impulsive generosity are numerous, a fact which makes it hard to understand how the legend of his meanness came to be spread about immediately after his death. No man, however rich he may be, is under any obligation to give money because it is demanded. He may not approve of the purpose for which it is intended, or he may suspect the beggar of incompetence to carry on a function with any hope of success, and have no wish to see good money thrown after bad. Whatever his motive for refusal may be, the money he has earned is his money, and he has a right to spend or withhold it as he pleases.

I will not tire my readers by citing numerous examples of his noble and spontaneous charity, and shall mention only those that are representative of his constant kindness.

Among the great variety of people who were his friends was a charming and unworldly French musician, Arnold Dolmetsch, who not only played but manufactured old-fashioned musical instruments, such as clavichords, harpsichords, lutes, viols, virginals and recorders, and gave concerts at which music composed for them was performed by him and his family. He had no sense of money whatsoever, and he spent so much time and devotion in making his instruments that he was generally out of pocket on his business transactions. Dolmetsch was, therefore, often in difficulties, from which he had to be rescued by G.B.S., who did not wait until the man was drowning before he threw him a lifebelt or jumped into the sea to save him.

On July 19, 1898, about six weeks after his marriage, G.B.S. wrote the following letter to Dolmetsch:

'I have just heard that you are going into the hands of the surgeons. As I have been in those hands myself for a couple of months, I know what that means—among other things, a lot of expense. You will need two nurses at first; for if you try to do with one, Mrs Dolmetsch will break down; and then matters will be worse than ever.

'Now, as you are not an opera singer, but an artist, the value of whose work is necessarily understood only by a very few people, I know, being an artist myself, that it is just as likely as not that all this expense is coming on you at just the most inconvenient moment.

'Consequently, you may as well know that I am rather in luck myself, as my last play has been very successful in America, and I have more money lying unused at the bank than I shall want this year. I pledge you my word that it will make absolutely no difference to me if I transfer £50 to your credit until you sell a harpsichord or get in your next season's harvest. The only person who will feel the loss will be my banker; and he can afford it better than either of us.

'If by good luck you are rolling in wealth, you will excuse me for proposing this arrangement, as I hope we need not stand on ceremony with one another. If not, send me a wire—with the address of your bank, and I will lodge the £50 (or more, if necessary) by return of post.

'As soon as you can be moved, get away into the country. It is the cheapest plan in the end, because you will mend so much faster in the fresh air.

'An operation, as I have found, is not so bad for an overworked artist as it is for most people. It stops the overwork and keeps one in bed. Most of us, after 20 years work or so, want six weeks in bed; and anything that forces us to take it is a blessing in disguise.

'Remember me to Mrs Dolmetsch and to Mlle Helene,
Yrs. sincerely,
G. Bernard Shaw.'

Observe the grace with which G.B.S. tries to make Dolmetsch believe that he will be conferring a benefit on his benefactor by accepting the money, as Dolmetsch did, a little too enthusiastically.

At the same time that he was helping Dolmetsch, he was helping several other distressed people to an equal extent, one of whom had no claim on his consideration beyond the fact that his brother had been G.B.S.'s friend. This old man formed the habit of asking for a 'loan' of £50 almost every month, and nearly always got it, though sometimes only half that sum was sent. 'Many', says the author of *Ecclesiasticus*, 'have reckoned a loan as a windfall, and have given trouble to those that helped them.'

An unfortunate poet, John Davidson, whose troubles eventually caused him to drown himself, was given £250 in one year to enable him to write a play without financial anxiety.

The Charringtons, like the Micawbers, were almost always on the verge of insolvency because of their total inability to cope with money.

In July 1893, G.B.S. wrote to Janet to tell her that he had been talking to May Morris a few days earlier about some enterprise which had left the Charringtons 'in very considerable difficulties'. 'The subject then dropped, but she must have seen that it was rather on my mind, as, indeed, it was; for to-day she asked me whether, if she cashed a deposit receipt for £10 which she happened to have lying idle, would you, as a matter of freemasonry between one artist and another, borrow it from her and pay her when you are next in luck. I said I'd try; and she there and then produced the enclosed note. . . .' In December, 1895, the Charringtons, according to custom, were again on the rocks. G.B.S., whose observation was exceptionally sharp, had noticed that Janet's wedding ring had disappeared from her hand; so he wrote to Charles:

> 'I have been relying on you to let me know if the financial situation became strained; but my faith in you is destroyed by the disappearance of the symbol of your union with Janet. The enclosed will make a difference to the bank, but not to me, as I expect to weather Xmas without sinking ten pounds of bottom—in fact, if I get in my cheques from the *Savoy*, *Chronicle* and *Saturday*, I shall be affluent enough to meet any further emergencies. When Providence begins to play such cards against one as typhoid fever, it is useless to waste delicacy and forbearance on it. I am prepared to observe the strictest duplicity with Janet if necessary. . . .'

Gilbert Chesterton, for whom G.B.S. had deep affection, was almost as unworldly about money as Arnold Dolmetsch, and never bargained with editors over the price of his work, with the result that he was generally underpaid. When G.K. died on June 14, 1936, G.B.S. wrote to his widow on the following day in these terms:

> 'It seems the most ridiculous thing in the world that I, 18 years older than Gilbert, should be heartlessly surviving him.
>
> 'However, this is only to say that if you have any temporary bothers that I can remove, a line on a postcard (or three figures) will be sufficient.
>
> 'The trumpets are sounding for him; and the slightest interruption must be intolerable.'

Mrs Chesterton was not in need, but she was deeply moved by G.B.S.'s instant thought for her when he heard of her husband's death.

He was greatly troubled when, for the only time in my life, I was threatened with an action for libel. He was convinced that I would incur heavy damages, and was infuriated because I refused to apologise in any way whatsoever; and he went to extraordinary lengths to save me from what he believed to be imminent ruin. The suit was settled out of court, but not by me, nor did I apologise or pay a penny, a fact which G.B.S. attributed to what he called my cursed luck, rather than to the truth, which was that the plaintiff lost his nerve and was glad to run away on easy terms.

I shall add to these examples of characteristic kindness and generosity, one of an entirely different sort.

When my wife and I were staying at the same time with him and Charlotte in the Hydro Hotel in Torquay where he wrote *Common Sense About the War*, we motored to Buckfastleigh to see the Abbey built there by the monks themselves. This was the sort of enterprise which interested G.B.S. enormously. A Belgian monk, who had probably never heard of him, showed us round, and in a few moments, he and G.B.S. were engaged in a discussion of the Authorised Version of the Bible, which the Belgian, with kindly condescension both to it and to G.B.S., acknowledged to be a good translation and seemed as if he might even admit that it is immeasurably better than the miserable Douai translation used by his own church, which is now, we may hope, superseded by the brilliant translation made by Father Ronald Knox, who has had the benefit of an upbringing in the Church of England and can, therefore, outwrite any priest who has not had that advantage.

At the end of our visit, Charlotte and my wife having already gone out of the Abbey, I realised, though he had said nothing, that he wished to be left alone, and so I walked ahead of him towards the door, taking care, however, to observe out of the corner of my eye, what he was doing. I saw him stuffing Treasury Notes into the box marked Building Fund.

113

His life may, for effective purposes, be divided into two periods: the forty-two years before his marriage, the forty-five years after it. The second period is far the more important.

G.B.S. is remarkable among writers for the lateness of his arrival at renown. The greater part of Shakespeare's work was accomplished before he was forty-two. According to Sir Edward Chambers in his *William Shakespeare* (Vol. I, pp. 270–1) all his plays, except *Coriolanus*, *Timon of Athens*, *Pericles*, *Cymbeline*, *The Winter's Tale*, *The Tempest*, *Henry VIII*, and whatever part he took in *Two Noble Kinsmen*, were written and had been performed by the time he was that age. These eight appeared within the next five years, which were followed by the five years of silence which preceded his death at the age of fifty-two.

Molière, who was a year younger than Shakespeare when he died, began to write plays at the same age as G.B.S. was when he commenced dramatist: thirty-six; but by the time he was forty-two, he had written twelve and part of *Tartuffe*. The remainder of his work, eighteen plays, the conclusion of *Tartuffe*, his share in *Psyche*, and several court pastorals, was written in the next nine years.

G.B.S. had written only seven plays when he was forty-two, one of which, *Candida*, may be described as a major work, though *You Never Can Tell* runs it fairly close: a surprising fact when it is remembered that Shakespeare at the same age was the author of nine major works: *Romeo and Juliet*, *Twelfth Night*, *The Merchant of Venice*, *Julius Caesar*, *Hamlet*, *Othello*, *King Lear*, *Macbeth*, and *Anthony and Cleopatra*.

The eleven plays written by Ibsen before his forty-second year include *The Vikings*, *Love's Comedy*, *The Pretenders*, *Brand*, *Peer Gynt*, and *The League of Youth*, all of them major works. Molière, at that age, was the author of three major comedies. *Les Précieuses Ridicules*, *L'Ecole des Maris*, and *L'Ecole des Femmes*.

After his marriage, however, G.B.S. began rapidly to produce major works, though the first of them, *Man and Superman*, which is one of the three great English comedies written in the last sixty years —the others are *The Importance of Being Earnest* by Oscar Wilde and *The Circle* by Somerset Maugham—was slow in coming. He began to write it in 1901. It was dedicated—the only one of his plays which was dedicated—to his friend and former colleague, A. B. Walkley, who had challenged him to write a play on Don Juan. The challenge was accepted with great gravity, and *Man and Superman*, which was finished in 1903, was the result. It was offered for publication to John Murray who refused it 'in a letter which really touched' its author:[1]

> 'He said he was old-fashioned and perhaps a bit behind the times; but he could not see any intention in my book but to wound, irritate, and upset all established constitutional opinion, and therefore could not take the responsibility of publishing it.'

This excuse for declining to publish *Man and Superman* seems odd when it is remembered that an earlier Murray—'My Murray'—had published Byron's work, though it, too, might have been expected to rouse adverse emotion in a respectable and old-fashioned publisher.

G.B.S. now decided to be his own publisher. 'By that time I could command sufficient capital to finance my books and enter into direct friendly relations with the printers (this began my very pleasant relations with Clarks of Edinburgh). I took matters into my own hands, and, like Herbert Spencer and Ruskin, manufactured my books myself, and induced Constables to take me "on commission",' an arrangement which lasted for the rest of his life.

Publication did not cause the West End managers to feel the

[1] See *The House of Macmillan* by Charles Morgan, p. 132.

slightest interest in *Man and Superman*. If the thought crossed the mind of one of them that this was an important piece, he kept the thought to himself. It is fair to say, however, that had any West End manager read the play when it first appeared in print, he could reasonably have pleaded that it was an impossible work to perform. Its third act would last for an hour, and each of the other three acts was almost as long. He could, too, have remarked with justification that it was a queer piece which could be produced, as its author suggested it should, with the whole of the third act omitted, though in making this statement he would certainly have exposed himself to the retort that *Hamlet* was habitually produced in a shortened form, as, indeed, were all Shakespeare's plays. *Man and Superman* takes no longer to act than *Hamlet* in its entirety.

G.B.S. recognised that there must be reason even in the production of plays, and *Man and Superman* was so written that the third act could be detached without causing the play to bleed. This is a peculiar fact about it. The first, second and fourth acts form a complete play in themselves. The third act is a philosophic interpolation which may be, and occasionally has been, performed by itself. The third act's detachability would seem to show that the play is not an organic whole; and the fact that it does not bleed when its substantial part is amputated, arouses the suspicion that it has no blood to shed. But these reasonable suspicions have no foundation in fact. The singular quality of the play is that it remains a complete play when it has suffered what in any other play would be mutilation. This being so, the critic may wonder whether the third act is superfluous, and find it in fault on the ground that it merely adds bulk to the play's body. But this also fails to be the fact. As a piece of craftsmanship, *Man and Superman* is probably the most remarkable comedy that has ever been written.

Those who have seen the whole of *Hamlet* acted must instantly realise how immeasurably greater it is in its entirety than it is when it has had parts of its body chopped away. Its grandeur makes the shortened version seem to be a different play on the same theme. And what is true of *Hamlet* is true of *Othello* and *Lear* and *Macbeth* and *Romeo and Juliet*. This is not to say that *Man and Superman* is superior to *Hamlet*. It is merely to say that Shakespeare's plays are more closely knit than G.B.S.'s comedy, a freak of a play which is, nevertheless, normal in its shape.

Man and Superman was the first important outcome of his happy marriage. For the first time in his forty-two years, G.B.S. lived in a well-regulated house, where the meals were ample and prompt and civilly served; and he greatly enjoyed his experience which was made the more pleasant by the fact that he was not a kept husband, but was earning enough money to be able to maintain the sort of home that Charlotte could inhabit. The single provision he permitted her to make in regard to himself was that if he should predecease her, she would make an allowance to his mother.

114

The year 1904 saw the beginning of his wide renown. In the spring, he had been adopted as a Progressive candidate for the London County Council, his running companion being Sir William Nevill Montgomerie Geary, fifth and last baronet, an Etonian and graduate of Christ Church, Oxford, who is described by Archibald Henderson as 'extraordinarily stern-looking and hard featured'. Geary, who was a Liberal, was a barrister and a landowner and had been a soldier. He was Attorney-General at Accra, Gold Coast, for two years; had tried to enter Parliament; and was the author of several law books. Their constituency was South St Pancras, which G.B.S. had represented in the Vestry and its successor, the Borough Council.

The supporters, the local Progressive Committee, issued a leaflet advocating their candidature, in which they paid the following tribute to G.B.S. :

'Mr George Bernard Shaw needs no introduction to South St Pancras. Many well-known authors seek election to Parliament; but there is no other instance on record of a man who, having attained a distinguished position in literature, has been found willing to devote six of the best years of his life to the homely work of a Vestry and Borough Council merely from a sense of its importance to his neighbours. Mr Bernard Shaw's practical business ability and commonsense surprised both his friends and opponents on the Borough Council. Although his Moderate opponents were in an overwhelming majority on the Vestry and Council during his years of service, he was placed in spite of his own protests against an excessive share of the work, on the Health Committee, the Parliamentary Committee, the Electric Lighting Committee, the Housing Committee and the Drainage Committee. His record, according to the last return by the Borough Council, was 192 attendances. These attendances were not merely nominal: each of them involved at least two hours' work at the Town Hall, and often three or four, Mr Shaw being admittedly one of the most active and diligent of Committee Men.'

The contest occupied the whole of February, but the meetings, Henderson states, were poorly attended: a strange fact when we remember how brilliant a debater G.B.S. was, how large were the audiences which, a few years later, assembled to hear him. The date of the election was March 5, and at the end of the day, Sir William and G.B.S. were at the bottom of the poll.

W. H. H. Gastrell (Municipal Reformer)	1,927 votes
F. Goldsmith (Municipal Reformer)	1,808 votes
G. B. Shaw (Progressive)	1,460 votes
Sir W. Geary (Progressive)	1,412 votes

Their defeat was due to several causes, the chief of them being G.B.S. himself. He declined to be a common party hack, and tried, but failed to make the majority of the electors take an intelligent interest in their own affairs. The fact that he received as many votes as he did, is surprising, in view of the trouble he took to alienate those who might have been expected to support him. But this conduct of the election was not capricious, as his old paper, *The Star*, asserted it was when his defeat was announced: it was entirely honourable to him and complimentary to the voters who were treated, possibly for the first time in their lives as electors, to reasonable argument. The shock of being taken seriously was too much for them; and so G.B.S. was defeated. He never contested another election.

The main point at issue concerned education, and on this point, G.B.S. lost the confidence of the Nonconformists. They were full of grievances as a result of the Education Act of 1902 which had been passed by the Conservatives and was largely drafted by Sidney Webb. Under this Act, subsidies were granted to sectarian schools, and the Dissenters were infuriated by the fact that they were rated and taxed to pay for Church schools. Their antagonism to these subsidies was such that they developed a stupid piece of political propaganda, called Passive Resistance, and refused to pay the Education rate. Many of them suffered distraint on their furniture which was sold by public auction, usually at absurdly small sums, so that the furniture could be returned to its owners at little or no loss.

This question of subsidies for sectarian schools still agitates the public mind, though not so sharply now as it did in 1904, when even The Fabian Society was so rent by it that Graham Wallas resigned his membership. The agitation to-day concerns mostly, if not exclusively, the Roman Catholic Schools, and the matter is not one that can easily be settled. Each party to the controversy has some reason on its side, though the reason is generally narrow. The Roman Catholics object to their childrens' attendance at mixed schools, and demand that they shall be provided with schools exclusively for their own faith. The ground of their demand is that they do not wish their children to be exposed to the danger of losing their faith and morals if they mingle in the same classes and playgrounds with Protestant children. They seem to reasonable men and women to pay their religion a poor compliment when they suggest that it can so easily be lost.

Neither Webb nor G.B.S. liked sectarian schools, for good and sufficient reasons, but they existed and were likely to exist for a long time, so it was essential that the children who were taught in them should not suffer from defective instruction because their parents were unduly attached to their sect. Moreover, in some places, such as villages, the only accessible school to many children was the Church school.

> 'What is it that we feel most strongly about the Church Schools?' G.B.S. said in his election address. 'Is it that the children are being taught the Church catechism? Not at all. What concerns us is that the children in the Church schools seldom win the County Council scholarships, that the school buildings are often inferior and insanitary, that there are not teachers enough, that what teachers there are are always underpaid and sometimes unqualified, and that the clergyman is forced to beg, often literally from door to door, to make both ends meet.'[1]

This was the common sense of the matter, and would seem certain to win general agreement, but the fact is otherwise. The Dissenters were infuriated by it. They were not alone in their fury. G.B.S., despite what seemed to him sweet reasonableness, succeeded in rousing the wrath of large numbers of voters of all sorts. The Nonconformists were not appeased when he had himself nominated by the wife of an eminent Methodist minister, a nomination which, incredible as it now appears, repelled some ministers of the Established Church. Publicans and Rechabites were antagonised by his suggestion that the drink trade should be municipalised, and the dairymen were filled with fury when he told the electors that they were poisoning their customers. His Socialism finished him with all but the Socialists. In these circumstances, his poll was surprisingly large.

The Webbs were displeased with him because of his defeat which was, they thought, due to his lack of electioneering gumption. He should, they said, have dissembled more. They were less scrupulous in revealing their intentions than G.B.S. was, and had no objection to manipulating facts to get votes. Frankness was all very well, but if it lost an election, it was folly. They even imagined that G.B.S.'s untimely candour was a form of conceit! . . .

115

His defeat was fortunate. Had he been elected, he would have wasted his time and energy in Council Committees when he should have been spending it on plays. Delivered from this thraldom, he set

[1] I have taken this extract from his election address from R. F. Rattray's *Bernard Shaw; a Chronicle*, pp. 155-6.

about his proper task. The Vedrenne-Barker season was to be in the autumn of 1904, and G.B.S. was urged to let them have a new play. Between March, when he was rejected by South St Pancras, and September, he wrote *John Bull's Other Island* and a one-act play, *How He Lied To Her Husband*, which was written as a curtain-raiser for *The Man of Destiny* in Arnold Daly's production in New York.

The history of the longer of these two plays is odd. W. B. Yeats had asked G.B.S. to write a play for the Abbey Theatre in Dublin, and so *John Bull's Other Island* was composed. It was not, however, accepted. The official excuse for its rejection was that it made demands on the Irish Players which they could not fulfil, but Yeats himself told me that he could not make head or tail of the play when he read it. In a letter, dated November 7, 1904, to Lady Gregory, he tells her that 'I have seen Shaw's play,' which had just been produced at the Court Theatre a week earlier: 'it acts very much better than one could have foreseen, but it is immensely long. It begins at 2.30 and ends at 6. I don't really like it. It is fundamentally ugly and shapeless, but certainly keeps everybody amused.'[1] But Yeats, to whom laughter was positively painful, had little or no critical judgment, and his opinions were generally wrong. The Players, however, had no difficulty in coping with it when, a few years after its successful production in London, it was performed in Dublin. Yeats was antipathetic to Shaw, despite his reluctant admiration for some of his work; and he was exceedingly obtuse and stupid about qualities which he himself did not possess. Shaw's energy seemed vulgar to Yeats, who confused langour and inertia with aristocratic calm and poise. Celtic Twilight and empty dreams and stale romance appealed not at all to G.B.S., who thought it was high time that Irishmen acquired a sense of fact and ceased to deceive themselves with the delusion that they were somehow superior to all other people.

G.B.S. had seen some of Yeats's bloodless plays, but I never heard him mention them or any of the poems. It would not surprise me to hear that he had not read a line of Yeats's verse.

John Bull's Other Island infuriated the routine-minded Irish, but it had a cathartic effect on those who were, like Dowson, sick of an old passion; and it gravely disturbed the complacency of English Liberals who were accustomed to regard all Irishmen south of the Boyne as walking archangels. There is a tendency, now that Eire is an alien republic, to regard the play as obsolete, but it is as true to the facts of Eire to-day as it was when it was first written; and it is remarkable for the revelation of G.B.S. himself in two characters, Larry Doyle, the expatriated Irishman, and Father Keegan, the unfrocked priest.

[1] *The Letters of W. B. Yeats.* Edited by Allan Wade, p. 442.

The year 1904 was an important time in the history of the English theatre. G.B.S. had at last come to his place. The Vedrenne-Barker productions profoundly affected the theatre, not only in Great Britain, but abroad. There was an extraordinary resurgence of dramatic literature. Repertory theatres were being founded everywhere in the two islands. The Stage Society, the most influential of all the private play-producing organisations, was incorporated in that year. The old theatre was collapsing, and the day of Pinero was almost done. The Continent began to be conscious of G.B.S. In November, 1900, a young Viennese, Siegfried Trebitsch, visited London to meet William Archer, who told him that the most important dramatist in England at that time was unknown on the Continent, and almost unknown in Great Britain. Trebitsch enquired for the name of this genius and was told. Archer was still doing good turns to G.B.S.

Trebitsch bought *Plays Pleasant and Unpleasant* and *Three Plays for Puritans*—and read *Candida* on his way home. This was the beginning of a long association with their author as his German translator, though Trebitsch did not meet G.B.S. until 1902, when he received permission to make the translations. The English drama at that time was little esteemed in Austria and Germany. Hermann Bahr, himself a dramatic critic and dramatist, denounced the work of Henry Arthur Jones and Arthur Wing Pinero and even Oscar Wilde as characterless melodrama, written in a wornout technique. After he had read Trebitsch's translations of G.B.S.'s early plays, Bahr wrote, 'Imagine my astonishment, my amazement, my delight when suddenly I discover before me English plays which comply with the highest demands of the French both in clarity and pliancy of form, and which for sheer, intellectual acuteness and subtlety of temper, fineness of tone, and grasp of human relations are excelled only by their power to transpose all actions into the key of pure intellect.'

This was the first recognition, apart from Trebitsch's, that G.B.S. had received in the German-speaking countries. But a little earlier than Bahr's recognition, came that of a renowned Danish critic, Georg Brandes, who had demanded in *Politkken* in December, 1902, that *Candida*, *The Devil's Disciple* and *Arms and the Man* should be performed in Copenhagen. It is, however, one thing to be recognised by discerning critics and a far different thing to be recognised by theatre managers and the general public. Despite the praise of Bahr, Trebitsch could not persuade a manager in Austria or Germany to produce any of G.B.S.'s plays; and it was not until February 1903, that *The Devil's Disciple* was performed at the Raimund Theatre in Vienna. *Arms and the Man* was to have been produced at an earlier date, but was banned by the Austrian censor because it was thought

373

to be offensive about the Balkans. Despite the warm reception given to *The Devil's Disciple* at the Raimund, the play ran only for four nights. (Long runs have always been rare in Austria and Germany, where a play which is performed 100 times in succession is considered to be a sensational success).

116

Arms and the Man was the first Shaw play to be performed in Germany. That was in 1903. The rise of his popularity in the German-speaking nations was slow, and it is the bare truth to say that but for the persistence and devotion of Trebitsch, the plays, despite their immense appeal to German minds since 1903, would have had as poor a fate in Germany as they have had in France.

It is an extraordinary and almost inexplicable fact that G.B.S. has so far failed to find much favour in France. He has sometimes been called the Irish Molière, a title which, added to the intellectual sympathy which has long existed between France and Ireland, would seem to prove that his work would appeal strongly to the French: though Molière himself is out of fashion with his countrymen to-day. The vitality and optimistic mood of G.B.S.'s work might have been expected to win favour with French men and women in these times when their own dramatists are devitalised and despondent, and their politicians rightly receive the world's contempt. If ever a nation needed a strong whiff of Shavian hope and vigour, France is the nation.

But although his work has been widely performed to packed houses in a large part of the world, France remains indifferent to it. At the end of 1904, Maurice Maeterlinck had never heard of G.B.S. 'Je l'avoue avec une profonde confusion.' Nor had Emile Fauget. When Archibald Henderson enquired into this strange matter, he was told by Jules Lemaitre and Jules Claretie 'that they had never discussed Shaw in their *Chroniques Théâtrales*'. That was in 1904. Augustin Filon, in his book, *The English Stage*, which was published in 1897, makes no mention of him. It was not until February 1907, that the first Shaw play to be produced before a French-speaking audience was performed at the Théâtre Royal du Parc in Brussels. This was *Candida*, which was produced three months later at the Théâtre des Arts in Paris. 'During the next five years,' says Henderson,[1] 'Shaw made no further advance in the French theatre,' despite the fact that his plays were beginning to be discussed in French reviews and magazines.

In 1912, *Mrs Warren's Profession* was performed eighty times at

[1] See his article, *Bernard Shaw and France*, in the winter issue of *Caroline Quarterly*, 1954.

the Théâtre des Arts, and was, Henderson asserts, 'undoubtedly a success', but this success did not provoke any general popularity for his work. 'During the next thirteen years, with varying fortunes but no marked success, five of Shaw's plays were produced: *On ne peut jamais dire* in 1913; *L'Homme et L'Héros* in 1912 and 1921; *Androcles* in 1921; *Le dilemme du medecin* in 1922; and *Pygmalion* in 1923.' It was not until May 1925, that he had what Henderson calls his 'one authentic triumph' in France: when Jean and Ludmilla Pitoeff produced *Sainte Jeanne* at the Théâtre des Arts, a production which G.B.S. disliked.

Despite the success of *Sainte Jeanne* in France, a success which reflects no particular credit on the French since the play has been a tremendous success all over the world, G.B.S. has still failed to capture the French playgoing public. Why? G.B.S. himself, who never at any period of his life felt much respect for the vaunted French culture, gave a characteristic answer in *Comœdia* in the spring of 1924:

'It seems to me that the theatre in France addresses itself less and less to an intelligent public; the public is in fact so stupid that an explanation of the play must be printed on the program to help the spectators to understand what they see. The other day I saw a program of *Arms and the Man* which carefully explains that the tragic figure of my play is a buffoon who must not be taken seriously. It is pitiful because an appreciation of my plays has become a proof of civilization, and up to the present France is almost at the bottom of the form. Nothing, however, can be done. I have educated London, I have educated New York, Berlin and Vienna; Moscow and Stockholm are at my feet, but I am too old to educate Paris; it is too far behind and I am too far ahead. Besides this, my method of education is to teach people how to laugh at themselves, and the pride of Paris is so prodigious that it has beaten all its professors from Molière to Anatole France and might even beat me. . . .

'My plays are mixtures of seventeenth century rhetoric, of modern thought and of that barbarous English humour which shocked Voltaire in Shakespeare. They are full of politics, religion, biology and all sorts of terrestrial things except adultery. They contain no traitors, no duels, no misunderstandings nor dramatic plots; and when the question of passion between the two sexes arises, it is the real thing, not the convention which holds its stead on your modest boulevards. The material which serves your talented dramatic authors for the construction of a play would not last me thirty seconds; the old-fashioned denouements are mere phrases in my plays, about half a dozen a page.'

The shallow-minded and obtuse may dismiss this argument as routine Shavian stuff, the pseudo-vanity of a man who is galled because he has failed to win French approval; but people whose minds are lively will wonder whether G.B.S. is not in the right of the matter. The world has lived for several centuries in the delusion that French civilisation is supreme over all other civilisations, and no people are more deceived by this belief than the French themselves. The first characteristic of a civilised society is its ability to govern and defend itself. The French ability to do so has steadily declined since the fall of the Bastille, and they can now do neither. The argument that the French, in failing to appreciate G.B.S., are thereby proving how superior they are to the rest of mankind will not convince anybody but overwrought Francophiles and the stupider French themselves.

117

Why is it, then, that G.B.S., who conquered most of the world, failed to conquer France?

The commonest answer returned to this question is that his translator, Augustin Hamon was incompetent: a charge which G.B.S. always repudiated with fury.

Hamon was not, in any reasonable sense of the term, a literary man or a man with any understanding of the stage. He was a sociologist who held what are called advanced views on politics: a mixture of Socialist and philosophical anarchist. His published works, apart from his translations of Shaw's plays, are concerned with hygiene, sociology, and collective psychology, according to Henderson, who thinks that his translations, as a result of practice, improved; he belonged to no literary circle; nor was he treated with respect by writers in general or by editors of important reviews. His style is about as exhilarating as that of the late Harold J. Laski. If we can imagine Laski translating Molière or Anatole France into English, we shall have some idea of what Hamon's translations of Shaw into French are like.

G.B.S. had known Hamon as a member of international Socialist Conferences. At the beginning of 1904, Hamon gave a young Frenchman an introduction to him, recommending him as a possible translator of *Man and Superman*. As the young man was an undergraduate, G.B.S. was not impressed by the proposal; and he suggested that Hamon himself should translate them. This suggestion stupified Hamon, 'whose knowledge of English was slight, his acquaintance with world literature sub-par, and his knowledge of the drama and acquaintance with the theatre of the boulevards infinitesimal'.[1] But G.B.S., who was liable to get bats of this sort in his belfry, would not listen to Hamon's reasonable objections. The very fact that he was not a literary man, was, in G.B.S.'s opinion, a good reason why he should translate his plays. G.B.S., for some unknown reason, had always been scornful of writers. His severest term of contempt was

---

[1] Henderson.

'the Savile Club lot'. This contempt probably sprang from a harsh experience in his young manhood, but he attributed it to what he considered to be their indifference to politics and sociology. One feels that he liked *The Deserted Village*, not because it is a good poem, but because it shows that Goldsmith had some knowledge of agricultural economy.

Hamon persisted in his argument that he was an unsuitable person to translate English plays into French, especially when G.B.S. told him that his translator 'must have the literary dexterity of a Victorian Sardou'. This was a dexterity which he did not possess, but G.B.S. was not easily diverted from his will, and at last Hamon, exhausted by his efforts to make him see reason, capitulated.

'I knew very well what I was about,' G.B.S. wrote to him when he was under violent attack for the faults in his translations. 'The dramatic liveliness of the reports you gave of some of the Socialist Congresses had satisfied me that you were the man to undertake a French version of my plays. As far as intimate knowledge of English was concerned, it was enough that Madame Hamon possessed this. You understood the modern social organism, you knew human nature; and it was these points that were essential.'[1]

It is easy to believe that Hamon's translations are the main, if not the sole, obstacle in the way of Shaw's popularity in France, and that this unpopularity will end when Hamon's exclusive right to translate the plays expires. But it is possible that there are profounder causes than this. Trebitsch, although he, too, is a dramatist of notable skill, has been accused of faulty translation into German, but these faults, if they exist, have not prevented G.B.S. from winning great favour in Germany. There may be profounder causes to his work than mistranslation. His habit of thought may be repellent to the French.

Mlle Mina Moore makes an interesting remark which may here be of help. She draws a distinction between authors who are in accord with the prevailing temper and those who are in discord with it.

> 'M. Bernard Shaw est l'illustration d'un cas plus rare. On commence par trouver le public résistant; loin de se laisser décourager par l'insuccès, on revient avec persistance à l'attaque, jusqu'à ce qu'on se soit imposé aux lectures, grâce à ses propres efforts. On ne se lasse pas de répéter ce que d'autres voudraient étouffer. Plein de la conviction que communique la passion du vrai, on les force à écouter, sinon à se rendre. Et l'hostilité, la non-compréhension ne font qu'aiguillonner la volonté jusqu'au triomphe des idées qu'elle défend.'

This, indeed, is a strictly accurate account of the war G.B.S. had to wage everywhere. It fails, however, to account for the singular fact

[1] The reader who is interested in this matter, will find Mlle Mina Moore's book, *Bernard Shaw et la France*, impressive. It was published by the Libraire Ancienne Honoré Champion, 5, Quai Malaquais, VIe, Paris, in 1933.

that France, alleged to be the citadel of civilisation, has not yet admitted G.B.S. to its roll of acknowledged great dramatists.

G.B.S. was an Irish Protestant Puritan, a very different person from an Irish Roman Catholic Puritan; and this substantial fact is almost certainly the chief cause of his lack of popularity in Roman Catholic countries. The reader will do well to ponder that fact that his plays are no more popular in Ireland, except among Protestants, than they are in France or Italy or Spain. The mind of an Irish Protestant Puritan is obviously remoter from the Latin people than it is from the English or the Protestant Americans or the Germans or the Northern Europeans. Then, too, G.B.S.'s attitude towards sexual love is not only remote from, but almost incomprehensible by the Latin mind.

Sexual excitement is intensely important to a Frenchman or an Italian or a Spaniard, despite the seclusion, less to-day than it was formerly, in which their young women are kept. An English girl has a freedom of movement which seems almost immoral to Latin parents; and it is notorious that many French fathers and mothers were deeply shocked in the First World War by the enlistment in the British Forces of young girls. There was a fairly wide belief in France that the Waacs were sent there to satisfy the sexual needs of our soldiers.

The coldness of G.B.S.'s women and the lack of passion in their lovers disconcerts the Latin mind. Vivie, in *Mrs Warren's Profession*, must appear to a Frenchman to be a female monster. The calculating character of Ann Whitefield, the deliberation with which she pursues her man and bags him in the end, make her appear repulsive to an Italian. The Frenchman has never allowed his intellect to interfere with his impulses and passions; and he has difficulty that is almost insuperable in understanding the Shavian man who does. It is notorious that Frenchwomen find Englishmen unsatisfying lovers. The French distaste for G.B.S.'s work, therefore, is more likely to be a matter of temperament than of translation. His insistence that intellectual passion transcends any physical passion alienates him from their liking or understanding; and their insistence that physical passion is more important than any other, since it stimulates the mind and elates the spirit, is merely disgusting to G.B.S.

A. B. Walkley, who, though he was one of Shaw's oldest friends, had little liking for his plays, offered an explanation of their unpopularity in France which Hamon, with considerable pedantic skill, attempts to refute.[1] The plays, he complained, are disorderly, and

---

[1] See *The Twentieth Century Molière: Bernard Shaw*. By Augustin Hamon. The English translation, by Eden and Cedar Paul, was published by Allen and Unwin, Ltd., in 1915. It has long been out of print, but copies may be found in some public libraries as well as in the London Library. The biographical part of this book is shockingly inaccurate, but the critical part of it is interesting.

reveal in their author a deep contempt for form. This disorderliness proves that G.B.S. is devoid of the French spirit. The French, Walkley contends, have a reverent regard for order and a powerful sense of form: statements which seem to have no relevance to fact. A nation so individualistic as France that it is unable to govern itself, cannot easily be accepted as an exemplar of form. Why an Irishman should be expected to possess the spirit of a Frenchman is hard to understand. Are the French so self-possessed that they cannot interest themselves in any spirit but their own?

Hamon denies Walkley's contention, and asserts with a lavish display of learning that Shaw is so far from being disorderly that he can be called a classic writer. Any disorderliness there may be in his work is to be found only in what he calls 'the material action', that is to say, in the physical construction of the plays. There is none of it in the characterisation or the intellectual action: and the disorderly material action is a classic characteristic of all comedy. He finds in G.B.S. a close identity of spirit with all the great comic writers from Aristophanes onwards, and maintains that G.B.S. is far nearer to the classic French dramatists from the time of Molière to that of Beaumarchais than all the French dramatists since the time of the latter. The French dramatists, beginning with Scribe and Sardou, deserted the classic style and substituted mechanical efficiency for spiritual elation. Their plays were well-made, but remote from life; and the reason why Shaw's plays are unpopular in France is that the French people, forgetting Molière, have become so inured to Scribe and Sardou that they cannot appreciate the classic style any longer, which is why G.B.S. and Molière are unpopular. Hamon insists that Shaw 'exhibits a close approximation to the French spirit', and that the Celt in his composition 'renders him far more closely akin to the French than to the English', an argument which is specious, for Walkley could justifiably have retorted to Hamon that the Celt in G.B.S., assuming there is one, which is very dubious, had not made his plays any more acceptable to the Irish than they are to the French.

It may be, as Hamon contends, that when the French have recovered the classic spirit and have ceased to be a nation of disorderly anarchists, Shaw will become as popular in France as he is elsewhere, but here we are in the region of unverifiable speculation. It must be enough that Hamon puts up a reasonable argument for his point of view.

118

The seasons at the Court Theatre established G.B.S. in English favour; and the public performance of *Man and Superman* made even the most sceptical critics admit that the play had genius. Its popularity has steadily increased, and the latest revival seems to surpass in public favour all the previous revivals. G.B.S. gives good measure in his work, not only to the public, but to the players. All the parts, even the small ones, are full of character, and they permit those who take them to win regard and recognition.

Enough attention has not been given to G.B.S.'s technical skill as a dramatist. Critics have applauded his dialogue, his wit and audacious thought, but few of them have applauded his immense ability in constructing his plays. He uses every available device to make his pills palatable. The settings are unusual and sometimes fantastic. The stage is filled with colour. Where the argument is severe, he lightens it in a variety of ways that take the strain off the playgoer's attention; as, for instance, in *Heartbreak House*, where he puts a character into romantic clothes for evening dress.

These devices are nearly always borrowed from life. The ship-shaped house in *Heartbreak House* is based on one built by Lena Ashwell's father, a retired naval officer, and the Arab robes worn by Hector Hushabye in the evening were borrowed from Wilfred Scawen Blunt. His most extravagant characters are based on actual people. When Ellen Terry refused to regard Lady Cecily Waynflete in *Captain Brassbound's Conversion* as a credible character, he was able to confound her by reminding her of Miss Mary Kingsley, the niece of Charles, whose remarkable book, *Travels in West Africa*, he recommended her to read:

> 'Listen to me, woman with no religion. Send to your library for two books of travel in Africa: one Miss Kingsley's (have you met her?) and the other H. M. Stanley's. Compare the brave woman, with her common sense and good will, with the wild-beast man, with his elephant rifle, and his atmosphere of dread and murder, breaking his way by mad selfish assassination out of the difficulties created by his own cowardice. . . .'

All his characters are remarkable people. The commonplace man or woman did not interest him. It was his sense of notability in people that enabled him to make all the parts in his plays distinctive; and *Man and Superman* is a brilliant example of his skill in this respect. The secondary parts are as well etched as the principal parts. John Tanner and Ann Whitefield are gifts to actors and actresses, but all the remaining parts, and especially that of Henry Straker, the chauffeur, are so finely drawn that any actor or actress must be pleased with them. Straker was one of the first, if not actually the first chauffeur to be put in a play, thus showing another Shavian characteristic: immediate interest in novelties.

The argument of *Man and Superman* is a flat contradiction of Tennyson's in most of his work. The poet saw woman as subordinate to man, made by him for his purpose; but the dramatist saw her as superior to man, who was made by her for her purpose. 'As the husband is, the wife is', according to *Locksley Hall;* and the theme is repeated and elaborated in *The Princess.* 'Man is the hunter; woman is his game.'

> Man for the field and woman for the heart:
> Man for the sword and for the needle she:
> Man with the head and woman with the heart:
> Man to command and woman to obey;
> All else is confusion.
> The woman's cause is the man's: they sink or rise together.

This is G.B.S.'s argument in reverse. To him, the female is the hunter, the male is the game. Woman, animated by an irresistible impulse to perpetuate the species, marks down her man and, by a variety of seductive arts, allures him to her bed so that he may fertilise her. That, according to G.B.S., is the sole purpose of his existence from her point of view. The male matters so little to the female, apart from his ability to fertilise her, that some creatures kill him when he has performed his function. The female spider eats her mate immediately after she has been impregnated. The Queen bee apparently suffers no pangs when her lover, after he has caught her in the air, dies at the end of their raptures.

The Shavian theory is that man, being a creative artist in one way or another, is less interested in the production of progeny than he is in expressing himself; and he can be diverted from his own purpose to that of the woman only by some exceptional excitement. That is why the sexual act has been made intensely pleasing to him, although it is often displeasing to her, who suffers it because her passion for posterity cannot be gratified without it.

Nietzsche carried this argument a little further. There was no reason, he said, why women should obtain any satisfaction from carnal concurrence, as Justin Martyr calls it. Her satisfaction is felt when she feels her baby nuzzling at her breast. We may suspect, however, that Nietzsche, who failed to satisfy several wives, was inventing a philosophic excuse for his virtual impotence. If pleasure in sexual intercourse is unnecessary for women, why did any of his wives desert him? And how did he account for the nymphomaniac?

It is probably true that if the sexual act had not been made extraordinarily pleasing and stimulating to the male, no male creature could ever have been induced to perform it, since the posture in which it is performed makes him appear ridiculous; but the conclusion

381

drawn from this premise by G.B.S. seems not to have much validity, since the passion for posterity, so far as we can determine, is as strong in men as it is in women. There are, indeed, women who have never had the passion at all.

In G.B.S.'s philosophy, the woman aided by the powerful urgency of nature, uses all her arts to seduce the man to her purpose. She adorns her body by devices that are often elaborate and alluring. The main purpose of her dress is not to keep her warm, but to excite desire in the male. She paints her face and her nails and her toes to provoke his emotional appetite; and she or her dressmaker, whether they acknowledge their motive or not, design her clothes so that they will concentrate his thoughts on her body.

The purpose of fashion, largely, is sexual allurement. When one style becomes ineffective through familiarity in rousing desire, another style, which may be in complete contrast, is immediately adopted. The present mode is for the girl to display as much of her bare body as the law will allow; but in an earlier age, when women were subtler than they are to-day, concealment and discreet revelation were the means employed. There are sages who say that greater desire was aroused by the long, voluminous skirts and manifold petticoats of the Victorian lady than can be stirred by a nearly naked body.

When Queen Victoria was a young girl, women displayed their breasts in day clothes more lavishly than the modern woman shows hers in evening dress. The sudden revelation of a woman's ankle in a shower of rain or the brief exhibition of a white petticoat or the rustle of a silk skirt was sufficient in the mid-Victorian time to evoke male desire. When concealed legs ceased to excite, legs were lavishly displayed. At the root of all spectacular entertainment is an attempt to rouse male passion. Every movement made by a chorus girl in a musical comedy is carefully designed to titillate male emotion, either in the callow youth or the dotard, and the debutante is dressed by her mother with a single intention, to make her as alluring as possible to some desirable and easily inflamed young man.

That is the theme or rather the theory of *Man and Superman*, and it is implicit in nearly all G.B.S.'s work. It may be said to be derived from the Book of Genesis in which Eve, instigated by the Serpent, tempts Adam to enjoy her body. But G.B.S., especially in the Garden of Eden act in *Back to Methuselah*, fails to observe that Adam had not created anything until he was seduced by Eve. Up to that enthralling moment, he had been no more than a spiritless gardener, dully tending a garden he had not made: about as creative as a ranger in a municipal park. The end of the Garden scene is odd. The Serpent refuses to make any vows. He prefers to take a chance. 'If I bind the future, I bind my will. If I bind my will, I strangle creation.'

This assertion draws a cry of protest from Eve. 'Creation must not be strangled. I tell you I will create, though I tear myself to pieces in the act.' But creation for her has only one meaning: the creation of children. Adam is afraid of uncertainty. He wishes to bind the future and to be delivered from fear. In his brooding moments, he is full of alarm in the world he inhabits, but does not know or understand. His imagination fills him with aspirations which frighten him as much as they excite him. That is why he demands certainty and wishes to know. He refuses to hear the Serpent's secret, and leaves his wife to hear it alone.

'Now the secret,' she exclaims. 'The secret.'

Then follows this strange and unconvincing stage direction. 'She sits on the rock and throws her arms round the serpent, who begins whispering to her. Eve's face lights up with intense interest, which increases until an expression of overwhelming repugnance takes its place. She buries her face in her hands.' But is it not more likely that she leapt with joy?

G.B.S. was revolted by my question, and he wrote me a vehement letter. 'I have just been reading your article in *The Observer*,' he said, and added, 'Think, boy, think.' He then estimates the possible number of Eve's grandchildren, adding that by the time she was three hundred years old, 'there were so many thousands that if it had been possible for them all to live within reach of her and keep up the acquaintance, she and Adam would have died of hunger if they had stopped working long enough to kiss the lot once a week.'

> 'And you complain because I have not represented her as a grand-mother spoiling her first grandchild!!! Blush for yourself. You contend further that I am a misogynic St Paul because I have represented a woman in a state of complete pre-sex innocence as making a wry face when it is explained to her that in consequence of the indelicacy with which Nature, in a fit of economy, has combined a merely excretory function with a creatively ejaculatory one in the same bodily part (she knowing only the excretory use of it), she is to allow herself to be syringed in an unprecedented manner by Adam. You say that I should have made her jump for joy. . . .
>
> 'It is true that the indignity has compensations which, *when experienced*, overwhelm all the objections to it; but Eve had not then experienced them. I am myself only too susceptible to them; yet I always feel obliged, as a gentleman, to apologize for my disgraceful behaviour; and I would be shot rather than be guilty of it in public.'

I interrupt him here to remark that any man would. The union is so personal and intimate that it must, so far as human beings are concerned, for no animal has any reticence about it, be conducted in solitude. G.B.S. goes on to say:

'In this I am the normal heterosexual man describing, in Eve, the normal heterosexual woman. Yet you describe me, in an ecstasy of reaction against Victorianism (contemporary with Eve's clothes, which I did not design) as a morbid and important Pauline monster. Stuff!

'You will have noticed that the arrangement leaves Eve unsatisfied. It leaves the red-blooded he-man Cain unsatisfied. You, in a hearty manner, imply that it leaves you unsatisfied; everybody is apologetic; we would all like to detach the ecstasy from the indecency. My suggestion is that the passion of the body will finally become a passion of the mind. Already there is a pleasure in thought—creative thought— that is entirely detached from ridiculous and disgusting acts and postures. Shakespeare could not have written of the ecstasies of St Thomas his sonnet about "the expense of spirit in a waste of shame". The Aberdonian[1] cannot say of the achievements of Einstein that "the position is ridiculous, the pleasure but momentary, and the expense damnable". There is no reaction, no disgust, no love changed to hate. The pleasure falls very short of the pleasure of sex in intensity but you have only to conceive an intensification of the pleasure of thought as it becomes more and more a vital necessity to evolving society and humanity, accompanied by a reduction of intensity in physically reproductive pleasure, to understand why, 30,000 years hence, the naked and physically comfortless Ancient says to the dancing, love-making boy that a moment of life lived as the Ancients lived it, in a chronic ecstasy of thought, would strike a boy dead. Also why the dancing boy cannot conceive how the Ancients can endure their (to him) apparently joyless existence.

'Grasp this, and you will not longer talk to me as the boy talks to the Ancient.

'When I began, Archer complained that my plays were reeking with sex. Now that I am ending, you complain that I am an anchorite. Women have never complained of me either way. *They* know that I know what I am talking about.

'After this, it seems an anti-climax to add that Charlotte is now out of bed after half-past twelve, and downstairs; but it is still very doubtful whether she will be able to come up to town this week. However, if she doesn't, I will: so you may expect me to lunch on Thursday any-how. We will keep you informed of her progress.

ever, G.B.S.'

On the day following the receipt of this letter, he sent me a post-card in which he said:

'After posting my letter, I amused myself by adding up the number of Eve's descendants available when she was 300 years old, assuming families of 10 and no deaths. It comes to four million, eight hundred

---

[1] I do not know what he means by 'the Aberdonian'. It was Lord Chesterfield who made the remark.

and eighty two thousand, two hundred and ten persons, allowing 33⅓ years per generation

4,882,210'

But a man who has seen seventy springs is not less enchanted by the seventieth than he was by the first of which he was aware. The descendants who brought their babies to Eve must still have had some feeling of family and blood-relationship with her, and where there is a feeling of family and blood-relationship there is, nine hundred and ninety times out of a thousand, a thrill of interest and love. These relationships cease to have any force when a family becomes an unorganised horde, though our sense of kindred remains strong enough in a nation which is conscious of itself. One's 4,882,210th descendant is not issue: it is sheer efflorescence, almost spawn; and unlikely to excite any more emotion in Eve than a cod fish feels on beholding one of the innumerable eggs it deposits on the ocean bed. The salient fact in G.B.S.'s life was that he had never enjoyed a family life, that after his fifteenth year, he had no family life at all until he was over forty, and that even this life was not a family life, but a very happy association with a good companion.

119

In the second scene, outside Eden, we find Cain, the vegetarian and first murderer, asserting the right his father had failed to assert, the right to conquer and rule. He tells his mother that 'the making of men' is her function in the world. 'You make my father here your mere convenience, as you call it, for that. He has to dig for you, sweat for you, plod for you, like the ox who helps him to tear up the ground or the ass who carries his burdens for him. No woman shall make me live my father's life. I will hunt: I will fight and strive to the very bursting of my sinews. When I have slain the boar at the risk of my life, I will throw it to my woman to cook, and give her a morsel of it for her pains. She shall have no other food; and that will make her my slave. And the man that slays me shall have her for his booty. Man shall be the master of Woman, not her baby and her drudge.'

Eve is infuriated by the pot valiant boast; and she denounces Cain as a beefy fool who imagines that he is exhibiting valour and independence of mind in his assaults on wild animals when he is merely the slave of a luxurious woman whose body he adorns with the pelts he takes from the creatures he kills. 'You fight because you think that your fighting makes her admire and desire you. Fool: she makes you fight because you bring her the ornaments and the treasures of those you have slain, and because she is courted and propitiated with power and gold by the people who fear you. You say that *I* make a mere convenience of Adam: I who spin and keep the house and bear and rear children, and am a woman and not a pet animal to please man and prey on them. What are you, you poor slave of a painted face and a bundle of skunk's fur?'

Eve is a disillusioned woman. The Serpent's secret has given her less happiness than she had expected to receive. Her descendants do not delight her. Life is a long series of dull repetitions, and she is tired of it and tired of her children and their children and their foolish bragging about their activities and deeds which are no more than the activities and deeds of Adam and Eve. 'Oh, I have heard it all a thousand times. They tell me, too, of their last born: the clever thing the darling child said yesterday, and how much more wonderful or witty or quaint it is than any child that ever was born before. And I have to pretend to be surprised, delighted, interested; though the last child is like the first, and has said and done nothing that did not delight Adam and me when you and Abel said it.'

Here G.B.S. fails to realise the beauty of repetition and regularity or the consolation which these bring to the man who lives in the knowledge and assurance that life is always essentially the same. How frightened, I suggested to him, Adam and Eve must have felt when they saw the first sunset. Their terror at the thought that they would never see the sun again must have been overwhelming. Were they to spend the rest of their lives in the dark? Their joy when they saw the sun rise must have been unbounded, as it was when they realised that this repetition and regularity of dawn and dark would never alter. I reminded him that his mother had never known the raptures of a grandmother, and that her indifference to children, therefore, had misled him into his shocking ignorance of a common fact, the deep and enduring love every grandmother feels for her grandchildren, who give her the pleasure, but none of the pangs of maternity.

G.B.S.'s belief that woman is the hunter and the man is the quarry seems to have been shared to some extent by Shakespeare. It is the women in *As You Like It* and *A Midsummer Night's Dream* who pursue the men. Portia was so determined to .marry Bassanio that she obviously arranged with Nerissa that he should choose the right casket; and there is good ground for thinking that Desdemona pursued Othello. Orlando is lovesick for Rosalind, but it is she, far more intelligent than he is, who sets out to find him, not he who sets out to find her; and she anticipates the modern girl by putting on the medieval equivalent of trousers.

G.B.S. was careful to choose only those analogies which seemed to illustrate his argument. It would be as sensible to choose the sow as a proof that the female of the species eats her young as it was to prove that the woman uses the man only for her reproductive purposes and is indifferent to him otherwise by citing the female spider who devours her mate immediately after he has fertilised her. The female spider is rare among insects just as the cuckoo is rare among birds. The higher the organism becomes, the deeper is its attachment to its mate and its devotion to its young. He seems never to have considered the possibility that the creation of a child is more satisfying to a man than the creation of a picture or a book or a piece of music.

To make a woman the mother of a child is surely a prodigious feat to which no normal man can feel indifferent: one, too, which has divided thought since the beginning of time on the question of which is the creator: the man or the woman. The patriarchs of the Old Testament had no doubt in their minds about this problem. The children of Israel were the seed of Abraham, not the seed of Sarah; and this belief seems, according to Gilbert Murray, to have been held by the Greeks. If the Greeks and the Israelites were right, then the mother's womb is the soil in which the father's seed is sown. The seed is not, as some people suppose, provided by the mother and fertilised by the father. The biological difference between these two beliefs is profound.

The artist man and the mother woman, the first creating and destroying, the second preserving and perpetuating, are shown in *Man and Superman* to be in a state of war. This is what used to be called the duel of sex. It denotes a difference between the purpose of the man and the woman so deep that it is difficult to believe, if it be true, that there can be any useful co-operation between the sexes. Tanner tells Octavius, the romantic poet who loves, but is not loved by, Ann Whitefield, that the woman is ruthless in her determination to create children. It is one of the signs of Tanner's stupidity that he does not realise that Ann is in love, not with Octavius, but with him. The following passages of dialogue illustrate his argument. He is warning Octavius that Ann means to marry him:

> Tanner: Tavy: that's the devilish side of a woman's fascination: she makes you will your own destruction.
> Octavius: But it's not destruction: it's fulfilment.
> Tanner: Yes, of her purpose: and that purpose is neither her happiness, not yours, but Nature's. Vitality in a woman is a blind fury of creation. She sacrifices herself to it: do you think she will hesitate to sacrifice you?
> Octavius: Why, it is just because she is self-sacrificing that she will not sacrifice those she loves.
> Tanner: That is the profoundest of mistakes, Tavy. It is the self-sacrificing women that sacrifice others most recklessly. Because they are unselfish, they are kind in little things. Because they have a purpose which is not their own purpose, but that of the whole universe, a man is nothing to them but an instrument of that purpose.

Octavius: Dont be ungenerous, Jack. They take the tenderest care of us.

Tanner: Yes, as a soldier takes care of his rifle or a musician of his violin. But do they allow us any purpose or freedom of our own? Will they lend us to one another? Can the strongest man escape from them when once he is appropriated? They tremble when we are in danger, and weep when we die; but the tears are not for us, but for a father wasted, a son's breeding thrown away. They accuse us of treating them as a mere means to our pleasure; but how can so feeble and transient a folly as man's selfish pleasure enslave a woman as the whole purpose of Nature embodied in a woman can enslave a man?

That conversation is full of question-marks. We make notes of interrogation against every sentence Tanner utters. If the woman is the slave of Nature, compelled by a power she cannot control or resist to force some man to fertilise her so that she may breed the posterity Nature demands, she is as much a victim as the man she seeks to enslave. This, surely, is the Higher Determinism which would scandalise Calvin? The villain of the piece is the Life Force, Creative Evolution, *élan vital*, Nature, God, whatever we choose to call it, from whose clutch no one can hope to escape.

The artist man is not less scrupulous in his determination to fulfil a purpose. He claims that it is his own purpose, but how does he know that it is not Nature's as much as the mother woman's intention to perpetuate her species is also Nature's? If this were not true, then the artist-man is guilty of the sin G.B.S. so sternly denounced, his refusal to be 'a force of Nature instead of a feverish, selfish clod of ailments complaining that the world will not devote itself to making him happy.'

'The true artist', Tanner tells Tavy, 'Will let his wife starve, his children go barefoot, his mother drudge for his living at seventy sooner than work at anything but his art. To women he is half vivisector, half vampire. He gets into intimate relations with them to study them, to strip the mask of convention from them, to surprise their inmost secrets, knowing that they have the power to rouse his deepest creative energies, to rescue him from his cold reason, to make him see visions and dream dreams, to inspire him, as he calls it. He persuades women that they may do this for their own purpose whilst he really means them to do it for his. He steals the mother's milk and blackens it to make printers ink to scoff at her and glorify ideal women with. He pretends to spare her the pangs of child-bearing so that he may have for himself the tenderness and fostering that belong of right to her children. Since marriage began, the great artist has been known as a bad husband. But he is worse: he is a child-robber, a blood-sucker, a hypocrite and a cheat. Perish the race and wither a thousand women if only the sacrifice of them enable him to act Hamlet better, to paint a finer picture, to write a deeper poem, a greater play, a profounder philosophy! For mark you, 'Tavy, the artist's work is to shew us ourselves as we really are. Our minds are nothing but this knowledge of ourselves; and he who adds a jot to such knowledge creates new mind as surely as any woman creates new men. In the rage of that creation he is as ruthless as the woman, as dangerous to her as she is to him, and as horribly fascinating. Of all human struggles there is none so treacherous and remorseless as the struggle between the artist man and the mother woman. Which shall use up the other? that is the issue between them. And it is all the deadlier because, in your romanticist cant, they love one another.'

This is a tremendous indictment of the artist man, unless we can prove that his purpose is superior to Nature's or that it is Nature's purpose and, therefore, he can no more help himself than the mother woman can help tempting a man to fertilise her.

But is it true? Are artist men as ruthless as Tanner asserts they are? G.B.S., in the passage about the man who lets his mother drudge at seventy to earn his living, is here repeating the romantic nonsense that he let his mother earn *his* living. The fact is otherwise. There are artist men, Balzac, for example, who behave like ravenous animals and are indifferent to the common claims of life, but these men are rare, and it is only among the criminal and evil-minded and mentally disturbed people that we find this unpopularity which Tanner insists is a common characteristic of the artist man. The higher and more civilised the creature becomes, the more careful of those dependent upon him, he is.

If the creation of life is the supreme form of art, we perceive that there is no war in any significant sense between men and women, each fighting for a dissimilar purpose, but an essential union not only of bodies, but of minds and spirits in a great effort to make the creatures begotten and conceived finer than the man who begot, and the woman who conceived them. The state of war, in short is ended: a state of alliance has begun.

This great comedy definitely marks a period in the history of the English theatre: the period in which philosophic thought in a large way was first dramatised. If G.B.S. had never written anything else than *Man and Superman*, his value to the theatre would still have been immense. For the first time in our history, an audience was found for the play of ideas. The multitude, of course, still went to musical comedies and pantomimes and spectacular pieces, just as it reads only detective tales and wild westerns and shockers. There is nothing surprising in this. The general mind is meagre. The abundant mind is rare. But it is the abundant mind which prevails over the general mind; and, in time, even the musical comedies and the shockers improve and the detective tale ceases to be a jigsaw puzzle and becomes intelligent enquiry.

120

Man and Superman had the singular effect of impressing men and infuriating women. The sentimental woman who saw herself simply as her husband's helpmate, a woman without will or purpose of her own, asserted that G.B.S. was ignorant of feminine charm and selfless nature; and she denied passionately that there was a word of truth in his statement that she hunted a man for her own purpose. But the realist, even when she resented the exposure of the woman's object, admitted that there was truth in the Shavian argument. R. F. Rattray says that his lectures on the subject were fiercely debated by women, one of whom 'blurted out, "We know it's true, but we don't like men to know it!" ' The supreme fact, however, is surely to be found in the woman's attitude towards her husband and children. If she has to choose between saving the life of the man or that of the child, which will she save? In nearly every case, the child. And she will save it because the child is the life that is to come, whereas her husband is the life that is nearly over. This distinction between the child and its father is made by all creatures. Even that most timid of fowls, the domestic hen, will fight fiercely for her chickens, though she will not lift a feather in defence of the cock.

It was in the preface to this play, that G.B.S. first definitely enunciated his belief in the Life Force, as he called it, which was derived from Bergson's doctrine of *élan vital* or Creative Evolution. There is a passage in this preface which has left a mark on the mind of every person who has read it, whether or not he shares G.B.S.'s creed:

> 'This is the true joy of life, the being used for a purpose recognised by yourself as a mighty one: the being thoroughly worn out before you are thrown on the scrap heap; the being a force of Nature instead of a feverish, selfish little clod of ailments complaining that the world will not devote itself to making you happy.'

In this statement, we have the focal point of his religion. But it is a statement which disturbs as much as it impresses the mind. It seems to suggest a noble abnegation of self, a deep desire to fulfil the purpose of the universe, but is it truly so? G.B.S. never came to a decision about the function and purpose of man that is clear and explicit. It is not easy to know what he meant by the Life Force. Did he believe in God? He certainly believed in something that can be compared with the general faith in a Supreme Spirit, but the Life Force must always seem insufficient to those who cannot exist without the hope of a God who knows what he is doing and why he is doing it. There is no assurance in G.B.S.'s doctrine that the Life Force has a clear understanding of its intention or that it can perform what it wishes to do.

The Life Force acts on the principle of trial and error. It tries to do universally what Sidney Webb tried to do terrestrially: establish a neat order of existence in which there will be a place for everything, and everything will be in its place.

The existence of evil is a proof, in the Shavian doctrine, that God is an imperfect being trying to become perfect. Evil, indeed, in this belief ceases to be evil in the sense of sheer malignance, and becomes merely inefficiency. A man who makes an experiment which is a failure is not a wicked man: he has failed for one reason or another to discover the right means to his end. George Stephenson was not an evil engineer, he was not even an inefficient engineer because The Rocket was a clumsy engine in comparison with The Capitals Express: he had made the best engine that he was capable of making in the conditions of his time.

The Life Force, seeking for a perfection it does not yet possess, had begun by using mindless creatures who were not aware of its intention. Found to be useless because they could not consciously assist the Life Force in the realisation of its intention, they were either scrapped, as were the mammoth beasts, or made servile to the needs of the finer creature the Life Force eventually evolved: Man.

Man differs from all the tools the Life Force had previously made in the supreme respect that he has a mind with which he can understand the purpose of the Force, and can, if he wishes, help or frustrate it. The creation of a thinking instrument established freedom, for freedom is essentially the right to choose. Man can help or hinder God. He can follow his own purpose and deliberately frustrate God's. But he will do this at his peril, for God, despite his great patience, will not consent to be patient for ever. If Man opposes him or refuses to help his purpose, then it is certain that God will eventually tire of Man and scrap him as he scrapped the sabre-toothed tiger and the dinosaurs. That done, he will seek to make another instrument more amenable to his will.

Certain conclusions, adverse to G.B.S.'s creed, may be drawn from this summary account of it. One is that there is no freedom of choice for man. He must either obey the Life Force or be scrapped. He will, indeed, be scrapped whether he consents or declines help. 'The true joy of life' includes 'being thoroughly worn out before you are thrown on the scrap heap', as if you were a chisel that has lost its edge and can no longer chip. There is, apparently, to be no participation by Man in the perfection achieved by his aid, assuming that it is achieved. Man's fate, in fact, will be that of the mammoth beast.

There is worse than this. For Man has no assurance that the Life Force will ever find or create the perfection it seeks. Why, then, should Man assist a Force which does not know what it wants, except to be perfect, and cannot give its creature the slightest assurance that it will ever be able to fulfil its intention? For what purpose is the perfection sought? If, as we must suppose from G.B.S.'s assertion that the instruments which enable the Force to become perfect are to be scrapped when they are no longer required, who and what will share this perfection? The Life Force alone?

This summary account of G.B.S.'s religious belief will make it seem to be heavy stuff for a comedy, and those who have neither seen nor read it may feel discouraged from doing either. If they are, they will miss a brilliant and delightful play which is full of the thoughtful laughter demanded by Meredith. It grows in popularity, drawing at each revival larger and larger audiences whose pleasure in its wit and audacious thought and finely drawn characters is abundant. The dialogue is swift and must be spoken swiftly. Speeches a hundred and more words long are common, and some of those spoken by Tanner are between three and four hundred words in length. If they are not spoken as swiftly by the actor as they were conceived by their author, they must lose about half their effect. Granville-Barker always instructed the players to remember that the Shavian manner was that of Italian opera, and he besought them to speak their lines as if they were being sung by impassioned baritones and tenors, sopranos and contraltos. Yet the lines are not laborious. They come swiftly and easily off the tongue, and even the reader finds the lines slipping quickly past his eyes.

Those critics who maintain that it is G.B.S.'s best play, have warrant for their belief. There had never been such a play on the stage before, and audiences took time to become accustomed to it, but when its style and thought no longer puzzled or shocked them they accepted it without question or demur. The long tuition of his audience was ended. He had taught people to like and enjoy his work, and they were now eager for it. His comedy established authority unfailingly over the audience from curtain rise to curtain fall, and it possesses that singular power which is shown only by great plays, the power to fuse an audience so that it ceases to be a collection of dissimilar individuals and becomes a united group of men and women with a single interest. This power is exhibited in plays so different from each other in all other respects as *The Trojan Women* of Euripides, *Hamlet*, and *The Wild Duck*.

121

About the time that *Man and Superman* was published, G.B.S. made the acquaintance of Robert Loraine, an acquaintance which was to quicken into friendship. Loraine, who was born at New Brighton in Cheshire on January 14, 1876, was the son of an actor, named Henry Bilcliffe, who had been disinherited by his puritanical father for becoming an actor. He was forbidden to use his own name on the stage, so he chose that of his mother: a name more pleasing than Bilcliffe. Robert Loraine, an uncommonly handsome young man, followed his father on to the stage and remained there, until, on the outbreak of the South African War, he enlisted as a trooper in the Imperial Herefordshire Yeomanry. Loraine, like T. E. Lawrence, was the sort of man who greatly interested G.B.S. He led a life of varied adventure. He fought in two wars, the Boer War and the First World War, and was a pioneer of aviation, nearly losing his life when an aeroplane in which he was flying fell into the Irish Sea.

On his discharge from the Army at the end of the war with the Boers, Loraine joined the American stage, where he quickly became popular. He was known as the handsomest actor in New York, a renown which displeased him and made him consider his situation in the theatre with great gravity. It was not his intention to become a matinee idol, and he decided that he must make a drastic change in the sort of play he produced. He had earned and saved enough money to be able to please himself. 'I was desperately considering some other way of making a living when, on a train journey from Boston to New York, I read *Man and Superman*. Whether I cried Eureka or no, I knew at once that this was a marvellous play—simply bound to succeed in the theatre—and danced a jig of delight up and down the corridor of the train, elated beyond bounds by the brilliance of the book itself, and rejoicing at the prospect of producing and acting in a masterpiece. Here at last, was a play, a play with a difference. Not only would I be rescued from the necessity of acting the comparative bosh that had been suggested, but I could do work in the theatre of which I would be proud. And I knew beyond doubt that fortune would come as well as fame.'[1]

But he had not reckoned with the managers of the New York Theatre, who were still as obtuse about Shaw as the managers in London. 'It did not enter my head for a moment that the managers who were seeking a play in which to "star" me, could fail to see the irresistible quality of *Man and Superman* as a commercial proposition; that is, as a Big Profit-making Success, quite apart from its merits as a

[1] *Robert Loraine, Actor, Soldier, Airman.* By his wife, Winifred Loraine, p. 75.

great and enlightening piece of work. And it was an absolute facer to me when they thought I was insane in suggesting it. "Not a play at all," they said. "Just talk." ' When he reminded them of the success Richard Mansfield had had with *Arms and the Man* and *The Devil's Disciple*, they explained it away by saying that it was entirely due to Mansfield's acting, who 'had done nothing to discourage this impression'. Loraine might have said that they were paying him a poor compliment by implying that he would fail to do what Mansfield was alleged to have done.

He read the play to fifteen managers, all of whom were eager to exploit him, but 'they would have nothing to do with it'. One manager, Lee Shubert, having heard Loraine read the play six times, suggested that the play might be tried out in a small town with a cheap company, on the principle, presumably, that since Loraine seemed to be infatuated with it, he must be indulged as inexpensively as possible. But Loraine demanded the finest theatre in New York, 'with a first-rate company', and insisted that the production must be lavish in fine scenery 'to take away any suspicion that it' was 'intellectual'.

That was the end of Lee Shubert. Nevertheless, Loraine persisted. G.B.S. would grant him the American rights for a payment of £200 in advance of royalties at 10% of the gross receipts, but this sum would make a hole in his savings, and, as he was unable to obtain any financial backing in New York, he decided to return to London to seek assistance. This was in 1905. The play had been put on at the Court Theatre for its first morning performances, and Loraine went to see it, and deeply disapproved of Granville-Barker's production. In the foyer of the theatre, he met Shaw for the first time. His description of G.B.S., with whom he lunched on the following day, is interesting not only because of the vivid style in which it is written, but because it expresses something of the feeling that the majority of people felt when they met him. Loraine was amazed 'at the vital and spiritual force of this astonishing man, so different from anyone else I have known . . . his wit and wisdom seem to me to be like the fresh and uncontaminated outlook on life of a baby, miraculously made supremely articulate. . . . I have a foolish self-assertive independence which fights against the idea of hero-worship, yet I was never free from the impression when Shaw was speaking to me that he might at any moment ascend to Heaven like Elisha on a chariot of fire.'

His meeting with G.B.S. was not the only encounter he had in London that summer. He was summoned to the presence of a charming old Jew, called Charles Frohman, who was drowned when the Lusitania was torpedoed by the Germans in May 1915. Frohman was

394

a man of such honesty of character that no one who worked with him had a contract. His word was enough for everybody. When Loraine left the Savoy Hotel, he had an agreement with Frohman to finance and manage a production of *Man and Superman* in New York that autumn. Frohman was the only American manager to whom Loraine had not read the play.

The rehearsals were not easy or amicable. Loraine was not content with second best. He would have best or nothing. 'He tried out and dismissed thirteen Strakers, four Tavys, history does not record how many Ann Whitefields, or, to take a tiny part, Papa Hector Malones.' He insisted on bringing a fine Anglo-Irish actor, J. D. Beveridge, to New York to play the last named part, although the cost of doing so was 'many hundred pounds' instead of a hundred dollars. At the end of the rehearsals, Frohman, who had never encountered producers like Loraine, was, probably for the first time in his life, frightened. He foresaw an expensive flop.

But his fears were groundless. The play was produced at the Hudson Theatre in New York, on September 4, 1905. It was an immediate success. A month after its first performance, the receipts were the highest in the history of that theatre. 'From that date on, the play took anything between 11,000 dollars to 12,359 dollars and 50 cents a week (equivalent to £2,500) and broke the Ziegfeld Follies takings for that season. This was an unheard of achievement for a non-musical play, let alone an "intellectual" play.' The extraordinary fact about the production is that while it was smashing the theatrical records of New York, the published play was banned from the New York libraries on the ground that it would pervert the morals of the young. The run lasted for eight months, ending only because the summer heat had begun. In the following September, Loraine took it on tour for a further seven months. In May 1907, he came to London and acted Tanner with the company at the Court Theatre. He now repatriated himself, living comfortably on the £40,000 he had made out of *Man and Superman* in America, and anticipating the time when he could make his own production of the play in London.

The opportunity did not come at once. He had first to play Bluntschli in *Arms and the Man* at the Savoy. It kept him there for five months. Then he created the part of St John Hotchkiss in *Getting Married* at the Haymarket. In the summer of 1908, he was the guest of the Shaws at Llanbedr in Wales where the Fabian Society was holding a summer school. It was during this holiday that both Loraine and G.B.S. were nearly drowned. There had been a fierce storm in the night, and the sea was rough, but G.B.S. decided that they should both swim as usual. They found themselves being floated out on the tide, and they nearly failed to get back. When at last, feeling exhausted, they flopped down on the shore, gasping for breath, G.B.S. remarked, 'That was a near thing', and then went off to fetch his sandshoes. On his return, Loraine asked him whether he had had the experience which the superstitious believe all drowning people enjoy or suffer, of seeing their whole lives flash through their minds in a few moments. 'He shook his head. Nor I,' .said Loraine.

> 'Did you think of God, or Hell, or Heaven?'
>
> 'No,' said Shaw. 'A man does not think of fairy tales within two minutes of certain death. I thought of nothing but pressing practical things. First, I wanted to tell you not to try to swim to shore, as it was of no use and the effort would exhaust you. The thing to do was to let the sea take you where it liked and keep afloat as long as possible. But the noise of the waves was too loud and you were too far away. Then I saw that we were being carried along the shore; and I considered whether the people there could help us if we sang out. But there were no fishermen there; only trippers who would have upset a boat if they had tried to launch it. Then I thought of Charlotte getting the news that I was drowned, and of how I had not altered my will and how she would never be able to understand my arrangements with my translators. Then I saw you were having a hard time when the big waves came, and thought of what a pity it was that you should be lost in the strength of your youth with the world before you, and that I didn't matter, as I had shot my bolt and done my work. Then I asked myself how many more strokes I could swim before the effort became too great, and I had rather drown than try any more. Then my foot struck a stone, and instead of saying, "Thank God!" I said, "Damn!" Then came a really awful moment. When I got on my legs you had vanished. It was my clear duty to dive after you and rescue you. I could not go home without you and say I had left you to drown. And then came the frightful humiliation of realising that I was utterly incapable of swimming another stroke. I had reached my limit. And then I found that you were standing close behind me. But, by God, it took the conceit out of me.'[1]

122

The Shaw vogue in the English-speaking world had now seriously begun. It coincided with an extraordinary revival of the theatre in Great Britain. Repertory theatres were starting all over England, and even in Wales and Scotland.

Amateur dramatic companies of a more responsible sort than had hitherto been seen in the country, were founded so rapidly that many dramatists were making good incomes from their performances. These

[1] *Robert Loraine* by Winifred Loraine, p. 95.

companies are now so numerous and, on the whole, adventurous that even highbrow authors are able to live on the fees their productions bring them. Plays of quality are performed by amateur societies which have never been produced in the West End, and there are now many able producers of plays whose experience has been gained exclusively in such societies. The days when amateur productions were servile copies of West End productions are over; and it is becoming rarer for authors to be asked to supply amateurs with a prompt copy of a play. The few who ask me for one, do not receive it. They are told to make their own productions.

G.B.S.'s renown was spread in the provinces by the repertory theatres, although his plays were not easy of performance in them. They demand uncommon skill in the cast, and settings which are sometimes beyond the financial and stage resources of the management. *Candida*'s popularity, in comparison with *Captain Brassbound's Conversion*, is partly due to the fact that it can be performed in ordinary day clothes in one interior set, and that it has only six characters, whereas there are fourteen characters and a number of supernumerary parts in *Captain Brassbound's Conversion*, which has three unusual sets, one of them outdoor, and requires semi-tropical as well as Moorish costumes and American naval uniforms. The cost of producing the second play is obviously much greater than the cost of the first. *Androcles and the Lion* is seldom performed by amateurs or by repertory companies because it almost demands a revolving stage in addition to a large cast, including an acrobat to play the Lion, and expensive ancient clothes. *Caesar and Cleopatra* is impossible for impecunious players.

Nevertheless, Shaw's plays brought health and strength to the repertory theatres and prepared the way for the work of other authors who, without his lead, could hardly have hoped for production. The entire character of the drama was transformed after G.B.S. Even Ibsen was not so influential in changing it. The historian of the theatre will be compelled to acknowledge very handsomely the debt the theatre in the first half of the twentieth century owed him. It was he, beyond a shadow of a doubt, who created an intelligent audience for intelligent plays and educated actors and actresses who could perform in them.

123

With increasing popularity, he became prolific. *Man and Superman* was written in 1903. It was followed in 1904 by a brilliant short play, called *How He Lied To Her Husband*, which is commonly considered to be a skit on *Candida*, and by *John Bull's Other Island*. In

1905, came *Major Barbara*, and in 1906, *The Doctor's Dilemma*. He worked at that rate for a large part of the rest of his life, in addition to the chores he did for The Fabian Society and the lectures he delivered in various parts of the country and his journalism.

None of these plays was routine. In each of them, people were put on the stage who were seldom seen there or seen only to be derided. If a member of The Salvation Army was among the characters in a play, he or she was almost invariably mocked and maligned. It is remarkable that only in a musical comedy, *The Belle of New York*, and *Major Barbara* are Salvationists treated with respect and as normal human beings. It was not G.B.S.'s habit to follow the derisive mob. He was prompt to recognise nobility in a person or an organisation, and was equally prompt in defending the derided from contempt and scorn.

Few religious bodies could have been more antipathetic in belief to G.B.S. than Booth's Army. It held, and still holds, a fundamentalist faith which was repulsive to him, accepting the Bible as an exact history of the human race as well as an infallible and inspiring guide to happiness; though Abraham and Jacob are not men who are fit to be regarded as models for anybody. A Salvationist is almost certainly a person who believes that the world was submerged, presumably to a depth of about five miles, by a flood which drowned the entire population, animal and human, with the exception of four men and four women and a small collection of beasts and birds. Questions of probability do not perturb his mind, and he has no difficulty in believing that Noah and his three sons were able to build an ark large enough to accommodate and provide an ample food supply not only for eight persons, but also for two animals of every sort. The congestion, to say nothing of the stench, must have been appalling in a vessel of no great size which included among its occupants two elephants, two rhinoceros, two hippopotamuses, two camels and two giraffes, in addition to a couple of lions, tigers, bears and other beasts. The Bible contains no hint of any increase, human or animal, in the population of the Ark, but there must have been some.

The obsolete theology of The Salvation Army, however, did not prevent G.B.S. from perceiving the simple beauty of the average Salvationist's life or the great power for good the Army is. He had praised its brass bands when superior persons were busy sneering at them, and he knew better than any other writer, because of the enquiries made by the Webbs, that their social work was immensely beneficial both to the individual 'rescued' and the community. The Army could influence men and women who were impervious to the calls of other religious bodies. That, to G.B.S.'s mind, was the essential

fact. Some years after he had written *Major Barbara*, I told him
story about a Salvationist which pleased him immensely. During
strike in South Africa which caused a good deal of distress, the
religious leaders called a meeting of the strikers so that their physical
needs, at least, could be satisfied. They decided that the strikers should
be grouped according to their sect. The Anglican clergyman stood up
and requested all those who belonged to the Church of England to
stand over there. He was followed by the Roman Catholic priest and
several Noncomformist ministers who gave a similar direction. Then
the Salvationist stood up, and said, 'All you chaps who don't belong
to anybody, come to us!'

The layout of *Major Barbara* was characteristic of his style. Who
but he would have opened *You Never Can Tell* in the surgery of an
impoverished dentist or have ended his first act by making the
dentist give a patient gas before he began to pull out a tooth? Would
any other dramatist have made the principal character in the play an
old waiter whose son was a member of the bar and a 'silk'? The
second act of *Major Barbara* is laid in a Salvation Army shelter in
West Ham, and a brilliant act it is: almost a complete play in itself.
The other two acts are laid, the first in a West End drawing-room and
the third, partly in the drawing-room and partly in a model ammuni-
tion factory town.

He was careless in writing the play, as lazy over it as Shakespeare
was over Henry VIII, which is one of the worst-bungled plays ever
written by a man of supreme genius. He had not made up his mind
about Barbara, nor had Shakespeare made up his mind about the
King. Who is the principal character in Henry VIII? Henry Irving
had no doubt about this when he produced the play. He took the
part of Wolsley. The title suggests that the King is the principal
character, but the Cardinal takes a more prominent part than Henry
does in the beginning of the play, though Cranmer looks like acting
him off the stage at the end. Queen Katherine lives in our minds as
vividly as her husband, and so, indeed, does that poor little creature,
Anne Bullen. The title of G.B.S.'s play predisposes us to regard
Barbara as the principal character, but her father, Andrew Undershaft, reduces her stature, as he reduces his wife's, every time he opens
his lips.

The play is curiously incoherent, and three of the characters are
little more than lumber: Stephen, the son; Sarah, one of the daughters;
and Charles Lomax who is Sarah's young man. Sarah is scarcely
alive. Lomax is a lay figure of fun. The best that can be said for him
is that he has some resemblance to Mr Tite Barnacle in *Little Dorrit;*
and he may be described as that bureaucrat's debilitated grandson.
Stephen, who starts off well enough, peters out. The scene between

399

him and his mother, Lady Britomart Undershaft, at the beginning
of the play is excellent fun and suggests that Stephen's inevitable
revolt against her will be important, but he falls to pieces thereafter
and does not appear in the second act. He is Philip Clandon in
You Never Can Tell run to seed. Lady Britomart herself is less clearly
realised than Mrs Clandon, and she, too, loses authority as the play
develops. She may be described as Ann Whitefield of *Man and Superman* in her middle age: still seeking and obtaining her own way while
pretending that her sole desire is to please other people.

One of G.B.S.'s beliefs was that a person living on unearned
income and ignorant of its source was worse than the person who
directed the source from which the polluted income came. This was
the main point in his first play, *Widowers' Houses*, and he makes it
again in *Major Barbara*, but less effectively. It is difficult to believe
that Stephen Undershaft does not know that he is living on the money
his father makes out of manufacturing armaments. It is harder still
to believe that he would have seen anything wrong in this. When we
are asked to believe that the lightminded Charles Lomax, who is
nearly brainless, is shocked by the nature of Andrew Undershaft's
business, reason revolts. Is it a sin to have shares in an armaments
factory in such a world as this? Ought Woolwich Arsenal and Devon-
port Docks to be scrapped?

There is a great theme in *Major Barbara*, though G.B.S. muffs it,
except in his brilliant second act. This is one of the plays about rebels
which is also a play about a great individual. Shaw calls it an example
of 'the conflict between real life and the romantic imagination', a
piece of 'tragi-comic irony', but he could better have called it the
tragedy of an idealist who discovers that her ideals are false, or cannot
be realised in her lifetime. Barbara is shaken to the heart's core when
The Salvation Army accepts money from brewers and distillers and
manufacturers of guns and shells, and, in her despair, throws up her
commission.

But her father, the wisest person in the play, restores her sense
of proportion in the last act when he answers her complaint that she,
who had so nearly saved the soul of Bill Walker, the guttersnipe of the
second act, had lost him through her father's gift of £5,000 to the
Army's funds. 'Does my daughter despair so easily?' he asks. 'Can
you strike a man to the heart and leave no mark on him?' His reply
sobers Barbara. 'You may be a devil,' she replies, 'but God speaks
through you sometimes!' She has learnt the lesson that truly religious
people with keen spiritual insight have always learnt, that God is not
particular about the instrument he uses: he is particular only about
the purpose he achieves with it. Abraham was undoubtedly a mean
and cowardly man whom we rightly suspect of consenting to his wife's

seduction by the Pharaoh, but God, nevertheless, used him for his purpose. William Booth would have said much the same to Barbara had she gone to him to complain that the Army had taken money from men who were the cause of sin. Why should he not use their wealth for *his* purpose? When reproved for singing hymns to music-hall tunes, he replied that he saw no reason why the devil should have all the best tunes.

The great moment in the play is when Barbara and her father exchange the speeches cited in the previous paragraph. But the imp of mischief which sometimes possessed G.B.S. and forced him to tear himself and his play to pieces got the better of him in the last act and made a farce of the rest of it. It cannot be called broken-backed, for the second act, which is the back, is superb, but it does not cohere. The strength is dissipated in knockabouts.

There are numerous obscurities in the play. We are not told what took Barbara, the daughter of a millionaire and the granddaughter of an earl, into the commissioned ranks of The Salvation Army. This is not in the least improbable. Booth attracted a number of men and women of good family and high position into his Army. One of his first Commissioners was a judge in India. Another had been an Anglican clergyman. A third, Adelaide Cox, belonged to a family of distinguished soldiers. A princess of the royal house of Sweden was one of his adherents. Our complaint is not that G.B.S. makes a woman of family do what we think a woman of family would not do, but that he does not account for her conversion. Some powerful force must have possessed Barbara's spirit to make her leave her fashionable home in Wilton Crescent and live in an Army shelter in West Ham. We are left to surmise what it was.

Major Barbara and *Caesar and Cleopatra* are said to be the only plays by G.B.S. in which there is any development of character. In all his other plays, the characters are static: exactly the same at the end of the play as they were at the beginning. But what do we mean by development or evolution of character? Is it a change of nature or a change of opinion? Human beings are rarely changed suddenly and entirely. Those who believe, as G.B.S. appears to believe in this play, that a person can completely disrupt himself in less than an hour, as Bill Walker does, are believers in magic and fairy tales, and may justly be described as superstitious.

Barbara's ignorance of her father, apart from her knowledge of his trade, is implausible. Would not a girl of her character and disposition have made at least one effort to redeem this stupendous sinner?

All the defects in the first and third acts, however, are made to seem trivial by the vivacity and vigour of the second which is full of veracious character and moving action. It is a trifling fault that Barbara is in command of a shelter to which men as well as women resort. The Army does not put a shelter where toughs are likely to be found, under the control of a woman, though young girl officers of the Army have often gone without a tremor into slum areas where the police dare not patrol except in pairs. But this is a minor fault in the play, and can be justified by its results.

The theme is akin to that of *Captain Brassbound's Conversion*, that a soft answer turneth away wrath. Lady Cicely Waynflete overcomes Brassbound and divests him of his ignominious passion for revenge by treating him civilly and sensibly. Barbara and the young girl officer, Jenny Hill, confound the ruffian, Bill Walker, by refusing to feel any grievance against him or to take the money he offers in compensation for his assault on Jenny. All they want from him is a broken and a contrite heart.

There is nothing indeterminate about the character of Bill Walker. Even the curious character, called Cusins, the professor of Greek who is engaged to be married to Barbara and joins the Army as a big drummer, does not seem implausible, a statement with which Professor Gilbert Murray would probably agree, for he was the original of this character. It was easy for G.B.S. to make Cusins attractive as well as plausible. He had only to take one look at Murray and the job was done.

It is in this act that the familiar Shavian theme is set out: Bill Walker is painfully disconcerted when he is told by Barbara that Jenny Hill, whom he has brutally beaten, is praying for him.

But this is not the only theme of the play. The wickedness of curable poverty is another and, perhaps, the main theme.

In his preface to the play, G.B.S. asks this question: Now what does Let Him be Poor mean? and answers it thus:

'It means let him be weak. Let him be ignorant. Let him become a nucleus of disease. Let him be a standing exhibition and example of ugliness and dirt. Let him have rickety children. Let him be cheap and drag his fellows down to his own price by selling himself to do their work. Let his habitations turn our cities into poisonous congeries of slums. Let his daughters infect our young men with the diseases of the streets and his sons revenge him by turning the nation's manhood into scrofula, cowardice, cruelty, hypocrisy, political imbecility, and all the other fruits of oppression and malnutrition. Let the undeserving become still less deserving; and let the deserving lay up for himself, not treasures in heaven, but horrors in hell upon earth. This being so, is it really wise to let him be poor . . . ? Suppose we were to abolish all penalties for such activities, and decide that poverty is the one thing we will not tolerate—that every adult with less than, say, £365 a year shall be painlessly but inexorably killed, and every hungry half naked child forcibly fattened and clothed, would not that be an enormous improvement on our existing system, which has already destroyed so many civilizations, and is visibly destroying ours in the same way?'

But would the system of compulsory comfort be an improvement on the system that existed when *Major Barbara* was written? We have achieved something like it in the Welfare State, but are we pleased with the result? One of the axioms of the Fabians was that men who are well paid, well fed, and well housed will work more conscientiously and do much better work than men who are badly paid, badly fed and badly housed. Is that axiom borne out in the practice of our time?

G.B.S. never faced the fact that two households, each living in the same street on the same amount of money, may differ profoundly from each other. In one house, may be a sloven and a slut who neglects her home, her husband and her children, while in the other may be a careful housewife, whose work is the foundation of a happy home. The economic argument is sound so far as it goes, but it does not go very far. It is the argument used by Undershaft in the great discussion with his daughter Barbara in the third act.

Undershaft describes the seven deadly sins: food, clothing, firing, rent, taxes, respectability and children. Nothing, he says, 'can lift those seven millstones from Man's neck but money; and the spirit cannot soar until the millstones are lifted.' He goes on to describe poverty as 'the worst of crimes'.

'All the other crimes are virtues beside it: all the other dishonours are chivalry itself by comparison. Poverty blights whole cities; spreads horrible pestilences; strikes dead the very souls of all who come within sight, sound or smell of it. What you call crime is nothing: a murder here and a theft there, a blow now and a curse then: what do they matter? they are only the accidents and illnesses of life: there are not fifty genuine professional criminals in London. But there are millions of poor people, abject people, dirty people, ill fed, ill clothed people. They poison us morally and physically: they kill the happiness of society: they force us to do away with our own liberties and to organize unnatural cruelties for fear they should rise against us and drag us down into their abyss. Only fools fear crime: we all fear poverty. Pah! (*turning to Barbara*) you talk of your half-saved ruffian in West Ham: you accuse me of dragging his soul back to perdition. Well, bring him to me here: and I will drag his soul back to salvation for you. Not by words and dreams; but by thirty eight shillings a week, a sound house in a handsome street, and a permanent job. In three weeks he will have a fancy waistcoat; in three months a tall hat and a chapel sitting; before the end of the year he will shake hands with a duchess at a Primrose League meeting, and join the Conservative Party.'

'And will he be the better for that?' Barbara demands. 'You know he will,' her father retorts.

> 'Don't be a hypocrite, Barbara. He will be better fed, better housed, better clothed, better behaved; and his children will be pounds heavier and bigger. That will be better than an American cloth mattress in a shelter, chopping firewood, eating bread and treacle, and being forced to kneel down from time to time to thank heaven for it: knee drill, I think you call it. It is cheap work converting starving men with a Bible in one hand and a slice of bread in the other. I will undertake to convert West Ham to Mahometanism on the same terms. Try your hand on my men: their souls are empty because their bodies are full.'

Undershaft seems to have the best of the argument. *His* was the best of the argument in 1905. But if he and Barbara were having that discussion to-day, might not Undershaft discover that his daughter really had the better of the argument when she asked her searching question? There is a hint of this in the end of the play when a transfigured Barbara exclaims to Cusins: 'My father shall never throw it in my teeth again that my converts were bribed with bread. I have got rid of the bribe of bread. I have got rid of the bribe of heaven. Let God's work be done for its own sake: the work he had to create us to do because it cannot be done except by living men and women. When I die, let him be in my debt, not I in his; and let me forgive him as becomes a woman of my rank.'

'Then', says Cusins, 'the way of life lies through the factory of death?'

'Yes,' Barbara replies ecstatically, 'through the raising of hell to heaven and of man to God, through the unveiling of an eternal light in the Valley of the Shadow.' She is about to return to the colours, slightly different now in hue, which she deserted in despair, crying out, to the great scandal of some of the dramatic critics, 'My God; why hast thou forsaken me?'

124

G.B.S. became more and more preoccupied by this economic argument until he reached the point at which he advocated equal incomes for everybody. His was not the only mind which was disturbed by it. John Galsworthy, who was essentially a Forsyte, was incapable of believing that a man could be poor and happy. There is no sign anywhere in G.B.S.'s work that he ever adequately realised that men are less interested in money than they are in power, though he had an object lesson of this fact constantly before him in the person of Sidney Webb, and a still more familiar example in himself. W. B.

Yeats, writing to Stephen Gwynn in June of 1906, said of him, 'Shaw does not care about money.' If, in his studies of The Salvation Army for *Major Barbara*, he had reflected on the singular career of its Founder, William Booth, his faith in the economic argument would have been severely shaken.

Booth, determined on his own method of redeeming the damned, separated himself from the Methodist Connexion, of which he was a minister, because those who were in authority over him insisted that he should cease to be an evangelist and become a pastor. He declined, and resigned from his ministry. He also resigned from his income, a serious resignation for a man who was the husband of a delicate saint and the father of a large family of delicate children. Having cut himself adrift, he went out one dark and dreary evening and took his stand on a patch of mouldy earth, called Mile End Waste, where, with no other apparatus than a Bible and an umbrella, he began what was to become one of the world's greatest religious organisations. The umbrella was not intended to protect him from the elements: it was waved in the air to call the attention of passers-by to the fact that a lonely and almost penniless man had a message from their Lord God.

At no time of his life had William Booth a larger income than £500 a year, and for a large part of it, his income was little more than a pound a week. But could he have done more than he did, had his income been £5,000 or £50,000 a year? It was not his monetary means that made him the man he was and enabled him to found his Army: it was the flame in his heart.

G.B.S. was quick to realise a source of danger to the Army in its growing activities. 'It is building up a business organisation which will compel it eventually to see that its present staff of enthusiastic commanders shall be succeeded by a bureaucracy of men of business who will be no better than Bishops, and perhaps a good deal more unscrupulous. That has always happened sooner or later to great orders founded by saints; and the order founded by St William Booth is not exempt from this danger.'

Here he was stating a profound and disturbing fact. The breath was scarcely out of the body of St Francis of Assisi before his successor was changing the spirit of his Order. Would Ignatius Loyola recognise in the contemporary Jesuits the Order he founded? The world has sore cause to realise how St Paul changed the society founded by Christ. The chief occupation of many prominent Salvation Army officers is the collection of money to finance their social activities. They have little time left for the salvation of souls, with the result that the Army is now far from being the one Booth founded, and is little more than a Charity Organisation Society on a large scale.

Despite percipience in this matter, however, G.B.S. could not rid himself of Andrew Undershaft's delusion, that you have only to make a working-man better off financially to make him a better man intellectually and spiritually. He was beginning to suspect that he had deceived himself a little while before his death, but the doubt was raised too late. There was nothing now that he could do about it.

125

In the year in which *Major Barbara* was written, G.B.S., on the solicitation of Charlotte, went to Ireland for the first time since he had left it thirty years earlier. He liked it no better than he had liked it then.

It was in the following summer, 1906, that William Archer complained in the press that G.B.S. had never written a tragedy, by which he meant a play concluding in death. A comedian is said to be less than a tragedian because tears are more universal in their origin than laughter. Archer doubted, indeed, if G.B.S. could dramatise death. If his doubt were substantial then G.B.S. was a small genius, a dealer only in gaiety, incapable of grief. It was while Archer's challenge was being deliberated that Granville Barker asked for a new play to be performed at the Court. Talking to Charlotte, Barker casually mentioned a doctor who was being treated for tuberculosis in a London hospital, and the conversation then turned to a general discussion on the vast trouble taken by medical men to preserve useless and even harmful lives. A murderer who attempts, but fails to commit suicide is tended with great care only to be brought to trial for his crime and subsequently hanged. The conclusion of the casual conversation was that such useless or harmful lives should be quietly ended. It was far too simple to be considered, for who can tell what is useful and what is not? Darwin seemed to his elders to be very idle at Shrewsbury and Cambridge because he spent too many hours searching for plants and butterflies, and was warned that if he did not amend his ways he might come to a bad end. Let him pore over his books so that he could take a degree that might make him an assistant master in a third-rate academy.

What ground have we for the belief that the care given even to the least worthy of men and women is wasted? An important discovery can as well be made on the body of an incorrigible scoundrel as on the body of shining saint, may, perhaps, be more likely to be made on the sinner's body than the saint's because his life has exposed him to greater variety of experience.

Charlotte, whose casual interjections in conversation were often the stimulant of great activity in her husband's mind, remembered that Sir Almroth Wright, a famous bacteriologist, while examining a patient at St Mary's Hospital in the London suburb of Paddington, was asked by an assistant if he could add another to the small number of people he could treat on his new opsonic system. Wright's reply was, 'Is he worth it?' G.B.S., the moment he heard Charlotte's reminder, immediately seized a notebook and began to write *The Doctor's Dilemma*. He worked so swiftly that the play, begun in the early summer, was performed for the first time at the Court on the 20th of the following November. Made in such haste, it might seem certain to be slap-dash in form and careless in invention, but it is not only one of the most brilliant of his plays, but one of the best-built. If the fifth act were omitted, *The Doctor's Dilemma* might well be regarded as his most skilfully constructed drama, without a waste word in it; but G.B.S. never knew when to leave off or let well alone, and he was liable to clutter his work with useless addenda. There is less excuse for the fifth act of *The Doctor's Dilemma* than there is for the Epilogue to *Saint Joan:* it is the nearest thing to irrelevant verbiage that its author ever wrote. Despite this act, however, the play, which is not a tragedy, but a comedy, is uncommonly compact, turning with skill on a vital theme, and people with brilliantly conceived characters.

Its theme is, which is the more valuable life, that of an a-moral artist of indisputably great quality in his craft or that of a mediocre doctor who is a good and decent man? The problem is not solved: it is merely stated; and Sir Colenso Ridgeon is allowed to save the commonplace doctor and sacrifice the unscrupulous artist for a wholly irrelevant reason: because he is in love with the artist's wife and wants her for himself. Ridgeon, on any moral principle that can be imagined, is guilty of murder. At the end of the play, we still do not know what, in G.B.S.'s opinion, Ridgeon should have done. Nevertheless, *The Doctor's Dilemma* displays him at the top of his form, a fact which makes his failure to solve the problem all the more reprehensible. A Christian, placed on the horns of such a dilemma, would have no difficulty in finding an answer to the problem. He would say there is no difference between one soul and another, and that the doctor should have made an effort to save both the patients: an assertion which would allow the doctor to retort that it is a meritorious act to release an immortal soul from a foul or defective body.

It is sometimes charged against G.B.S. that his characters were all fictitious: that is to say, that they were whimsical conceptions rather than authentic people. The charge is false. He was more interested in unusual men and women than he was in routine people, though, like the author of the apocryphal *Ecclesiasticus*, he was well aware of the value of the 'rude mechanicals', as Shakespeare called the proletariat, who, though they are seldom fit to seat themselves on the bench of judgment, maintain the state of the world. His unusual characters were not in the slightest degree figments of his imagination: they were solidly founded on fact; and the two principal people in *The Doctor's Dilemma*, Sir Colenso Ridgeon and Louis Dubedat, were faithful, not only in detail, but largely in substance, to men he had known with some intimacy. All his unusual characters, indeed, were so founded; and he drew them with such skill that their acquaintances easily recognised them. Sir Almroth Wright and Dr Edward Aveling, a man now remembered only by very few and very old people, were the originals from whom G.B.S. derived Colenso and Dubedat. There is a little of Aubrey Beardsley, an artist with a delicate sense of line and morbid, almost macabre imagination, in Dubedat. It was Beardsley, no doubt, who gave Dubedat his profession.

Almroth Wright was the most renowned of the five sons of the Rev. Charles H. H. Wright, an Ulster Episcopalian, who had held cures abroad as well as at home, and his Swedish wife, Ebba, a daughter of Nils Wilhelm Almroth, the Master of the Mint in Stockholm. The Wrights formed one of those rare families in which all, or nearly all, the members have notable careers. Four of their sons became distinguished, one of them, the second, being a near genius. They were Eric Blackwood, who went to the Bar and became Judge of the Supreme Court of Trinidad and Tobago, ending as Legal Adviser to the French Section of the Ministry of Munitions in 1920: Almroth Edward, who was renowned for his researches into pathological parasites and his work on vaccines and toxins; Charles Theodore Hagberg, a distinguished scholar who became London Librarian; and Major-General Henry Brooke Hesgstromer, an Engineer whose work in Egypt and Palestine during the First World War was remarkable both in the skill with which it was done and the ingenuity with which it was conceived. His blunt speech made enemies for him and prevented him from obtaining the higher recognition that was his due. Almroth and Charles were knighted: Henry almost certainly, but for his unruly tongue, would have been. The fifth son, Ernest, followed his father into the Anglican church. Doctors, more than parsons, prevailed among the Wrights, and their record in medicine is probably unique. Almroth is the son who concerns us here. G.B.S.'s portrait of him in *The Doctor's Dilemma* is so faithful, even in his quirks and idiosyncracies, that his kindred, when they saw the play performed, were full of laughter as they recognised them.

Aveling was a very different character. This almost totally a-moral man had only one fidelity: his faith in socialism. How he, who had no compunction in any other matter, contrived to maintain this fidelity with the courage of a Christian martyr is one of the insoluble mysteries. His borrowings and betrayals were so familiar to the early Fabians that all of them, seeing *The Doctor's Dilemma*, knew without any hesitation who was the original of Dubedat. His marital adventures were extensive and peculiar. He deserted his first wife to live with Eleanor Marx, the daughter of Karl, but when his wife died, he went off almost capriciously and married another woman than Eleanor who, left gravely in the lurch, committed suicide. Fact, in his career, was so much stranger than fiction that it seemed to have changed places with fiction.

Oddly enough, *The Doctor's Dilemma*, which was performed for the first time in New York at Wallack's Theatre on March 26, 1915, when Granville-Barker was the director, as a producer is called in America, has been less seldom revived than one might expect so fine a comedy to be. It is a gift to actors, but not to actresses. That, perhaps, is why. Yet, even with this defect, it should be the most frequently revived of all G.B.S.'s plays, if justice were done not only to a superbly composed piece, but one which offers actors of quality the opportunity of their lives.

126

We may pause for a moment to note that some of G.B.S.'s political and social forecasts were falsified by time. In the preface to *John Bull's Other Island*, he states that 'Home Rule will herald the day when the Vatican will go the way of Dublin Castle, and the island of saints assume the headship of her own church. It may seem incredible that long after the last Orangeman shall lay down his chalk for ever, the familiar scrawl on every blank wall in the north of Ireland, "To hell with the Pope"—he exaggerates the extent of its familiarity—will reappear in the south, traced by the hands of Catholics who shall have forgotten the traditional counter legend, "To hell with King William." ' It not only seems incredible: it is.

'Let us suppose that the establishment of a national government were to annihilate the oligarchic party by absorbing the Protestant garrison and making it a Protestant National Guard. The Roman Catholic laity, now a cipher, would organise itself; and a revolt against Rome and against the priesthood would ensue. The Irish Roman Catholic Church would become the official Irish Church. The Irish Parliament would insist on a voice in the promotion of churchmen; fees and contributions would be regulated; blackmail would be resisted; sweating in conventual factories and workshops would be stopped; and the ban would be taken off the universities. In a word, the Roman Catholic Church, against which Dublin Castle is powerless, would meet the one force on earth that can cope with it victoriously. That force is Democracy, a thing far more Catholic than itself. Until that force is let loose, the Protestant garrison can do nothing to the priesthood except consolidate it and drive the people to rally round it in defence of their altars against the foreigner and the heretic. When it *is* let loose, the Catholic laity will make as short work of sacerdotal tyranny in Ireland as it has done in France and Italy.'

Never was forecast so false. The Protestant population of Eire is now less than half what it was in 1901, and, if the decline continues at its present rate, there will not be a single Protestant left in Eire at the end of the century. So far is the Eirean Government from having a say in the promotion of priests that it has actually less influence in this respect than the British Government had. Not a single one of the reforms prophesied by G.B.S. has been made. On the contrary, the position in each case has deteriorated.

The thought that Ireland, thirty years after it had been given self-government, would still be partitioned, one part an alien Republic that was almost an enemy alien republic in the Second World War, and one part included in the United Kingdom, seems never to have entered G.B.S.'s head, even if the thought of any partition had ever occurred to him. It had never occurred even to Webb! . . .

Formerly, an Eirean could crack his fingers under the nose of his priest, and sometimes did, but he would be a bold man who did this to-day. There is a passage in the preface, under the cross-heading of The Revolt against the Priest, in which G.B.S. sets out a list of priestly oppressions under which the Irish Roman Catholic was then suffering. Every one of those oppressions is still, but more intensely, suffered by him. When Mr Costello's first Government introduced a Public Health Bill into the *Dail*, the Archbishop of Dublin summoned the Prime Minister and other members of his Cabinet to his house where they were severely reproved for their audacity and told to withdraw the Bill, which, almost abjectly, they did, the Minister of Health, Dr Noel Browne, being virtually dismissed for his offence.

Can we conceive of the Archbishop of Canterbury ordering Sir Anthony Eden or Mr Gaitskill to visit Lambeth Palace to be admonished for introducing a Bill into the House of Commons without his approval, and demanding that it shall be scrapped? Can we conceive of either of them obeying the command if the Archbishop were foolish enough to give it?

Man and Superman changed the general attitude of intelligent people to G.B.S. Previously, he had been regarded as a devilishly clever and amusing Irishman who had not a scrap of responsibility in his composition, a man who made fun of everything and thought, as Max Beerbohm caricatured him, that, standing on his head, he could see more clearly than people who were standing on their feet. *Man and Superman* changed that opinion. The published play was his first book success. Five impressions of it were sold in two years. Prior to its publication, he had thought that if a book of his sold a thousand copies, he had done very well.

He had now settled down to a routine of playwriting, lecturing less and writing fewer articles for the press. An extraordinary vogue in Shaw began. He was much sought after, and he went often to small parties, which he enjoyed, but seldom to large ones, where he was invariably bored, and never to late parties or to parties exclusively for men, if he could avoid them, because, as he said to me, the guests at such parties got drunk and threw bread about. He liked a regular life, and, as he grew older, became more and more inclined for his own and Charlotte's company. He had been gregarious in his bachelor days, seeking male companions, such as William Archer and Graham Wallas, for long argumentative walks. But now, solitary walks were more pleasing to him, though he still liked an occasional companion. My disability prevented me from ever walking with him, but he walked with my wife, who, like Lady Astor, pleased him because she never made any attempt to flirt with him. On one of their walks, they talked about religion, and she told him that she sometimes felt ashamed of herself because she never prayed to God unless she wanted something.

But why should she feel ashamed of that? God, he assured her, probably exclaimed, 'I'm sick of these people who flatter me with their prayers and petitions all day long. Now, there's that nice woman, Nora Ervine, who never bothers me unless she wants something! . . .'

He enjoyed his popularity and took immense pleasure in being photographed, chiefly, no doubt, because he had what the film people call a photogenic face. The frequence with which his portrait appeared in the press, added to his height and tawny beard, now beginning to be brindled, made him easily recognisable, and it was common to see people turning to stare as he strode along the street, swinging his arms and taking long strides, while his eyes, as quick as a sparrow's, darted glances in every direction as if he were afraid of missing some sight he ought to see. I doubt if many men got as much out of a walk in the street as G.B.S. did.

His curiosity was insatiable. He liked to know how one amused oneself. How did one do this? How did one do that? To walk with him was to discover very quickly how kind and courteous he was. He had an extraordinarily happy and unexpected way of paying a compliment, which made those who received it, feel attached to him for ever.

I can illustrate this habit by my own experience. My first full length play, *Mixed Marriage*, had been performed in London for the first time by The Irish Players. It happened that I had been asked to address a public meeting then, and soon after I started to speak, I was surprised and a little dismayed to see G.B.S. enter the hall. At the end of the lecture, he took part in the discussion, for no other reason, apparently, than to tell the audience about my play, which, he said, was almost as good as one of his. After he had departed, a man said to me, 'Shaw paid you a great compliment. He came up from the country to hear you!' But I think he came because he wished to do me a good turn.

128

Simultaneously with this activity in the theatre and on the platform, G.B.S. was conducting an active resistance movement to the reform of the Fabian Society by H. G. Wells. Wells, who had joined the Society in 1903, was one of those restless men who live in a continual state of upheaval. His sociological works are based on discontent for the sake of disturbance, seldom have any relevance to needs, and are often unrelated to substantial fact. He waved his arms about, but quickly tired of application to the problem he urged other people to solve. He was essentially a journalist, so far as sociology was concerned, always on the alert for a popular grievance to exploit. Like Lloyd George, whom he resembled in upbringing, character and habit, he was impatient of detail and could not continue long in one thing. Sustained and dull effort bored him. He liked quick decisions, regardless of whether they were right or wrong.

On February 9, 1906, H.G., as his friends called him, opened his campaign for the reform or, as it seemed to 'the Old Gang', total disruption of the Fabian Society. On that date, he read, very badly, a paper entitled 'Faults of the Fabian', in which he complained, chiefly, that the Society was 'still half a drawing-room society', lodged in 'an underground apartment' or 'cellar', with one secretary and one assistant.[1] 'The first of the faults of the Fabian, then, is that it is small, and the second that strikes me is that, even for its smallness, it is needlessly poor.' He, too, suffered the fatal disease of imagining that big things are better than small ones, and that nothing worth doing can be done by one or two, but only by mobs. The fact is made

---

[1] I have taken some of this information from *The History of the Fabian Society*, by Pease.

plain in the following passage from his paper. 'The task undertaken by the Fabians', he said:

'is nothing less than the alteration of the economic basis of society. Measure with your eye this little meeting, this little hall: look at that little stall of not very powerful tracts: think of the scattered members, one here, one there. . . . Then go out into the Strand. Note the size of the buildings and business places, note the glare of the advertisements, note the abundance of traffic and the multitude of people. . . . That is the world whose very foundations you are attempting to change. How does this little dribble of activities look then?'

The puerility of this statement is plain. All changes in any social system are conceived in single minds and begun by small organisations. There is no exception to this rule. If Wells had been a bright young Jew in Israel in the first quarter of the Christian era, and had encountered a footsore band of workmen toiling up the long dreary road from Jericho to Jerusalem, he would have addressed them substantially as he addressed the Fabians. One can see him, his fine bright eyes full of laughter, buttonholing Jesus and saying, 'My dear chap, what do you and this lot of fishermen and whatnots think you're up to? Use your eyes, man, when you get to Jerusalem. Look at the Roman soldiers in the streets. Go into the Temple and take a look at the Chief Rabbi. See the Romans and the Israelites busy on the well-laid roads . . . and then ask yourself how you think *you* are going to change all that. My *dear* chap! . . .'

Wells scoffed at everything. He denounced the Society's Basis: 'ill-written and old-fashioned, harsh and bad in tone, assertive and unwise.' Their numbers were few. They must increase the membership by thousands. The fact that the Fabian Society was largely responsible for the foundation of the Labour Party and that its despised tracts were eagerly read by people who would have disowned the name of Socialist, and were profoundly influencing the minds of politicians in the Dominions as well as at home, and that the whole conception of municipal government, whether we approve of the change or not, was being reconstructed by the Fabian Tracts, seems not to have been known to Wells, whose schoolboy love of big parades was the operating factor in his intellectual outlook.

The upshot of this jejune lecture was the appointment of a Committee of members and non-members of the Executive Committee 'to consider what measures should be taken to increase the scope, influence, income and activity of the Society'. Neither Webb nor G.B.S. were members of it, probably because they thought they could be more adroit, as, indeed, they were, outside; but Charlotte was a member, and so was Mrs H. G. Wells, who acted as Secretary.

From the outset, Wells was a defeated man. He had neither the training nor the application nor patience to make himself effective in a revolution of the sort he wished to make: and he was in opposition to two men, Webb and G.B.S., who were highly trained in the management of meetings, and uncommonly skilful in debate. The Special Committee—Wells's—made a report, and a copy of it was sent to every member of the Society, together with a copy of a Report by the Executive Committee of the Society, 'drafted by Bernard Shaw and incomparably superior to the other as a piece of literature'.

The one substantial suggestion made by the Committee was the promotion of a weekly review; and this proposal, some years later, was made effective, but not by Wells. Webb and G.B.S. were the chief influences in the foundation of *The New Statesman*. The discussion of the Wells Report began on December 7, 1906, and was continued until March 8, 1907. In these discussions, G.B.S. was admittedly the prevailing force. He played with Wells as a master swordsman plays with a clumsy and inexperienced opponent. Pease, in his *History of the Fabian Society*, asserts that 'Bernard Shaw's speech' in the opening debate, 'was probably the most impressive he has ever made in the Society', and it 'was delivered to a large and keenly appreciative audience in a state of extreme excitement'.[1] Some minor reforms were made in the constitution of the Fabian Society as a result of the Wells Report, but most of them would have been made if he had never conducted his campaign. The membership of the Society had begun to increase before he read his paper on *Faults of the Fabian*, and it rose considerably before he made his Report. His mortification at his defeat rankled, and in September 1908, he resigned from the Society, ostensibly for other reasons, but really because he still felt exceedingly sore at his defeat by Webb and Shaw. He took a poor revenge by painting a ferocious picture of the Webbs, as the Oscar Baileys, in *The New Machiavelli*.

What Wells never realised or wilfully ignored was that G.B.S., who seemed to be his most powerful opponent in the debates, was sincerely his friend and doing his best to prevent him from being mortified by defeat. He would have succeeded had Wells been less obstinate and obtuse. G.B.S. had an immense admiration for H.G.'s imaginative gifts, and was eager to retain them for the benefit of the Fabian Society. But Wells was unwilling to be helped, and insisted on going headlong to his fall. The fact that he was personally antipathetic to Pease, for whom his dislike was intense, did not help to mend matters. Pease was a 'difficult' person, but he was far from being ill-natured, was, on the contrary, a man of high and fine character, who bore no rancour against Wells that I could discover,

---

[1] 'A long report' of this meeting, 'pacifically toned down by Shaw himself, appears in *Fabian News*, January, 1907.' See Pease, p. 174.

and I knew him fairly well. He was not tolerant of fools, nor did he hesitate to tell them of their folly, but he was not vindictive, as H.G. certainly was, and although he had ample cause to feel resentful of Wells's attitude to him, he never, in my knowledge, expressed it with any bitterness.

129

In these respects, he differed deeply from H.G., whose temper was quick and violent and his manners downright bad, although he, too, had uncommon charm when he chose to display it. During this row in the Fabian Society, he behaved badly to everybody, especially to Pease and the Webbs, so badly that G.B.S. took him to task in a long letter which will appear in the following section, together with H.G.'s reply. In these letters, the character of the two men is plainly revealed. G.B.S. was severe on Wells, more severe than was wise, and he displayed signs of that intellectual cruelty in his nature which he would have done better to suppress. He should have known that a man as quick-tempered as H.G. would not feel conciliated by it, would, as indeed, he did, explode into ill-bred wrath; but in his defence it may be said that he and Webb had endured far more than they should have been asked to endure through H.G.'s misbehaviour. Had Wells offended only G.B.S., the letter would not have been written in the terms it was; but H.G. had publicly and almost brutally affronted Webb, and was habitually offensive to Pease; and G.B.S., always prompt to rush to the aid of his friends, was scandalised by this attack. It is essential in reading them to bear in mind that H.G. was jealous of G.B.S., who could do easily, gracefully and well all the things that H.G. wished, but was unable to do.

G.B.S. was tall and had a distinguished look and manner. H.G. was stumpy and, except for his fine eyes and forehead, undistinguished looking: his arms depended from his shoulders as if they were an afterthought by his creator who had hung them very carelessly. G.B.S. had a brilliant platform manner, was prompt and nearly always effective in retort, and his voice was full of pleasant notes. H.G. spoke badly on platforms, was, indeed, almost inaudible, and his voice was thin and reedy, nearly a squeak. He was slow in retort, and he had little wit, though he was a good conversationalist. His ineffectiveness as a public speaker was such that even in broadcasting he was almost inaudible. He was useless in committee because he could not control his temper, was vulgarly rude, and was impatient with detail and routine. G.B.S. was an unusually able committee man, attentive and patient, regular in attendance, always ready to yield speech to others, and unfailingly courteous. It was only in his old age when garrulity took possession of him that G.B.S. ceased to be a good committee man.

Neither of them influenced the general public opinion as much as they might have been expected to, though their influence on individuals, a much more important influence, was immense; but that is a characteristic, especially in politics, of public life in England, where a second-rate politician or a man who manufactures tacks on a large scale will receive deference that would be fulsome if it were offered to an archangel. G.B.S. wisely declined invitations to become a candidate for parliament: he had more important things to do than waste his time in Westminster; but H.G. stood as a candidate for London University, and was defeated. They were writers, a fact which was evidence against them, and G.B.S. was witty and provocative and accustomed to utter embarrassingly true remarks. Neither of them was likely to become a servile party man.

Each, however, took himself with right and proper respect, and they were both offended by the general attitude of the public to men of their sort. G.B.S. was eager to become a member of the Irish Convention which was appointed by Lloyd George in 1917 to try to make peace in Ireland: a task which is unlikely to be performed by human beings. Meeting the wife of an eminent politician in Bond Street one afternoon, he mentioned his ambition to her, in the hope that it would be repeated to her husband, and was angered by seeing a look of amazement in her eyes as if she could not believe her ears. She hurriedly fled from him, and no more was heard of the matter. When he related this incident to me, his resentment was deep. 'I could see she regarded me as an amiable buffoon who was welcome at her parties in Downing Street, but would be out of place in a serious committee!'

His resentment was justified. He was a man of long and varied political experience. He had worked in many committees, where he had been exceedingly useful; and he had drafted, with great skill, reports and pamphlets on political problems which were widely read and influential. He had been largely instrumental in founding the Labour Party, and had been assiduous in attendance at Labour Party Conferences. He had lived in long and close contact with able men and women in every sort of social and political organisation, and was a popular and exceptionally fine public speaker, in addition to being a man of genius with the acute understanding of affairs that belongs to the man of genius and is never possessed by the ordinary man of politics or man of business or man of learning. He was, moreover, much more intelligent and perceptive than the political lady's husband. In addition, he was an Irishman who, in his youth, had had exceptional experience of land questions and was an intimate friend of Sir Horace Plunkett who subsequently became Chairman of the Convention. There can be no doubt in the mind of any reasonable person that he would have been a useful member of the Convention, but he was not appointed to it because the routine politicians did not take him seriously.

At the bottom of all his complaints about Great Britain and his gibes at the English is his anger at this unjust belittlement, his feeling that he was prevented from serving his country in offices where he could have been of great value. He was entitled to resent the assumption that he was inferior to the inert Asquith and the half-educated Lloyd George whose chief and almost only literature was Wild Westerns which he read every night in bed, leaving the light on after he had fallen asleep lest he should frighten the wits out of himself by waking up in the dark.

130

The letter to Wells runs as follows:

'My dear H.G.W.
        'There are various things that you are forgetting.
        'Imprimis, you have chucked Women's Suffrage out of the (Fabian) basis as well as all the other democratic implications of Socialism; and this would make it impossible from the start to get through without amendments.
        'Further, you are forgetting your committee manners—if a man can be said to forget what he never knew. Just consider what you have done. When the Committee was formed, Webb and I got to work at once; and within a fortnight we had spent a day together down here at Ayot over the job and sent you a draft for discussion. This remarkable document you absolutely ignored, saying you were too busy to be bothered about it and would do a proper basis yourself later on when you had finished your book, we to await your convenience in the meantime. The meantime proved to be just a year, during which we had to read through your confounded book for you and neglect our own immortal works for your sake. Then you send us a new basis with the proposal, not that we shall consider it, but that we shall immediately send it out to the Fabian groups in order, as you naively tell us, that they may override the committee by an overwhelming rally to the side of your popular pen.
        'Now I don't mind this. But if I were an opponent desiring to thwart you, and at all hostile to you personally, I might seize the opportunity to take serious offence and put you hopelessly in the wrong before the society. You will remember (or rather forget; for you never remember anything) that one of the reasons why I gobbled you up so easily at the Special Committee corobbery was that you insanely accused us of deliberately and maliciously delaying the report when

417

as a matter of fact we had done in six weeks what you had dawdled over for months. This time the proportion is more glaring still—Shaw and Webb, less than a fortnight, and the strictest consideration of you as our committee colleague; Wells, over eleven months, and the gross insult to his colleagues of absolutely ignoring their work and proposing to send his draft to the groups and the society without meeting them or discussing with them.

'Now I tell you you mustn't do these things. You can treat me privately without the least ceremony; and though you annoy Webb extremely by your unruliness and by your occasionally *cold* civilities, he has to put up with you. But in public work we must proceed on publishable lines. I can't get up at Fabian meetings and put the matter to them as a series of private larks between us. We must proceed in proper form. You may call us all the fools, liars, egotists and nincompoops you can lay your tongue or pen to; but you must be careful all the time not to take liberties of a technical kind. You may draw caricatures of us; but you must not copy our signatures at the foot of cheques. There is an art of public life which you have not mastered, expert as you are in the art of private life. The fine part of private life consists almost wholly in taking liberties: the art of public life consists fundamentally in respecting political rights. Intimate as I am with Webb, I should no more dream of treating him as you have treated him than of walking into the House of Lords and pulling the Lord Chancellor's nose. It was your duty—your DUTY, Herbert George— to send that draft of yours with the intimation that you were now ready for a meeting to collate it with my draft and discuss it; and when we asked you to let it stand over until we were through with some pressing work, you should have cordially awaited our convenience as we did yours.

'Also, though this does not touch our committee, when you address a public meeting, you must do so according to the forms of public meeting, and not publicly insult the chairman by not only assuming his duties and privileges, but actually thrusting him bodily out of his place. You may do that with impunity with worms who know no more about "order" than you do. But have you any idea of what would happen to you if you tried it on with, say, Lord Courtney, or with the Speaker of the House of Commons? Learn, rash egotist, that if you were a thousand H. G. Wellses, there is one sacrosanct person who is greater than you all, and that is the chairman of a public meeting. To be ignorant of this, to fail in respect to The Chair, is the lowest depth of misdemeanour to which a public man can fall.

'I have yet another technical lesson to give you. When you first spoke at a Fabian meeting, I told you to hold up your head and speak to the bracketed bust of Selwyn Image on the back wall. To shew that you were not going to be taught by me, you made the commonest blunder of the tyro: you insisted on having a table; leaning over it on your knuckles; and addressing the contents of your contracted chest to the tablecloth. I will now, having tried to cure you of that by fair means in vain, cure you of it by a blow beneath the belt! Where did you get that attitude? In the shop. IN THE SHOP. At the New Reform Club, when your knuckles touched the cloth, you said unconsciously, by reflex action, "Anything else to-day, madam?" and later on, "What's the next article?" Fortunately you were inaudible, thanks to the attitude. Now I swear that the next time you take that attitude in my presence I will ask you for a farthing paper of pins. I will make a decent public man of you yet, and an effective public speaker, if I have to break your heart in the process.

'And this brings me to a matter of immediate importance! As I, thank heaven, am an ORATOR, and not a mulish draper's assistant, the announcement that I am to speak at the Queen's Hall on Tuesday has sold the whole house out like a shot, without a single advertisement. Clear profit, at unnecessarily low prices, over £100. I think it possible that if you were to undertake another such oration, and stand on your heels instead of on your knuckles, you might do the same. Remember, there is a good deal to be made as a professional lecturer if you prefer to emancipate yourself from Fabian auspices and simply let the Lecture Agency take you on as a speculation. They implore me at brief intervals to let them make my fortune and their own. But if you prefer to do as I do, there is still the fact that you can become a platform athlete in propaganda if you choose to. When there is no table handy, you are already a very tolerable speaker: and the rest is only a matter of practice and of a little daily exercise over the alphabet. What is more, when you become a rhetorician, you will have acquired a new literary power. Why is it that you can't write a play, and I can? You think it is because you don't choose. Yah!'

There is more of the letter,[1] but it is irrelevant to this book. H.G.'s undated reply, which begins with a comment on the irrelevant passage in G.B.S.'s letter and includes one of the comic caricatures with which he sometimes adorned his correspondence, goes on as follows:

'. . . . For the rest, your letter is just bosh! I think I wrote and told you in the matter of the Basis (though not exclusively) you are an ass. I consider that is my contribution to the discussion. You and Webb have as much capacity for running an educational propaganda as—Bland. If you were modest and respectful instead of being resentful, suspicious, greedy and constitutional (*sic*) and habitually red-haired, you might supplement my obvious, beautiful, gigantic and attractive defects, and the world would have a splendid lesson in the superiority of 2 to 1 plus 1, of which the sense of your fundamental inferiority to me, a thing for which I am in no way to blame and which I do my utmost to mitigate by speaking always with my chin down, wearing frock coats too long for me and pins in my lapel, *gnaws*. You are obsessed more and more by

[1] I am indebted for it to Professor Gordon N. Ray, of the University of Illinois, who is writing a life of H. G. Wells, and is already well known in Britain for his brilliantly edited volumes, *The Letters and Private Papers of W. M. Thackeray*, and a life of Thackeray.

the craving to be disrespectful to me, to be impertinently familiar, to point to the frock coat and pins (which everyone can see). You shindy about and try to distract people from me, when nobody is looking at me. You strike attitudes and play for effects upon me when you know as a matter of fact that I can see you. You invent explanations of me and subtle unnecessary detractions. What good is all this liveliness? Here I am.

'If you want the present hopeful expansion of Fabian influence and Socialist training to go under the most favourable conditions, you must alter the Basis. You can get this done, I can't. It isn't in my line of aptitude. I've given you indications. You can prevent it being done or you can do it wrong. I regret to say I don't care a damn, such is my faith (?) in God. I have done what I can and I'm ready to come and lose my temper thoroughly when you and Webb are free to discuss the matter further.

'We went to hear your play. I have always thought and spoken highly of your plays. They lack characterisation and modelling and the last act of *The Doctor's Dilemma* was disgraceful. But I know of no other playwright quite like you.
'God bless you both.

H.G. (followed by a vast flourish)
'(Just compare this beautiful signature with your thin scratchy G.B.S. Note your middle class habit of the surname. You are G.B.*S*. I am H.G.)'

One must not allow one's attachments to deflect one's judgment, even when it is transparent that Wells was inferior in almost every respect, in breeding, manners and mind, to Shaw, but it is not partiality which, in this exchange of letters, makes the superiority of G.B.S. to H.G. seem obvious. His brief career as a dramatic critic did not give Wells the slightest understanding of drama. He could not have said that G.B.S.'s plays 'lack characterisation', if he had known what he was talking about. The plain fact is that Wells knew in his bones and blood that G.B.S. was his intellectual and social superior, and was deeply galled by his knowledge. He never *answered* Shaw's letters in any serious sense of the term, but dodged about like a frightened ferret, throwing anything that came to his hand. 'Fundamentally,' he writes in a letter dated August 23, 1907, 'you are a weak man. You and I know it. No advice of mine will save you from a fourth act and too much. You will probably die about 1938— obscurely.'

No one behaved to Wells with so much chivalry as G.B.S. did, defending him when defence seemed impossible. It is pleasant to be able to record H.G.'s belated recognition of this fact at a time when he was in grave trouble. Wells, who had the slovenly habit of not dating his letters, probably because, unlike G.B.S., he had never had any responsible business training, wrote to him towards the end of August 1909—the letter is marked in G.B.S.'s handwriting, 'received 25/8/09 at Parknasilla'. The end is too private to be quoted, but the beginning is as follows:

'My dear Shaw, Occasionally you don't simply rise to a difficult situation, but soar above it, and I withdraw anything you would like withdrawn from our correspondence of the last two years or so! . . .'

But even H.G. never knew what a superb fight G.B.S. had put up for him.

131

In 1908, the first of what G.B.S. called disquisitory plays was produced at the Haymarket Theatre. This was *Getting Married*, a long conversation, conducted mainly by a remarkably able and benign bishop, drawn from Mandell Creighton, the Bishop of London, and finely acted by Henry Ainley.

London was not yet accustomed to disquisitory plays, indeed, it still is not accustomed to them, and the play was not a financial success. But it is interesting to people who like good conversation and are not terrified by hearing ideas discussed. The matter under enquiry is marriage. George Meredith had suggested a system of leasehold marriage, the period of contract to be seven years. At the end of that time, the parties to the contract, if they found it unsatisfactory, could terminate the engagement and make a fresh one! . . .

This was the sort of proposal that leads nowhere. Marriage is not a business arrangement in which a man and woman undertake to carry on a factory for the production of children: it is a highly complicated relationship in which emotion and physical experience, of which one, and perhaps, both of the partners, except in theory, may be ignorant, play a supreme part. The early years of marriage are the most difficult. The partners are young and inexperienced, and have to adjust themselves to each other without much, if any, instruction.

In America, where success is expected from the start of any adventure, it is fairly common for a marriage to collapse at the end of two or three years; but in European countries, where the absurd demand that success shall be immediate is seldom or never made, the majority of men and women manage with fair success to overcome the trials and troubles of a difficult relationship in which young affections are sometimes badly bruised.

G.B.S., who never quite ceased to be a journalist and was always interested in human problems, set himself the task of trying to settle the business as if it were a subject for discussion at a Fabian meeting. A solicitor, turned priest, was brought in to draw up a perfect marriage contract with the result, obvious from the start, that the young couple whose imminent marriage had started the argument, slipped out of the Bishop's palace and got themselves married in the ordinary way. The effort to make an ideal marriage had hopelessly failed. Couples must continue to solve their problem for themselves by the method of trial and error, with each making large allowances for the other and bearing in mind that there are third parties to almost every marriage whose interest in the preservation of the contract is intense, though it is less seriously considered than it ought to be.

Getting Married was no more helpful than Meredith's proposed septennial contract. Marriage has always been, and will always be, difficult; and it is certain to become more complicated as women's economic independence, either by inheritance or earnings, becomes more assured; but it will still have mixed up with its purely commercial arrangements, an amount of emotional agitation which no contract can possibly cover.

Marriage is not a sacrament: it is an arrangement for the comfortable increase of mankind; and no thinking man or woman supposes that it will not, as it had been in the past, be subject to changes and diversions which may be drastic. As late as the middle of the nineteenth century, wealthy women, especially if they were widows, preferred to live with a man as his lover rather than his wife because her fortune, on her marriage, passed into the possession of her husband, to be disposed of as he pleased. We may yet see unmarried women proudly bearing babies without the slightest reproach from any one.

But even in such arrangements as these, the emotional factor will be profoundly influential, apart altogether from the desirability of a child having the benefit of intimate association with a father as well as a mother. It is this element of love in marriage for which G.B.S. makes insufficient allowance because, perhaps, it is often a transient emotion. To him, affection, which is more durable than love, is the important element. There is much wisdom and wit in *Getting Married*, but the play is more likely to become a library piece than a piece for the stage.

Its popularity in the library will be increased by the pleasure the reader can obtain from the preface, in which G.B.S. applies his powerful mind to a long study of marriage. The pious citizen feels horrified when the sanctity of marriage is called in question, falling into a fury with the questioner who asks what system of marriage he means; and is appalled to learn that there are almost as many systems of marriage as there are nations. 'In the British Empire we have unlimited Kulin polygamy, Muslim polygamy limited to four wives, child marriages, and, nearer to home, marriages of first cousins: all of them abominations in the eyes of many worthy persons.' He might have added that the Irish peasant dispenses with the passion of love, basing his marriage entirely on pounds, shillings and pence, and feeling no more love for the woman he buys than a cock feels for the hen he treads.

The general assumption, certainly in Britain, is that monogamous marriage is the only virtuous form, and that all nice-minded men and women believe in monogamy. But the fact is that there are many polygamous men and polyandrous women, few of whom will publicly declare their preference because to do so will cause them to be reprobated by their neighbours, even when their neighbours are as polygamous or polyandrous as themselves.

The main purpose of marriage, however, is the production of children, and no amount of sentimental tosh can conceal that fact. It has subsidiary purposes, such as agreeable companionship, the maintenance of a pleasant home, and so forth; but we are liable to sentimentalise some of these subsidiary purposes and to think that what is called a good mother is better for a child than what is called a bad mother. There is an increasing belief among sensible people that a doting mother may do her son infinitely more harm than an indifferent and neglectful one; since the children of the former are always looking around for support, while the children of the latter soon learn to fend for themselves.

G.B.S. later in the preface remarks that 'experience shews that women do not object to polygamy when it is customary: on the contrary, they are its most ardent supporters. The reason is obvious. The question as it presents itself in practice to a woman, is whether it is better to have, say, a whole share in a tenth-rate man or a tenth share in a first-rate man.' The operative word in this matter is 'customary'. If polygamy were the common practice, nobody would feel ashamed of it. The deserted wife suffers less from the loss of her husband, of whom, indeed, she may be glad to be rid, than she suffers from the loss of her pride. She is humiliated by the thought that the wives who still possess their husbands are sneering at her as the woman who failed to keep her man.

A deplorable defect in modern society is that an increasing number of able women are deprived of 'their right to maternity' because they will not pay its price by taking a husband and abandoning their work. The ability these women possess is not passed on to posterity. It is dissipated in loose arrangements with lovers, strictly on the understanding that their sexual relations shall not result in offspring. A woman of conspicuous ability who allowed herself to become an unmarried mother would almost certainly lose her job; though a man of conspicuous ability who becomes an unlawful father does not lose his.

The harm caused by this injustice cannot be calculated. We are not so rich in mind and spirit that we can afford to throw any of it down the drain. It is probably true that the best life for a child is to be found in a home where he is influenced both by a father and a mother, and that one in which the influence is either entirely female or entirely male—a public school, for example—is deleterious in the extreme; but we may well believe that as the economic position of women becomes less and less dependent on their ability to capture men who will keep them, a solution of this problem will be found.

The plain fact is that the majority of marriages are successful and happy. If this were not true, marriage would long ago have been abandoned or so drastically changed that it no longer seemed to be marriage. But the main purpose of marriage will compel us to revise the institution so that we shall not waste any useful woman, expecially if she is a woman of notable ability. It is a significant fact that there are no 'unwanted women' in polygamous countries. These derelicts are to be found only in countries which are monogamous; and they represent, less to-day, perhaps, than formerly, sheer waste of mother-power. Even as things are, the 'unwanted woman' is still doomed to lead a solitary life, unless she has an illicit lover, and can contemplate old age and retirement only with dismay.

132

Getting Married, which may seem to be a more important play to our descendants than it seemed to those in whose time it was first performed, was followed by two short plays, written in 1909, both of which were banned by the Censor. These were *Press Cuttings* and *The Shewing-up of Blanco Posnet*. The first was banned because it contained characters obviously based on eminent persons: Mitchener and Balsquith. The Censorship had, indeed, been instituted in the eighteenth century by Walpole to protect politicians from exposure by dramatists; and an immediate result of it was that Fielding was put out of business as a dramatist, but, to the great benefit of his country, went immediately into business as a novelist.

Press Cuttings is a topical piece, but like all G.B.S.'s work, informed by matters that are permanent. It was privately performed on July 9, 1909, at the Court Theatre by a society created solely for that purpose. The longer play was banned because words were put in the mouth of Blanco Posnet, a rough prairie bad hat, about the Almighty. 'He's a sly one. He's a mean one. He lies low for you. He plays cat and mouse with you. He lets you run loose until you think you are shut of Him; and then, when you least expect it, He's got you.' These words profoundly shocked the respectable solicitor, George Alexander Redford, who had been appointed Reader of Plays in the office of the Lord Chamberlain, and was, virtually, controller and dictator of the English drama.

The banning of these small plays had a large result. *The Shewing-up of Blanco Posnet* was performed at the Abbey Theatre in Dublin because the Lord Chamberlain's writ did not run in that city. Any play could be performed there without let or hindrance, unless its performance resulted in a breach of the peace, in which event, the Lord Lieutenant could order its withdrawal. W. B. Yeats and Lady Gregory, who were the Directors of the Abbey Theatre, immediately offered G.B.S. the hospitality of their theatre; and the play was produced on August 25, 1909, in the presence of a large number of London critics who had crossed the Irish Sea in the delusion that they were about to witness something very shocking. Their disappointment when they found themselves witnessing the performance of a religious tract was deep; and some of them expressed their disappointment by attacking, not the Reader of Plays, but the author.

Dissatisfaction with the licensing of plays had been growing for some time when *Press Cuttings* and *The Shewing-up of Blanco Posnet* were banned: a dissatisfaction which was chiefly provoked by Redford, a man of small and narrow mind, who would have been better placed as Clerk to a Diocesan Board than as a judge of literature or morals.

The upshot of this increasing dissatisfaction was the appointment of a Joint Select Committee of the House of Lords and the House of Commons on Stage Plays (Censorship), by the Liberal Government in July 1909. Herbert, afterwards Lord, Samuel was the chairman.

The result of its enquiries and deliberations were published in a Blue Book in November 1909, at the price of 3s 3d, as cheap a volume as has ever been issued, considering that it contains lengthy statements by Redford himself, William Archer, Bernard Shaw, Granville Barker, Sir James Barrie, Forbes Robertson, John Galsworthy, Laurence Houseman (one of the Censor's victims), Beerbohm Tree, Sir William Gilbert, A. B. Walkley, Lena Ashwell, Professor Gilbert Murray, George Alexander, George Edwardes, once famous for the production of musical comedies, The Speaker of the House of Commons, Oswald Stoll, who built the Coliseum, the Bishop of Southwark, Hall Caine, Israel Zangwill, Sir Squire Bancroft, Sir Arthur Pinero, and G. K. Chesterton. Such a galaxy of mind and wit had never appeared in a Blue Book before, nor has it been seen since.

As a result of this Committee, the licensing of plays was sensibly changed; a change that was considerably assisted by the fact that a later Lord Chamberlain, the Earl of Cromer, administered his office with great tact and intelligence. The opponents of any censorship were, of course, disappointed that the office had not been abolished;

but there can be little doubt in most minds that it is better to live under the aegis of the Lord Chamberlain, who, for a reading fee of two guineas, tells the theatre manager in advance of performance whether or not he will license the play, than to endure the expense and misery of having the theatre raided by the police, the play's performance suspended, and the entire cast taken off to prison for acting in a play regarded by the constabulary as immoral.

This is what happens in New York. The system, too, is superior to that of licensing by local authorities, whose Watch Committee may include among its most active members some sour-faced fellows who regard the theatre as a sink of iniquity and are prepared to do any thing, fair or foul, to ruin it.

A sensation was caused by the Committee's decision, after hearing part of a statement made by Shaw, not to hear the rest of it. The advertisement this decision gave his statement was immense, and it resulted in more people reading what G.B.S. had not been allowed to say than would have read it if the whole statement had been accepted. He was not guiltless of misbehaviour. He used words and phrases in his statement which he must have known were likely to be misunderstood by careless or shallow-minded readers of the popular press. People of quality knew exactly what he meant when he described himself as 'a specialist in immoral and heretical plays', and went on to say that his 'reputation' had 'been gained by' his persistent struggle 'to force the public to reconsider its morals'.

But people without quality, that is to say the vast majority of the population, accepted his description of himself in the common meaning of immorality, especially when he said that he regarded 'certain doctrines of the Christian religion as understood in England to-day with abhorrence'. Every member of the Bench of Bishops knew what he meant by these phrases, but who could tell what thoughts they roused in the minds of country curates and suburban vicars, apart from the great horde of spiritual and intellectual strap-hangers throughout these islands?

To these people, G.B.S. appeared to be a pornographic atheist, shamelessly boasting of his iniquity. Two minutes after he had started to give evidence, his cause was ruined so far as the general public was concerned. But only temporarily, though temporarily, so far as the mob is concerned, usually means permanently. Amendment of the law was achieved in the end. The Blue Book, which contains nearly four hundred pages of foolscap size, is too long to be read by the general reader, despite the richness of its material, but G.B.S. gives a just summary of it in the preface to *The Shewing-up of Blanco Posnet*, together with some portraits of members of the Committee, which are uncommonly entertaining.

Eventually, the ban on *The Shewing-up of Blanco Posnet* was lifted, and it is part of my pride that I was the means of removing it. While I was managing the Abbey Theatre, I took the Players to the Repertory Theatre in Liverpool; and it occurred to me that if I could get the ban on *Blanco Posnet* lifted, the benefit to us would be considerable. I therefore wrote to G.B.S. to tell him that I proposed to apply for a licence, and he very skilfully drafted a letter to the Lord Chamberlain which I dispatched. To my surprise and delight, the play was licensed, and it is now performable anywhere in Great Britain and Ireland as it was written by its author. It has never, in my knowledge, excited the slightest resentment.

It was followed by three short plays, *The Glimpse of Reality*, *The Fascinating Foundling*, and *The Dark Lady of the Sonnets*, the last of which was written to help the funds of the National Theatre, a building which still does not exist, but has reached the length of a foundation stone on the south bank of the Thames. It was written in 1910, and is as lively to-day as it was when it was first performed.

In that year, too, was produced another of the disquisitory plays, *Misalliance*, which is, perhaps, the least liked of the lot. It formed part of the programme of an abortive repertory theatre founded by Charles Frohman at the Duke of York's Theatre in 1910, a theatre which began in hope and ended in debt. It ought to have been a permanent success, and might have been but for a divided policy which dithered between popular and excessively intellectual plays. The acting was superb. So was the production, which was done by Dion Boucicault and Harley Granville-Barker, but some of the plays fell short.

The time, too, was unfortunate for such an enterprise. The second and third generation of the mercantile class were now in possession of wealth, while the aristocracy were declining in authority through penal taxation. The rich and expensively educated young men whose great-grandfathers had been mill hands were destitute of culture. Their gods were golf, motor cars and money. Musical comedies were their dramatic entertainment. They read little or nothing, and the little they did read was rubbish. They heard no music, saw no pictures, were uninformed even in a small degree about fundamentals of any sort, and they ate and drank lavishly. They were flashy, rootless men, who liked ornate hotels in which they drank too many cocktails. Their houses were monuments of vulgarity and desolation, full of 'lounges' and billiard rooms unless they had had the luck to marry a woman of family and taste who knew how to provide them with homes in which civilised people could live.

The cultivated classes were comparatively poor. If they were middle-class, they retired to the suburbs where they gardened and read. The theatre was too much for them in the matter of money. If they were aristocrats, they stayed on their estates as long as they could, hoping that a turn of the wheel might enable them to resume their former position.

Misalliance is about such people; for G.B.S. had keen sight and could see signs and wonders long before they were even dreamt of by other people. The play opens brilliantly. In about fifteen minutes of acting time, we are introduced to five characters, each of whom is clearly and vividly revealed in nature and outlook on life. The skill with which the characters are differentiated is exceptional even for G.B.S., who could display a nature in less than a hundred words of dialogue.

Johnny Tarleton, a wealthy mercantile man, who thinks that morality is drawing a line and making other people toe it, and Bentley Summerhays, the neurotic son of a gentleman, are drawn so firmly that in less than five minutes after the curtain rises, the audience knows them intimately. The distinction between Johnny's father, Tarleton of Tarleton's Underwear, and Lord Summerhays, is made with so little effort that the untrained playgoers do not notice how skilfully it is done, though the experts in characterisation realise immediately that this is character-drawing of genius.

Tarleton's wife is sharply contrasted with her designing daughter, Hypatia. But the superb character of the play is Tarleton: a man of mercantile genius who behaves like a mixture of Casanova and a ringmaster in a circus: a florid, demanding, expansive, vain, promiscuous, but extraordinarily shrewd and likeable man. He is superficially based on three rich mercantile men: Andrew Carnegie, William Whiteley, and Gordon Selfridge, more on Whiteley than on the others. But the foundation is slight. Tarleton is not any one of them, and their aspects are no more than those that were known to many people. It is doubtful, indeed, if G.B.S. ever set eyes on any of them, though he may have met Selfridge casually.

A character in a play who is a millionaire and has the habit of lavishly building and endowing public libraries, as Carnegie did, and is as promiscuous as Whiteley, who thought he had the right to bed any desirable woman assistant he employed, and is menaced with a revolver by one of his reputed bastards—Whiteley was murdered by one—and is genially florid and munificent in his social manners and addicted to living in the mansion of a marquis who can no longer afford to live in it himself, as Selfridge was, and has a superficial culture, is likely to be thought an exact reproduction of any one of them. But G.B.S. created his own people using only such facts from life as were helpful in making verisimilitude. Tarleton is not Carnegie or Whiteley or Selfridge, though he has habits that each of them had:

he is entirely a Shavian creation. Hypatia, who seems at first to be a cod fish of a woman with an eye to the main chance, turns out to be a girl greatly bored by her idle existence and pining for a romantic affair: an affair which is soon experienced when an aeroplane tumbles out of the sky, wrecking some of Tarleton's 'glass' and adding two characters to the cast: one Joseph Percival and a figure in a masculine uniform who turns out to be a woman, a Polish acrobat and juggler, Lina Szczepanowska, who greatly discomposes Mrs Tarleton by demanding, among other requirements, a Bible and six oranges.

The demand is reasonable. Lina wishes to test the state of her nerves after the crash. She, therefore, opens the Bible at the Psalms, props it in front of her, and begins to juggle with the oranges, keeping all six simultaneously in the air until she can not only read a Psalm, but understand it. That done, she knows that she is in full possession of herself.

Another character appears: a neurotic clerk whose mother is a cast-off mistress of Tarleton, though Tarleton is not this class-conscious young man's father. He announces himself as John Brown, though his true name turns out to be Julius Baker. This youth has convinced himself that it is his duty to avenge the seduction of his mother, Lucinda Titmus, on the general principle that it was a bourgeois act and a natural result of capitalism, though there seems to be no doubt that Lucinda had no objection to being seduced and that she thoroughly enjoyed herself while she was Tarleton's mistress. Brown, however, is disarmed and made to appear the little squit somebody calls him, though his self-respect is soothed by the kindness he receives from Mrs Tarleton.

That is all we get in the way of a plot, though there is a theme somewhere in the play which loses itself in torrential talk. *Misalliance* proves the argument of some critics, notably Mr Frank Swinnerton, that G.B.S. had the makings of a remarkably fine novelist in him, despite the total failure of the novels he wrote in his nonage. All the disquisitory plays, except *Heartbreak House*, would have been more impressive as novels.

133

Misalliance was succeeded by *Fanny's First Play*, which surprised its author by running longer than any other play he had yet had performed in London: 624 performances; a longer run than any of his subsequent plays has enjoyed. He called it a pot-boiler, but there must be many dramatists who wish they could write a play as good as this one. Its long run, however, means less than it seems. The play was produced at the Little Theatre on April 19, 1911, but the Little, as its name denotes, is very small, seating only 377 people. It is obvious that a run of 624 performances in the Little is very different from the same number of performances in the Haymarket which seats 900 or Drury Lane which has, approximately, room for 2,247. Had *Fanny's First Play* been performed to no more than 377 people at each performance in the Haymarket, the theatre would have been less than half full, and the play would have been a failure. But the probability is that in the larger house, it would have drawn a larger audience, and its qualities suggest that its run would have been long and profitable. It is well, however, that the reader should not be misled by the length of the run at the Little. *Saint Joan* was performed 244 times at the New, which seats 938 people, and 321 times at the Regent, a much larger theatre, when it was revived there about a year after its withdrawal from the New. Obviously, the run at the Little was not much, if any, longer, in terms of receipts and persons present, than the run at the New and was considerably less than the run at the Regent.

Its form is interesting. The play is literally Fanny's. She is the daughter of an obsolete romantic who runs away from life because it seems sordid and ugly. This is a preposterous Irishman, one O'Dowda, a Count of the Holy Roman Empire, who, when at home, always dresses 'with studied elegance a hundred years out of date'. There was, oddly enough, a prototype in reverse of O'Dowda, living in Dublin some years after *Fanny's First Play* was performed, who provided another instance of G.B.S.'s prescience about odd characters. O'Dowda lives mainly in Venice where he tries to forget the sordid realities of every day existence. 'I find England ugly and Philistine. Well, I don't live in it. I find modern houses ugly. I don't live in them: I have a palace on the grand canal. I find modern clothes prosaic, I don't wear them, except, of course, in the street! . . .' O'Dowda, in short, is a coward who cannot face life, but must live in a state of make-believe: a Peter Pan of fifty.

His daughter silently revolts against her father's absurd pretence of living; and induces him to send her to Cambridge. When he asks her what she wishes for a birthday present, she tells him that she has written a play and will be grateful if he will pay for its performance in private with several representative dramatic critics in the audience. Four London critics are induced to attend. One of them, Flawner Bannal, has to be bribed to be present. He represents the vulgar press and its vulgar readers, and is a composite character. The remaining three, who attend without payment, are Mr Trotter, Mr Vaughan and Mr Gunn, and are amusing caricatures of A. B. Walkley, of *The Times*, E. A. Baughan of the *Daily News*, and Gilbert Cannan of *The Star:* all of whom appeared to have been flattered by their representation. Walkley, indeed, allowed Mr Claude King, who took his part in the play, to study him closely for purposes of make-up.

O'Dowda feels confident that his daughter's play 'will be like a Louis Quatorze ballet painted by Watteau. The heroine will be an exquisite Columbine, her lover a dainty Harlequin, her father a picturesque Pantaloon! . . .' The shock he sustains when he discovers that her play is a modern realistic piece, so up-to-date and removed from romance that it has a Suffragette in its cast, is almost fatal to him. The characters are suburban middle-class people, very respectable and routine in their habits, except that one of them, Mrs Knox, is a religious mystic. Mr Gilbey, the father of Bobby Gilbey, and Mr Knox, the father of Margaret Knox, are partners in business, and the intention is that Margaret and Bobby shall marry and keep the business in a family compound of the Knoxes and Gilbeys. But the young people have views of their own on this subject.

Bobby has entangled himself with a good-natured prostitute, called Darling Dora, who, while slightly intoxicated and in a jocular mood, knocks a policeman's helmet over his eyes, with the result that she and Bobby are taken before the magistrates: she is sent to prison for a fortnight, and the unfortunate Bobby, who is innocent of offence, is sentenced to pay a fine of four pounds or to go to gaol for a month. He has no money, so he goes to gaol. Dora, now released, is eager to have him delivered, which can be done by paying the fine; and she seeks help from his parents. They, half distracted by his disappearance, are almost completely maddened by their discovery that he is in prison and is mixed up with such a young person as Darling Dora.

One of their chief concerns is to conceal the news of their son's disgrace from the Knoxes, who, they fear, will break off their daughter's engagement if they hear of it. But the Knoxes themselves are in dire trouble. Their splendid daughter, Margaret, one of the finest young women in the whole Shavian drama, has also been missing for a fortnight. She has spent the time in Holloway Prison.

Margaret, 'a strong, springy girl of eighteen, with large nostrils, an audacious chin, and a gaily resolute manner, even peremptory on occasions', had been taken to a Salvation Army Festival at the Albert Hall by a pious aunt. 'The meeting got on my nerves somehow. It was the singing, I suppose: you know I love singing a good swinging hymn; and I felt it was ridiculous to go home in the bus after we had been singing so wonderfully about climbing up the golden stairs to heaven. I wanted more music—more happiness—more life. I wanted some comrade who felt as I did.' So she descended from the bus at Piccadilly Circus, walked into Leicester Square, and paid five shillings to enter the promenade of a music hall, where she found herself standing next to a Frenchman, M. Duvallet, to whom she spoke. The time was Boat Race night, and the West End was choked with drunken undergraduates from Oxford and Cambridge, all busily engaged in proving that when it comes to hooliganism, the lower classes have nothing on their social superiors.

Duvallet, who naturally misunderstood Margaret's occupation when he was accosted by her in a promenade frequented by expensive whores, invited her to drink champagne, but Margaret, remembering her upbringing, thought that this frivolous and over-rated wine would be much too dear, so she refused the invitation, but wished she could dance. They went to a dance-hall, where, in addition to dancing, she drank some champagne. Unluckily, the hall was invaded by the flower of England's intellect, the drunken undergraduates. There was a ferocious row, quelled very roughly by the police, one of whom received an almighty biff on the ear from Duvallet's boot, for the Frenchman, forgetting he was in England, gave him 'a magnificent *moulinet*' that almost laid him out. Margaret, inflamed by champagne and piety, used her fists with considerable force and skill, with the result that she and Duvallet were each sentenced, he to a fine or a fortnight's imprisonment, she to a fine or a month. On his discharge, he discovered that he could have Margaret set free by paying her fine, which he did.

This is the plight in which the Knoxes are at the very moment that the Gilbeys are in a similar plight through Bobby and Darling Dora. Each, unaware of the other's misfortune, is terrified of what the other will say.

Her experience has released Margaret from her repressions. She had been brutally used by the police when they dragged her to the station:

> 'They kicked me with their knees; they twisted my arms; they taunted and insulted me; they called me vile names; and I told them what I thought of them, and provoked them to do their worst. There's one good thing about being hard hurt: it makes you sleep. I slept in that filthy cell with all the other drunks sounder than I should have slept at home. I can't describe how I felt next morning: it was hideous; but the police were quite jolly; and everybody said it was a bit of English fun, and talked about last year's boat-race night when it had been a great deal worse. I was black and blue and sick and wretched. But the strange thing was that I wasn't sorry; and I'm not sorry. And I don't feel that I did anything wrong, really. Now that it's all over I'm rather proud of it; though I know now that I'm not a lady, but whether that's because we're only shopkeepers or because nobody's really a lady except when they're treated like ladies, I don't know!'

The last remark is characteristic of G.B.S.'s belief. The Flower Girl in *Pygmalion* behaved like a lady when she was treated like one.

Margaret behaved as if she were not a lady because she was not treated like one. The first performance is more probable than the second. We can all follow a good lead: we do not all follow a bad one. When Mrs Knox, lost in wonder, asks Margaret why she had behaved in this extraordinary manner, the girl replies, 'The prayer meeting set me free somehow. I should never have done it were it not for the prayer meeting.' The reply horrifies her mother. 'I know that prayer can set us free . . . but it sets us free for good, not for evil.' 'Then', Margaret replies, 'I suppose what I did was not evil; or else I was set free for evil as well as good,' which is sound Christian doctrine.

At the end of her talk with her mother, Margaret exclaims that hell is now as real to her as a turnip. She will never again make pretences about anything. 'What's the good of pretending? That's all our respectability is, pretending, pretending, pretending. Thank heaven, I've had it knocked out of me once for all.'

Mrs Knox is deeply agitated by her daughter's remarks, which sound cynical to her, though Margaret imagines them to be frank and honest; and she tells the girl how she had brought her up in the hope that she would learn the happiness of religion. 'I've waited for you to find out that happiness is within ourselves and doesn't come from outward pleasures. I've prayed oftener than you think that you might be enlightened! . . .' To which Margaret makes this profound and deeply impressive reply:

> 'You shouldn't have prayed for me to be enlightened if you didn't want me to be enlightened. If the truth were known, I suspect we all want our prayers to be answered only by halves: the agreeable halves. Your prayer didn't get answered by halves, mother. You've got more than you bargained for in the way of enlightenment. I shall never be the same again. I shall never speak in the old way again. I've been set free from this silly little hole of a house and all its pretences. I know now that I am stronger than you and Papa. I haven't found that happiness of yours that is within yourself; but I've found strength. For good or evil I am set free; and none of the things that used to hold me can hold me now.'

In the last act, she pays a visit to Bobby who does not know that she has been in Holloway, nor does she know that he has been in Wormwood Scrubbs. Bobby is shocked when he hears Margaret declaring that she was in one of her religious fits when she knocked out two of the policeman's teeth. 'I've got one of them,' she says exultantly. 'He sold it to me for ten shillings.' If she had said that she'd gone out on the loose for a lark, Bobby could have understood her, and would not have been much perturbed; for that was how he landed himself in gaol. But to hear her saying that she went on the loose on principle horrifies him. 'To talk about religion in connection

433

with it; to—to—well, Meg, I do find that a bit thick, I must say.' Their engagement ends, and as it ends, Darling Dora enters the room, and immediately recognises Margaret as No. 406 from the next cell to hers in Holloway.

Bobby develops all the talents for respectability of a Gilbey. Everything Margaret says and does upsets him. The foundations of his dull and pretentious life have been shaken, not by Darling Dora's pavement manners, but by Margaret's new morality and her refusal to feel shocked by the little pavement tart. 'I do think it's not quite the same thing my knowing her and you knowing her,' he says, and the remark makes her call him a skunk.

'Well, dearie,' Dora remarks philosophically, 'men have to do some awfully mean things to keep up their respectability . . . I've met Bobby walking with his mother; and of course he cuts me dead. I won't pretend I liked it; but what could he do, poor dear?' 'And now,' Margaret exclaims, 'he wants me to cut you dead to keep him in countenance. Well, I shan't: not if my whole family were there. But I'll cut him dead if he doesn't treat you properly. I'll educate you, you young beast,' she concludes as she turns on Bobby.

The play proceeds to its end, and during its progress the discovery is made that Juggins, the Gilbey's manservant is the brother of a duke: a typical Shavian diversion. Mr and Mrs Gilbey and Mr and Mrs Knox are themselves upheaved by their experience of recent events, and are almost inclined to break loose from their routine respectability. Mrs Knox explains their upheaval. 'We find out then that with all our respectability and piety, we've no real religion and no way of telling right from wrong. We've nothing but our habits; and when they're upset, where are we? Just like Peter in the storm trying to walk on water and finding he couldn't.'

The Frenchman, Duvallet, delivers a long rhapsody on the beautiful liberty enjoyed by the English girl, an oration in which the familiar argument that anything done in France is better than anything done in England is brilliantly reversed. The general expectation that Duvallet, having got himself imprisoned on Margaret's account, should make him and her respectable by marrying her is disappointed by his revelation that he is already married and the father of two daughters. However, Margaret had fallen in love with Juggins when she thought he was a footman, and so she pairs off with him, while Bobby engages himself to Darling Dora, and the play ends, except for an epilogue in which Count O'Dowda tells the dramatic critics how horrified he is that his daughter could have written this piece of raw realism and not a work of romance. He will return to Venice at once and never show his face in Britain again.

The play's purpose, G.B.S. proclaims in the short preface, is to convince people that 'mere morality, or the substitution of custom for conscience' is a damnable thing: and that 'the young had better have their souls awakened by disgrace . . . than drift along from their cradles to their graves doing what other people do for no other reason than that other people do it, and knowing nothing of good and evil, of courage and cowardice, or indeed anything but how to keep hunger and concupiscence and fashionable dressing within the bounds of good taste except when their excesses can be concealed.' 'I hate to see dead people walking about: it is unnatural. And our respectable middle class people are all as dead as mutton.'

Androcles and the Lion, which was performed for the first time in Berlin in 1912, was the next play. On September 1, 1913, it was produced at St James's Theatre by Granville-Barker. Max Beerbohm had made a caricature of Barrie reading *Peter Pan* to a group of adults and children. The adults were delighted, but the children were all asleep. G.B.S. apparently shared Max's comic delusion about *Peter Pan*, for he told Hesketh Pearson[1] that he had written *Androcles* 'to show what a play for children should be like. It should never be childish; nothing offends children more than to play down to them; all the great children's books, *The Pilgrim's Progress*, *Gulliver*, *Robinson Crusoe*, *Andersen*, *Arabian Nights*, and *Grimm's Fairy Tales*, were written for adults.' G.B.S. could twaddle like the rest of us, and this passage is twaddle almost from start to finish. The great children's books, as he calls them, are not presented to children in the form in which their authors wrote them, but in shortened and sometimes bowdlerised versions. No child has read *Gulliver's Travels* as Swift wrote it. We may imagine the dismay of a mother on finding her infant reading how Gulliver put out the fire in the Empress of Lilliput's apartments! . . .

Peter Pan was performed for the first time at the Duke of York's Theatre on December 27, 1904, and it has been revived almost every year since that time: that is to say, it has been performed once a year, except, perhaps, during the World Wars, for fifty years and shows no sign of ceasing to be revived. *Androcles and the Lion* ran at St James's Theatre for eight weeks, and has been twice briefly revived several times. The play is short: in a brief epilogue and two acts, the second being divided into three short scenes; but it is written in a very extravagant manner in which no expense is spared.

It is probably the most costly short play to produce in the whole history of the drama; for it not only requires a revolving stage for the speedy production of the second act, but also some fifty performers. There are seventeen speaking parts in the play, including the Lion, a part which requires an actor who is a combination of animal imitator and acrobat: and, in addition, a large number of supernumerary

[1] *G.B.S. A Postscript*, p. 75.

actors, Roman soldiers, captive Christians, gladiators, servants, the Emperor's suite, menagerie keepers, speciality performers and slaves. The costumes alone are a serious expense.

There can be no doubt of the entertaining quality of the play, though the critics, after their fashion, either affected to feel superior to its simple affirmations of faith or deeply shocked by its blasphemy. A distinguished Congregational minister, the Rev. James Morgan Gibbon, controverted its moral, which, like that of *Major Barbara*, proclaimed the defeat of Christianity by the men of blood and iron.

This intelligent attack provoked G.B.S. to reply in a letter to the *Daily News*, where it was published on September 29, 1913. As it reveals G.B.S.'s mind on religion and the general situation of the world, I quote it almost in full. He begins by defending Mr Gibbon from what he supposes to be misrepresentation by the interviewer. He cannot believe that Mr Gibbon, because he is a Christian, can demand that every play shall end with the triumph of Christianity over its adversaries, without regard to the facts:

'When I travel about Europe and see Germany studded with colossal images of the Man of Blood and Iron, the latest being also the hugest and the most irresistibly suggestive of Dagon and Moloch; when I read the recent history of the triumphs of Mars in Tripoli, in Morocco and the Balkan States; when I see compulsory military service rapidly becoming universal and Mars achieving the miracles of the submarine and the aeroplane in a few years, while Christ cannot in as many centuries get rid of even such a blazing abomination as the mixed general workhouse, I really cannot see how any sane man can allege that Christianity has gained an inch since the Crucifixion.

'If you dramatise the world movement as a struggle between Christ and Mars, Christ is down and out, despised and rejected of men, spat upon, nailed up, laughed to scorn, not even allowed the right not to be kicked when He is down. He is not allowed to say to Mars—though it is true—"Kick away, my friend, crucify me, spit on me, hammer your nails in, laugh at me with what side of your mouth you can, you must, nevertheless, allow me to point out, first, that you cannot kill me, and, second, that no mess could possibly be worse than the mess you are making of the world."

'Now, I am not going to say—because I do not know—whether this state of things is desirable or undesirable. Nobody who is not in the literal and Scriptural senses of the two words a damned fool, can possibly see *Androcles* and mistake the direction of my sympathies; but my sympathies may be diseased and sentimental and cowardly. Most men who take the blood and iron pose would say so.

'But of one thing I am absolutely certain, and that is that nothing but mischief can be done by pretending that Mars and Mercury, Militarism and Commerce are Christianity, or that the ladies and gentleman who sit under Mr Morgan Gibbon in Stamford Hill are Christians living in a Christian country. The simple fact that they are not in prison proves that they are not Christians; and it would be an enormous gain to intellectual clearness and honesty of soul if they would say so.

'Ferrovius in my play is an honest man. When he finds that when it comes to the point he glories in war, and is proud of his pride, he recognises that his real faith consists in the assumptions on which he acts, and not in the words he repeats when nothing is happening to him. If he had been an Englishman he would have said that the Lord is a Man of War, who came not to send peace on earth, but a sword. And he would have knocked down anyone who said he was not a Christian or refused to cheer Lord Roberts. . . .'

I have not cited Mr Gibbon because my purpose is solely to show the state of G.B.S.'s mind on the subject and to illuminate the motive which made him write *Androcles and the Lion;* but it is common justice to point out that the minister might fairly and impressively have reminded G.B.S. that Jesus, in his actions and often in his words, was far from being a pacifist who never answered back or answered vehemently and even abusively.

134

It was not a pacifist who scourged the moneychangers in the Temple who were lawfully performing a useful service to pilgrims, nor was it a man who turned away wrath with soft words who rebuked the High Priest and denounced the Scribes and Pharisees because they said one thing and did another. In comparison with the terrific tirade of abuse which Jesus applied to these people in the 23rd chapter of St Matthew's Gospel, anything G.B.S. wrote in his play was mild and inoffensive.

What would be said and written about a man who should walk into St Paul's Cathedral as the Archbishop of Canterbury was about to begin a sermon, and call him a whited sepulchre, outwardly beautiful but inwardly full of dead men's bones and all uncleanness, a hypocrite who strained at a gnat and swallowed a camel, denouncing the villainies of his predecessors who slew prophets when he himself and all his followers were guilty of persecutions not less foul? And addressed him and the robed clergy in the choir as vipers who could not hope to escape the damnation of hell? Such a person would, we should feel, rightly be flung into the street and arrested for brawling in church.

War is a calamity from which we may well pray to be delivered, but it is idle to think that we are yet in a state in which any nation can wisely and safely divest itself of armaments or rightly refrain from going to war. Would it have been good for mankind had Hitler won the Second World War? Would this earth have been a better place had the North Americans silently consented to slavery and disunion? In reading his reply to Mr Morgan Gibbon, we may warrantably assume that Mr Gibbon had a case, even if we feel that it was well met by G.B.S.

When the play was published, it was preceded by a long preface, more than a hundred pages, with a note of five pages at the end: a heavy burden for a small play, even when it is overcrowded with characters. But G.B.S. was becoming more and more inclined to use the published plays as an excuse for a public pronouncement which might, but need not, have some relevance to the work which it prefaced. This particular preface excited a good deal of resentment, some of it singularly stupid, which has not yet died down.

It would be absurd to expect that any statement made by G.B.S. would fail to raise the dander of a fairly large number of people. He wrote too plainly and frankly to hope to escape censure from someone, nor did he make much effort to avoid censure. It was not his purpose to soft-soap anybody. He had things to say, and he meant to say them in terms that could not be misunderstood. Saints and prophets do not mince or measure their words, nor do they mind very much whom they upset. 'The words of the wise are as goads,' says the author of Ecclesiastes, 'and as nails fastened by the masters of assemblies.'

Unless we bear continually in mind the fact that G.B.S. had an apocalyptic mind, and that art interested him much less than social reform, and that he thought Sidney Webb was not less important than works of Beethoven and Michelangelo, we shall profoundly misunderstand his character and purpose in life. He had, no doubt, the human desire to be liked, but not at the cost of his conscience; and he sought within the limits of his powers to speak what he believed to be the truth.

Despite occasional follies, however, the preface is profoundly interesting and impressive. G.B.S. examines the Gospels exactly as they might be examined by an intelligent person who had recently heard of Christianity and was eager to discover its history and doctrine and effect on human society. Obviously, any exceptional mind, when such a task is undertaken, is likely to display fresh thought about it, and this fresh thought must be valuable even when it shocks the routine-minded people who have taken their religion on trust and have never examined it.

135

The reader will do well to keep prominently in mind the fact that the Christian concept of Christ has changed drastically during the long period that has elapsed since the Crucifixion: even in such matters as his personal appearance, which, in all ages, has been fanciful. Would it, one wonders, have been a benefit to Christianity if Josephus, a Jew who was a contemporary of Jesus, had written a detailed account of him? There is value in mystery which cannot be too highly esteemed. To know the founder of a faith intimately may be to ruin the faith.

It is an extraordinary fact that the Gospels contain no account of the looks or physique of Jesus. The conventional portrait is the result of rules laid down by the Roman Catholic Church in which the features were mathematically set out. This was done because artists were painting the Lord according to their own fancy; and the church rightly feared that the faith of simple-minded people might be shaken by portraits differing widely in the facial features. But we must conclude even from a cursory reading of the Gospels that Jesus was a man of exceptional wiriness and nervous strength when we perceive how undaunted he seemed to be by long walks through hard and stony country in great heat. Anyone who has taken the journey from Jericho to Jerusalem must feel impressed by the physical endurance of a man, reputed to be slight in body, who could walk up that long, ascending road between hard black mountains without apparently feeling fatigue; and even more must the reader feel impressed by the fact that he was able to make his disciples take it, too.

Jesus has been portrayed by the romantics as a handsome and aristocratic-looking European, carrying, as G.B.S. remarked, an expensive lantern, as, for example, in Holman Hunt's famous picture, 'The Light of the World'; but the eremites, who were not any more realistic than the romantics, revolted from this conception of their Saviour, which must have convicted them of self-desecration in neglecting their bodies. They, therefore, invented the legend that the Son of God, when he decided to appease his Father's anger against the human race by assuming human shape and suffering a cruel and ignominious death for the redemption of mankind, humiliated himself further by taking on the appearance of an ugly, mean and insignificant Jew. There was, indeed, a passion for this form of self-denial that was felt long before the eremites went into the desert. St Paul tells the Corinthians that his bodily presence is weak and his speech contemptible, yet who travelled more or suffered greater hardship or was more often assaulted and put in danger of death, until at last he was decapitated by his powerful enemies?

439

These variations in belief about the person of Jesus are of no consequence, nor, indeed, are the variations in the Gospels about matters of fact. What is important is the point, on which G.B.S. insists, that out of these insufficient and contradictory documents emerges a figure which has taken complete possession of a large part of the world's imagination. If anything is clear in the preface to *Androcles and the Lion* it is the respect and reverence G.B.S. feels for Jesus Christ. Discussing the choice between Barabbas and Our Lord, a choice which the world may be said to have been making since the beginning of time, he says, at the outset, 'The question seems a hopeless one after 2000 years of resolute adherence to the old cry of "Not this man, but Barabbas".'

'Yet it is beginning to look as if Barabbas was a failure, in spite of his strong right hand, his victories, his empires, his millions of money and his moralities and churches and political constitutions. "This man" has not been a failure yet; for nobody has ever been sane enough to try his way. . . . We have always had a curious feeling that though we crucified Christ on a stick, he somehow managed to get hold of the right end of it, and that if we were better men we might try his plan. . . . I am no more a Christian than Pilate was, or you, gentle reader; and yet, like Pilate, I greatly prefer Jesus to Annas and Caiaphas; and I am ready to admit that after contemplating the world and human nature for nearly sixty years, I see no way out of the world's misery, but the way which would have been found by Christ's will if he had undertaken the work of a modern practical statesman.'

He is impressed, as intelligent people always are, by the fact that Jesus seemed to resent being asked to perform a miracle, and that when he consented to perform one, he besought the healed not to tell anybody about it. G.B.S. gives the obvious explanation, namely, that Jesus had a gospel to preach, and that he was more concerned to preach it than to gain a reputation as a miracle-monger.

'But the deepest annoyance arising from the miracles would be the irrelevance of the issue raised by them. Jesus's teaching has nothing to do with miracles. If his mission had been simply to demonstrate a new method of restoring lost eyesight, the miracle of curing the blind would have been entirely relevant. But to say "You should love your enemies: and to convince you of this I will now proceed to cure this gentleman of cataract" would have been, to a man of Jesus's intelligence, the proposition of an idiot. If it could be proved to-day that not one of the miracles of Jesus actually occurred, that proof would not invalidate a single one of his didactic utterances; and, conversely, if it could be proved that not only did the miracles actually occur, but that he had wrought a thousand other miracles a thousand times more wonderful, not a jot of weight would be added to his doctrine. And yet the intellectual energy of sceptics and divines has been wasted for generations in arguing about the miracles on the assumption that Christianity is at stake in the controversy as to whether the stories of Matthew are false or true. According to Matthew himself, Jesus must have known this only too well; for wherever he went he was assailed with a clamour for miracles, though his doctrine created bewilderment.'

This is undoubtedly the fact. But it is possible that Jesus felt afraid of miracle-mongering, not so much because it might divert the minds of people from his doctrine, but because he feared that he might fail to repeat a success, and his doctrine would, therefore, suffer.

H. G. Wells, in *Tono-Bungay*, makes Ponderevo say about his patent medicine, 'We're minting faith, and by Jove we've got to keep on minting!' Obviously, a man whose sight has been restored would be more likely to listen to the doctrine than a man whose sight had not been restored. So would his friends and relations and all those who saw the miracle performed. It is not wicked to wish to be well. It is wicked to remain ill if you can obtain a cure. Was there any reason, apart from his fear of failure, why Jesus should not have performed such cures as he could in addition to preaching his gospel? They were part of his process of 'minting faith'.

The supreme fact about The Bible is that it is substantially a history of the growth of the idea of God. The idea visibly changes several times in the Old Testament, and is entirely different in the books of those who, very queerly, are called the Minor Prophets, from what it was in the Pentateuch. The teaching of Jesus has so little relevance to the teaching of Moses that it can only be associated with it by treating it as the climax of a series of developments as large and extensive as those between a sedan chair and a Rolls-Royce.

In the evolutionary process, man becomes conscious at last that he is a son of God, divine because he has been divinely created, and that life does not end: it is passed on. The logical conclusion of this belief, according to G.B.S., is the establishment of Communism with equality of incomes. The logic of this deduction is not apparent to everybody. Does the kingdom of God on earth depend on each of us receiving, say, a pound a week? Is not G.B.S. falling into the delusion from which John Galsworthy suffered, that it is impossible for a poor man to be happy, and inviting us all to believe that the problems of existence are soluble only on an economic basis?

When he says that 'the late Mr Barney Barnato received as his lawful income three thousand times as much money as an agricultural labourer of good general character', and then invites his readers to 'name the principal virtues in which Mr Barnato exceeded the labourer three thousandfold; and give in figures the loss sustained by civilisation when Mr Barnato was driven to despair and suicide by the reduction of his multiple to one thousand', he is manifestly setting a

441

sum which has no relevance to any moral principles worth mentioning.

No one has ever asserted that a rich man is superior to a poor man in mind or morals because he is rich or, indeed, that he is superior to the poor man in any respect. But there are degrees of ability. The Fabian Society, indeed, was in the habit of demanding the Rent of Ability. And no society that the mind of man has yet conceived has been or can be conducted on any other basis than that of difference of income. Barnato was probably paid too much. The agricultural labourer certainly was paid too little. But the essential values of the two men would not be changed by any system of payment, equal or unequal; and it is the essential values that must be considered in the allotment of authority in any society that may be substituted for the one in which we live.

In a community in which the highest income allowed to anybody is £1,000 a year, the man who draws that sum will be a millionaire in comparison with the man whose income is only £100 a year; and if incomes were equalised and no one received more than a pound a week, the millionaire would be the man whose authority was the highest. Increasingly we perceive that what matters is not money, but power and authority.

A fact which G.B.S. does not face is that Jesus, after he had been baptised and had come out of the wilderness to begin his mission, made no effort to earn a living. Not only did he cease to work as a carpenter, but he persuaded other men to give up their jobs, sometimes with great inconsideration. It is true that in the first paragraphs of the preface G.B.S. says 'I have no sympathy with vagabonds and talkers who try to reform society by taking men away from their regular productive work and making vagabonds and talkers of them too,' but that is as far as he goes in condemnation of the band of missionaries who wandered up and down Israel, living on the land.

He has no rebuke for the sons of Zebedee who responded to the call of Jesus with such precipitation that they left their old father to cope alone with boats and nets while they hurried off to redeem suffering humanity. He makes a slip when he says 'the disciples, like Jesus himself, were all men without entanglements': St Peter was a married man with a dependent mother: but this rough-tongued, quick-tempered, commonplace and semi-illiterate fisherman was allowed to desert his wife and home without, apparently, making any provision for them or even sending word to say that he was joining the roving evangelists.

It is all very well to say that Jesus found family ties tedious and obstructive of his purpose, but G.B.S., as a good Fabian, would have had Jesus in the dock pretty soon had he and his companions lived in the twentieth century and had casually and callously abandoned their families. St Paul receives harsh treatment from G.B.S., and we may agree with much that he says about this irascible rabbi, but he did at least earn his living as a tentmaker while he went about, enduring great hardship, trying to evangelise Europe.

Shaw manifestly does not believe that Jesus was divine in the sense that is expounded in the Apostle's creed; or that he is more distinct from other men than a genius is from a routine person. Who is greater, a man who aspires to be a god or a god who reduces himself to the level of a man? May we not justifiably believe that one who fans the divine fire in himself and inspires other men to find their own fire, is a god more worthy of worship than a third part of the Trinity who spent some thirty years in human flesh, well aware that he would rise again from the dead and resume his place in the god-head? We can follow the example of the man who reaches out to divinity, but what example is there to be followed in a god who descends to flesh?

The preface ends, as, indeed, it had to end, inconclusively, but it fulfills a great purpose: to make its readers examine their minds and hearts and justify their faith. A man who reads it with care must feel a keener interest in his belief than he felt before he read it, even if he disagrees with almost every word G.B.S. writes. It offers us a vivid example of the stimulating effect G.B.S. had on people. Those who had previously taken their faith on trust and were Anglicans or Roman Catholics or Nonconformists for no other reason than that they were born in a particular bedroom, were compelled after they had read the preface to try to know what their faith was and why they held it. And what better service can one man render another than to make him understand his creed?

136

In 1912, G.B.S. wrote a one-act play, called *Overruled*, which was performed in the same year. It is a slight, desiccated thing, done in the mood of *The Philanderer* and full of the embarrassing skittishness which he was apt to display when sex relations were involved. He had long been terrified of his own emotions and sought to allay them by laughing them off; but the laugh was always forced. The last twenty years of his life were full of fear of women, and this fear, after Charlotte's death, degenerated into something like mortal terror. *Overruled* is the laughter of a man who is frightened out of his wits.

It was in this year that he began his comic relations with Mrs Patrick Campbell, who preferred temperament to talent, and threw away a career as a great actress so that she might provide slight people with topics of conversation because of her whims and wham-sies. How tiresome she was is made plain in a letter written by W. B. Yeats to his father in 1909.[1] He had written *The Player Queen* for her, and at the end of November went to her house to read it. He was invited to lunch at 1.15. At 2, she appeared, and lunch was eaten. The first act, much interrupted by comments from a parrot, was read and received with enthusiasm. As Yeats was about to begin the second act, a musician arrived to play incidental music in some production in which Mrs Campbell was about to act. 'This won't delay me more than ten minutes,' she said to Yeats. 'And then,' Yeats tells his father, 'began an immense interminable quarrel with the musician about his music', which must have been especially tiresome to Yeats who loathed music.

The row lasted for an hour and a half, and Yeats suggested that he should telephone to a friend and cancel an engagement to dine. At 6.30, the musician departed, and the second act was begun. 'A deaf man sat there whose mission was, it seemed, to say irrelevant enthusiastic things to Mrs Campbell. I got through Act 2. Mrs Campbell still enthusiastic. Then there came in telephone messages and I was asked to stay to dinner and read it afterwards. . . .

'After dinner arrived Mrs Campbell's dressmaker, this would only take a few minutes.' But it went on and on and on. 'At half past ten there was a consultation in the drawing room as to whether somebody shouldn't go up and knock at Mrs Campbell's door. It was decided that somebody should, but everyone declined to be the one. I wanted to go home, but I was told on no account must I do that. At half past 11, Mrs Campbell came down, full of apologies, it would only be a few minutes longer. At twelve, young Campbell's wife, who is an American heiress, and therefore independent, announced that she was going home and did, taking her husband. . . . At half past twelve Mrs Campbell came in so tired that she had to lean on her daughter to get into the room.'

Yeats told her that he must go home, but Mrs Campbell insisted that she should hear the end of the play on the same day that she had heard its beginning. So Yeats resumed his reading. 'She did not know one word I was saying. She started to quarrel with me! . . .'

It was not until 1912 that G.B.S. began to take serious notice of her. There had been intermittent correspondence between them, mainly about possible productions of plays, especially of *Caesar and Cleopatra*, but the letters were sometimes separated by long intervals, two of which were each about five years. *Pygmalion* was written for her, and when it was ready, he began his attempt to secure her interest by writing the extravagant letters that he habitually wrote to actresses whom he wished to act for him.

[1] *The Letters of W. B. Yeats.* Edited by Allan Wade, p. 539.

'Many thanks for Friday,' he writes to her, 'and for a Saturday of delightful dreams. I did not believe that I had that left in me. I am all right now, down on earth again with all my cymbals and side drums and glaring vulgarities in full blast; but it would be meanly cowardly to pretend that you are not a very wonderful lady, or that the spell did not work most enchantingly on me for fully 12 hours.'

The old showman, the circus barker was at it again, telling the woman to walk up, walk up and see the wonderful performance! . . .

This pseudo-romance was pure salesmanship: he had a play to sell, and he was using all the pedlar's wiles with the capricious kitchenmaid. The relationship was as innocent as dewdrops on brambles. Another man, writing to Mrs Campbell, with far more cause for passionate asseveration than G.B.S. ever had, would have written, 'I greatly enjoyed meeting you on Friday', but G.B.S., with his eyes on his wares, wrote and behaved as if he had just stepped out of *The Arabian Nights* after intense and delightful dalliance with the Sultan's favourite. This was his version of Neon lights.

His second piece of paper passion is dated July 3, and although it begins with 'beatricissima', it is little more than a sound business letter, in which he tells her plainly and very sensibly that a single star company is a hopeless enterprise financially, and that the only sound theatrical companies are those in which there are two stars: an actor and an actress. 'O Stella Stellarum, there is nothing more certain in the suns than if you attempt management on the single star system, nothing—not even my genius added to your own—can save you from final defeat. Male and female created He them. Your public is more than half feminine: you cannot satisfy their longing for a male to idealise; and how can they idealise a poor salaried employee pushed into a corner and played off the stage. Do you want to be a Duse? A hammer without an anvil? A Sandow with paper dumb-bells?'

There never was a man who could tear a passion to tatters as effectively as G.B.S. when he was writing a purely business letter. 'I could not love thee, dear, so much, loved I not money more,' he tells her. 'I must go now and read this to Charlotte. My love affairs are her unfailing amusement: all their tenderness recoils finally on herself.' Charlotte probably rocked with laughter as he read it to her, and assured him that he was an unscrupulous and mercenary devil who led poor actresses up the garden path and, pretending to passion, induced them to sign contracts for plays.

Mrs Pat herself was aware of his purpose. When, perhaps in a fit of remorse, he told her to shut her ears tight against 'this blarneying Irish liar and actor', who would fill 'his fountain pen with your heart's blood and sell your most sacred emotions on the stage', she replied, 'You didn't *really* think that I believed you came to see me because you were interested in *me*. I knew it was Liza,' the flower girl, 'and I was delighted that you should be so businesslike in such a bewilderingly charming way. . . .' One of her friends, she tells him a year later, had warned her against him. 'He walks into your heart with his muddy galoshes, and then walks out, leaving his muddy galoshes behind him. . . . His love is epistolary. . . . He has no respect for the feelings of those who love him. . . . Don't give him affection: he will surely hurt you.'

The singular fact about their relationship is that what had begun as a piece of business blarney suddenly turned serious, so far as G.B.S. was concerned, and became a source of trouble to Charlotte. The jester, selling his wares to the girl at the back door, found himself infatuated with her. He talked about her wherever he went, boring his listeners intensely. Sidney Webb, who disliked her, considered his 'subsequent infatuation as a clear case of sexual senility',[1] but as the passion of love could not be scheduled and indexed and placed neatly on a file, Sidney was unlikely to regard it as anything else.

Charlotte began to feel alarmed. Mrs Pat, galled, perhaps, by Charlotte's indifference to her, was acutely eager to make her acquaintance. In 1912, by chance more than design, they met briefly, and Charlotte treated the irresponsible and tempestuous creature with 'high courtesy', as G.B.S. said.

> 'She has a calm way of taking it for granted that no woman can resist me; and when her affections and interest are not engaged her feeling seems to be an odd mixture of shrugging her shoulders at them because they can't; and being indignant and contemptuous if they can. She doesn't care much for women; and she hasnt found you out yet. . . .'

In May 1913, Charlotte accidentally overheard a telephone conversation between G.B.S. and Mrs Pat which deeply disturbed her. Telling Mrs Campbell of this, G.B.S. wrote 'the effect was dreadful. It hurts me miserably to see anyone suffer like that. I must, it seems, murder myself or else murder her. . . . Well, I daresay it is good for us all to suffer; but it is hard that the weak should suffer the most. If I could be human and suffer with a suffering of my own, there would be some poetic justice in it; but I can't: I can only feel the sufferings of others with a pain that pity makes, and with a fierce impatience of the unreasonableness of it—the essential inhumanity of this jealousy that I never seem able to escape from.

> 'And it is a comfort at least that you also have the unquenchable gaiety of genius, and can stand anything. . . . I throw my desperate hands to heaven and ask why one cannot make one beloved woman happy without sacrificing another. We are all slaves of what is best within us and worst without us.'

[1] See Introduction to *Our Partnership* by Beatrice Webb, p. 9.

He was not deceived by his infatuation. He knew the woman well enough, how calculating she was, how careful about the lengths to which she would go; and he knew in his heart as well as in his mind that she was a delusion and a sham, a thing of greedy appetites, incapable of honest passion and reckless desire. While this grotesque love affair was in spate, she became engaged to be married to George Cornwallis-West, and the entanglement turned comic when Cornwallis-West and G.B.S. discovered that they liked each other immensely. 'Therefore, though I like George (we have the same taste) I say he is young and I am old; so let him wait until I am tired of you.

> 'That cannot in the course of nature be long. I am the most faithless of men, though I am constant too: at least I dont forget. But I run through all illusions and trample them out with yells of triumph. And about you I am a mass of illusions. It is impossible that I should not tire soon: nothing so wonderful could last. You cannot really be what you are to me: you are a figure from the dreams of my boyhood—all romance, and anticipation of the fulfilment of the destiny of the race, which is thousands of years off. I promise to tire as soon as I can so as to leave you free. I will produce *Pygmalion* and criticise your acting. I will yawn over your adorably silly sayings and ask myself are they really amusing. I will run after other women in search of a new attachment; I will hurry through my dream as fast as I can; only let me have my dream out. . . .'

They began to meet at his sister Lucy's house at Denmark Hill. Lucy and Mrs Pat had so much in common that they instantly became good friends; and Lucy, no doubt, still sore from Charlotte's distaste for her, took pleasure in conniving at deception. It amused her, perhaps, to think that Charlotte thought G.B.S. was paying a fraternal visit to his ailing sister when it was to meet Mrs Pat.

But the violent end to this thunder and lightning affair was swiftly approaching. A man as romantic as G.B.S. could not continue in thrall to a calculating woman. Early in August 1913, when she was staying at The Guildford Hotel at Sandwich, G.B.S. decided to join her there. His intention was, I do not doubt, to consummate their love; but he had forgotten, if he had ever known, that she was the supreme egotist, the man-teaser in excelsis, the woman with her eye firmly fixed on her own advantage and on nothing else. On August 10, horrified at finding him in Sandwich and terrified by the thought of what the effect of this visit would be on her impending marriage, she sent him this note:

> 'Please will you go back to London to-day—or go wherever you like but don't stay here—if you won't go I must—I am very very tired and I oughtn't to go another journey. Please don't make me despise you. Stella.'

On the following day, he found another note awaiting him at her hotel. She had fled. 'Goodbye. I am still tired—you were more fit for a journey than I—Stella.' The reaction was swift and terrible. The wild love turned instantly to wilder loathing. He sat down and sent her a letter that must have torn even her complacency to pieces:

'Very well, go. The loss of a woman is not the end of the world. The sun shines: it is pleasant to swim: it is good to work: my soul can stand alone. But I am deeply, deeply, deeply wounded. You have tried me: and you are not comfortable with me: I cannot bring you peace, or rest, or even fun: there is nothing really frank in our comradeship after all. It is I who have been happy, carelessly happy, comfortable, able to walk for miles after dinner at top speed in search of you, singing all the way . . . and to become healthily and humourously sleepy afterwards the moment I saw that you were rather bored and that the wind was in the wrong quarter. Bah! you have no nerve; you have no brain: you are the caricature of an eighteenth century male sentimentalist, a Hedda Gabler titivated with odds and ends from Burne-Jones's ragbag: you know nothing, God help you, except what you know all wrong: daylight blinds you: you run after life furtively and run away or huddle up and scream when it turns and opens its arms to you: you are a man's disgrace and infatuation, not his crown 'above rubies': instead of adding the world to yourself you detach yourself, extricate yourself, guard yourself: instead of a thousand charms for a thousand different people you have one fascination with which you blunder about—hit or miss—with old and young, servants, children, artists, Philistines: you are a one-part actress and that one not a real part: you are an owl, sickened by two days of my sunshine: I have treated you far too well, idolised, thrown my heart and mind to you (as I throw them to all the world) to make what you could of: and what you make of them is to run away. Go then: the Shavian oxygen burns up your little lungs: seek some stuffiness that suits you. You will not marry George! At the last moment you will funk him or be ousted by a bolder soul. You have wounded my vanity: an inconceivable audacity, an unpardonable crime. Farewell, wretch that I loved. G.B.S.'

His fury was unabated on the following day, and he wrote to her again, the letter being headed, 'Sandwich. Darkness.'

'Oh my rancor is not slaked: I have not said enough vile things to you. What are you, miserable wretch, that my entrails should be torn asunder hour after hour. Of that 57 years I have suffered 20 and worked 37. Then I had a moment's happiness: I almost condescended to romance. I risked the breaking of deep roots and sanctified ties; I set my feet boldly on all the quicksands: I rushed after Will o' the Wisp into darkness: I courted the oldest illusions, knowing well what I was doing. I seized handfuls of withered leaves and said, "I accept them for gold". And now there is that desolate strand, and the lights of Ramsgate that might have been the camp fires of the heavenly hosts on the Celestial mountains. I said, "there are seven stars and seven sorrows and seven swords in the heart of the Queen of Heaven: and for myself I want seven days." They began; and I held back: I was not greedy: for I wanted the last to be the best. And you yawned in my face, and stole the last five to waste in some desolate silly place with your maid and your chauffeur. Oh, may you be bored until in desperation you ask the waiter to walk out with you! You are worse than that fiend of a woman: she could at least hate and stick to it: you are neither love nor hate. Wretch, wretch, how will I, an Irishman know this Roman Catholic product, this precociously forced erotic sentimentality, this narrow mind, this ignorance, this helplessness that longs to be forced because it can imitate [? initiate] nothing, will nothing, change nothing, that has no power except the power of endearment and no appeal except the appeal of beauty. These are the things you set up against me when I drag you out into freedom and fellowship. Give me, oh my critical mind and keen eye, a thousand reasons for treating this light creature as she deserves, if such a monstrous retribution is possible. Come round me all the good friends I have neglected for her. Even her slanderers shall be welcome: I shall say "Spit your venom; heap up your lies; vomit your malice until the air is poison; you will still fall short of the truth." And to her friends, her dupes, her adorers, I will say, "All that you say is true and not half good enough for her; and yet it is all nothing: she would tear the strings out of an archangel's harp to tie up parcels: she has done that with my very heart strings." And this is the wretch whom I shall have to drive through a play which she will do her utmost to ruin, whom I shall have to flatter, to conciliate, to befriend on occasions when she is about to run violently down a steep place into the sea. Stella, how could you, how could you? . . .'

Like Shakespeare, he had met and been sorely wounded by his Dark Lady of the Sonnets, the little wanton woman without a heart or a mind, to whom money was the most important thing in the world, who wanted to play with incombustible fire. He was still sore and bleeding on the third day after her flight. 'I want to hurt you because you hurt me. Infamous, vile, heartless, frivolous, wicked woman! Liar! lying lips, lying eyes, lying hands, promise-breaker, cheat, confidence trickster! . . .'

His taunts stung her little wizened heart into retaliation. 'You with your eighteenth-century ribaldry habit. You lost me because you never found me.—I who have nothing but my little lamp and flame —you would blow it out with your bellows of self. You would snuff it with your egotistical snortings—you elegant charmer—you lady killer—you precious treasure of friendship—for you do I keep my little lamp burning for fear you may lose your way in the dark! . . .'

But the fire had been raked out and the cinders were cold, and her maudlin drivel about her little lamp could not rekindle it. The correspondence dragged on for several years, but a listless, dead correspondence about plays and performances. The vehemence of his reproaches had almost kindled a passion in that cold bosom, but he had thrown away the torch. He had done with the woman. She could continue to amuse him. He could still pretend a passion when he meant only a business deal, and he could evoke gales of wrath from Charlotte by seeming to be still attentive to her. Writing to Mrs Pat from Valence-sur-Rhone in September 1913, he says: 'Charlotte is happy in the prospect of joining Lena [Ashwell] in Biarritz: and that after two perfectly frightful scenes with me, in which she produced such a case against my career and character as made Bluebeard seem an angel in comparison, she quite suddenly and miraculously—at a moment when murder and suicide seemed the only thing left to her— recovered her intellectual balance, her sanity, and her amiability completely, and became once more (after about two years) the happy consort of an easygoing man.'

The end of all that passion was a nagging old woman, whom no one would employ any more because of her tantrums and affectations and her dreary repetitions of stale emotions. She wished to publish G.B.S.'s letters so that she could make money out of them. He had always helped her when she was in trouble, but this was a trouble of a different sort. She wanted publicity as well as money. He tells her that their correspondence must not be published in Charlotte's lifetime, but she repeats with idiot iteration her demand that it shall. The poor old temperament is wearing very thin now, and it pleases nobody, not even her. She knows that her 'lines' are stale and cannot stir a single pulse. She had performed all her tricks too often, and the audience was tired of them and wanted new tricks. Her marriage to Cornwallis-West, which had taken place on April 6, 1914, collapsed, as was inevitable, and she drifted, jobless, about, calling for help from G.B.S. and anybody else who could assist her.

She went off to Hollywood, and, in that place of faked emotions and spurious passion, she rattled the old bones of her temperament again, but no one was amused. Even there, she failed of effect. It was soon after her departure from New York that G.B.S. asked me one morning if I knew where she was. The question convinced me that she no longer mattered much to him, a poor old woman who might need help. That was all. 'Yes,' I replied. 'She's in Hollywood, trying to get jobs in moving pictures. All they can do with her is to make her climb up ladders!' 'Oh,' he muttered. 'Well, I suppose I'll have the usual S.O.S. before long!'

She left America to come home, but the Customs officers would not allow her to bring her dog, Moonbeam, into the country until it had been in quarantine. So she went on to the Continent, from which came appeals full of self-pity. She moaned and sighed and whined and snivelled. 'If only you could write a true book', he tells her candidly and brutally, 'entitled, WHY, THOUGH I WAS A WONDERFUL ACTRESS, NO MANAGER OR AUTHOR WOULD EVER ENGAGE ME TWICE IF HE COULD POSSIBLY HELP IT, it would be a best seller. . . . As to bringing you over. I had as soon bring the devil over. You would upset me and everybody else. You don't know how I have blessed that wretched little dog. . . .'

In her last letter to him, dated June 28, 1939, she tells him that she is 'getting used to poverty and discomfort, and even to the very real unhappiness of having no maid to take a few of the little daily cares from me, and give me an arm when I cross the road carrying Moonbeam through the terrifying tearing traffic.' But he remains inexorable to her wheedling, reminding her in the last letter he wrote to her, that Gabriel Pascal had had to give her part in a film to Marie Lohr because she 'would not be separated for six months' from Moonbeam. His last words are like the sound of a knell. 'I am too old, too old, too old.'

She died in Paris on April 9, 1940. Her age was 75. 'Yes, she is dead;' he wrote to Mrs Ada Tyrrell on April 17, 'and everybody is greatly relieved; herself, I should say, most of all; for the last pictures of her are not those of a happy woman. She was not a great actress but she was a great enchantress, how or why I dont know; but if she wanted to capture you, you might as well go quietly; for she was irresistible. Unfortunately, she was professionally such a devilish nuisance that nobody who had been through a production with her ever repeated the experience if it were possible to avoid it. She made a great success for Pinero and another for me; but though we both wrote plays afterwards containing parts that would have suited her to perfection, we did not cast her for them. She did not know how to live with real people in the real world. She was a hybrid, half Italian, half suburban Croydon; and the transition from one to the other was bewildering. Though her grandfather ran a circus and her mother rode in it and was never anglicised, there must have been a strain of nobility on the Italian side; for she could behave finely on occasion. She enchanted me among the rest; but I could not have lived with her for a week; and I knew it; so nothing came of it. She was kind to Lucy, who, in some ways, could walk round her. Orinthia in *The Apple Cart* is a dramatic portrait of her. R.I.P.'

137

But the most powerful factor in the breaking up of this romance was the imminence of war; and we must therefore go back a year or two. He had been writing articles and letters to editors on what should be done to avert this disaster, and his letters to Stella were largely light relief from this anxiety. The German people, under the rule of Bismarck, had changed from a sentimental, music-loving race into a jack-booted and military-minded nation, spoiling for a fight. France was in its customary state of disruption, while Russia was tottering into revolution under the rule of a weak and visionary Tsar.

Division was wide in England. The Tories had not yet recovered from the degeneration into which they had sunk after twenty years of power, and the Liberals, steeply divided into groups ranging from Liberal Imperialists to Radicals on the verge of Socialism, were led by flabby intellectuals whose habit, when trouble arose, was to retire to bed in tears or take to the bottle or wave their arms wildly while they babbled about the Welsh mountains as if they were their private property. Foreign affairs, on the principle that the man who knows least about a thing is the most suitable person to whom to entrust it, were under the direction of Sir Edward Grey, who had not even the schoolboy's knowledge of French, and was convinced that foreigners could very well be done without. Periodically, this nice, amiable man was torn away from fishing and bird-watching and told that there was trouble in the Balkans about which he must do something! . . .

The signs of impending trouble were already visible and were rapidly thickening.

Early in 1912, G.B.S. proposed that a pact should be made between Britain, France, Germany and the United States in which these nations should assert plainly and without any equivocation that any country which made war on a neighbour without submitting its grievance, if it had one, to the judgment of the Powers, would instantly find itself also at war with the Great Four. No attention was paid to his suggestion, a neglect that was, two years later, to cost Europe and, indeed, the whole world very dear. He was to issue warnings increasingly in the next twelve months, with as little effect, and so he turned his mind to a play he had mentioned in a letter to Ellen Terry in 1897 while he was busy on *Caesar and Cleopatra:* a play about an 'East End dona in an apron and three orange and red ostrich feathers'. This was *Pygmalion*.

138

But before we come to its production we must take note of the death of G.B.S.'s mother, who had taught music at the North London Collegiate School for Girls until she was an old woman, not because she had need of money—her son had seen to that—but because she had need for work. She was eighty-two when, on February 19, 1913, she died. She had outlived her husband by nearly twenty-eight years. Granville Barker, who went to her cremation, was amazed at G.B.S.'s gaiety during the ceremony. He was delighted with the spectacle of his mother's body enveloped in garnet flames, and imagined her spirit anxiously regarding the workman who separated her ashes from the remains of the coffin as if she feared that he would make a mistake.

'You certainly are a merry fellow,' Barker dryly remarked.

It was odd that he, who knew him well, should not have realised that G.B.S. was once more hiding his emotion under an air of raillery. Was it callous of him to think that his mother would take pleasure in the brilliant colours in which her worn-out body was consumed? Was this not a finer end for it than slow and foul decay in sodden earth?

G.B.S. continued his campaign about the imminent danger of war. An article, entitled *Armaments and Conscription: a Triple Alliance against War* was published in *The Daily Chronicle* on March 18, 1913, in which he restated his proposal that the Powers should ally themselves against aggressors:

'Our first step . . . should be to propose to France and Germany a triple alliance, the terms being that if France attack Germany, we combine with Germany to crush France, and if Germany attack France, we combine with France to crush Germany. . . . The alliance would guarantee, further, that if any other Power were to attack France or Germany, the three would line up together against that Power. From this starting-point we might enlarge the combination by accessions from Holland and the Scandinavian kingdoms and finally achieve the next step in civilisation, the policing of Europe against war and the barbarians. . . . If we cannot have an effective army for all purposes, we may as well shut up shop as far as foreign policy is concerned until we make an end of war; and that we can only do by being prepared to make war on war. . . . As a Socialist I am very strongly in favour of compulsory service. All income tax returns and insurance cards should in future have a column for chest measurements and age; and all able-bodied persons should be obliged to give the country 35 years' service, of which a few would be devoted to military training.'

He was to continue his admonitions and warnings to a careless and neglectful people, as we shall presently see, up to and after the outbreak of the First World War.

It was on May 12, 1913, that the first number of *The New Statesman* appeared. It was founded by the Webbs, with money from various people, including £1,000 from G.B.S. and a substantial sum from H. D. Harben, a millionaire Fabian and the grandson of a director of the Prudential Assurance Company. The editor was Clifford Dyce Sharp, with Jack Collings (now Sir John) Squire as literary editor, Desmond MacCarthy as dramatic critic, and a very able and likeable, but physically delicate, don at the London School of Economics, Charles Mostyn Lloyd, as foreign editor.

A deep and irreconcilable difference soon developed between Sharp and G.B.S., in which each of the parties had some right and some wrong, with Sharp rather more in the right than G.B.S.

G.B.S. had always been very independent in his attitude to editors, taking the view that a contributor of notable quality should be given liberties of an exceptional sort. Even in *The Star* days, when he was still known only to a restricted circle of readers in London and was almost totally unknown outside the capital, he behaved with audacious independence to T. P. O'Connor. O'Connor, indeed, was a good deal of a humbug, using his charming Irish voice very much in the way that Mrs Patrick Campbell used her strong sex appeal, for personal advantage; but he was an uncommonly good journalist, though not so good an editor, except that his ideas were excellent, and he was disinclined to be brushed aside even by G.B.S., who felt for him the contempt he felt for Irishmen in general; and although he realised how valuable a contributor G.B.S. was, he let himself be sufficiently exasperated by him to send him a letter in which, as G.B.S. records in his diary, he told him he could very well be done without. The row with Sharp was a repetition on a much larger scale than the row with T.P., and it became bitter, so far as Sharp was concerned.

Sharp, the son of a solicitor, was educated in engineering at University College, London, but his bent was for journalism, and he made no effort to become an engineer. He had a fair amount of mediocre talent, but had none of the brilliance which distinguished H. W. Massingham, the editor of *The Nation*, though he was, perhaps, more balanced in his beliefs. He was ambitious and obstinate, and he had a considerable amount of moral courage. A less bold and courageous man would not have made so strong a stand against G.B.S. as he did.

He received such training in journalism as he had, first, as assistant editor of *The New Age*, under A. R. Orage, an erratic man of quality who was never quite sure whether he was editing a paper or founding a new religion or being a public nuisance; and, second, as editor of the Webbs' propaganda sheet, *The Crusade*, which was the organ of their society to promote the success of the Minority Report on the Reform of the Poor Law. His training, it will be noticed, was slight, sufficient to enable him to 'put the paper to bed', but no more than that. He had never worked on a daily newspaper, nor been connected with any magazine, other than one of small circulation.

Rattray, referring to the quarrel between Sharp and Shaw, refers to the former as 'this young man in his twenties', but Sharp, at the time of his appointment to *The New Statesman*, was thirty and was about two years older when the quarrel was made. He had married Rosamund, a daughter of Hubert Bland, the Treasurer of the Fabian Society, who reviewed novels for the paper, and was more of a Tory Democrat than a Socialist.

The situation was a peculiar one. G.B.S. realised that his opinions carried less weight with the public than they ought to have done, partly because he seemed to routine people to be perverse and irresponsible, but mainly because he had wit and could think quickly. Winston Churchill spent years in the wilderness because he had imagination, wit, humour and style. Neville Chamberlain was preferred in his place. It took a World War to shake the English out of this strange stupidity, to which, however, they returned as soon as the War was won. Clement Attlee was put in Churchill's place.

Shaw's knowledge of this fundamental fact about the English made him eager that his contributions to *The New Statesman* should be published, not as individual articles under his name, but as editorials. Why he thought that his style could be disguised so skilfully, even by him, that the readers of the paper would think that his articles had been written by Sharp, whose style was as heavily pedestrian as a policeman's feet, is a mystery. His demand was a severe blow both to the Webbs and Sharp, who, naturally, hoped that signed contributions by him would be highly beneficial to the paper's circulation.

But G.B.S. was adamant. His contributions must be editorials. There is, however, a considerable difference between an editorial and a signed article. The first is supposed to be the deliberate opinion and policy of the paper: the second is strictly the opinion of the contributor, who alone is responsible for it. Sharp was bold, but not bold enough to accept responsibility for all G.B.S.'s opinions or to let them be regarded as the policy of *The New Statesman*. Despite his disappointment at G.B.S.'s refusal to sign his articles, he consented to print his editorials, subject, however, to the right every editor justly claims, of revising them so that they should conform to the policy of the paper. He revised them almost savagely. Desmond MacCarthy, in his book on Shaw, says, 'I know of no other literary man of anything like' G.B.S.'s 'eminence who would have taken such treatment' as Sharp's 'goodnaturedly'.

Here Sharp was deeply in fault, as Mrs Webb admits in her *Diaries, 1912-24*. Having right on his side, he promptly put himself in the wrong by behaviour which, in an undistinguished man of his age, was insolence when offered to a man of G.B.S.'s age and distinction. He should have gone to Adelphi Terrace and argued his irrefutable point, that an editor has the right to edit his paper, and

G.B.S. would probably have yielded to it. If the worst had come to the worst, he should have declined to print the article. He should not have hacked it to pieces.

It was not until November 1916, that the break between G.B.S. and *The New Statesman* was made. G.B.S., who prophesied that Sharp would one day shed Webb, a prophecy which was fulfilled, could no longer continue to work with his overweening editor, who now declined to publish even his signed articles. 'Clifford', Mrs Webb says in her *Diaries* for 1912–17, page 70:

> 'is a hard-minded conservative collectivist, who obstinately refuses to condemn either measures or men unless he has an alternative plan or an alternative Government to propose. He is also a materialist, a despiser of all ideals which cannot be embodied, in the near future, in social machinery to improve the conditions of life. Sentimentality is said to be the Emotion of the Unimaginative—but Sharp has neither imagination nor emotion. Unless he can see through a question or all round it with his intellect he refuses to admit that the question exists. Above all, he loathes the professional rebel. When he does not see the collectivist solution, he remains stolidly conservative. . . .'

There is a long letter in her *Diaries* from G.B.S. in which he puts his case against Sharp, and an equally long one from Sharp in which he puts his case against Shaw.

'As to Sharp,' G.B.S. writes, 'you must bear in mind that this conscription business is exceedingly trying to the nerves. Men of military age have to pretend to take it nonchalantly; but I have observed it pretty closely for some months and found that the suspense of playing for exemption is far worse than actual service. Sharp is a man of late hours and plenty of strong coffee; and he is ten times a better man in peace than in war. He is not very good at the technical business of literature: that is, he cannot bring all his personal qualities to literary expression: for instance, nobody who knows him personally would say that he is destitute of humour and generosity; but he cannot get those qualities into the paper, though he may later on, when the strain of the war is over. Meanwhile, he is a shaken man; and it was really this that determined me not to sit on the Board as a deadhead and make the nervous strain worse for him. His fundamental opposition to you will develop *unless you exercise his support of you strenuously*. . . . Three years ago, the *N.S.* was young; to-day it is about eighty.'

Sharp, in the final passage of his letter to Mrs Webb, puts the substance of his complaint against G.B.S.:

> '. . . I think you are quite right in saying that I am not very sensitive as regards individual hardships and injustices. I strongly believe in economising as it were one's capacity to protest and never using it

except when an important principle (as distinguished from a person) **is** involved and *where protest has a reasonable chance of producing concrete results. . . .'*

He had a considerable case against G.B.S., but he seemed not to realise that his own egotism was little less than Shaw's, without a tenth of Shaw's excuse. He was, by this time, beginning to be regarded as an important man. Herbert Samuel and Edwin Montague asked Graham Wallas to take a message to him. Would he make *The New Statesman* the organ of the Opposition? Sharp dined with Samuel, to discuss the proposal, but nothing came of it. The most that Sharp would consent to do was to take part in consultations and receive what he called 'Communications'.

In 1917, he was called up for military service, and posted to the artillery. Within a few weeks, he was withdrawn from the Army and sent to Stockholm, 'nominally', says Mrs Webb, 'as an independent journalist, but really as the agent of the Ministry of Intelligence to fathom Swedish opinion and to pick up information from foreign socialists.' This was a fairly foolish act on the part of the War Office, which had much better have left Sharp in his editorial chair than employ him in work for which he had no qualification whatsoever. At the end of the War, he returned to *The New Statesman*, his reputation undiminished. He felt so sure of himself that he refused the editorship of *The Daily News* when A. G. Gardiner resigned.

But things were not quite what they had been. There must have been some defect in his character which was not obvious even to those who knew him well. He seemed suddenly to go to pieces, and he had to resign from *The New Statesman*. His career became murky, and he, who had declined high positions in Fleet Street, began to crawl round the newspaper offices asking for a book to review. In 1935, he died in obscurity. His age was fifty-two.

139

Pygmalion, more than any other play that G.B.S. wrote, illustrates the curious habit of accumulation that went to the making of his work. Attention has already been drawn to a letter he wrote to Ellen Terry in 1897 while he was writing *Caesar and Cleopatra*. He told her of an idea he had for a play for Forbes Robertson and Mrs Patrick Campbell, a play about an 'East End dona in an apron and three orange and red ostrich feathers'. R. F. Rattray suggests that it was while he was in Rodin's studio that the idea of *Pygmalion's* statue was remembered, and that he also recalled a play by W. S. Gilbert, entitled *Pygmalion and Galatea*. The opening scene, under the portico of St Paul's Church in Covent Garden on a wet and windy night, was suggested by an incident of which he was a witness. It is described in *Music in London, 1890–94*, Vol. III, p. 142:

> 'Some time ago, happening to be caught in a pelting shower in St Martin's Lane on a gloomy evening, I took refuge in the entry to a narrow court, where I was presently joined by three men of prosaic appearance, apparently respectable artisans. To my surprise, instead of beginning to talk about horses, they began to talk about music— pure vocal music, and to recall old feats of their own in that department, illustrating their conversation by singing passages in which certain pet singers of theirs had come out wonderfully. This led to a discussion as to whether they could remember some work which had been an old favourite of theirs. Finally, one of them pulled out a pitch pipe; the three sang a chord; and away they went, *sotto voce*, but very prettily, into a three-part song, raising their voices a little when they found that the passers-by were too preoccupied by the deluge to notice them. They were wholly untroubled by any consciousness of the distinguished critic lurking in the shadow a few feet off, greatly pleased with the performance but withal sufficiently master of his business not to be surprised at this survival.'

The foundation of the play, however, was laid in the lodging-house in Dublin to which G.B.S., when he was a youth, went to live with his father after his mother migrated with her daughters to London. It was there that his interest in phonetics was evoked by Chichester Bell; an interest which he maintained until the day of his death, and is amply demonstrated in his last will and testament.

Pygmalion was performed for the first time on any stage at the Hofburgertheater in Vienna on October 16, 1913, with immense success, which was repeated when, on November 1, it was performed at the Lessingtheater in Berlin. This was the beginning of a long career of success wherever it was produced.

The choice of Vienna for its *premiere* was partly a compliment to its translator, Trebitsch, but mainly because the routine depreciation of his plays by the London dramatic critics had created a good deal of prejudice against his work among Continental managers. He decided, therefore, that *Pygmalion* should be seen first in Austria so that it might reach the German stage untarnished by doubt of its value. This policy was fully justified by its result; for when, six months later, the play reached the West End, the London critics, knowing how popular the play had been abroad, were less condescending in their comments than they would otherwise have been. Sheep are the model for most of us. How successful *Pygmalion* has been will appear from the fact that it has been revived in London alone six or seven times, and that it is the subject of a highly popular moving picture.

It was produced in London at His Majesty's Theatre on April 11,

1914, with Beerbohm Tree and Mrs Patrick Campbell in the principal parts. Tree was miscast as Professor Henry Higgins, but G.B.S. had to accept him because Mrs Campbell, for whom the part of Eliza Doolittle was written, was under contract to him. Its success was notable, and it ran until the end of the third week in July, and would have run for a longer time but for the fact that on June 28, the Archduke Francis Ferdinand, heir to the Austro-Hungarian throne, and his morganatic wife, the Duchess of Hohenberg, were killed by bombs in Sarajevo, the capital of Bosnia. Five weeks later, the First World War began: a week, that is to say, after *Pygmalion*, because of the fear in every heart, was, like many other plays, withdrawn. It was produced at the Park Theatre, New York, on October 12, 1914, with Mrs Patrick Campbell in the cast, and ran there until the spring when it went on a long tour.

140

A play about phonetics would seem certain to be a failure, unlikely, even, to obtain production, but G.B.S. was too deft a propagandist not to know how to coat his pill with plenty of agreeable jam; and the entertainment value of *Pygmalion* is great. The present generation will not easily be able to understand why it caused such a sensation in London when Eliza Doolittle, the transformed flower-girl, on being asked by Freddy Eynesford Hill if she intended to walk across the park, replied, 'Walk! Not bloody likely!'

The theatre world was full of gossip about the shocking word Mrs Patrick Campbell would have to utter; and a vast amount of windy argument was heard on the subject. Some people, ignorant of the fact that *bloody* had been heard in other plays, especially in one by Lennox Robinson, without any member of the audience appearing to be in the least perturbed by it, assured all who would listen to them that the Lord Chamberlain would ban it or that Beerbohm Tree would forbid Mrs Patrick Campbell to say it. It was also foretold that if the word were used, there would be a frightful scene in the theatre, the performance might be stopped, and the play would probably be withdrawn. . . .

None of these prophecies was fulfilled; and the astonishing fact is that although every member of the audience at the first perform-ance appeared to know that Mrs Campbell would say 'Not bloody likely', the whole audience behaved as if it had not had the slightest idea that such a phrase would be uttered. As the words came off Mrs Campbell's lips, there was a great gasp, followed in a few moments by an extraordinary roar of laughter, a brief silence, and then by what is technically known as the double laugh: a renewal of the

459

laughter even stronger than the first. G.B.S. had taken the colour and vigour out of the word *bloody* by making it a term no more awful than *dash* or *bother*. To-day, genteel girls use it without turning a hair or suffering any rebuke.

G.B.S. sometimes regretted that he had written the line, not because he thought it was wrong, but because it diverted attention from the theme of the play. Its use, however, demonstrated a fact about him which is insufficiently perceived, that he knew the temper of his time and the liberties that could be taken with an audience far better than people who professed to be his superiors in knowledge.

Pygmalion is not a major play. Its theme excites little interest, nor are many people impressed by the plea for an extended alphabet. The transformation in six months of a guttersnipe into a lady able to adorn the drawing-room of a duchess is achieved by pure fairy-tale methods and not by an elaborate display of phonetic instruction; but the diversions caused by the characters themselves, and especially by the intrusion into the cast of Eliza's rapscallion father, Mr Doolittle, the dustman, who is 'one of the undeserving poor', and proud of it, make an entertainment that is immensely pleasing.

It is not the phonetics which impress those who read or see the play: it is the fine sentiment, that the flower girl will behave like a lady when she is treated like one; and that a woman who is only technically a lady is not a lady at all. Expensive education can produce a person who is formally at ease in polite company and, at the same time, has the mental and spiritual outlook of a slut. It was not a course of phonetics which made Eliza display good manners in a world which was not a social and intellectual slum, but an inward grace which, like a seed hidden in the soil, germinates only when the conditions are right.

The published work is followed by an account of Eliza's life after the play ends. It convinces nobody who reads it. G.B.S. would not have it that Eliza married Professor Higgins, and was wrath with Beerbohm Tree who, as the curtain fell on the last act, threw her a flower; and he took enormous pains to prove that she married the helpless and incompetent Freddy Eynesford Hill and earned his living and her own by starting a flower shop adjacent to the Victoria and Albert Museum. But the facts of the play cry out against its author. The end of the fourth act as well as the end of the fifth act deny the laboured account of the flower girl's future, and assure all sensible people that she married Henry Higgins and bore him many vigorous and intelligent children.

141

The War profoundly affected G.B.S.'s thoughts. It is essential to bear in mind that any war was to him a public calamity. I remember, when someone asked him why he had written *Common Sense about the War*, he replied, 'Because I have always loathed war!' But war, like force, is a fact, and will not be ended merely by loathing it. Popular feeling about it has changed very drastically in my life time. We no longer hear subalterns moaning lest a war shall end before they have a chance of taking part in it.

Wars, so far as the British were concerned, were fought mainly at a long distance, and did not interfere much, if at all, with the life of people at home. The Boer War was waged more than three thousand miles from these islands, and, except for the mourning clothes that began to be seen more and more in the streets, and the humiliation of the first defeats, it scarcely disturbed us. The First World War changed that. We were all in it, even our daughters and our sisters; and we had the shocking experience of being bombed and bombarded. The hope that war will soon cease to be a fact of human life is so slight that no responsible person can entertain it. There are people who like war, and are stimulated by it, whose only hope of fulfilling themselves is that there shall be war. But although war is not likely to end or to be greatly reduced in the lifetime of any person now alive, it is reasonable to try to prevent or limit it; and G.B.S.'s proposal that the Great Powers should agree to fight aggressors is the most likely means of ending war that we have yet discovered.

Common Sense about the War appeared as a supplement to *The New Statesman* on November 14, 1914. It excited little attention at first, though 75,000 copies of it were sold, nor was much, if any, resentment of it shown until its effect elsewhere than in Great Britain became known. The Germans naturally made the most of it, and opinion in America was noticeably shaken by it.

G.B.S. was not a man who hated people, but so far as he was capable of hating anybody, he detested that simple-minded country gentleman, Sir Edward Grey, who roused a fury in him that was almost ungovernable. It took him to the absurd length of calling Grey a Junker. This description of the Foreign Secretary bewildered the British. A German Junker had a clear and unmistakable meaning for the majority of people: it denoted a square-headed, thick-skulled Prussian with a bloody mind, who encouraged his sons to swagger about the pavements of Berlin in military uniform, pushing civilians into the gutter. There was nothing in Sir Edward Grey to suggest a figure so repulsive. But G.B.S. could not be persuaded to believe that

Grey was other than the most devious-minded man who ever bedevilled international politics.

His thoughts, indeed, were wholly unreasonable on this subject. He could not decide whether Grey was a stupid country bumpkin who floundered into matters beyond his understanding or a diabolical example of Machiavellian intriguers, who allied his country to France without breathing a word of what he was doing to his Cabinet colleagues. Even in this respect, he was so devious that he left the French Ambassador in such doubts about his intentions that that unhappy gentleman did not know until the penultimate moment whether Britain would support France or Germany or remain neutral. G.B.S.'s attitude to Grey resembled his attitude to the English people who were somehow to blame for all that went wrong on two contradictory grounds: first, that they were too thick to see beyond their noses, and, second, that they were so cunning that they saw beyond all the noses in Europe and America, and used their cunning discernment exclusively for their own advantage.

When, in the middle of the First World War, a gang of half-baked schoolmasters, surly shop assistants, incredibly bad poets and platoons of schoolboys began what must be the shabbiest rebellion in the whole history of insurrection, G.B.S. took up the attitude that all the outrages and atrocities in Ireland were committed by the Black and Tans who fell furiously and brutally on mild-mannered and saintly Sinn Feiners who were quietly walking about in the cool of the evening, saying, perhaps, a little prayer for the conversion of England, when, suddenly, they were assailed by bloody-minded soldiers who hacked and slew men, women and children, all of whom, as they drew their last breath, prayed that their murderers might be pardoned! . . .

There had been a political campaign against what is called 'secret diplomacy' before the war began, and Sir Edward had become identified as an active agent of such negotiations, and, indeed, had made an arrangement with France which was unknown to some of his colleagues in the Liberal Government. G.B.S. advocated 'open diplomacy', which is pure nonsense. Diplomatic negotiations cannot be conducted in public, any more than a national or local authority can negotiate for the purchase of a building or a piece of land in open debate.

Even those who felt some sympathy with the opinions expressed by G.B.S. in this pamphlet, were agreed that its publication was untimely. This was the supreme example of his habit of saying the right thing at the wrong moment. It confirmed the generality of people in their increasing suspicion that G.B.S. was essentially anti-British and was incapable of finding any good thing to say about the country he inhabited. This belief was absurd. A man does not spend the greater part of his life in a country he hates. Nearly all G.B.S.'s friends and intimates were English. His Irish friends were few, and he was not intimate with them. His knowledge of Ireland was slight, and most of it was derived from political arguments and not from experience. When, after the establishment of the Eirean Republic, he yielded to Charlotte's sentimental importunities and became a registered citizen of the Republic, he was appalled to learn that he had made himself an alien in the country he had no wish to leave. The thought of repatriating himself in Ireland was abhorrent to him.

Those who charge him with incurable anti-British feelings, misunderstood his character. He was under greater obligations to the American nation than he was to the people of Great Britain, but he was no kinder in his reference to the former than he was to the latter. He was the sort of man that Jeremiah was, a man compelled to speak his mind when he felt that his people were erring. It was more important to him that the British people should be right than that the French or the Germans or the Bashi-Bazoucks should be right; and he was highly contemptuous of the doctrine, my country-right-or-wrong. His country had no right to be wrong. This is, I insist, the fundamental fact about him; and it is one which is certain to make a man gravely misunderstood and cordially detested by his countrymen. John the Baptists are not popular, however much we may admire them after we have put them to death.

The First World War did undoubtedly frighten, though it did not daunt, the British people. German efficiency seemed about to be justified. The Retreat from Mons looked like a total defeat, and it was announced in terms that made it appear to be one, just as, two years later, the Battle of Jutland was announced by the Government as if it had been a victory for the German Fleet. A 'victory' which sent what was left of that fleet scurrying to ports from which it never emerged until the end of the War, is very rum.

An accumulation of feelings caused the English to change their attitude towards G.B.S. abruptly. They had previously regarded him as that clever and amusing chap. The discovery that he was an earnest and passionately sincere man upset and angered them. His hatred of war was treated as hatred of England. The arguments he used were insufficiently considered. His assertion, for example, that Grey should have made it plain to the Germans that we would fight them if Belgium were invaded and France assailed, was not considered at all. It is conceivable that if Grey *had* warned them, the Germans would still have invaded Belgium and France, but in that case there would be no complaint of duplicity on our part.

It should be remembered that even the French were not certain that we would support them until the penultimate moment. If the

463

French Ambassador could feel doubtful of our help, is it not reasonable to suppose that the Germans thought we would remain neutral, especially as some of our newspapers, for example, the *Daily News*, were imploring the Government to stay out of the War, and were enforcing their argument with the suggestion that we could make a great deal of money by selling supplies to both sides?

The fact that Grey was doing his utmost to prevent the war was unknown to G.B.S., but this ignorance, when he became aware of it, merely strengthened his argument against 'secret diplomacy'. Ramsay MacDonald, who was sent into the wilderness even by the Labour Party at this time, was as strongly opposed to 'secret diplomacy' as G.B.S. was, yet no man was ever more secretive, even furtive, in all his negotiations than MacDonald, who had all the reticence and love of intrigue and mystery which characterise the Highlander.

G.B.S. became intensely unpopular. His plays were no longer performed. His appearance at any public function caused the instant departure of many of those present. Some of his friends disowned him. His statement that England was not fighting in defence of 'little Belgium', but in defence of herself, infuriated people who failed to notice that exactly the same statement was made in a very popular and widely read book, *Ordeal by Battle*, by F. S. Oliver. It may be said that England's ultimate reason for entering the War was her own security, though why this should be regarded as an unworthy excuse is hard to understand, but it certainly is true that it was the invasion of Belgium which made many people, who, at first, were unwilling to enter the war, support our entrance. It is not unfair to say that if Belgium had not been invaded, we might have remained neutral.

The Belgians felt no ill-will against G.B.S. He was invited by the Government to state their case against Germany, and he did so in *An Open Letter to President Wilson*, which appeared in this country in *The Nation* on November 7, 1914. What effect it had on Wilson is not known. He gave no sign of having read it or, indeed, of knowing anything about G.B.S. But Archibald Henderson, who deals very severely with G.B.S.'s views on these matters, is confident that historians will one day recognise how influential those views were on Wilson's mind: in such matters, for example, as the Fourteen Points, The League of Nations, the Freedom of the Seas, direct dealing with the German people, and the Treaty of Versailles.

It must have seemed to many people, unaccustomed to the detachment of G.B.S.'s mind, that he was either perverse or afraid of the storm he had raised and eager to ingratiate himself with his countrymen again, when he agreed to a proposal by A. E. W. Mason, the novelist, who was then engaged in Secret Service work in the

464

Mediterranean area, that he should write a counter-blast to the German use of *Common Sense about the War* for circulation among the Moors. The result was an Epistle to the Moors which is said to have been effective in keeping them quiet. This was not the only problem G.B.S. set people. They found him hopeless when he stated that whatever party had been in power in 1914, 'we must have drawn the sword to save France and smash Potsdam as we smashed and always must smash Philip, Louis, Napoleon, *et hoc genus omne.*' That being so, why all the fuss with *Common Sense about the War*?

We need not labour the point that G.B.S. showed great moral courage in writing his pamphlet, but his moral courage was no greater than Clifford Sharp's in publishing it. The fact that it was written and published at all is, perhaps, the highest proof of the freedom of the British people. What other country, in such a time, would have allowed it to appear? If a German had written a similar work in 1914, would he, had he been left at liberty or alive, have been invited to visit the Front as the guest of the Commander-in-Chief of the German Army, as G.B.S. was invited to the British Front by Sir Douglas Haig in 1917?

142

During the War, a servant of the British Crown, Sir Roger Casement, an Ulsterman from County Antrim, who had done invaluable work in exposing atrocities in the Congo, became mentally unbalanced. This statement is not made offensively or in a partisan spirit, but as a fact. His biographer, Denis Gwynn, in a work entitled *The Life and Death of Roger Casement*, asserts his belief that Casement, in the last years of his life, was out of his mind. Had this plea been made and substantiated, he could not have been hanged, as he was in 1916.

Casement, in his lunacy, 'went native', as Ulstermen say of an Ulster Protestant who becomes an Irish Republican; and in October 1914, he began a campaign to secure the 'freedom' of Ireland by German aid. He gained admission to Germany, and, as part of his campaign, endeavoured to seduce Irish prisoners of war from their allegiance. They were to serve in a German Army as soldiers seeking to set Ireland free. This was a poor performance for a man of honour and some distinction, and it is inexcusable on any ground save that of insanity. It is idle to say that Ireland was suffering from great wrong. All Ireland's grievances at that time were academic, and could have impressed only men whose minds were divorced from reason.

The country was as contented as Ireland is ever likely to be; the government, especially in local affairs, was substantially in the control of the people who were either owners of their land or in process of becoming owners. There was a larger degree of general prosperity than there had ever been; and that prosperity was increased enormously during the War. It was, indeed, an argument used for rebellion by Patrick Pearse, an incompetent schoolmaster whose bankrupt school was maintained to a great degree by Irish-Americans on condition that he trained his pupils in riot and disturbance. He told his associates that Ireland was now so prosperous that the people were no longer interested in Home Rule.

Casement tried to persuade the Germans to send arms and troops to Ireland to help the malcontents to create a diversion there substantial enough to hamper the Allies in France. They were reluctant to do this because they could see in it no particular advantage for them. Casement had failed to seduce the prisoners of war from their allegiance. Except for two or three men, they refused to listen to him otherwise than with scorn and derision. If they were typical of the Irish people, then any hope the Germans might have been persuaded by Casement to hold would turn to dust and ashes. In the end, they agreed to send him and two companions to Ireland in a submarine and land them on the coast of Kerry. They promised to supply rifles at a later date: a promise which, even if they had intended to fulfil it, could not be kept because of events.

Casement, who, by this time, had lost faith in the Germans, was landed on April 30, 1916. The Rebellion was to begin three days later. But the British Intelligence officers knew more than they were thought to know; and Casement and his companions were arrested immediately after they had landed. Our concern is with him: his companions were men of little or no account. He was taken to London where he was tried for treason, was found guilty, and, after he had been deprived of his knighthood, was hanged.

Efforts were made to obtain a commutation of his sentence by people who had no sympathy with his actions, but were mindful of his good services in connexion with the Congo atrocities and were convinced that he was mentally deranged when he committed his treasonable acts.

Among those who took up Casement's cause was Mrs J. R. Green, the widow of the historian, who was in distress because she could not persuade any distinguished counsel to defend her protégé. Sir John Simon would not accept a brief, nor would Tim Healy. Sir Charles Russell, a Roman Catholic and son of Lord Russell of Killowen, refused to help in any way. When Gavin Guffy consented to act for him, his partners are said to have repudiated him. But even if a counsel of the first quality had been willing to defend Casement, the cost of defence in a High Court trial was certain to be heavy; and so Mrs Green, who had given £200, sought aid from people better off than herself. It was in the hope of obtaining money from G.B.S. that he and Charlotte were invited to lunch with her next-door neighbours, the Webbs, to meet her.

Mention has already been made of Mrs Webb's deep dislike of her husband's best friend. She was a woman very apt to dislike people. When she discovered that she could not manipulate G.B.S. for her purposes, she conceived a cold hatred for him which she periodically displayed in her conversation and in her diaries. Her account of the luncheon party, will be found in *Beatrice Webb's Diaries*, 1912–24, at pages 62–3. It is painful reading, not only in its display of bitter rage against G.B.S., but because she shows no percipience of any sort. She saw the surface of things, and even that was wrongly seen.

She had no knowledge of the fact that G.B.S., though he had tried in his peculiar way, to stir public feeling in favour of Casement, was shocked not only by his action in Germany, but by the rumour that was spread round London, that he was a sodomite. Beatrice Webb had never perceived the fact about G.B.S. that though he had the common failing of being hard in some respects, he had a far wider and deeper sympathy for unfortunate people than most of us have; and it was his fear of being submerged in his own emotions which made him behave as if he were callous.

'But G.B.S. as usual had his own plan. Casement was to defend his own case; he was to make a great oration of defiance which would "bring down the house". To this Mrs Green retorted tearfully that the man was desperately ill; that he was quite incapable of handling a court full of lawyers; that the most he could do was the final speech after the verdict. "Then we had better get our suit of mourning," Shaw remarked with an almost gay laugh. "I will write him a speech which will thunder down the ages." "But his friends want to get him reprieved," indignantly replied the distracted woman friend.'

The luncheon party was a failure. The Shaws refused 'to waste our money on lawyers', and G.B.S. went off to write his speech from the dock. 'Alice Green retired in dismay, and I felt like a fool for having intervened to bring Irish together in a common cause.' Such is Mrs Webb's comment, in which may be detected her sense of personal affront when anybody declined to fulfil her wish. It is followed by this bitter denunciation of a friend who had done much for her and her husband, and who, never in his life, allowed a harsh word about either of them to escape from his lips or his pen.

'Alice has been heroic; her house has been searched; she herself has been up before Scotland Yard; she is spending her strength and her means in trying to save the life of her unfortunate friend. The Shaws don't care enough about it to spend money; and Shaw wants to compel Casement and Casement's friends to "produce" the defence as a national dramatic event. "I know how to do it," was G.B.S.'s one contribution to the tragedy-laden dispute between the weeping woman friend and the intellectual sprite at play with the life and death of a poor human.'

I interrupt her to remark that there is not one word in this statement to show that Beatrice Webb was aware of the grave plight in which her country was at that time, how near, indeed, we were to defeat, or even that she knew what was the crime with which Casement was charged. Casement, indeed, was 'a poor human' and Mrs Green's 'unfortunate friend'. Was he not also a British subject and a servant of the Crown who had shown no interest whatever in Ireland until the last years of his life? And had not this 'poor human' attempted to cause the defeat of his country in war by persuading its enemy to help in raising a rebellion? Was not his effort to seduce prisoners of war from their allegiance a mean and paltry act? Is there any country in the world which would have behaved differently in such a case from the way in which Great Britain behaved?

Mrs Webb resumes her confidence to her diary:

'And yet the man is both kindly and tolerant, but his conceit is monstrous, and he is wholly unaware of the pain he gives by his jeering words and laughing gestures—especially to romantics like Alice Green. He never hurts my feelings because I am as intellectually detached as he is. He sometimes irritates Sidney with his argumenta-tive perversities, but there is an old comradeship between them, and G.B.S.'s admiration for Sidney's ability has become part of his *amour propre*. And there is this to be said: if everyone were as intellectual and unemotional as he is—as free from conventions in thought and feeling—his flashes might alter the direction of opinion. There would remain his instability of purpose. He is himself always in a state of reaction from his last state of mind or generalising from his most recent experi-ence. A world made up of Bernard Shaws would be a world in moral dissolution.'

But was G.B.S. as vain and foolish on this occasion as Beatrice Webb asserts he was? Mrs Green's tears are of no importance in this matter. She was one of those overbearing, bossy women—Beatrice was another—who start off with the assumption that what they want is what everybody should want. Was it wrong of Scotland Yard to make enquiries about her activities at this grave time in her country's history? If she chose to associate conspicuously with a man who had behaved as Casement had, what else could she expect?

There were only two pleas that could honourably be made for, or by, Casement: one, that he was insane; the other that he gloried in what he had done. The first plea seems not to have been considered by Mrs Green or the Webbs, or, indeed, by G.B.S. The second, suggested by G.B.S., was obviously based on the behaviour of Robert Emmet when he was in a similar situation to Casement's at the beginning of the nineteenth century. Emmet's speech from the dock has a fine peroration, which is, I suspect, the only part of it anyone, but myself, has read. The rest is fustian and clap-trap.

The speech drafted by Shaw to be delivered to the jury by Casement before they retired to consider their verdict, was privately published in twenty-five copies by Clement Shorter, a notable journalist in his time, and a passage from it is cited by Henderson on page 647 of his life of G.B.S. The passage runs as follows:

'Almost all the disasters and difficulties that have made the relations of Ireland with England so mischievous to both countries have arisen from the failure of England to understand that Ireland is not a province of England, but a nation, and to negotiate with her on that assumption. If you persist in treating me as an Englishman, you bind yourself thereby to hang me as a traitor before the eyes of the world. Now as a simple matter of fact, I am neither an Englishman nor a traitor: I am an Irishman, captured in a fair attempt to achieve the independence of my country; and you can no more deprive me of the honours of that position, or destroy the effects of my effort, than the abominable cruelties inflicted 600 years ago on William Wallace in this city when he met a precisely similar indictment with a precisely similar reply, have prevented that brave and honourable Scot from becoming the national hero of his country. . . . I am not trying to shirk the British scaffold: it is the altar on which the Irish saints have been canonised for centuries. . . .'

The argument in this passage is specious. Casement was not treated as an Englishman: he was treated as a British subject. As a servant of the Crown he had taken an oath to serve his sovereign faithfully, which oath he had broken for no discoverable reason, except that, on his retirement from his sovereign's service, he had developed into some sort of a Sinn Feiner, though he had no grievance, nor had he ever, until shortly before the outbreak of the war, displayed any interest in Ireland other than that of a man who had been born there, but had spent a large part of his life abroad.

Had he been a member of a Nationalist and Roman Catholic family, there would have been some sense in the argument G.B.S. tried to put into his mouth, but as he was a member of an Ulster Protestant and Unionist family, there was none. If he was a sane man, then, beyond a shadow of a doubt, he was a traitor. He had not disowned his allegiance or made any attempt to shed his British nationality. He kept the title his sovereign had conferred upon him.

469

The analogy between him and Wallace is a false one and has no relevance to fact. But Casement was not sane, and should not have been executed. In the middle of a war, however, when the situation seems desperate and defeat likely, men do not turn from their efforts to change the situation to enquire very closely into the sanity of a man who deserts his country and invites its enemy to invade it.

G.B.S. was not happy at this time. The bitter feelings he had roused by his sustained detraction of his country in its time of trouble, were wide and deep; and some of his closest friends withdrew their friendship from him. Henry Arthur Jones, who had been one of them, attacked him almost virulently; and induced the Dramatists' Club to tell him that his presence at their meetings was distasteful. He thereupon resigned his membership, and Granville-Barker, loyal to his friend, resigned his.

Jones, who was old and ill and no longer a popular dramatist, but was a good-natured, kindly, though irascible man, had ample excuse for the vehemence with which he denounced G.B.S. He was in America when *Common Sense about the War* was published there, and saw its effect on many American minds. He could hardly have been expected to feel complacent about it. There were Fabians who felt enraged by G.B.S., too much enraged to notice that a good deal of what he said was sound. But it is the fate of those who are solitary in their wisdom and thought, to be misunderstood.

Anyone who believes that G.B.S. was a pro-German or a pro-anything else but what he believed to be best for civilised society, fundamentally mistakes his purpose. A man who believes war to be a disaster to mankind, (and who is there now who believes anything else?) cannot justifiably be condemned for lashing out in anger when he finds the world landed with a gigantic war because Sir Edward Grey would not tell the Germans plainly that we would fight them if they violated Belgian neutrality and attacked France. We may, at least, acknowledge that there was high moral courage in a sensitive man, warmly attached to his friends, who proclaimed his faith in the face of all people when, had he been more politic and careful of his interests, he would have remained silent. He had, he said, demanded 'the establishment of a Hegemony of Peace, as desired by all who are capable of high civilisation, and formulated by me in the daily press in a vain attempt to avert this mischief whilst it was brewing. Nobody took the slightest notice of me; so I made a lady in a play say "Not bloody likely", and instantly became famous beyond the Kaiser, beyond the Tsar, beyond Sir Edward Grey.' This was written out of his heart's bitterness, and who will deny that he had cause?

During the war, G.B.S. wrote little but journalism, mostly about war, but he relieved his mind with some one-act plays, *O'Flaherty*,

V.C., *The Inca of Perusalem*, *Augustus Does His Bit*, and *Annajanska*, *The Bolshevik Empress*. The second was sent to the Abbey Theatre which I was then managing. While we were rehearsing it, a letter was sent to W. F. Bailey, a Land Commissioner and a Trustee of the Theatre, by the General Officer commanding the Dublin District, in which he stated that he had heard that the play was to be performed. My recollection of the letter, typical of the sort of communication that is written by a not very intelligent soldier, was the statement that, knowing the sort of man G.B.S. was, he wished to warn us that if there were a riot in the theatre as a result of the production, the theatre's licence would instantly be cancelled. As the play was written by G.B.S. to promote recruiting in Ireland, this was almost comic.

But it was also grave. The Abbey, like all theatres, was working under great difficulty. We lived from hand to mouth. A wet night would send our receipts almost galloping down. Summary closure of the theatre would be ruin. Yeats was in London, and Lady Gregory was in America. I had no one to give me counsel, except Bailey, an excitable little man, whose advice was that the play should be withdrawn, for the present at any rate. So we withdrew it, a decision I now deeply regret; for there is little in this very entertaining piece that can be called inflammable, although, heaven knows, the Irish do not need much to set them on fire. The play, I should add, was presented to the Abbey for performance in Ireland free of royalty.

G.B.S., early in the war, began a long play. This was *Heartbreak House*, which is said by many distinguished critics to be his best play. It is described as 'a Fantasia on English Themes in the Russian Manner', and was the beginning of his despair about the world. The Victorian belief in mechanical progress from bad to good, from good to better, from better to best, though it was derided by Edwardians, was sufficiently powerful to influence even them. The Webbs truly believed that if men and women were sensible enough to entrust their affairs to well-trained civil servants, Morris's Earthly Paradise, with the poetic nonsense omitted, would be established. H. G. Wells was certain that, barring cosmic disaster, progress was assured. G.B.S., too, shared this belief up to the time of the First World War. Thereafter, however, his faith was no longer firm, though it was not shattered. It was his hope that it could be sustained which attached him so closely to Communism.

Wells, convinced that all progress was made by the accumulated activities of large groups of innominate people, ran about the earth looking for leaders, and then, convinced that there were none, died in despair. Beginning with the belief that wilful man could achieve everything, he ended in the belief that wilful man could achieve

471

nothing. There was enough 'knowledge and imaginative material' scattered about the earth to turn 'the whole world into one incessantly progressive and happily interested world community. All that' was 'needed' was 'to assemble that scattered knowledge and these constructive ideas in an effective form.'

All? One puts the point to the Muslim and the Hindu, the Jew and the Arab, the Bulgarian and the Greek, the Yugoslav and the Italian, the people of Brazil and the people of the United States, the white and the coloured people. *Is* that all? It may be that as communication becomes quicker and easier, the feeling, already weakening, that people of one colour have against people of another, the white, black, brown and red people of the world will be replaced by a people of one hue, a tawny-coloured people, who will have no race prejudice of any sort, but this is unprofitable speculation in any practical sense, since such a fusion of races is unlikely to happen for a long time.

Wells, at any rate, became less optimistic than he had formerly been. The desirable state of lofty and perpetual picnic he desired, was, he maintained, prevented from establishment here and now only by wilful, rather than will-full, people. 'Mankind, which began in a cave, and behind a wind-break will end', he says dolefully in *The Fate of Homo Sapiens*, 'in the disease-sodden ruins of a slum. What else can happen? What other turn can destiny take?' His despair deepened in his last book, *Mind at the End of Its Tether*, as its title indicates.

The book, which was begun in 1945, the year in which the Labour Party, of which he was an unruly member, came into effective power for the first time, shows that this important change in British politics, roused no hope in him, nor did it diminish his despondency. 'The end of everything we call life is close at hand and cannot be evaded.' This end was to occur 'within a period to be estimated by weeks and months rather than aeons'. 'Our universe is not merely bankrupt; it is going clean out of existence, leaving not a wrack behind. The attempt to trace a pattern of any sort is futile.'

Even the Webbs had begun to despond. Ferociously opposed to Soviet Russia at first, they suddenly collapsed into devotion to it. They had lost heart about the Labour Party. So, indeed, had G.B.S. Writing to Augustin Hamon in 1914, he defined the purpose of the Fabian Society to be 'the detachment of Socialists from the Labour Party, which is not a Socialist Party, but a radical wing of the Trade Unions'. He maintained this argument for the rest of his life.

> 'The Labour Party is good in that it represents labour, but bad in that it represents poverty and ignorance, and it is anti-social in that it supports the producer against the consumer and the worker against the employer instead of supporting the workers against the idlers. The

Labour Party is also bad on account of its false democracy, which substitutes the mistrust, fear and incapacity of the masses for genuine political talent, and which would make the people legislators instead of leaving them what they are at present, the judges of legislators.'

Mrs Webb was vehement, even violent, in her denunciation of the Labour Party. Ramsay MacDonald, she says in her Diary for 1914, 'with his romantic figure, charming voice and clever dialectics, is more than a match for all those underbred and under-trained workmen who surround him on the platform and face him in the audience. . . . Owing to his personal distinction and middle-class equipment he is superior to all his would-be competitors.'

On the following page, 18, she returns to the attack. 'The Labour members are a lot of ordinary workmen who neither know nor care about anything but the interests of their respective Trade Unions and a comfortable life for themselves.' MacDonald, she continues, 'is bored by his Labour colleagues'. On page 23, she writes, 'The cold truth is that the Labour Members have utterly failed to impress the House of Commons and the constituencies as a live force, and have lost confidence in themselves and in each other.' And then, on page 50, her hands go up. 'I am haunted with the fear that all my struggles may be in vain; that disease and death are the ends towards which the individual, the race and the whole conceivable Universe are moving with relentless certainty.' Despite her personal dislike of Wells, she was a Wellsian.

On page 65, she refers to 'the colossal stupidity of the Trade Union rank and file, and the timidity and "smugness" of the Trade Union leaders'. On page 109, she is very fierce.

'The position of privilege, irrespective of capacity—a position occupied by many Trade Union officials—is becoming the most scandalous circumstance of the Labour Movement. It makes one despair of the Labour Party as an organ of Government. These men are not only incapable of doing the work themselves; they are not fit judges of other men's capacity. . . . The cleavage between the somewhat neurotic intellectuals of the I.L.P. and the Trade Union leaders is becoming more marked.'

Her brother-in-law, Lord Parmoor, who had seceded from the Conservatives to join the Labour Party, gets a rap from her on page 115. 'It is a rare joke to see our dear brother-in-law posing to himself and to the revolutionaries of the Labour Movement as a believer in democratic liberties.' On pages 116–7, there is a diatribe about the Central Office of the Labour Party, which is too long to quote. It ends what is a recurrent refrain in her remarks about the Party. 'Unless the two old parties have completely lost their cunning, it is difficult to imagine that such a crazy piece of machinery as the existing Labour Party will play a big part in the reconstruction of the U.K. and the British Empire after the war.'

So she wails her way to the last damning entry about the Party on page 208, where she states that 'the manual workers, organised as producers, cannot find men of sufficient character and intellect to lead them in the higher ranges of statesmanship. That is the plain truth. The Trade Union officials are not "fit to govern": they are not even equal to their own extremely limited business of collective bargaining with the strike as the sanction.'

The Labour Party has never forgiven Winston Churchill for saying it was unfit to govern, but it appears not even to know what Mrs Webb said far more ferociously to the same effect.

143

G.B.S. had kept a resolute heart, but even he was now beginning to wilt. He had passed his sixtieth year when he finished *Heartbreak House*, which he had begun to write earlier in the war. Heartbreak House is England as it was seen by G.B.S. in 1913, a ship drifting on to the rocks in total disregard of the warning beams from the lighthouse and the signals from the solitary guards on shore. 'And this ship we are all in,' Hector Hushabye says to Captain Shotover, 'this soul's prison we call England?'

> Shotover: The Captain is in his bunk, drinking bottled ditch-water; and the crew is gambling in the forecastle. She will strike and sink and split. Do you think the laws of God will be suspended in favour of England because you were born it in?
>
> Hector: Well, I don't mean to be drowned like a rat in a trap. I still have the will to live. What am I to do.
>
> Shotover: Do? Nothing simpler. Learn your business as an Englishman.
>
> Hector: And what may my business as an Englishman be, pray?
>
> Shotover: Navigation. Learn it and live; or leave it and be damned.

This is the substance of the play, which is full of wisdom and beauty, as if the prophet Isaiah had turned dramatist, and was crying to the players, 'give them beauty for ashes'.

But if there are beauty and wisdom in the play, the same cannot be said for its preface. The play was not performed for the best part of ten years after it was written, because of the war and, almost as bad, the war's after effects. So it was published in 1919, and immediately provoked great anger by what seemed to be wanton levity.

Re-reading it to-day, one finds in it a great deal of personal anguish. His sorrowful feeling about the war periodically interrupts his argument and sometimes makes him say things that ought not to have been said at all. There are passages in this preface which infuriated, and rightly infuriated, those who read them. It was monstrous to write that when the Lusitania was sunk by the Germans, 'an amazing frenzy swept through the country', and 'men who up to that time had kept their heads now lost them utterly. "Killing saloon passengers! What next?" was the essence of the whole agitation.'

Those words, which were not spoken on the spur of the moment, but were written, and, therefore, must have been deliberated, were brutally false. Even when we read the subsequent sentences, 'To me, with my mind full of the hideous cost of Neuve Chapelle, Ypres, and the Gallipoli landing, the fuss about the *Lusitania* seemed almost a heartless impertinence', and make allowance for his feeling, the preceding passage remains brutally false.

> 'When I asked those who gaped at me whether they had anything to say about the holocaust of Festubert, they gaped wider than before, having totally forgotten it, or rather, having never realised it.'

Heartbreak House is in a shape and style that was unfamiliar to playgoers everywhere. G.B.S. had had little or no success with his disquisitory plays, *Getting Married* and *Misalliance*,[1] and had not yet educated the West End audience well enough to make them enjoy this play. It was modelled on the work of Anton Chekhov, whose plays, when they were first performed, received as little favour in Moscow and St Petersburg as *Heartbreak House* received in London. Chekhov, indeed, felt so discouraged by their reception that he contemplated suicide. But no criticism, had it been as fierce and vicious as Lockhart's criticism of Keats, could ever have induced G.B.S. to that depth of despair.

The play was originally to have been performed at the Lyric in Hammersmith, but Nigel Playfair and Arnold Bennett stoutly maintained that a charming Irish actress, Ellen O'Malley, was miscast in the part of Ellie Dunn. She was, they thought, too old for it, and they wanted to engage a younger and more ingenuous actress. Playfair dallied so long over the dispute that when James Bernard Fagan, an Ulster dramatist who was directing a season at the Court Theatre, asked if he might have the play, G.B.S. consented. It was produced on October 18, 1921, just under a year after it had been performed 125 times with great success in New York by the Theatre Guild.

My criticism of the production brought me the only letter from G.B.S. that I resented. I cite him, not on that account, but because the quotations I shall make support the argument I have maintained

---

[1] But *Misalliance* when it was televised in 1954 was very successful. The disquisitory plays broadcast so well that one feels that G.B.S. had foreseen broadcasting and written them for that medium.

throughout this book, that he was an exceptionally kind man who would do more for his friends than they would do for themselves. On October 23, 1921, he wrote to rebuke me for my remarks about Miss O'Malley's miscasting. 'You give a dig at poor Ellen O'Malley which I connect with the fact that you were talking to Arnold Bennett between the acts.' This is the statement that angered me. He seemed to be suggesting that I had been 'briefed' by Bennett when I had formed my opinion before A.B. spoke to me.

G.B.S. goes on to say:

'I did not cast Ellen for Ellie Dunn. I wrote the part for her; and it fits her like a glove. Nobody else on the stage could play it in the proper way except Kate Rorke (or Mary); and they are both too old,' which was part of the criticism I made of Miss O'Malley. 'Unfortunately for her, she got taken up as an ingénue because she had golden hair, delicate hands and so forth (being Irish), and a general air of being born to say "Mary had a little lamb". As an ingénue, she was about as interesting as a steam hammer closing licked envelopes. She was nice and respectable, like an Irish lady (a thing abhorrent to the Englishman speculating on a Friday to Tuesday at Brighton); but she was unexciting and finally disappointing. She married a very good sort of man (they really deserved one another and were an ideal couple) but the war took him abroad, and he died on his way back, leaving Ellen a widow and, professionally, that most forlorn of actresses, a dud ingénue. There hasnt been a worse run of luck on the stage since Mrs Siddon's beginnings.

'Then, with my eye on her, I wrote *H.H.* Lillah McCarthy came after it; Nigel Playfair and Bennett came after it; and finally Fagan came after it. But I did not care to risk Lillah's money on it or encourage her to manage (it is not her strong point); and when I informed Nigel that Ellen was indispensable, he said she was too old, and no use as an ingénue; but he could not take it in: he had made up his mind that Ellie must be a sweet little sexual attraction and that Hesione (Mrs. Hushabye) was the heavy part. He said I should have to give in about it, and bided his time. Result: Fagan got the play; and it became a point of honour with Nigel and Arnold to maintain that I had ruined it by my casting. . . .'

'Ellen can go slow or fast, poetic or prosaic, to order; and I dont want to have another false tradition started on her. So stick up for her all you can as for a woman with a first-rate punch who has been wasted on patting kittens when she should have been playing Lady Macbeth, and who can, on occasion, get into another world than the West End one, like Keegan in *John Bull* and the clairvoyant in *Getting Married*. Only an Irish critic will understand without a lead.'

When I protested against his suggestion that I had no mind of my own, but allowed myself to be told what to say by Arnold

Bennett, he dropped that argument, but maintained his assertion that Miss O'Malley alone could play the part of Ellie, as if a play of any worth contains characters that only a particular person can act. If this were true, then the death or permanent disablement of that person would mean the death of the play. He dared me to name any actress who could perform the part better than Miss O'Malley had performed it, and told me that Nigel Playfair had wanted to cast Moyna MacGill, who would, in age at least, have been more suitable, and would have performed it well. 'Bennett', he concluded, 'would probably have liked Iris Hoey', whose performance would certainly have been impressive.

The play was a failure in London, partly because of miscasting, but chiefly because the London audience was a failure. I have a postcard, dated November 14, a month after the first performance, in which he tells me that 'this afternoon at Hammersmith I was making for you in the interval when Fagan intercepted me to discuss whether it was worth while to go on with *H.H.*, which drew £39 yesterday. I told him to announce a disgraceful failure, and we agreed that the notices should go up on Saturday.' And that, for the time being, was the end of a work of genius.

G.B.S. took the failure with less fortitude than he commonly showed in adversity, which is not surprising, for it contains much of his best work. The characters are superbly depicted and the dialogue is rich with human nature. It flows with greater ease than the dialogue in any other play he wrote. For the first time in his life, he let his mortification be seen.

But the pioneers have to fight their way through the jungle, and cannot hope to reach their goal unscathed. They are lucky if they reach it alive. *Heartbreak House* did not die of discouragement, as do the Ancients in *Back to Methuselah*, and it will in due time rise from its dust and ashes as *The Cherry Orchard* and *The Seagull* rose, and will be acclaimed for the noble work it is.

144

On March 27, 1920, G.B.S. went to Denmark Hill, the suburb in South London near which Browning was born, in which Ruskin spent his youth, to visit his sister, Lucy, whom he found ill and dejected in bed. She was now sixty-seven years of age, three years older than her brother. 'When I had sat with her a little while, she said, "I am dying". I took her hand to encourage her and said, rather conventionally, "Oh, no: you will be all right presently." We were silent then; and there was no sound except from somebody playing the piano in the nearest house (it was a fine evening and all the windows

477

were open) until there was a very faint flutter in her throat. She was still holding my hand. Then her thumb straightened. She was dead.'

When the doctor arrived, G.B.S., who had to register her death, said he supposed the cause of her death was tuberculosis, a disease she had developed after an attack of pneumonia, and was astounded to hear him reply, 'Starvation'. She had been cured of tuberculosis.

'I remonstrated, assuring him that I had provided for her better than that.' But the doctor maintained his statement. Her appetite had failed since the First World War, and he had never been able to persuade her to eat enough. She had been badly shell-shocked when, during an air-raid, an anti-aircraft gun which had been planted outside her garden, broke all the windows and crockery in her house. She had been removed to Devon, but had never recovered her appetite. Lucy was the white-haired child of her family, destined, in her mother's belief, to become a prima donna, but she rose no higher than the principal part in a provincial tour of the light opera, *Dorothy*. Her life had been a failure in almost every respect.

She had moved from disappointment to disappointment, and was totally dependent on her brother whom she had demanded should be put out of her mother's house when he was trying to make a writer of himself. The ugly duckling, once again, had proved to be the royal swan, while the white-haired child who was to ride the world as if it were her hobby-horse, faltered and failed.

145

The year of her death was the year in which he finished his long, metabiological pentateuch, entitled, *Back to Methuselah*. This, he thought, was his best play, an opinion which nobody shares. It takes at least three nights to perform. Such a monstrosity of a play could be produced only by a powerful theatrical organisation which was not afraid of losing money on a spirited enterprise, or by a philanthropic lover of the theatre. Luckily, G.B.S. found the one and the other.

It was produced for the first time by the Theatre Guild of New York at the Garrick Theatre in that city on February 27, 1922, in cycles of a week each. Although the American audience has more curiosity than the British, the season was unsuccessful. Few people were able or willing to go to the theatre every night for a week, and the Guild lost $20,000 on the production; which, according to Lawrence Langner, one of the founders of the Guild, greatly upset G.B.S., who hated to think that anyone had incurred loss through him. Langner tried to console him by telling him that a run of nine weeks for such a play with a loss of only $20,000 did not denote failure, but success, especially as the Garrick was a small theatre. 'If we had had a theatre twice the size, there would have been a profit instead of a loss.' Langner assured him that the loss would soon be retrieved. 'Most of the materials, etc., which we used can be used over again, and, anyway, the Guild is not the least bit worried about it. In having ventured to tackle so big a job, we have made a tremendous number of friends and shall have nearly double the number of subscribers for the coming season as we had for this season, so it will all come back to us eventually.'[1]

It cannot often have occurred in the history of the theatre that a dramatist received such a letter from a manager whose company had just lost $20,000 on his play. In a short time, G.B.S.'s spirits revived, and when another American manager, Lee Shubert, suggested that his fees were too high, he proved to him that the value of his name on a playbill was worth $10,000. The Theatre Guild had expected to lose $30,000, but had lost only $20,000, thus making a clear profit of $10,000 through the magic of his name alone!

Langner, who is an uncommonly good negotiator and would make a first class ambassador for the United States, obtained a concession from G.B.S. over *Back to Methuselah* which has never been obtained by any other person. In obtaining it, he had the help of Charlotte, whose quiet remarks that were almost asides, were immensely influential with her husband. *Back to Methuselah* is not one play: it is five; and the Guild wished to cut *The Tragedy of the Elderly Gentleman*, 'which contained one of the most long-winded parts ever written, and the strain on the audience listening to the play was excessive'. William, the Negro doorman at the Garrick Theatre, when asked by a Director of the Guild, how the play was going, replied, 'Fine! Less and less people walk out every night'.

Temerariously, Langner broached the subject of cuts, for G.B.S. was reputed to be ferocious about them, and he had little hope of succeeding in his mission. I had suggested to him that he should make cuts and say nothing about them, but Langner replied that there was a lady in New York, so devoted to G.B.S.'s work that she attended every performance of his plays, taking a copy of the play with her, and if a line were dropped by a forgetful player, she immediately reported the crime to G.B.S.

Luckily for Langner, Charlotte was present at the interview, and when G.B.S. began to talk about his principles, she quietly remarked that 'perhaps the Americans don't always know what the Elderly Gentleman is talking about. There's a long piece about John Knox and the Leviathan; hardly any English people know about that, either.' Langner promptly followed her lead, and presently G.B.S. was not only consenting to the cuts proposed by him, but 'took out

[1] See *The Magic Curtain*. By Lawrence Langner. Chap. 13.

at least half as much again as I had originally hoped for.' The whole play would be much better and compacter if the elderly gentleman's tragedy had been cut entirely.

146

The point of the play is that the term of human existence is not long enough for man to profit by his experience. When he knows enough to be able to cope with life, he dies. To become effective, he must extend his life: a statement which *The Wisdom of Solomon* sagely disputes. 'For honourable age is not that which standeth in length of time, nor that is measured by the number of years. But wisdom is the grey hair unto man, and an unspotted life is old age.' But whose life is unspotted? It was one of G.B.S.'s cardinal beliefs that man can do whatever he desires if he wills it hard enough: a belief he derived largely from Lamarck and Samuel Butler, and especially from the latter's *Life and Habit*. His complaint against Darwin's *Origin of Species* was that it banished mind from the universe, leaving in its place only a vast mindless machine whose cause we do not know nor can we guess with much, if any, satisfaction to ourselves. The problem of evil is sufficient to confuse every mind. If God be omnipotent, why does he permit pain and poverty to exist when he could easily abolish both? If he be omniscient, why did he create the world when he must have known that evil, with its attendants, pain and poverty, would appear?

The question of Free Will seems to have no relevance to this problem; for the animals, which have no decision in their own lives and are in no way guilty of sin against God, suffer even more than men and women; though Butler, from whom G.B.S. derived much of his faith, held the singular belief that animals, in proportion to the degree of development they have attained, share man's responsibility for the existence of evil. They are hunted and exterminated when they are inedible, or bred only to be beasts of burden or slaughtered as food. When they can no longer bear our burdens, they are killed, and their flesh is given to the dogs. The domestic animals, indeed, have had no decision in their own development. Their form has been modified or extended, not for their benefit, but for ours. This horse has been bred for speed, that for strength. The hog is fed on a system which has no relevance to his advantage, but solely to satisfy our taste in pork. The cow is deprived of her calf which is taken to the butcher, so that we may have the cow's milk and the calf's veal. Animals which do not serve any useful purpose for man are kept as exhibits in zoos, to amuse our children or to gratify the curiosity of zoologists.

480

On any ground that a thinking man or woman can conceive, God must appear to be capricious, if not cruel, when, having the power to remove evil from the world, he permits it to exist. Driven from this belief by our need for a loving God, we are compelled to believe that God is not master of his universe, that Satan has at least as much authority in it as he has.

G.B.S. answers these questions by turning aside from Darwin, or, rather, from the neo-Darwinians and denying the statement that the world is a mindless machine operated by a mechanic who does not know what he is doing or why he is doing it or, at all events, does not care so long as he gets his wages; and he prefers Lamarck to Darwin. He turns, too, from the belief of the fundamentalist who feels certain that God dictated the entire contents of the Bible to a small and insignificant group of people living in a small and insignificant part of a peninsula, most of it desert, on the eastern shores of the Mediterranean. Why should God have chosen the Jews when he had much finer people, the Greeks and the Romans, to choose if he was searching for a great race to fulfil his wishes? What justification had he for choosing that cowardly, greedy and extremely superstitious peasant, Abraham, for his friend when there was Socrates in Greece?

The answer G.B.S. makes to these questions is that God is not all-powerful and all-knowing, but is seeking to become so; that he has no other means of effecting his purpose than that of Trial and Error, so powerfully advocated by Sidney and Beatrice Webb, and that he has spent the whole of time in making instruments to enable him to achieve his purpose. When he finds that an instrument is either useless or no longer sufficiently powerful to be effectively used or is replaceable by another instrument that is better adapted to his purpose, then he scraps that instrument with as little concern as a mason burns a mallet which is falling to pieces or a carpenter discards a chisel which has lost its edge.

147

G.B.S., agitating himself throughout his long life over problems that the rest of us cease to examine in our early manhood because we feel there is no solution to them, concluded that man *has* decision in his own life and *can* alter the shape of things for the better if he wills its alteration. An intelligent and conscientious people will not be content with a shoddy, ramshackle society, but will seek to make it a substantial society which is worthy of respect. His arguments were mystical more than they were scientific, a statement which would not have disconcerted him, though he would have claimed to have a good deal of science on his side and to know more about it than some scientists who are as liable to be routine-minded as anybody else. Were we not, while this passage was being written, profoundly shocked to learn that the Piltdown skull, which had taken the place of the Tables of the Law for scientists, was a fake? Have we not some ground for thinking that a good deal of what scientists believe has no more veracity than the applewoman's belief that God made the world in six of our days? Have we, indeed, so much? The applewoman at least founds her faith on the belief that God is omnipotent. If he is, then he could have made the world in six of our minutes had that been his wish.

G.B.S. asserts that civilisations collapsed in the past for no other reason than that those who peopled them failed to fulfil their creator's purpose.

> 'The rich are instinctively crying "Let us eat and drink; for to-morrow we die," and the poor, "How long, O Lord, how long!" But the pitiless reply is that God helps those who help themselves. This does not mean that if Man cannot find the remedy, no remedy will be found. The power that produced Man when the monkey was not up to the mark, can produce a higher creature than Man if Man does not come up to the mark.'

The comment that can be made on this extract from the preface, is, first, that the monkey has not been scrapped and may, therefore, be presumed to be of some use to its Creator, and second, that although we have no ground for believing that the remedy will be found, if *we* refuse to search for it, neither have we any ground for believing that it can be found at all. A limited God, in short, seems even more incomprehensible than a God who is unlimited.

G.B.S. then reveals his plan for altering this dead-end existence. The average duration of life is not long enough, a fact which God, most surprisingly, had not realised, despite thousands of years of experiment, until G.B.S. mentioned it. Indeed, if we may believe the Book of Genesis, the term of life has been reduced, presumably because God thought he could do better work with short-livers than with long-livers. Adam lived to be 930 years of age; Methuselah, the oldest man in recorded history, died when he was 969 years; Noah lived to be 950. Nine centuries was the average duration of life then. But God suddenly and irritably reduced the duration to 120 years; and by the time the Psalmist was reached, the average life was three score years and ten. Now, however, we are pushing it up again, and it is common to meet men and women of eighty and ninety and even a hundred and more years.

It is not unlikely that the duration of life may be extended so that every man and woman, barring accidents, will have a reasonable expectation of becoming a centenarian; 'nobody', says G.B.S. 'can explain why a parrot should live ten times as long as a dog, and a turtle be almost immortal. In the case of man, the operation has over-shot its mark; men do not live long enough; they are, for all the pur-poses of high civilisation, mere children when they die. . . . Presum-ably, however, the same power that made this mistake can remedy it. If on opportunist grounds Man now fixes the term of his life at three score and ten years, he can equally fix it at three hundred, or three thousand.'

But can he? Did he fix his own term of life? If, as Weismann pointed out, death was invented so that the population of the world could periodically be weeded out and the danger of vast overcrowd-ing averted, how are we to rearrange the terms of life so that our years may be lengthened without any danger of overcrowding?

The population of Ireland in the year of its union with Great Britain, 1800, was about four millions. It was doubled in less than forty years, and abruptly and brutally halved again by the Famine which filled the land with pestilence ten years before G.B.S.'s birth. It is now about what it was 150 years ago. There were over sixteen million people in the British Islands in 1801. There are over fifty millions to-day. Yet families were large in 1801, and are small to-day. But there is no relation between the statistics and the quality of the population; nor do we find the children of the comfortable classes are superior in physical strength to the children of the proletariat.

They are often, indeed, less physically fit than the sons and daughters of the poor. It is a notable fact that prize-fighters come from working-class areas and even from slums, and seldom or never from the homes of well-to-do and wealthy people. The Irish people, despite the poverty of their diet which was almost restricted to potatoes and milk, were physically more robust than the English people, who were better fed, for a large part of the nineteenth century. It was they who supplied Great Britain with the majority of their navvies when the railways were being built. It was not the Famine which killed them: it was the pestilence which followed the Famine.

148

We now possess one of the healthiest populations in the world; but are perturbed to find that the increase in our physical well-being has not been accompanied by an equal increase in our in-telligence or sense of responsibility. It is arguable that the general level of intelligence is less to-day, despite the Welfare State, than it was seventy years ago when a Welfare State was not even thought of. It is even more arguable that a highly mechanised and physically fit population is more likely to be a disaster than a blessing. We have produced a people with fairly fit bodies, but have still to produce one with minds as fit.

To G.B.S., the problem is entirely one of longevity. By the time we have learnt how to live a reasonable life, we begin to decline and droop, and then we die; and all the experience we have gained is wasted. But is longevity in itself enough or nearly enough? G.B.S. would have answered, "Not enough, but the beginning of enough,' and would have cited Thomas Hardy in his support:

> Sophocles, Plato, Socrates,
>   Gentlemen,
> Pythagoras, Thucydides,
> Herodotus, and Homer—yea
> Clement, Augustin, Origen,
> Burnt brightlier towards their setting-day,
>   Gentlemen.

But was John Keats, who died when he was twenty-six, a lesser poet than Alfred Austin who lived to be seventy-eight? Will anyone believe that Austin was three times the poet Keats was because he lived three times as long? Is not G.B.S., in demanding an extension of the duration of life on the ground that we do not live long enough to learn how to live sensibly, falling into the mechanistic heresy which he denounced in the neo-Darwinians? The Swiss mystic, Amiel, remarks in his *Intimate Journal* that 'numbers make law, but goodness has nothing to do with figures'. He might have said the same about length of years. The goodness that was in Hardy's Ancients was born in them. If it had not been in them from the beginning, they could not have created it had they lived ten times as long as they did. All we know about Methuselah is that he lived for 969 years. Had he done anything in that time that was worth mentioning, it would have been mentioned.

149

Lamarck said that 'living organisms change because they want to', and G.B.S. accepts this statement as if it had been confided to him by God himself, though God is not a word for which he has any liking. A personal God, the only credible kind of God, as Wells once remarked, was not to G.B.S.'s taste. He preferred an abstraction, such as Bergson's Elan Vital or, as G.B.S. named it, Creative Evolution. The living organism need only wish hard enough to become whatever it wants to be.

'If you have no eyes, and want to see, and keep trying to see, you will finally get eyes. If, like a mole or a subterranean fish, you have eyes and don't want to see, you will lose your eyes. If you like eating the tender tops of trees enough to make you concentrate all your energies on the stretching of your neck, you will finally get a long neck, like the giraffe.'

This may be true, but it is certainly far more fantastic than the belief that the giraffe got its long neck because its creator gave it one. The metaphysics in this quotation are surely extravagant if not actually false. If a species has no eyes, never has possessed eyes, is unaware of sight or of the fact that there are sights to be seen, how can that species desire sight or will itself into the possession of eyes?

We can only will what we need. We cannot desire anything unless we have knowledge of our need of it and knowledge, too, of the fact that it exists or can be made to exist. Man knew about flight long before he could fly. Insects and birds were familiar objects. He could see leaves and pieces of paper blown about by the wind, whirling up into the air, falling back to the earth. He made kites and hauled them into the heavens. He filled sacks of silk with gas and used them to raise him above the earth, and was even able to propel himself some distance through space. At last he achieved the internal combustion engine and invented aeroplanes, and to-day, the poor little creature, maddened by the lust for fast movement, flings himself about the earth and the sky as if he were a frantic angel who had lost his way to heaven and was afraid of falling into hell.

But if he had never had any conception of flight, if he had never seen any creature fly, if he had never had the faintest idea that it was possible to lift an object heavier than air into the sky, a feat which Kelvin had declared to be impossible, and keep it there, he could not have invented an aeroplane. Samson, eyeless in Gaza, had the memory of eyes to sustain him while he waited for the moment when he could seize the pillars and pull the temple down about the ears of the Philistines; but if he had been born without eyes, and had no conception of sight, how could sight have been imagined or desired, apart from being achieved? 'If', G.B.S. says, 'you can turn a pedestrian into a cyclist and a cyclist into a pianist or violinist, without the intervention of Circumstantial Selection, you can turn an amoeba into a man, or a man into a superman.'

Can you?

It is one thing to make a cyclist, but a far different and harder thing to make a pianist or a violinist. Balancing on two wheels is a feat practically every human being can perform, even if he has lost a limb; but only a small number of people are able to play the piano or the violin well. Who is the *you* who can turn an amoeba into a man? Has any human being ever performed the feat? How can an amoeba become a man of its own volition when it has not the faintest notion of what a man is?

Is progress possible?

The thought throughout this preface has all the fine confusion attributed to Scotch broth. G.B.S. has not made up his mind whether he is a free man or a slave, a victim of his environment or the creator of it. He tells his readers that he wrote what he modestly calls pot-boilers, such as *Pygmalion*, *Fanny's First Play*, and *You Never Can Tell*, works which would be other men's masterpieces, when his evolutionary appetite craved for sterner stuff: a statement which indicates some powers of election, an ability to choose between one thing and another; but he has no sooner made it than he adds, 'I do not regard my part in the production of my books and plays as much greater than that of an amanuensis or an organ-blower', which suggests a reversion to the less intelligent forms of Calvinism which were professed in Dublin when he was a child.

'An author', he says, 'is an instrument in the grip of Creative Evolution, and may find himself starting a movement to which in his own little person he is intensely opposed.' This sounds uncommonly like blasphemy, the very blasphemy against which the whole of *Back to Methuselah* is a vehement protest. Darwin's crime, according to Samuel Butler and G.B.S., was that he banished mind from the universe, replacing it by mindless mechanics. But if man is not a conscious creature, capable of choice and election, acutely aware of what he wants and what he is doing, and able to decide whether he shall write pot-boilers or immortal works to satisfy his evolutionary appetite, then he is no more than a mindless termite, if, indeed, he be so much.

Surveying man in this preface, G.B.S. cannot definitely make up his mind about him. Is he becoming better or worse? Are we now suffering birth pangs or death throes? Is Man marching forward or marching back or standing still or merely revolving?

> Progress is
> The law of life, man is not
> Man as yet

says Browning, announcing himself to be an optimist as he says it; and G.B.S.'s demand that human beings shall improve themselves implies both a conviction by man that he is in need of improvement and an assurance that the improvement can be made.

But if man cannot or will not offer a foothold for divinity, then, divinity can do nothing for or with him. That, indeed, is the warning which G.B.S. continually sounds in his work. 'If man will not serve, Nature will try another experiment.' Caesar, reproaching Cleopatra for the murder of Pothinus, is made to complain of the endless exactions and repetitions of revenge, 'And so, to the end of history, murder shall breed murder, always in the name of right and honour and peace, until the gods are tired of blood and create a race that can understand.'

The young shepherd Amos uttered a similar complaint when he, too, put words into the mouth of God. 'Bring me no more vain oblations: incense has become an abomination to me: the new moons and sabbaths, the calling of assemblies, I cannot away with them; it is iniquity, even the solemn meeting. . . . And when ye spread forth your hands I will hide mine eyes from you, yea, when ye make many prayers, I will not hear; your hands are full of blood.' The Temple had become a slaughterhouse, reeking with the blood of young lambs and cattle, slain by sadistic priests, in a pretence of piety, and the House of the Lord God of Israel was no more than a butcher's shop.

G.B.S., like others before him, believed that man has a foothold for divinity or is capable of making one. He demanded that it should be used or devised. That is the exhortatory part of his evangel.

In *Back to Methuselah*, he advances, despite the contradictions he publishes on the way, from indignant exhortation to detail and decision. Man not only can and must develop himself, but is told how to do it. He is something more than an amanuensis or an organ-blower, and has the power of election and choice. He is called, not to repentance, but to conscious purpose and effort and firm decision.

G.B.S. uses, as already noted, the familiar illustration of the giraffe's long neck, and decides that of several possible causes, the most probable is that the giraffe made up its mind to lengthen its neck and lengthened it. We are to imagine a herd of giraffes browsing on the branches of trees in primitive times. Some of them have short necks, some have necks of medium length, and others have long necks. Obviously, the leaves on the lower branches of trees will be eaten first because they are accesssible to all the giraffes, whatever the length of their necks may be; but when the lowest leaves are eaten, and the giraffes become dependent on the higher and highest, the low-necked will die of hunger since they cannot reach them . . . unless, of course, they can find a supply of other food which will sustain them. The medium-necked giraffes will survive as long as the higher leaves are available, but they, too, will be in peril when these are eaten; and the presumption made by the neo-Darwinians is that, in the end, it is only the long-necked giraffes, able to feed on the highest leaves, who will survive.

G.B.S. rightly disagrees with the last argument, which implies or asserts that the long-necked giraffes will breed only long-necked off-spring. Giants can produce runts, and handsome parents raise a plain and even ugly family. Sopranos do not necessarily produce sopranos: they may produce children who are tone-deaf or detest music or have voices like corncrakes. Characteristics are not easily acquired, if, indeed, they can be acquired at all. If, as G.B.S. points out in this preface, characteristics could in time become part of the general inheritance, Chinese women would now be born with tiny feet, since their feet have been bound for many generations. But, except for the few who are malformed in the womb, every Chinese girl is born with normal feet.

G.B.S. plumped for election. Giraffes, observing how useful long necks are, willed themselves into long necks for all giraffes, a willing which ensured that the long-necked giraffes, whose chances of survival in the world of varied necks were greater than those of short-necked giraffes, now had no more chance of survival than the rest of the herd! The leaves on the trees, low and high, would be eaten by the whole herd and not only by a part of it, and the food supply, unless it could somehow be augmented, would therefore be much less than it had formerly been.

There are, G.B.S. tells his readers, 'nearly two hundred different sorts of dogs, all capable of breeding with one another and of producing cross varieties unknown to Adam.'

But is it not probable that in the beginning, just as, according to Genesis, there was one sort of man, so there was one sort of dog, and that, just as man began to vary as he dispersed himself about the earth in all sorts of climate, so dogs began to vary when they, too, were dispersed? This is the theory expounded by Buffon in his *Histoire naturelle, général et particulière*, and cited by Butler in *Evolution, Old and New*. Many creatures, from mammoths to mice, have had their physical being drastically changed by climatic alterations or by the general differences between one country and another. Some creatures, indeed, have disappeared because they could not adjust themselves to these changes. There must, Buffon asserts, have been many animals in the world of whom we no longer have the slightest knowledge: they vanished because of their inability to adapt themselves to changed conditions.

'It is probable then that all the animals of the new world are derived from congeners in the old, without any deviation from the ordinary course of nature. We may believe that having become separated in the lapses of ages, by vast oceans and countries which they could not traverse, they have gradually been affected by, and derived impressions from, a climate which has itself been modified so as to become a new one through the operation of those same causes which dissociated the individuals of the old and new world from one another; thus in the course of time they have grown smaller and changed their characters. This, however, should not prevent our classifying them as different species now, for the difference is no less real whether it be caused by time, climate and soil, or whether it dates from the creation. Nature, I maintain, is in a state of continual flux and movement. It is enough for man if he can grasp her as she is in his own time, and throw but a glance or two upon the past and future, so as to try and perceive what she may have been in former times and what one day she may attain to.'

It is immaterial to our argument here whether or not Buffon's theory is still regarded as sound. Our concern is solely with the fact that G.B.S. accepted it, and based his belief on it. We can adduce in its favour that a great deal of the variety in animals has nothing whatever to do with their own desire or natural environment, but with the whim of an entirely different creature, man, who has changed the animals to satisfy his needs or gratify his pleasure much in the manner of the horrible experimenter in H. G. Wells's novel, *The Island of Dr Moreau*.

150

G.B.S. could not be shaken from his belief in man's ability to choose his own destiny and make himself whatever he desired to be; and he was convinced that this ability to manipulate the world was severely limited by the brevity of existence. He had made the discovery every person of quality makes, always with surprise, although it was very old when the author of *Ecclesiastes* made it, that man has not time enough to do all he wishes to do or is capable of doing. Methuselah probably complained of the shortness of his life, as bitterly as Cecil Rhodes, dead at forty-eight, complained of his. 'From the cradle to the grave, what is it?' he exclaimed to W. T. Stead. 'Three weeks at the seaside!'

But is the beautiful, brief life of a butterfly, the short season of a flower, worthless to them or to us? The life of a tortoise is almost interminable, but who wants it?

G.B.S. having convinced himself that life should be longer, next convinced himself that man had only to will long life to achieve it; and he supported his belief by citing the vital statistics which prove that the average duration of existence in England has been extended by about twelve years in the last century, entirely through improved sanitation and a higher standard of living. He either ignored the decrepitude which comes with advancing age or took it for granted that longevity would be accompanied by prolonged physical and mental energy, without which, indeed, long life would be a burden, if not a disaster.

But he gave no thought to the fact, apparent even in these times, that the longer men live in a state of activity, the longer it will be before the succeeding generations achieve authority; and that a day may come when the young will destroy the old as savages threw their aged people to the crocodiles, not because they are useless passengers on the public car, but because they will not get out of the way of youth or relinquish their authority.

He seemed to himself to settle the problem, but very unconvincingly to the rest of us, by prolonging the period of juvenility and aesthetic emotion far beyond the present time school-leaving age, and by withdrawing the Ancients from any participation in public affairs. There is, indeed, no proof in *Back to Methuselah* that the state or anything else is managed by anybody. It appears to run itself. The supreme pleasure in life to him was *thought:* and he was scornful of those whose ideal delight was *feeling*.

When we argued the matter, he wrote to me that 'it is not our experience of life, but our expectation of life that determines our conduct, our attitude, and the effort we call upon ourselves for. . . . Men certainly develop during their whole life on certain lines. Listen to Beethoven's Septet for wind instruments and then to his Ninth Symphony, and all discussion on the point seems absurd.

'But the mischief is that the physical lifetime, which determines one's power of endurance, is not coincident with mental lifetime. In fact, there are several physical and mental lifetimes which overlap more or less, but are not coincident. A sprint runner, in his prime at 18, is hopelessly too old at 20. Carpentier and Dempsey will soon be on the shelf. Actors and opera singers last longer than boxers: public speakers last longer than tenors. But their understanding of their work and of themselves may improve to the end. Carpentier at 50 will be a more formidable boxer than he is now—for fifty seconds. . . .

'I can be as young for five minutes as you can be for a week. There are things that I cannot do that I could do years ago; but there are also things that I was never clear about that I am quite clear about now. I am still growing while I am decaying. It is the physical decay, with its reduction of my powers of endurance in every department that is beating me and will presently kill me. When a man dies of old age, he kills a lot of mental babies with which he is pregnant.

'In *Methuselah*, I could not show the life of long livers, because, being a short liver, I could not conceive it. To make the play possible at all I had to fall back on an exhibition of shortlivers and children in contrast with such scraps of the long life as I could deduce by carrying a little further the difference that exists at present between the child and the adult, or between Reggie de Veulle (or whatever his silly name is) and Einstein. I cannot contemplate the portrait of Descartes in the National Gallery and believe that the late George Edwardes was a much happier man.'

I interrupt him here, to remark that George Edwardes was a widely-renowned producer of musical comedies, whose name was associated chiefly with the Gaiety Theatre and Daly's.

G.B.S. continues:

'I defy you to say that you would prefer the conscience of the average sensualist of Piccadilly to the conscience of Descartes. If you had to choose between celibacy with intense intellectual activity and a life of voluptuous adventure with perfect health but without intellectual exercise, you would not hesitate; you would recognise that intellect is a passion; that is, an activity of life, far more indispensable than physical ecstasy or reproduction. Shakespeare grudged the vital cost of the sexual ecstasy: he immediately begins to talk of expense and waste with it—"expense of spirit in a waste of shame, etc." Do you seriously think you enjoyed that very clever letter in *The Times* the other day so little that you cannot conceive the Ancients living in a permanent ecstasy of that sort of enjoyment raised to powers of which we have no experience? I can understand an Englishman being depressed by the Ancients, because the religion of the Englishman today, as the reviews of *Methuselah*, show, is simply Phallism; but you ought to know better.'

It was easy to dare me to deny that I should prefer the conscience of Descartes to the conscience of the average sensualist of Piccadilly, because the feeling experienced by the latter is not, in my meaning of the term, passion at all, but mere satisfaction of momentary appetite; but G.B.S. could not convince me, nor do I believe that he convinced himself, that the passion of a man for a woman he loves is inferior in its intensity or its positive value to his passion for intellectual activity.

Thought without action is sterile, and the thought of the Ancients in *Back to Methuselah* is not related to any activity. They wander about, solitary and morose, hairless and unhappy, thinking, but doing nothing. An Ancient, taunted with his miserable appearance by a Youth, replies, 'Infant: one moment of the ecstasy of life as we live it would strike you dead.' But we have only his word for that: there is no proof of it in his appearance or his behaviour or in any result he achieves.

Later in the play, a She-Ancient claims that the Ancients possess 'a direct sense of life', though she complains a page or two later, that she is still 'the slave of this slave, my body', and, like St Paul, asks who will deliver her from the body of this death. When The Newly Born girl enquires, 'What is your destiny?' the She-Ancient tells her, 'To be immortal'.

> The She-Ancient: The day will come when there will be no people, but only thought.
> The He-Ancient: And that will be life eternal.

But is thought bombinating in the void more attractive or exhilarating than any other sort of bombination?

At the end of the preface, a remarkably provocative piece of writing, provocative of dynamic thought, even when it rouses resentment and creates disagreement, he states the case for himself as a dramatist: his serious exposition in all his work of a religious intention. Referring to the high spirits of *Man and Superman*, he says, 'the effect was so vertiginous, apparently, that nobody noticed the new religion in the centre of the intellectual whirlpool:

491

'Now I protest I did not cut these cerebral capers in mere inconsiderate exuberance. I did it because the worst convention of the criticism of the theatre current at that time was that the theatre is a place of shallow amusement; that people go there to be soothed after the enormous intellectual strain of a day in the city: in short, that a playwright is a person whose business is to make unwholesome confectionery out of cheap emotions. My answer to this was to put all my intellectual goods in the shopwindow under the sign of *Man and Superman*. That part of my design succeeded. . . .

'Since then the sweet-shop view of the theatre has been put out of countenance; and its critical exponents have been driven to take on intellectual pose which, though often more trying than their old intellectually nihilistic vulgarity, at least concedes the dignity of the theatre, not to mention the usefulness of those who live by criticising it. And the younger playwrights are not only taking their art seriously, but being taken seriously themselves. The critic who ought to be a newsboy is now comparatively rare.'

All that is strictly true. G.B.S. was not to know that the disaster of the First World War, in which the British alone lost a million of their most valuable men, would be followed within a quarter of a century by the Second in which, though the loss of life was much less, the loss of mind and spirit was enormous.

151

The quality of *Back to Methuselah* is remarkably unequal. The play about Adam and Eve, is full of fine thought and feeling, especially in the second act, and there is a despondent beauty in the final play, *As Far as Thought Can Reach*, but, very surprisingly the plays which are nearest to our own time, are the least impressive, though *The Gospel of the Brothers Barnabas*, which belongs strictly to the time between the two wars, is full of fun, even when the fun comes near to being slapstick, and its portraits of Asquith and Lloyd George, under the names of Lubin and Joyce Burge, are brilliant, so like their originals that they almost horrify us.

What is most striking in the Garden of Eden play is the fear and distress with which Adam contemplates immortal life. When Eve reproaches him for his morosity and his habit of slinking off to solitary reflection, and infers from both that he hates her in his heart, he tells her that she is wrong, that he feels appalled by the 'horror of having to be with myself for ever. I like you; but I do not like myself. I want to be different; to be better, to begin again and again. . . . I am tired of myself. And yet I must endure myself, not for a day or for many days, but for ever. That is a dreadful thought. That is what makes me sit brooding and silent and hateful.'

The play begins with their discovery of death. They find a fawn with a broken neck. It is the first dead creature they have ever seen. And they are both frightened and appalled by it. In all their conversations, they find themselves inventing words to fit their experiences, most of which are new. Eve says the word *dead* as she looks at the fawn, and it startles Adam, whom it should have pleased, since it offers him an escape from the immortality he dreads.

It is the Serpent who gives Eve the knowledge which will enable her and Adam to get rid of the burden of everlasting life. She had discovered death before she had heard of birth, and although the thought of death had brought comfort to Adam, not only bored by, but terrified of, immortality, it had brought little or none to her, whose desire for perpetuation and fulfilment was greater than his.

How could the human race acquire everlasting life without the misery of personal immortality?

The Serpent told her. 'You imagine what you desire; you will what you imagine; and at last you create what you will.' Then, in Adam's absence, he whispers the secret of sex in her ear. By this means, Eve will obtain all that her imagination desires. She will be exalted emotionally by physical union with her mate, and she will also be exalted emotionally, intellectually and spiritually by the knowledge that in her body a new life is growing to replace hers and Adam's.

'Life must not cease,' says the Serpent. 'That comes before everything,' and he tries to excite her by telling her that she can have what she wants if she only wants it hard enough. 'You do care,' he tells Eve. 'It is that care that will prompt your imagination; inflame your desires, make your will irresistible; and create out of nothing.' When Eve contradicts the last remark, saying 'there is no such thing as nothing, the Serpent is struck by her profundity. 'That is a great thought,' he tells her. 'Yes; there can be no such thing as nothing, only things we cannot see.'

Everything is here, already in existence, waiting only to be discovered. We have only to draw the curtain, and we shall find what we want.

Throughout the play, women seem to have the best of the argument. It is natural, no doubt, that a man who was brought up in a home ruled by a determined woman, a home in which the man was insignificant and feckless, though possessed of some charm, and occasionally wise, should attribute greater authority to women than to men, but the balance between the sexes is disproportioned. Not only are the wisest words given to women in *Back to Methuselah*, but the last word is given too, and it is insufficient. 'It is enough', says Lilith, 'that there is a Beyond.' But *is* that enough?

Eve's most assertive child is Cain, whose boast is in slaughter, whose ambition is to be perpetually at war. Some of her children please her. One of them is Enoch who walks on the mountains alone, 'and hears the Voice continually, and has given up his will to do the will of the Voice, and has some of the Voice's greatness'. Others are artists and thinkers and dreamers; 'and when they come, there is always some new wonder, or some new hope: something to live for. . . . And then you, Cain, come to me with your stupid fighting and destroying, and your foolish boasting; and you want me to tell you that it is all splendid, and that you are heroic, and that nothing but death and the dread of death makes life worth living.'

The last speeches of the Eden play are full of sombre beauty, and the best of them are Eve's. When Adam, spitting on his hands and beginning to dig again, asserts that life is long enough for digging, Eve exclaims, 'Yes, to dig. And to fight. But is it long enough to dig for other things, the great things? Will they live long enough to eat manna?' 'What is manna?' Adam asks. 'Food drawn down from heaven,' answers Eve, who makes the last speech:

'Man need not always live by bread alone. There is something else. We do not yet know what it is; but some day we shall find out; and then we will live on that alone; and there shall be no more digging nor spinning, nor fighting nor killing.'

All of which can be found in the words of Jesus Christ.

Lines pregnant with wisdom are abundant in the play. They sometimes seem to slip out of their author's mind without his knowledge. In reply to a question by a parlour-maid, who is eager to be assured of her respectability, one of the Brothers Conrad makes a profound remark, in which the whole business of marriage and social relations is summarised.

'My good girl, all biological necessities have to be made respectable whether we like it or not; so you needn't worry yourself about that.'

Women can squeal like white mice about their respectability and their social position without having the slightest effect on Nature, who, it has been truly said, is not interested in chastity. But she is interested in perpetuation; and if she cannot get the children she needs in one way, she will get them in another.

152

It is interesting in reading G.B.S.'s plays to notice how much he is addicted to dialogue in which the characters utter sentiments which most of us feel, but do not express. When the abounding Welshman, Joyce Burge, protests that the Brothers Barnabas, in their plea for legislation to promote longevity, are wasting his time, Conrad

Barnabas immediately retorts, 'Is your time of any value?' a remark that almost stuns the ebullient Celt. Blunt utterances of this sort abound in the Shavian drama, causing most of the laughter when, that is to say, they are not causing most of the shock.

G.B.S. himself, despite his great kindness and courtesy, was often so blunt that he seemed to be brutal. When a sensational newspaper tried to exploit a navvy who had written good verse, and employed one of its cub-reporters to take him to see Shaw who was in the middle of a rehearsal of one of his plays, G.B.S., irritated at being interrupted, asked the reporter why he and his companion had come. 'Well, Mr Shaw, this is So-and-so, the working-man poet!' 'Why doesn't he do some work?' said G.B.S., as he went back to his.

But the play, despite its fine comedy, advances nothing. We are told by Franklyn Barnabas that when longevity has been achieved, 'it will begin with the best men', but, in fact, in the succeeding play, we find that the first long-livers are the parlour-maid who was so concerned about her respectability, and a light-minded clergyman whose main contribution to any conversation was the word 'Price-less!'

But these two, in *The Thing Happens*, are shown in a considerable state of intellectual improvement; and their improvement appears to be due entirely to their long life. Experience, apparently, teaches. and the personal quality of the taught is unimportant. But how much is experience able to teach? No man undergoes exactly the same experience in exactly the same way twice in his life; and nearly all the vital decisions have to be made without time to look up the records and see what was done the first time trial was endured. Most of our life is spent in improvisation, and if our wits are slow and dull, we shall suffer severely.

The argument G.B.S. sets out to prove seems to be abandoned when he makes his first long-livers out of comparatively commonplace and mindless people like the parlour-maid and the tittering curate. Longevity, in the play, is not the result of will, but of chance, and might have happened, as, indeed, Conrad Barnabas, in contradiction of his brother Franklyn, asserted, to 'the loudest laugher of them all'. The respectable parlour-maid, seeking safety, remarks that she has only one life and must make the most of it: but she still has only one life when, without her volition, she finds herself a tricentenarian. To spend a period as a Lapp or a Finn, another as a Frenchman or an Arab, a third as a Bashi-Bazouck or a Basuto, and a fourth outside human society altogether, as a limpet or a lion, would be an interesting experience, even if it were nothing else; but to continue for centuries in one mind and shape would surely be a futile performance?

495

The Ancients assert that they spend their lives in a whirlpool of pure thought, but they give no proof of this existence nor any evidence that it is worth the trouble it causes. Thought which has no relation to activity is as empty as activity which has no relation to thought. The Ancients are destitute of rational activity, and must perform infantile antics with their bodies to keep themselves from going out of their minds: increasing the number of their members, six heads instead of one, four arms instead of two. In the end they degenerate into silence so total that they will not speak even to one another, and they long for death from discouragement.

It is saddening to find that an extraordinarily bold endeavour to dramatise not only the history, but the aspiration and future potentiality of mankind should come to no more than this, that to live a long time is, in itself, unimportant; and perhaps the most caustic comment on this pentateuch is that G.B.S., who lived longer than any other great man in the whole world of literature, found old age irksome, and died, not of discouragement, indeed, but of an accident.

He was sixty-five and full of honour when *Back to Methuselah* was published. But he felt, as he told me, that he was finished. I derided him for talking such nonsense, and reminded him that William de Morgan, a very competent novelist, had not yet begun to write at that age. But obviously the play had taken a good deal of his energy out of him; and it was not until 1923 that he began to write *Saint Joan*.

Its beginning was odd. His friend, Sir Sydney Cockerell, who was curator of the Fitzwilliam Museum at Cambridge, had read T. Douglas Murray's *Jeanne D'Arc* and felt certain that there was a play in the highly dramatic records of Joan's trial. He, therefore, passed the book on to G.B.S., who, however, showed no very great interest in the matter.

It was Charlotte who suggested that he should write the play, and she worked on her suggestion with great wiliness: she left books about Joan lying in every room he was likely to inhabit. He found himself periodically picking up one of these books and reading in it, until one day he suddenly exclaimed to the wise and smiling Charlotte that he had thought of a good idea for a play. What is it, she demanded, and was told that it was about Joan of Arc. How interesting, said Charlotte! . . .

His model for the girl saint was a most likeable middle-aged woman, Mary Hankinson, who managed Summer Schools for The Fabian Society, and was the sister-in-law of Francis Brett Young, the novelist. 'Hanky', as her numerous friends called her, was a woman of unusual good sense, a remarkably self-controlled woman, and so full of personal charm that people meeting her for the first time felt

496

certain that there must be some terrible flaw in her character, since no human being could possibly be so devoid of disagreeable characteristics: only to learn, as they became better acquainted with her, that she was the one human being anybody knew who was so composed. When the play was published, G.B.S. sent a copy of it to 'Hanky', with this inscription, which is cited by Rattray, 'To Mary Hankinson, the only woman I know who does not believe that she is the model for Joan and the only woman who actually was.'

153

Opinions on which of his plays is G.B.S.'s best vary remarkably. He himself had no doubt on this point: *Back to Methuselah*, for him, surpassed all the rest. But there are acute judges who prefer *Man and Superman*, which he, too, once, preferred; and there are many people who acclaim *Saint Joan*. It is, at least, his most popular play. It would be nearly faultless if G.B.S. could have controlled his passion for giving information or had ever realised that any audience at a play about The Maid brings some knowledge of her into the theatre. The natural end of the play is the concluding speech made by Warwick at the end of the sixth scene when, in reply to the Executioner's remark, 'You have heard the last of her,' Warwick, with a wry smile, retorts, 'The last of her? Hm! I wonder!' There is no need to add another word.

But G.B.S., who wrote as if he believed that his audience was ignorant of the most elementary facts, would not admit that the play was complete without the Epilogue in which the audience is told that Joan has been canonised. To deny the need for the Epilogue is not to disregard its beauty, and especially of the superb litany which almost ends it.

The noblest of Joan's utterances is the great speech on solitude with which the fifth scene ends. She has been abjured by the tedious Archbishop and even by her friend, Dunois, to submit to the authority of her spiritual and political betters: the priests and the politicians. If she refuses to do so, she will stand alone. No one can save her from the fires to which the English wish her to be condemned.

But Joan is bold in her belief. 'Where would you all have been now if I had heeded that sort of truth? There is no help, no counsel in any of you:

> Yes: I am alone on earth: I have always been alone. My father told my brothers to drown me if I would not stay to mind his sheep while France was bleeding to death: France might perish if only our lambs were safe. I thought France would have friends at the court of the king of France; and I find only wolves fighting for pieces of her poor torn

497

body. I thought God would have friends everywhere, because He is the friend of everyone; and in my innocence I believed that you who now cast me out would be like strong towers to keep harm from me.

'But I am wiser now; and nobody is any the worse for being wiser. Do not think you can frighten me by telling me I am alone. France is alone; and God is alone; and what is my loneliness before the loneliness of my country and my God? I see now that the loneliness of God is His strength: what would He be if He listened to your jealous little counsels?

'Well, my loneliness shall be my strength too: it is better to be alone with God. His friendship will not fail me, nor His counsel, nor His love. In His strength I will dare, and dare, and dare, until I die. I will go out now to the common people, and let the love in their eyes comfort me for the hate in yours. You will all be glad to see me burnt; but if I go through the fire, I shall go through it to their hearts for ever and ever. And so, God be with you.'

G.B.S. was not afraid to put his audience to a severe test of endurance. He filled his plays with speeches, each of which was almost as long as an act in the featherweight comedies of some of our playboy-dramatists. Such a speech is the great oration on heresy delivered by the Inquisitor in the sixth scene. It fills nearly two and a half pages of close print, and takes about seven minutes in delivery. But it never loses its hold on an audience.

When The Maid, temporarily overcome by the Court, recants what it calls her heresy, and then is told that she will be sentenced to spend the rest of her life in solitary confinement in a prison, her great heart protests and she tears up her recantation and affirms her faith. 'My voices were right . . . they told me you were fools, and that I was not to listen to your fine words nor trust to your charity:

You promised me my life; but you lied. You think that life is nothing but not being stone dead. It is not the bread and water I fear: I can live on bread: when have I asked for more? It is no hardship to drink water if the water be clean. Bread has no sorrow for me, and water no affliction. But to shut me out from the light of the sky and the sight of the fields and flowers; to chain my feet so that I can never again ride with the soldiers nor climb the hills; to make me breathe foul damp darkness, and keep from me everything that brings me back to the love of God when your wickedness and foolishness tempt me to hate Him: all this is worse than the furnace in the Bible that was heated seven times.

'I could do without my warhorse; I could drag about in a skirt; I could let the banners and the trumpets and the knights and soldiers pass me and leave me behind as they leave the other women, if only I could still hear the wind in the trees, the larks in the sunshine, the young lambs crying through the healthy frost, and the blessed, blessed church bells that send my angel voices floating to me on the wind. But without these things I cannot live; and by your wanting to take them away from me, or from any human creature, I know that your counsel is of the devil, and that mine is of God.'

That is the moment when the rage of the sadistic celibate priests bursts in horrible fury, and The Maid is declared to be a relapsed heretic and sent to the market place to be burnt alive.

Of the moving quality of the play, the most moving work G.B.S. wrote, there is no doubt. It is lamentable that this powerful scene is followed by the Epilogue, though we should have lost the fine character of the English soldier who tied two sticks to make a cross, and gave them to Joan as she was hurried to the pyre.

The preface of the play, however, is another matter. Here he leaves the world of creative imagination and enters the world of legal and historic fact. He was so eager to be the devil's advocate, an honourable trait in his character, that he sometimes became unfair to those whom the devil has harmed. His main argument in the preface is that the Church of Rome behaved with scrupulous legality in its condemnation of The Maid, and that those of its servants who were implicated in the trial were really lion-hearted men, tenderly seeking to release an ignorant girl from the peril in which she was wilfully floundering.

The judgment contradicts that of the Church of Rome, made in the lifetime of some of the members of the Court, and, more importantly, by The Maid's canonisation on April 19, 1909. The Church could hardly have put a halo on her head if it had thought she had been justly condemned by her judges.

The historians, too, dissent from G.B.S.'s belief. Dr G. G. Coulton, who had few equals and no superiors in his medieval studies, does not fail to distinguish between the debater and the dramatist in *Saint Joan*. Admiring the play immensely, he had a poor opinion of its preface. In a note to his book, *Inquisition and Liberty*, he says, 'Though Mr Shaw's *Saint Joan* is a fine dramatic success, and his picture of Joan herself is practically true to the records, his long Introduction must be dismissed as childish. The itching for cheap paradox has overmastered him; and he flounders blindfold among the documents.' These are hard words which I am not competent to confirm or refute, but they are the words of a man who can tell the difference between an artist and a propagandist.

Against them, however, may be set Renan's opinion that the whole truth about an historical figure is not to be found in documents. 'To what', he says, 'would the life of Alexander be reduced if it were confined to that which is materially certain? Even partly erroneous traditions contain a portion of truth which history cannot neglect.' He points out that those who rely entirely on documents will find themselves in a pretty pickle when they have to contend with documents, such as the Gospels, which 'are in flagrant contradiction one with another.' G.B.S. consulted the documents in Joan's history and came to conclusions that seem infantile to Dr Coulton; but who will dare to say that the vision of a man of genius is less authoritative than the recordings of confidential clerks? The supreme fact about *Saint Joan* is that a great and inspiring figure emerges from it. We do not know, nor do many of us care, that this or that interpretation of a document is disputed. It is enough for most of us that we have been shown into the presence of nobility and have felt ourselves the better for the sight.

Dr Coulton denies that Joan received a fair trial. Rehearsing the facts in his twenty-third chapter, he concludes that she 'did not really get a fair trial, even if we make allowance for the spirit of her age, and admit the general justice of inquisitional law and procedure'. His argument is supported by W. P. Barrett of King's College, London, in his work, *The Trial of Jeanne d'Arc*, in which he publishes the first full translation of the documents of the trial. His considered judgment is that:

> 'The case against her was weak. The protraction of the trial, from January until near the end of May, when all parties, the University, the Church, and the English were anxious for her conviction, is proof enough of that.
>
> 'But at this time the machinery of the Inquisition was at the height of its perfection: every security of justice was removed, and no person in the situation in which Jeanne found herself, accused of witchcraft and heresy in a hostile ecclesiastical court, had the faintest chance of a fair trial.
>
> 'By the time the preparation of the articles of accusation was complete, Jeanne had been in prison, heavily ironed, for nine months. This, in itself enough to weaken her spirit, was the least of her sufferings.
>
> 'Before she was led to her judges she demanded permission to hear Mass, and the right to have among her assessors ecclesiastics of her own party equal in number to the representatives of the English, but both requests were denied. She was continually refused the consolation of religion, and through harsh treatment in gaol grew seriously ill.
>
> 'The account gives little idea of the tempestuous nature of the trial. A session would last anywhere from three to four hours, during which she was subjected to the continual and agonising strain of a pitiless and unfriendly cross-examination. Many of the questions were purposely confusing, designed with cunning ambiguity to entrap her, however she answered. . . .
>
> 'At times the judges all spoke at once in passion or anger, so that she protested, "Good my lords, speak to me one at a time". Towards the end of the proceedings she was threatened with torture, every nigh three soldiers slept in her cell, though she needed little watching, since her legs were doubly fettered. . . .

'In accordance with custom evidence was admitted against her which she was not allowed to see, and, with the miserable exception of Catherine de la Rochelle, she did not even know the names of those who testified. She was entirely without aid, her party scarcely lifted a finger to save her, and she was unable to call witnesses in support of her case. . . .'

The tale need not be continued. It is long and distressing. G.B.S., in his eagerness to side with the authorities and officials against the individual of genius who will not be bound by petty rules and regulations and little laws laid down by dull men of routine mind and behaviour, to whom Clause A, section B, sub-section C is more than the word of God, manipulated the evidence to establish his strange case.

Nevertheless, nobility emerges from the play. Few people who see it, come away unmoved by the fortitude and valour and greatness of mind and spirit they have seen displayed on the stage. It is immaterial that the priests are whitewashed and the little legalists and pedlars of Clause This and Clause That are treated with undeserved respect. What is supremely material, what makes the play stir rich emotion in those who see it, is that here, unmistakably, greatness and nobility are revealed, and the human heart, eager for signs of divinity in itself, finds them in the dramatic story of a young girl who rose up from the muddy fields of France and glorified mankind.

154

The first performance of *Saint Joan* was given at the Garrick Theatre in New York on December 28, 1923. A brilliant American actress, Winifred Lenihan, played the eponymous part with great distinction. This production is remarkable for the fact that the American playgoers were much quicker than the New York dramatic critics to realise that they were witnessing the first performance of a masterpiece. Despite a cool, and, in some quarters, downrightly stupid reception in the press, the public thronged to the theatre in such numbers that the play had to be transferred to a larger theatre soon after its first night. Dr Alice Griffin, in a lively and well-informed article in *The Shaw Bulletin*, the official organ of The Shaw Society of America for January, 1955, gives an impressive and entertaining account of the reception.

Dr Griffin asserts that had the power of the dramatic critics in New York 'been as great as it is to-day, one wonders whether *Saint Joan* would have made the grade'. Mr Percy Hammond, a critic of some quality and considerable standing, denounced it in the *Tribune*. 'Mr Shaw's chronicle of Joan of Arc makes the life and works of that sainted maiden duller though more probable than legends have taught us to believe,' and he insisted that the play was 'just another example of Mr Shaw's gift for interminable rag-chewing'. He did not wait to see the Epilogue, probably because the need to get an account of the play into the next morning's paper compelled him to leave the theatre early, but he reported to his readers that, according to his informants, it was 'tiresome'. He was to repent of his opinion when, in March 1936, Katherine Cornell revived the play. 'Although he found the play this time "a bit loquacious", he said of the final scene: "When in the epilogue (Joan) vanished in a happy ending tableau . . . I said to myself, here is the Theatre in one of its most consecrated moments".'

The late Alexander Woolcott found 'greatness' in the play, despite 'its grogginess' and its tendency to 'falter and go raucously astray', and his final judgment was that it was 'beautiful, engrossing and, at times, exalting'. Mr Kenneth Macgowan, one of the arty-and-crafty critics, who worked for the *Theatre Arts Monthly*, felt certain that G.B.S. had passed his prime. 'Age seems to be withering the scorn of this iconoclast, tarnishing the perverse brilliance of his mind, and taming his wit.' According to him the dialogue lacked brilliance, and 'the inspiration and divinity of Shaw have departed'.

The most discerning critic in New York then was Mr Walter Prichard Eaton who realised the fact which was so surprisingly over-looked by some of his colleagues, that 'Shaw is not only one of the keenest minds in the world to-day; he is one of the most religious of men . . . *Saint Joan* is the work of a religious soul.'

The most impressive comment on this production, however, was made by the great Italian dramatist, Luigi Pirandello, who happened to be in New York then and was asked to record his feelings about the play in *The New York Times*. 'Had an act as powerful as the fourth act of *Saint Joan* been produced on any one of the numerous Italian stages,' he said, 'all the people present would have jumped to their feet, even before the curtain fell, to start a frenzied applause.' Since that time, the play has been revived three times, each time with immense success.

When the play was produced in London three months later, on March 26, 1924, at the New Theatre, with Sybil Thorndike nobly and beautifully in the part of the Maid, its reception by the public was more cordial even than that given to it by the American people. It was performed 78 times in New York—its second theatre there was a large one—and 244 times in London, where it has been revived at least seven times. The New York critics, at revivals of the play, were, on the whole more discerning than their predecessors at the first production. Mr Gilbert Gabriel and Mr John Mason Brown had no doubt about the genius in the play, and Mrs Edith

Isaacs, the editor of *The Theatre Arts Monthly*, atoned for the juvenile imbecilities of Mr Macgowan.

Mr Brooks Atkinson, criticising the Cornell production, wrote that 'a generous share of the modern theatre's grandeur is now on display', and, after some justly expressed fault-finding, concluded that 'if *Saint Joan* offered nothing except the solemn trial scene and the compassionate wisdom of the inquisitor's speech, it would still rank with the best in the modern theatre.'

An odd fact is that, in London, the play is now less warmly received than it was at its first performance. Mr Kenneth Tynan, who gives curious exhibitions of himself in *The Observer*, went so far in his antic performances as to describe it as 'Shaw's bleak masterpiece', in which, he brightly remarked, the first signs of senility could be detected.

The play has been highly successful wherever it has been performed. Trebitsch, who made the German translation, says in his *Chronicle of a Life*, that its *première* at the Deutsches Theatre in Berlin 'was the greatest theatrical success that I have ever known'. The producer was Max Reinhardt, and The Maid was Elisabeth Bergner. Its reception at the Deutsche Volkstheater in Vienna, where the Joan was Annemarie Steinsieck, was equally fervent. Even in Paris, where Shaw had failed to impress playgoers, the play, with Ludmilla Pitoeff as Joan, was popular.

The Epilogue excited the most singular dispute in literary controversy. On one side was G.B.S., determined that it should not be cut: on the other was almost everybody who saw it in performance, as determined that it ought to be cut. But the matter is not so simple as this statement of opposites suggests.

G.B.S. was not only an obstinate man, resolved to make every point in his argument, even when the point was obvious to everybody: he was also a man with a message to those who now venerate The Maid more, perhaps, than any other saint in the Calendar. And that message was that we do not like saints even when we worship them; and that the prospect of their return to life fills us with fear and apprehension.

Some of the critics, not unwarrantably, complained that G.B.S. failed in imagination and sensitiveness in parts of the Epilogue, especially in the passage in which a priest in the clothes of 1920 appears and announces The Maid's canonisation. Certainly, the sight of this priest in a silk hat and a frock coat gravely disturbed the mood the play had created, which was, indeed, maintained with great power and beauty until the priest's appearance.

But there is noble writing in the Epilogue, which is moving to read, and it contains many passages and sentences of lovely wisdom: such as the speech in which Cauchon cries out in anguish 'must then a Christ perish in torment in every age to save those that have no imagination?' The spirit is stirred and the heart deeply touched when Joan, as the midnight bell begins to toll and she is left alone in a white radiance, cries out, 'Oh God that madest this beautiful earth, when will it be ready to receive Thy saints? How long, O Lord, how long?' It is conceivable that in this matter, G.B.S. is right, and that all the rest of us are wrong.

155

The year 1924, which G.B.S.'s world renown firmly sealed, was also the year in which he suffered an irreparable loss. William Archer, his benefactor and candid friend, who had gone into a nursing home for an operation which seemed to him less serious than it turned out to be, died on December 27. G.B.S. was then on holiday abroad. On December 17, Archer, obeying some instinct which may be called the equivalent in a Rationalist of 'making his soul', wrote the following letter to his old friend:

'My dear G.B.S.,
  'Since I wrote you, I have learnt that I shall have to undergo an operation one of these days—I go into a nursing home tomorrow. I don't know that the operation is a very serious one, and as a matter of fact I feel as fit as a fiddle, so I suppose my chances are pretty good. Still, accidents will happen, and this episode gives me an excuse for saying, what I hope you don't doubt—namely, that though I may sometimes have played the part of the all-too candid mentor, I have never wavered in my admiration and affection for you, or ceased to feel that the Fates had treated me kindly in making me your contemporary and friend. I thank you from my heart for forty years of good comradeship. . . .

Ever yours,
W.A.

Archer's death deeply distressed G.B.S., who, in his first transports of grief spoke and even wrote harshly about doctors and surgeons, almost accusing them of having killed his friend. The word, indeed, was harsher than that; and even in his last years, long after Archer's death, he still declared that Archer had been 'murdered'; but this was only the outcome of his strongly emotional nature and should not give serious offence to anyone. The important fact is that Archer and G.B.S., men so dissimilar that they might have been expected to feel antipathetic, had a deep affection for each other that could be called love. 'When I returned to an Archerless London,' G.B.S. wrote, 'it seemed to me that the place had entered on a new age, in which I was lagging superfluous. I still feel that when he went, he took a piece of me with him.'

156

In 1926, when he was seventy, G.B.S. was awarded the Nobel Prize for Literature. It put him in a quandary. He had always refused titles and honours on the ground that if he had any worth, his books and plays would be his monument: if he were without worth, then the sooner he was forgotten the better.

He declined honorary degrees from Universities because, he said, it was unfair that men who had worked hard for degrees should be humiliated by finding that men who had not worked at all should have them given to them in circumstances of high honour. The argument is fallacious, and G.B.S. would have been one of the first to complain if honours had been withheld from men of genius or distinction. He declined to be made a member of the Order of Merit, a reprehensible act for which his friends rightly reproved him.

The only honours he accepted were the Freedom of Dublin, where he was born, an odd acceptance since he hated the place, and the freedom of the borough of St Pancras in which he had lived, of which he had once been a councillor. He also, very strangely, became a Freeman of the City of London.[1]

His disinclination to accept the Nobel Prize was due, partly, to his odd reluctance to accept any honour, but mainly to the fact that the prize was a substantial sum of money. He was now a man of considerable wealth, and had no need of more money. It was not until he realised the he could use the prize, 118,165 Swedish kronor, roughly the equivalent of £7,000, for a laudable purpose that he consented to accept it.

The whole of the money financed a society for making Swedish literature available in English. This was the Anglo-Swedish Literary Foundation, which has the Crown Prince of Sweden for its Patron, and is under the direction of three Trustees, who were, at the time of the foundation, Viscount Burnham, Admiral H. Lindberg, President of Svensk-Engelska Foreningen in Stockholm, and Baron Erik Palmstierna, who was then the Swedish Minister in London.

The first translation, a volume of four plays by August Strindberg, was published by Jonathan Cape in 1929. By 1939, seven other works,

---

[1] He received the freedom of London on June 20, 1935, as a member of the City Company of Stationers and Newspaper Makers.

The honorary freedom of Dublin was conferred on him on August 28, 1946. As he was then 90, the Roll was taken to him for signature at Ayot St Lawrence. He was shown the signatures of his father and grandfather, both of whom had been freemen.

The Borough of St Pancras made him its first honorary freeman on October 9 of the same year. Intending to be present at the ceremony, he was unable to do so because of a weakness in his legs which made him liable to fall. But the speech he had meant to make was recorded at his flat in Whitehall Court and was broadcast that evening.

including three more volumes of Strindberg's plays had been published. After the Second World War was ended, publication was resumed in 1952 with a translation of *Carl Linnaeus* by Knut Hagberg. Another volume, issued in conjunction with The American-Scandinavian Foundation, was published in 1953. This was Selma Lagerlof's fine novel, *Gosta Berling's Saga*.

An immediate result of this award was a great number of begging letters. 'After the executors of the inventor of dynamite awarded me the Nobel Prize, some fifty thousand people wrote to me to say that as the greatest of men I must see that the best thing I could do with the prize was to give it to them. Instead, I gave it back. Then they all wrote again to say that if I could afford to do that, I could afford to lend them £1500 for three years.'

157

He seemed now, so far as the drama was concerned, to have written himself out. But he was not idle. His sister-in-law, Mary Stewart Cholmondeley, the wife of Brigadier-General Sir Hugh Cecil Cholmondeley, had asked him to write a few notes to enable her to explain Socialism to the local Women's Institute.

She got much more than she had asked for: *The Intelligent Woman's Guide to Socialism and Capitalism;* 470 closely printed pages containing nearly a quarter of a million words. What the Women's Institute made of it has never transpired. It took him three years to write: a considerable feat for a man who was nearly seventy when he began to write it. The book which was handsomely made and bound, had a considerable sale, despite Rattray's statement that it is difficult to read: a difficulty which I have not discovered. Rattray adds that it 'has been, and probably will be, uninfluential'.

How he knows this, is not stated, but a book which is widely read, though it does not cause a revolution in thought, can scarcely be said to have had no influence on its readers. Even if we believe that it failed to change the mind of a single one of them, it may still have had a considerable effect on their thoughts. The value of a book is not to be measured by the converts it makes to the author's opinions, but by the extent of the thought it evokes; and it is inconceivable that any person could have read this remarkable work from cover to cover without finding his mind greatly stimulated, if not in agreement, at least in dissent.

Rattray himself supplies an impressive, if over-stated refutal of his opinion when he quotes Ramsay MacDonald's remark to Trebitsch that, 'after the Bible, this, in my estimation, is humanity's most important book'. Had G.B.S. been in a mood of levity, he might have paraphrased Whistler and exclaimed, 'Why drag in the Bible?' Against MacDonald's opinion, may be set that of Miss Patch who asserts in her odd volume, *Thirty Years with G.B.S.*, that 'he would be an uncommonly devoted Shavian who to-day would cheerfully set out again to read through *The Intelligent Woman's Guide*. . . .' Does Miss Patch imagine that a book cannot influence anybody's mind unless it is read and re-read?

To have read a long closely-argued work of this sort once is a considerable feat, and few people perform it. There cannot be many men or women who have read Adam Smith's *Wealth of Nations* or Darwin's *Origin of Species* twice, but no one will have the hardihood to deny their importance on that account. The lives of millions of men and women who never read a line of *Das Kapital* by Karl Marx have been profoundly and, perhaps, permanently changed by it.

The book suffers, as any book of its sort by G.B.S. was certain to suffer, from his partisan point of view. A man who begins a book on Socialism and Capitalism with the assumption that Capitalism is inept and wicked and that Socialism is sensible and sanctified, obviously cannot treat the subject with the dispassion that it requires. But, allowance being made for that defect, it is a brilliant work, written with all the verve and vigour that one expects from its author, and with all the vivacity that can be put into a work of its kind.

It is absurd to think that a book on the social and economic organisation of a community can be written in a bright and breezy manner. Its influence would be slight if it were; and we may justly believe that when a person finds a serious work on a serious subject heavy going, he is condemning, not the work, but himself. A man or a woman with a trivial or slightly-furnished mind ought to have enough sense to realise that a book which is difficult for him or her to read is not, therefore, unreadable or dull. Its readability depends on the amount of intelligence and knowledge its reader brings to it, and if the reader is stupid or ignorant or shallow-minded, he or she will almost certainly put it down after reading the first page.

G.B.S. was given to over-simplification. An example of this may be found on page 29, where he states that 'a shop-keeper or a coal merchant may not pick your pocket; but he may overcharge you as much as he likes'. In theory, he can, but in practice he bankrupts himself if he does. His ability to charge a price is limited by the capacity of his customer to pay it, and also by the fact that he has rivals who may, and probably will, undersell him. The customer is at the mercy of the shop-keeper only when the shop-keeper has no competitors within reach of the customer; but that is an argument, not against capitalism and enterprise, but against socialism and monopoly.

Choice in marriage

When the socialist argues that it is wasteful for several milkmen to purvey milk in one street, he overlooks the important fact that the customers are able to make a choice and to chasten an extortionate or careless milkman by transferring their custom to one of his rivals. Where the supply of milk is a monopoly, either of a syndicate or a municipality, the power to chasten the purveyor disappears. Since the end of the Second World War, we have had ample experience of the defects of monopoly in purveying goods of any sort; and even the Labour Party is beginning to wonder if it is not time to call a halt to the nationalisation of industries.

When G.B.S. comes to intimate and personal matters, such as marriage, he finds the State useless, though he still maintains his belief that the range of choice in marriage will be greater in a community where there is equality of income than in one where there is inequality. 'Miss Smith and Miss Jones have finally to make up their minds to like what they can get, because they can very seldom get what they like; and it is safe to say that in the great majority of marriages at present Nature has very little part in the choice compared to circumstances.'

But is it safe to say anything of the sort? Miss Smith and Miss Jones, in the majority of cases, have as much power of obtaining the mates they want as anyone is ever likely to possess; and much more than a royal lady.

A working-class girl probably has a wider range of choice than a girl of the upper class, because her mind is less bound by thoughts of money and because she has a more extensive acquaintance than her social superior. A village girl who has been to the same school and has played in the same streets and is familiar with the same people as the boy whom she marries, knows far more about her husband than any upper class girl who has picked her husband or had him picked for her simply because he has enough money to keep her in the style to which she is accustomed or wishes to become accustomed.

G.B.S. rejects the state control of mating, such as that which was exercised in Sparta, by asserting, first, that men and women cannot be mated for breeding purposes as we mate bulls and cows, mares and stallions, sows and boars, without giving them some choice in the matter. Here he overlooks historic fact. Such mating not only can be, but has been, done. Moreover, the children born of such marriages are as likely to be satisfactory as the children born of love matches. G.B.S. was himself a proof of the fact. His mother had no love or even feeling of affection for his father. She married him to escape from intolerable domestic conditions, and she soon repented of her escape. But she conceived a genius by her unloved and unsatisfactory husband.

He gives a second reason why men and women should not be mated as if they were animals whose mating is made, not for any purpose of their own, but for the purposes of animals of an entirely different species: for the better production of beef or mutton or milk or wool, fat bacon or lean bacon, speed or strength. This reason is that we do not know what sort of human being we want to breed. We know that we have no wish to breed neurotics or drunkards, and that we *do* wish to breed strong, healthy, intelligent, honourable and courageous men and women.

But we have no notion of how this is to be done. Is there a family on this earth which is free from some sort of taint? If we were to insist that no person who has had a criminal or a lunatic in his ancestry should be allowed to have children, there would be no marriages at all, and the human race would abruptly end.

Are we, indeed, fit to decide who is suitable and who is not? 'Considering that we poisoned Socrates, crucified Christ, and burnt Joan of Arc, amid popular applause . . . we can hardly set up to be judges of goodness or to have any sincere liking for it. . . . As to moral excellence, what model would' our political authorities, if we were childish enough to let them control our matings, 'take as desirable? St Francis, George Fox, William Penn, John Wesley, and George Washington? or Alexander, Caesar, Napoleon, and Bismarck? It takes all sorts to make a world; and the notion of a Government department trying to make out how many different types were necessary, and how many persons of each type, and proceeding to breed them by appropriate marriages, is amusing, but not practicable.'

158

Yet this is precisely what Bertrand Russell, in *The Scientific Outlook*, thinks is likely to happen in the future. The whole scheme of marriage, he believes, will be revolutionised in a comparatively short time. The revolution, indeed, began on the day when the Married Women's Property Act was passed in 1882, and it was enormously accelerated when women became economically independent of men. Russell foresees a day when the father will either be excluded from the family or admitted only on sufferance, tolerated only by the mother for as long as she thinks him fit to fertilise her.

He forecasts a great regimentation of people in the future, a regimentation which is more credible to us with our knowledge of what has been accomplished in totalitarian states in recent years and is in common practice in communistic countries to-day, but would have seemed incredible to our fathers and grandfathers. There will, Russell asserts, be a highly trained governing class, whose members 'will be selected, some before birth, some during the first three years of life, and a few between the ages of three and six. All the best-known science will be applied to the simultaneous development of intelligence and power.'

Forecasts of the future are generally, though not invariably, statements of personal desire. If Russell were able to make a world, the world he forecasts is probably the world he would make. He seems to like a specialised people and to be contemptuous of men and women of general character. He even wishes to specialise some women in maternity. 'If the simultaneous regulation of quantity and quality is taken seriously in the future', he writes on pp. 261–3, 'we may expect that in each generation some 25 per cent of women and some 5 per cent of men will be selected to be the parents of the next generation, while the remainder of the population will be sterilised, which will in no way interfere with the sexual pleasures, but will merely render these pleasures destitute of social importance:

> 'The women who are selected for breeding will have to have eight or nine children each, but will not be expected to perform any other work except the suckling of the children for a suitable number of months. No obstacles will be placed upon their relations with sterile men, or upon the relations of sterile men and women with each other, but reproduction will be regarded as a matter which concerns the State, and will not be left to the free choice of the persons concerned. Perhaps it will be found that artificial impregnation is more certain and less embarrassing, since it will obviate the need of any personal contact between the father and mother of the prospective child. . . .
>
> 'Fathers would, of course, have nothing to do with their own children. There would in general be one father to every five mothers, and it is quite likely that he would never even have seen the mothers of his children. The sentiment of paternity would thus disappear. . . .'

It is not surprising that Russell foresees a total disappearance of art and literature. 'In such a world, though there may be pleasure, there will be no joy.' In the world foreseen by G.B.S. in *Back to Methuselah*, the joy of sexual union will not be experienced by anybody, not even by brood mares and stallions: animals, indeed, seem to have disappeared from his Utopia, for there is no suggestion in the play that they exist. The prospective child will be hatched from an enormous egg, though there is no indication of the source of the egg. The He Ancients and the She Ancients, despite the assertion that they will live in an ecstasy of pure thought, will feel neither pleasure nor joy. They will drift about the world, looking like the picture of misery, waiting and hoping for a fatal accident or a grave bout of discouragement to rid them of their dismal lives.

But G.B.S., though he demands a great increase of social regulation, does at least object to the specialisation of men and women in the Russell manner. 'There is nothing for it but to let people choose their mates for themselves, and trust to Nature to produce a good result.'

Utopias are usually desolating states, but a reader of William Morris's *News from Nowhere*, G.B.S.'s *Back to Methuselah*, and Bertrand Russell's *The Scientific Outlook*, will have no difficulty in making up his mind about which of the utopias described in them he would care to inhabit: the first far the foremost; and the decision about any form of society will be made, not by little men with microscopes in laboratories, but by the general desire of the whole community.

The problem which will confront the practical politician in the future will be that of securing the whole people in the means of life: a problem which is already in process of solution; and of preserving the people thus secured from demoralisation because they are kept, not by their own exertions, but by the benevolence of their neighbours. We have practically solved the problem of production, and need only solve the problem of distribution to have the whole matter of securing the population in the means of life settled. The harder problem will be the second. The world will be worse than it is if, as a result of a greatly extended Welfare State, the entire population degenerates into a crowd of Gimme, Gimme men and women with extended hands, none of whom has the slightest sense of personal responsibility. The practical politician, in short, will have to concern himself a great deal more with the soul of man than the politicians who set up the Welfare State dreamt of doing. The problem is not how to produce healthy people, a problem that can easily be solved, but how to produce an intelligent people who are full of spiritual grace.

> 'The rule that subsistence comes first and virtue afterwards is as old as Aristotle and as new as this book,' G.B.S. says on page 94. 'The Communism of Christ, of Plato, and of the great religious orders, all take equality in material subsistence for granted as the first condition of establishing the Kingdom of Heaven upon earth. Whoever has reached this conclusion, by whatever path, is a Socialist.'

But this argument will not do. Socialism is much more than a system of feeding and housing the hungry and homeless: it is an elaborate scheme for the regulation of society; and G.B.S. does not tackle the problem of how people are to live in liberty and extensive regulation simultaneously. The first Christians established their simple Communism because they believed that the end of the world was imminent, and were convinced that at any moment Jesus Christ would ride out of the heavens to claim his own. Why, then, should they take thought for the morrow?

Misstatements of fact

Plato was foolish enough to accept an invitation to tutor Dionysus II of Syracuse, and off he went to show the young monarch how men should be governed. The experience was fatal to his reputation as a practical philosopher, and he scurried back to Athens to revise his *Republic*. It is a comforting thought that we need only put these bossy people into places of authority to see them expose their total incompetence to govern anything. Plato's *Republic*, had it been established, would have perished of inanition: as all Socialist and Communistic communities will perish.

There is no health in any of these closely organised societies, even when they are religious, for they are barren of fertile spirit. Monks and nuns have renounced the world, unaware that it regards them as people who have shirked their share of its responsibilities. They are dedicated people whose way of life cannot be taken as an adequate guide to ordinary social life. There is no convincing ground for the belief that Jesus himself held the communistic beliefs professed by his first followers after the Crucifixion.

Some of G.B.S.'s arguments in favour of a highly socialised society must have left the Intelligent Woman derisive. When, for example, he tells here that the good kind Government provides her with an army, and a navy, a civil service, courts of law and so forth at cost price or more nearly at cost price than any commercial concern would, he fails to tell her that if the commercial concern could extract the entire expense of these services from the public in the form of taxes, they, too, could provide them at cost price. He is disingenuous when he says that 'the Government takes a vast sum of money every year from the whole body of the rich, and immediately hands it back to those who lent it money for the war.' But those who receive the low rate of interest paid on War Loans, are taxed at the high rate levied on unearned increment. The Government has no rivals with whom to compete, and it can do very nearly what it likes.

There is a shocking misstatement of the facts on page 120, where he says that the Americans improved the morals of their country by closing the saloons or public houses. They 'found immediately that they could shut up a good many of the prisons as well'. He must have known that Prohibition was such a curse in the United States that it had to be repealed because it had created a large criminal class and caused wide-spread drunkenness. He treats rent as if it were entirely profit to the landlord of the house, omitting to mention that out of it has to be paid the cost of repairing the house; and he also fails to state that although private landlords were forbidden for many years to raise rents, and were maintaining their property at a severe loss, municipalities were allowed to raise the rent of Council Houses.

Following the habit of H. G. Wells and other theorists on the

512

composition of a community, he announces the inefficiency and impending ruin of the small shop-keeper because of the competition and better service of the multiple store. 'These ruined shopkeepers may think themselves lucky if they get jobs in the multiple shops as shop assistants, managers of departments, and the like, when they are not too old to change.' If H. G. Wells, who derived his knowledge of small shopkeepers from his inefficient father, a man who could not have conducted an ice-cream barrow with any hope of success, had no expert knowledge of the matter on which he laid down the law. Because his father was a failure in the hardware shop he kept in Bromley, an occupation for which he had neither training, taste nor talent, *all* small shopkeepers were destined to become bankrupts.

This belief pervades the whole of his work, imaginative, sociological and speculative. It is the foundation of *The History of Mr Polly*, who, was, surely, Joseph Wells? 'It is manifestly written out on the scroll of destiny', he says in *New Worlds for Old*, 'that the little independent butcher's shop, buying and selling locally, must disappear. . . . This is equally true of a milk-seller, or a small manufacturer, or a builder, of a hundred and one trades. They are bound to be incorporated in a large organisation: they are bound to become salaried men where formerly they were independent men, and it is no use struggling against that.' G.B.S.'s words might have been lifted out of H. G.'s book. Thirty-two years later, unaware, seemingly, that there was not the slightest sign of his forebodings being fulfilled, Wells repeated his doctrine of economic determinism in *The New World Order* in words that would have scandalised Calvin and the Bishop of Hippo and made Pelagians of them both.

Wells had had some experience, as a child, of a shop-keeper's life, but it was a limited and exceptional experience, entirely in failure; G.B.S. had no knowledge whatsoever of such life, apart from the single encounter with any member of the shopkeeping class which he mentions in one of his prefaces: when his father forbade him to play with the son of a Dublin shopkeeper who could have bought and sold Mr Shaw several times.

'I remember thinking when I was a boy how silly it was that my father, whose business was a wholesale business, should consider himself socially superior to his tailor, who had the best means of knowing how much poorer my father was, and who had a handsome residence, with ornamental grounds and sailing-boats, at the seaside place where we spent the summer in a six-roomed cottage with a small garden. The great Grafton Street shopkeepers of Dublin outshone the tailor with their palaces and yachts; and their children had luxuries that I never dreamt of as possible for me, besides being far more expensively educated! . . .'

Did it never occur to G.B.S. that the owners of these large shops were the children or grandchildren of men who had owned little shops?

He has the audacity to tell his Intelligent Woman that Socialism 'will be more elastic and tolerant' of private enterprise than Capitalism, 'which would leave any district without a carrier if no private carrier could make it pay'. Yet the fact was staring him in the face that when the railways were nationalised, all the unprofitable branch lines which had been maintained by the private companies for the benefit of the public in small areas, were promptly scrapped.

But he corrects himself later on in *Everybody's Political What's What*, where he reminds his readers that 'Socialism may prove more corrupt in corrupt and ignorant hands than a simply selfish plutocracy', and tells them that 'it has repeatedly occurred that State railways have been allowed to fall into ruinous disrepair and scandalous inefficiency through the Government using the money paid by the public for transport to reduce taxation instead of for necessary repairs and maintenance of the service at optimum efficiency, and devoting the profits, if any, to cheapening it or improving the conditions of its operatives.'

But these are minor matters in a work of considerable virtuosity. Although he is an advocate, pleading a cause in the manner of a partisan, he does not conceal adverse facts as lesser men would do; and some of his shots into the future are shrewd and have been justified by time. 'At present,' he says, 'the propertied classes are looking to capitalist Trade Unions to save them from Socialism. The time is coming when they will clamour for Socialism to save them from capitalist Trade Unionism: that is, from Capitalised Labour. Already in America Trade Unionism is combining with Big Business to squeeze the sleeping partner.'

He is more fair-minded than a propagandist is expected to be. He does not restrict his warnings to the efforts of mine owners to get their industry subsidised by the tax-payers, but warns his readers that 'if miners, or any other workers, find that the local authorities will confiscate the incomes of the ratepayers to feed them when they are idle, their incentive to pay their way by their labour will be, to say the least, perceptibly lessened. Yet it is no use simply refusing to make these confiscations. If the nation will not take its industries out of the hands of private owners it must enable them to carry them on, whether they can make them pay or not. If the owners will not pay subsistence wages, the nation must; for it cannot afford to have its children under-nourished and its civil and military strength weakened, though it was fool enough to think it could in Queen Victoria's time. Subsidies and doles are demoralising, both for employers and proletarians; but they stave off Socialism, which people seem to consider worse than pauperised insolvency.'

514

159

In October 1927, the Shaws removed from Adelphi Terrace, where they had lived since their marriage, where Charlotte had lived for some time before their marriage; and took a flat in Whitehall Court which had formerly been occupied by Lady Russell, the charming and popular Elizabeth of the German Garden, Bertrand Russell's sister-in-law. The Adelphi flat was uncomfortable. It had no proper bathing facilities, and its kitchen, which had been improvised in one of the attics, was difficult to work. I had listened often to Charlotte's complaints about Adelphi Terrace, as I had listened to her complaints about Ayot St Lawrence and her assertion that G.B.S. was thoroughly tired of both, without, however, much hope that they would ever remove from one or the other.

They had to leave Adelphi Terrace, which was to be demolished to make way for the barbaric building which houses the Shell Mex Company; and a great hullabaloo there was about this necessity.

It happened that Elizabeth, who was my next-door neighbour in Whitehall Court, had decided to give up her expensive flat, and when she told me this, I thought that it would suit the Shaws admirably. I therefore walked round to Adelphi Terrace and told Charlotte that Elizabeth was eager to get rid of it, and suggested that she should go to tea with her and come to some arrangement. Charlotte, who had the odd delusion that people disliked her and G.B.S., was reluctant to do this because she felt certain that Elizabeth was unfriendly. So I went back to Whitehall Court and talked about the matter to Elizabeth, who declared that she was so far from disliking the Shaws that she could be said to love them, which, of course, was nonsense, since she scarcely knew them, and I therefore suggested that she should invite Charlotte to tea, which she did.

Within a few weeks, Elizabeth removed herself to Virginia Water, where she complained to everybody that I had evicted her from her beautiful flat so that I could have the Shaws for my immediate neighbours.

G.B.S. was not fond of Whitehall Court, but Charlotte loved it. It was exactly the sort of place, next to a hotel, in which she liked to live: with no more housekeeping troubles than an inspection of the restaurant menu every morning. For eighteen months, G.B.S. and I lived side by side. Then I went to America for several months and afterwards settled in the house in Devon which was being built for me while I was in New York; and G.B.S. told everybody that after inveigling him into Whitehall Court, I ran away and left him to it. But even he was happier there than he had been in Adelphi Terrace.

It was in the same year that Barry (now Sir Barry) Jackson founded the Malvern Festival, mainly for the purpose of producing plays by G.B.S. The immediate outcome of this Festival, so far as he was concerned, was *The Apple Cart*, which was the first play he had written for five years.

160

The Apple Cart is badly articulated. The skeleton is loose and shapeless, and some bones are missing, but the play, nevertheless, is uncommonly good entertainment, and it reveals the political faith of G.B.S. more plainly than any other piece he wrote. The middle act of the three seems to have little or no relevance to the other two, but it is, in effect, the main-spring of the play, apart from being an almost literal transcript of a scene he had with Mrs Patrick Campbell, when that singular woman tried to prevent him from keeping an appointment with Charlotte.

This book will have failed in its purpose if it has not made the reader fully aware of the fact that G.B.S. had a deep love for Charlotte, who was as deeply devoted to him, and that he never failed to treat her with the greatest courtesy. Any promise he made to her, however slight it might be, was punctiliously kept. If he had said he would be home at six, he would step into the flat at that hour, though Charlotte had probably forgotten that he had made the promise, and would not have minded had he broken it. He paid her numerous small attentions that were significant of a happy marriage in which the partners are well aware of each other's idiosyncracies and fond of them. Charlotte liked to eat an orange after her lunch; and every day G.B.S. peeled one for her, and broke it into slices which were then passed to her. It was a pretty piece of ritual, and it was never, in my knowledge, omitted.

When Mrs Campbell discovered how particular he was in this respect, she resolved that he should break at least one promise to Charlotte, and so, when he rose one afternoon to leave her house, she first tried to make him stay longer, and then, in her determination to have her way, caught hold of him to detain him. In the struggle, they both fell on the floor, and while they were lying there, the door opened, and a maid, who was about to enter, gave one swift glance and hurriedly shut the door. This scene forms the second act of *The Apple Cart*.

161

The Apple Cart surprised all concerned in it by being remarkably successful when it was first produced, and surprised G.B.S.'s admirers by maintaining its popularity when it was revived. It surprised them still more by its exposure of the foibles and follies of Labour Cabinet Ministers and its apparent advocacy of the monarchical system. The latter aspect of it, however, should not have caused any surprise, for G.B.S. had little use for pseudo-democracy and had immense and often absurd admiration for dictators. An able king, even if he were an absolute monarch, was more to his liking than a Cabinet of scrapings from the Trade Unions' barrels.

Like H. G. Wells, he believed that all the world's fine achievements were the work of exceptional individuals, and that highly intelligent people were to be found in all classes. 'At present,' he says in the preface to *The Millionairess*, 'only about 5% of the population are capable of making decisions of any importance; and without many daily decisions, civilisation would go to pieces.'

King Magnus, who upsets the democratic apple-cart in this play, is a man of ability and great astuteness, confronted by a cabinet of windbags, spineless bureaucrats and neurasthenics, leavened by some members who have brains. At least three of the ministers are drawn from life: Ramsay MacDonald, John Burns and Harry Quelch. The King, manifestly abler than any of his ministers, disagrees profoundly with the policy of the Government, and his solution of the trouble is that he shall abdicate and, as a private person, seek election to the House of Commons as the representative of Windsor: a prospect which flings the Labour Cabal into a great flurry and enables the King to obtain his way. That, substantially, is the theme of the play which is adorned with wit and sagacity and a high sense of human character and dignity.

Its attraction for playgoers is unfailing in its strength, and it offers actors opportunities of displaying their talent which they are eager to take. Sir Cedric Hardwicke and Mr Noel Coward, actors totally dissimilar in talent, have each been highly successful in the part of King Magnus, Mr Coward being, in my judgment, the subtler of the two in delineating the king's character. Sir Cedric's Magnus seemed to make his decisions almost without thought: a man whose mind was so well ordered that he had no need to take counsel with himself. But Mr Coward, with uncanny skill, showed us the man encountering difficulties and thinking his way out of them.

The play was performed for the first time at the Polsky Theatre, in Warsaw, on June 14, 1929, with great success, and it was the last production made at the Deutsches Theater in Berlin by Reinhardt. Barry Jackson, having founded the Repertory Theatre in Birmingham, decided to hold a festival season of plays at Malvern, and the first of these seasons was opened by *The Apple Cart* on August 19, 1929, with Hardwicke as Magnus and Edith Evans as Orinthia. The play was then taken to the Queen's Theatre in London, where it opened on September 17, and was performed 258 times.

It was produced in New York on February 24, 1930, by the Theatre Guild, but was not successful: the depreciation of pseudo-democrats was not, perhaps, to the taste of the American people, who moreover, were not inclined to like remarks such as the one made by Lysistrata when the suggestion that Great Britain should be absorbed by the United States was made: 'It's no use pretending that the America of George Washington is going to swallow up the England of Queen Anne. The America of George Washington is as dead as Queen Anne. What they call an American is only a wop pretending to be a Pilgrim Father.'

162

G.B.S. was now beginning to slacken; and there was a perceptible decline in the quality of his plays. Formerly, he had been prolific and speedy in his output, but now he began to take things more easily. He was 73 when he wrote *The Apple Cart*, which was the first full length play he had written since *Saint Joan*. He did not make another play until, somewhere between Corsica and Sardinia, he began to write *Too True to be Good* on March 3, 1931. It was finished at Ayot St Lawrence on June 30, and soon afterwards he departed for Moscow, accompanied by Lord and Lady Astor and Lord Lothian, who was more widely known as Mr Philip Kerr.

The Communists received him with immense fervour, but the honours of the occasion were won by Lady Astor, who, having no veneration for dictators nor any awe of eminent persons, frightened the wits out of the interpreters during an interview with Stalin by asking that cunning Caucasian why he had slaughtered so many Russians. The interpreters were loth to translate it, nor did they do so, until Stalin, observing their fearful embarrassment, demanded to be told what Lady Astor had said. He took it very quietly, replying that some slaughter is inevitable when the constitution of a country is fundamentally disrupted. The violent death of a large number of people was necessary before the Communist State could be firmly established. The reply was not unreasonable. Many Englishmen, including King Charles, had to be killed before Cromwell could be sure of his Commonwealth.

Despite the applause G.B.S. received in the streets of Moscow, most of it carefully arranged by the authorities, he meant little even to those Russians who had some knowledge of him. Many of his plays had been translated and performed in various parts of the Empire before the fall of the Tsar, but, apart from *Mrs Warren's Profession*, none of them had been widely popular. The critics knew so little about him that they described him, according to Archibald Henderson, as 'a typical middle-class Englishman', a description which must have made his Irish blood boil. They considered him old-fashioned almost to the point of being reactionary; and a Liberal paper, the *Retch*, dismissed *Mrs Warren's Profession* as a characteristic English middle-class play, full of 'false sentiment and melodrama', a foolish description, even for a Russian intellectual to make.

Another newspaper, the *Russ*, remarked that although he was thought to be 'an *enfant terrible* in England', he was, in Russia, 'only a writer who is not absolutely devoid of advanced ideas. In our opinion his play belongs neither to the Extreme Right nor to the Extreme Left of dramatic literature; it is an expression of the ideas of moderation which belong to the Centre, and the proof of this is the production of it at our State supported theatre, which in our eyes is the home and shelter of what is retrograde and respectable.' The reader must remember that this criticism was made *before* the Russian Revolution.

At the time of the visit to Moscow, however, the intellectuals, having been sobered by the discovery that the revolution they had desired was making short work of them, joined in the official applause with which G.B.S. was received. Litvinov, who had spent a long exile in London and had married Ivy Low, the niece of Sir Sidney Low, the author of a standard work on the English Constitution, *The Governance of England*, was now an influential member of the Soviet Government, and he, probably, took care that the crowds in the street applauded very heartily when G.B.S. appeared.

Apart from his enjoyment of public applause, however, G.B.S. seems to have played *piano* in Moscow. He spoke once or twice, astounding some of the proletariat by telling them that Communism was a religion. Remembering his reputation for wit, they thought this remark was one of his jokes, and they laughed very amiably at it, but they became uneasy when he insisted that he meant what he said, for religion, they had been told, was dope and must, therefore, be abolished. The general impression of the Russian intellectuals, each of whom behaved as if he were a Chekhov character, was that G.B.S. was a good man who had fallen among Fabians and that he was no longer a significant figure in a world of high-minded Commissars.

When his short play, *Great Catherine*, was produced in Russia, the critics, Henderson tells his readers, jeered at it. It marked 'a falling-off in' his 'creative powers'; 'the fine satirist has become a vulgar buffoon': 'Shaw apparently considers this a joke.' He did, and it was. The little Russian robots dared not say anything else. Liquidation would have been their lot had they done so.

519

This was not the first time that G.B.S. had incurred the displeasure of the half-baked intellectuals who now ruled Russia. Seven years earlier, in December 1924, he had published an article in the Moscow paper *Izvestia*, taking care that a copy of it should also appear in *The Daily Herald* simultaneously, for, in spite of his clamant admiration for the Muscovites, he knew them too well to trust them not to uppress and even distort what he had written. He had addressed them more candidly than arbitrary Commissars are accustomed to being addressed, and they disliked the liberties he took with them. They were bluntly told that Mr Zinovieff, who was seeking to bind them to the Third International, was not only making an ass of himself, but was making asses of them:

'But I must add—and here my opinion may embarrass *Izvestia*—that the Soviet Government would do well to dissociate itself from the Third International as speedily as possible, and to tell Mr Zinovieff plainly that he must choose definitely between serious statesmanship and cinematographic schoolboy nonsense if the Soviet Government is to be responsible to Europe for his proceedings, which will, otherwise, make Mr Rakovsky's position here almost impossible. . . . The constitution of the Third International has been translated and published in the London *Times* newspaper; and the bourgeois idealism and childish inexperience of men and affairs which it betrays in every line have given a severe shock to the friends of the Soviet in England.

'From the point of view of English Socialists, the members of the Third International do not know even the beginning of their business as Socialists: and the proposition that the world should take its orders from a handful of Russian novices, who seem to have gained their knowledge of modern Socialism by sitting over the drawingroom stove and reading the pamphlets of Liberal Revolutionists of 1848–70, makes even Lord Curzon and Mr Winston Churchill seem extreme modernists in comparison.'

There was more in the same strain, and it made Mr Zinovieff squeal like a stricken guinea-pig. He delivered a long speech to a congress of school teachers in Moscow which was reported in *Pravda* on January 22, 1925. Most of it was a virulent denunciation of G.B.S. who was, he declared, the best example he knew of 'petty bourgeoise intelligence'. Shaw's attitude to the root questions of the revolution and Marxism, the furious Bolshie declared, was that of 'the remotest provincial Philistine'. The school teachers were defied to find anywhere in Russia an educated man 'with such ossification and Philistinism and such enormous blinkers on his eyes as G.B.S. had. G.B.S. might be a talented exponent of *belles lettres*, though Zinovieff did not appear to be certain of this, but in politics he was 'a desiccated bourgeois to the marrow'.

'Bernard Shaw is a fossilised Chauvinist, a self-satisfied Englishman through and through. It seems to him that, sitting in the British Empire, he is invulnerable and can lay down the law about all the rest of the world. History evidently presents itself to him in the same forms as to Lord Curzon. In fact, from Curzon to MacDonald and from MacDonald to Shaw on some questions you have a single front.' If G.B.S. were to be put side by side with Karl Marx, 'no one would notice this pigmy, this blade of grass called Bernard Shaw'. There were eight columns of this stuff in one issue, and more of it was promised in the next.[1] The brotherly love, it seemed, was to continue.

On his return to London after his nine days' visit, G.B.S. announced that heaven had been established in Russia. When asked why, that being so, he had not remained in heaven, he said that it was his duty to rescue the suffering British from the hell in which they were interned! . . .

163

The year 1931 was largely devoted to travel and tidying. The Standard Edition of his works was begun in this year, and a book of great charm and value, *Ellen Terry and Bernard Shaw: a Correspondence*, which was ably edited by Miss Christopher St John, appeared. The critics were astonished and delighted to discover that Miss Terry, though not so voluminous a correspondent as G.B.S., was no less pleasing; and the reading public enjoyed the volume immensely, though it was perplexed by the fact that letters of such affection and intimacy could pass between a man and a woman who had never met until after almost the last of the letters had been written.

164

On December 29, 1931, the Shaws sailed for South Africa where they had a serious misadventure and a maladroit meeting with General Smuts at a luncheon party given by a distinguished novelist Mrs Sarah Gertrude Millin.

The conversation at this party was uneasy. Smuts and G.B.S. had not much in common, apart from high intellectual quality, and their interests seemed not to touch anywhere. The fact that they were absorbed in politics might have been thought likely to set their tongues wagging, but it was a political remark which ruined any hope of agreeable discourse between them. Smuts, making conversation, had talked about guerrilla warfare, without awaking G.B.S.'s

[1] I have taken my account of the incident and the tirade from Zinovieff from various sources, *The Daily Herald*, *The Manchester Guardian*, and *The Daily Telegraph*, between December 9, 1924 and January 27, 1925.

interest, another odd fact, considering that Colonel T. E. Lawrence, a brilliant guerrilla warrior, was now an intimate friend of G.B.S. and Charlotte. It would have seemed simple to mingle the memories of Smuts with the experience of Lawrence.

Instead of talking of the Lawrence Smuts knew, G.B.S. diverted the conversation to the Lawrence of whom Smuts had scarcely heard: D.H.; and insisted on talking about *Lady Chatterley's Lover*, a work of which Smuts, who was not a novel-reader, was totally ignorant. 'Every schoolgirl of sixteen should read *Lady Chatterley's Lover*,' said G.B.S. oracularly, and Smuts, wondering what this work was, politely murmured, 'Of course, of course!'

The conversation was wilting when suddenly G.B.S. remarked that a country which went off the Gold Standard, was guilty of robbery. South Africa at that time was suffering severely from the maintenance of the Gold Standard, and Smuts was agitating for its abandonment. G.B.S., unwittingly, was, in effect, accusing Smuts of being a robber: a remark which did not please the field-marshal at all. The conversation died an unnatural death, and the luncheon party ended almost abruptly.[1]

The misadventure was a graver business. G.B.S., like H. G. Wells, drove motor-cars very badly, but imagined that he drove them well. While on his way with Charlotte and Commander Newton to Port Elizabeth, he made a mistake about the accelerator, treading firmly on it when he should have taken his foot off. The result was that the car leapt a bank, carried away a vast quantity of barbed wire, and almost ripped the veldt to pieces, and would, undoubtedly, have done so, had not Commander Newton suggested that G.B.S. should take his foot off the accelerator. G.B.S. and Commander Newton were unharmed; Charlotte, who had been hurled about with the luggage in the back seat, was badly injured, and was laid up for a month. Her first question, when she was taken out of the car, was whether G.B.S. had been hurt. Her temperature when she was taken to Knysna was 108! . . . 'Her head was broken, her spectacle rims were driven into her blackened eyes, her left wrist was agonisingly sprained; her back was fearfully bruised; and she had a hole in her right shin which something had pierced to the bone! . . .' So G.B.S. wrote to Lady Astor.

While Charlotte was recovering from her wounds, G.B.S. wrote a long fable, entitled *The Adventures of The Black Girl in Her Search for God*. In this fable, which is one of his shortest works, he succinctly set out the development in the world's mind of the idea of God; and the book, which was published in December 1932, and was brilliantly illustrated by Mr John Farleigh, had an extraordinary success. Over

[1] See Mrs Millin's account of it in *The Spectator* for November 17, 1950.

200,000 copies of it were sold within a year. It was ferociously attacked by the religious press which has never been distinguished for intelligence or generosity of mind, and some people, unaccustomed to think seriously about their religion, were deeply offended by it. It was banned from the public libraries of Cambridge. Dr W. R. Matthews, the Dean of St Paul's, wrote by far the best reply to it, *The Adventures of Gabriel in His Search for Mr Shaw*, which would have been effective if he had not committed the grave fault on his last page of seriously under-rating G.B.S.'s importance.

We belittle ourselves when we belittle our opponents. Victory over people of no consequence is itself of no consequence; and defeat is ignominious, proving that we are incompetent.

The Adventures of The Black Girl in Her Search for God is not a major work: but it performed the useful task of consolidating loose beliefs into an organic doctrine. No one who has lived through the years that have elapsed since Mr Forster introduced his Education Bill into the House of Commons in 1870, can fail to realise that a vast change has taken place in the religious belief of the people of Great Britain: a change which has been brutally facilitated by two World Wars. It is not possible to say definitely what that change is. Superficially, there is less regularity of worship than there was, but before we can accept the appearance as significant, we must first prove that regularity of worship in former generations was in itself a sign of piety. A large part of it was purely formal. The number of truly religious men and women in any age is not large. The saints are few and generally disliked. The rest of us are herd-like in our habits: going to church when it is fashionable to go to church, abstaining from it when abstention is fashionable.

The probability is that the piety of the devout to-day, when indifference to religious observation is common, is deeper than it was in the days when almost everybody went to church as a matter of course. But this probability, if it can be substantiated, will not seem to some people adequate compensation for the loss of faith in the mass of the population, and, especially, in the working-people. It is a grave act to take away the religion of simple men and women when we have nothing to put in its place. The Welfare State is not an adequate substitute for the Kingdom of Heaven. Highly educated people can compensate themselves for their lapse from Christianity or any other religion by consolations of all kinds, but the proletariat and the unlearned have not these resources; and so, when they have lost or thrown away their rudder, they are at the mercy of wind and water, and can only drift helplessly from one futile point to another.

The Russians soon learnt sense about this. Having abolished Christianity as dope, they found themselves obliged to tolerate its observance since material satisfaction was not enough. Man needs something more than three square meals a day to reconcile him to existence: he needs hope more than he needs food.

G.B.S., while Charlotte was convalescing, remembered a fact about the Bible which the majority of people overlook. Although it is the most widely distributed book in English—some three million copies of it are sold every year—it is unique among literary works in this respect, that it is seldom read in the way that any other book is read: that is to say, from the first word on the first page to the last word on the last page. It is read in bits and pieces, when it is read at all; and it is true to say that the number of men and women who have read it straight through is small.

The Black Girl, living the artless life of a simple naked Negress in Africa, receives a Bible from a woman missionary, and sets out to find God, only to discover how elusive He is. When she has caught up with the God in Genesis and found Him insufficient, the pages of the Bible in which He appears shrivel into dust. *That* God has ceased to exist. A large part of the Old Testament, indeed, fades away as she comes into the presence of the evolving God it describes. The God of Job destroys the God of Genesis, and is destroyed by the God of Micah.

How is it possible to believe in Job's God who, knowing the fidelity of his servant, wilfully and cruelly torments him to prove to the Devil how faithful His servant is, although the Devil knows the fact as well as God does and is so little interested in the demonstration that he does not stay to the end of it?

But although G.B.S. conducts his Black Girl through the several stages of man's conception of God, he leaves her at the end of his fable as little informed as she was at the beginning of it. She does not find God. She finds only ideas about God; and, very sensibly, G.B.S. suggests, since the discovery is impossible, she decides not to bother her head any more about divinity. She marries a white man who bears a remarkable resemblance to G.B.S. himself, and bears him several coffee-coloured coons; and is reasonably happy. She knows no more about the Almighty at the end of her quest than her Mother Eve knew in the Garden of Eden. That, perhaps, is all that any of us are ever likely to know.

Dean Matthews strikes G.B.S. in a vital part when he derides his doctrine of The Life Force with Gabriel's question, 'Does the Life Force know where it is going?' In all other conceptions of deity, the devout start off with the conviction that God, whatever name He may bear, does know where He is going and what He is trying to do, and has every hope of fulfilling His intention. It is this assurance which wins faith in Him.

Despite its extraordinary popularity, *The Adventures of The Black Girl in Her Search for God*, encountered adverse comment, most of which, apart from Dean Matthews, was on the paltry side. The Cambridge Public Library Committee banned it. *The Universe*, a Roman Catholic weekly paper, refused to advertise it, but gave it much wider publicity than it could have received from paid advertisement, by announcing its action in its editorial columns.

The oddest opposition to the book was provided by the County Wexford Bee-Keepers' Association, a body of which G.B.S., for a reason which passes all understanding, was a life member. At a meeting of this Association in Enniscorthy on December 29, 1932, an angry doctor, one Greene, solemnly proposed that 'the name of Mr George Bernard Shaw' should be removed from the list of members of the Association in consequence of his 'blasphemous statements concerning Christ and His Apostles' in *The Adventures of The Black Girl in Her Search for God*. The doctor was supported by a Mr McDonald who did not wish to be associated with an infidel.

The proposal was adjourned until the Annual Meeting on January 26, 1933, when the Bee-Keepers behaved with great dignity. The Chairman, Mr C. W. Lett, remarked that he 'did not pretend to be able to fathom one of the greatest minds of our time', but he had noticed that G.B.S., when mentioning his own feelings respecting the Deity, did so with 'becoming reverence'. Mr Lett regretted that 'our little brotherhood should have earned contempt and ridicule by presuming to deal with a matter which, if deserving of notice at all, should have been left to others better qualified' to deal with it.

The Association, on a show of hands, declined to hear Dr Greene speak on the subject, and he, after handing a letter of resignation to the Secretary, remarked that the Association seemed to prefer Bernard Shaw to Jesus Christ. He then stalked out of the room.

The common belief that the Christian Church has always held the entire Bible in the highest reverence is unfounded. Martin Luther, for example, thought less of the Synoptic Gospels than he thought of St John's Gospel, and would willingly have dispensed with them. He thought the Epistle of St James was 'a thing of straw', and had a poor opinion of the Epistle to the Hebrews. He rejected the Epistle of Jude, and was doubtful about the Revelation of St John, which is described by G.B.S. as the work of a drug addict. He thought the story of Jonah and the whale 'a lying invention', which, if it had not been in the Bible, he would not have believed, though why he should believe 'a lying invention' because it is in the Bible is hard to understand. The book of Esther was not, in his opinion, fit to be in the Bible at all.

A candid reader of the Old Testament must wonder why God made a friend of Abraham, whose entire life was contemptible, and have great difficulty in admiring Jacob, who cheated his dying father and swindled his brother Esau, a far finer man than Jacob, whose beloved Rachel meanly robbed her rascally parent. Joseph's only distinction is that he was the first man to make a corner in wheat.

G.B.S.'s argument is that men are foolish when they restrict their religious belief to an ancient and outworn creed. Why should they suppose that God had communicated all He had to tell man in His talks with Abraham and slightly informed Israelites who lived thousands of years ago? 'You see,' he said in New York, 'I do not, like the Fundamentalists, believe that creation stopped six thousand years ago after a week of hard work. Creation is going on all the time'; a remark which eventually became part of the dialogue of a pleasant comedy, *In Good King Charles's Golden Days*. We forget that the world starts again on the day every baby is born.

G.B.S. believed that the calendar of saints is ampler than the Christian Church realises, and he would have agreed with Erasmus that Socrates and Plato and Cicero should be included in it.

165

In the meantime, *Too True to be Good*, after a preliminary tour, was performed in New York on April 4, 1932, by the Theatre Guild. It was not a success there, or, indeed, anywhere else, for despite some deepening of his sagacity, G.B.S. displayed in it an indifference to form which made hay of his theme. The play is loose and incoherent, and its three acts seem irrelevant to each other. The first act, although it contains an amusing and ingenious character, a measles microbe which complains bitterly that its hostess will overeat and underwork herself and thus bring ill-health on *him* as well as on herself, could easily be cut. The reader has the feeling that G.B.S., when he wrote it, allowed his pen to put down what it liked.

The play is notable mainly for the inclusion in its cast of a character named Private Meek, who is based on Colonel T. E. Lawrence of Arabia. The character, however, is slightly drawn. He does not apear in the first act, and only insignificantly in the third. If G.B.S. had redrafted his play, cutting the whole of the first act, and making Meek the central figure, he might have given us one of his most important works. But he was seventy-five when he wrote it, and his energy was beginning to decline.

His prefaces now had little more relation to the plays they preceded than the fact that they both appeared in the same volume. He used them for the discussion of any ideas that happened to be in his head; and the idea that dominated his mind when he wrote *Too True to be Good* was that the rich were miserable and that the poor, by comparison with them, were fortunate. This is an ancient delusion, and it has almost no foundation in fact. The rich are not noticeably unhappy, and if any of them are, their unhappiness is not the consequence of their wealth.

But G.B.S., even when he was careless, could not compose a play which was without wisdom and impressive characters. The Sergeant and the Elder in the third act are as well-drawn as any people in his best work, and confirm the writer in his conviction that if the play had been thought out instead of dashed off, it would probably have been a major work.

When the play received its second production, this time in Warsaw, the Censor passed it for performance without reading it, and was dismissed for doing so, because of what the Sergeant said. Having read a passage from *The Pilgrim's Progress* to the woman character called Sweetie, in which the Pilgrim says, 'I am for certain informed that this our city will be burned with fire from heaven, in which fearful overthrow both myself, with thee my wife, and you my sweet babes, shall miserably come to ruin, except some way of escape can be found whereby we may be delivered,' the Sergeant remarked, 'Well, London and Paris and Berlin and Rome and the rest of them will be burned with fire from heaven all right in the next war: that's certain. They're all Cities of Destruction. And our Government chaps are running about with a great burden of corpses and debts on their backs, crying "What must we do to be saved?" '

The Sergeant and the Elder are strongly contrasted characters, each distinct and disillusioned, the one *into* faith, the other *out* of it. The Sergeant is the rough, excessively masculine soldier, who tells Sweetie when she begins to be amorous, that her love is of no consequence to him. 'A man of my figure can have his pick.' But the Bible and *The Pilgrim's Progress* have set him thinking, and when a soldier starts to think, things are certain to happen. Women are all very well in their way, conveniences for men, and the Sergeant has nothing to say against that. He enjoys a woman as much as any man. But women are not only conveniences for the relief of men's needs: they also, or some of them, have minds, and are fit to be talked to about other than bed matters. Sweetie is forced to listen to remarks she detests, just when she is pining to have her body used. The Bible makes her feel melancholy mad. What she wants is to be handled a bit roughly by a strong soldier! . . .

As they are about to enjoy amorous dalliance, they are interrupted by the Elder, a rational Determinist who had thought his world was finally fixed by Newton, but has seen it suddenly disrupted by Einstein.

In Newton's universe 'the stars in their orbits obeyed immutably fixed laws; and when we turned from surveying their vastness to study the infinite littleness of the atoms, there too we found the electrons in their orbits obeying the same universal laws. Every moment of time dictated and determined the following moment and was itself dictated and determined by the moment that came before it. Everything was calculable: everything happened because it must. . . . And now—now—what is left of it? The orbit of the electron obeys no law. . . . All is caprice: the calculable world has become incalculable. . . .'

His consternation is complete when his son, who has become a thief, tells him, when he is reproached for his crimes, that stealing a pearl necklace is nothing to the things he did, with everybody's approval, as an airman in the war.

'I was hardly more than a boy when I first dropped a bomb on a sleeping village. I cried all night after doing that. Later on I swooped into a street and sent machine gun bullets into a crowd of civilians: women, children, and all. I was past crying by that time. And now you preach to me about stealing a pearl necklace. Doesn't that seem a little ridiculous?'

When the Sergeant interrupts him with the assertion, 'That was war, sir,' he replies, 'It was me, sergeant: ME. You cannot divide my conscience into a war department and a peace department. Do you suppose that a man who will commit murder for political ends will hesitate to commit theft for personal ends? Do you suppose you can make a man the mortal enemy of sixty millions of his fellow creatures without making him a little less scrupulous about his next door neighbour?'

The Sergeant fails to make the obvious answer: that you can. It is true that all wars are followed by outbreaks of crime; but civilised society is coherent enough to cope with these aberrations, and it does so in a remarkably short time.

The substantial fact is that the young aviator can drop bombs on a sleeping village without becoming an incorrigible crook, and is able to meet his enemy after the war on friendly terms. If war, which has been a common fact of human history for countless ages, manufactures criminals out of decent men, as the Elder's son suggests it does, why is it that there are any honest and kindly people now alive? Ought not all virtues and kindliness long ago to have become extinct? This play, it must be remembered, was written seven, and published five years, before the outbreak of the Second World War, so that G.B.S. was not being wise after the event. He lived to see the flames of the burning city of London almost illuminating Ayot St Lawrence.

The Polish Home Secretary was present at the first performance at the Theatre Polski on June 4, 1932, and was greatly distressed by the response the audience made to the Sergeant's statement and other references to the horrors of war. He sent for the manager of the theatre, and, after a long argument, insisted that seventy-two lines should be cut out of the third act. The Censor was then reinstated in his office, presumably with a caution to be more careful in licensing plays by Shaw, and the performances were allowed to go on.

It was not until September 13, that *Too True to be Good*, which had been performed at the Malvern Festival earlier in the year, reached London. The Malvern production was upset by a ludicrous incident at the first performance. An arrangement was made by Sir Barry Jackson to bring the London dramatic critics to Malvern by air. Weather conditions were adverse, and the aeroplane was late in landing. At the end of an hour after the advertised time of beginning, the critics had still not arrived, and so the play began without them. They turned up in the middle of the second act, some of them in a dilapidated condition as they had been ill on the way, and almost immediately after they had entered the auditorium, one of them collapsed.

Their experience did not put them in a fit state to witness any play, especially one demanding some exercise of the mind, although one might pardonably have thought that men who were accustomed to seeing about four plays in a week in the theatrical season, many of which were nauseating, could have soared through the heavens without the slightest discomfort. For a reason which eludes understanding, some of them attributed the blame for this melancholy business to G.B.S., and one of them, according to Rattray,[1] asserted as he staggered out of the aeroplane, 'I am going to bash Shaw!'

The play drew about £1,000 a week at the New Theatre in London, which, however, is not enough in the West End, and it was withdrawn after a short run.

166

Charlotte had always had a passion for travel, a passion which was not shared by her husband. 'If I had been let alone,' he said, 'I should have died in the house I was born in.' I have already noted the extraordinary fact that although he disliked his house at Ayot St Lawrence, as Charlotte did, he bought it when he was told that he must either buy it or leave it.

On December 16, 1932, Charlotte took him aboard the Empress of Britain on a tour around the world. Hesketh Pearson asserts that these excursions were necessary to give her a holiday from double

[1] *Bernard Shaw: a Chronicle*, p. 245.

house-keeping in London and Hertfordshire, but as Charlotte, who loathed domesticity, never did any housekeeping, leaving it entirely to highly efficient housekeepers and, during the tenancy of the service flat in Whitehall Court, to the manager of the restaurant, there is nothing in this assertion. She had been a traveller for the greater part of her life, and, after her marriage, had visited America long before she could induce G.B.S. to go there.

His general attitude to travel is revealed in a letter, dated June 29, 1908, to Edward McNulty.

'On Saturday next, I am going to let my wife drag me by main force across the North Sea in belching misery to Sweden, a country which I do not particularly want to see, and of the language of which I cannot speak a word, simply because there I shall be out of reach of post and telegraph, the platform and committee room, the theatre with its endless rehearsals, and the paralysing arrears of literary work that I cannot keep my hands off at home. Every year, the same struggle arises two or three times—the eternal "You must come away" and "Oh, leave me alone: I haven't time: you know I loathe travelling." I am actually buying a motor car, the very mention of which brings out a cold sweat of terror on me, so as to be able to substitute a common mechanical worry for the subtler worries of my work. I can at least choose my time to drive the thing, whereas the emergencies with which I have to deal (my life is one long string of emergencies) always come as the last straw that breaks the camel's back.

'Of course I make the best of it: enjoy it: am vain about it; say that it is better to wear out than to rust out; argue that life is nothing but action, and that the idle man does not live, etc., etc; but there is reason in everything; and at such moments as the present, at the end of the season, the only effect of the gospel of the strenuous life is to make me feel inclined to brain the man who preaches it.'

The cruise gave him little pleasure. Tropical heat distressed him, and he was not the sort of person who enjoys organised excursions; nor was he a good sailor. He was happiest in New Zealand, so happy that Charlotte, on their return to London, told me that he and she had seriously thought of settling there.

It was during this cruise that he made his only visit, a remarkably brief one, to the United States. He visited William Randolph Hearst in San Francisco, a visit which, according to Lawrence Langner, gave great offence to Left Wing New Yorkers. On April 11, 1933, he reached New York, where he spent one day. Early in the morning, he paid an unheralded visit to the Guild Theatre. None of the directors was present. They had not been told of his arrival. In the afternoon he went to Metropolitan Opera House to deliver a long lecture in aid of a woman's society with the grandiloquent title of The

Academy of Political Science: an organisation which had escaped notice by anyone except its members until it suddenly found fame in this fashion. The lecture had been arranged before the cruise round the world was begun. G.B.S. had been beset by requests to lecture immediately the news was announced that he would visit New York, and he chose this society solely because of its name, imagining it to be much more important than it was.

The barren Bowery intellectuals of New York had agreed among themselves that this old man—he was seventy-seven—even if he was a man of genius, 'wasn't gonna put nuthin over on them'. It would take a bigger guy than this Mr George Bernard Shaw to put anything over on guys as slick as they were. (*Guy* is the only word an American has to describe a human being). So they 'razzed' him, as they call the process of belittlement and denigration in their barbarous speech. They filled their columns with assertions that the lecture was dull, and who did Shaw think he was anyway?

One educated man among the critics, the late John Anderson, protested against this scurvy treatment, but his voice was not heard in the manufactured din.

The lecture, which was published in 1933, under the title of *The Political Madhouse in America and Nearer Home*, reads well enough. No doubt, G.B.S., in preparing it for the press, tidied any loose ends there might have been in it, but, as one who heard many lectures by him, I have no doubt in my mind that it is a fair report of what he said. It is not a great lecture—the occasion did not call for one—but it is excellent for a mixed popular audience, characteristic of G.B.S.'s manner and thought, and greatly superior to the stuff that the Bowery intellectuals themselves were accustomed to deliver. His audience had assembled to hear a funny man being funny; and were disappointed by hearing themselves taken seriously as people who were interested in political science.

It was while he was on his way from Cherbourg to Southampton that he was interviewed by Mr Ritchie Calder. A report of the interview appeared in *The Daily Herald* on April 20, 1933. In its course, he complained with justifiable bitterness of the tales invented about him by cub reporters:

'They accused me of having insulted Helen Keller. How absurd,' and Shaw leaned forward in his evident distress. 'I remember meeting her in London, as they say in their attacks, at Lady Astor's. Conversation was difficult, as you would suppose, considering that she is both blind and deaf and everything has to be spelt out by someone else on her fingers. She "sees" you by feeling your face. It was rather embarrassing. It would have been in the worst possible taste to ignore her condition. I remarked, by way of a compliment, that she was wonderful, and added, jokingly, that she could see and hear better than her countrymen, who could neither see nor hear.'

I interrupt him here to remind the reader that he had just been roughly handled by New York reporters. A full account of his treatment by them will be found in *The Magic Curtain* by Laurence Langner.

'Someone takes a joking remark meant in all kindness and says I insulted Helen Keller by saying, "Oh, all Americans are deaf and blind and dumb anyway". I tell you I have been misquoted everywhere, and the inaccuracies are chasing me round the world.'

During the cruise, he wrote a charming 'comediettina for two voices', in three 'conversations', entitled *Village Wooing*. He wrote it, according to a note in the printed version, 'in the Sunda Straits'. The small play is full of the fragrance which was one of his most prominent characteristics, none the less so because he tried, unsuccessfully, to conceal it under an appearance of gruffness and bad manners.

A writer finds himself seated in a deck chair on 'the Empress of Patagonia' next to a garrulous young woman, 'presentable but not aristocratic', who interrupts him, while he is working, with comments and questions. She turns out to be a village postmistress from the Wiltshire Downs who has won a prize in a newspaper competition, and is 'blueing' the whole of the money on a cruise.

The second 'conversation' occurs in the Post Office in the following summer, where the writer, who has forgotten the garrulous young woman, meets her again.

G.B.S. had an irritating habit of leaving his characters unnamed in the text of a play until their names were mentioned. In this play, he calls the man A and the woman Z, and we never learn what their names are, with the result that it is occasionally difficult to identify them, despite the skill with which their conversation is individualised.

Z recognises A at once, and before he has finished the business which brought him into the Post Office, she has informed him that he is just the man for her and proposes marriage. In the third 'conversation', we find them running the village shop together, with immense benefit, physical and intellectual, to him. But they have not yet married. When she hints that marriage would be good for him, and says 'You'll find that you have senses to gratify as well as fine things to say,' he denies her statement indignantly.

'Senses! You don't know what you're talking about. Look around you,' he says. 'Here in this shop I have everything that can gratify the senses: apples, onions, and acid drops; pepper and mustard; cosy comforters and hot water bottles.

'Through the window I delight my eyes with the old church and market place, built in the days when beauty came naturally from the hands of medieval craftsmen. My ears are filled with delightful sounds, from the cooing of doves and the humming of bees to the wireless echoes of Beethoven and Elgar.

'My nose can gloat over our sack of fresh lavender or our special sixpenny Eau de Cologne when the smell of rain on dry earth is denied me. My senses are saturated with satisfactions of all sorts.

'But when I am full to the neck with onions and acid drops; when I am so fed up with medieval architecture that I had rather die than look at another cathedral; when all I desire is rest from sensation, not more of it, what use will my senses be to me if the starry heavens seem still no more than a senseless avalanche of lumps of stone and wisps of gas—if the destiny of Man holds out no higher hope to him than the final extinction and annihilation of so mischievous and miserable a creature?'

To which Z retorts, 'We don't bother about all that in the village,' which he denies. 'Yes, you do. Our best seller here is Old Moore's Almanac; and next to it comes Napoleon's Book of Fate. Old Mrs Ward would never have sold the shop to me if she had not become persuaded that the Day of Judgment is fixed for the seventh of August next.' But Z does not believe such nonsense. She tells him as plainly as a well-brought-up village girl can that he needs a woman and she needs a man, and that sooner they hurry off to lawful bed, the better. Z then telephones to the vicarage and asks for the banns to be published on the following Sunday.

A bald summary of the play cannot convey the peculiar fragrance it possesses, but audiences everywhere respond to its charm unfailingly.

167

On the Rocks was begun immediately after *Village Wooing* was finished, and while he was still cruising. It was produced at the Winter Garden on November 25, 1933, but without success. The play is inferior to its preface, and it ends inconclusively. More than any other play he wrote, it marks the beginning of G.B.S.'s despair about mankind. He becomes even more apocalyptic than St John the Divine whom he had denounced as a drug addict; and in the preface to *On the Rocks*, as well as in a following play, *The Simpleton of the Unexpected Isles*, he demands something like the wholesale slaughter of all those who fail to live up to his standard. He had always advocated elimination of the unfit, and had once proposed that every human being should periodically be brought before a tribunal and asked to justify his existence. It is obvious that a vast number of men and women of every class would fail to do so; but it is equally obvious that no tribunal that the mind of man is capable of conceiving, could be fit for the responsibility of deciding who should be slaughtered and who should be permitted to survive.

What is the survival value of Beethoven, Shelley, Lord George Gordon, Napoleon Bonaparte, Peter the Great, Nelson, Voltaire, Robespierre, Frederick the Great, Goethe, George IV, Mrs Siddons, Balzac, Torquemada, any Pope or Archbishop of Canterbury, and a butler, a footman, a carpenter, a tramp, and a shiftless fellow who drifts from job to job?

Goethe would not have admitted that Beethoven had any value. Byron had little respect for Shelley's poetry. The Pope thinks that the Archbishop of Canterbury is in serious danger of hell fire, though the Archbishop admits that the Pope will be saved. An editor of *The Times* thought that George IV was a common blackguard, as, indeed, did many of his subjects, but this belief did not prevent many people from asking God to save him and grant him long life when their most ardent desire should have been for his early demise. John Morley thought that W. B. Yeats's work was incomprehensible stuff and advised Macmillan not to publish it; but they, remembering their mistake when they had taken his advice not to publish G.B.S., had the good sense to publish Yeats.

Balzac was a genius, but how many of us would welcome him as a guest? A host of people believe that butlers are sycophants who ought to be scrapped, although it is plain to those who are informed that a good butler, like a good head waiter, is a man who has more organising ability, a clearer head and a quicker power of decision than the majority of people. Put a commissioned army officer in charge of the dining room of a hotel, and see what a mess he will make of it.

In all his apocalyptic diatribes, G.B.S. never once defines fitness to survive nor does he state the qualifications necessary in those who are to judge who shall survive and who shall be slaughtered. The nearest he gets to the definition of fitness is that each man and woman shall earn his or her living. Any person, a landowner, for instance, or a *rentier* or a common loafer, is to be condemned out of hand on the ground that he or she is living on other people's labour. The fact that a man may be a highly skilled carpenter and a bad husband and worse father is not considered.

He was contemptuous of democracy, and could not contain his scorn for the Government which had enfranchised every man and woman from the age of twenty-one. His admiration for dictators was almost unbounded. Hitler, Mussolini, Kemal Ataturk, Stalin— all these absolute rulers received his admiration. He had nothing but disgust for the effete people who formed Cabinets in Great Britain. He gave three hearty cheers when Mussolini referred to the decaying corpse of democracy, and wished that there were a Mussolini in every country. It must have bewildered him when he saw the dictators collapse before the patient resistance of the puerile democrats of Britain and America. What had happened that Mussolini's countrymen should string him upside down like an untrussed turkey and fill his body with bullets, and that Hitler, at last aware of his ruin, should order a soldier to blow the back off his head lest he should fall into the hands of the Allies?

168

The preface to *On the Rocks* begins with the assertion that 'extermination must be put on a scientific basis if it is ever to be carried out humanely and apologetically as well as thoroughly.'

> 'That killing is a necessity is beyond question by any thoughtful person. Unless rabbits and deer and rats and foxes are killed, or "kept down" as we put it, mankind must perish; and that section of mankind which lives in the country and is directly and personally engaged in the struggle with Nature for a living has no sentimental doubts that they must be killed. As to tigers and poisonous snakes, their incompatibility with human civilisation is unquestioned. . . . The sin is in the cruelty, and the enjoyment of it, not in the killing.'

This is the note struck through the preface: its connexion with the play is not apparent. It is the note he was to strike for a large part of the rest of his life. It was, however, no new notion, hastily conceived as the theme of a preface to a play. In a long Introduction to *English Prisons under Local Government*, by Sidney and Beatrice Webb, which was written in December and January, 1921–2,[1] he sets forth his views on the subject of punishment, and comes to some very queer conclusions which, however, are substantially the same as those set out in the preface to *On the Rocks*: conclusions which are sometimes irreconcilable with each other.

He begins with the assertion that 'no single criminal can be as powerful for evil, or as unrestrained in its exercise, as an organised nation', a statement which leaves the reader with the feeling that it is useless for any group of people even to try to co-operate. If the collective wisdom of mankind is no better, is even less, than the wisdom of the individual member of the community, what point is there in maintaining a collective society? When G.B.S. goes on, as he very properly does, to remind us that reformers and philanthropists have done as much harm as good by their well-intended beneficence, our despair deepens.

[1] It is included in *Doctors' Delusions* in the Standard edition of the works of Bernard Shaw.

'It is just such reformers who have in the past made the neglect, oppression, corruption, and physical torture of the old common gaol the pretext for transforming it into that diabolical den of torment, mischief and damnation, the modern model prison.' With those words burning holes in his brain, the reformer, who knows how true they are, may well abandon hope and decide to let the world go to its damnation in its own way. John Howard and Elizabeth Fry were full of good intentions, and were even apprehensive of the value of the system of imprisonment they advocated as an alternative to the system which prevailed in the eighteenth century. Of the damnability of that system there can be no doubt. Young children who were imprisoned for small infantile offences, were thrust into gaol to mingle promiscuously with old lags of every sort, including women of the pavement, habitual burglars, and murderers. No wonder the minds of good people like John Howard and Elizabeth Fry revolted against such a deformatory.

But what was the alternative they proposed? Separate cells in which the prisoners were immured for sixteen out of the twenty-four hours of the day. The gaolbird was deprived of conversation and company and compelled to live in almost total silence and, for most of his time, in solitude. The remedy was worse than the disease. It drove the gentle and highly sensitive John Galsworthy to write *Justice* in which the horrors of the silent system and solitary system were, movingly revealed.

Soon after the beginning of his preface, G.B.S. makes this terrible indictment of organised communities. 'Now, not only does society commit more frightful crimes than any individual, king or commoner: it legalises its crimes, and forges certificates of righteousness for them, besides torturing anyone who dares to expose their true character.' Yet it is to this cruel and oppressive society that G.B.S., nudged to it by the Webbs, would have us entrust not merely a part of our lives, but the whole of them!

The argument is bedevilled at the beginning by nonsense about life itself. 'The vast majority of our city populations are inured to imprisonment from their childhood. The school is a prison. The office and factory are prisons. The home is a prison. To the young who have had the misfortune to be what is called well brought up, it is sometimes a prison of inhuman severity.' At the end of this passage, the entire world appears to be a prison, but as we can do nothing about it, except commit suicide, we are left to make the best of our despondency.

169

But is this belief that all men and women are prisoners in a loath-some gaol true? None of us asked to be born, nor had we any say in the choice of our parents, our colour or social condition or sex. We were not asked whether we wished to be rich or poor, brilliant or stupid, naturally gay or naturally morose, successful or unsuccessful, healthy or unhealthy, long-lived or short-lived. All the major aspects of our existence were arranged before we were born. To that extent we are prisoners—immured in ourselves and our heredity. Wherever we go, we have to take ourselves with us. But we manage to survive and even to feel happy. This prison is not beyond our control. We have modified it, and hope to modify it still more.

If, as G.B.S. says, 'the freedom given by the adult's right to walk out of his prison is only a freedom to go into another or starve', why does anyone remain alive, why does every creature strive hard to defeat death?

That brings us to the problem which still baffles the mind: what is Man? Is he only an advanced animal or an image of God? His similarity to the animal is striking, but it may be no more than similarity, for the difference between any human being and any animal is more striking. Consider how helpless an animal is in certain simple circumstances in which a man is completely at his ease. If a dog is shut in a room, he cannot escape from it. The most he can do is to howl until he is released. If there is no person in the house, he must remain in the room until someone comes home; and if nobody comes, he will die of hunger.

There is, then, a profound difference between men and animals: a difference which cannot be explained by saying that it was an accident of evolution that man, one of the weakest of all creatures, developed a mind and made himself largely the master of the world. If we may believe the biologists, man's brain was not much more than that of an animal; and there are some matters in which he is less able and adroit even than insects. He is more at the mercy of the elements than any other creature, and he is helpless in his infancy. He comes to maturity more slowly than most animals. How simply and yet how skilfully a spider or a bird makes itself a home, how ingenious both are in supplying themselves with food. A man spends at least a third of his life in learning what almost any other creature, from an earwig to an elephant, learns in a few days or weeks.

But when we have admired the ingenuity of animals, we realise that the greatest feats they perform are slight in comparison with the works of man, who has thought of poetry and mathematics and music and imagined his own mind and soul. No animal can laugh, though we sometimes see a look on a dog's face that seems to suggest laughter, and we know how sensitive all dogs are to derision. We have learnt how to soothe pain and to bear it with fortitude. An animal cannot set a broken limb, but a man can set it for him. An animal is easily lost, but a man can find his way home by a hundred means, from gazing at the stars to asking the first person he meets in the street.

Men have lengthened their eyes and ears and tongues. They can sit in a village in the Hebrides and listen to a man talking in Australia; and before very long everybody in the world will be able to turn a small knob in a small box and see and hear people in Africa or Asia. We marvel at the beaver's dam or the spider's web or the bird's nest, but what are these in comparison with Chartres or the Bridge at Sydney or the Mersey Tunnel or the aeroplane or the motor-car or the power to take the guts out of a sheep and tie them tightly to screws on a thin box and play music composed by a man who died many years ago? Michelangelo mingles oil and pigments, and makes a picture which excites the awe and wonder of the world.

Man alone is capable of abstract thought. He can imagine a means of satisfying a need, and then invent it.

He is, then, extraordinarily different from any animal, so much different that his resemblance seems slight and unimportant. Our perception of this fact compels us to believe that man is unique, as no animal is unique, that he is, in a remarkable degree, separate from all living things; and especially in one vastly important fact, that he has a sense of sin. Animals have no sense of sin. A dog which takes the meat off a plate does not know that he is a thief, though he knows that man, to whom he shows a deep and unaccountable affection, has some queer complex about the matter and will beat him for taking it.

How, then, did man acquire his sense of sin? It is not enough to say that the common facts of life have taught him that a society can exist only on a basis of trust, and that he knows that unless he has respect for other people's property, there will be little, if any, respect for his. Animals live in packs and herds, but they have not learnt to respect each other's rights. They do not know what rights are, and can be deterred from taking the food out of another animal's mouth only by fear and force.

An animal has no idea of its purpose in being alive. How horrified our herds would be if they were to realise that they are bred and maintained to provide their owners with food. If a pig or a sheep or an ox can think at all, it probably tells itself how fortunate it is to have a kind farmer to look after it and grow food for it and keep it warm and sheltered in byres and sheds and styes. Every day, this faithful servant leads the herd or flock to a green pasture, where it feeds on rich and juicy grass, and in the evening he leads it home again and gives it sweet hay to munch or a warm mash. What existence could be pleasanter? Not for a moment does the pig or the ox or the sheep suspect that this kind and assiduous servant will one day lead it to a slaughter-house, and that there is a butcher's shop in nearly every street.

Can we doubt what a stampede of appalled and bewildered beasts there would be if the slightest suspicion of the farmer should enter their mind. What horse that has been gelded so that he can be put between shafts and worked hard from dawn to dark, would refrain from kicking his stable to pieces if he were to realise that when he can work no longer, he will be led to a ship and taken across the sea to be slain for food for men and dogs?

All people, at some time of their lives, have pondered these facts, and it is not vanity which makes them believe that they have been chosen for some purpose far transcending that of any animal, and that they may not have ascended from the animals, but have descended from the gods. This belief compels man to believe that he has somehow defiled his divinity, for how, otherwise, could he, the child of God, have fallen into the plight in which he finds himself? So he comes to have a sense of sin; and on this sense of sin his social system is founded.

170

A civilised society lives in the confidence each one of its members feels that he can walk down the street in the sure belief that he will not be robbed or murdered. If we did not feel this confidence, we could not live together, and no man could venture from his house without a pistol or a sword, nor would any woman go out unescorted lest she should be raped. Take this confidence away, and civilised society collapses.

The malefactor violates our sense of security. He destroys or at least upsets our confidence in our ability to walk abroad unafraid, knowing well that, except for some mischance, we shall return as safely as we set out. G.B.S. talks nonsense when he accuses us of retributory motives in punishing lawbreakers, and of displaying nothing but mean motives of revenge. It is based on our assurance that this complicated organisation we call society cannot be held together if we are liable at any moment to be assaulted and robbed or slain.

What, we have learned to ask, is an undesirable? Is physical fitness essential in those who are desirable? If so, Keats and Chopin would not have been allowed to live. A physically fit man may be morally and mentally inept. Is moral rectitude essential? If so, what is moral rectitude? How can we draw a distinction between what is moral in the eyes of God and what is moral only in the eyes of policemen and politicians? Morality meant very different things to Tolstoy and the Tsar.

Are we prepared to admit that there are moral standards for one set of persons which are different from those for another set? If, for example, we insist that a royal person shall marry for purely political reasons, can we reasonably complain if that prince keeps a mistress or this princess has a lover? And if we tolerate marital irregularities among princes, at what level of society do we forbid them? Can we, in short, regard morality as a line we draw and make other people toe, as one of G.B.S.'s characters says? If so, what qualifications do we demand in the man who draws the line?

G.B.S. reminds us that 'all Revolutions have been the work of men who, like Robespierre, were sentimental humanitarians and conscientious objectors to capital punishment and to the severities of military and prison discipline; yet all the revolutions have, after a very brief practical experience, been driven to Terrorism . . . as ruthless as the Counter-Revolution of Sulla. Whether it is Sulla, Robespierre, Trotsky, or the fighting mate of a sailing-ship with a crew of loafers and wastrels, the result is the same: there are people to be dealt with who will not obey the law unless they are afraid to disobey it, and whose disobedience means disaster. It is useless for humanitarians to shirk this hard fact and proclaim their conviction that all lawbreakers can be reformed by kindness.'

He then tells a story which points his moral with immense force:

> 'The late G. V. Foote, President of the English National Secular Society, a strenuous humanitarian, once had to persuade a very intimate friend of his, a much smaller and weaker man, to allow himself to be taken to an asylum for lunatics. It took four hours of humanitarian persuasion to get the patient from the first floor of his house to the cab door. Foote told me that he not only recognised at once that no asylum attendant, with several patients to attend to, could possibly spend four hours in getting each of them downstairs, but found his temper so intolerably strained by the unnatural tax on his patience that if the breaking point had been reached, as it certainly would have been in the case of a warder or an asylum attendant, he would have been far more violent, not to say savage, than if he had resorted to force at once, and finished the job in five minutes.'

The moral of this story is inescapable.

171

But G.B.S. makes too much demand on our sense of social security when he asks us to exterminate those who do not, as he says, fit into the community without some sort of guarantee that we shall not be delivering highly desirable men and women to the executioner. The dissentient is entitled to express his dissent and to propose methods which he believes to be better; but has he the right, some of us may ask, to raise a revolution to enforce his opinions? According to the people in power, he has no such right, and may justly be put to death.

The philosophic politician will say that the dissentient may preach his doctrine without let or hindrance, but that he must be content with the government in power until he has persuaded the great majority of his countrymen to share his opinions; though Bertrand Russell, in *The Scientific Outlook*, foresees a time when even this right will be generally denied. Unfortunately, the mob has no philosophy, nor have fanatics. No man, however noble he may be, is immune from the belief that he is right and his opponents are wrong; and he will require little persuasion to believe that his opponents are wicked men and women who will be better dead. 'I am more merciless than the criminal law', G.B.S. says:

> 'because I would destroy the evildoer's delusion that there can be any forgiveness of sin. What is done cannot be undone; and the man who steals must remain a thief until he becomes another man, no matter what reparation or expiation he may make or suffer.'

Here he flatly contradicts the essential spirit of Christianity, whose Founder enjoined us to forgive until seventy times seven. Despite this argument, however, he reaches the singular conclusion that 'we have no right to punish anybody', a statement which denies society the right to protect itself against those who would wreck it, and is irreconcilable with his belief that impossible people had better be 'returned to the dust from which they sprang'.

He recognises this right on the next page, when he reminds the citizen that Rousseau was wrong when he declared that man is born free, but is everywhere in chains. 'No Government of a civilised state can possibly regard its citizens as born free. On the contrary, it must regard them as born in debt; and as necessarily incurring fresh debt every day they live.' Civilised society is possible only by the consent of highly different people to accept some limitation of their liberty so that all, whatever their sort may be, shall have some freedom. One man can do what he likes only if another man is prevented from doing anything he likes; and the case against the criminal is that he breaks faith with his fellows and violates the only conditions in which it is possible for people to live together in comfort. There is no society under heaven in which it is possible to treat the criminal as if he were not a criminal, nor can anybody justify a system which puts the lawabider at a serious disadvantage in comparison with the lawbreaker. We may develop enough intelligence to be able to exterminate criminals, but none of us will consent to a system which enables a tyrant to get rid of those who resist tyranny by accusing them of unfitness to live in a community. Man has fought a long and hard and bitter fight to escape from such oppressions: he will not willingly return to them even in the interests of a well-ordered Webbian world.

172

'The extermination of whole races and classes has been not only advocated but actually attempted.' G.B.S. mentions Hitler's attempt to exterminate the Jews, and he might have reminded his readers of the French Papists' brutal effort to extirpate the Huguenots, and the equally brutal attempt of the Spanish Papists under Ferdinand and Isabella to destroy the Spanish Jews. What he fails to mention is that all these attempts at extermination recoiled gravely on the exterminators.

Spain began to decline after the expulsion of the Jews, and has not yet recovered from the effects of its crime. The loss the French sustained by the murder or deportation of the Huguenots is incalculable. The nations which received the expelled Protestants benefited enormously by their act of mercy. My own people in Ulster have good cause to know this. Hitler, when the Second World War came, soon discovered what injury he had done Germany when he killed or exiled the Jews; for he found that he had deported many men whose ability would have been of immeasurable value to him in waging his war. Lenin nearly ruined the agriculture of Russia by his misuse of the Kulaks, who were the ablest farmers in the country, and it was not until he recovered the use of his brains and brought the Kulaks back to their land that he was able to repair the great damage he had done.

G.B.S. never copes with the fact that there is a vast difference between killing an habitual criminal and killing a man whose general belief about life differs from ours. There is, indeed, a point at which the two men cannot easily be distinguished from each other; and crimes no less repulsive than those of the criminal are committed by people whose moral sanctity is sickening. Misled by the Webbs, G.B.S. believed in a world in which there is no variety. He pretended to believe, for he was too intelligent to accept it as anything but a partisan assertion, that extermination has been 'a real and permanent feature of private property civilisation', a statement which any slave-owner in the Southern States of America could have disproved to him in a couple of minutes, since the slave-owner either supported his slaves and their families when he had no need of them or sold them to some person who could use them. It was not until the slaves were liberated that their former owners could employ them only when they were needed, and could throw them on the labour market to get other work or starve.

It is untrue to suggest as G.B.S. does in this preface that the employing class were carefully educated to ignore the salient facts of inadequately organised business or, when these facts could no longer be ignored, offer as remedies for them war or emigration or Birth Control. People change their mind about the way of life just as they change their style of dress, and a man's idea of a well-governed society is seldom his father's and never his grandfather's. The history of this nation in the past hundred and sixty years shows that the Conservatives were as eager to remove slums and abolish poverty as the most turbulent member of the Socialist Party of Great Britain. The Earl of Shaftesbury was not a Labourite or a Radical, but he did more to raise the level of life for working-people than Bright or Cobden. The whole conception of a well-conducted factory had been changed by such men as the Cadburys, the Rowntrees, and the Levers, who had little or no knowledge of the Fabian Society; and the change was caused by their experience or by their nature or their general outlook on life.

173

G.B.S.'s passion for bureaucrats had become a mania, and he asserted that the Jews in Jerusalem and the Roman Governor had as much right to 'exterminate Jesus' as they had to 'exterminate the two thieves who perished with him'. Only a man who has been maddened by legality could maintain that doctrine. The community has no right to do wrong, and it must learn to tolerate Socrates and Christ and to protect Priestley and Einstein, even when its own existence is threatened by them. For men do not live by rules and regulations laid down in offices remote from market-places, but by the life blown into their nostrils by the Almighty. Verlaine spoke the simple fact when, lying ill in hospital, he was badgered by an official. 'A stroke of the pen made you, but I was made by the breath of God.'

It is hard to reconcile G.B.S.'s beliefs in this matter with any sort of reason. He condemns what he calls 'retributory punishment', as if it were merely the gratification of sadistical lust. He would not send a man to prison, but he would, if the man continued to commit crimes, take away his life. The misfit in society or the rebel against it must answer 'essential questions: are you pulling your weight in the social boat? are you giving more trouble than you are worth? have you earned the privilege of living in a civilised community?' But how can the questioned expect their answers to be treated with respect when their judges are convinced that they are not pulling their weight, are giving more trouble than they are worth, and have not earned the privilege of living in a civilised community?

His argument at this point is shocking sophistry. Himself an exceptionally kind man who had a deep abhorrence of cruelty and would, if he had lived in the age of Torquemada, have protested against the Inquisition as organised villainy, he let himself be humbugged by his belief in Communism into asserting that what would have been villainy in Spain was virtue in Russia.

'I dislike cruelty, even cruelty to other people,' he says, 'and should therefore, like to see all cruel people exterminated. But I should recoil with horror from a proposal to punish them.' The argument here is confused and peculiar. Extermination *is* punishment. But apart from the fact that if all who were guilty of cruelty were to be put to death, the population of the world would probably be devastated, there is the question of what is cruelty to be considered. A man can be more cruel with his tongue or his pen than with his fists or his feet. Is the cutting remark to be tolerated and the brutal blow forbidden?

G.B.S. misunderstands or pretends to misunderstand why society punishes instead of exterminating the wrongdoer. He is punished in the hope that he may amend his ways, a hope which implies that he is capable of amending them. But a man who is exterminated is denied the opportunity of amendment. All hope of amendment is extinguished by death. Are all incorrigible offenders to be exterminated, whatever their offence may be, the petty pilferer no less than the swindler and the murderer? Is the man who is resolved to change the form of government to be put to death because he habitually advocates some sort of revolution? Are we to preserve only the spiritless and servile? Is the dissenter from the established religion to be destroyed? Is no one to be permitted to change his belief about anything?

His readers are told that 'the Russian proletariat is now growing its own professional and organising class', but he does not pause to wonder how long it will be before that class begins to exact rights that are not shared by the proletariat: an exaction that was being made even while he was writing his preface. Commissars are better paid than proletarians, and enjoy privileges that are denied to others. He displays a simplicity of mind in some passages of the preface which is almost incredible in a man with a quick and discerning mind. One reads with amazement this astounding passage. Could G.B.S. have written it or was it slipped into the text by an enemy?

'I have no sooner read in *The Times* a letter from Mr Kerensky assuring me that in the Ukraine the starving people are eating one another, than M. Heriot, the eminent French statesman, goes to Russia and insists on visiting the Ukraine so that he may have ocular proof of the alleged cannibalism, but can find no trace of it.'

Innocent Heriot, but much more innocent G.B.S.! Did either of them imagine that the Russian guides would lead Heriot straight to the places where Ukranians were dying of hunger or would allow them to see the starving people eating human flesh?

174

But even at his most partisan, he could not long keep reason out of his writing.

'It is true', he says, 'that in the generations of men continuous high cultivation is not expedient: there must be fallows, or at least light croppings, between the intense cultivations; for we cannot expect the very energetic and vital Napoleon to be the son of an equally energetic father or the father of an equally vital son. Nobody has yet calculated how many lazy ancestors it takes to produce an indefatigable prodigy; but it is certain that dynasties of geniuses do not occur and that this is the decisive objection to hereditary rulers (though not, let me hasten to add, to hereditary figure heads) There is a large field for toleration here: the clever people must suffer fools gladly, and the easy-going ones find out how to keep the energetic ones busy. There may be as good biological reasons for the existence of the workshy as of the workmad. Even one and the same person may have spells of intense activity and slackness varying from weeks to years.'

Why did he not perceive that this passage cancels the whole of the twenty-three pages which precede it?

He continues to lapse, even after this passage. He even talks of the need for a standard religion, though he must have known as well as anybody that a large part of the world's trouble is due to the several attempts that have been made to establish a standard religion. He even goes so far as to say that he has 'no illusion of being free to say and write what I please'. We may doubt if any man has ever written more freely and provocatively than G.B.S. habitually did; and we may feel certain that in no other country than Britain, except, perhaps, America, would he have been allowed to publish *Common Sense about the War*. He was not only given all the liberty that is good for a man, but he took liberties that few people but himself would have been allowed to take, and nobody banned or jailed him. Had he been a German or an Italian, Hitler or Mussolini would have hanged him out of hand for writing a tenth of what he wrote unmolested in Britain.

How little regard he paid to fact, how much he paid to his party principles is apparent from his complaint that 'our papers are silent about the supression of liberty in Imperialist Japan, though in Japan it is a crime to have "dangerous thoughts" '.

Two comments may be made on that statement: the first is, that our papers were not silent on the subject. How did G.B.S., how did any of us know about these suppressions and the belief about 'dangerous thoughts' if they were not to be read about in the press? The second comment is that 'dangerous thoughts' are criminal in Russia no less than they were in Japan, that G.B.S. in one part of his preface applauds such suppressions, and in another part condemns them.

> 'In my native Ireland, now nominally a Free State,' he remarks, 'one of my books is on the index; and I have no doubt that all the rest will follow as soon as the clerical censorship discovers their existence. In Austria my chronicle play *Saint Joan* had to be altered to please Catholic authorities,' as it had to be in Poland to please political authorities, 'who know less about Catholicism than I do. In America, books which can be bought anywhere in Europe are forbidden. The concentration of British and American attention on the intolerances of Fascism and Communism creates an illusion that they do not exist elsewhere; but they exist everywhere, and must be met, not with ridiculous hotheaded attacks on Germany, Italy, and Russia, but by a restatement of the case for Toleration in general.'

But none of G.B.S.'s books is banned in Great Britain. He did not utter a moan when the Polish Minister for Home Affairs ordered the removal of seventy-two lines from the third act of *Too True to be Good*, although he had done no more than forecast accurately what would happen in the next European War; but he made a tremendous song and dance when the Lord Chamberlain ordered him to remove six words from *The Shewing-up of Blanco Posnet*. Books are undoubtedly banned in America and in Great Britain, though to far less extent than in Eire or Russia, but is any human society conceivable in which some books will not be banned? Does any reasonable person believe that the British were wrong to forbid Suttee in India when fanatical widows eagerly sought the funeral pyre?

175

The concluding part of the last cited passage from the preface to *On The Rocks* is positively comic. Here is G.B.S. pleading for Toleration in a preface which is largely devoted to denying the need for it. 'The essential justification for extermination', he asserts, 'is always incorrigible social incompatibility and nothing else.' John the Baptist was incompatible with Herod and Herodias, and lost his head for saying so; but does the fact that he was executed by an arbitrary king prove that he was wrong and that Herod was.right?

G.B.S., on his own argument, ought to have been exterminated long before the date of his death. He dissents from the conclusion of John Stuart Mill's *Essay on Liberty*, 'that self-regarding actions should not be interfered with by the authorities', which, he declares, 'carries very little weight for Socialists who perceive that in a complex modern civilisation there are no purely self-regarding actions in the controversial sphere.'

The idea of a totalitarian state is not new. It is as old as sin. Plato liked the idea. So did Dante. Shakespeare, taking a tip, perhaps, from Herodotus, describes the state that is dear to the heart of the dictator, when he makes the gardener in *Richard II* say to his assistants:

> Go thou, and like an executioner,
> Cut off the heads of too fast growing sprays,
> That look too lofty in our commonwealth;
> All must be even in our government.

'Nowhere else in Greece', says Jowett:[1]

> 'was the individual so completely subjected to the State' as in Sparta; 'the time when he was to marry, the education of his children, the clothes he was to wear, the food which he was to eat, were all prescribed by law. . . . The "suprema lex" was the preservation of the family, and the interest of the State. The coarse strength of military government was not favorable to purity and refinement; and the excessive strictures of some regulations seems to have produced a reaction.'

Yet 'of all Hellenes, the Spartans were the most accessible to bribery; several of the greatest of them might be described as having "a fierce longing after gold and silver".'

Alexander, Julius Caesar, Louis the Fourteenth, Napoleon Bonaparte, Mussolini, Hitler, Lenin and Stalin—all these men sought to make a uniform world: a uniformity which would be imposed upon it by one nation. But the whole trend of life is towards diversity. Nature is lavish and wasteful and various, spilling a thousand acorns to get a single oak; and the centralisers and uniformists cannot thrive since they are moving against the current of creation.

---

[1] *The Dialogues of Plato.* Translated into English by B. Jowett, M.A. Vol. III. *The Republic.* Introduction, p. clxx.

It might be more convenient to arbitrary people if all trees were alike in size and shape and texture. How tiresome it is that there are so many to be named and numbered and noted in the card index. Is it not a nuisance that there is a great variety of colour and shades of colour: dark green and light green; green that is almost black, and green that is almost blue, and green that is almost yellow; the green of young grass and old leaves and falling water? Why cannot soil everywhere be more or less the same? How much easier farming would be if all fields were alike! . . .

In their large work, *The Science of Life*, H. G. Wells and his collaborators, Julian Huxley and G. P. Wells, assert that the number of governing minds in the world is small:

> 'They are in perpetual conflict with hampering traditions and the obduracy of nature. They are themselves encumbered by the imperfections of their own trainings and the lack of organised solidarity. By wresting education more or less from its present function of transmitting tradition, they may be able to bring a few score or a few hundred millions into active co-operation with their efforts. Their task will still be a gigantic one.'

Yet G.B.S. would have placed this understanding minority of rebellious people who wish to depart from the routine of existence and to make changes in all conditions of life, under the dominion of a close gang of wilful and irresponsible bosses who could, if they felt so inclined, exterminate them.

176

We must remember in making up our minds about these matters, that although there are many important services which can be done better by the state than by any individual, there are other services, not less important and, in the belief of many people, much more important, which the state cannot render at all. No one but Shakespeare could have written *Hamlet*. Committees cannot create works of art, nor can they invent or discover new methods of working or devise beliefs about the purpose and function of mankind.

The pioneering man, the innovator, the rebel, the man with a new message, the man who wishes to grasp this sorry Scheme of Things entire and shatter it to bits and then remould it nearer to the heart's desire, has always had opposed to him the vast inertia of the dull and easily contented mob. He had to fight the experts in authority who could not admit his claim that change was essential, since to do so would have been to confess that they had failed to perform their function, which was to keep the community in good condition, and had also failed to observe that change of some sort was desirable.

Harvey, who discovered the circulation of the blood, was called a lunatic by his contemporaries in medicine. Lister's use of anaesthetics earned him the dislike and enmity of the London Surgical Society—and also the scorn and contempt of G.B.S. In the year 1787, the Lords of the Admiralty refused to make a grant to Lord Stanhope for an experiment with a steamship because they were unanimously of opinion that it would never be possible to move a vessel without the aid of wind and tide. In 1907, the Lords of the Admiralty, who had not, apparently, learnt their great-grandfather's lesson, rejected the offer of co-operation in the manufacture of aircraft made to them by the famous aviators, the Wright Brothers, because their experts were satisfied that aeroplanes could never be of use.

When John Smeaton, in 1756, proposed to build Eddystone Lighthouse with stone, he was called a crank, and was told that the only suitable material for a lighthouse was wood: and if he had not been so determined to use stone that he refused to accept the contract unless he were allowed to have his way, Eddystone would have been Eddywood.

When the first railway was opened at Liverpool, wise and impressive men went about remarking that no good could come of this invention, and clergymen preached vehemently against it. Stage coaches, they said, already travelled at the nerve-shattering speed of eight or nine or even ten miles an hour, and if an attempt were made to surpass that rate, the respiration of the passengers would become difficult, if not impossible. They had horrifying visions of trains rushing along at as many as fifteen miles an hour, while cries and moans issued from compartments full of people with bursting lungs.

The assertions of experts in warfare have been so comic and illusory that merely to call a man an expert is to hear him damned for mediocrity if not for plain imbecility. Goering told the Germans at the beginning of the Second World War that no British aeroplane would ever reach Berlin. A high officer of the R.A.F., in a speech delivered at a public dinner in London about the same time, informed his audience that although he could not say that the Germans would not penetrate the defences of the capital the first time they made a raid, he could say they would not penetrate them a second time. The wrecked streets of London must have mocked that man when he saw them. After Dunkirk, the experts told us that the German Army would not be able to move further into France for at least three weeks, as they would require all that time, and probably longer, to rest and reorganise their troops. But in three weeks' time, the Germans were in Paris, and France had fallen.

What wretched folly was it that made G.B.S. abandon his high
and saintly conception of society for a neatly-regulated Webbian
world from which all discordant elements, such as Socrates and Jesus
Christ, should be eliminated, leaving only tidy little obedient men
and women, metaphorically touching their hats to the Commissars
and assuring Stalin that whatever he said was quite right, sir, and
anybody who dissented from his words ought to be done in, sir? What
had he in common with the hard-faced Lenin, who said 'It would
not matter a jot if three-quarters of the human race perished; the
important thing was that the remaining quarter should be Communist', or with the bloated Nazi, Goering, who told his countrymen
that 'heads will simply be chopped off if men do not obey the inspired
Hitler and submit to his decrees'?

Man has not yet found, and may never find, the form of government that is faultless; but even if such a government could be found,
the natural development of our resources would compel us periodically to make changes of some sort. The world in which we are living
is moving so fast that people in their middle age are astounded at the
revolutions that have been made in their own life time. I have seen
the pony trap and the brougham and the penny-farthing bicycle give
place to the motor-car, the motor-bicycle and the aeroplane. The
wireless and television and the moving-picture have all come into
operation in a short part of my life. In my childhood, bathrooms
were rare, and young servant girls had to carry pails of hot water up
long flights of stairs to bedrooms, and then, when the 'tubs' were
taken, carry the whole lot downstairs again. I cannot remember
seeing a telephone in any private house, except a doctor's, before the
year 1911.

All these changes cause other changes no less influential or
drastic. The language has been enriched or debased, according to our
fancy, by new words made necessary by new machines and gadgets.
If my father, who died in 1886, could be raised from the dead and
were told, on entering a room, to switch on the wireless, he would not
know what the words meant. There was no electricity in Belfast when
he died, and the only illuminants he knew were candles and paraffin
oil lamps and gas.

The sight of numerous vehicles of all sizes and shapes moving
about the streets without any visible means of propulsion would
terrify him, who had never seen any vehicle, except a railway carriage,
that was not drawn by a horse or an ass. He may have seen a telephone, but he never saw a bicycle with pneumatic tyres or a moving

picture or an aeroplane or a submarine or a motor-car and would have thought that a man was mad who prophesied that I, then a baby, would one day be not only heard, but seen by people miles away from the room in which I would be sitting and talking. It is absurd to suppose that such changes as these do not profoundly affect our lives, intellectually as well as physically and socially, and must create needs that will be resisted by those who are old and set in their ways or arbitrary and self-satisfied.

178

On The Rocks, which was the excuse for this preface seems to have little, if any, relevance to it; though it was intended, no doubt, to reveal the defects of democratic government by making the Cabinet, and especially the Prime Minister, a collection of noodles and neuropaths.

The scene is laid in the Cabinet room of 10, Downing Street, and the play opens with the Prime Minister, Sir Arthur Chavender, idling over a late breakfast and *The Times*, although Whitehall is congested with processions of unemployed workmen. Sir Arthur is about to dictate some notes for a speech about the Sanctity of the Family to his secretary when he is interrupted by his rather silly family, his wife and son and daughter, who seem to bounce in and out of the Cabinet room whenever they feel like it.

Lady Chavender describes herself as 'not born for wifing and mothering'. What she *was* born for, she does not state. Her daughter, Flavia, is an ill-conditioned creature of 19, who bawls at the top of her voice, as she enters the room, 'Papa: I will not stand Mamma any longer. She interferes with me in every possible way out of sheer dislike of me. I refuse to live in this house with her a moment longer.' Her brother, not less indisciplined than his silly sister, is aged 18. He, too, has a few words to say about his mother. 'Look here, Mamma. Can't you leave Flavia alone? I won't stand by and see her nagged at and treated like a child of six. Nag! nag! nag! everything she does.'

Quite a pleasant little family! . . .

In the midst of this brawl, Sir Arthur's secretary comes in to ask if he had arranged to receive a deputation from the Isle of Cats. She has no note of it. Sir Arthur had made such an arrangement, but had forgotten it! . . . This is poor stuff. G.B.S. knew far better than that. Prime Ministers do not make casual engagements, nor do they keep any engagements they make entirely to themselves. The reception of deputations is not conducted in a haphazard fashion: it is carefully arranged by efficient secretaries.

So far, the play has all the appearance of a clumsy farce written by a cub reporter on the staff of a seaside newspaper. One would not suspect that its author had ever been inside 10, Downing Street, and was fairly familiar with Prime Ministers and their families. Several of his personal friends were or had been members of Cabinets, and he might have been expected to know how such people behave.

But he was determined to make democratic government seem absurd, and he was not very scrupulous about his exposure. What he overlooked was the fact that the foibles he derided are not inherently democratic, but human, and that they would be displayed by dictators no less than by popularly elected politicians. They are, indeed, more likely to be found in dictators than in democratic leaders. Hitler's behaviour, according to those who knew the man, was that of a highly temperamental prima donna on the verge of a nervous breakdown. A democratic leader would not have the folly or the insolence to conduct himself as Mussolini was accustomed to behave.

The deputation has come to enquire what the Prime Minister intends to do about the unemployed. When Sir Arthur asks the Mayor what he can do for them, the Mayor replies, 'Well, Sir Arthur, as far as I can make it out the difficulty seems to be that you can't do anything. But something's got to be done,' which is as nice a *non sequitur* as anybody has ever uttered. It is apparent that none of the deputation has the faintest idea of what should be done, but, filled with the strange notion which possesses almost everybody in the world that people in political power somehow or other know better than the rest of us what should be done in any state of emergency, they expect Sir Arthur to produce a remedy for trouble as promptly as a conjuror produces a rabbit from a hat, without even having had time to put a rabbit *into* the hat.

Their expectation provokes the Premier to one of those outbursts of frank speech with which G.B.S. enriches his dialogue in a startling fashion. 'What can I do?' he exclaims. 'Do you suppose that I care less for the sufferings of the poor than you do? Do you suppose I would not revive trade and put an end to it all to-morrow if I could? But I am like yourself: I am in the grip of economic forces that are beyond human control. What mortal man could do, this Government has done. We have saved the people from starvation by stretching the unemployment benefit to the utmost limit of our national resources! . . .'

This act ends with a visit to the Cabinet Room of a mysterious lady who turns out to be some sort of a neurologist. She receives those who are on the verge of nervous collapse into her nursing home in Wales, and there Sir Arthur, now dithering, is removed. In the second act, we find him completely cured, as he himself believes, but madder than ever, according to his colleagues, proposing a programme for his party which might have been drawn up by The Fabian Research Department after a long outburst of emotional oratory by Mr Aneurin Bevan.

G.B.S. had thrown up his hands. Democracy was down and out. There is a line in *England, arise*, which runs, 'Faint in the east behold the dawn appear.' For G.B.S. the east was Russia, and the dawn was a dictator-dominated commune. Mussolini had begun as a Socialist agitator, and so had Hitler; and both of them had become, as Lenin and Stalin became, ruthless bosses. That, seemingly, was what the world would have to come to. So G.B.S. thought. He had put up his hands.

There is a passage in the preface to *On the Rocks*, in the imagined trial of Jesus, when Pilate and Our Lord, rising to the height of great argument, discuss the word and the act. Here it is:

> *Pilate:* In the mouth of a Roman words mean something: in the mouth of a Jew, they are a cheap substitute for strong drink. If we allowed you, you would fill the whole world with your scriptures and psalms and talmuds: and the history of mankind would become a tale of fine words and villainous deeds.
>
> *Jesus:* Yet the word came first, before it was made flesh. The word was the beginning. The word was with God before he made us. Nay, the word was God.
>
> *Pilate:* And what may all that mean pray?
>
> *Jesus:* The difference between man and Roman is but a word; but it makes all the difference. The difference between Roman and Jew is only a word.
>
> *Pilate:* It is a fact.
>
> *Jesus:* A fact that was first a thought: for a thought is the substance of a word. I am no mere chance pile of flesh and bone: if I were only that, I should fall into corruption and dust before your eyes. I am the Word made flesh: that is what holds me together standing before you in the image of God.
>
> *Pilate:* That is well argued; but what is sauce for the goose is sauce for the gander; and it seems to me that if you are the Word made flesh so also am I.
>
> *Jesus:* Have I not said so again and again? Have they not stoned me in the streets for saying it? Have I not sent my apostles to proclaim this great news to the Gentiles and to the very ends of the world? The Word is God. And God is within you. It was when I said this that the Jews—my own people—began picking up stones. But why should you, the Gentile, reproach me?
>
> *Pilate:* I have not reproached you for it. I pointed it out to you.
>
> *Jesus:* Forgive me. I am so accustomed to be contradicted! . . .
>
> *Pilate:* Just so. There are many sorts of words: and they are all made flesh sooner or later. Go among my soldiers and you will hear many filthy words and witness many cruel and hateful deeds that began as

553

thoughts. I do not allow these words to be spoken in my presence. I punish those deeds as crimes. Your truth, as you call it, can be nothing but the thoughts for which you have found words which will take effect in deeds if I set you loose to scatter your words broadcast among the people. Your own people who bring you to me tell me that your thoughts are abominable and your words blasphemous. How am I to refute them? How am I to distinguish between the blasphemies of my soldiers reported to me by my centurions and your blasphemies reported to me by your High Priest?

Jesus: Woe betide you and the world if you do not distinguish! . . .

I break off because the superb debate is too long for quotation, and because Jesus in the passage I have cited answers the nonsense put into Sir Arthur Chavender's mouth by G.B.S. about·talkers in ignominious comparison with doers. Here we have the hinge on which the world turns. The thought precedes the word: the word precedes the action. There is no movement or performance without thought. The mind is the mainspring of life.

And it is because thought and speech are of the first importance that his admirers are entitled to complain of G.B.S.'s despondent betrayal of words spoken by the wise in the interests of deeds done by violent despots. Out of his great wisdom, G.B.S. told us that if revelation is not continuous, there is no such thing as revelation; and that creation is going on all the time. But how can revelation continue and creation be carried on, if the revealers and the creators, who by their very nature, must be in rebellion against established things, are to be exterminated by the gang that happens at the moment to be in power?

179

In 1934, Charlotte and he went to New Zealand, where a guide who showed him through the Roturua district, said he had never accompanied a man who walked as quickly as G.B.S. His age then was seventy-eight. It was during this excursion that he wrote *The Simpleton of the Unexpected Isles, The Millionairess* and *The Six of Calais.*

A letter he wrote to my wife while he was on board the *Rangitane*, sailing from Wellington to London, and dated May 12, 1934, may serve as an introduction to these plays:

'My dear Nora,

'This is in reply to yours of the 7th February last, which just managed to reach me on the ship before it cast loose at the Albert Dock. Consequently it has been half way round the globe and back with me. I have written two plays on the double voyage. The second is only just finished; and now comes your turn.

'When I say finished, I mean that the first wild draft in shorthand is finished. The first play was interrupted by a month in New Zealand. When I resumed it I had forgotten it to such an extent that I had to send a wireless to my secretary to remind me of the names of the characters—the only point on which—in my plays—continuity is necessary.

'Playwriting is becoming a Platonic exercise with me. *On the Rocks*, which of course meant nothing except to a little congregation of Fabians and their like, started (at half prices) at £600 a week, dwindled to £400, and perished. The congregation is more enthusiastic than ever, especially the mouldier section of it; but it does not grow. Old age is telling on me. My bolt is shot as far as any definite target is concerned and now, as my playwright faculty still goes on with the impetus of 30 years vital activity, I shoot into the air more and more extravagantly without any premeditation whatever—*advienne que pourra*. The first of these two plays, which were written mostly in the tropics, is openly oriental, hieratic and insane. The second, by reaction, is quite commonplace in form: three acts in the metropolitan area, and the theme quite stuffily matrimonial; but the dialogue is raving lunacy from beginning to end. I shall not ask any manager to waste gambling on either of these dotings.

'I have seen no newspapers except N.Z. ones since I left three months ago, and don't know what St John has been doing. The daily bulletins on the ship dont go into such matters. All I have is a general impression that everybody's dead, and that I ought to be. Elgar, with whom we have of late years become specially intimate, was the most world-shaking death; but we knew before we left that it was imminent. That was on my musical side, which is so important in my development that nobody can really understand my art without being soaked in symphonies and operas, in Mozart, Verdi and Meyerbeer, to say nothing of Handel, Beethoven and Wagner, far more completely than in the literary drama and its poets and playwrights.

'I still remain faithful to St John; but we do not see much of you, partly because you lurk in Honey Ditches far from London, and partly because, as we are verging on our eighties and you are in the prime of life, we are growing shyer and shyer of inflicting ourselves on you. I still talk too much, and am probably one of the ship's most dreaded old bores. However, we are glad to be taken notice of: so you need not be shy.

'As this letter cannot find any other means of conveyance than this ship, it will go ashore at Plymouth and be delivered to you the following morning some hours before we are dumped at Tilbury and forwarded to Whitehall Court, where we shall hear all the news before going down to Ayot St Lawrence on Saturday as usual.

'You and St John ought to go round the world. It makes a difference. Charlotte and I, bad sailors enough, have now been six months at sea without missing a meal. And on a long voyage you have to work or go mad. You looked wretched the last time I saw you; but I attribute that to the idotic arrangements which prevented us from sitting together at the Grein dinner when that was obviously the correct juxtaposition. I was equally disappointed.

Ever

G. Bernard Shaw

The Simpleton of the Unexpected Isles was produced for the first time on February 18, 1935, by the Theatre Guild of New York, but was coldly received by the critics and was soon withdrawn, though Lawrence Langner still has faith in its quality and foresees a day when it will become popular. 'I believe it contains some of Shaw's most inspired writing . . . a magnificent allegory,' he says.

The theme is the Day of Judgment. Its first performance in Great Britain took place at Malvern on July 29, 1935, and, after a short run at the Arts Theatre in London, it was transferred to the Princes' Theatre, where, however, it failed to attract audiences, mainly because the theatre was too large. Langner's opinion of it is not shared by many of G.B.S.'s admirers. E. Strauss, in an interesting essay, *Bernard Shaw: Art and Socialism*, dismisses it as 'not only generally dull', but as 'a particularly sad instance of the decline in Shaw's dramatic powers'. This is a severe, even a harsh, but not an unjust judgment.

The play is poor in conception and execution, and The Simpleton himself is a mindless curate who spends much of his time in apologising for his existence. Parsons suffer severely in G.B.S.'s hands, except in *Getting Married*, where the bishop and the solicitor turned priest are impressive and, in the case of the Bishop, pleasing. Yet G.B.S. met many parsons who must have seemed to him to be men of fine quality.

Stewart Headlam was his colleague on the Fabian Executive Committee for many years; he knew Conrad Noel and Percy Dearmer well; R. J. Campbell, Ensor Williams and Dr Clifford were among his friends. His respect for Dean Inge was immense. When he and Dr Barnes, the late Bishop of Birmingham, lunched in my house in Devon, they found themselves notably congenial to each other. I met him coming out of Westminster Cathedral once, and asked him what he was doing in there. 'Oh,' he replied, 'I was listening to Ronnie Knox. I always go to hear him preach when I can.' As, indeed, any sensible person would do. His general experience of clergymen of all denominations was amiable. He liked them, and they liked him. That is why it is odd to find so few of them in his plays who are admirable.

The play suffers from an old fault in his dramatic technique. He had always decorated his plays extravagantly so that the audience might have pleasant relief from argument; and as he grew older, he became increasingly reckless with adornment. Even in his one act plays, he would shift the scene from one elaborate set to another, and fill the cast with many characters, thus making the plays difficult in production. The short play has disappeared from the West End stage, a grave piece of misjudgment on the part of managers, and it is now performed mainly by amateur actors, who cannot afford elaborate sets and have not enough acting members to supply casts for the numerous characters in the majority of G.B.S.'s short pieces. *The Six of Calais* is one of his shortest plays, and it has only one set, but this set is elaborate and demands a good deal of stage room. There are at least eighteen characters in the cast, with a number of supernumerary characters. This is a typical example of his extravagance in casting and decorating a play.

The prologue to *The Simpleton of the Unexpected Isles* is divided into three short scenes, the first laid in an emigration office in the tropics, the second on a grassy cliff top overhanging the sea, and the third on a shelf of rock half way down a cliff. The whole of the Prologue could be cut with advantage to the play. It takes up time and space that could have been put to better use in the play itself. The satire is ingenuous and biteless. His shafts seldom hit the target and never pierce it. The play, too, is full of that fantastic farce to which he became increasingly addicted as he grew older. There is a large element of slapstick in all his work, and he himself could suddenly abandon the serious side of his nature and become very larky. His face, more than most people's, reveals his divided nature very clearly. It was a remarkable face, growing in distinction as he grew in years, and it was full of grace. Two men, highly dissimilar from each other, found a Christlike appearance in his head: G. K. Chesterton, in his book on G.B.S., and Rodin, who made a great bust of him. Rodin's is the more impressive opinion because he knew little or nothing about G.B.S. when he made his bust, whereas Chesterton was his familiar friend. The French sculptor, so his secretary, A. M. Ludovici, states 'was struck by the Christlike quality of his appearance'. This impression, which was shared by Madame Rodin, seemed absurd to Ludovici, who was familiar, because of his previous long residence in London, with the G.B.S. legend. But Rodin maintained his opinion. 'C'est une vrai tête de Christ,' he declared. Ludovici knew the Shaw legend: he did not know Shaw. Rodin knew Shaw, but did not know the legend.

He was liable in his relations with people to display his slapstick moods when they were least to be expected, but this liability is more apparent in his plays than in his personal habits. He was well aware of it, even afraid of it, and he once told the students at the Royal Academy of Dramatic Art that the Joey in him was always popping out when he was least wanted. In nearly all the plays he wrote after

557

Saint Joan, Joey had greater possession of him than ever before. Joey is far too prominent in *The Simpleton of the Unexpected Isles*, which is disfigured mainly by the fact that The Simpleton himself is only a simpleton, and not, as the fools in Shaw no less than Shakespeare, almost always are, the wisest of men.

'Life, as we see it', G.B.S. writes in the short preface to *The Six of Calais*, 'is so haphazard that it is only by picking out its key situations and arranging them in their significant order (which is never how they occur) that it can be made intelligible.' This is a truth so profound that we wonder how he came to overlook it in writing *The Simpleton:* it is the foundation of all art.

The lack of reality in the play is made more remarkable by the fact that in the concluding passage of the preface to it, he casually remarks that an experiment in group marriage which is an important part of the action and development of the theme is not to be taken seriously. As this group marriage is the cause of the threatened hostilities in the second act, its dismissal in this airy manner seems curiously trivial. It is true that the experiment of group marriage is handled very slightly, the interrelations of six people, three men and three women, resulting only in the birth of four fantastic children who appear to be the offspring of one mother; but why was it made an important part of the end of the play if it was only G.B.S.'s fun, and not to be regarded as a serious suggestion?

180

His next long play, *The Millionairess*, a remarkable piece of bravura, was offered to the Theatre Guild, which, very stupidly, declined it. It was, however, produced by Langner in his own private theatre at Westport with Jessie Royce Landis as Epifania. 'The play', Langner says, 'is delightful and was extremely well received by the audience.' Its first performance on a public stage was given at the Academy Theatre in Vienna on January 4, 1936, by the company from the Burgtheater in that city, and its first performance in England was made by a repertory company, the Matthew Forsyth Players at the Pavilion in Bexhill on November 17, 1936, a fact which is surprising in itself.

G.B.S. was the greatest dramatist of his day, yet he had to depend for the first performance of a very diverting farcical comedy on a little known organisation. *The Millionairess* is one of the lesser Shaw plays, but it is good entertainment; and two brilliant actresses eventually played the principal part: Dame Edith Evans and Miss Katherine Hepburn.

The play may be described as a sequel to the first play G.B.S.

wrote: *Widowers' Houses;* and to deal with the later life of Blanche Sartorius, now enormously rich: the sort of woman who runs through husbands as easily as mindless young men run through fortunes. It is a study of indiscipline. Epifania has all the predatory instincts of a dictator. She grabs what she wants, and is surprised and indignant when she encounters resistance. The woman is full of vitality for which she has insufficient outlet, and she seems to have inherited some of her father's ability, though her inheritance is not very skil-fully revealed, and her successful conduct of a hotel can be said to be due less to her ability than her wealth. By the time it was written, G.B.S. had become exceedingly careless in making his plays, and he was liable to waste time on irrelevant scenes.

Such a scene occurs in *The Millionairess:* the scene in the sweaters' cellar. This scene is not even plausible in the context of the time in which the play is laid. G.B.S. had forgotten that sweat shops such as he describes had ceased to exist long before *The Millionairess* was written. Beatrice Webb's courageous adventure into one, when, dis-guised as a working-girl, she took a job in an East End shop where tailoring garments were finished, had not failed of effect, as he ought to have known. The year is 1935. There were no women working in sweat-shops then for twelve hours a day at 2½d an hour, earning any-thing from twelve to fifteen shillings a week. The whole of this scene could be cut. Any value it has as a revelation of Epifania's character is made much more effectively in the succeeding and final act.

But the dialogue is full of the old buoyancy, and the play moves at tremendous speed. There is character in every line of it, even when the character is extravagant. When, half a minute after curtain rise on the first act, Epifania enters the office of Julius Sagamore, and utters her first speech, the pace and quality of the play is set, and it never drops. 'Are you Julius Sagamore, the worthless nephew of my late solicitor, Pontifex Sagamore?' she says, an enquiry sufficiently unusual in Lincoln's Inn Fields to rouse the curiosity of the audience about what is to follow.

It is not all extravagant. G.B.S., in his wildest scenes of slapstick, never forgot humanity; and he had the rare gift, not only as a dramatist, but as a public speaker, of setting a large audience in a roar of laughter, and then, in a moment, silencing it with a grave remark, spoken almost casually in his pleasant Irish voice which, while it had no great oratorical notes in it, such as adorned the speeches of Gladstone and John Bright, was not only clearly articu-lated, but highly evocative of deep and thoughtful response from an audience.

The Millionairess is undoubtedly a minor Shaw play. That fact, in itself, is sufficient to condemn it in the eyes of those singular

persons who feel surprised when a man of genius, even in his old age
—he was seventy-nine when he wrote it—produces a work which is
less than immortal. They seem to think that the works of great
writers must all be masterpieces, and that his latest work must be his
best. But Shakespeare did not produce works on an ascending scale
of greatness any more than mankind marches steadily upwards.
Milton wrote *Paradise Lost* and then wrote *Paradise Regained,* which
convinces those who read it that paradise was better lost. Sheridan,
after he had written *The School for Scandal,* was silent for twenty years.
He then produced his single tragedy, *Pizarro,* causing his admirers to
wish he had remained mute.

If great men can rise higher than the rest of us, they can also fall
lower. They have further to fall. That is what dismays the undiscerning on finding them short of greatness. The genius, we say, must
not make poor jokes, nor may he disport himself in a Bank Holiday
mood. His home is on the heights, where he must remain. If he
descends to the plains, he will be hooted and derided; and humour-
less prigs and bright cub reporters will go about asserting that he is
gaga.

But great men have always been ready to crack bad jokes. Earnest
schoolboys at Oxford and Cambridge blush for Shakespeare when
they think of the knockabout humour in which he so often indulges.
He is partial to puns, and he laughs at behaviour which makes
serious people feel embarrassed. He cracks jokes, such as that surprising one made by Cloten to the musicians in the third scene of the
second act of *Cymbeline.* . . . So different, so very different from the
delicate wit one hears in Common Rooms! But we must take men of
genius as they choose to be taken. It is not we who should give orders
to them, but they who should give orders to us. The minor work of a
genius is likely to surpass the best work of a mediocrity. *The Millionairess* is below the level of *Man and Superman, Heartbreak House* and
Saint Joan, but it is superior to the masterpieces of whatshisname who
flashed for a short while and then went out. It is provocative of
thought, and it is full of fun and larks.

G.B.S. throughout his life was preoccupied by two problems: the
quality of people and how to get them rightly governed; and these
preoccupations appear in *The Millionairess.* We need no great profundity to realise that a large number of men and women are infants
walking about in the bodies of adults. Like all intelligent people,
G.B.S. brooded over these problems, of how we are to improve ourselves and how we are to maintain the comity of civilised society while
we are making this improvement. It was absurd, he thought, that
the fate of mankind should depend on the whims of a half-educated
and short-memoried mob of men and women who can easily be

stampeded and are so unintelligent that many of them, after nearly ninety years of compulsory education, cannot make a simple mark on a ballot-paper without spoiling their vote.

His main idea, reasonable enough, was that a disciplined democracy, which the world badly needs, can be achieved only by the labour of exceptional people. This is why he was attracted by the idea of dictators. But he was not oblivious of the fact that dictators are likely to be incontinent and may become demented. Those who are empowered to indulge all their desires, tend to believe that there can be no authority superior to theirs. Hitler, in *Mein Kampf*, asserts that his 'conduct is in accordance with the will of the Almighty Creator', and almost suggests that even God hesitates to contradict or oppose him. The fall of France in the Second World War and its deplorable state since its liberation makes even those who feel no sympathy with Fascism or Communism feel that there can be too much deference to mob minds and uninstructed opinion.

But the statesman realises that no policy can be effective finally unless the mob understands and approves of it. Who will entrust a machine to a man who knows nothing of its function? It will soon cease to work if he does not know that it must be oiled. Existence for any ruler would be easy if he were never criticised or questioned or asked to justify his policy. Such claims as this are made only by inefficient, arbitrary men who think that genius is mainly emotional and can dispense, therefore, with proofs and justification. Even Lenin and his gang of commissars soon realised that efficient industrial workmen cannot be made out of ignorant peasants by order or decree; and that skilled men, even if they have to be sought among capitalistically-minded foreigners, must be employed to train them.

In *The Millionairess* we are shown an able woman who has no control of herself because she has never been subjected to any discipline, her own or anybody else's. All her whims were indulged by her doting dad, yet she finds herself frustrated by her uncontrolled authority, and there is a poignant passage in the play in which she asserts how sorrowful her life has been because there is no one whom she can trust, no one whose approach to her is selfless. It is only when she meets a man who has subjugated himself that she finds any hope of fulfilling her function in the world.

Because she is a millionairess, she cannot keep her husband, her lover, or anything but her money. When her solicitor begs her to be reasonable, and asks if anyone can live with a tornado, an earthquake or an avalanche, she replies that thousands of people live on the slopes of volcanoes, in the track of avalanches, on land thrown up only yesterday by earthquakes, but no one can live with a millionairess who seeks to fulfil her destiny and wield power given to her by her money. 'Well, be it so. I shall sit in my lonely house, and be myself, and pile up millions! . . .'

But at last, the unhappy, indisciplined Epifania meets a man whom she can respect, a Moslem doctor whose disinterest in money is total, but who is deeply interested in leaving the world better than he found it. To him, riches and poverty are curses. 'Only in the service of Allah is there justice, righteousness, and happiness.' Epifania is dumbfounded when she finds herself treated with indifference by this Egyptian doctor who rebukes her for her self-indulgence and money-worship. When she tells him that she wishes to marry him, he says he is married to Science and does not desire any other bride; and when she becomes importunate, he tells her that he made a vow to his dying mother that if any woman sought him in marriage, he would hand her two hundred piastres and tell her that unless she could go out into the world with nothing but that and the clothes in which she stood, and earn her living alone and unaided for six months, he would never speak to her again.

Epifania soon settles that business, and the play concludes with a dithyramb on marriage. 'And I tell you that in the very happiest marriages not a day passes without a thousand moments of unfaithfulness. You begin by thinking you have only one husband: you find you have a dozen. There is a creature you hate and despise and are tied to for life; and before breakfast is over the fool says something nice and becomes a man whom you admire and love; and between these extremes there are a thousand degrees with a different man and woman at each of them. A wife is all women to one man: she is everything that is devilish: the thorn in his flesh, the jealous termagant, the detective dogging all his movements, the nagger, the scolder, the worrier. He has only to tell her an affectionate lie and she is his comfort, his helper, at best his greatest treasure, at worst his troublesome but beloved child. All wives are all these women in one, all husbands all these men in one. What do the unmarried know of this infinitely dangerous heart-tearing everchanging life of adventure we call marriage?'

The Millionairess may be an extravagant farce, but it is a farce with a considerable difference; one that would make Ralph Lynn and Robertson Hare stare their eyes out.

181

The moral he draws in the preface is the old one of the need for economic equality. But we are more than wage-earners, and our ability to live together depends on far more important things than money. We seek our friends among those whose tastes we share:

we do not seek them among those whose incomes equal ours. Millionaires do not hobnob only with millionaires. They generally dislike each other.

The preface contains what seems to me a profound misstatement. 'It is always', he says, 'the greatest spirits . . . who are communists and democrats', and he adds that it is only 'the commonplace people who weary us with blitherings about the impossibility of equality'.

The examples of the great spirits he cites in support of his argument disprove it. They were all exclusive men. Jesus, for example, who is named by G.B.S. as one of them, was more intimate with a few of his disciples than he was with the rest. If we were to judge his relations with his Twelve Apostles as they are reported in the Gospels, we might imagine that he never exchanged a word with the majority of them. Simon the Zealot must have been a man of exceptional character and experience, yet there is no record in the New Testament of Our Lord ever having spoken to him. We know only that Peter and James and John were his intimates, and that he talked to Peter more than to any other person: and that he sometimes made a remark to Judas Iscariot.

The discipleship of the Zealot is inexplicable. The Zealots were a group of irregular Jewish soldiers, almost bandits, who harassed the Romans exactly as the Sinn Feiners harassed the British. It was their habit to assassinate not only unwary or isolated Romans, but to murder any Jew who was friendly with Romans. There is a legend that the Zealots were attracted to Jesus at the beginning of his ministry, thinking that he might lead them, but this attraction, if it ever existed, ended abruptly when they were told that the kingdom of Jesus was not of this world. Theirs was.

Simon may have been the intermediary between Jesus and the leaders of the Zealots. He may have become converted to Our Lord's belief. But why is it that this singular man, whose physical courage and general attitude to the world must have distinguished him among the Twelve, seems to have been an insignificant member of the Apostolate? Why, too, did this brave guerrilla soldier join the frightened Apostles in their flight from their Lord after his arrest? We should have expected him to be more faithful than any of them. He returned to the following after the Crucifixion: he is one of those named in the first chapter of *The Acts of the Apostles;* but what became of him after that strange assembly is not known. He is not mentioned anywhere in the New Testament again.

The economic arrangements of Jesus and the Twelve Apostles are nowhere described. We know that Judas Iscariot was the purse-bearer, but are not told how the purse was filled or replenished. Presumably, people who listened to Jesus made gifts either of food or of money to him, but there is no description of any transactions of this sort, apart from the meals he and the disciples ate in private houses. The life of Our Lord and the Twelve can, by an abuse of words, be described as communistic, but it certainly was not communistic in any sense that would have been understood by Lenin or Stalin. Stalin could hardly have withdrawn from the seminary where he was studying to become a priest of the Russian Orthodox Church, if he had believed for a moment that Jesus was an Early Marxist.

182

There was another cruise, this time in the Pacific, in 1936, and in February of that year, G.B.S., passing through the Panama Canal, began to write *Geneva*, which was first performed on August 1, 1938, at Malvern, and was transferred to the Saville Theatre in London on November 22. It was a moderate success. The Theatre Guild of New York declined it. An important factor in their decision is entitled to sympathy. Almost the whole of the directors of the Guild were Jews, and there were sentiments and speeches in *Geneva* which filled them with profound resentment.

Langner, who was now a fairly close friend of G.B.S., was especially infuriated by G.B.S.'s light and airy dismissal of 'Hitler's heartless treatment of the Jews—a treatment which was later to culminate in the killing of over four millions of them in the concentration camps of Buchenwald and Oswiecim.'[1] He wrote a long letter to G.B.S. in which, with great courtesy and dignity and skill, he remonstrated with him on this matter. It will be found among the appendices to *The Magic Curtain*, where will also be found G.B.S.'s unimpressive reply.

The Jews, not unnaturally, are highly sensitive to derogatory references, and are inclined to take offence where little or none is intended. Their history has given them this touchiness. It makes them resent Fagin in *Oliver Twist*, though Dickens has been more unmerciful to many of the Gentiles in the story. Is Bill Sykes let off more lightly than Fagin? Sensible Jews will not complain because one of them is portrayed as a blackguard, since he knows that there are rogues in all races. Those who call themselves the Chosen Race, should not feel surprised if other people, unconscious of any inferiority to them, resent the ascription.

Geneva was not only untimely, but seemingly callous. It was distressing to his friends at this period of his life to find G.B.S. making excuses for barbaric deeds, which, had Americans or Britons committed them, would have made him furious. Gentiles were as angry as the Jews about these aberrations; and no ingenuity of argument

---

[1] *The Magic Curtain*. By Lawrence Langner, p. 293.

could convince them that he was right in defending and applauding the dictators. In the preface to *Geneva* in the Standard Edition of his Works, he complains that Great Britain 'made no protest when' Mussolini's 'star was eclipsed and he was scandalously lynched in Milan'. But why should Britain have protested against the downfall of her enemy? Ought we to have held a memorial service for him and Hitler in St Paul's?

He was sufficiently impressed by Langner's protest to make some excisions and modifications in *Geneva;* but his partisan spirit had given his mind some of the consistency of ferro-concrete, and it is still saddening stuff to read. As a play, it dissatisfied him; for the version which appears in the Standard Collection has four acts instead of three as in the original version. The additional act improves it, but it is almost certain to be thrown into the discard, so far as performances are concerned.

The preface was not written until 1945, seven years after the first performance at Malvern. G.B.S. was then eighty-nine. His age is apparent in the quality of the preface, which is far below his general quality. If it had been written when the play was written, he could hardly have composed the passage which appears on page 18:

> 'The Hohenzollern monarchy in Germany, with an enormous military prestige based on its crushing defeat of the Bonapartist French Army in 1871 . . . was swept away in 1918 by the French Republic.'

Did G.B.S. not realise, one wonders, that if it had not been for the British participation in the First World War at the start of hostilities, the French would have been defeated in the first six weeks of the War, as they were in the war of 1870. Had the British remained neutral, the German Navy would have had an unimpeded voyage to the French coast, and the debacle which is known as Sedan would have been repeated in the English Channel.

Who was it that collapsed in 1940, who was it that fought on unaided?

It is the fashion among some silly people to jeer at Sir Winston Churchill when he reminds us that we, fighting alone in 1940, withstood the Germans for a year; but this is not sentimental assertion and patriotic claptrap. It is solid and irrefutable fact. If Great Britain had thrown in her hand when France fell, the Second World War would have been lost by the Allies, and the American people would have been in a grave position, with a victorious Germany commanding the Atlantic and a victorious Japan in serious control of the Pacific.

General Marshall, who was Chief of Staff to the United States Army, making his biennial report for 1943–5 to the Secretary of War, recognised this to be a fact:

'Hitler's first military set-back occurred when, after the collapse of France, England did not capitulate. According to Colonel General Jodl, Chief of the Operations Staff of the German High Command, the campaign in France had been undertaken because it was estimated that with the fall of France, England would not continue to fight. The unexpectedly swift victory over France, and Great Britain's continuation of the war found the General Staff unprepared for an invasion of England. Although the armistice with France was concluded on 22 June 1940, no orders for the invasion of Britain were issued prior to 2 July. Field Marshal Kesselring stated that he urged the invasion since it generally was believed in Germany that England was in a critical condition. Field Marshal Keitel, Chief of Staff of German Armed Forces, however, stated that the risk was thought to be the existence of the British Fleet. He said the army was ready but the air force was limited by weather, the navy very dubious. Meanwhile, in the air blitz over England the German Air Force had suffered irreparable losses from which its bombardment arm never recovered.'

General Marshall, later in the same report, makes a further statement which must have disturbed American minds very gravely:

'There can be no doubt that the greed and mistakes of war-making nations as well as the heroic stands of the British and Soviet peoples saved the United States a war on her own soil. The crisis had come and passed at Stalingrad and El Alamein before this Nation was able to gather sufficient resources to participate in the fight in a determined manner. Had the U.S.S.R. and the British Army of the Nile been defeated in 1942, as they well might if the Germans, Japanese, and Italians had better co-ordinated their plans and resources and successive operations, we should have stood to-day in the western hemisphere confronted by enemies who controlled a greater part of the world.

'Our close approach to that terrifying situation should have a sobering influence on Americans for generations to come. Yet, this is only a prelude of what can be expected so long as there are nations on earth capable of waging total war.'

183

Mussolini figures more prominently in *Geneva* than Hitler. G.B.S., indeed, esteemed the Italian more than the German, exalting Mussolini because he seemed to be a man of mind, depreciating Hitler because he seemed to be a man of emotion. How did it happen that this strange, hysterical creature, Hitler, went through the whole of the First World War without reaching any higher rank than that of a corporal at a time when the Germans, like all the other combatants, were combing their ranks for commissionable men, and yet lived to be the supreme commander of the Germany Army and the dictator of the docile Huns? This is a mystery which no one has yet solved, nor is there any sign in *Geneva* that G.B.S. perceived what a mystery it is.

To regard Mussolini as superior to this mixture of mystic and missionary was a surprising gaffe for G.B.S. to make. The fact that the Duce had compelled the Italians to bring their trains to their destinations on time, and that Hitler had abolished unemployment by setting jobless men to making roads, seems to have satisfied the Fabian in Shaw that they were great men. The singular worship he felt for Webb forced him to believe that achievements which men like Joseph Chamberlain had made in Birmingham without anyone being struck dumb with astonishment, denoted that Mussolini and Hitler must be statesmen of the highest order.

The most impressive character in the play is not a dictator: he is Sir Orpheus Midlander, the elegant and seemingly inert Englishman, a mixture of Arthur Balfour and Austen Chamberlain, who quietly, almost casually deflates the dictators when they become bombastic. Unobtrusively, he tells the dictators just what will happen if they perform monkey tricks. He does not pretend to understand the dictators or their intentions:

> 'Their remarks are most entertaining: every sentence is an epigram: I, who am only a stupid Englishman, feel quite abashed by my commonplaceness. But if you ask me what their intentions are I must frankly say that I don't know. Where do they stand with us? I don't know. But they know what England intends. They know what to expect from us. We have no speculative plans. We shall simply stick to our beloved British Empire, and undertake any larger cares that Providence may impose on us. Meanwhile, we should feel very uneasy if any other Power or combinations of Powers were to place us in a position of military or naval inferiority, especially naval inferiority. I warn you—I beg you—do not frighten us. We are a simple well meaning folk, easily frightened. And when we are frightened we are capable of anything, even of things we hardly care to remember afterwards. Do not drive us in that direction. Take us as we are; and let be. Pardon my dull little speech. I must not take more of your time.'

This speech, which is almost pure Arthur Balfour, makes Hitler-Battler remark 'Machiavelli', and no wonder. Bombardone-Mussolini exclaims, 'A most astute speech. But it cannot impose on us.' The Judge, however, being wiser than either of them, says, 'It has imposed on both of you. It is a perfectly honest speech made to you by a perfectly honest gentleman: and you both take it as an outburst of British hypocrisy.' Hitler and Mussolini were to realise just what the speech meant when they joined issue with the 'easily frightened'

British. The streets of Berlin and Hamburg still bear the marks of what that 'fear' produced.

The play has no conclusion other than a futile hope. At the end of the third act, the Judge, replying to the despondent Secretary of the League of Nations, who feels certain that the Dictators will not attend the conference, asserts that 'They will come. Where the spotlight is, there will the despots be gathered.' At the end of the play, the Judge remains optimistic. The Secretary, pessimistic as all officials are, finds comfort only in the fact that 'this farce of a trial' has been broken up. 'Not a farce, my friend,' the Judge replies. 'They came, these fellows. They blustered: they defied us. But they came. They came.' There he was wrong. They came, not to confer, but to wreck the world. And they very nearly succeeded.

184

Geneva was followed by a very pleasant play, *In Good King Charles's Golden Days*, full of rich, sagacious and witty lines, lines such as Kneller's 'Man: artists do not prove things. They do not need to. They *know* them.' The characters are mature and brilliantly drawn, each full of his own idiosyncrasy, each stamped with the ineradicable lines of life.

The play is in two acts, the first, laid in the house of Sir Isaac Newton, very long, and the second, laid in the boudoir of Catherine of Braganza, very short; and the majority of the characters are notable people: Charles II, who is drawn with such grace and distinction that he almost makes us pardon the Scots for the greatest injury they inflicted on the English, the Stuarts; Newton, George Fox, Godfrey Kneller; James, Duke of York, the stupidest of the Stuarts, Nell Gwynn, Barbara, Duchess of Cleveland; Louise, Duchess of Portland; and Catherine of Braganza, the Queen. The skill with which G.B.S. seizes on the essential characteristics of each of these men and women is extraordinary.

A vast amount of windy trash has been written about his inability to depict people, his habit of using men and women as ventriloquist's dolls for the utterance of his own opinions. It is true, to some extent, that every writer, whatever his quality, makes his characters in his own image, cannot, indeed, make them in any other, since he can only describe what he himself sees; but this fact does not exclude distinction and differentiation of people. God is said to have made all men in his own image, but his creation has not resulted in uniformity or failure to separate man from man, and, more difficult still, woman from woman; nor, unfortunately, has it made men like gods.

It is only in the second act that Charles begins to talk like G.B.S., and even in this act, he remains regal and wittily wise. But although he is made in G.B.S.'s image, he has his own accent and knows his own mind. The King may have heard his author muttering to himself, 'In every nation there must be the makings of a capable council and a capable king three or four times over, if only we knew how to pick them. Nobody has found out how to do it: that is why the world is so vilely governed,' but he manages by some alchemy to change the words into his own speech.

The riddle of how to choose a ruler is still unanswered; and it is the riddle of civilisation.

'I tell you again there are in England, or in any other country the makings of half a dozen decent kings and councils; but they are mostly in prison. If we only knew how to pick them out and label them, then the people could have their choice out of the half dozen. It may end that way, but not until we have learnt how to pick the people who are fit to be chosen before they are chosen. And even then the picked ones will be just those whom the people will not choose. Who is it that said that no nation can bear being well governed for more than three years?'

We may doubt if Charles would ever have talked like that. He knew too much to spout like a lecturer at a Fabian Summer School, and he realised that a collection of saints, philosophers, dons, slim ecclesiastics and well-informed civil servants could make as great a mess of their country's affairs as a collection of trade union leaders and earnest members of the Independent Labour Party.

Jesus set the example we shall be wise to follow. He chose the first twelve men he met and made them his Apostles. We choose our juries on that system, too, and any lawyer knows that a common jury, chosen in this fashion by the Clerk of the County Council, is better than a Grand Jury of select persons. We have got rid of the Grand Juries, but we still retain the common jury.

Could Charles have foreseen the Russian Commissars, as G.B.S. here makes him foresee them, he would have foreseen also that these clever little men with their dispatch cases and their neat minds and their smart intriguing habits and their love of rules and regulations are quickly approaching the time when the uncouth, cunning and deeply religious peasant will rise up in wrath and sweep them from the earth.

There is a passage of dialogue between Charles and Catherine which demands to be cited. In it, we find the essential wisdom of G.B.S.

Catherine: Our consciences, which come from God, must be all the same.

569

Charles: They are not. Do you think God so stupid that he could invent only one sort of conscience?

Catherine (shocked): What a dreadful thing to say! I must not listen to you.

Charles: No two consciences are the same. No two love affairs are the same. No two marriages are the same. No two illnesses are the same. No two children are the same. No two human beings are the same. What is right for one is wrong for the other. Yet they cannot live together without laws; and a law is something that obliges them all to do the same thing.

Why, one wonders, did G.B.S., who knew this, and put the words into the mouth of Charles, lose himself in the world where everything must be the same, the little robots repeating their ritual opinions, in the manner approved by Sidney and Beatrice Webb. One, two, three, get up. One, two, three, go forth. One, two, three, come back. One, two, three, go to bed. One, two, three, get up! . . .

185

This charming comedy, full of mind and grace, was written while G.B.S. was sickening severely, though, in the beginning, the nature of his sickness was not clear. He became lethargic and, more alarming, irritable. It was his irritability which alarmed his friends, for his serenity of temper was almost inhuman. It seemed impossible to rattle him or to upset his spiritual balance. This is not to say that he could not behave with severity. It is simply to say that he lost his geniality with some people only when he meant to lose it, and that he seemed to be devoid of any illwill or rancour.

But in 1937, I saw, for the first time in my long knowledge of him, signs that his temper and patience were wearing thin. Charlotte became worried about him. She thought he was overworking, as, indeed, he nearly always was; and when we suggested to her that Sidmouth might benefit him, she repeated our suggestion to him, and, to her surprise, found him jumping at it. 'A line in haste for post,' she wrote to my wife in March, 'to tell you G.B.S. has actually fallen for Sidmouth. Before I could tell him he caught at the idea and said he was worn out and must get away, and Sidmouth sounded just the place to go to.'

Their requirements were more than those of most married couples. They wanted two bedrooms and a sitting room large enough for them not only to recreate in quiet, but for G.B.S. to work. My wife vetted the hotels for them, and eventually we settled them in the Victoria where the manager, the late Mr Fitzgerald, who was Irish, and his wife were particularly attentive to them and won Charlotte's unending regard because of their efforts to make G.B.S. feel at home. 'Oh, Nora dear, bless you,' she wrote in April. 'I am so glad to have that settled. The Victoria of course, it is. And their letter is so nice. You *have* been a friend in need, Yours Charlotte.' They arrived in Sidmouth towards the end of April, staying for several weeks, and were so happy that they returned to the care of Mr and Mrs Fitzgerald at a later date.

But there was no doubt that he was ill. It was plain in his manner. His shyness became more pronounced as his illness developed, so pronounced that he hated to pass through the entrance hall of the hotel where he was certain to be gaped at, and took to leaving and entering his sitting-room by the fire escape, causing some agitation to elderly women who saw his long, lean figure suddenly appearing outside their bedroom window.

Our main task was to distract him from his illness, and we took him to various houses up country. During one of these visits, to lunch with the late Admiral and Mrs Parker,[1] I saw him more abashed and disconcerted than I had ever seen him since the evening when, at a meeting of The Fabian Society, Anatole France publicly kissed him on both cheeks. Admiral Parker called him Sir. To be addressed in that style by an admiral shook him. He could not have felt more over-come if the Queen had dropped a curtsey to him.

One morning, when Charlotte and we were waiting outside the Victoria for him to go with us to tea at Ashe, in Musbury, the house where the great Duke of Marlborough was born, Charlotte complained to me that she had spent years trying to make G.B.S. be present in his drawing room to receive his guests, but she had failed utterly. He waited until they were assembled, and then he made an entrance. Herself entirely at ease with people, she could not understand his shyness in meeting anybody until he had, so to speak, worked up an entrance. 'You know, St John,' she said, 'I think G.B.S. rather likes publicity!' There can hardly ever before have been uttered such a superb example of under-statement.

His interest in Ashe House was less than his interest in its archery range. I do not think he cared very much where the great Duke of Marlborough was born, but he was extraordinarily interested in the places where bowmen had practised their great game.

It was on that afternoon that we realised how little was his interest in natural beauty, though he always denied that he lacked this interest when teased about it. Yet he said that all trees looked alike to him. During our journey from Sidmouth to Musbury, we stopped to admire the beautiful valley in which Seaton sits. We had passed

[1] Now Dame Dehra Parker, Minister of Health and Local Government in the Northern Ireland Parliament.

along roads that seemed to be floating in a blue mist, so thick were the bluebells in the hedges. Charlotte turned to him and said, 'Did you see the bluebells, G.B.S.?' and he replied, 'What bluebells?'

There are few references to natural beauty in his work, as I once remarked to him, but he would not agree that this denoted lack of interest in it. Why should he spend his space in descriptions of it when the scene-painter could enable the audience to see what he wished it to see. The reply was artful, but unconvincing. His pleasure was in thought, his delight was in argument. He was indifferent to his surroundings and could have lived quite happily in a bare cell without the slightest sense of dis-ease.

One of the happiest engagements we made for him was a visit to the late Sir Matthew Nathan at West Coker in Somerset. Sir Matthew had been Permanent Under Secretary for Ireland at the time I was at the Abbey Theatre, and had met G.B.S. at Sir Horace Plunkett's house at Kilteragh. Just why it gave him so much pleasure, I do not know, except, perhaps, that it gave him a chance to talk about Ireland. It was during this visit to Devon, that, coming into my drawing-room late in the afternoon, I found him fast asleep on a sofa. I knew that he napped a little while after lunch, but now he was in a deep slumber and did not awake until Charlotte came to rouse him. That incident made me feel more troubled about his health than I had been before.

Despite his illness, he was full of concern for me when, during a visit to another country house, I became acutely distressed by bronchial trouble. It was on such occasions as this that one realised vividly and fully the beauty of his rich and generous nature, how completely he could forget his own distress in contemplating other people's. His stay in Devon did, I like to think, divert his mind from his illness, and we found him a good companion. But then I had always found him a good companion.

He still wore his old panache, and was still capable of larking. Coming into his sitting-room one morning, I found him making his will. 'I'm always making it,' he said. 'People die on me, and I have to have the whole thing redrawn. You know, I used to feel sorry when I heard of the death of an old friend, but now I take a fatuous pride in survival. "What!" I say, "old so-and-so, younger than I am, is down and I'm still up!" ' And then he went off into one of his comic huddles of laughter.

It was this geniality which made me all the more disturbed when I saw signs of irritability in him, even with Charlotte, to whom he constantly displayed a gracious courtesy. In all the years I had known him, I had never seen him in a bad temper. He could speak with indignation and vehemence, and his writing is full of strong and extravagant language, but he remained, even in the sharpest discussion, completely in control of himself, and never failed in courtesy to his opponents, although they sometimes failed in courtesy to him.

186

Despite the benefit he had derived from his stay in Sidmouth, his illness continued and worsened. The general belief that his health was good, a belief which he encouraged people to hold in the hope that hearing how healthy he was on vegetarian diet, they would abandon their carnivorous habits and become graminivorous, too, was far from the fact.

Toward the end of May 1938, Charlotte, who was becoming gravely alarmed, insisted on a consultation with Mr Geoffrey Evans, a distinguished doctor to whom she took a great liking. The report was very disturbing. There was no organic disease, but there was 'most alarming anaemia', which could scarcely be regarded as a tribute to a vegetarian diet. The patient must 'do nothing, and see no one for a week or ten days at least'. We had been invited to lunch in the period in which seclusion was required, but of course we cried off. Charlotte, however, wrote to my wife that G.B.S. had said, 'I'd like to have them for lunch. St John will talk for us both.' By the time we got to London, however, he was much worse, and so we did not see him.

His cure included a course of liver injections, a treatment which caused him much mental agitation, for liver injections obviously involved the slaughter of animals. . . .

Charlotte settled that problem. If liver injections were essential to his recovery, then he should have them, no matter what his principles might be. And he had them. She would herself have forced them into him if he had remained obstinate. Charlotte did not often display her fighting mood, but when she did, submission was the result of it. She fought a good fight. She always fought well when her blood was up, and nothing fetched it up so quickly and ferociously as the threat of injury of any sort to G.B.S.

Only once during his grave illness did she lose her equanimity. That was when, in the midst of her troubles, there was a threat of billeting twenty-five children on her. 'Then I spoke up,' she wrote to my wife. The thought of dumping so many children on a man and woman who were well over eighty years of age, the man suffering from pernicious anaemia, could have occurred only to an unimaginative bureaucrat, a fact which, when he was well enough to stand it, I rubbed into G.B.S. Had the state he desired been established then, those twenty-five children would almost certainly have been billeted on Charlotte, even if he had been at his last gasp.

In June, responding admirably to his injections, he began to mend, though he was still far from well and he tired easily. 'I am really in good spirits,' Charlotte wrote to my wife in the middle of the month. 'I have suffered such agonies of late, seeing him get weaker and weaker and whiter and whiter—and seeing no way out. Now I have help, and most efficient help.' Geoffrey Evans, to whom she directed me when a little later I, too, was gravely ill, and Dr Hewsman and a pathologist, Cuthbert Dukes, one of a brilliant band of brothers, who include Ashley, the dramatist, were the help.

By the middle of July, G.B.S., who had now been removed from London to Ayot St Lawrence, was considerably better, though still weak and easily tired. It may be said here that he never fully recovered his strength after this illness, though he recovered more than any of his friends believed he would. The doctors had promised that he would be fit to go to the theatre by the end of August, and he was, but the old flare had gone. Pernicious anaemia on top of eighty-two years takes the stuffing out of the most vital of men. It happened that about this time, I published in *The Observer* a long review of Frank Harris's *Oscar Wilde*, in which I drew comparisons between Wilde, Harris and G.B.S. On the morning after the first part of it appeared, I received a letter from Charlotte, who had an intense dislike of Harris because of his revelations of his sex life in his autobiography:

'Dear, dearest St John, *thank you*, THANK YOU, THANK YOU! That's a splendid article, and has sent my spirits up by leaps and bounds. We've had a dreadful time. Poor G.B.S. just returned from death's door, trying to get peace here—and messenger boys arriving in motor cars, telegrams six pages long, telephone unceasing and Mr K. arriving without warning at 8.30 at night. G.B.S. forced to write letter after letter when he could hardly hold the pen! You can realise how grateful I am to you who *understand*.

'It will be all right now. G.B.S. is really getting better by leaps and bounds—the way he has stood all this fuss. I hope we will meet soon now. I am so rejoiced you are better. Our loves to you both,
Yours C. F. Shaw.'

At the end of October, he went to Droitwich, and was 'really quite well again', according to Charlotte, who added, that 'the doctors are amazed at him.'

In that year, 1938, I was ill too, and in addition had to have an operation to my right eye. The retina had become detached. This, I was told, was another result of my war wounds, but whether it was or not I cannot tell. The effect of the illness and the operations—I had two, but both were unsuccessful, and I am blind in my right eye —was that I saw less of G.B.S. and Charlotte than I had seen for a long while; and by the time I was fit for company, the Second World War had begun. Charlotte herself, now that her anxiety about G.B.S. was ended, suddenly collapsed. 'I have been in rather low water lately,' she wrote in April 1939, 'a long story, not worth telling, and I hope soon now I shall be perfectly well. G.B.S. is marvellous. . . . Everyone's first exclamation is, "How well he's looking".'

In April 1940, she wrote a sad letter to my wife. 'Nora dear, I was so delighted to get your letter this morning. We think of you both and speak of you *often*. But we have tumbled over into real old age and got into a dreadful groove and have neither strength of body or mind to get out of it. First, G.B.S. was very ill with pernicious anaemia. I think you know about that'—her memory was failing fast then—'and when he got well I went down. The doctors said it was the shocks I got with him. I had a "nervous breakdown". What that is I cannot tell you, but that is what I have got. I was fearfully bad. That was about a year ago. I was an invalid all the winter and am just beginning to trot about now. We still do the omnibus round we always used to do: up to London by car on Wednesdays and down again to Ayot on Saturdays. You will have heard about King Charles' Golden Days,[1] I expect—the play G.B.S. did for last year's Malvern Festival. I got a great deal of joy out of it, for I like it extremely. . . . I am so thankful St John is well. A horrid gossipy woman told me last week he was "very ill" and I hated her and was sure it wasn't true. . . . He really must manage to come to see us. At our age our friends must not foresake us.'

The last letter we had from her was in July. 'We would so greatly like to see you again. . . . I am better and can manage something like an ordinary life—crawling about!'

The rest of her time was full of pain. This good and kind woman, whose love and devotion for her husband was unbounded, deserved a quieter and happier end than fate awarded her. She developed *osteitis deformans*, and was tormented by it. The single pleasure she enjoyed during her last years was to hear G.B.S. playing music for her. He would arrange his organ at the foot of the stairs so that she could hear it as she lay in her room, and sometimes he sang to her; and always she was pleased by what she heard. Sir Barry Jackson, who was their close friend, went to see them one evening, when they were at Whitehall Court, and found them sitting side by side on a sofa, while he turned over the pages of a book of pictures for her.

In a letter written about a year before her death, he tells me, 'We keep up our affectionate interest in you and Leonora; but we are too old to presume on our ancient attractions. Charlotte's

[1] It was the last play by him she saw performed.

575

osteitis deformans is incurable: she is often in pain, and moves about very slowly and not far. I was vetted lately and pronounced sound; but that means only that when I go I shall go all at once. We are both deaf; and the number of familiar names that we cannot remember increases: in short, we are considerably dotty. I have resigned everything, committees, chairmanships, etc., and work on my book as hard as I can lest I should not live to finish it. I seldom go outside the curtillage, and for exercise just saw firewood for an hour or less in the garden. I can still write a bit; but that is all. Unlike Ibsen I can still remember the alphabet. . . . Altogether we have reason to feel very grateful to you for not dropping our acquaintance. Forgive senile garrulousness, Ever Yours, G. Bernard Shaw.'

The journeys to Whitehall Court were still made as long as Charlotte could travel, but her memory had almost faded away, and sometimes in the flat, imagining that she was at Ayot St Lawrence, she would ask G.B.S. to carry her upstairs to her room. Towards the end, her mind failed. On September 12, 1943, she died at Whitehall Court. Her age was eighty-six.

Her death knocked down all the barriers which kept G.B.S.'s emotions under strict control, and he was overwhelmed with sorrow. And, as was customary with him, he moved from one form of emotion to another with such rapidity that those of his friends who did not fully perceive how he strove to keep his deeper feelings dark, imagined that he was hysterical or callous when, after shedding tears, an act of which he was supposed to be incapable, he would begin to sing almost hilariously. This was the grief which is abandoned. His life after Charlotte's death was empty. He missed her far more than he had ever imagined he could miss anybody; and he gradually sank into a quietness at Ayot St Lawrence with his memories of her to sustain him through the solitude that was to last for seven years.

A vast number of letters and messages of condolence were sent to him, far too numerous for an old man to answer; and so he published a general reply in the Personal Column of *The Times:*

'Mr Bernard Shaw has received such a prodigious mass of letters on the occasion of his wife's death that, though he has read and values them all, any attempt to acknowledge them individually is beyond his powers. He therefore begs his friends and hers to be content with this omnibus reply, and he assures them that a very happy ending to a very long life has left him awaiting his own in perfect serenity.'

She was cremated at Golders Green, and G.B.S. was accompanied to the crematorium by Lady Astor and his secretary, Miss Patch. There was no religious service. The organ played Elgar's *We are the Music Makers* and Verdi's *Libera Me* from the Requiem.

During the cremation, Handel's *Largo* was played, followed by *I Know That My Redeemer Liveth*, and as the end of the anthem approached, G.B.S. stretched out his hands and sang the words softly to himself. He had lost his best comrade. She had wished her ashes to be scattered on the Three Rock Mountain outside Dublin, but war-time conditions made this impossible. They were kept, and when in due course G.B.S. himself died and was cremated, hers and his were mingled and scattered in the garden at Ayot St Lawrence where he and she had lived so long.

187

Her will, which was dated September 2, 1937, began by stating her desire that she should be cremated and her ashes scattered on Irish ground, that no flowers should 'be sacrificed' for her and 'no black clothes worn' and 'no memorial service held at' her 'funeral'. It devised £154,967. She made a number of bequests which were free of all duties, including one of £1,000 to 'Sidney James Lord Passfield', and several to her servants. 'To my gardener Harry Batchelor Higgs the sum of One Hundred and fifty pounds and to his Wife Clara the sum of One hundred and fifty pounds, but if either of them shall die before the date of payment the legacy of the one so dying shall be payable to the survivor.'[1] She left a similar legacy to her chauffeur, George Frederick Day and his wife, and an annuity of £52 each to her housemaid, Emma Hodgman, and her sister, Kate, the parlourmaid, which was increased by an annuity of an equal amount in G.B.S.'s will, and she left an annuity of £156 to her housekeeper, Margaret Bilton, which was increased under G.B.S.'s will by a further annuity of the same amount. Should Mrs Bilton predecease her, an annuity of £104 was to be provided for her daughter, Alice, this annuity being increased by G.B.S. to £260.

The remainder of her estate was to form a Trust Fund, out of which two bequests were to be fulfilled: a sum of £20,000 was to be raised for the benefit of her niece, Cecily Charlotte Colthurst, who was to receive the income from it during her life. On her death, the interest was to be paid to Mrs Colthurst's daughters, Mary Penelope Hamilton and Shournagh Dorothy Combe. The rest of the income from the Trust was to be paid 'to my husband if he shall survive me during his life.'

When all these bequests had been settled or the beneficiaries of

[1] This bequest was reinforced by one made by G.B.S. of an annuity of £156. G.B.S., who had erected a monument to Mrs Higgs, arranged that this monument should be completed when Higgs died by the addition of the date of his death, the cost to be paid out of his estate.

incomes from interest on the Trust Fund had died, then the revenue was to be devoted to a purpose which seemed important to Charlotte, and was a very sensible arrangement. But it brought odium on her grave, cast there chiefly by sour-minded Irish-American Roman Catholic priests who foamed at the mouth after their fashion when the terms of the bequest were announced.

It will be best to state the terms of the bequest as they appear in the Will:

19 (i) 'WHEREAS:

'(*a*) I am desirous of promoting and encouraging in Ireland the bringing of the masterpieces of fine art within the reach of the Irish people of all classes so that they may have increased opportunity of studying such masterpieces and of acquiring a fuller and wider knowledge thereof, and

'(*b*) In the course of a long life I have had many opportunities of observing the extent to which the most highly instructed and capable persons have their efficiency defeated and their influence limited for want of any organised instruction and training for the personal contacts whether with individuals or popular audiences without which their knowledge is incommunicable (except through books) and how the authority which their abilities should give them is made derisory by their awkward manners and how their employment in positions for which they have valuable qualifications is made socially impossible by vulgarities of speech and other defects as easily corrigible by teaching and training as simple illiteracy and whereas my experience and observation have convinced me that the lack of such training produces not only much social friction but grave pathological results which seem quite unconnected with it and that social intercourse is a fine art with a technique which everybody can and should acquire

(ii) 'Now with a view to furthering and carrying out the objects which I have at heart I HEREBY DECLARE that the Irish Bank shall stand possessed of the ultimate Trust Fund as and when so transferred to and vested in the Irish Bank UPON THE TRUSTS and with and subject to the powers and provisions following that is to say:'

And here she sets out the objects on which she wishes the Irish Bank, which was to possess absolute discretion in the matter, to expend the revenue from her Fund.

Grants were to be made to public bodies to enable them to bring 'the masterpieces of fine art within the reach of the people of Ireland of all classes in their own country'; and for the teaching, promotion and encouragement in Ireland of self control, elocution, oratory, deportment, the arts of personal contact, of social intercourse, and the other arts of public, private, professional and business life; the establishment and endowment 'of any educational institution or any Chair or Readership in any University College or Educational

Institution now existing or coming into existence for the purpose of giving instruction in or promoting the study by the general public of the subjects mentioned in Clause 19.'

The expression 'masterpieces of fine art' was declared to mean and include 'works of the highest class in the fields of orchestral and classical music painting sculpture fine printing and literature produced or originating not in any one Country exclusively but in any Country in the world and by or among people in any age period or date whether ancient or modern.'

188

One may criticise this will on several grounds. It was, surely, a strange thing that Charlotte should limit the territory to which her bequest was to apply 'to the existing Irish Free State and any other future extension of it that may take place'; unless, of course, she thought that Ulstermen were in no need of such education: in which case, of course, she was sound. The fortune came to her through her mother, whose family was English, and it was odd of her to bequeath it to Eire, a country in which she never showed any wish to live. But she had a right to make that limitation if it seemed fitting to her, and it is nobody's business to complain of it. It may be said, too, that some of the purposes on which she wished the income of her Trust to be expended are not achievable and might be undesirable if they were. How are an emotional people to be taught 'self control'? What does 'self control' mean? No one knows by what alchemy an excitable Celt can be changed into a phlegmatic Saxon, and few people are willing to believe that the change should be made. Can we believe that the world would be better than it is if every Italian were drilled into the frozen calm of a Finn?

But these objections remembered, what is wrong with Charlotte's will? Who does not know beyond a shadow of a doubt how many men of good quality have been disabled in public life by uncouth manners? Is it not one of the chief blessings of a University life that it enables young men and women to rub off their awkward angles and become at ease in the world? Even in Universities, at all events in former times, the poor scholar was at a serious disadvantage because he could not mingle with his richer fellows owing to his straitened means.

The whole intention of Charlotte's will was wise, even if some of its details were impractical, and it was sad to see this kindly, generous-minded good woman grossly insulted soon after her death by Irish-American celibates who howled like infuriated and demented banshees at the 'insult' she had offered Ireland. G.B.S. came in for some of their back-street wit. Charlotte, they said, could only have conceived the thought that high-souled Eireans were in need of civilising influences through her life with him. The poor, uncouth Dublin jackeen she had married, had to be taught how to behave himself, and the deluded Charlotte, though she herself was partly Irish and was born in Ireland, could not rid her mind of the belief that all Irishmen resembled her husband. But no one who had ever spent five minutes in his company could have believed that he was anything else than a proud Irish Protestant gentleman whose manners, at once natural and cultivated, were as fine as any man's, and better than most.

The Irish-American celibates, however, were less numerous than the Eireans who promptly wrote to G.B.S. to ask if they could have something on account of their share of the spoil.

A codicil to the will, made on November 27, 1940, bequeathed 'the letters which were written to me by Colonel T. E. Lawrence and which are at present in safe custody at the British Museum to the British Museum absolutely.' It also included bequests to two servants: Robert Studman, at Whitehall Court, who received £100, and Maggie Cashin, Charlotte's maid at Ayot St Lawrence, now married, who received £50.

This section may fitly be ended by a passage from a letter, dated July 27, 1944, addressed to 'my dear St John and Leonora', in which G.B.S., writing from Ayot St Lawrence, sums up the situation:

> 'I live a bachelor's life here, never going to London except when I must, arranging Charlotte's affairs and my own affairs, and getting rid of as much of them as possible, which means getting rid of as much of my property as possible. Charlotte left £150,000 to me for my life. It has not enriched me by a single farthing; and I have given £20,000 of it to her niece, and paid more than £50,000 in death duties and other expenses, in addition to the war taxation, which is enormous. All of which does not trouble me in the least, though it greatly increases the proportion of business to the literary work I have on hand. Other men retire long before they approach 80: I cannot retire and have more and more to do the nearer I approach 90. I am giving away my Irish property to the nation which doesn't know how to take it. I have had to devise a way, and am now trying to convince Eire that it is the right way. I wish the property were in Belfast instead of Carlow: the Protestant boys would grab it fast enough.

> 'I make dozens of blunders every day, and am a bit groggy on my legs through giddiness; but I keep up a stage effect of being exceptionally ablebodied and ableminded for my age. But it is only acting. Charlotte's complaint was "You're always acting".'

He was, but he always gave a good performance.

189

G.B.S.'s life was now almost entirely withdrawn from the world in which he had flourished with so much vigour and vivacity and gay abundance of mind and experience. All his contemporaries, with the exception of Edward Pease, were dead. Even some of his immediate juniors with whom he had argued and debated, Gilbert Chesterton and H. G. Wells, were dead, too. Only Hilaire Belloc, among these juniors, survived him.

In 1942, Sidney, Lord Passfield, was stricken beyond hope of recovery by a severe stroke, though he lived longer than any of his friends believed he would. He outlived Beatrice, who died on April 30, 1943. She was eighty-five. Her mind had been haunted by the fear that she would die before he did. In August 1922, they had both been seriously ill: he had had a severe nervous breakdown, she had had equally severe colitis. One day, during the previous winter, while walking up a hill in her company, he had suddenly become purple in the face and so faint that she had to lay him on the ground. He was unconscious for several minutes.

This breakdown began with an attack of vertigo in the night, followed by dizziness. The local doctor who examined him, found every organ healthy. There was no blood pressure. His arteries, for a man of his age, were 'very young'. But the dizziness and weakness and uncertainty of walking 'continued and even got worse, and the doctor became seriously concerned'. A rest of four months' abstention from all work was ordered.

'What troubles me,' Beatrice wrote in her diary on August 9, 1922, 'is not my own health:

'I don't believe my life is a good one, and I don't want to drift into a long senility. But what would Sidney do without me if he became an invalid . . .? There is no one to look after him and he is so absurdly dependent on me. However, the Lord will provide. We have had a good life together: we leave finished work; and the one who is left behind for a few years more life, will have, as consolation, the memory of a perfect marriage. What more can a human being expect or demand? One of us *must* go before the other. It is for the one who is left to rise to the height of the gratitude due for our superlative good fortune.'

It was she who went first; he survived in total dependence on attendants.

Sydney, Lord Olivier, died on February 15, 1943. He was eighty-four. H. G. Wells died on August 13, 1946. Webb lingered on, no longer fit for any work, until October 13, 1947. His age was eighty-eight. These deaths alone must have given G.B.S. a deep sense of desolation. But they were not the only deaths among his contemporaries and his near contemporaries that helped to sadden him. The beloved Archer had died in 1924; and Gilbert Chesterton, no less beloved, had died in 1936. H. G. Wells, expecting to outlive him, has predeceased him by four years: in 1946, just under eighty. There was none of the Old Gang of the Fabian Society left, except Pease and himself, and Pease lived at Limpsfield in Surrey, a long way from Ayot St Lawrence in Hertfordshire; too far for old men approaching their nineties to drop in or make visits.

He had lived too long, as he himself often declared. The demand for great increase of life made in *Back to Methuselah* now sounded hollow. It was not long life that Jesus desired: it was abundant life; and G.B.S. had had abundance. The Labour Party, which he, as much as any man, had helped to create, had obliterated the Liberals, who, bouncing into overwhelming power with a Cabinet of all the talents in 1906, found themselves torn in pieces by their most popular leader, Lloyd George, and reduced to such a state of impotence in the constituencies that the monotonous iteration of their defeat in General Elections became comic: 'the Liberal candidate forfeits his deposit'.

The Labourites were once more in power, real power this time, and an inconspicuous member of the Fabian Nursery, Clement Attlee, was Prime Minister. If either of the Webbs was aware of Attlee's existence at the end of the First World War, they successfully concealed their knowledge. There is not a single reference to him in Mrs Webb's published diaries, though the latest of them carries her records up to 1924.

It should have been satisfying to G.B.S. that he had seen the fruit of his political labour gathered and stored, apart from his personal renown as a dramatist; but it was not. The Labour Party, he declared with bitterness, was an oligarchy of Trade Unionists who were no better, if no worse, than an oligarchy of Victorian industrialists or eighteenth-century landlords. The Fabian argument that if workmen were better paid and had more leisure, they would not only do finer work with greater heart, but would use their leisure to increase their culture, had proved delusive. Instead of better work, there was worse work. There was actually a decline in the intellectual quality of the proletariat, whose most absorbing interest remained the winner of the two-thirty! The man in the street, Chesterton wisely said, was less interested in the equality of man than he was in the inequality of horses.

So far were they from an increase of higher and finer thought, that there was a grave decline in common honesty, a steep decline in consideration for the rest of the community when an advantage could be snatched. Lightning strikes were deliberately arranged so that they might inflict the greatest hardship on the whole community in the hope of provoking the crowd to such exasperation that the employers would be compelled to yield to the workers' claims. The whole apparatus of collective bargaining was upset by unruly proletarians who repudiated agreements made by their leaders almost whimsically, though similar behaviour, had it been displayed by their employers, would have provoked vast quantities of stinking breath from Labour orators at every street corner in the country.

Soon after Charlotte's death, G.B.S. suffered a further loss in the retirement of two devoted servants: Clara Rebecca Higgs, his cook-housekeeper, and her husband, Harry Batchelor Higgs, his gardener. They were both septuagenarians, and had long wished to retire, but, in deference to Charlotte, who was greatly attached to them, they had consented to stay with her until after her death, though Mrs Higgs herself was in ill-health. She was succeeded by Mrs Alice Laden, who continued to be his cook-housekeeper until his death, and, at the request of the National Trust, acted as custodian of Ayot St Lawrence for some months after his death. The Higgs, handsomely pensioned, retired to Windlesham, near Camberley in Surrey, where, on August 4, 1948, Mrs Higgs died.

The Shaws had the rare ability of winning the liking and deep regard of their servants, to whom G.B.S. behaved with the same courtesy and consideration that he would have shown to any man or woman of any rank. None of them left their employment, except to marry or retire because they were too old to continue in service. Miss Patch, in her book, *Thirty Years with G.B.S.*, states that their chauffeur, Frederick Day, 'normally not a talkative man, once remarked to' her 'that he "would do anything for Mr Shaw"', and he was devoted to Charlotte, too.'

When Mrs Higgs died, G.B.S. raised a memorial stone to her in the churchyard at Windlesham; and he took as much trouble over its design and erection as if it were a tribute to his most intimate and dearest friend. He commissioned Mr John Easthaugh, sculptor and stonemason, at Windlesham, to make the memorial, and Mr Easthaugh has allowed me to read their correspondence. Always particular about payment, G.B.S. asked Mr Easthaugh if he 'would like the money in advance as I am 92 and may not live long'.

The sculptor felt perturbed when he found that G.B.S. had ended a sentence in the inscription with a preposition, and, in his dismay, suggested that instead of carving 'thereby setting him free to do the work he was fitted for', he should carve 'free to do the work for which he was fitted'. He received a postcard in reply:

> 'Stick to my text; it will save cutting five letters. I never use these "for whiches" and "and whiches". . . . "he was fitted for" is genuine vernacular English "for which he was fitted" is schoolmaster's bad English.'

So the stone was carved in accordance with G.B.S.'s wishes.

190

In 1944, G.B.S. published another political work, clumsily entitled *Everybody's Political What's What?* on which he had been engaged for almost the whole period of the Second World War. In this work, as in his prefaces to his plays and *The Intelligent Woman's Guide to Socialism*, he makes no attempt to be philosophically impartial: he is an ardent advocate of a cause.

When, for example, at the outset of the book, G.B.S. compares what he calls the Old School Ties with the German and Italian dictators to the disadvantage of the Old School Ties, he overlooks the fundamental fact that the Old School Ties defeated the dictators. 'Democracy', he says at the beginning of his fifth chapter, 'means the organisation of society for the benefit and at the expense of everybody indiscriminately and not for the benefit of a privileged class,' and he goes on to say that 'a nearly desperate difficulty in the way of its realisation is the delusion that the method of securing it is to give votes to everybody which is the one certain method of defeating it. Adult suffrage kills it dead.'

But how can we hope to have a well-governed country unless there is a residuary wisdom in its people which will enable them to keep their heads in times when heads seem certain to be lost? Countries which are ruled by exuberant persons, convinced that God tells them what to do, lack the stability of countries whose governments depend on an adult suffrage based on the right of the elector to choose between one set of politicians and another.

The Russian system of adult suffrage is a complete negation of the principle of democracy, since it deprives the electors of the first condition of freedom, which is the right to choose, and compels them to maintain the corps of commissars who are in power and cannot be displaced, except by successful revolution. The Russian electors are presented with a catalogue of candidates, all of whom support the people in power. No other candidates can be nominated. The right to choose is restricted to the choice of one of these government-chosen candidates! . . . This, apparently, was the electoral system G.B.S. liked. Its advantage to the people in power is obvious. They can remain in office for the whole of their lives, provided they do nothing to annoy their leader.

We shall delude ourselves if we suppose that this system of government is repulsive to all our countrymen, or that only an Irishman could approve of it. Advanced thinkers, as they are strangely called, have not concealed their belief that freedom is a questionable matter, and that most of us would be better with less of it. Even that ardent

Liberal, John A. Hobson, in a small book, entitled *Democracy*, tells his readers that:

> 'A democratic State will recognise "a right to work" or, alternatively a "right to subsistence", on the part of all its members, but not a right to work in any occupation or on any terms each member chooses. As soon as it is recognised that the value of all work is determined by the needs and well-being of society, it becomes evident that a worker has no longer full liberty to choose his work or to insist upon the particular conditions under which he does it. Over his "right to work" must be set the right of society that he be set to do the work which he can do in the best interest of society.'

That is a receipt for slavery. Hobson, who, like G.B.S. and all Left Wing thinkers, denied that workmen had any right to strike and would have had society so arranged that all strikes would be illegal, was asserting a belief about life which is more explicitly described in a work, entitled *Problems of a Socialist Government*, published by Victor Gollancz in 1933. The contributors to this symposium included Sir Stafford Cripps, Mr Attlee, and Mr G. D. H. Cole, each of whom stages his extraordinary opinions and political desires with admirable candour.

Cripps asserted that a Socialist Government must exact the right to prolong its period of power 'for a further term without an election', an exaction which would give it the right, if it chose to take it, to continue in power for as long as it liked; which is practically the position in Russia.

Any attempt to dispute the authority of the Socialist Government would, according to Cripps, be 'quelled by force': a strange doctrine to be held by a man who was a pacifist. The power of the Courts to challenge the right of any particular Parliament to change the entire character of the constitution 'must be taken from the Courts, and the sole right to challenge such orders must rest with Parliament', which will, as we have noted, previously have given itself the right to remain in power as long as it pleases without an election.

Mr G. D. H. Cole is less reticent on this subject than Cripps. He boldly proposes that the country shall be divided into Regional Development Councils, and that these bodies shall be 'dominated by Socialists', and that Socialists shall be 'in the key positions among their staffs of officials'.

> 'It will be best, as soon as Parliament has conferred on the Government the necessary emergency power, for it to meet only as often as it is needed for some clearly practical purpose, leaving the Socialist administrators to carry on with the minimum of day-to-day interference. There will be no time for superfluous debating while we are busy building the Socialist commonwealth,'

which is a pretentious name for a state of slavery.

Cole, whose spiritual father was Simon Legree, insists throughout his remarkably frank confession of faith, that the Socialist government shall be arbitrary, and that no person known to dissent from Socialism shall be employed in any position of power anywhere in the community. All industries will be controlled by 'managing boards consisting each of a few men of undoubted drive and technical competence, combined with Socialist conviction'.

Mr Attlee is not less harsh. He longs for Commissioners, or, as the Russians would call them, Commissars. He does not, indeed, disguise his admiration for the Russians in this respect:

'Thus I conceive the district commissioner as something more than a public servant. He is the local energiser and interpreter of the will of the Government. He is not impartial. He is a Socialist, and therefore in touch with the Socialists in the region, who are his colleagues in the campaign. It may be said that this is rather like the Russian plan of commissars and Communist Party members. I am not afraid of the comparison!'

Among the frankest of the Socialist commentators on a collectivised society was the late Lord Allen of Hurtwood who, in his book, *Britain's Political Future*, tells his readers that:

'Whatever may be their ultimate intentions, the first generations of men who accept economic equality cannot expect to retain much personal liberty. Socialists who believe that the system of private profit-making must be eliminated, and an equalitarian society established, in order that poverty may be abolished, cannot deny that this new form of society would require every citizen to take his orders from a vast network of authorities: local, national and industrial. We must acknowledge frankly that this might involve a diminution of personal liberty.'

The word *might* in the final sentence ought to be *will*. Lord Allen, almost sadly, adds that:

'All men may, it is true, be equal, but none are likely to be free, except, perhaps, the politicians who will have been entrusted with the task of government. Whether it will be possible for our future governors in such an elaborately-planned equalitarian society to keep their hands off liberty of thought and expression, I do not know.'[1]

This was the state that satisfied G.B.S. in theory, for I have not the slightest doubt that if he had had the misfortune to live in such a society, he would have been the first rebel to be hanged or shot.

He tells us on one page that the congenital criminal 'should be pitied and painlessly killed without malice as a mad dog is killed',

---

[1] Page 130.

and is justifiably cross with the 'half thinkers' who blither about reforming him when it should be plain to them that it is impossible to reform a *congenital* criminal; and then, on another page, hopes that Adolf Hitler will escape the fury of the Germans he has tormented and 'enjoy a comfortable retirement in Ireland or some neutral country, as Louis Napoleon did at Chislehurst and the Kaiser at Doorn'.

But why was this 'mad dog' to be thus indulged? Are we to put a congenital criminal who has murdered one or two people to death, and permit a congenital criminal who is responsible for the persecution and brutal murder of a multitude of his own countrymen, apart from the suffering and death he has caused in other nations, to escape with no more censure or punishment than a wagged finger, while he reclines comfortably in a South American villa, living on a substantial pension provided either by the people he has tortured or by the people who have had to fight him to save themselves from the slavery he imposed upon his own race?

G.B.S. says he cannot endure to see 'animals performing unnatural tricks at the command of trainers . . . whom I should shoot at sight if I could be sure of a verdict of justifiable homicide', forgetting that any trick or task that an animal performs for the benefit of man is unnatural. A horse does not 'naturally' draw a cart or carry people on its back. One of the most unnatural organisations in the world is a farm which, if it were left to Nature, would soon become a jungle. The farmer spends his life forcing land into shapes it abhors and compelling it to fulfil, not its own purpose, but his.

Hanging, which is considered by many responsible people to be the most merciful and least barbarous form of execution, is to be abolished; and the murderer is to be poisoned without warning on the ground that this is a humane form of execution. But is it? Will not the condemned man look with suspicion on every meal he eats and every drink he sips before he receives the fatal dose? Execution cannot be made tolerable to the condemned, nor is there any reason why it should.

Karl Marx, he says with apparent approval, asserted that British prisons were the cruellest in the world. How did Marx know? He had never been inside a British prison, nor was he acquainted with all the world's prisons. Yet G.B.S. accepts Marx's statement as if it had been personally delivered by the Holy Ghost.

His credulity was surprising. William Archer had long been familiar with it, and, indeed, reproached him with it in a letter dated June 12, 1923.[1] 'The trouble with you', he wrote, 'is that you are incurably credulous. Someone comes along and tells you that wool

[1] See *William Archer*. By Lt-Colonel C. Archer, p. 391.

is the only wear; and instantly you go in for woollen boots, which lead, in due course, to a course of crutches. . . .'

How credulous or obstinate in holding an absurd opinion he could be will appear from an incident in which I was involved. There is an old story of a verger in Westminster Abbey feeling shocked when he found a worshipper at prayer. The sex and even the nationality of the worshipper varies in the several variations of the tale. In G.B.S.'s version, which appeared originally in his preface to *Three Plays by Brieux*—Charlotte had translated one of them—and was republished in *Prefaces by Bernard Shaw* in 1934, the cause of the verger's distress was a Frenchman, 'who, in Westminster Abbey, knelt down to pray:

> 'The verger, who had never seen such a thing happen before, promptly handed him over to the police and charged him with "brawling". Fortunately, the magistrate had compassion on the foreigner's ignorance; and even went to the length of asking why he should not be allowed to pray in the church. The reply of the verger was simple and obvious. "If I allowed that," he said, "we should have people praying all over the place." And to this day the rule in Westminster Abbey is that you may stroll about and look at the monuments, but you must not on any account pray.'

This tale, which I took to be one of his jokes, seemed to me to be out of place in the serious argument he was conducting in his preface, and I teased him about it in *The Observer*, where I reviewed the *Prefaces* in one of my weekly articles.

I was amazed to receive a long letter, dated August 23, 1934, in which he was obviously very angry with me. He first rebuked me for deriding him because of a denunciation he had made of habits which he treated as exclusively English when they were universal, and then chided me for doubting his story of the verger in Westminster Abbey:

> 'You imply that I have invented a ridiculous story about a verger "admonishing" a foreigner. . . . If you care to hunt up the newspaper evidence you will find that a pious Frenchman who knelt down to pray in Westminster Abbey was not admonished by the scandalised verger, but there and then handed over to the police and charged at the Westminster Police Court with brawling. . . . The magistrate discharged the foreigner with a caution. The foreigner's reflections on the English character were not reported.'

As he did not give the date of the alleged incident, I did not propose to spend the rest of my life in the British Museum searching files of newspapers for a report which I felt certain had never appeared about an incident which had never occurred; but I was a little shaken by his evident belief in the truth of his tale and by the detail with which it seemed to be supported. So I wrote to the then Dean to enquire about it. Neither he nor any person connected with the Abbey had ever heard of it, and there certainly was no rule forbidding any person to pray there privately: a piece of news I did not need to be told.

Later on, when my friend, Canon Charles Smyth, became Rector of St Margaret's, Westminster, and a member of the Abbey Chapter, I told him the story, but he, too, was ignorant of it and derisive of G.B.S.'s credulity. It was not until several years later, that I came on the origin of the story, but by that time, G.B.S. was dead.

In one of the numerous volumes of Mr Ivo Currall's Shaviana, I found what I wanted in, of all places, the pages of *The Freethinker*, where, in two issues, dated February 28 and March 7, 1943, Mr W. Kent, reviewing Mr Hesketh Pearson's book on G.B.S., derided the 'absurd story' and gave an earlier version of it which he believed to be the original version. While reading a work, entitled *Safe Studies*, by the Hon. Lionel Tollemache and his wife, Kent had come across the following passage on page 379:

> 'The Dean (Stanley) told a story about Westminster Abbey which tends to show that this house of prayer used to be regarded, if not as a den of thieves, at least as a monopoly of beadles. Not long before his appointment, a lady, contrary to the Protestant fashion, knelt down in sacred edifice to say her private prayers. A veteran beadle, shocked by the innovation, interrupted her devotions; he told her that if such irregularity were permitted, there would be no end to it: she must join the party of sightseers or else leave the Abbey.'

This, of course, is the sort of ribald story that canons are liable to tell in the privacy of a Chapter where no one is expected to believe it. The fact probably is that the lady had knelt down in a part of the Abbey where she blocked a passage, and that the verger asked her to say her prayers in a less inconvenient spot. Dean Stanley obviously told the story as a piece of amusing dinner-table conversation and without the slightest idea that anybody would accept it literally. He would have been amazed and probably disturbed if he had known in what shape it would be when G.B.S. had finished with it. The daunting fact about it is not that G.B.S. had made this extraordinary version of it, but that he believed it to be true. He could not deceive others, but he deceived himself.

He tells his readers on page 149, that civilisation cannot be maintained by 'everybody doing what everybody else does', and reminds them of the historic fact that where nobody is allowed to advocate and initiate changes, 'civilisation will fossilise and perish.' Without law and order, convention and etiquet (his spelling) 'there can be no civilisation; yet when these are established there must be privilege for sedition, blasphemy, heresy, eccentricity, innovation, variety and change, or civilisation will crash again by failing to adapt itself to scientific discovery and mental growth.'

'Governments have to persecute and tolerate simultaneously: they have to determine continually what and when to persecute and what and when to tolerate. They must never make either persecution or toleration a principle. British mistrust of principle and logic is rooted in the wisdom of this rule.'

How shall we settle the boundary between what is tolerable and what is intolerable in a state? Is there any form of government that the wit of man has yet devised which will ensure a Cabinet which is wise enough to decide what the people shall believe, what they shall disbelieve? If the community is to be ruled by a collection of self-appointed and arbitrary commissars instead of a haphazard group of popularly elected members of parliament chosen by men and women over the age of twenty-one, how can we ensure that toleration of change which G.B.S. agrees is essential to the progress of mankind, assuming, that is to say, that there is any progress?

Perhaps the most saddening part of *Everybodys' Political What's What?* is to be found in a passage on page 262 where he confesses that The Fabian Society was a failure. Payment of members of parliament, he says, made 'the House of Commons more and more an alms-house for retired Trade Union secretaries who called themselves Socialists only when they were told to, without knowing what the word meant:

'The supposed conversion of Britain to constitutional Socialism by the Fabian Society made even less change than the conversion of the Roman Empire to Christianity by Constantine. The triumph was not to the Fabian Society but to the dead Disraeli, who, as Conservative leader, had taken the first serious step in the enfranchisement of the proletariat, then called the working class, because in his early days as a revolutionist to whom the House of Commons refused a hearing . . . he had learnt that the bulwarks of Conservatism were not in frivolous Mayfair but in poverty-stricken Mile End. The more the franchise was extended the more hopeless the situation became, until at last, when complete adult suffrage was consummated by the enfranchisement of women, votes for everybody made the oligarchical Victorian parliaments of Disraeli and Gladstone seem hotbeds of revolution compared to the parliaments of Baldwin and Ramsay MacDonald.'

A note of arid determinism had crept into his thought, and he, who had always maintained that man could do what he willed, now began to think that man could only do what he was told. 'A really good man', he writes on page 326, 'is one who is good because he likes being good. His good life is a life of self-gratification, not of self-denial. He is made that way; and the credit for it belongs not to himself but to his maker, whether we call his maker God or Creative Evolution.' But if that be true, the bad man does not deserve condemnation, which belongs only to his maker, God or Creative Evolution.

This passing despondency was immaterial in comparison with his intense belief that man could, if he chose, improve himself and achieve the stature of a god. The Creator, or whatever one chooses to call the energising impulse that has made the universe, 'is not infallible: it proceeds by trial and error; and its errors are called the Problem of Evil. It is not omnipotent: indeed it has no direct power at all, and can act only through its creations. Its creations are not omnipotent: they proceed by guesses; and evil arises when they guess wrong with the best intentions. It has neither body nor parts; but it has, or rather is, what we call a soul or passion, forever urging us to obtain greater power over our circumstances and greater knowledge and understanding of what we are doing.'

We must make a greater effort than we have hitherto made to secure good government and 'to select fit operators for the brain work of democracy. If that fails, we shall become part of the Problem of Evil, and be exterminated like the mammoths and mastodons by some new species of greater political capacity. For we have no reason to suppose that we are the Creator's last word.'

'In my childhood,' he says, 'I heard a pious Irish mother say to her adult son, when he warned her that she was in danger of losing her train, that she would catch it "with the help of God". His reply was "Yes; but you will have to look pretty sharp yourself".' In that moment, G.B.S. learnt the substance of his faith.

'When democratic Socialism has achieved sufficiency of means, equality of opportunity, and national intermarriageability for everybody, with production kept in its natural order from necessities to luxuries, and the courts of justice unbiassed by mercenary barristers, its work will be done; for these, and not a mathematical abstraction like equality of income, are its real goal. The present stratification of society will be levelled up until the largest possibilities of human nature are no longer starved; but it will still be human nature with all its enterprises, ambitions and emulations in full swing, and with its pioneering superior persons, conservative average persons, and relatively backward inferiors in their natural places, all fully fed, educated up to the top of their capacity, and intermarriageable. Equality can go no farther.'

And so we perceive that the advanced thinker, G.B.S., was an old-fashioned Christian who could, quite easily, have been one of the little band of men who wandered up and down the hills and plains of Israel, serenely indifferent to the pomp and power of Imperial Rome, but, unknown to themselves, laying the charges that would one day make that mighty empire reel and tumble in the dust.

191

In 1946, he reached his ninetieth year, and, very much to his surprise, discovered that he was regarded with affection as well as with awe and wonder. The young man who had bombarded publishers in vain was now the admired of almost all beholders, despite his extraordinary capacity for rubbing them up what they thought was the wrong way. His ability to anticipate the future was now plainly discernible even by the obtuse: his plays might have been written for broadcasting, so apt were they to this medium, and they were not less apt to the moving picture.

In that year, he began to write his last completed play, *Buoyant Billions:* a work in which there are good conversations, but little or no drama. It displays the remnants of a mind, but they are the remnants of a great mind. In his ninetieth year, he could still think of large themes and write good dialogue and turn a witty phrase, as when Mrs Secondborn, hearing a solicitor say, 'We really must not be personal,' replies, 'Whatever is not personal is not human.' But he could no longer assemble his theme with his old skill, and he tired quickly. The play was published in 1948, and he anticipated the commonplace criticism that he was old and should retire to the chimney-corner, with the pathetic retort, 'As long as I live I must write. If I stopped writing I should die for want of something to do.' In this disjointed piece, in which he repeats his old trick of adorning argument with brilliant decoration, he states as best he can the religious argument that had sustained his life. Man must be a creator.

When Miss Buoyant, afraid of the life force which is seeking to make her marry, asserts that 'the day of ridiculous old maids is over. Great men have been bachelors and great women virgins,' her lover replies, 'They may have regretted it all the same,' and the solicitor reminds her 'that though many women have regretted their marriages there is one experience no woman has ever regretted, and that experience is motherhood. Celibacy for a woman is *il gran rifiuto*, the great refusal of her destiny, of the purpose of life which comes before all personal considerations: the replacing of the dead by the living.'

There is a passage in the third act which truly concludes the play. Mrs Thirdborn has remarked that 'Sir Ferdinand's law has failed us. Dick's science has failed us. Fiff's boyish dreams have failed us: he has not yet bettered the world. We must leave it in God's hands.' Her husband adds his comment. 'It always comes to that: leave it to

God, though we do not know what God is, and are still seeking a general mathematical theory expressing him. All we know is that He leaves much of it to us; and we are making a shocking mess of it. We must be goodnatured and make the best of it.'

The act concludes with a remark made by a priest. 'The future is with the learners.'

In 1949, he wrote a little book, called *Farfetched Fables*, and in that year, too, he published *Sixteen Self Sketches*, a sprightly work in which there is much biographical stuff and much serene wisdom. Religion was still his hope for the world, a faith that would make men work with selfless passion for betterment. No other force could move the stubborn heart so quickly and so powerfully. 'I know as a hard fact,' he wrote, 'that Methodism which is saturated with abhorrent superstition, changed our colliers and their wives and mothers from savages into comparatively civilised beings,' and there was no other means, under heaven, whereby this could be done. His next work, a little puppet play, entitled *Shakes versus Shaw*, was written to pass the time. His last play was entitled *Why She Would Not*, but it scarcely got beyond an unfinished scenario. The final words of the unfinished sixth scene are: 'The world will fall to pieces about your ears.'

One of his hobbies was photography, and the last book he published was a little rhyming guide to Ayot St Lawrence which was illustrated by photographs he had taken of the village. He had scarcely finished it when he met with the accident which ended his life. Why he should have chosen to prune trees is hard to say. He had a good gardener, able to do the job far better than he could, but he had an inflexible belief, first, in the need for exercise, and, second, that he could do almost anything as well as anybody. So he went into his garden at the age of ninety-four, and began to prune his trees. It may be said of him, and with affection, that, like Nelson, he died of showing off.

As he stepped back from a tree, he slipped and fell on the uneven ground and broke a leg.

He was taken to a hospital in Luton where he was so well treated that he seemed, at first, likely to recover. But kidney trouble brought him down, and he was weakened by operations. His spirit remained high, and he chaffed his nurses with the kindly banter he had displayed throughout his long life. Would one nurse kindly give him a certificate that she had washed him thoroughly and did not need to be washed again! . . . He was, however, failing and would not recover. He had a sudden desire to go home to Ayot, and was removed from the hospital. A fancy for clotted cream possessed him, and Mrs Musters wrote to my wife to ask if any could be bought in Devon. But there was no cream obtainable in Devon then, though Mrs

Musters was luckily able to get some nearby; and Ivo Currall had some sent to him from the Isle of Man by air. He remembered the doctors in Luton, and sent each of them an autographed copy of one of his books.

The postman was kept busy delivering letters and telegrams, and Mrs Musters sorted them out and read to him only those she thought he would especially enjoy. It gives me happiness that one of them was from me, telling him that it would take more than a broken leg to finish him. Mrs Musters read it to him, and, as she wrote to me afterwards, he smiled and murmured, 'Oh, St John!'

An extraordinary serenity settled on him as he slowly dropped out of life. Rattray says, 'a friend who saw him in Luton hospital told me he would never forget the radiance that Shaw gave him'. He had done his work, and the world, so far as he was concerned, had come to an end. All his comrades, except Pease, were dead; and he had lost Charlotte. There is no solitude so severe as that of a man who has outlived his contemporaries, unless it be that of an intelligent man or woman condemned to live among fools. G.B.S. had a long record of various work behind him. He had lived to the top of his bent. He had known nearly all the distinguished men and women of his time, and he himself was world-renowned. What more could he do? It was time for him to pack up and go. So he went, and, true to his form, in one of the greatest blazes of publicity that the world has ever known.

There was an extraordinary demonstration on the day his death was announced. The Indian Cabinet adjourned; the lights on Broadway were briefly extinguished; *The Times* gave him its first leader; the press, everywhere, was full of him. There was a singular sense of loss. Detractors were not wanting. Detractors never are. Among them was one which was distressing to those who knew detractor and detracted.

The Daily Express had commissioned H. G. Wells to write G.B.S.'s obituary notice for that paper, but Wells had died first. Nevertheless, his article was in the paper's files, and the editor asked H.G.'s elder son if he had any objection to its publication. Young Mr Wells, suffering, perhaps, from a sudden fit of insensitiveness, had none. The result was that a piercing scream from the grave appeared in *The Daily Express*, in which H.G. discharged all the rancour and jealous rage against G.B.S. that had seared his mind for a large part of his life. His wrath had made him incapable of understanding even a plain and simple fact, and he dazed those who knew them both fairly well by accusing G.B.S. of callous disregard of Mrs Wells's last illness and of a flippant attitude towards her suffering.

This was a monstrous misunderstanding, explicable only by the fact that H.G. was so ill himself that he was incapable of reason on the subject. It happens that I met G.B.S. about the time to which H.G. refers. His attitude to Jane's illness was his lifelong attitude to all illness. 'Everybody goes to Easton with a long face and depresses her, when they should put on their most cheerful looks and make her feel she is getting better. If I were H.G., I'd throw the gloomy ones out of the house and admit only those who will tell her jokes and make her laugh.' How could H.G. misunderstand the man who made that remark? His son should have had the grace of spirit to prevent the publication of that horrible howl.

192

Rattray complains that the Dean and Chapter of Westminster Abbey did not offer burial ground for G.B.S., but the complaint is not substantial. The third paragraph of his will made his wish about his ashes plain, and it was decisive.

> 'I desire that my dead body shall be cremated and its ashes inseparably mixed with those of my late wife now in the custody of the Golders Green Crematorium and in this condition inurned or scattered in the garden of the house in Ayot St Lawrence where we lived together for thirty five years unless some other disposal of them should be in the opinion of my Trustee more eligible. Personally I prefer the garden to the cloister.'

This paragraph is so worded that his Trustee could have accepted, had an offer of burial in Westminster Abbey been made. But G.B.S.'s preference is plain.

The fourth paragraph of the will almost forbade the offer to be made or accepted.

> 'As my religious convictions and scientific views cannot at present be more specifically defined than those of a believer in Creative Evolution I desire that no public monument or work of art or inscription or sermon or ritual service commemorating me shall suggest that I accepted the tenets peculiar to any established church or denomination nor take the form of a cross or any other instrument of torture or symbol of blood sacrifice.'

Westminster Abbey is a Christian church: it is not a public cemetery or a Pantheon without religious affiliations. Is it reasonable to suggest that G.B.S.'s ashes should have been carried into the Abbey in the absence of the Dean and Chapter and without a recital of the Burial Service? While his body was being cremated, Sir Sydney Cockerell, an old and valued friend, read the passage in *The Pilgrim's Progress*, a book which had profoundly influenced G.B.S.'s mind since he was a boy of ten, in which Mr Valiant-for-Truth's end is described.

595

193

He left a large fortune of £367,233 13s, the net value of which was £301,585 7s 5d: one of the largest fortunes ever left by a writer, and contrasting sharply with the £6 he earned in his nine years of adversity. The ravenous and wasteful state confiscated £180,571 1s 4d of this sum; but as G.B.S. approved of community extortion, no complaint can be made of that, except that the more sensible objects of his munificence could have used the money to far better purpose. Bequests were made to the few aged relatives who survived him, and his servants were provided with substantial annuities. The residue was to be spent on a scheme for reforming the English language, a devise which excited derision among the large body of persons who know better than we do how our money should be spent. Why should a man not endow his hobby if that be his pleasure? His interest in the reform of the alphabet had developed in his boyhood in Dublin, and it had remained one of his chief interests for the rest of his life.

But the devise was not made to be meat and drink for lawyers; and the will included a clause under which, if his intention in regard to the language could not be fulfilled, the residue should be divided equally between the National Gallery of Ireland, where he had learnt most of what he knew about pictures; the British Museum, which had been his library and club in his poverty; and the Royal Academy of Dramatic Art, as a sign of grace and remembrance to the great band of actors and actresses who had performed in his plays. He was still being grateful for benefits received. His testament is one of the most public-spirited documents in the whole history of bequest.

194

In the four years after his death there was a small reaction against him which was smaller than the shrillness of those who led it made it appear to be. Unluckily, the total failure of an ill-advised effort to raise a vast Memorial Fund in his honour seemed to justify the leaders of the reaction. The proposal was that a sum of £250,000 should be raised for three objects: first, to provide subsidies for young authors, musicians and playwrights to assist them in obtaining performance or publication of their work; second, to ensure 'the worthy presentation of Shaw's plays in appropriate Festival settings and, if possible, the formation of a repertory company to perform them here and to tour the English-speaking world': and third, to maintain the fabric of Shaw's Corner at Ayot St Lawrence. G.B.S. had given the house to the National Trust, but had failed to provide means for its maintenance.

Mr Ivor Brown was asked to become Chairman of the Shaw Memorial National Committee; and he invited me to join the governing body of this Committee. I gave him several reasons why I felt disinclined to do this. There was no likelihood that £250,000 could be raised.

The English have never had the slightest desire to honour their great artists, preferring, instead, to build memorials to politicians, soldiers, sailors and wealthy merchants who endow orphanages. Had it not been for the generosity of America, the Shakespeare Memorial Theatre at Stratford-on-Avon would probably not have been built. The single out-of-doors tribute to Shakespeare in London is a miserable statue in Leicester Square.

Moreover, G.B.S. had always resisted attempts to ennoble him with honours on the ground that he would either be remembered as a dramatist 'as long as Aristophanes and rank with Shakespeare and Molière, or I shall be a forgotten clown before the end of the century.' His argument is, I think, fallacious, since honours for great men are not intended to settle the judgment of posterity, but to indicate the respect felt for him by his contemporaries. True or false, however, the argument demanded attention.

The purpose of the Memorial Fund seemed objectionable to me. Subsidy nearly always is sought by people without quality, and is ruinous to those who possess it. The Royal Literary Fund exists to help authors who are distressed by illness or misfortune, but its Committee is beset by persons demanding grants whose merits as authors are so slight that they are indiscernible. I remember an occasion when a grant was requested for the widow of a retired Civil Servant whose contributions to the literature of his country were letters of topical interest which he had written to a suburban newspaper! If this object of the Memorial Fund were to be established it would result in endless cadging by unmeritable people seeking sums of money they had not the ability to earn.

Shaw's plays were able to take care of themselves. They required no bolstering from public funds. If they fell out of favour, they would, as G.B.S. himself always asserted, be getting their deserts, and efforts to foist them on the public would not only be ineffective but reprehensible. The history of the plays since his death proves beyond a doubt that their popularity remains undiminished. In less than five years, seven of his plays were very successfully revived, and in the United States his vogue was even greater.

The single respect in which money might well have been given to the Fund was the maintenance of the house at Ayot St Lawrence. But no such sum as a quarter of a million pounds was required for that. A number of writers, of varying merit, expressed antipathy to this proposal. The house, they said, was a commonplace villa. These sensitive souls seem to have thought that writers were accustomed to choose for their homes houses which were superb examples of fine architecture. G.B.S. alone had lived in a house which compelled exquisite persons to shudder at the very thought of it. But writers, like other people, have to live where they can, and there is no ground for thinking that the houses they inhabit give greater cause for artistic pleasure than the homes of meat packers or chartered accountants. Our interest in Shakespeare's house is not in its architecture, but in the fact that Shakespeare lived in it. No one suggests that Wordsworth's cottage should be demolished because it is unimposing, and our interest in The Pines at Putney is entirely due to Swinburne's residence there. Mr T. S. Eliot, whose manner becomes more and more apostolic, frowned heavily on the proposal because, apparently, he disapproved of G.B.S., and several solemn celebrities of lesser degree shook their heads.

Mentioning my doubts to Mr Brown, I was surprised to hear him say that he felt certain the money would soon be raised. He had been urged to take the Chairmanship of the Committee by Mr Attlee, a fact which made me feel that perhaps the Labour Party, which G.B.S. had been influential in founding, was prepared to support the appeal for funds in a highly practical manner, though Mr Brown gave me no cause to believe that this was so; and so, full of doubts and disapproval, I let myself be persuaded to support the scheme. It was a dire failure. The Committee asked for £250,000: it received £407. This result was substantially due to the publication of G.B.S.'s will. The generality of people, forgetting that a man should not be expected to pay for his own memorial, thought that an estate of more than £300,000 could easily have provided the money for maintaining Shaw's Corner without any public support other than the cost of admission. G.B.S. may have thought that in giving the house itself—and the complainants fail to remember that it has a considerable money value—was enough, and, knowing how much his estate would be reduced by taxation, have felt that he must give the residue to the cause he had most at heart: the reform of the language. Here, however, we are speculating without hope of solution. We know only that G.B.S. bequeathed the whole of his property to public purposes: a feat which his detractors are unlikely to perform.

195

Had there been a decline in the public interest, this would, surely, not have been surprising. The world has not yet produced an author whose popularity remains constantly high, nor has it produced one whose work is always on the same great level. Shakespeare suffered periods of neglect, and some of his plays are poor. There would be nothing singular, therefore, in a decline in G.B.S.'s popularity. It is absurd to suppose that so vivid a mind will fade out of general knowledge and become unknown except to pedants and historians.

It is hard to believe that G.B.S. will out, out like a brief candle. Somewhere in the corridors of time, his flame will still burn brightly and steadily. His influence on his own age was immense, on those who railed against him no less than on those who clapped their hands. He was generous and kind and compassionate, and he had a deep love of social order which forbade him to tolerate poverty and maimed lives and curable distress. He served his country faithfully to the full extent of his great ability, and when he died he left all he had earned for a public purpose. Considerate for others, he sought no consideration for himself, but took with courage and fortitude the blows he had to bear. Prompt with help for those who needed it, he took no help himself, but fought his fight cleanly and courageously. He sometimes lacked wisdom, but he never lacked charity; and when he gave, he gave without reproach or condescension. His heart was large: it contained multitudes. His courage, his candour, his unfailing faith, and his fearless announcement of the truth as he saw it, made him a beacon in a time of intellectual darkness. And that flame still brightly flares.

INDEX

601

Index

Campbell, Rev. R. J., 556

Campbell-Bannerman, Sir Henry, 227, 354

Canada, proposed exchange for Guadeloupe, 356

Candid Friend, The, 31, 32

Candida, play discussed, 277–82; suggested production by Ellen Terry, 260; read to Charles Wyndham, 339; produced in provinces (1897–1898), 277, 341; accepted for America but abandoned at rehearsal (1897), 339–40; published (1898), 327–30; produced in America (1903), 341; in London, 338, 341, 342, 347; in Belgium and France, 374; original of character, 32; Janet Achurch in name part, 162, 277, 320, 339–40; American view of, 277–8, 279; popularity with amateurs, 397; mentioned, 257, 291, 367, 373

Cannan, Gilbert, 430

Cape, Jonathan (publishers), 505

Capital, nationalisation of, 105

Capital punishment, 587

Capitalism: *see Intelligent Woman's Guide to Socialism and Capitalism, The*

Capone, Al, 95

Captain Brassbound's Conversion, play discussed, 337–8, 402; original title, 332; Irving refuses to produce, 263; Ellen Terry and, 332, 336–7, 380; performed by Stage Society (1900), 285; published (1901), 332; produced in London (1906), 337; originals of Drinkwater, 86; difficulties for amateurs, 397

Carlyle, Jane Welsh, 101, 102

Carnegie, Andrew, 428

Caroline Quarterly, 374

Carpenter, Edward, 124

Carr, Rev. Edward, 8

Carr, Frances: *see* Shaw, Frances (grandmother)

Carr, Rev. George Whitmore, 6

Carr, J. Comyns, 272–3

Carroll, Emily, 37

Carroll, Rev. William George (uncle and cousin), 7, 26, 37

Carson, Murray, 341

Casement, Sir Roger, 465–70

Cashel Byron's Profession, written (1882), 15, 98, 104; original of character, 23; Meredith recommends rejection, 64; Robert Louis Stevenson on, 76, 186; Fisher Unwin and, 196; published (1886), 186; copy sent to Janet Achurch, 162

'Cécile': *see* Bennett, Arnold

Cellier, Alfred, 197

Censorship and licensing of plays, *Mrs Warren's Profession* banned by Lord Chamberlain, 251–2, 259; ban lifted (1925), 256; rules governing production of plays, 251–3; history of censorship in England, 251–3, 424; plays by G.B.S. banned in England; books banned in Eire, 279, 546; *Mrs Warren's Profession* denounced and company arrested in America (1905), 347–8, 426; *Arms and the Man* banned in Austria, 373–4; book of *Man and Superman* banned from New York libraries (1905), 395; *Press Cuttings* and *The Shewing-up of Blanco Posnet* banned (1909), 424–7, 546; dissatisfaction with the licensing of plays, 425; Samuel committee's report (1909), 425–6; G.B.S.'s evidence before committee only part-heard, 426; changes in licensing, 425–6; Polish censor orders cut in *Too True to be Good* (1932), 527, 529, 546; views of G.B.S., 546

Central Model School, Dublin, 29–31

Chamberlain, Austen, 567

Chamberlain, Joseph, and Henry George, 105; G.B.S.'s forecast about, 187; and Beatrice Webb, 218, 225; Tariff Reform campaign, 303; mentioned, 202, 355, 356, 567

Chamberlain, Neville, 455

Chambers, Sir Edward, 366

Champion, Henry Hyde, 112–13, 119

Champion, William, 242–3

Chaplin, Charlie, 264

Chapman and Hall (publishers), 64

Characterisation of plays: *see* Construction and characterisation

Charity Organization Society, 213, 218

Charrington, Charles, 107, 162, 257–8, 364–5

Charrington, Janet: *see* Achurch, Janet

Chatto and Windus (publishers), 64

Chekhov, Anton, 249, 475, 477, 519

Chesterton, G. K., commentary on G.B.S., viii; attends lecture by G.B.S., 96; friendship with G.B.S., 114, 174, 292, 365; and the Webbs, 127; laughter, 184; no ear for music, 193; unworldly about money, 365; evidence on censorship, 425; on 'Christlike' appearance of G.B.S., 557; on the man in the street, 582; death (1936), 365, 581; G.B.S.'s letter to Mrs Chesterton, 365

Childers, Erskine, 279

China, Fabians and, 359–60

Index

Ibsen, Henrik (*cont.*)
and, 176–7, 179, 231–2, 241; G.B.S.'s *The Quintessence of Ibsenism* (1891), 231–8, 240, 310; contrasted with G.B.S., 231–7; London production of *A Doll's House* and *Rosmersholm* (1891), 240; critics' abusive reception of *Ghosts* (1891), 241–4, 251, 259; Nora in *A Doll's House*, 247, 250; Danish critic's remark 'no specific talent for writing plays', 249; Henry Irving and, 263, 292; G.B.S. on *Rosmersholm*, 274; G.B.S. and, 277, 280; plays performed at Court Theatre (1904–07), 337; plays written before his forty-second year, 367; influence on the character of drama, 397

Immaculate Conception, G.B.S. and the, 96

Immaturity, novel discussed, 70–71, 75–77, 83, 84, 95; G.B.S.'s own experiences in, 61, 74–75; written in 1879, 64; rejected by publishers, 64–65, 68, 97; pirated edition published in America (1921), 64; first British publication (1930), 64; characters appear in other novels, 76, 83; failure, 80; compared with Shakespeare's first work, 109; preface quoted, 5, 27, 57, 74

Imperialism, 354–9

In Good King Charles's Golden Days, 526, 568–70, 575

Inca of Perusalem, The, 471

Incest as theme for play, 252, 253

Income tax, G.B.S. and, 314

Incomes, equality of, 404, 441–2, 508, 591

Independent Labour Party, 217, 244, 305, 473, 569

Independent Theatre, 240, 247, 251, 259, 277

India, British withdrawal from, 359; Cabinet adjourns on announcement of G.B.S.'s death, 594

Industrial remuneration, conference on (1885), 149

Inge, Dean W. R., 114, 193

Intelligent Woman's Guide to Socialism and Capitalism, The, 319, 506–14, 584

International rights of travel and trade, Fabians and, 359–61

Ireland (*see also* Dublin), in 1856, 3; Famine of the Forties and plague, 3, 206; Irish emigration to America, 4; decline in population, 4, 410, 483; populated by three groups (Roman Catholics, Ascendancy and Ulster Protestants), 4;

Ireland (*cont.*)
G.B.S. leaves (1876), 56; G.B.S. revisits (1905), 57, 273–4, 406; Casement's campaign for 'freedom' by German aid (1914–16), 465–9; G.B.S.'s attitude to Black and Tans, 462; G.B.S.'s attitude to, 462–3; attitude to G.B.S., 279, 378; books by G.B.S. banned, 279; and the British Commonwealth, 358–9; British claim to govern, 360; G.B.S. becomes registered citizen of Irish Republic, 110, 463; suggested honorary British nationality for Eireans, 110; puritanical prohibitions in, 222; priestly oppressions on Roman Catholics in, 409–10; decline of Protestant population, 410; partition, 410; G.B.S.'s plays popular among Protestants, 378; physical condition of population, 483; disposal of G.B.S.'s property, 580

Irish Convention (1917), 416

Irish Nationalists, 204

Irish Players, 372, 412

Irishmen, dislike of Ireland and each other, 273; delusion of superiority, 372; G.B.S. and, 454

Irrational Knot, The, novel discussed, 76, 80–85, 95; scene used in *The Apple Cart*, 83–84; written in 1880, 85; rejected, 97; preface quoted, 100

Irving, Sir Henry, G.B.S. sees in Dublin, 50; G.B.S.'s antagonism to, 114, 171, 202, 261–3, 276–7, 284–5, 289–91, 297–8, 300–1; G.B.S. praises performance in *King Arthur* (1895), 272; G.B.S. in direct contact for first time, 284; early difficulties, 284; relations with Ellen Terry, 287; G.B.S.'s unsuccessful efforts to persuade him to produce *The Man of Destiny* (1896), 288–92, 297, 300, 304; implications of drunkenness in G.B.S.'s criticism (1897), 294–6; Irving's reply, 296; accident to knee, 295–6; letters drafted by Austin, 301; Ellen Terry's efforts to persuade him to produce G.B.S. play, 300–1; leaves for America (1899), 336; as actor and producer, 343; in *Henry VIII*, 399; quarrel with G.B.S. complete, 297, 300–1; death (1905), 298; G.B.S.'s obituary article, 298–9

Irving, H. B., 285

Irving, Laurence (son of Sir Henry), 114, 285

Irving, Laurence (grandson of Sir Henry), 295, 296

Isaacs, Edith, 502–3

610

Index

Index

Shaw, George Bernard
(religion, attitude to) (*cont.*)
knowledge, 26; attempt to read
the Bible through, 27; nominally
member of Episcopal Church of
Ireland, 29; sent to school with
Roman Catholics, 5, 29–30; discussions at home, 36; wish to found
new religion, 49; profound interest
in religion, 51, 92; letter on evangelism, 51–53; on character of God,
149; his beliefs, 390–2, 440–3, 481,
525–6; on prayer, 411; summary
of his faith given in *The Shewing-up
of Blanco Posnet*, 424; respect for
Jesus Christ, 440; will quoted, 595
Residences: *see* Synge Street, Dublin;
Hatch Street; Harcourt Street;
Victoria Grove, Fulham; Fitzroy
Street; Osnaburgh Street; Fitzroy
Square; Adelphi Terrace; White-
hall Court; search for country
house, 361; move to Ayot St
Lawrence, 361–2
Secretaries, 327
Servants' regard for, 583
Sexual love, attitude to: *see* Sexual love
Sheets, dislike of, 309
Shyness and nervous temperament,
58, 67, 87, 93, 147, 571
Smoking, attitude to, 309
Son, Granville-Barker legend, 344
Speeches, ability to write, 72; plat-
form delivery, 73, 93, 107–8; first
public speech (1879), 87; as an
orator, 419
'Sponging' on his parents, charge of,
68, 78, 99–104, 178
Systematic in habits, 363
Teetotaller, fanatical, 21, 169, 309
Testimonial from Townshend's, 54,
66
Travel, loathing of, 305–6, 529–30
Vegetarianism, 97, 98, 106, 169, 309;
liver injections during illness, 573
Walking, liking for, 314, 411, 454
War, hatred of, 461, 470
Will, 596
Wit and sardonic humour, inherited
from his father, 185
Women, early lack of interest in
girls, 47–48; need of woman friend,
70–71; relations with women, 114–
118, 145–7, 151–66, 170–3, 304,
445–50; 'six affairs on his hands'
(1888), 157, 158; the 'seduced not
the seducer', 158; his fear of women
in later years, 443
Shaw, George Carr (father), ancestry,
3–7; birth and early life, 8–12;
marriage, 14; relations with his

Shaw, George Carr (father) (*cont.*)
wife, 15, 17, 322, 508; financial
position, 15–17, 27, 39, 42; gentility of home, 20–21; tippling
habits, 13, 21–22; frightened into
sobriety, 34; G.B.S.'s recollections
of, 35–37; wife and daughters
emigrate to England (1872), 37,
42–43; allowance to wife, 43, 100,
150; lodgings with G.B.S. in Harcourt Street, 43, 48; visits wife in
London, 43; contemplates suing
for divorce, 51; asks Townshend
for reference for G.B.S., 54, 66;
G.B.S. leaves him behind in Dublin, 55; G.B.S. charged with sponging on, 99–104; reads *An Unsocial
Socialist*, 119; G.B.S. inherited wit
and sardonic humour from, 185;
and *You Never Can Tell*, 322–3;
G.B.S.'s attitude to, 323; death
(1885), 8, 150, 185; effect of death
on G.B.S., 150, 293
Shaw, Dr and Mrs G. F., 22–23
Shaw, Lucinda Elizabeth (*née* Gurly)
(mother), ancestry and early life,
3, 10–14; marriage, 14; no love for
her husband, 15, 17, 322, 508;
married life in Dublin, 16–20;
children born, 16, 25; attitude of
children to, 17–20; G.B.S.'s recollections of, 18–19, 25, 48; love of
music, 20, 22, 24–26; becomes acquainted with Lee, 22, 26, 28–29;
friendship with Mrs G. F. Shaw,
22–23; voice trained by Lee, 22,
26, 38; declares herself an atheist,
24, 28; dabbles in spiritualism, 28,
320; attended by Lee in illness, 34;
G.B.S.'s attitude to, 36, 37, 42, 51,
57, 78, 323; leaves husband and
follows Lee to London (1872), 37,
42–43; fails to correspond with
G.B.S., 43; encounter with Emily
Carroll, 37; relations with Lee, 42,
51; allowance from husband, 43,
100, 150; estimate of income, 43;
husband contemplates divorce, 51;
G.B.S. joins in London (1876), 57;
breaks with Lee, 62; receives news
of Lee's death, 63; portrayed in
Love Among the Artists, 77, 78;
parties frequented by, 80; London
residences (1881–87), 96–99, 156–7;
isolated during G.B.S.'s smallpox
(1881), 98; daughter Lucy leaves
home, 98, 198; G.B.S. charged
with sponging on, 99–104; income
from bequests to children, 103;
allowance from G.B.S. 104; G.B.S.
breaks with her friends, 105, 114;

DATE DUE